STONE ALONE

THE STORY OF A ROCK 'N' ROLL BAND

Bill Wyman

with Ray Coleman

FROM THE LIBRARY OF

A SIGNET BOOK

SIGNET
Published by the Penguin Group
Penguin Books USA Inc., 375 Hudson Street,
New York, New York 10014, U.S.A.
Penguin Books Ltd, 27 Wrights Lane,
London W8 5TZ, England
Penguin Books Australia Ltd, Ringwood,
Victoria, Australia
Penguin Books Canada Ltd, 10 Alcorn Avenue,
Toronto, Ontario, Canada M4V 3B2
Penguin Books (N.Z.) Ltd, 182-190 Wairau Road,
Auckland 10, New Zealand

Penguin Books Ltd, Registered Offices:
Harmondsworth, Middlesex, England

Published by Signet, an imprint of New American Library,
a division of Penguin Books USA Inc.
Published by arrangement with Viking Penguin.

First Signet Printing, October, 1991
10 9 8 7 6 5 4 3 2 1

Dedication

A few weeks before Christmas 1962 I joined an unknown group of guys in Chelsea who were learning to play blues music. They called themselves 'The Rollin' Stones'. Four months later, a small provincial newspaper wrote an article about us; I kept it. A month after that a music paper wrote another article; I kept that too. Slowly, more articles followed; I kept them. Then we made a single, which did moderately well. More press articles followed; I kept them. We did a few radio shows and then some television.

I have a son, Stephen, who was then eighteen months old. I was proud of him, and wanted him to be proud of me when he grew up. I decided to keep some small mementoes of my limited success for him to see when he was old enough to understand. I wanted him to know that once I had played in a small musical group that had been on radio and TV a few times, and had made a couple of 'not-so-bad' singles.

I bought a scrapbook, which was soon filled. I bought another, and in a few weeks that too was full. I bought another—and another and another. Items were coming thick and fast—too fast for me to keep up with them in my limited free time. I put everything in a small trunk, but soon that was full. I bought another trunk—and another and another. Still the items kept on arriving.

Stephen didn't really show much interest in my career until he was seven years old. During his first week at boarding school a boy asked the invitable question: "What does your dad do?" Stephen replied in all innocence: "He's in the Rolling Stones." When Stephen arrived home the next weekend he pulled me aside and said shyly, "I didn't know you were *that* famous!"

Neither did I, son, neither did I!

I dedicate this book to Stephen, who has, unwittingly, made sure I never feel *that* famous.

Contents

List of Illustrations

With Stephen, Kenilworth Court, 1965 (*Bent Rej*)

Diane, Stephen and me in Paris, April 1965 (*Bill Wyman*)

Touring—Mick and Keith playing Monopoly in flight, 1965 (*Bill Wyman*)

Brian with Bob Bonis on our first US tour (*Marty and Rita Rowe*)

The Times Square billboard for *December's Children* (*and Everybody's*), October 1965

Stephen, 1965 (*Bill Wyman*)

SECTION II

Me with my MGB outside Keston, June 1966 (*Courtesy: Gered Mankowitz*)

Keith outside Redlands, summer 1966 (*Courtesy: Gered Mankowitz*)

Charlie outside the Old Brewery, Lewes, summer 1966 (*Courtesy: Gered Mankowitz*)

Brian in his Elm Park Lane flat in the summer of 1966 (*Courtesy: Gered Mankowitz*)

Andrew Oldham, Allen Klein and us in New York, June 1966

Peter Frampton at Pye Studios, London, 1966 (*Bill Wyman*)

Judging a beauty competition, May 1967 (*Courtesy: Express Newspapers*)

Ian Stewart, Stones founder member, road manager (*Bill Wyman*)

Mick and Robert Fraser at Redlands, June 1967 (*Courtesy: Michael Cooper Collection*)

Brian at the US Embassy in London, 1967 (*Courtesy: Michael Cooper Collection*)

Me and Keith at the *Satanic Majesties* photo session (*Courtesy: Michael Cooper Collection*)

Jimmy Miller and Mick, Brian, and Brian, Keith and me at the Rock 'n' Roll Circus rehearsal, December 9, 1968 (*Eric Hayes*)

Rock 'n' Roll Circus, December 10, 1968 (*Eric Hayes*)

December 1968: the *Beggars' Banquet* press launch

Mick and Marianne arriving at court after their drugs bust, May 1969 (*Courtesy: UPI/Paper Photos*)

Astrid at Gedding Hall (*Bill Wyman*)

Astrid and Stephen in Denmark (*Bill Wyman*)

Brian's home—Cotchford Farm (*Bill Wyman*)

Brian's funeral, July 1969 (*Courtesy: Hulton Picture Collection*)

Mick Taylor, autumn 1969

Charlie, Mick Taylor, Mick Jagger, Keith and me just before our Hyde Park Concert (*Courtesy: Hulton Picture Collection*)

Every effort has been made to contact all copyright holders. The publishers would be interested to hear from any copyright holders not here fully acknowledged.

Introduction

'Age does not matter unless you are wine.' So runs the truism, embroidered on the cushion that Astrid Lundström gave Bill Wyman on his fiftieth birthday; it faces him every day in his office in Chelsea, London, and it neatly summarizes his attitude to life; being fifty-something doesn't count to a man with his level of energy, self-discipline and concentration.

The world of rock 'n' roll has produced many thousands of consummate musicians whose lives away from the stage are unfocused. Bill Wyman is from a rarer breed, a man who insists that orderliness should surround his life and work, a man who plans his movements and remembers events in microscopic detail. Some of his friends find his exceptional precision unnerving, but that very steadfastness has made this book possible. And it is that same characteristic, plus a keen sense of humor, that has been essential to his survival since he joined the world of the Rolling Stones back in 1962.

It was pop music then: young, innocent, a clarion call to youth. The songs and sounds had a huge impact and so, too, did the attitudes engendered by the Stones, their friends the Beatles and a host of others. The Stones were a crucial component in the fabric of the sixties, a decade that continues to be analyzed, glorified and—by some—vilified. In that period of high energy, Something Happened—and it is that Something, plus a whole lot more, that Bill, as the Rolling Stones' historian, captures in this book.

Bill Wyman was a boy of the wartime 1940s, a teenager of the blossoming 1950s, a pop star of the 1960s and beyond. This autobiography therefore has several facets to which he brings a unique strength in recapturing those eventful years: a truly incredible memory and an enormous archive of memorabilia from which to draw self-portraits of the schoolboy, the conscript in the Royal Air Force, the office clerk and, most importantly, the pop star in love with his music. The reader will quickly realize the extent of Bill's diaries as the story unfolds.

My mind travels back more than a quarter of a century, to a moment in 1963 when, as a reporter, I was interviewing the just-emerging Rolling Stones in a Mayfair café. Their disparate personalities, which coalesced so well into that fractious entity that was the Stones, struck me forcefully even then. Mick Jagger seemed the most pragmatic, Brian Jones the most charismatic, Keith Richards the most dogmatic, Charlie Watts simply phlegmatic. Smoking excessively, saying little but absorbing everything, Bill was, I wrote, one to watch. His warm, wry smile and barbed wit concealed a mathematical mind. He said little but when he spoke it was something meaningful, direct—and meticulous.

He hasn't changed. Watching him before huge crowds in Los Angeles during the Stones' 1989 tour, I saw him play the same role—the perfect, rock-solid musical foil for the band's gymnasts.

In the years since the Stones first found scandal and glory, Bill Wyman has stayed true to his original aims. Notorious he may now be, but the life and style of a jet-setter often sits uncomfortably on him. Pop stardom and what came as a result of stardom was always an enjoyable by-product of doing something he earnestly believed in and therefore intended to execute efficiently. It is easy to accept what his mother recalls of his early days as a Stone: that all he expected from their success was a nice house and a car. Certainly Bill did not expect to be author of a history book on the subject at the start of the 1990s.

The text names the friends, relatives and Stones associates who have assisted Bill and me in assembling this book and ensuring its accuracy; I thank them all warmly. I would also like to thank my lawyer Roger Samuels. Above all, on behalf of many thousands of Rolling Stones supporters, thanks to Bill Wyman for his commitment and for his unfailing and endearing candor, which shine through this memoir.

RAY COLEMAN

I would like to thank the many people who have helped me with this book over the last twelve years: all the friends and colleagues who have been interviewed, including my parents, my brother Paul and my sister Judy; the Stones fans around the world who have sent me memorabilia; Roy Carr, whose book *The Rolling Stones* was so helpful; Astrid Lundström for her special help; my wife Mandy for her support; my son Stephen for his years with me on the computer; my assistant Karen Kearne; my lawyers Paddy Grafton-Green and Howard Siegel; my agent Mort Janklow; and from Penguin Books Tony Lacey and Judith Flanders.

Finally, I would like to thank my fellow Rolling Stones for twenty-eight unforgettable years of wonderful music.

BILL WYMAN

1

Flash Forward

It was the biggest rock tour in history: three and a quarter million fans in sixty shows gave us a triumphant 1989 return to the concert stage on our four-month trail across the United States. Grueling, intoxicating, momentous and moving, it was the most exhilarating period in the turbulent life of the Rolling Stones. The incredible tensions that had so often threatened to tear the Stones apart were finally converted into a glorious strength.

I never believed that that great tour could happen—or that we would go on to play two other great tours in 1990, in Japan and Europe. Now, standing on stage in those gigantic stadiums night after night watching the interaction and dynamism between Keith and Mick was like witnessing the embrace of blood brothers. Yet for three years before the tour we all felt the twenty-five-year-old Rolling Stones rock 'n' roll band had reached the point of no return. A battle between Mick and Keith had turned bitterly personal, seemingly out of control. Instead of speaking to each other they were slugging it out in the newspapers. Asked repeatedly whether the band would re-form, my reply was simple: only if Mick and Keith could patch up their quarrel. It ran very deeply in both their egos . . . and, paradoxically, their fight centered on the very factor that eventually brought us back together: loyalty to the Stones.

Despite the fact that he screwed up the band with his drug problems for about ten years, Keith has always claimed devotion to the Stones. A mere two personnel changes in over a quarter of a century reflect our exceptional team spirit. An unwritten law of this band has always been that whatever any player's other interests, private or professional, *the Stones takes priority*. The rest of the band believed Mick broke that bond, committing the cardinal sin of putting another project ahead of a band effort. Keith was angry that Mick's solo album would feature his own songs—to the detriment of his regular collaborations with Keith. The battle began during the recording of our 1986 album *Dirty Work*. Mick seemed preoccupied with finishing and promoting his solo album *She's the Boss*, and Keith became resentful. This turned to fury when Mick didn't want to tour with the new Stones album but over the next few years poured his energy into a second solo album and tours of Japan and Australia. The final straw for all of us was Mick doing a supposedly solo tour that was totally dominated by Stones songs. Two childhood buddies started a battle neither could win. The biggest loser was the band.

Dozens of people around the band had encountered crises, but this was our lowest ebb. Everything looked black. Communications between all of us throughout the eighties had been irritable, patchy or non-existent. The Stones seemed to have gone on hold as we all became immersed in private projects. But nobody expected a rift between Keith and Mick to cut so deep that Keith went ahead and did a movie with Chuck Berry, a solo album and a solo tour of the States. And on *his* solo album, Keith hit back at his old mate and songwriting partner—a song called "You Don't Move Me." (This was a theme he had begun on the *Dirty Work* album with such songs as "Had It With You.")

Band relationships continued to deteriorate until we met in London in May 1988 to decide our future. So many people, including me, believed the Stones to be dead and buried. Others clung to the romantic notion that we all needed each other, whatever the problems. I'd felt strongly that we should not trickle away into the sunset. How tacky to end like that. As Keith says: "You can't hire a band like the Stones on the street corner."

At this meeting Mick told us of his plans to do tours of Japan and Australia in support of his second solo album. Keith said he was starting work on *his* solo album at that time, with *his* tour of America; but we all felt intuitively right for getting back as a band. It all centered on whether Mick and Keith could gel again after all that bickering. Like us or not, the Stones are inimitable, centered on music at least as much as on style. Keith got it exactly right when, patching up his fight with Mick, he told him: "Darling, this thing is bigger than both of us." Keith pointed out that people don't bother to sustain a fight with enemies. And that was the basis of his healing process with Mick that enabled us to return so successfully to the American stage.

However, Keith's and Mick's solo projects ran longer than anticipated and they didn't get together until January 1989 in Barbados. Perhaps the earlier tension between them provided an impetus, for they worked with amazing speed. They swept aside all their grievances and quickly got on with turning out fine songs. In February Charlie went out, to put some rough demos down. And then in early March, Ronnie and I joined them for rehearsals in Eddy Grant's studio. On March 21 we broke for ten days and everyone went home—except me; I holidayed in Antigua; my son Stephen flew in from London to share my holiday, as did a girlfriend, Melissa, from New York. As well as this crucial reunion of the Stones, I had a pressing personal issue on my mind. I had to resolve my relationship back in Britain with a certain Mandy Smith.

When the Stones reassembled in Montserrat on March 30 the transformation in our chemistry was remarkable. Probably because of the long layoff, it was like a young band again. We got on marvelously well—playing pool, table tennis and socializing—and the music felt good. The Stones were back, and the word was out that an enormous and enthusiastic audience was waiting for us in America for a marathon tour later in the year. But it would be a race: it depended on finishing the album in five weeks (unheard of since the early sixties!). Miraculously, we did—and the tour of America was on for the autumn.

Many successful rock bands had split up on the basis of only a fraction of the aggravation encountered by the Stones. The aura of disaster, negativity, in-fighting and intrigue that had always plagued us seemed to intensify as we became older, more rigid, less vigilant about the band's survival and geographically split to the corners of the world.

Children of the sixties, we had been swept along by the euphoria and optimism of a decade in which youth smiled with satisfaction. Reviled, and then busted for drugs at the peak of our breakthrough, we were made scapegoats for the social revolution that had been spearheaded by our music, despised as an "evil influence." The harsh reality of the seventies ravaged the Stones and we seemed fated to end in a whirlpool of deaths, drug overdoses and wrecked lives. How and why did a great little rock 'n' roll band attract such a catalogue of doom as the Stones always did? More amazingly, how could five men survive— and return to the stage stronger than ever, to the clear pleasure of those millions of Americans who bought tickets to see us: children, their fathers and their grandfathers all nominated us, still, "the world's greatest rock 'n' roll band," a title we never claimed, but never denied.

There had always been band tensions. Imagine a family in which a child and parents are at loggerheads, keeping a terrible silence so that the air is never cleared. That was the Stones in the mid-seventies to early eighties. For about eight years, for example, Keith and I hardly spoke—he was heavily into drugs and I could not relate to him. Ronnie Wood, who replaced Mick Taylor in 1975, was the peacemaker on this as on so many occasions; he brought Keith and me together in 1978 in a hotel room on a US tour. Keith insisted I had never liked him—and it was like two kids making up after a fight. "I never disliked you, Keith," I answered. "Remember when you went to live in Switzerland [for a drug cure]—I wrote you letters, and you sent me a lovely letter back with pressed flowers in it? It was *you* who never made any attempt to keep a relationship going . . ." "Oh well, let's be mates now then," he said. And we were. Woody is a great catalyst.

Against myriad problems like that, an immutable strength kept the Stones together. We have been feuding for years—taunting each other in private and in public; making solo records; getting married; jet-setting; tending to our families; some taking drugs, others painting; gardening; collecting antiques. And yet somehow, after a seven-year break, we were harmoniously back, musically valid with a strong new album, *Steel Wheels;* with bruised egos but with the damage repaired. The atmosphere was like a carnival and we bounced off each other beautifully as we took the stage in Philadelphia on August 31, 1989, for that huge American tour. Despite the cushion of our private jet and luxury hotels, this was a physically tough schedule for men past their youthful prime. Yet the critical acclaim we received for every show, from Boston to Los Angeles, from Montreal to Miami, talked of our exuberance, our mystique, our armory of hits, our accent on showmanship and our timelessness when measured against newer bands. And this was the same band that had been nearly torn apart so many times.

The end of the sixties was indeed the end of innocence. That golden decade, during which the Stones and so many other major bands were formed, carried a vibrancy that has never been equaled. The fallout from that period is still powerfully around us as the nineties dawn—a whole army of British acts including Paul McCartney, Elton John, The Who, Rod Stewart, the Bee Gees and Eric Clapton are touring with renewed success. A major reason is that, like the Stones, they had served their apprenticeships in the sixties, when British rock 'n' roll was in such a formative, energetic mode.

Pop music was never meant to endure, but the best of the rock 'n' roll born in the sixties survives well. There are two main reasons. First, we young musicians were mining gold, the rich source of our inspiration being black or black-inspired music. That wellspring of our fervor seemed lost on the generation of rock bands that succeeded us. To them, *we* were the Establishment, and they took their cue from us with little knowledge of our heritage. They had superior technology, but their sources were secondhand. Secondly, bands like ours blossomed alongside important social change. Battles were fought and won in the sixties. The fifties, when the Stones were teenagers, had been gray years in Britain, when we paid the price of wartime and we had no real voice. By the start of the sixties, we were ready to assert ourselves forcefully: long hair became OK; an anti-Establishment attitude among teenagers suited the Stones perfectly; experimentation with drugs became prevalent, if controversial, entering the lives of many rock musicians; and with the permissive society came the arrival of the birth-control pill.

For these years of revolution, the Stones helped provide the soundtrack. They were heady and combative times, when the sun shone on us and we carried a torch for individuality against conservatism. In the final year of the decade came two warning shots that signaled the start of the Stones' dramatic New Dawn. On July 3, 1969, the founder of the Stones, Brian Jones, was found dead in the swimming-pool of his home, aged twenty-seven. And on December 6, 1969, came Altamont.

America was always joyful for Stones tours. The birthplace of the music that inspired us, it also offered hundreds of musician friends and uninhibited audiences producing tremendous atmospheres for our concerts. In November 1969 we crisscrossed the country performing twenty-two shows and breaking many attendance records. Our chosen support was Chuck Berry, B. B. King and his band and the noted British singer Terry Reid. As a gesture of thanks to American fans for this great tour we planned a free concert in a style similar to our very successful Hyde Park free concert four months earlier. After tremendous hassles about the location, we settled on Altamont Speedway at Livermore, California. Our fourteenth American album, *Let It Bleed,* was released on the day of the concert, featuring titles that could later be seen as evoking the blackness that Altamont gave to Stones history: "Gimme Shelter," "Midnight Rambler" and "You Can't Always Get What You Want." We had filmed much of the American tour, and the footage from this giant free concert was to provide a grand finale. Or so we thought.

The Woodstock festival four months earlier symbolized the love, peace, flowers and bells of the hippie generation. We hoped Altamont could be similarly gentle but it quickly became obvious, as we helicoptered in from our San Francisco hotel, that tension was in the air. The Grateful Dead, one of the opening acts, had suggested that Hell's Angels "police" the concert, but they seemed only to increase the uneasiness in a crowd of 300,000, which suffered from too much bad dope and terrible congestion. Jefferson Airplane's Marty Balin was knocked out on stage by an Angel, and the group's singer, Grace Slick, pleaded with everyone to cool out.

As we began to play, Hell's Angels beneath the stage began manhandling fans with pool cues. Mick's appeal for them to relax fell on deaf ears. Halfway through our set a teenage black kid ran towards the stage, brandishing a gun. Leather-jacketed Angels closed in on him—and pretty soon Mick was calling out for a doctor. Meredith Hunter, eighteen years old, had been stabbed to death.

We played on, with frequent breaks as fights continued during the songs: "Under My Thumb," "Midnight Rambler," "Little Queenie," "Brown Sugar" and, finally, the now all-too-relevantly-titled "Street Fighting Man." Finally we were rescued and flew out to San Francisco in the last overcrowded helicopter, which could only just take off. It was then that the grim news sank in: the Rolling Stones' gesture of goodwill had turned into rock 'n' roll's Armageddon. It was a heartbreaking end to the epochal sixties.

Blinking into the harsh daylight of the seventies, the Stones faced a stunning truth. We were broke. I had a bank overdraft of £12,000, a figure at which it had hovered for several years, and though we all had houses as assets, the press tag of us as millionaires jarred as a sick joke. The only millions we knew about were the records we sold all over the world.

1970 began positively enough with the recording of a new studio album, and in September we began an extensive European tour covering Finland, Sweden, Denmark, West Germany, Holland, France, Austria and Italy. We released the live album from the US tour, *Get Yer Ya-Yas Out,* and the film from the tour *Gimme Shelter.* 1970 was also the year when we ended our six-year association with Decca in the UK and London Records in America.

This precipitated an important chapter in the Stones story. Since the exit of the managers who launched us, our business affairs had been controlled by the infamous New Yorker Allen Klein. His predatory desire for British acts was legendary and his forceful arrival into the Beatles' company Apple made him the world's most notorious manager. When the Stones became represented by him in 1965, I was the lone voice to express reservations.

Two years later our finances were in a farcical mess; Andrew Oldham had quit during the recording of *Their Satanic Majesties Request.* At the Stones office the telexes crackled with requests for cash from Klein's New York office—the only way we had to pay our bills. Responses were frustratingly vague. Significantly, the several record and songwriting advances Klein had secured for us from London Records and Decca had been skillfully structured so that he received the advances and paid the money out to us in small amounts over many years. We had been convinced by him that we would, through this system, not fall victim to the problem of making a huge sum of money over a two- or three-year period, paying 83–93 per cent in tax and then finding we'd got absolutely nothing if we weren't successful in the future. It was a "steady income." But I felt as if we were also effectively wage slaves; it all boiled down to the fact that we seemed to be technically employed by Klein.

Engulfed by Klein's fiscal ingenuity, our future was clear. We would be the world's most famous bankrupts unless we severed our relationship with Klein—who had originally told us he would overturn the age-old relationship between record companies and musicians, and retrieve our just rewards of millions of dollars. Our decision to quit Klein was swift and unanimous. The problem was a monumental: *how?* His contracts with us were watertight in his favor. Who would take on the Herculean job of extracting the poverty-stricken Rolling Stones from the jaws of such a plausible, street-wise accountant who knew all the angles and appeared to have locked us up for years?

Throughout the rise of the Stones, Mick had always mixed at parties in rarefied social circles some distance from the rock 'n' roll set. At one such event in Kensington in 1969, his befriending of a man who was descended from Austrian royalty was to be our biggest ace in the exhausting job of exorcising Klein. Prince Rupert Loewenstein, the managing director of the London merchant bankers Leopold Joseph, had already taken care of a few deals for Mick when Mick asked him to examine the Stones' affairs in depth.

Such an approach by a Rolling Stone had undertones of humor for Loewenstein. Rock 'n' roll was, in the late sixties, the bastard child of the entertainment world. While the Beatles had a semblance of credibility in the corridors of London's financial district, the Stones were considered drug-ridden, sex-crazed young upstarts without pedigrees. After our early publicity as dirty layabouts, we were *personae non gratae* as precursors of what the Establishment still considered our unacceptable revolution. Loewenstein was, however, impressed by Mick's grasp of the seriousness of our financial albatross. (Mick was, after all, a student at the London School of Economics before pop music claimed him.) Loewenstein recalls that when he received Jagger's call, he believed he might be facing the pleasant duty of investing surplus funds for a highly successful pop group. When Mick and later Keith, Charlie and I met him, Loewenstein was appalled to discover that we were all flat broke, that our assets did not even cover our debts, our mortgage payments nor our daily expenses. And Klein's contract with us ran until the summer of 1970, arguably beyond.

It was a complex legal web, with Klein's grip on our services so tight that we could simply not wriggle free. What had happened with Klein was simple: he controlled our masters and copyrights. Our songs were the products of our creativity. Loewenstein's advice was straight, direct—and dangerous. We should drop Klein and drop out of England—a heavy gamble, but the only way, for Klein would certainly not willingly give us our freedom. We acted. Leaving England was the easy part—a tactical move that was later made by many to avoid the crippling income tax of those years. If we had stayed in England, we stood no chance of paying off our outstanding tax bills of over £100,000 each. In March 1971 we announced we were going to live in France. Earlier, on July 30, 1970, Klein was instructed that he had no authority to make any new deals for the Stones; next day, our Decca contract expired and Loewenstein sought a new deal for us. But ditching Klein to sign with our new "home," Atlantic Records, was a break fraught with danger: technically, would we now own our future product?

On March 22 Klein was fined $15,000 in New York for failing to submit quarterly federal tax returns for his employees. Rolling Stones Records, which we had formed to license our product, signed a world deal with Kinney, the umbrella company for Atlantic, on April 6, 1971. During all this mayhem we had also done a ten-day British tour.

Over the next few years litigation with Klein reached spectacular heights. Our relationship degenerated from an attempted settlement to court battles. At one stage we filed suit for $29 million in damages in the New York Supreme Court, claiming Klein had used his position for "his own personal profit and advantage." Atlantic Records was not able to indemnify us against any claim by Klein that he owned the first one or two records we made for Atlantic. And as the battle raged, Klein said that many of the songs we had said were completed after 1970 were in fact written previously—and claimed a slice of them. It was very ugly. To this day, Klein owns the pre-1970 Rolling Stones masters, and administrates the publishing of the Jagger–Richards songs of those early years, as well as those of our group songwriting name, Nanker-Phelge.

The signs were that the Klein suit would be lengthy and exhausting. Finally Mick and Rupert phoned me with a summary of the proposed settlement with Klein. We had two options—of taking Klein to court and maybe spending two years in litigation with enormous legal costs and having our money frozen—or settling with him for what I thought was a ridiculously low figure. Our advisers led us to believe that Klein owed us a minimum of $17 million, maybe more. Mick and Rupert told me we should get rid of him and settle for $2 million, $1 million of which was for Mick's and Keith's songwriting publishing, the other to be split between the four of us and Brian Jones's estate.

I asked why Charlie and I were paying a fifth of the costs when we were due to receive a tenth of the whole settlement; Charlie and I would end up with about $160,000 each—practically an insult. Charlie and I discussed this, and then I asked for a better deal. Mick and Keith agreed via Rupert that legal costs would be split equally in ratio to what we each received and Mick and Keith would jointly give us an additional $50,000 each. We agreed. Later Charlie bought me a beautiful painting and wrote a letter of thanks for protecting his interests. On May 9, 1972, we announced "settlement of all outstanding difficulties" with Klein after a marathon, non-stop thirty-six-hour session in a New York lawyer's office.

These days relationships between the Stones' financial director, Prince Rupert Loewenstein, and Allen Klein are businesslike. Even during our 1989 tour of America there were still issues they needed to discuss—since Klein's ownership of our pre-1970 work gives him a piece of the cake in perpetuity.

It's only rock 'n' roll. Is it really?

After a short tour that ended in London on March 14, we returned to the Marquee Club on the 26th to film a special for television and, true to his image, Keith arrived unshaven, hours late—and caused a rumpus. The manager of the Marquee, Harold Pendleton, had been an old jazz adversary of the Stones since 1962. When Keith saw a large sign saying "Marquee Club" behind our stand, he insisted it be removed. Pendleton insisted it stay—and Keith let rip, swinging his guitar in an attempt to hit him. Fortunately he didn't connect. Our views on Pendleton dated back to the earliest days of the Stones, when the jazz crowd tried to impose a "closed shop" on rock 'n' roll and block our progress. And we never forgot.

As a true Englishman I viewed exile in the south of France with misgivings. I love my roots, and swapping my beautiful country home, Gedding Hall in Suffolk, for an alien territory and culture didn't promise much. But my reluctance to go was overridden by our desperate financial state.

With Stephen happily established at boarding-school Astrid Lundström and I settled initially from April 1, 1971, in a rented house in Grasse, while the dispute with Klein lumbered on. Keith lived in Cap Ferrat, and I saw him quite a lot. Mick lived about twenty minutes away from me in Biot and Charlie too far away—past Marseilles. Ironically—because his predecessor Brian Jones had been my best mate in the Stones—I saw most of our "new boy," Mick Taylor, who had no idea when he came to us in 1969 that he was joining a band that was destitute! He and his wife Rose arrived with a baby daughter born on January 6, 1971, and rented a house near me. I wasn't allowed to return to Britain for the first year, and as Astrid recalls: "It all felt very temporary at first, almost as if all the Stones were on holiday as one group, playing house, meeting in restaurants." Keith would drop by for dinner at my house with about ten people in tow, and we'd sometimes drift over to his or Mick Taylor's houses.

Women around the Rolling Stones have always provided feasts and fantasies for voyeurs and the tabloid newspapers. We made it easy for them: in the sixties, Marianne Faithfull and Anita Pallenberg, plus Brian Jones's unending parade of girls, formed an integral part of our story. The banner headlines that surrounded my romance with Mandy Smith in the mid-eighties topped everything as an international scandal; but way back in the seventies, just as we settled into France, it was Mick's turn.

After our Paris Olympia concert on September 23, 1970, he was introduced to a girl named Bianca Rose Perez Moreno de Macias.* Their romance was intense and swift: within two months Bianca had moved in with Mick. After we were all exiled to France, Mick sprang the news on us: he was to marry Bianca in St. Tropez on May 12, 1971. We were even more shocked to find that apart from Keith, none of the Stones nor our ladies was invited to the wedding—and only to the celebrity-packed St. Tropez reception by a casual call from Mick the day before. Their daughter Jade was born on October 21, 1971. It was a stormy marriage and Mick and Bianca divorced on November 5, 1980; Keith, who had been the best man, was openly critical of Mick's professionalism during the marriage.

Astrid was a tower of strength and support to me in our first year in France. She flew back several times a month to visit Stephen for weekends out at Gedding or to bring him to France for holidays and return him.

I was homesick for England but quickly noticed a distinct improvement in our acceptance compared with my home country. In France a successful rock musician is treated with respect, placed in the same category as a poet, writer, painter or sculptor. France was good for our confidence. I was welcomed as a creative and successful person—contrasting with Britain, where the Stones were pigeon-holed as unkempt, empty-headed rock musicians. Away from Britain we might have been, but we were determined to make it profitable; it was a very prolific period for the band. A hot new single, "Brown Sugar," and an album, *Sticky Fingers*—both on our new Rolling

*Born in Nicaragua, Bianca at seventeen won a scholarship to study at the Institute of Political Science in Paris. Before meeting Mick she had hit the headlines with Michael Caine.

Stones Records label—were highly acclaimed on their release. Perhaps, I thought, it could be a refreshing chapter in our lives. I should have known better—with the Stones, you grow to expect the unexpected.

Our sessions for the album that became *Exile on Main Street*—in our mobile studio at Keith's house—marked a very tense period to be around the Stones, and were eventually immensely damaging to the band and everyone close to us. Practically everyone dabbled in drugs at that time, including Keith and Anita, Mick Jagger and Mick Taylor, producer Jimmy Miller, session musician Bobby Keys, and Keith's friend Gram Parsons. Gram and Keith's photographer friend Michael Cooper both died from drug overdoses in 1973. I was particularly saddened to discover much later that Astrid had been experimenting with drugs and this became a major factor in our split ten years later. The only people who seemed to be regularly straight were Charlie, Ian Stewart, our road manager, keyboard player Nicky Hopkins—and me. Apart from some pill-popping and occasionally smoking joints back in the mid-sixties, I'd always steered clear of drugs because I'd seen their effect on too many people around us. Drugs took people to a place I didn't want to go; I preferred reality.

My lack of interest in drugs had been a recurring problem in the Stones. Mick, Keith and Andrew Oldham particularly mocked my straightness and there were many attempts through the years to turn me on.* But with me it's all or nothing. I was much more acutely aware of the dangers than many of my friends were, but my feeling of rootlessness while living in France must have prompted

---

* For example, in Los Angeles on October 24, 1969—during a US tour—they threw a party at the house of Stephen Stills of Crosby, Stills, Nash and Young to celebrate my thirty-third birthday. Someone had made a hash cake and Mick, Keith and Mick Taylor, who were staying there, looked on smilingly as they saw me innocently eating. I became stoned very quickly, felt awful and panicky, and spent a lot of time in the bathroom splashing my face trying to get straight before leaving the party early. Ian Stewart drove Astrid and me back through the hills at great speed; sitting in the back, I felt claustrophobic and panicky and wanted to jump out. This disturbing experience made me even more determined not to experiment with drugs.

my immersion in smoking marijuana. Astrid, whose memory of the period is crystal clear, recalls: "Bill had given up smoking cigarettes and we were told the police would never bust our houses as they had Stones homes in England. It was like pressing a button—I've never seen anybody smoke hash like him—he would have a joint before his morning cup of tea. And quickly he was chain-smoking pot, because Bill has a very addictive personality. He got completely into it, but his life changed from being very organized, predictable and rigid into a slide. If he'd had one or two joints a day it might have been a different story, but this was *all the time!* The change was extreme and after a year of substituting pot for cigarettes he realized he'd become too laid back and unproductive. He went and buried his remaining hash in the garden and said: 'That's it!' It was amazing he could give up just like that—but that's Bill. He said he would never try cocaine or stronger drugs because if he liked them he would do that all the time too."

During that pot-smoking year of 1972, Mick and I were interviewed in July in New York by Dick Cavett for his TV chat show. We had a great exchange and he repeatedly asked me if I smoked. Sitting with a joint in my hand, which was captured by the camera, I said no. "But you *are* holding a cigarette," said Cavett. I was able to deny this truthfully, despite his persistence. I returned to cigarettes after about a year; at the time of writing, I intend to stop—and fail about thirty times a day.

"The straightest rhythm section in rock 'n' roll," they called us. Yet if Charlie Watts and I hadn't been so understanding, forgiving, conscientious and tolerant of other people's excesses, the Stones wouldn't have existed in this form for more than the band's first five years. The greatness of the front line is beyond question, but living with them hasn't been easy.

This book's story of the Stones in the sixties is redolent with drugs, but the seventies became even heavier. Immediately we entered France I found Keith impossible to relate to because of his addictions to cocaine, heroin and other narcotics. He's always been incredibly honest, and admits now that he screwed the band up for that period and beyond; it became extremely difficult to tour because of his and Mick's drug convictions. In March 1972 Keith was in such bad condition during the mixing of *Exile on Main Street* in Los Angeles that he had to be flown to Switzerland to undergo a drug cure at a clinic. And the pressure on him from the police was relentless. Around the time that *Exile on Main Street* and the "Tumblin' Dice" single were released, French police arrested a drug ring in Marseilles which led them to Keith's house. Police wanted to question us all.

And so Charlie and I, the only two then in France, appeared before a Nice judge on September 7, 1972, formally charged: suspects arrested in Marseilles alleged they had seen the Rolling Stones taking drugs in Keith's house. All five Stones were listed as suspects at ports of entry into France and other countries, but we denied everything and the judge said that until the case came to trial he would remove our names from the lists.

Feeling free, I went to London to see my son Stephen but when Astrid and I returned to Nice we were astonished to be arrested at the airport and detained for three hours. The airport immigration authorities had failed to remove my name from the suspect list. We were treated appallingly: when I wanted to visit the toilet, I was frog-marched by two policemen. I had to make a long statement, detailing every conceivable identifying mark on my body, before finally being free. Later, I formally complained and requested an apology from the authorities but this was ignored.

It often seemed to me that when there was a hazard facing the band, either by accident or design, I would be used as a guinea-pig. I was the first Stone in for questioning by a judge when the four of us met in Nice on November 2. He was hostile, and adjourned the case against us for a month. Next day, having returned to London, Mick phoned me to warn me to be prepared to leave France at very short notice, because of the judge's attitude.

We had work on our minds, anyway: on November 23 we all flew to Jamaica to record tracks for the album that would become *Goats Head Soup*. A week later we discussed with lawyers the French problem. We flew to London on December 2, meeting Rupert Loewenstein and British lawyers before flying to Paris, an airport easier to deal with than the one at Nice. While there,

Mick excused himself from the situation, going off with Bianca to see a Paris lawyer, while the rest of us went to Nice to face the music.

At the court case in Nice on December 4, which we had to attend, we all faced charges arising from the alleged use of heroin and hashish at Keith's villa. But the case against us collapsed when five witnesses for the police said they had been browbeaten into saying they had seen the Stones taking drugs at Keith's home. Despite persistent attempts in cross-examination to make them indict us, they insisted the police had made them sign false statements. We were cleared.

But even when pronounced innocent, we suffered: reports traveled the world saying the Stones were jailed in France, and when fake stories of a Stones heroin bust reached Japan and Australia, both governments blocked our entry. Australia later relented and we toured there from February 8. But we were still marked men—airports at Sydney and at Hawaii on our return journey put us through extensive body searches.

Touring the US looked out of the question; we knew we wouldn't get work permits. Then, after the Nicaraguan earthquake of December 1972, we decided to do a benefit concert. Mick favored a Los Angeles venue, since this could help our status with the US government.*

Still, the catalogue of trouble around Keith was seemingly endless. With Anita and their friend Stash, who had been busted alongside Brian Jones in the sixties, Keith was busted at his Cheyne Walk, Chelsea home on June 26, 1973. Between them they were charged with possessing cannabis, Mandrax and heroin. Keith was additionally charged with possessing a revolver and ammunition. They were bailed for four days—when, mysteriously, a fire gutted Keith's Sussex home, Redlands. Because of this, the case was adjourned. Two months later Keith was found guilty of all charges and fined a total of £275. Anita was conditionally discharged for possessing Mandrax,

---

*Our show at the Forum on January 18, 1973, raised £350,000 for earthquake victims and Mick and Bianca flew to Washington on May 8 to be presented with a Golden Key for this achievement. I thought it rather odd that the other Stones didn't get a letter or a word of thanks.

and Stash was found not guilty. Next day Keith fell asleep in the Londonderry House Hotel, Hyde Park Corner, accidentally setting fire to his room. The Stones were immediately banned from there, having used it extensively since 1969.

We were in Antwerp nearing the end of a European tour when, on October 15, 1973, Keith's French bust was heard in a Nice court. Found guilty of the use, supply and trafficking of cannabis, he received a one-year suspended sentence. On a similar charge involving heroin he was fined 5,000 francs. Keith invariably emerged from his crises with incredible luck.

Our long-running battle with authority, which had of course been a feature of our lives in the sixties, in fact continued soon after we entered France, with Shirley, Charlie's wife, being arrested at Nice airport on February 16, 1972, for allegedly hitting and swearing at customs officials. In her absence she was sentenced on June 2 to six months in jail. She appealed on August 9 and received a fifteen-day suspended sentence. That little episode was nothing when compared with what followed, a tumultuous decade between the Stones and the law.

At Aylesbury magistrates court on January 12, 1977, Keith was fined a total of £1,000 for possessing LSD and cocaine. This was serious enough, but it paled into insignificance when compared with the Toronto bust six weeks later, during our visit to the city for rehearsals.

With their eight-year-old son Marlon, Keith and Anita had, with the rest of us, checked into the Harbour Castle Hotel in Toronto on February 27. While they slept Royal Canadian Mounted Police raided their suite, discovering large quantities of heroin and cocaine. This stemmed from Anita arriving in Toronto a few days after us and being busted at customs for possessing a spoon which had traces of cocaine on it: less than a week later she was found guilty in court of possessing heroin and hashish and fined $200 on each count. At this time Ronnie Wood had a liaison with the Canadian prime minister's wife, Margaret Trudeau, diverting public attention from Keith's scandal: the press mistakenly assumed her link was with Mick. Keith went to court on March 8 to be bailed on $25,000 for cocaine possession. The quantity of drugs found on Keith was so large that police thought he might have plans to traffic; the maximum sentence for that was life in jail.

This was a disastrous period for Keith. He was in such an appalling physical state. I'll never forget going to his room with Woody to find him writhing on the floor, vomiting. We tried to give him pills but he threw them up. Woody said to me: "What can we *do?*" I said: "Well, we've obviously got to get him some heroin, haven't we?" I feared he would otherwise have died. Nobody seemed to be looking after him. And so Woody and I went out of the hotel, which was riddled with plain-clothes detectives, and scored some heroin to get him by. I've never done that for anybody before or since, but he simply had to have it at that point.

It was a scary time to be a Stone and hell for Keith. He was given a visa to enter America to take a drug cure—on condition that he returned to Canada for trial in October. He agreed and flew straight to America for detoxification and therapy treatment. An important part of Keith's cure was his introduction by fellow addict Eric Clapton to a pioneering London doctor, Meg Patterson, whose "black box" treatment transmitted an electrical signal to the brain to restore normality without cravings during withdrawal.

The long US tour of June and July 1978 started—and nearly ended without me. In St. Paul, Minnesota more than two weeks before the end of the tour, after completing a very successful show, as we were leaving the stage—running in the dark behind the equipment—I jumped to reach some fans who were hanging over the balcony, lost my balance on some power cables and fell nine feet into darkness, knocking myself unconscious.

Everybody else jumped into the waiting cars and were ready to speed away when Astrid said I hadn't come out. One car stayed behind and I was finally found, still unconscious. I was taken to the local hospital for the night. The doctor said I was very lucky—X-rays showed I had only broken a knuckle on my left hand, plus a cut head and a torn shoulder muscle. Lucky? He said I had to rest for a month—and we had another nine shows to do.

I discharged myself the next morning after discussing with the others whether or not to cancel that night's show. But we flew on to St. Louis and after physiotherapy

I played with my middle two fingers taped up—and continued that way for the rest of the tour. On the last night Keith suggested I be nominated for the purple heart. A brief and not very pleasant diversion: we had been constantly aware that at the end of the tour Keith might go to jail.

He finally appeared in court in Toronto on October 23, 1978, pleading guilty to possession of heroin (a charge of possessing it with intent to traffic was dropped). He received a one-year suspended sentence with an order that he make regular visits to a probation officer. Other conditions were that he would continue treatment for heroin addiction at the Stevens Institute in New York and that he give a benefit performance for the Canadian Institute for the Blind within six months, either alone or with a band of his choice. We all rallied once again to Keith's support and played that show in Toronto on April 22, 1979—one day before the court order expired. Opening the show for us was Woody's newly formed band, the New Barbarians, with whom Keith also played; he then went on to tour America with them, and later England.

It was Ronnie Wood's turn in February 1980 while he and Jo were holidaying on the island of St. Martin. Five grams of cocaine were found in their apartment and they were jailed for five days before being deported to America; they were never charged.

The miracle was that we got any work done but, with the perversity that marks the entire Stones story, we were quite productive. One of our most innovative and successful albums, *Some Girls,* was released on June 1, 1978, and sold over 8 million copies.

In retrospect I suppose it was hardly surprising that the only new member of the band to join us since our formation had been affected by what he saw and experienced. Mick Taylor just stood there, on stage and in the studios, like me, unanimated, and made music . . . but he was wonderful, a technically great, inspired guitarist. Like me, also, he had a non-assertive personality and grew to resent the lack of recognition of his contribution to the band generally and some songs in particular. On the plane returning to London from Jamaica on December 14, 1974, Mick's wife Rose told me he was disillusioned with the Stones, mostly because he was not encouraged to write songs—the stranglehold by Mick and Keith was too strong. I understood exactly how he felt; Rose said Mick was seriously considering joining another rock band, Free.

As we entered the studio to record the album *Black and Blue* in Munich that month, Mick quit. We thought he was possibly bluffing to demonstrate his frustrations, but we accepted the resignation, even though it left us in a quandary—we had to cut an album and tour America. Competition for the position of Stones guitarist was enormous; guitarists who came to record with us included Jeff Beck, Rory Gallagher, Wayne Perkins and Harvey Mandel. Stu and I suggested Peter Frampton, an old friend and gifted musician, and even Eric Clapton was mentioned. Among those who moved in to fill the temporary void on the *Black and Blue* album session was Ron Wood, guitarist alongside Rod Stewart in the Faces. After four months of negotiations, on April 14, 1975, Ron was confirmed our new man. He brought musical vitality and a powerful, likeable personality into our ranks. Crucially, too, Ron has always been a positive influence in soothing tensions in the band. He's able to hang out with us all in turn. Acting as a foil for both Keith and Mick, on and off stage, couldn't have been easy. He had a tough baptism two weeks after he joined when on May 1 we began a three-month American tour. During this, on July 7, Keith, driving in Fordyce, Arkansas, was charged with reckless driving and carrying a concealed weapon (a knife). He was once again cleared of charges, a week after the tour ended.

Although France was my base, I was scarcely there for the first five years of exile. We worked feverishly hard and traveled widely. Only when I had put down roots, in 1976 moving into the house I'd built above Vence, did I meet a poet, André Verdet, who introduced me to many of the impressive artists who lived in the area (sadly I missed meeting Picasso by about a month), and I derived great pleasure from stepping outside the rock world, visiting churches, the observatory, going to exhibitions, collecting prints. One day we went for tea with Marc Chagall, and for a few years I visited him regularly. My first encounters with him were amusing. He spoke little English and I little French. He was about ninety then, a legend, and he kept telling me to get my hair cut, saying it "wasn't original." He'd seen so many pictures of rock musicians, and bracketed the Stones with the rest. I enjoyed putting him right: "But we were the *first* ones in England or anywhere to ever grow long hair!" This impressed him—he demanded originality in everything: "Oh well, then you should keep it."

André decided to write a book with him and, having seen some of my photographs, suggested to Chagall that I might take pictures. It would have been an imposition to ask someone of Chagall's stature to pose for portraits, so I took a long-distance lens to his house, shooting from the other side of the room and in the garden while he spoke to André. The book, *Chagal mediterranéen*, became a three-way collaboration, and was published in 1981.

A decade in exile suggests an attitude of "dropping out," but in fact these years in France became positive for me, artistically. Blues music, our original inspiration, is particularly popular in Europe and on July 27, 1974, I drove to the Montreux Jazz and Blues Festival. Promoter Claude Nobs had called me to ask me to put together a rhythm section to join Buddy Guy, Junior Wells and Pinetop Perkins in supporting Muddy Waters, after the first set by Buddy Guy and Junior Wells. I used Dallas Taylor on drums, and my old friend Terry Taylor on rhythm guitar and myself on bass. Next day, during brief rehearsals with Muddy, I was pulled aside by Buddy and Junior who told me they didn't like their backing group and would we back them? We did the first set backing them and after the interval we all backed Muddy. There were lots of encores during this stimulating evening. Some years later, after many musician friends had praised the show and video, I acquired the audio and video tapes and put together a live album, *Drinkin' TNT 'n' Smokin' Dynamite*, which did exceptionally well for a blues album, particularly in the UK and USA. Again in 1977 Dallas and I sat in with Muddy Waters' band at the Montreux Jazz Festival. During the Stones' 1981 American tour, Mick, Keith and Woody all sat in with Muddy at Buddy Guy's club in Chicago, the Checkerboard.

Hard work has always been the basis of my life and despite the Stones' heavy schedule I stretched myself, becoming the first member of the band to make a solo album. *Monkey Grip,* released in 1974, brought together about twenty guest musicians including notable Americans Danny Kortchmar (guitar), Dr. John, Dallas Taylor, Leon Russell (keyboards) and back-up singers George McRae, his wife Gwen and the great Betty Wright. The album did well, entering the charts, before Atlantic seemed to pull away from promoting it, realizing it would clash with the imminent Stones album *It's Only Rock 'n' Roll.* My second solo stab, *Stone Alone* in 1976, attracted about forty musicians. I was rubbing shoulders with eminent artists like Van Morrison, Dr. John, Joe Walsh, Sly Stone, the Pointer Sisters (singing back-up) and the Tower of Power Horn Section. The buzz around the album was great, but again there was no supporting promotion. I'd call up the Stones office about those two albums and get replies like: "I can't deal with setting up interviews for two or three days, Bill—I'm looking for a nanny for Keith!" I didn't show my pique, but I felt it. My confidence bruised, I decided to put my solo work on hold as we embarked on another British and European tour.

It was never easy to help the decision-makers inside the Stones, and often the band lost out. Rolling Stones Records had a talent-seeking policy and in 1978 on holiday in Barbados after a seven-week tour of America I heard Eddy Grant for the first time. Excited, I phoned Mick and Keith in New York, predicted a big success for him, and said we should sign him. No, they said; they'd already signed one reggae artist, Peter Tosh, and another would be too much. Eddy's success has proved which artist we should have acquired. It was always frustrating to me to have good instincts rebuffed in that way.

The Stones were always my spiritual band but I'd never lost my love of good pop music. And looking back on our long periods of inactivity in the eighties, it was propitious that I struck out around that time with a parallel solo career. Far from feeling marooned in France, I probably saw more concerts by visiting British artists (and others) than many people who lived in England: I saw French shows by Elton John, Eric Clapton, Police, XTC, UB40, the Average White Band and Muddy Waters.

1980 was a year of bleak inactivity for the Stones. We released one album, *Emotional Rescue;* I was still suffering neck and shoulder trouble, after effects from my fall from the stage a full two years before. Mick went to South America to film *Fitzcarraldo*, a project that threatened to take so long that he aborted it. Charlie reverted to his first love, jazz, for his solo fancy, joining a group called Rocket 88, with Ian Stewart on piano. We were dispersed mentally and physically—probably a reaction to being in each other's pockets for so long. Woody was living in Los Angeles, Keith in New York. As I said at this time, there was little unity in the band when we weren't working: "It's more a coming together once, twice or three times a year—like brothers and sisters. When you grow up, you get married and move away—but it's great to see each other at Mum's at Christmas!"

With the Stones a closed shop to my songwriting I felt an urge to develop beyond rock 'n' roll. I didn't rate myself a good singer or lyricist, so at home in France at my four-track recording studio I began experimenting with electronic instruments. My thoughts turned vaguely to writing for something like a television documentary—perhaps on a subject close to me, say, Stonehenge or archaeology in Egypt, as I'd always been interested in those subjects. However, my career broadened in a direction I could never have expected—by writing a film soundtrack.

I had begun writing some light-hearted songs, South American in flavor, and after about a year of my doodling a friend said someone who was putting together a film might be interested. So I took a couple of demos over on a cassette to Jack Weiner, the producer of the film *Green Ice*. He covered himself so he could reject my offer: he didn't want disco or rock 'n' roll. When he played the tape he said the sounds were nostalgic yet fresh, just what he was seeking.

Over a period of five months I constructed the soundtrack for the movie, which starred Ryan O'Neal and Omar Sharif. I played drum machine, synthesizer, keyboards, bass, percussion and harmonica. Movie writing perfectly suited my disciplined method of working.

It was at this time that I made a vital move towards independence. During the writing of the movie score, songs started flowing freely and I decided to make my third solo album. I had no faith in Rolling Stones Records for my own product so I formed my own company, Ripple, as an umbrella for all my solo activities—and signed a record deal with A & M.

Very speedily, in July 1981, my debut album for them, called simply *Bill Wyman*, yielded a huge hit that went Top Ten in most countries. "(Si Si) Je Suis un Rock Star" was a parody of myself as a recognized musician in exile in France; to the present day this remains the biggest solo hit by a Rolling Stone. It was followed by two other top forty singles, "Come Back Suzanne" and "A New Fashion." After two decades in the shadows, people began to take an interest in my creativity.

Immediately after this, from September 25, 1981, the Stones undertook a mammoth three-month tour of America, where we performed to 2.5 million people, followed by what was then the biggest-ever European tour by any act—running for two months from May 26. By the spring of 1983, after eleven years in France, it really felt like time to go home. I missed England, and its taxation system had been relaxed enough for me to return. Astrid and I took a three-month trip around the world, visiting Los Angeles, Maui, Hawaii, Fiji, Australia and Bali, ending with a month in Japan before returning to the beauty of Suffolk. Shortly afterwards we bought a London home in Mulberry Walk, Chelsea.

Then Astrid and I split up after nearly seventeen years together. We'd never married because we never seemed to agree what was the right moment to do so . . . and Astrid is a very indecisive person. The legality of getting married, with the red tape surrounding a Swede and an Englishman living in France, was a deterrent too: we simply never bothered to deal with it.

Astrid had had an alcohol and drug problem for some years. From 1966, when we met in London, she was as firmly against dope as me, but after a year in France she began experimenting, believing as potential addicts often do that dabbling could be confined to social occasions. Within a few years she was hooked on cocaine and sampling heroin; in 1977 she had a breakdown which put her in a clinic; in 1981 she went for detoxification in America. We'd been strong partners but I found her descent impossible to take. I hated the fact that after avoiding drugs all my life, I had a partner to live with who was into it. Astrid now freely admits that her use of drugs contributed to the decline of our relationship, but adds: "Bill's infidelities in turn triggered my addictions. So it's very much half and half with us. My drugs and alcohol use made me very irrational, but there were other contributing factors." She felt I "got too busy: we gave up communicating, even though with Stephen we had developed a very close family unit."*

Our split finally came in 1983 during the making of my autobiographical video feature, *Digital Dreams*.† Astrid was still strung out on drugs, alcohol and pain-killers; the parting was combative, but now she is cured and our relationship is harmonious.‡

The seventies had been a double-edged decade for the Stones. We worked hard and achieved solvency, but neither our creativity nor the general mood (with the arrival of the punks and Glam Rock—all image and little music!) allowed us to declare it a vintage period. The whole rock 'n' roll movement went through self-examination and bands like ours, born in the sixties, had to sit it out and tolerate sneers and denigration by younger bands who described us as dinosaurs. But in 1983 the dinosaurs signed with CBS in what was then the biggest ever record deal.

As the Stones dispersed, we found ourselves regularly involved in individual projects. Charlie and I played in the all-star band assembled by Glyn Johns that raised

*Astrid had dedicated herself to her ongoing role of helping me to bring up Stephen, who went on to achieve ten O-Levels, and two A-Levels (in physics and math). He later went to Aston University, where he gained an honors degree in managerial studies; he runs the computer organization at my office and has given this book invaluable assistance.

†This featured Astrid and me, James Coburn, Stanley Unwin, and Richard O'Brien, with animation by Gerald Scarfe. It was filmed on location at my Suffolk and Chelsea homes.

‡From her vantage point alongside me, traveling on every Stones tour and going to most recording sessions from 1967, Astrid developed a razor-sharp observation of the chemistry of the Stones and she has given considerable help in this book.

money for Ronnie Laine (formerly of the Faces) and the Action Research for Multiple Sclerosis charity in America, along with Eric Clapton, Jeff Beck, Joe Cocker, Stevie Winwood, Paul Rodgers, Kenney Jones, Ray Cooper, Jimmy Page, Andy Fairweather-Low and many other excellent musicians. After two shows at London's Royal Albert Hall in September 1983 (one before the Prince and Princess of Wales), we played nine American concerts, in Dallas, San Francisco, Los Angeles and New York, where Woody joined us for two shows. These were hugely enjoyable and successful. But sadly we learned later that most of the million dollars we raised mysteriously disappeared and that ARMS failed to benefit as expected.

In 1984 the Stones seemed to go on hold again, with only one hit compilation album, *Rewind,* and a single, "Miss You." For *Rewind* I thought of putting together a one-hour video special of early footage and link pieces, also called *Rewind*—they promoted each other and were highly lucrative. But there was little intensity around the band and the Stones seemed preoccupied by family life and domesticity. Ronnie and Jo Howard had a baby boy, Tyrone, born on August 20, 1983; Mick and Jerry Hall, who had met at a New York party in 1977, had a daughter, Elizabeth Scarlett, on March 2, 1984, and a son, James, on August 28, 1985.

Rewarding solo projects included Mick recording in New York with Michael Jackson; Keith playing with Jerry Lee Lewis on American TV; my own *Willie and the Poor Boys* album in March 1985, plus a half-hour video special to promote it. The project starred Jimmy Page, Paul Rodgers, Andy Fairweather-Low, Charlie Watts, Terry Williams (Dire Straits' drummer), Kenney Jones, Chris Rea and Ringo Starr and was critically acclaimed as one of my most inventive projects. I donated all profits to Ronnie Laine and his ARMS charity. Mick and Tina Turner appeared at the Live Aid extravaganza in New York on July 13, 1985 (after the band had unanimously agreed in Paris *not* to perform!). Keith and Woody then accompanied Bob Dylan in the show's finale. Keith presented Chuck Berry with his Rock 'n' Roll Hall of Fame award on January 23, 1986, and later went on to be musical director and perform in Berry's film *Hail, Hail Rock 'n' Roll.* The next month the Stones received a Grammy lifetime achievement award from our friend Eric Clapton in London, the ceremony being beamed by satellite to the States on February 25, 1986.

These were isolated, important events, but still the Stones lacked a cohesive spirit. The rigors of two frenzied decades, plus our individual lives, splintered the band. But we were suddenly jolted back to a reminder of our roots with the death on December 12, 1985, in London of Ian Stewart.

Pianist in the band from its formation in 1962, our road manager and our best friend, Stu died, aged forty-seven, after a massive heart attack. With him went our conscience. A unique and crucial figure in our chemistry and our evolution, Stu was a natural and knowledgeable musician, guardian of our blues roots and a fierce and valued critic when we stepped out of line. It was almost impossible to contemplate the Stones without him at our side—on the road, in the studio, in hotels, at rehearsals, or driving us and our gear in our van around Britain back in our struggling early days. How could we ever forget his immortal words in hundreds of dressing-rooms as we waited to go on stage: "Come on, my little shower of shit—you're *on*!"

We were all at his funeral at Randalls Park Crematorium, Surrey, on December 20, together with Eric Clapton, Jeff Beck and Glyn Johns, and we knew that Stu's death would leave a huge gap. As Keith said to Woody at the funeral: "Who's gonna tell us off *now* when we misbehave?" And Keith meant it; we were heavily choked up. We played a memorial tribute to him at London's 100 Club on February 23, 1986, and were joined on stage by Clapton, Beck, Jack Bruce, Pete Townshend and Simon Kirk.

The eighties seemed dominated by solo projects by the Stones. When the band decided to give up collective ownership of our mobile studio, active since 1968, I took it over. I then launched AIMS—Ambition, Ideas, Motivation, Success—and together with sponsorship from Pernod we were able to give free recording facilities to fifty bands, out of 1,200 applicants in England. My purpose was to encourage young live bands in an age when producers were taking over. This project was climaxed by a charity concert at the Royal Albert Hall on February 20,

1988, featuring the five top bands plus compère Jim Davidson, the Bad News Band, the Chris Rea Band, Elvis Costello and Chrissie Hynde, and my own All-Star Band featuring me, Ronnie Wood, Phil Collins, Terence Trent D'Arby, Eddy Grant, Ray Cooper, Kenney Jones and Ian Dury. Harvey Goldsmith presented the concert and we raised almost £30,000, which we gave to the Great Ormond Street Children's Hospital. Harvey sent the check . . . and Harvey got the letter of thanks.

During 1986 Charlie also plunged into a project very dear to his heart, forming his own orchestra of over thirty top British jazz musicians. He toured with them in America, Britain and Europe and I organized the shooting of a video of the band at Fulham Town Hall.

While Mick was on his solo tour of Japan in the spring of 1988, Woody was also there touring with Bo Diddley, and he continued to tour with him through Europe during the summer. Meanwhile in America, Keith was working on his first solo album, *Talk is Cheap*.

After Mick's solo tour of Australia and Keith's solo tour of America, the Stones were inducted into the Rock 'n' Roll Hall of Fame in New York on January 18, 1989. Charlie and I didn't attend. It seemed ridiculous to me that we were being honored by the Establishment of show business so late in our careers and I'd have felt hypocritical at a formal dinner as a Stone, dressed in tuxedo and bow tie, an image we had vigorously opposed throughout our career.

Mick, Keith, Ronnie and Mick Taylor (who lives in New York) were there to receive the Stones' award—and Pete Townshend, who helped in the ceremony, seemed to have an inkling of our imminent tour when he told the guests at the Waldorf Astoria Hotel: "It won't be easy for the Stones next time around, and if it wasn't for the vast sums of money they can make they wouldn't bother at all, really. Or at least Mick wouldn't. So it's lucky for us fans that Mick has such expensive tastes. Because the Stones feel to me as if they still have a future. Guys, whatever you do, don't try to grow old gracefully. It wouldn't suit you."

Describing our impact on him in the sixties, Townshend said: "Without you, there wouldn't have been a London rhythm-and-blues scene . . . so much of the musical blood of Jimmy Reed and John Lee Hooker runs in this band, as it does from the other black artists the Stones ripped off . . . I had no idea then that so much of what I got from the Stones I was getting secondhand!" He added that the "shocking, riveting, stunning Stones" changed his life, and continued: "The Beatles were fun but the Stones made you wake up. The Beatles had screaming girls; the Stones were the first to have a screaming boy."

Replying, Mick Jagger pointed out that it was "slightly ironic that tonight you see us on our best behavior, but we're being rewarded for twenty-five years of bad behavior. And then, there's a bit of music on the side . . . but we're not quite ready to hang up the number yet." Mick and Pete paid tributes to Brian Jones's pioneering work in the Stones in the sixties, plus the contribution of Ian Stewart. Touchingly, Keith Richards told the audience: "I still feel like I'm working for him. It's his band . . ."

Often, it's not necessarily those who finally appear center stage who contribute everything to a major act. If Brian Jones was the original heart of the Stones, then Ian Stewart was the band's spine. Both were vital to our existence, at the eye of the hurricane that propelled the Stones into orbit back in the sixties. Rock 'n' roll was young and fresh but it spawned too many copyists whose sounds lacked commitment to anything except easy money. The Rolling Stones' foundation of originality stemmed primarily from Jones's and Stewart's idealism, which unfolds in this book.

In and out of the Stones, I've always kept a low profile, helped by my interests away from rock 'n' roll. I'm very lucky at any sport or game I put my hand to, with a good track record. In Chicago in 1972 Hugh Hefner taught me to play backgammon at the Playboy mansion, and I immediately beat him in two consecutive games. On tour in Spain in 1976 I beat the former Spanish table tennis champion without knowing his identity. And in recent years, after a gap of nearly thirty years, I returned to cricket—successfully, too, playing with many famous county and international players in charity and benefit games, as well as in charity matches with Eric Clapton's XI. I scored my first half century, and was particularly proud of bowling out international players John Emburey, Michael Holding and Graeme Hick in one season.

My energy level remains high: I average about five hours' sleep a night. I regard sleeping as an essential waste of time. I don't exercise, take vitamins or eat health foods, and I've smoked cigarettes since I was seventeen; I now consume about thirty a day. Eating is functional, too: breakfast is two cups of tea and two cigarettes. I don't go hunting gourmet food. But in May 1989 I did open my own restaurant in Kensington, London, and called it Sticky Fingers. This gave me the opportunity to display on the walls some of the huge collection of Stones memorabilia I had collected since the band began. 1989 was quite a year. I prepared a solo album which was shelved when the Stones swung into action; we rehearsed and finished the *Steel Wheels* album. And I got married.

I was at the Lyceum in London on February 21, 1984, where, at the *Daily Mirror* British Rock Awards, I was to present a posthumous award for Alexis Korner to his wife. Normally, I don't like glitzy showbiz events—they always seem so phoney. But Korner was a musician who was a major catalyst in the formation of the Stones, and I was delighted that his importance was being recognized at last.

I'd gone that night with Julian Temple, who had worked on the Stones' videos and later directed *Absolute Beginners*. We sat together watching bands, and the kids dancing to them. The organizers had invited them from various London clubs to ensure that the event had some youthful atmosphere. I saw two stunning girls leaving the dance floor and my heart just jumped. She took my breath away. I felt like I'd been whacked over the head with a hammer. I immediately said to Julian: "I've *got* to meet that girl, *got* to talk to her. Can you go and invite them over?"

The older girl came over and introduced herself as Nicola Smith. On inquiring, I was amazed when told they were not twins and that she was the elder by two years. "Well, you must be about twenty," I said. "No, I'm fifteen," she answered, "and Mandy's thirteen." "*What?*" I said. We just could not believe it. Mandy then joined us briefly; they were still at school but said they wanted to meet people to try to get established in modeling. As I knew one of the owners of Models One agency in London, I offered to arrange an appointment. "Give me your number and I'll give you a ring with some details."

I was totally besotted with Mandy from the moment I saw her. But I was playing it cool and, knowing her age, I wanted to be careful and particularly open from the start with her mother. Two days later I got them a meeting at the modeling agency.

They were told they were rather young and should return in a year. Over lunch, I said I was anxious to meet their mother. Two weeks later, on March 8, I drove over with flowers and chocolates; we all had a fine evening. After dinner, as I walked from the kitchen to the living room, Mandy and I met in the passage. I grabbed hold of her and gave her a big kiss. She was a woman at thirteen, and she certainly looked like the twenty-year-old I had originally believed her to have been. When I asked her mother if I could take Mandy out to dinner, I was told she had been going to clubs and pubs for a year and a half; there was no objection.

We began going out a few times a week and I took her to various restaurants and clubs like Tramp, where she was introduced to all my friends. Everyone accepted her as an adult without question.

In January 1985 the Stones started recording the *Dirty Work* album in Paris and during the six months we were there Mandy frequently flew over with my assistant Karen Kearne. All the Stones tried to warn me off— "You're asking for trouble . . . treading on dangerous ground . . . this could explode in your face." I knew *that* only too well—but there was nothing I could do. Logic told me one thing, my feelings another. Emotions always win in the end, so that was it. I was in love.

For two and a half years we were an incredibly well kept secret. However, a problem developed. I could only take her for quiet rendezvous where we would not be seen, while she naturally wanted to be with me all the time—at the more visible, glamorous nights out, too. She understandably resented the fact that I had to be seen with other girls on my arm to divert attention. I tried to reassure her that while I was serious about her, she needed some freedom too.

And so Mandy frequently went to Glasgow and twice to Marbella and met up with a boy with whom she continued a relationship while we were together. I also continued other relationships—because I was terrified of getting hurt when the inevitable break came. The tension and uncertainty of our relationship led to quite a row: this occurred on her sixteenth birthday, July 17, 1986, during a long phone conversation from my Gedding home to Mandy in Marbella. We decided to go our separate ways. And yet we got on too well to stop talking: she would call me for chats and advice about her singing and modeling career and I phoned her occasionally.

I went to Paris with a girlfriend on July 23 for a week, after which we drove down to my home in Vence. I'd been there only a short time when the story of my relationship with Mandy exploded all over the *News of the World* on August 3 and in Monday's daily papers. All hell broke loose. My phone did not stop ringing. Mandy had innocently mentioned our friendship over dinner in Marbella with a party of people who included her boyfriend, Keith, her new manager Maurice Boland and, unknown to her, a reporter. What hit the British tabloids was the inference that she had sold her story of her liaison with Bill Wyman, which was not the case. When the news erupted, scores of journalists poured into Marbella to chase Mandy and parked themselves outside my gates in Vence for weeks. I decided it was my responsibility to get her out of Spain to avoid the madness, so I arranged a quiet departure—and was immediately accused of surrounding her with the "Stones Mafia!"

My lawyer told me there was the possibility of criminal charges and I should stay in France until things cooled down. Although I'd left England over two weeks before, the papers said I'd "rushed off and hidden in the south of France" to avoid them! Everyone said the hubbub would last two or three days, but the story was still front-page news a year later.

It was a nightmare. I didn't think I'd done her any harm, whatever her age. Quite the reverse. I was deeply upset at being in the limelight like this, because I'd looked after Mandy and treated her honorably: I'd tried to encourage her to continue her education when she'd flunked out; I'd tried to help her career; I hadn't introduced her to alcohol or drugs. I simply wanted to be with her.

I stayed in France for eleven weeks before deciding to return to London to face the music. During this time I had tremendous support from my son Stephen, my assistant Karen and friends who were in France on holiday, including Tramp boss Johnny Gold and family; Mike and Angie Rutherford who lived nearby and frequently invited me for dinner along with their guests Phil Collins and their manager Tony Smith. I found them, and many others, highly supportive—but there was hardly a word from any of the Stones. Shortly after my return on September 28 I contacted the police, who said the director of public prosecutions was not really interested: "We've interviewed the mother and the daughter. They don't want to press any charges. There's nothing we can do. Thank you very much. If we need you we'll be in touch." And that was the end of that.

Or so I thought. The papers wouldn't let go, of course. Members of Parliament who wanted their names in lights were speaking out, and would not let the matter drop. Many of the gutter press libeled me, stating wild inaccuracies—like the "fact" that I offered Mandy and her family £250,000 to keep their mouths shut. The press were able to publish what they fancied with the certainty that I could not retaliate.

It was an impossible situation for Mandy and me. Many old girlfriends and my ex-wife Diane told their stories to the gutter press. True to her style, Astrid refused huge sums of money for her "revelations," and continues to do so.

My two-year split from Mandy coincided with the biggest watershed in the history of the Rolling Stones. We'd survived all the years of fame and financial crises, management troubles, drug busts and internal battles, but nothing compared with the vicious confrontation between Mick and Keith. That trouble stemmed from their individual pride and their solo work. Keith sniped at Mick for not putting the band first and for assembling a band of "Stones clones" to tour Japan and Australia. Mick attacked Keith over his personal problems that had contributed so heavily to putting the band on the edge of disintegration. It was heartbreaking to watch two guys who were basically so close, like brothers, degrading themselves in public, dragging the band down with them.

I was pessimistic, despondent and bored at the wrangling that affected the lives, careers and incomes of Charlie, Ronnie and me. Unlike people who had watched us from the sidelines for many years, I thought it was really the end for the band—and what a terrible way to go. But I was busy writing songs for my new solo album and planning the opening of my restaurant. I was also finalizing work on a book on the work of photographer Michael Cooper, published during our American tour; and heavily involved in completing *this* book.

Astrid, who had always said the Stones would re-unite, was proved right. With the uncanny momentum that has ensured our survival, everything fell into place with lightning speed. Mick and Keith patched up their differences and agreed on the big issue: "This band is bigger than both of us." By an uncanny coincidence, the Stones were flickering back into action just as Mandy and I were resolving our future.

On March 8, 1989, the night before I flew to Barbados, Mandy visited me at my Fulham flat. We'd been in touch and had spent occasional evenings together for a year or so, and I told her I'd like to have another attempt at our relationship. I was delighted to learn that she felt exactly the same. We had both been too proud, shy or reserved to admit it to each other. As I was flying away next day, we decided to think it over for a while. After I reached Barbados, Mandy and I spoke by phone several times, believing we both needed to make a firm decision about the future. In a conversation on March 26, I said simply: "Well, how do you feel about getting back together?" She answered: "I would like a more serious situation. I don't want to be just mates, girlfriend–boyfriend, with an open relationship. I'd prefer more of a commitment by both of us. Why don't we get engaged?" I agreed instantly. A couple of days later, when Mandy phoned to say she'd seen a ring she liked, we decided that if we were going to get engaged, we might as well get married! "Let's do it in the spring of 1990," I said, "after I've done the Stones' American tour." "Why wait?" Mandy said. "Let's do it *before* the tour." We decided to get married in early June.

Mandy was almost nineteen by the time our plans to marry were announced at the end of March 1989; I was in Antigua while Mandy, in London, spoke happily to reporters about our excitement and happiness. The newspapers had a field day with headlines like "Old Bill and Me," "Why I'm Going to Marry My Randy Stone" and "I'm Glad Mandy's Rolling Me Down the Aisle!" Absolutely elated, I said: "The time is right to marry again—and Mandy is the perfect girl."

One aspect of all the media madness irritated me: despite the fact that we'd given them the hottest love story in years, some writers still wouldn't stop taunting us. Some of my old girlfriends talked to the *Sun* in a feature headlined "The Wonder of Wyman . . . by beauties he charmed," which was predictable, while the *Daily Mail* enlisted the aid of a psychologist to attempt to analyze the attraction between "the ageing pop star and his child lover." Insisting that the thirty-three-year age gap didn't matter, Mandy spoke out: "I don't think about it. I love him and that is all that matters. Bill has never really acted his age anyway!" The worst onslaught came from the *Daily Mirror,* where on March 31 Christina Appleyard wrote sourly about Mandy's "clingfilm tight dresses, endless legs and long blonde hair." Appleyard, the paper's woman's editor, had the nerve to call me geriatric, and declared that I was old enough to know better even if Mandy wasn't. She even had the audacity to imply that we were timing our wedding to coincide with massive publicity for the Stones' reunion tour! How absurd.

With a pack of journalists flying in from England the band was concerned at the possible disruption to the sessions and insisted that I should fly to Antigua to fend them off with interviews and photo sessions. I decided to give a series of interviews at the Coconut Grove restaurant in Antigua so that the subject could be closed and the band could continue working.

I explained how, quite simply, the power of love had changed my life, how the suddenness of my decision was alien to me as an organized person who liked everything planned: "I've got bloody goose-pimples, like a kid with a new toy . . . it's like Christmas and I can't wait to see her again." Laying my feelings bare, I also admitted that in dating Mandy I'd defied my conscience, which had been overtaken by my emotions. It was "like finding religion; if it happens once or twice in your life, you're lucky." Summing up my views of Mandy, I declared: "She has every quality I admire, style, beauty and intelligence. She loves to travel, and loves to be at home. She loves to sit and read. She is just so easy to get on with. She loves nature and animals, as I do; she loves kids; she is just a really, really nice girl." I pointed out that Picasso was seventy-five when he married a thirty-five-year-old: "That marriage lasted and there's no reason why ours shouldn't be the same," I added.

Falling in love and planning a wedding was heady enough; I was working abroad and Mandy threw herself into the organization of the wedding with gusto. But there was a shock awaiting me at Gatwick airport on May 4. I was aware that Mandy was suffering from multiple allergy problems but was distressed to find her frighteningly underweight. She reassured me that, being under medical treatment, she would be fine for the wedding. There was no indication then of the extent of the problem, which continues to the present day and has caused yet more stress to our marriage.

It was coincidence that another major event for me should occur with the wedding imminent. Five days after my return, Sticky Fingers opened. A great turnout of friends gave the restaurant launch party a terrific atmosphere. They included Ronnie and Jo Wood, Emma ("Dynasty") Samms, race ace James Hunt, Patti Boulaye, Anita Pallenberg, Jim Davidson, Barbara Bach, Michael Winner and Jenny Seagrove, John Keeble of Spandau Ballet, boxer Gary Mason, "Bungalow" Bill Wiggins, Tim Rice and Elaine Paige, Steve Winwood, Kenny Lynch and Queen's John Deacon.

By now, the press was breathless with anticipation of the marriage and Mandy and I were all over the media next day. The mood was now slowly but surely changing in our favor as editors sensed that "Mandy and Bill" was an interesting story; and that Bill had finally "done the right thing." "An Old Stone's Bride and Joy" said *Today* newspaper on May 10, reporting that we had stepped out with our wedding plans the previous night at the restaurant launch. Here, I was described as "the wrinkly Lothario and sometime bass player with the Rolling Stones" —comical, in view of the album we had just cut and the slog that lay ahead on the band's American tour. Mandy didn't escape the jokes, either: she was called my "altar ego" as she revealed that couturier Louise Hamlin-Wright would design her wedding dress and that the royal jewelers Asprey would provide our rings.

We had had less than a month in which to plan the wedding. A full church wedding was not possible because I was divorced, so we secretly arranged a register-office wedding on Charlie Watts's and my brother Paul's birthday, June 2, at Bury St. Edmunds, close to Gedding Hall. We really wanted a peaceful ceremony away from the glare of publicity that had always surrounded us, so we went down to Gedding the night before and early next morning we were married quietly, with only Stephen and Mandy's sister Nicola as witnesses. We then had a wedding breakfast at the Crown Hotel, Bury St. Edmunds, where we were joined by Mandy's mother Patsy and my brother Paul and his wife, over from New York. Although invited, my parents declined to attend; they were incensed at not being at the actual wedding.

But the *Sun* newspaper realized that the church booked for June 5 could only be a blessing, since I was divorced; they correctly deduced that we would have to be formally married first in a register office and checked all the ones within a large radius of my home. When we stepped out after the ceremony, their photographer got pictures that appeared on the front page next day. We were stunned that they had discovered us. As a kind of compensation, they later sent us an album of all the photos taken—our only wedding photos. Full marks for enterprise! That afternoon we returned to London and appeared on the Terry Wogan show. This had been booked for a month and Terry was elated to find that we had been secretly married that day.

The church blessing followed by the reception on June 5 went off beautifully. Stephen was my best man and Mandy was given away by her uncle at St. John's Anglican church, near Hyde Park. Mandy looked stunning in her satin gown of white with touches of peppermint green

and pink, with full headdress and train, while I wore a
pearl-gray suit made by Tommy Nutter. Father Thaddeus
Birchard, who put us at our ease and conducted the
service with a wonderful touch, told us he had consulted
our star signs. To Mandy, a Cancerian, he said: "A change
of domestic circumstances will be in your best interests."
And to me, a Scorpio, he said: "You will be happier
when a loved one agrees to an exciting idea."

Keith and Patti, Mick and Jerry, Charlie and Shirley
and Ronnie and Jo all came to the party for 400 guests
that afternoon at the Grosvenor House Hotel. Andy
Fairweather-Low, Gary Brooker and Georgie Fame provided great music. We had some fabulous gifts, but the
one that everyone loved came from Spike Milligan, a
friend of many years. He presented me with a walking
frame: "To help Bill get through the honeymoon!" We
had earlier planned to spend our honeymoon in Turkey,
where Atlantic Records president Ahmet Ertegun had
generously offered us the use of his house and boat.
Somehow the press got on to this and started camping
out at London airport awaiting our departure. So after
hiding for three days we changed our plans, reluctantly,
and instead drove to our house in the south of France for
a honeymoon that lasted five weeks.

On July 8 Mandy returned to England and next day I
flew to New York to prepare for the marathon American
tour. Mandy and I had planned that she would frequently
visit me on tour, but her health deteriorated and caused a
painful separation of five and a half months that lasted
right through to Christmas. Again the press had a field
day, now suggesting the marriage was on the rocks.

We organized the running of the tour and rehearsed
until we opened in Philadelphia on August 31. In four
months we performed wonderful, sold-out shows, high-
lighted by four massive concerts at Los Angeles Coliseum
(78,000 a show), and six others at New York's Shea
Stadium (67,000 a show). It was great to have our friend
Eric Clapton sit in with us for "Little Red Rooster" on
several occasions.

The American tour was a vindication of the Stones,
and of rock 'n' roll as an enduring art. And we killed the
idea that guys heading for fifty were past producing worthwhile music in this idiom. As for me, on October 24, 1989,

I celebrated my fifty-third birthday feeling great. My assistant Karen organized a "secret" party and as well as all the tour people, my parents and Stephen flew in to New York. The band gave me a pool table and shipped it back to London.

We ended the eighties stunningly, with a degree of band harmony, energy and musical strength stronger than any of us would have dared to predict. Amid all the cynicism about our age, and gibes about "the wrinklies of rock," one important factor could not be overlooked: sixties acts seem built to last. Exactly what it took to be a Rolling Stone in that memorable decade is the theme of this book.

2

Roots and Routes

Could anything prepare anyone for a life as a Rolling
Stone? For twenty-eight years, we've been pilloried and
praised, faced anger and adoration, earned the respect of
our fellow musicians—but always, despite our success,
we've been forced outside the Establishment. "Subver-
sive," "decadent," "dirty," "the Great Unwashed" and a
"bad influence on the young" were taunts we learned to
live with, and shrug away. As we entered the gladiatorial
arena in the sixties it was difficult to persuade our critics
that we all had traditional family backgrounds, and had
grown up amid much the same childhood traumas as
those who cast us as inhuman and insensitive.

Rock 'n' roll is not merely a sound: it's an attitude.
From Elvis Presley and Buddy Holly to the Beatles and
Elton John, fans expect powerful personalities that match
their music. The most successful artists have been the
ones who drew strength from their environments: for
Presley, the influences of the great Mississippi blues men;
for the Beatles, the salty flavor of Liverpool. The Stones,
too, are made up of powerful personalities with tangible
and strong roots.

The great strength of the Stones is that we combine a
clean directness about our sources of music with five
complicated personalities. Blues music was our trump
card: in Britain in the early sixties few groups wanted to
take that minority music as seriously as we did. And
the almost palpable chemistry between these guys from the
south of England helped form a perfect response to the
bland sounds that then stifled British pop.

In the sixties, as now, the Stones were based on an
outlook and a commitment. Passionate, cynical, ruthless,
sensitive, this band battled through hatred and ridicule to
reach the huge audience we knew was waiting. Today, as

yesterday, we're utterly different characters coalescing into unity on stage and in the studio. We've been to hell and returned because we love the *entity* of the Stones— even more than we love each other. How did we survive a quarter of a century on this helter-skelter path? Our backgrounds provide the best clues. In the beginning, we were all pretty spiky kids.

My childhood was scarred by poverty, which I was able to convert into a strength, and by the lack of a good education, which I earned but was denied me. The bumps of childhood taught me that the best way to survive is through optimism and cheerfulness. I learned the positive strengths of self-discipline—and humor, absolutely essential in the raw framework of my growing up. As the eldest of six children I bore the brunt of Father's frustration as his pay vanished every winter. Food was scarce, the house was freezing and there were no luxuries whatsoever.

For our weekly bath my mother boiled water in the copper and in pots and pans. I took the large zinc bath down from the back-garden wall and placed it in the kitchen, where we filled it with water and, starting with the youngest, we bathed in turn, washing our hair with a large slab of soap. I naturally ended up in filthy water, emerging almost dirtier than when I got in, attempting to dry off with a wet, five-times-used towel that hung on the back of the door.

We shared one toothbrush between the whole family and we all suffered bad teeth. Toothpaste was expensive, so we used salt. New clothes were rare—we handed down everything possible to the next brother or sister. We each wore one pair of socks a week; by the time we changed, on Sundays, they almost *stood* beside our beds at night!

Our street was wild, one of the roughest in southeast London. Everyone was violent, and some were really wicked; the gangs in our street were legendary.

Once my sister Anne got up in the middle of the night and looked out of the window to see two guys a couple of doors away breaking into a safe they had obviously stolen. There were crooks all around us, but our parents brought us up to be honest and respectable citizens. We weren't a particularly religious family, but were expected to "do the right thing." With my brothers and sisters I went every week to the Sunday School at the Tabernacle Church in Maple Road, Penge, where I joined the Wolf Cubs.

My father was out of work a lot, but he didn't go around stealing. My parents brought us up with a strong moral code, and in the criminal environment of our district, that was an achievement. I'm sure that background of stability has had a big effect on my level-headedness during my time in the Rolling Stones.

Without doubt, my father's treatment of me was traceable to his own austere background and to the insecurity and tough times of raising a family in wartime. The second of ten children, William Perks was born on January 16, 1914, at 18 Miall Road, Lower Sydenham, a three-bedroom council house with gas lighting and a toilet in the back garden. It was a typical working-class family of the time. The gas-works were at the bottom of the road, fifty yards away; it was here that his father and most of the menfolk of the area worked. Hearing stories of my father's childhood was like being told a Charles Dickens story—and often it seemed as unbelievable.

His father, Alfred Henry Perks (known as Harry), was born in 1882—a small, stocky laborer, as hard as nails, with a short, bristling moustache. Keen on sport, he befriended Edgar Beard, the south of England barefist boxing champion. Conscripted into the army during World War I, Harry became a machine-gunner. He lost his right eye at Salonika, Greece in 1918 and returned to military hospital in England, to be discharged that year with an empty eye socket and a small pension for his efforts. He began to breed pigeons in his garden, racing them and winning many prizes; the house was adorned with paintings of his famous winners. All his earnings went on this hobby.

Although the children were sometimes given pigeon eggs for breakfast or tea, my grandfather was a tyrant at home, and they suffered. He was a great admirer of music-hall stars, and after his tea, on Saturday evenings in the gas-lit kitchen, with his beer and cigarettes, he would demand that the children take it in turns to dress up. They stood on the kitchen table and sang songs, imitating the likes of Harry Champion, Marie Lloyd and George Robey. As soon as they had completed their acts, accompanied by laughter, cheers or boos, they were whisked upstairs to bed, often with a slap around the legs with his belt.

Father's mother, Alice Roberts, the sixth of seven children, was born on Christmas Day 1890 at Porthcawe Road, Lower Sydenham. She spent most of her childhood in an orphanage in Anerley, south London. A hard, thin, pinched woman, she chain-smoked throughout her life and died in 1977 at the age of eighty-seven. Her sister Kate emigrated to Perth, Australia in 1924; I visited her there on Rolling Stones tours in 1965, 1966 and 1973.

Dad's childhood was tough: at Christmas the kids would hang up their stockings, only to find each one filled with a beer bottle, with maybe a nut or apple at the bottom, but never a gift. His father and mother ruled the children with iron hands. Dad was often beaten with his father's belt for scuffing his shoes or for being a few minutes late getting home. Attending Haseltine School, Lower Sydenham from the age of four, he became good at arithmetic and sport. He played cricket and football for the school team. He remembers being made to walk miles with a wheelbarrow before school, delivering my grandfather's wicker baskets of pigeons to various railway stations in London— and then getting the cane for being late for school. Dad left school at the age of fourteen and became an apprentice bricklayer, remaining in the trade all his working life. As a teenager he taught himself piano, and later bought himself a piano-accordion. He became very adept at both instruments and was much sought after for parties.

In January 1935 William Perks celebrated his twenty-first birthday by going with his mate to the Penge Empire to see the music hall. They sat next to two girls and in the interval got talking. One was Kathleen May Jeffery, aged seventeen, known to her family and friends as Molly. At the end of the show the boys asked if they could see the girls home. Undecided about which girl to take, they tossed a coin. William called tails, and took Molly home. My parents' courtship began.

Molly, the fourth of six children, was born on September 2, 1917, and lived at 36 Blenheim Road, Penge. Her father, Herbert Henry Jeffery, a rather grumpy little man, had, in his youth, been very clever. He would later remember riding by horse between Penge and Beckenham, which was then all fields. But in 1917, at the age of thirty-six, he was disabled in an accident at work. After remaining in a coma for twenty-eight days he partially recovered, but he had to be retaught everything, and he never returned to his former self. Eventually he worked as a stove and kitchen-range fitter.

Molly's mother, Florence French, one of five children, lived in Beckenham and attended school in Penge. Later her family moved to Wells Park Road, Upper Sydenham, next door to the renowned cricketer, W. G. Grace. She went into service after leaving school. A very intelligent woman, she spent all her time reading, and she could hold her own on a multitude of subjects. When my mother left school in 1932, aged fourteen, she too went into service.

In mid-1935, some six months after their first meeting, William and Molly went on a day's outing to Margate and there they became engaged. They married at Christ Church, Penge on Christmas Day, moving into a tiny flat in Forest Hill. Dad was twenty-one, Mum eighteen. From Burts department store in Peckham they bought furniture for the entire flat for under £70. Four months later they moved to 38 Miall Road, Lower Sydenham, a terraced house with a small front garden and hedge, gas lighting, no bathroom or hot water and a toilet in the back garden.

I was born at Lewisham Hospital at 11:25 p.m. on October 24, 1936, and named William George, after my father. I was in excellent company—it was a period when many rock legends were entering the world. A year earlier, Elvis Presley, Buddy Holly and Jerry Lee Lewis had been born; in 1936 itself Roy Orbison and Bobby Darin; 1937 brought us singer Sam Cooke; in 1938 Eddie Cochran, Duane Eddy and Tina Turner were born—quite a roll-call of names who would be my future influences. My grandmother picked me up when I was a fortnight old, and announced seriously to my mother: "This child is going to be world-famous."

I was apparently a child who cried a lot; neighbors in our street grumbled so much that my parents walked me round the area in a pram until I'd gone to sleep.

Two years later a baby brother arrived, on October 15, 1938—Brian John, always known as John; he was my mother's favorite. He was followed on December 11, 1939, by Anne Rosemarie.

In April 1940 my mother and we three children were evacuated to the safety of Pembrokeshire, Wales. After a first wondrous train journey we arrived to a lovely, quiet countryside. But mother was not happy there and we returned to London after only a few weeks. On the way to the railway station, Mother gave us our very first bananas. Hungry, we ate them quickly—including the skins!—and were all horribly sick. But we simply didn't know when to stop!

Back home in Sydenham, we returned to a normal life. Occasionally I would go on the 75 bus from Sydenham to Penge to visit my mother's mother, Florrie Jeffery, staying there for short periods to ease the strain on mother, who was having problems coping with three small children. My grandmother was very affectionate and I loved her dearly. She taught me the basics of reading and writing, my times tables and how to recite the alphabet backwards. It was just a simple rhyme—ZYX—W—V, UTS and RQP, ONM and LKJ, IHGF—EDCBA. When I started at infants school, aged three and a half, the teacher asked if anyone knew the alphabet. I replied that I knew it backwards, which seemed to stun her. I casually recited it to the class and sat back down again, impressing everyone. My grandmother's tuition provided my first moment of glory.

Some mornings in Sydenham I would help the milkman with his deliveries in our street and he'd give me a few coins. But this little earner ended abruptly after my brother John, almost two, fell in front of the three-wheel cart. The front wheel ran over his arm, breaking it, and that marked the end of my help for the milkman.

Among my vivid childhood memories is also the day I accidentally swallowed a torch bulb. Mother rushed me to the South London's Children's Hospital around the corner where I was persuaded to eat a sandwich of bread with wads of cotton wool between the slices. The sensation of trying to bite into it, pulling it apart with my teeth, chewing it then swallowing it, live on with me today—I've had a revulsion for touching cotton wool ever since!

The Battle of Britain began in August and continued

until the end of October. I vividly remember everyone standing in the street, looking up to a sky completely filled with formations of German bombers. Among them were the white trails of our fighter planes. Everyone was cheering—it was great to be British.

I began my romantic experiences at the tender age of four, falling "in love" with Mary Tappington, the girl next door. We played under the bushes in her front garden and exchanged kisses, with our mothers looking on.

Some nights at my grandmother's house we all slept in the air-raid shelter in the back garden, where I shared a big mattress with my three aunts, Kath (15), Dolly (13) and Bessie (11). When we went to bed, I would innocently go exploring under the sheets and play, fascinated by the strange but pleasant smells and the body hair I discovered. My aunts would just giggle, make jokes and humor me during these bedtime games.

For a few months, Dad's two youngest sisters, Dolly and Bessie, would take me each Saturday morning on the tram, a wonderfully wild, windy, noisy contraption with wooden seats, from Catford to Honor Oak Park, where I took piano lessons from a Miss Oppenheimer for a shilling a lesson.

By this time I had acquired a bicycle. I had been running errands and doing odd jobs for months, giving the local shopkeeper everything, which he marked down in a savings book. One day I took my usual few coins down to the shop. To my astonishment the shopkeeper informed me with a wide smile that I'd saved £3 10s. and the bike was mine. I proudly pushed the tiny two-wheeler home, not knowing how to ride it. My mother accused me of stealing it and promptly beat me, insisting I return it to the shop. There the man explained the savings scheme to my mother. Drying my tears, I kept my bike.

In June, as Germany invaded Russia, Father was sent to Nottingham to work on building airfield hangars. We were evacuated with Mother 150 miles north to join him, moving into temporary accommodation in Sherwood Street, Mansfield Woodhouse. Playing in the communal back yard with all the other kids, we were teased about our Cockney accents. We were always asking for bread and buppy (butter) and so we were promptly nicknamed "The Buppy Kids."

After the summer holidays, in September, I started school there. I had to walk a good mile with my schoolmates across the edge of town, through country lanes that bypassed fields and a farm with animals. This was all very exciting and new to me. Shortly after that we settled into our own house across the yard, at 122 Coke Street, where I celebrated my fifth birthday.

The British offensive was launched in the Western Desert in November and on December 7, 1941, the Japanese Air Force attacked Pearl Harbor, destroying most of the American Pacific fleet. The next day Britain and America declared war on Japan. On December 18 Dad passed a military medical examination in Mansfield, and was on his way into the army.

1942 began with huge snowfalls in Nottingham. People dug passageways through deep drifts. Near the station there was a large waste area. Everybody took sledges and made tremendously long slides on which both children and adults played.

By February, when the snows had cleared, Singapore had fallen to the Japanese; but young William Perks had bigger problems. I was going through a bad time at school, where the teacher ridiculed my Cockney accent and urged me to talk in the local dialect—hitting me when I wouldn't. I did what any five-year-old would do and often played truant with friends, hiding away in an old disused church, making bonfires to keep warm.

I have wonderful, magical memories of that long walk to and from school during the late spring and early summer, the expeditions into lanes and fields nearby, finding frogs, lizards and birds' nests. Once we were playing around a disused mining area, where water had settled into a thick black swamp. My sister Anne, not yet three, stepped into it and couldn't escape. We finally dragged her free, leaving her shoe to vanish into the murky depths. We made her hop home, crying.

Yet even in rural Nottinghamshire the war was never far away. I was woken up one night in summer by the sound of a plane crashing nearby. The whole room lit up with an eerie red glow.

All this came to an end in August 1942. Because of my unhappiness at school, it was arranged that I should return to London to live with my grandmother Jeffery at her home in Penge. Gran, then fifty-two, and Grandad lived there together with Nobby Everett (a lodger and family friend) and Aunt Dorothy, Mum's younger sister.

It was a cosy home for a five-year-old. Gran grew a few vegetables like runner beans, peas, lettuce and mint and also grew her favorite flowers, sweet peas and pansies. I helped her in the small garden. There were two bedrooms, a kitchen and a scullery. The toilet was outside in the garden, and everyone used chamber pots under the beds. The place was gas-lit, and the only heating came from the kitchen fire and stoves. An air-raid shelter in the garden was shared by several families.

Grandad, who was sixty-one, repaired boots and shoes for the neighbors. He was also an expert at slaughtering chickens, ducks and rabbits. I sat fascinated as he brought them clucking or quacking into the scullery, and then wrung their necks. I helped him put them in hot water and then pluck them, before cutting them open and gutting them. Once he opened up a chicken and took out a whole string of eggs, some almost full-size, some like tiny peas. Right up until I was about sixteen, chicken or duck was a special treat, kept for Christmas dinner. A particular feature of those years for the British kids was sitting outside a pub with a lemonade while the adults went in. My Grandad and Nobby spent most evenings in the Lord Palmerston in Penge, playing darts and dominoes while I waited, with a lemonade and an arrowroot biscuit with the other kids.

My second sister, Judith Cecelia Grace, was born in Mansfield Woodhouse on October 20, 1942—John's and my birthdays were also only a few days' away from Dad's. A few days after her birth, the German and Italian armies were defeated at El Alamein. During November, Dad was called up. He reported to Matlock Bath, Derbyshire for his six weeks' basic training. While there, he carved me a wooden plane, which he sent to me at Gran's house for my Christmas present. At this time the Number One record in the USA was Bing Crosby's "White Christmas," which was to become the biggest-selling single record of all time.

As 1943 arrived and the remnants of the German army surrendered at Stalingrad, we were taught fire- and air-raid drills at Melvin Infants School. The importance of the basics of safety came home with alarming speed: the air-raid sirens went one lunchtime as my friend Derek Stuttley and I got to the top of our road. A German fighter-bomber roared towards us between the roof-tops, machine-gunning the length of the road. We ran down between the houses and the small coping walls as it zoomed overhead. Derek went on to his house further down while I rushed into Gran's upstairs flat where she was waiting for me. She hurried me down the back staircase towards the air-raid shelter in the garden—but the plane returned before we could get there, and through the skylight window we saw it tearing past, very low. We stood quaking until it had gone and then raced to the safety of the shelter. It was petrifying—but naturally, the kids turned it into an adventure. After the all-clear we went up and down the street collecting bullets, digging them out of the walls. Later that day we heard that it was one of the German planes that had bombed and machine-gunned a girls' school in nearby Lewisham, killing twenty-three children and four teachers.

Soon Mum and the other kids returned to live in Miall Road, Sydenham where I rejoined them. Dad had been posted near Chiswick, west London, where he passed a short driving course before being posted by the Royal Electrical Mechanical Engineers to Norwich. My first indirect exposure to popular music came around this time, when I was six. While visiting my grandfather I was given the job of taking some accumulator batteries to a shop for recharging, and then on my return to the house I became aware of radio. I was fascinated to see my aunts grouped around it, listening and singing along to all the songs, swooning over dance bands and singers. At this time trumpeter Harry James and the Glenn Miller band were among the big names in America and Frank Sinatra was just emerging as a solo singer.

In April 1943 we moved into a first-floor flat at 32 Mosslea Road, Penge. Three families shared the house and the air-raid shelter in the garden. John and I walked daily to Melvin School a mile away. All the kids were enthusiastically collecting and swapping pieces of shrapnel that we would find all over the streets after air raids. We were issued Mickey Mouse gas masks and shown propaganda films. One I remember particularly was about anti-personnel weapons the German planes were dropping: something called a "Butterfly Bomb." The film showed a little boy in his garden finding one, stooping down to pick it up, and "presto" . . .

One weekend my father took me to his barracks where I met all his soldier friends; they showed me their bunks and rifles, and how they were loaded and used. We went to Maidenhead and visited a friend of his who lived in a large house on the river. The family invited me to stay for the weekend; there were three children who all slept in one big bed—and I joined them. I snuggled up to the eldest, a girl aged ten, and we kissed and cuddled until we fell peacefully to sleep. I was six years old—and briefly in love.

Summer was coming in every way—the Allies won the final victory over the U-boats in the Atlantic, and the German and Italian armies surrendered in Tunisia. My father, now stationed at Winchester as a vehicle mechanic, once returned home on leave with a dead pheasant. We had never seen one before, and were fascinated by its beautiful colors. We helped pluck it ready for the oven, and kept all the best feathers.

The reality of a tough life for any kid in Anerley and Penge was rammed home to me when at age seven I began junior school at Oakfield Road. The classes were huge, with forty or fifty pupils in each, many of them spoiling for a fight—any fight. During playtime on my first day I was confronted in the toilets by a big boy named Jimmy Pearce, who asked me if I wanted to get bashed up. Small for my age, I was scared and didn't want to fight—but he continued to threaten me. Suddenly, in panic, I swung out, hitting him on the nose by sheer luck. Bleeding heavily he rushed out of the toilet, crying. After school he was waiting for me. I expected a real fight but instead we became friends. He assured me that if I had any trouble from anyone he would defend me. By coincidence we later served together in Germany in the Royal Air Force.

Yet although I made friends, school days at Oakfield Road were marked by horrible memories that will never leave me: dental treatments at the school clinic, which consisted of pulling out teeth or of drilling and filling them, neither with anaesthetic; treatment against scabies, which involved stripping naked and being immersed in a bath of sticky liquid. After leaving the bath we were not allowed to dry off but were made to put our clothes on and return to class like that. Then there were the recurring attacks of fleas. Every few days Mother sat the kids down at the kitchen table, with a newspaper in front of each, and combed out our hair with a flea-comb.

But it is the sounds of wartime that live on in my mind. During the frequent air raids, trucks with pom-pom guns went up and down the roads, firing shells at German planes. There were floating barrage balloons in every park and wasteland area. One day our milkman, making his deliveries during an air raid, walked into an explosion and was blown up a flight of stairs, only to walk down again, completely unharmed. I remember one night raid when we had no time to get to the shelter. Mum threw herself over us children, all sleeping in one bed, as she heard the bombs fall. I suddenly realized that she really cared for us.

In early June 1944, when Rome had been captured and the Allies had landed in Normandy, Germany began its flying-bomb (V1 rocket) attacks on London. A neighbor, Mr. Wheeler, took me out into the garden and showed me a flying bomb going over, with flames pouring from its back. Within a few weeks, we had our worst experience. We had gone to the shelter one day as the sirens sounded yet again. Mum had made sandwiches and drinks and we settled down in the damp, musty shelter to await the arrival of the flying bombs. We sat silently listening to the menacing drone, praying that they would pass overhead. The noise suddenly stopped right above us. The few seconds of silence seemed to last forever. Then a tremendous explosion made the ground shake. Dust and dirt, leaves and tree branches, were blown into the shelter. When the all-clear sounded we reappeared to a very different back-garden, with bushes and trees smashed, debris everywhere. Looking back at our house, we saw our huge French windows lying in the garden. The flying bomb had glided down two streets away, flattening about twenty houses. Inside every piece of furniture we had had been flung to the walls nearest the explosion.

My father was given five days' enemy-action leave and came home to arrange for mother and John, Anne and Judy, to be evacuated temporarily to Mansfield Woodhouse. I returned to my grandparents in Blenheim Road, Penge.

Shortly after this, when a flying bomb fell on Laurel Grove, just around the corner, I went to look with other kids, and found both sides of the street flattened. We rummaged through the rubble, picking up toys and books until we were chased off by air-raid personnel. It was only the next day at school that the harsh truth hit us: two girls in our class had been killed by that bomb.

It was a period when history was being made and a generation of kids had vital events etched on our subconscious minds, never to be completely forgotten. I remember a particularly exciting day earlier that year when all the local schools turned out and the children lined Maple Road. Winston Churchill visited us in a convoy of cars; he stood waving, making his victory sign and smoking his big cigar. He also made a short speech from one of the cars. We were all very impressed.

I was equally impressed with the chewing gum I got from American servicemen who took my Aunt Dorothy out. She took me along with her dates to dances at Purley and Croydon, where I'd watch them jitterbug; but I was more interested in the dance band.

In September 1944 the family returned south and I rejoined them. It was a very bleak time; food rationing was in force and the Perks family was very short of money. After school John and I went to the market in Maple Road to pick up damaged apples and vegetables thrown out by stall-keepers, taking them home to swell mother's meager supplies. She sent us to the Cooperative bakery in Royston Road to buy stale loaves cheaply, and, while the man was getting it, we'd steal a fresh loaf. The stale loaf, soaked by Mum in water and then rebaked, came out as new, and we ate it with dripping, lard or sugar. If we had meat it was usually horsemeat or whale.

I was all the while becoming much more aware of girls, and we played kiss-chase on the bombed sites on the way home from school. I fell madly in love with Marjorie

Baker, who lived behind us and was in my class. Sitting on the grass in Penge Recreation Park, she would comb my hair for hours. While all this romancing was going on for seven-year-old William Perks, Brussels was liberated, the battle of Arnhem took place and the first V2 rockets landed on England. Two months after I celebrated my eighth birthday, the famous bandleader Glenn Miller disappeared forever while crossing the English Channel by plane.

At Christmas, big parties organized by Mum and Dad (who was home on leave) and Aunt Dorothy were attended by American servicemen and neighbors and there were sing-songs, with Dad on the piano. On these nights all the Perks brothers and sisters were packed into one bed, some at one end, some at the other, like a tin of sardines.

In April 1945, Mussolini was executed and Hitler shot himself in Berlin—but I was much more interested in a pretty, dark-haired girl, Jessie Brown. She lived in Anerley, but visited her grandmother who lived near us. I was madly in love with her and she knew it; she kept me hanging on a string for years.

On Tuesday, May 8 World War II ended in Europe. We celebrated with a wonderful street party and an enormous bonfire in the middle of the road. Whole staircases were burned, plus doors and beams from the bombed houses. Men were running up the stairs on one side, through the fire, and then down the stairs on the other side. It was a fabulous, exhilarating moment.

My second brother, Paul Edgar, was born on June 2, 1945, at Blenheim Road—obviously conceived nine months earlier on Mum's birthday, September 2. Many years later I suddenly realized that John, Judy and I had all been conceived on Dad's birthday, January 16.

I started going out regularly with Betty Southby, who lived in Arpley Road. Dating Betty was hazardous: her road was among the most dangerously violent in a vicious area: you didn't go down Arpley Road unless you really had to. Our street was tough enough, and some of the kids from it later ended up in reform school or prison. Local gangs from Blenheim Road would occasionally attack Arpley Road with bottles and stones, but astonishingly nobody was ever seriously hurt.

By now Mum and Dad were giving us each sixpence a week pocket money, which we saved for our weekly treat at the Saturday-morning children's cinema at the Odeon or the Kings Hall. I was mesmerized by the cowboy serials (Tom Mix, Hopalong Cassidy, Roy Rogers and Bill Boyd), cartoons, and my favorite, Flash Gordon.

Upon returning to school in September, David Eastwood and I were so advanced that we were moved up an extra year in class and were asked to look after some of the backward pupils during lessons.

Mum and Dad seemed to be taking a lot more interest in us and taught us kids how to knit and embroider, and how to make rugs from canvas and old rags that we cut into thin strips.

On October 24, 1945, I celebrated my ninth birthday and on the 26th, Dad came home for twelve days' leave. As he had become skillful with a newly bought fretwork machine, he made me a wonderful fort for Christmas, one with castle battlements, a gate with a portcullis, a moat with mirrored glass for water and a drawbridge. The big disappointment was that he could not afford soldiers to accompany it. This was one of his very rare presents. Twenty-three years later, I scraped together enough to put down a deposit on an English manor house, Gedding Hall in Suffolk, which uncannily resembled that fort. And one of my hobbies became collecting military artifacts, including models of Scottish soldiers— probably a subconscious reaction to what I hadn't had as a child.

Discharged from the army in May 1946, Dad immediately set to work trying to improve our living conditions. There were rats and mice in the garden and under the floorboards of the house which our new ginger wire-haired terrier, Sandy, helped keep at bay, but we were also overrun by bedbugs. Dad went all over the beds and springs and all the walls and woodwork in the bedrooms with a blow-lamp about once a month.

In midsummer our whole family went on holiday to a rented bungalow in Jaywick Sands, Clacton. We children collected winkles, whelks, mussels and crabs, brought them back to the bungalow and filled the bath with them, much to our parents' annoyance. One day John and I were playing beside the breakwater, where one of the main posts entered the sand. We were in about two feet of water and, as I stepped forward to the post to collect some winkles, the sand suddenly fell away. I slipped down into a deep hole formed by the waves. When I tried to regain my balance the sand gave way and I couldn't get out. I couldn't swim, and I couldn't pull myself out because the wood was slimy with weeds. I was drowning. Dad miraculously appeared to drag me out, spluttering and coughing saltwater. I was badly scared. Since that day I have hated water.

Two years later terror struck me at Beckenham Grammar School when I heard we were to have swimming lessons every week. I begged and pleaded with my parents and eventually, complaining of bad pains in my shoulders and back, I went to the doctor. He diagnosed rheumatism and excused me from swimming for the rest of my schooldays. I never learned to swim properly, and I will still do anything to avoid it.

Back in Penge, my father devised a foolproof method of filling the large fish tanks he kept in the garden. At weekends he went by night with his mate to Keston Ponds. They took a large net on a pole, and torches and bricks. Then they walked around the ponds looking for large sleeping carp. When they discovered one, they gently put the net behind it, then dropped a brick in front of it. The fish would turn and swim straight into the waiting net. They brought the carp home wrapped in wet rags and deposited them in the tanks. Dad assembled a great collection of fish this way. When he was at work, we kids would fish in the tanks with bent pins on string, and worms we had dug up from the garden—then get whacked if Dad found out. He usually did, since all the fish ended up with frayed mouths!

As well as fishing, soccer was to become another passion in my life. My first experience of a professional match came in October 1946 when my father took me to Selhurst Park to see Crystal Palace. They were in the Third Division South, doing very badly. They lost and I remember Dad saying that they couldn't beat a blind school. They became my team from that day on, and over the years I've seen them rise to the First Division.

In November, together with some of the boys at school, I joined a church football team in Anerley. We always seemed to play when it was raining, but there was a great feeling of freedom in running all over a water-logged pitch for ninety minutes, getting muddy and soaked to the skin. We played with an old-fashioned leather football, which soaked up water like a sponge, and trebled its weight in minutes. It took some effort to kick it any distance, but when it was kicked into the air, we all jumped to head it. The unfortunate one who connected would have a headache for the rest of the game.

Just before Christmas, John and I helped Dad finish constructing a beautiful dolls' house for Anne and Judy. It had windows, staircases and fires with lights that ran on batteries. All the rooms were filled with miniature furniture, even curtains and mats that he and Mum had made. It was a work of art.

But the new year of 1947 began with heavy snow and Britain was paralyzed by huge drifts up to fourteen feet deep. This spelled disaster for the family income: Father's work as a bricklayer was non-existent during bad weather. As money became scarce he became very irritable and bad-tempered. We all suffered. My father recalls: "People cannot believe how bad things were financially. As a bricklayer, winter was the worst for money because of the weather, and one Christmas we had twelve shillings to live on—with five children."

My brother Paul: "Dad was breaking his back every day, getting frostbite or being laid off work. That's when he got nasty. The summers were great for him and consequently for us; the winters were violent because he didn't have any money and he would take it out on us.

"There wasn't enough food to go round, so he'd hit a couple of us, send us to bed without any dinner. That meant the rest of the family could eat. In his own mind he probably kept track of who hadn't eaten the day before and sent two others to bed without dinner the next day. That was a regular occurrence.

" 'Get to bed, don't argue!' Then you'd get hit, kicked up the stairs—vroom, that was it. That happened frequently. And in the house we lived in, you didn't *want* to go to bed. It was freezing cold, really nasty, with ice on the inside of the windows and bedbugs that drove us crazy.

"Bill always had the hardest time. He was the first to

get hit at the dining-room table because he was the closest to my father. I was always the last to get hit because I was the farthest away—and being tiny I could duck better. Bill's probably got the worst memories because he got treated more tough, being the eldest."

My sister Judy: "Dad was a Victorian father, tolerant about some things, strict about little things, and very heavy-handed. There was limited cash and, living in a very rough area, trying to keep everyone on the straight and narrow was probably a terrific worry to him. My mother had a temper but she was much lighter and easier. She enjoyed family parties."

I have always had an orderly outlook. My parents recall that when they returned from visiting the cinema, I would have the house immaculately tidy, with all toys put away, a tray of tea ready for them. "We praised and thanked him," says my father, "but years later we discovered that he had made all the other children clear away with the promise of a treat for the first one to finish the jobs he had given them. The treat was that they were the first one allowed to go to bed. He organized the children, catalogued all their books, and they weren't allowed to read them unless they got permission from Bill to get them from his 'library.' "

To bring some cash in Mum took on the task of peeling onions at home for a pickling company. All of us were called on to help; we peeled dozens of sacks between us. After a few days our hands turned yellow. We had to give up this small money-earner after about a month because nobody would come near us. We became very unpopular in the street and at school. It took weeks for the stains to disappear and to get rid of the smell in the house and on our clothes.

We all tried to do our bit to boost the family income. I worked on a milk-round in Penge and Beckenham every morning with M. A. (Mickey) Reed, a man with a hook in place of his left hand. From my six shillings a week, I would have to give Mum half, but at least I now had a little spending money.

My baby brother David Raymond was born at Blenheim Road on April 8, 1947—with yellow jaundice from which he never recovered. After spending all four months of his life in hospital he died on August 15 and was buried at

Elmers End cemetery, Beckenham, in an unmarked grave. That morning I went round to the market and bought a small bunch of flowers for him. At ten, I was heavily cut up about such a family tragedy. Mum reacted quietly and submerged her sadness; the children did not attend the funeral, but all had a cry.

Born and bred in the poorest part of southeast London, I was one of only three eleven-year-olds, from a class of fifty-two, to gain a scholarship to the prestigious Beckenham and Penge Grammar School, starting in September 1947. What should have been an encouraging start in life quickly became a trauma for me, both at school and at home.

The contrast between my background and the other pupils was vast. Ninety per cent came from upper- or middle-class homes in the expensive parts of suburban Kent. Penge, my home, was definitely the wrong side of the tracks. I was inhibited by what other kids called my "working-class" accent, and a sense of inferiority prevented me from inviting them to my small and spartan home because most of them lived in big, detached houses. I was short (four feet two inches tall) and the skinniest kid in a class of twenty-eight. However, I made friends quickly. Academically I was fine at the start of my grammar-school days. I was put into Form 1B, where we concentrated on French and German. God knows why I was chosen for this course: I hated languages. Outside class, I made friends very quickly and was nicknamed "Willie," because I was so small. I compensated for my size by excelling at playground football—you play hard when the odds are stacked against you. We were not allowed to play football in games, but had to play Rugby instead, which everyone disliked. We had a wonderful class teacher, Mr. Sharp, who was kind to all the boys, but was taken advantage of because of this. By contrast, our math teacher, a vicious little man called Mr. Bowman, lifted us out of our seats by the hair if we couldn't answer a question. He also cracked us on the head with his knuckles, giving the recipient a headache for the rest of the day.

On the way home I spent hours looking in the bike shop, wishing for one. I finally set my heart on a three-speed Hercules with drop handlebars, priced at 18 guineas. The only way to buy this was to earn the money myself. By the next summer I finally managed it, by taking on various milk-rounds and paper-rounds.

At school we all had to run the mile in under 7 minutes 30 seconds by the end of term. I managed it in 6 minutes 33 seconds at the age of eleven and felt quite proud. In my second year I managed to get it down to 6 minutes and 8 seconds. I was no good at sprints but excellent at longer distances. Metaphorically, that's been the story of my life; it may go some way to explaining why I stayed in a mad rock 'n' roll band for a quarter of a century!

I was given 2s. 6d. (twelve new pence) per week by Gran for school dinners. Like most of the boys in the class, I just kept it, going without food during the day. Instead, we bought sweets and chewing gum and all the boys' comics like the *Hotspur, Champion, Rover,* and *Wizard.* Composed of great stories on sport, war and adventure, they were full of fictitious schoolboy heroes; my favorite was Wilson, the mysterious athlete who lived wild on the Yorkshire Moors, and broke just about every world record at athletics. I've got a good collection of comics featuring him; his character still fascinates me.

If my integration at school was tough, the pressure at home became intense. A pre-teenage kid tries to merge into his environment, but when I tried to speak in the smoother style of the other grammar-school boys people all around me—parents, relatives and old friends—called me a snob. I started to have rows with my father particularly. He thought me "stuck-up" because of my changing speech. He saw it as a determination to discard my background; I saw it simply as "mixing in," being influenced by my new friends.

Local kids in Penge threw bricks at me, mocking my grammar-school blazer and cap (which my father could ill afford to buy), taunting me: "Getting too big for your boots!" Even though I knew it was jealousy, I was in a no-win situation. If I went to school and spoke normally, they would poke fun at my working-class accent, but if I tried "talking posh" as they called it when I got home, I was mocked by everyone around me.

In midsummer things became unbearable at home and I returned to live with my grandmother Jeffery in her new home, 23 Garden Road, Anerley, where there was the luxury of a long garden and a tiny television set with a six-inch screen—the first I'd ever seen.

My grammar school progress was generally good and in the autumn of 1948 I moved up to Form 2B, doing well in mathematics, art and music. I also enrolled for clarinet lessons, which I continued for two years. I'd already had piano lessons with Mr. Choat near Gran's home, and also joined his choir at Holy Trinity Church, Penge.

My mother recalls my piano teacher visiting them to declare, "Bill's body is alive with music." Later, when my parents could no longer afford the teaching fees, my grandmother took over paying for them. In May 1949 I passed my primary examination on piano at the Royal College of Music in London. Later that year I returned and passed my preliminary exam too.

My brother Paul: "Our parents sent all the family except me to music classes. Everyone else, especially Bill, according to Dad, abused it, so I didn't get the privilege, being the youngest. Bill learned piano, John violin, Judy the trumpet, Ann something else. The whole house was full of music all the time. Bill was the talented one, but he'd return from his piano lessons and jazz it all up—I remember he did a brilliant jazzed-up version of *Orpheus in the Underworld*. And my father used to beat the hell out of him. It was funny—we used to encourage it because we liked to see Bill get beaten up. We'd set him up for a beating: we'd ask him to show us how he could play and my father would come storming into the room and smack him around because he wasn't following the right style. Father wanted him to become a classical pianist."

I received small amounts of cash for singing in the church choir, with bonuses for singing at weddings; we wore cassocks, surplices and starched, ruffled collars for the services.

Returning to school for the new spring term, I began to get bad headaches. Gran took me to an optician who prescribed reading glasses. I hated them and didn't wear them, although I was constantly badgered by Gran and my parents. I conveniently lost them, had them replaced, and lost them again. After that it was all forgotten. The headaches disappeared and my eyesight has been perfect ever since.

Three months later, I suffered from repeated stomach pains and I was finally diagnosed as having a grumbling appendix. At the South London Children's Hospital, Sydenham, I underwent an appendix operation. The resulting scar was quite long and appeared to be two separate incisions as though somebody had missed the first time; it took eleven metal clips and three stitches to close. I was told that there was nothing wrong with my appendix but they took it out anyway. I was in hospital for about three weeks, and struck up a romance with the girl in the next bed, who was also thirteen.

I have since realized that, around this time, I was going through puberty, and I felt strange most days. Sometimes I would find myself talking or being talked to, and I would not know what was being said. I can only describe the feeling as one of being miles away, looking at everything from a great distance, like in a dream. I wish that somebody could have explained it to me at the time.

In May, I joined the youth club at Christ Church, Beckenham with my schoolfriend John Blagden. It was here that I developed a lifelong interest in table tennis. John and I struck up a friendship at the club with a polio victim who was confined to a wheelchair. Maureen Lovelock came from a well-to-do family and we spent many happy days at their house in Beckenham. Maureen was a Crystal Palace fan and we would push her for miles in her wheelchair to many of the home matches.

John Blagden recalls: "I remember the kindness Bill showed Maureen, walking her round the park in her wheelchair; we would then return to her house to play Doris Day records. I remember thinking later that the Bill I knew in 1952 was very different from the image he acquired as a Rolling Stone."

Later, I fell head over heels for Anne Ford, a girl at the youth club. I followed her home day after day, cycling up and down her road hoping for a glimpse of her. She totally ignored me. Depressed, I wrote her many love letters but I didn't post any. I never did get to know Anne properly.

In 1950 my grandfather became very sick and I moved back to my parents. Life became less happy at school. Although I went into Form 3D, finally dropping languages in favor of art, music, woodwork and metalwork, my interest in learning was decreasing. This was a much lazier class and bad for me. I was regularly chastised by my parents, and my social integration, or disintegration, became a large problem. I felt I didn't belong anywhere: the school was wrong to expect me to change my accent and lift me out of my working-class background. And my parents were at fault for condemning my attempt to merge into school society. I compromised, speaking to suit my audience, and as a result, although my social life was balanced, from the age of fourteen my schoolwork plummeted. I was relegated to Form 5X, a class for academic outcasts. I was rebelling against everything and my life seemed directionless. Towards the end of the summer term of 1952 I performed poorly in the mock examinations for the General Certificate of Education exam due to take place a year later. In mathematics, art, music and geography I was fine, but I failed miserably in all other subjects.

At home, the five kids were pretty close. On dry days we would climb out of our bedroom window, swing over on to the window ledge by hanging on the gutter above, and then pull ourselves up on to the flat roof at the back of the house. We never realized the dangers. We would then have picnics on the roof. Sometimes we would steal Dad's air pistol and pellets and sit there shooting holes in the washing hanging on the neighbors' lines over our back fence. The old women would go mad.

We played for hours in the garden. There were lots of tea chests and boxes about, and two wooden sheds. Once we built a stagecoach: the inside was made with a large metal water tank. When we were getting in, it collapsed and the tank fell on Paul's head, splitting it open. In hospital he needed sixteen stitches; he still has the scar.

John and I used to get up at 5 a.m. and go fishing in the Crystal Palace grounds, sneaking in, avoiding the keepers, and fishing with hand-lines and bread paste in the breeding pond. We filled large tins with small carp and gudgeon, climbing over the fence and returning home to empty them into Dad's fish tanks.

Sometimes we spent a whole day exploring the grounds. We never had any food, and we experimented by eating various leaves and plants: Spanish rhubarb was quite bitter but it filled us up. We even ate acorns, and berries from the hawthorn bushes, and hawthorn leaves—which we called "bread and cheese."

But gradually, girls and music were becoming my prime interests. A young, very pretty girl in our street, Pamela Clarke, had a crush on me. She would run after me, throw her arms around me and try to kiss me, which embarrassed me in front of all my mates. She was about three years younger than me and in later years became a real beauty. By then, she totally ignored me, more's the pity.

(My brother Paul, nine years younger, recalls: "My first memory of Bill with girls was when he was dating a girl named Jessie; he was thirteen, I was four. I clearly recall that because when he was seeing Jessie, he fixed me up with a partner to accompany them—her sister Maureen. And I was in a pushchair!")

When I was asked to become the choirboy *soloist* in church, I felt inhibited. I refused, lost interest and quit the choir shortly afterwards. The clarinet was more difficult, but I was holding my own. For today's rock fans, the way I grew up hearing music must sound prehistoric! My father's mother had a record-player and records, 78 rpm, and to be allowed to play them on her manual wind-up record-player was a great treat.

The popular music in England at the time was incredibly bland and lacking inspiration. Listening to the BBC in those days was pointless: it offered nothing to young people. Radio Luxemburg—the only commercial station—was the one for us, but the charts were completely dominated by adult interest. Nat "King" Cole was becoming very popular in Britain, while in America the big names included Perry Como, Patti Page and Rosemary Clooney. It was mostly ballads—"moon in June" stuff—without any balls.

All the news in pop came from the States. In October 1950, as I celebrated my fourteenth birthday, Al Jolson died. That was the year a man named Sam Phillips launched Sun Records in Memphis, a move which was later to begin the career of Elvis Presley.

But 1951 began with a great sound catching my ear: "How High the Moon" by Les Paul and Mary Ford. Here was the first example of electric guitar, played imaginatively, and it must have influenced thousands of kids of my age. The record had terrific verve, proof at last that pop music had something more than love songs; that it could provide stylish instrumental inventiveness. Les Paul was the first person to turn me on to the guitar sound.

But that January brought another low in the Perks household. The appalling, snowy winter meant that, once again, my father's work as a bricklayer was nil. He had some savings, but eventually my parents ran out of money. They asked to borrow some from my post office book, which had £17 10s. in it, slowly saved up for me by my grandmother from the time I first lived with her. That equaled about two weeks' wages for Dad. They took me to the post office in Penge, where I drew out the lot. A couple of years later, I asked when they would repay me. Dad turned on me instantly, giving me a beating for being "ungrateful and cheeky." They never repaid me the money.

I continued to date, but with slightly less intensity. There was one girl from the girls' grammar school in Beckenham, who I certainly couldn't take home because she would have been considered "snooty"; and I saw Jessie on and off in Anerley. There was much petting in the back rows of cinemas. Then I took out Shirley, who lived in Maple Road. For fifteen-year-olds, we behaved quite romantically, visiting Crystal Palace recreation grounds, walking around the boating lake, lying on the grass, petting. Freckle-faced, trim and pretty, Shirley was the first girl to let me see her breasts.

Another great passion, which intensified at age fifteen, was cricket. For two whole seasons, John Blagden and I wangled weekend jobs together as scorers for the Lloyds Bank cricket team at Beckenham. Traveling to away-games in a coach was great, and I particularly relished the lunches and afternoon teas. Good players, great games—and the social aspect of the job was wonderful. I became an obsessive follower of the game, visiting my grandmother's house to watch the Test matches on her tiny TV. India was touring and I spent many happy hours with Gran, who loved the game too.

A great day in my life was June 21, 1952, when John Blagden and I went to Lord's cricket ground for the first time to watch the third day's play of England versus India. I saw England's wicketkeeper Godfrey Evans score

98 runs before lunch and complete his century immediately afterwards.

I continued going out with the crowd from the youth club and started dating Jeanette McNaire, who lived in Beckenham. She was very well endowed, and it affected me deeply.

Popular music also suddenly made a deep impression on me, when on television I saw Johnnie Ray mobbed during a performance at the London Palladium. The emotion in his voice as he sang "Cry" gave me a tingle of excitement that I got from no other performer at this time except Lloyd Price, when he sang "Lawdy Miss Clawdy"—probably the first rock 'n' roll record.

The Big Smog fell on Britain at the end of December 1952. You could actually *taste* this foul weather. When we blew our noses the handkerchiefs would be black. Everyone got lost, even on a walk around the corner to the shops. A trip to school was a dangerous expedition. And I had no inkling that my schooldays were numbered.

The bleakness outside was matched by the mood at home. My father decided with a work-mate to launch a building company doing subcontract assignments for large firms. This went so well that after a few weeks they had twenty employees. My prowess at figures was useful; Dad asked me to do the bookkeeping and work out the men's wages. The business was profitable very quickly, but suddenly my father's partner disappeared with all the money. Dad was left to carry the debt and needed all his savings, plus borrowed cash, to pay the men their dues. After closing the business he was in debt for months.

Relationships disintegrated at home. It was odd: as the eldest child, one who had won the chance for a fine education, I might have expected the family to take some pride in me. Instead my ambition to succeed seemed to increase my father's unease. The reality of his eldest son hoisting himself into a more hopeful future seemed to embarrass Dad. I found myself polarized between loyalties to my parents and my school horizons. My parents seemed resentful of everything I did, and we argued continually. Nor was there much space for individuality to emerge: I shared a bed with my two brothers and had to be home by ten o'clock every night: Father was a disciplinarian.

As 1953 began, there were two pluses for British kids. The British Top Twenty charts began in January, heralding the passion for popular music that ignited our interest in American sounds, and the wartime sweet-rationing we'd endured for eleven years ended in February. There were crazy scenes in the shops, which were stripped bare within days. It took weeks for things to settle and for us to accept the freedom of being able to buy sweets whenever we liked.

Despite all the pressures at home, I tried hard to improve my schoolwork and began to turn the corner with my grades. But a thunderbolt was unleashed on me by my father. He wrote to my headmaster, L. W. "Jumbo" White, in March 1953, saying that I would be leaving school at Easter, just two months before I was to sit the GCE examinations—the major reason for being at such a fine school. Father said he was pulling me out of school because he'd found me a job working for a London bookmaker. There was a big future for me there he said, and eventually, with my expertise at figures, he could open his own betting company.

I was dumbfounded, but had no say in the matter. Dad was always a man of decision, especially in family matters. On March 26, 1953, my headmaster replied, asking him to change his mind and leave me at school until I had completed the exams. Father could not be persuaded. I kept that letter because it marked my life: having to leave school was a bitter blow to my confidence.

It was therefore a very nervous William Perks who, reluctantly discarding grammar-school uniform, started work just after Easter 1953. From Penge East station to Victoria and then by underground with hundreds of commuters, I headed for Bond Street tube-station. Just around the corner, at 71 Duke Street, was the City Tote office where I began as a junior clerk at £3 10s. a week. This well-run betting office had a staff of fifty; bets were conducted only by phone, of which there were about a hundred. There was a little sunshine to lighten my confusion: I was welcomed by three other boys of my age, a very funny guy named Ian Fernley, a pure Teddy Boy from Stepney named Kenny Scrutton and John Hayes, from Mile End. They quickly accepted me into their ranks and we soon became good work-mates.

One of my tasks was to take films of telephoned betting slips to be developed near St. Paul's. I was shocked to see that everywhere was still completely flattened by the war's bombing; the reconstruction of the City was only just beginning. Postwar spirit manifested itself in various ways: on May 29 Edmund Hillary and Sherpa "Tiger" Tensing Norkay became the first climbers to conquer Mount Everest. And four days later Elizabeth II was crowned Queen of England.

There was a spirit of optimism and adventure in the world but it didn't stretch to my pocket. My wages went nowhere as I was made to give mother £2 10s., leaving me a pound a week. From this I had to travel to work, have a cheese roll and coffee for lunch, either at Lyons teashop in Oxford Street or a café in Duke Street, and buy my clothes and entertainment. Cigarettes, available in five or ten packs, were also mercifully sold individually to people like me who often could not afford full packets.

My tastes in music were becoming defined: I hated the syrupy sounds of Mantovani and his orchestra or Eddie Fisher, but I listened out for songs with rhythm. I wanted a record-player and records, so, one Saturday in July 1953, I took my stamp collection that Gran had helped me assemble to a shop in West Norwood and sold it for £3 10s. It was worth far more, but I badly needed the money. I went straight to a record shop in Anerley where I bought an old secondhand wind-up record-player and a box of needles for £2 10s., and my first two precious records: Les Paul and Mary Ford's "The World is Waiting for the Sunrise," which was not new but featured Les Paul's marvelous, revolutionary multi-tracked guitar playing; and Frankie Laine's punchy ballad "I Believe," which went to Number One in America and Britain.

Soon afterward I became friendly with Albert Stone, a fireman's son who lived close by. We began going out to coffee bars, which were very popular in the fifties among teenagers; and we began taking dancing lessons at Beckenham Ballroom. When Albert began dating a girl, I made up a foursome with them and her girlfriend, Anne. She was fifteen, still at school, but had the biggest boobs in town. We began dating regularly.

There was music in her family, and through her elder brother I heard my first jazz records: Dizzy Gillespie,

Gerry Mulligan and a band called Kenny Graham and his Afro-Cubans. This first exposure to jazz fascinated me. On the radio we were still being subjected to such bores as Guy Mitchell.

But after Christmas I broke off from Anne. She had become increasingly jealous and possessive; I was also embarrassed because everywhere we went people stared at her breasts. My next record purchase, a mildly satirical song by Johnnie Ray called "Glad Rag Doll," could have been dedicated to Anne; the words suited her perfectly.

I wasn't footloose for long. Within a month I began a friendship with a girl called Janice Jacks, from Anerley, and we petted quite heavily on the rare occasions when we could arrange for some privacy. The lucky nights were when we baby-sat for a couple she knew.

Though I was active with girls, I was reminded of a childhood romance one morning as I was dressing for work. I looked across our back garden to Marjorie Baker's house and saw her standing naked at the window of her bedroom, brushing her hair. She looked wonderful. Making inquiries, I discovered she was "going steady." But I continued to see her from a distance in the mornings, admiring her beauty and so wishing I still knew her.

In the spring of 1954 Bill Haley recorded "Rock Around the Clock" in America; this was released on April 12 in the USA, but in Britain we were not to know about it for another year.

All the Perks kids, including me, were getting into a radio show which has since become legendary among my generation. The Goons featured Peter Sellers, Spike Milligan and Harry Secombe, and with my usual concentration on detail, I remember all the zany jokes and episodes well, particularly "The Toothpaste Mines" and "The Dreaded Batter-Pudding Hurler." Great, timeless humor.

My father often came up with schemes that would put him "in the money," but they all seemed to fail. After the building-company collapse a few years earlier, he'd again become solvent, but then spent all his hard-earned savings on financing a pet-shop stall in Penge market. He bought goldfish, canaries, budgerigars, tortoises, terrapins and many other animals, food, seed, cages, tanks.

But this never paid, and he was left with many birds on his hands.

He then decided to breed them, and enter them in shows for profit. He kept them in the upstairs scullery. Soon he bred some baby bullfinches, and we took it in turns to feed them food placed on the tip of a matchstick. They grew up to be very beautiful birds and he won many prizes—everything seemed to be working at last. Then one day he went upstairs only to find that our cat Sooty had killed or eaten practically every one of the fifty birds in the room. Dad went crazy and kicked the cat. Sooty went flying down the stairs with a birdcage bouncing after him. We all rushed up the passage to see what was happening. The cat raced for the back door, but Dad was close behind, and the door was shut. Dad picked him up, opened the back door and kicked him over the fence. From that day onwards, Sooty never came in the house when he was there, but sat on the back fence and just looked at him.

Dad then started taking me to Catford to see the greyhound racing. He always managed to come home with a few pounds in his pocket, and never seemed to lose. A short time later he bought a greyhound called Robin for some considerable sum and started to train him. But one Sunday Robin strolled past the dinner table just before dinner, took the whole joint off the table and ate it. Dad got rid of him shortly afterwards.

As my eighteenth birthday neared, I joined many of my mates in fearing the arrival of the dreaded call-up papers for my compulsory two years' National Service in the army, RAF or navy. But no worries could stop me celebrating that birthday in some style, with a big party at home. Among the lads I invited from work were Ian Fernley and Kenny Scrutton, who brought half a dozen of his Teddy Boy friends from Stepney, a notoriously tough part of east London. As they came silently through the front door, the atmosphere became pretty tense. I sensed we could be in for some trouble. Father and some of my uncles looked grim and started preparing for a fight. But as the evening wore on, things loosened up. They proved to be great guys, very friendly and extremely funny. Everyone liked them, danced with them and chatted happily, commenting when they'd left what a nice bunch of guys I'd invited.

My National Service papers arrived in January 1955. The only good thing was that I was conscripted into the RAF, as I'd requested. I told my bosses at the betting-office the bad news and they promised my job would be waiting for me when I returned in two years. In fact, they were not doing me any favors: holding a person's job for his return was the law.

On January 20 I reported for duty at RAF Cardington. To the authorities bundling me and other unfortunates into a truck at the station I would no longer be a name or a person but a number and rank: 2745787 Air Craftsman 2 Perks, W. G.

My pay was 28 shillings a week. At Cardington we were kitted out; after a few days I was posted to RAF Padgate, near Warrington in Lancashire, for my eight weeks' basic training and drill. This was reputed to be the hardest camp of them all. We were billeted in three huts, twenty boys in each. We each had a metal bed, and a large and a small bedside cupboard. In the center of the hut was an old metal coal stove. The winter was very cold and so were we. We were allowed to use the stove but were rationed to one bucket of coal a day. The problem was that every morning at 6 a.m. it had to be completely clean and polished, both inside and out. In addition, the stove surrounds had to be whitewashed. The cleaning was such a chore that after a few days we decided that it was easier not to light it, and freeze instead. The hut was supervised by a tough corporal who had his own small room and he would instruct us to go and steal coal for him.

The medical officer inspected us after a couple of days. We stood by our beds, naked, shivering with the cold, while he walked along the line, lifting our cocks up with his stick, checking us for VD. It was all very embarrass-ing and humiliating. We then had various injections, and our arms stiffened painfully. We had to keep the floor so highly polished that we walked everywhere in socks on cotton dusters. Hardly able to move our arms, we were still forced to polish and clean the floor daily. And if you didn't move enough, the corporal would grab your arms and swing them for you: agony.

We were inspected every morning at seven o'clock. Only perfection was acceptable. If clothes were not folded to the right dimensions, or a mug was supposedly dirty, they would be thrown across the room, accompanied by a mouthful of oaths from the inspecting sergeant-major, "Big Jim," a terrifying man. We soon learned to keep one set of clothes for show only, supported inside with cardboard. Drill and training were very demoralizing. We were not allowed to leave the camp at any time during our eight weeks there, and we were subjected to daily drills, parades, physical training and inspections.

Anything that didn't meet with the approval of the NCOs was punished with guard duty and cookhouse fatigue. We were warned that if we didn't pass out after eight weeks we would join a new squad, and we could possibly do our entire two years' service here. In fact there was a guy called Parrott in our squad who had been there for over a year and was on the wrong side of everyone. He gave us lots of tips on how to get by. He also told us that one recruit had become so depressed that a few weeks earlier he had hanged himself. This kind of news terrified us. Those early RAF days were sheer purgatory.

During February, we did our rifle and bren gun training, lying on the range in the snow, just wearing boiler suits. After shooting we were allowed to light a fire with the broken-up ammunition boxes. Once some unused bullets were accidentally put into the fire and started to explode—I've never seen twenty people scatter so quickly. After rifle training I contracted frostbite on my left hand, which was treated at the medical section for some time. We always had to take cold showers which I hated, and were supervised to make sure we did. It was a miserable time.

During March we did various guard duties. We also did parades, where we were made to stand to attention for hours, until we could hardly move our arms with the cold and cramps.

On March 21, I passed out of basic training and was given a few days' leave at home. It was like coming out of eight weeks of prison and seeing the world again. I heard that I had been posted to RAF Credenhill, Hereford for trade training as a clerk progress. We were told that this was a nice relaxed camp, and much more bearable.

I left home and reported for duty on March 26, 1955, and settled in quickly. Over the next month I got a couple of weekend passes and I was able to return home. I hitchhiked to London and then went the rest of the way by train. From camp we went into town, chatted to the local girls and sampled the scrumpy, or local cider, which was very potent; then we staggered back to camp well-soused.

In our hut we had a radio speaker, and we would listen to the popular records on British Forces Network. We liked Tennessee Ernie Ford's "Rain" and Perez Prado's "Cherry Pink," which was Number One in England and America. Eartha Kitt and the Crewcuts were also good, but we didn't care much for ballad singers like Joan Regan, Dean Martin, Ronnie Hilton, Doris Day or Tony Martin, the other Top Ten artists.

One warm May day I decided to sign on for an extra year's service, which would bring better pay, a better uniform, more leave and passes, apart from getting me much better treatment. On July 9, the very day that Bill Haley's "Rock Around the Clock" went to Number One in America, I left RAF Credenhill as a clerk progress. My rank was now AC1 (Air Craftsman First Class). I was told that I had been posted to West Germany, and nine days later, with my kit-bag over my shoulder, I went by train to London. At Liverpool Street station I caught the train to Harwich, together with many other RAF servicemen and army personnel. At Harwich we were transferred to a flat-bottomed troop ship and ushered down into the bowels. Here we settled into three-tiered bunks and set sail for the Hook of Holland, the nearby engines throbbing in our ears, the atmosphere hot and stuffy. It was a smooth passage and we docked at 7 a.m. and transferred to a train that took us through Holland, across the German border to RAF Gock, the reception station where we stayed the night. This was my first trip out of England. We continued our train trip, and later in the day pulled into the station at Oldenburg, where we were met and driven to the camp in lorries. There I was assigned to a room for five guys, and joined Jim Bottrell (from Birmingham), Ron Aldous (Essex), Taffy Lewis (Wales) and Ken Steans, a Scouser. Everyone was friendly and helped me to settle in happily. Next day at the motor transport section I was given my duties.

During August I got myself sorted out. I was working in an office with a Corporal Ryan and two German civilians called Walter and Rudi. The camp was set up for three fighter squadrons of Hunter jets (23, 26 and 33 Squadrons). There were 4,000 servicemen altogether in the camp. We were on a permanent four-hour alert to evacuate the camp, being only about eighty miles from the Russian border. My job was to give out slips for fuel and repairs, control detailed accounting of all vehicles on the camp and send quarterly returns to the RAF head-quarters in West Germany. There was a lot of maths, charts and graphs involved, which I was good at.

On September 3, as Mitch Miller's "Yellow Rose of Texas" went to Number One in America, I joined the MT section football team. It was here that I became mates with a guy named Lee Whyman, a fabulous player in the style of the great Rodney Marsh. We also started making a few excursions to town. We would look around the shops, stopping for wonderful cheap snacks at the food-stalls on the streets, where they sold the tastiest Bockwürste and Bratwürste sausages and delicious bowls of mock-turtle soup. Occasionally we would eat in small bars—just fried eggs and potatoes, but they melted in our mouths, washed down with German beer.

It was easy to get news from around the world through American Forces Network radio: we heard that in America James Dean had died in a car crash in California. On September 22 in England, Independent Television was launched, but the English Top Ten was very dull.

We all clubbed together and bought a good radio for our room. At last we were able to listen whenever we wanted: mostly to AFN Radio—BFN was pretty boring by comparison. We would wake up at 5:30 to country music on a program called "The Stick Buddy Jamboree," which was wonderful. We also began to hear singers like Elvis Presley, Bill Haley, Fats Domino, Little Richard for the first time. In England they were still listening to Jimmy Young and Rosemary Clooney. Next door they had a record-player, and records that included the Humphrey Lyttelton Band playing "Bad Penny Blues." I also heard skiffle for the first time, by the Chris Barber Band, featuring Lonnie Donegan. Like thousands of other young guys, I was immediately hooked on skiffle's energy and rhythm; Donegan and Barber inspired thousands of British musicians, who later got into rock.

I was promoted in November to LAC (Leading Air Craftsman) and returned home for ten days' leave. I managed to wangle a lift in an RAF truck to Ostend, and crossed to Dover with other military personnel. After going through customs, we caught the train for Victoria Station, London, which passed through Penge East station, just a mile from my house. When it stopped at the entrance to the Crystal Palace Tunnel I jumped on to the tracks and the boys threw my kit-bag down. I was immediately stopped by station officials who took me to an office to charge me, but after a chat they decided to let me go. I walked home and surprised the family. When my father saw me, he said: "Hallo, Bill, home again? When do you go back?"—the perennial question to servicemen on leave. At the end of my leave I walked the mile to Penge East station by myself. None of the family volunteered to see me off, which was a disappointment. I went to Liverpool Street station and caught the train to Harwich, where we got on the troopship for the Hook of Holland. We sailed in very rough weather; nearly everyone on board was seasick on the seven-hour trip, including me, but we weren't allowed on deck and just sat it out below, trying to find a vacant toilet or sink. I'd never felt so miserable before in my life. At last we docked, and continued on to Oldenburg by train.

Here when we went out of the camp, we often ended up in a German bar/dancehall called the Grünewald, where quite a few girls hung out with the servicemen. A jukebox featured all the latest rock 'n' roll records from America, which was wonderful. Once, trying to be flash, three of us ordered a full bottle of cheap rum, which we proceeded to drink rapidly. We barely made it back to the camp. I spent most of the night hanging out of the billet window being violently sick. The feeling stayed with me, on and off, for almost a week and every time somebody talked about food, I would be sick again. I've never drunk rum since.

During the year there were five million-selling records by Fats Domino. But rock 'n' roll had arrived in the shape of Elvis, and the generation gap which the Rolling Stones would encounter later was beginning. Summing up the events of 1955, the *Encyclopaedia Britannica* appraised rock music thus:

> The rowdy element was represented by "Rock Around the Clock," theme song of the controversial film *The Blackboard Jungle*. The rock 'n' roll school in general concentrated on a minimum of melodic line and a maximum of rhythmic noise, deliberately competing with the artistic ideals of the jungle itself.

January 1956 was so cold that we were all issued with sleeveless leather jerkins with fur collars. Walter, the German who worked with me, invited me to his house for a Sunday afternoon and evening. I was introduced to his family, who were very welcoming; I enjoyed the day very much and visited them regularly after that.

At the Grünewald bar my mates and I became friendly with a bunch of girls and went back into town with them. Everything was closed and there was nowhere to go to be alone. We wandered down to the railway station, where we found a train in the sidings. We got into some of the carriages and spent a few hours fooling around with the girls, keeping warm as best we could.

I was now completely mad on Elvis Presley, whose "Heartbreak Hotel" went to the top in America in April. I found a great photo of him, drew Elvis on the back of my jerkin and was called "Elvis" around the camp. Musically, things were changing. As Tennessee Ernie Ford's "Sixteen Tons" went to Number One in England, Lonnie Donegan's great "Rock Island Line" entered the Top Ten, beginning the mania for skiffle that soon enveloped Britain.

One day I was walking to work on the camp, with my hands tucked into the arm-holes of my leather jerkin, when a sergeant yelled at me, asking me if I were a girl. "No, sergeant," I said, assuming he was referring to my hair needing cutting. "Well," he bawled, "if you ain't got a pair of tits in there, what are you doing with your hands?" I walked away trying to keep a straight face.

In May I went back to England on leave. I went straight to Hull to visit Sue, a girl whose address I'd been given by a fellow-airman; we had been writing to each other for a while. I stayed on holiday there with her, her widowed mother and young brother. She was sixteen and quite pretty. I made love for the first time when she came to my room on the second night of my stay. We continued throughout the week. I'm sure her mother must have known what was going on.

When I went to London to see my family, I bought Presley's "Heartbreak Hotel" and played it with the windows to the street open until it wore out.

In July I returned on leave again to find that my parents had bought a secondhand sofa-bed for me to use in the front room—far better than sleeping with my two brothers upstairs. With a very fashionable flak jacket, impressing the girls was high on my list and I decided to contact another girl I'd been writing to from camp. Anne Worsall, a nurse, lived near West Wickham, Kent, about five miles away. We arranged to meet at her house. Blonde and very pretty, Anne had one eye slightly off-center, which strangely made her more attractive to me. After a few dates, I invited her over to Penge and took her to the Regal Cinema, Beckenham, to see a film. By the time we got to my house it was too late to get her home. Everybody was asleep and I decided that we should sleep in the front room in my bed. In the morning I heard Dad's alarm clock go off upstairs, woke Anne and told her that my father *never* came into my room before going to work—she was safe. Of course, on this day he did. We just lay there with our eyes shut, hoping he hadn't noticed. After he'd gone out without saying anything, I went to the kitchen and told Mum what had happened. She just cooked breakfast for us both before I took Anne home. I never did find out whether Dad had actually noticed us.

On my return to RAF Oldenburg, I went to town and bought myself a cheap Spanish acoustic guitar and fooled around with it, tuned to a chord.

Around this time, we bought tickets to see the modern jazz of the Stan Kenton Band perform in Bremen. This was a great concert, and I particularly loved "Peanut Vendor" and "Artistry in Rhythm," where whole groups of horn players stood up and down in sequence, to play all those great discords.

I was still seeing the girl from the Grünewald, but I had nowhere to take her at the end of the evenings. Then one night in October, she invited me to go home with her for the first time. She said she lived with her grandmother. We took a late train to her village, just outside of town and walked to her house. It was about one in the morning. She let herself in and then opened the ground-floor window for me. I climbed in and found myself in her bedroom. We undressed, jumped into bed and made love for ages. I was half asleep a little later, when I heard a bump on the floor upstairs; she woke up, really scared. It was her dad, getting ready for work; I had to leave—and quickly. I rushed into my clothes, said goodbye, jumped out of the window, walked to the station and waited along with the other commuters, knowing that her dad was among them. I returned to the camp happily.

On November 3 Elvis Presley's "Love Me Tender" went to Number One in America, but more mundane matters were on my mind in Germany: all the guys in our room suddenly started scratching: we all had first doses of the crabs. We went to the medical officer and he prescribed a white lotion that burned like hell but killed the little buggers. When we checked, we found that this was a very common problem in the camp.

In January I started taking driving lessons and had training on three-and-a-half ton trucks. I became a "B" driver (which meant I could drive military vehicles in convoy but not civilian vehicles) and went on a number of day and night convoys, driving in the snow and ice on the cobbled streets, which was an exciting experience. After that I would make trips to other camps for a few days.

Tommy Steele appeared in England with "Singing the Blues" and went to Number One in the charts, but I wasn't impressed by him or his music. I preferred grittier stuff.

While working at the MT section, I got to know Lee Whyman a lot better. He was a refueling driver for the fighter planes, and always looked really funky. He made quite an impression on me with his style.* At this time too Jimmy Pearce, the boy from Penge whom I'd hit at

---

*In 1964 I adapted his name and changed mine by deed poll.

school ten years earlier, arrived at RAF Oldenburg and we renewed our friendship.

Returning to London on leave, I contacted Anne Worsall, but by this time she was going out with a boy she really liked. This was disappointing, but she introduced me to a few of her nurse friends at Swanley Hospital, Kent. I made a date with one and took the train from Penge East to Swanley. We went to the cinema, then to a small café and, when we got back to the hospital, we went down to the side wall and petted for a while. By the time she left, it was too late to get a train or bus, and I was twenty-three miles from home.

I went to the local police station to ask for help. They gave me a cup of tea and went out on to the bypass and flagged down a lorry that took me as far as Lewisham. The walk back from there took me a few hours and I got home quite late. A few nights later the same thing happened. Back at the police station they said, "Not *you* again!" But once more they got me a lift, this time to Lee Green. I walked from there, another long walk, but well worth it, I thought. A few days later my girlfriend and I ended up in the Oxo sports ground, where we made love naked on the grass. I dropped her back at the hospital and was once again too late for my train home. I dared not go to the police station a third time and decided to walk all the way home. I started off down the road, stealing milk from the doorsteps on the way. I walked along the Sidcup bypass, on down to Eltham, through Lewisham, Catford, Sydenham and finally to Penge, arriving home at eight o'clock. As I walked into the kitchen Mum said, "Bill, you're up early this morning."

On October 4, 1957, the Sputnik 1 was successfully launched and on the 14th the Everly Brothers' "Wake Up, Little Susie" went to Number One in America. That same day I returned home on leave to celebrate my twenty-first birthday, but the celebrations turned sour when father's brother, Freddie, died suddenly of pneumonia.

In mid-November, I was back at RAF Oldenburg, where I started a skiffle group with Casey Jones, a Liverpudlian who Eric Clapton was later to play with briefly. Buddy Holly and the Crickets' inspirational "That'll be the Day" went to Number One in England. During the year there had been 6 million-selling records by Elvis

Presley, three each by Fats Domino and Little Richard, and two each by Chuck Berry, Sam Cooke, the Diamonds, the Everly Brothers, Buddy Holly and the Crickets and Jerry Lee Lewis. Rock 'n' roll was here to stay!

But the backlash was starting too. *Contacts*, the Catholic youth center's newspaper, demanded of all God-fearing Christians: "Smash the records you possess which present a pagan culture and a pagan concept of life. Check beforehand the record which will be played at a house party or a school record dance. Switch your radio dial when you hear a suggestive song."

I flew back to England to be demobbed. A few days later, I returned home a civilian to live with my family at 60 Blenheim Road, Penge. For some weeks I went around with my Aunt Bessie and Aunt Joan, both about five years my senior. I took an old girlfriend, Shirley, out a few times too and I started to fall for my Aunt Joan, the widow of my father's brother Freddie. We got on well, but we both felt it was too close to home.

A major impact on my life came when at the Regal Cinema in Beckenham with some friends I saw the film *Rock Rock Rock*. All was as normal until suddenly Chuck Berry appeared in a white suit, singing "You Can't Catch Me." As he started doing what was later to be known as the "duck walk" the whole audience started to laugh. They seemed to think it was a comedy number, but my hair stood up on the back of my neck and I got cold shivers all over. I've never been so affected before or since. This was *it*! I became a dedicated Chuck Berry fan from that moment. His records were not available in England at that time so I would order them direct from America. Singles would take a month to arrive and I patiently waited three months for his album, *One Dozen Berries*. Suddenly, it seemed, *our* music was everywhere. Jerry Lee Lewis's "Great Balls of Fire" went to Number One in England and then was replaced by Elvis Presley's "Jailhouse Rock."

In February I decided to get a job again, and I went back for my old job at City Tote, where I'd previously worked. I was interviewed by the boss, John Hammond, but he wouldn't re-employ me. I was shocked: he acted like he'd never seen me before. Because I'd done more than my National Service requirement he no longer had to take me back. So I started looking around for work. I went for interviews for jobs with insurance and elevator companies, but as soon as they heard that my last job was for a bookmaker, it was all over. Finally, I managed to get a job working in the offices of W. Weddell and Company, meat importers, in the Royal Victoria Docks, East Ham for £6 10s. a week. Initially I traveled there by train and bus but owing to my low wages I soon started to journey the twenty-six miles by bicycle.

My social life was busy: I started going with friends to the Royston Ballroom, Penge, which was run by the famous dance team, Frank and Peggy Spencer. One night, sitting having coffee in the balcony, a friend pointed out some girls he knew. I said how much I fancied one of them. She was dark-haired, rather Spanish in appearance. We invited them up for coffee and I began chatting to her. Discovering that she liked jiving, I asked her for a dance. I began taking her out regularly and we became enthusiastic jive-dancers, winning competitions.

The girl was to become my wife. Diane Maureen Cory, born in February 1941, lived with her widower father and younger sister in Kirkdale Road, Upper Sydenham. Her mother had died when she was a kid, so she had become used to running the house from an early age, and was a good cook. She had very black, curly hair, a cheerful personality and enjoyed a laugh. In fact she did turn out to have Spanish blood, through a grandparent. Diane had a well-paid job as a bank clerk at Barclays, Millbank, preparing statements—these were still the days before computers.

We didn't have enough money to go out every night, so when we couldn't afford the cinema, we watched television either at her house or mine, or visited her relatives in Dulwich, Beckenham and Bromley. They were good fun, very amusing, and we had a pleasant time.

Diane was a sports fan—she was long-jump champion at school, played netball and followed Crystal Palace like me. Our main social life revolved around the eight boys and girls who went to dances and spent evenings at the Three Tuns Hotel, Beckenham.

Diane had been brought up under the iron hand of her father in a well-behaved, middle-class family, and she believed in virginity before marriage. We indulged in heavy petting but no actual sex took place during our courtship. It wasn't a big issue to me at the time, but the sexual aspect of our relationship was to surface as a major problem later.

At this time the seeds of a British rock 'n' roll movement began unwittingly to be sown when—on April 13, 1958—the Marquee Jazz Club opened in London, promoting modern jazz. The jazz world was buoyant and the prospect of this venue playing host to groups such as the Stones were to become was unthinkable. Rock 'n' roll was far too teenage-orientated: on May 24 Jerry Lee Lewis opened his English tour at the Edmonton Regal and the next day the Sunday papers broke the news that his thirteen-year-old cousin, Myra Brown, had been bigamously married to Lewis for two months. Diane and I went to see him perform the following week at the Granada, Tooting. This was his last show before the tour was canceled because of adverse publicity. He returned home to America, where his new single "High School Confidential" was banned by almost all white radio stations in America and his career nose-dived, before he resurfaced and became a legend.

Around this time, I saw a Lonnie Donegan show and got so excited I danced in the aisles for the first and only time in my life. He was brilliant. But he was to slag off and insult the Stones in later years, a mean characteristic of so many of the old jazz musicians we eclipsed in popularity.

In September, I left W. Weddell and got a job at John A. Sparks (Diesel Engineers) at Streatham Hill, as storekeeper and progress clerk for about £11 per week. At first I traveled there from Penge by bus or train, but six months later I was able to buy my first car, a secondhand 1938 Morris 10, for £30. I had to spend a lot of time doing it up before I could travel to work in it each day.

After a row with her father which resulted in her getting a black eye, Diane moved in with my family in Blenheim Road. We were now winning the jiving competitions most weeks; our prize was free tickets for the next week's dance. We would also go to dances at the Beckenham Ballroom, where drainpipe trousers were banned. My mother remembers: "Bill had a good sense of humor. Once he went to a dance with Diane and was turned away because his trousers were too tight. So the next week he went along again, wearing a fairly wide pair of trousers. They let him in and he went straight into the toilets to take them off. Underneath were the same pair he had worn the week before."

After being together for eighteen months, Diane and I seemed virtually to drift into marriage, following the custom of so many of our friends. The pattern was so different in the late fifties: then, you left school, got a steady job, found your girl and settled down, mainly to escape from your family. And so on October 24, 1959, I celebrated my twenty-third birthday and married eighteen-year-old Diane at Christ Church, Penge. We moved into lodgings in Woodbine Grove, Penge, an inauspicious start to a doomed marriage.

During November, England's first motorway, the M1, opened. Diane and I went up it on a brief honeymoon, planning to visit my old RAF friend Jim Bottrell in Smethwick, Birmingham. Half-way up the motorway we realized that we had left his new address at home. Since we had enough petrol money for only one trip, we continued to Birmingham and drove to Smethwick. Now the challenge began! First, I drove to the center of town. I remembered that the house had a high number, so I looked for a long road. I took the first one we saw. I then drove half-way down that road. I stopped and approached an old woman sweeping her steps. I asked her if she knew my friend, who'd just moved in a week ago. She said that two doors down was a couple with a new baby—they had just moved there. I walked down and knocked on the door and Jim Bottrell opened it, proving that miracles really do happen!

3

How the Stones got the Blues

1960 was a remarkable year. I remember taking an interest in the USA's Little Joe 4 Spacecraft. The first Playboy Club was opened in America. And the Beatles were playing the tough clubs of Hamburg, unwittingly beginning a revolution for young people. But there was no way of predicting that the sixties would be such a momentous decade for hundreds of guitarists like me, who had grown up with rock 'n' roll. At the start of the decade I was twenty-three, had been married for three months and was in a regular, routine job. Diane and I, although desperately short of cash, wanted to set up our own home. All kinds of tensions were affecting the marriage. We were lodgers in a small house, continually worrying about money for rent and food. Unknown to me Diane told my mother of our shortages, and Mum gave her groceries. Perhaps because of these worries the marriage was not working sexually: three months after the wedding it was still not consummated.

My life was as conventional as that of many guys in their early twenties. I went to the Wallington public hall with a friend named Stewart Wealleans and saw a rock 'n' roll band called Neil Christian and the Crusaders. They had a bass player with white boots (quite daring) named Bootsie Slade. In the same hall, a few weeks later I saw a well-known act called Nero and the Gladiators. Pop music was still simply an interest, although my knowledge of it, and firm opinions on what was good and bad, was growing and developing.

Fantastic pop records that would live on forever were pouring out: the Everly Brothers' "Cathy's Clown" reached Number One in America. In Britain, Johnny Kidd and the Pirates went to the top with "Shakin' All Over," to be replaced by the Shadows' "Apache." A sad moment came when it was reported that Eddie Cochran, aged twenty-one, had died in a car crash in Wiltshire. In the States, the twist dance craze was spearheaded by Chubby Checker's single, "The Twist," which went to the top and soon repeated its success, both as a record and a dance, in Britain and the rest of the world.

My domestic life changed that autumn. After a year in lodgings Diane and I found a ground-floor flat at 40 Birbeck Road, Beckenham. The only thing in its favor was privacy. The place was smelly and consisted of a living room (with a big hole in the wall that I temporarily blocked off with the sofa), bedroom (damp, and almost impossible to be in) and a kitchen and scullery. The hallway was so damp the paper was peeling off. The toilet was in the garden and there was no hot water, no bathroom nor central heating. We had to wash in the kitchen sink, just as I had at my parents' house. Well, at least we were on our own. For this sordid accommodation, we paid £2 10s. a week rent.

Just after my twenty-fourth birthday and our first wedding anniversary I quit the job I'd held for nearly two years over a pay dispute, and I began a new job locally at Duponts department store in Penge High Street with lower wages but saving on food and travel.

The pop charts were alive with great stuff: Roy Orbison's "Only the Lonely" was top, while in America Ray Charles's "Georgia on my Mind" was Number One. At work music entered my life unexpectedly: I became friendly with a colleague, Steve Carroll, who played the guitar. Inspired by his interest, I bought my first electric guitar, a Burns, for £52 on hire-purchase. The seeds of my first pop group were sown when I introduced Steve to Chuck Berry records and we began practicing with my sister Anne's brother-in-law, Cliff Starkey.

We decided to form a group in Beckenham. At Duponts, another colleague, Len Holdaway, said he would consider managing us if we did get it together. Regular practice sessions began with Steve Carroll and Cliff Starkey at my flat and at Len's house in Beckenham.

My pay was £10 a week and after deductions I took home £8 10s. With rent and hire-purchase for furniture totaling about £6, that left little for extras. We allowed ourselves £1 5s. a week for everything else. What remained was a 15-shilling float for things we had to save for, like clothes. There was not even any money for cigarettes. But over Christmas 1960 I decided that if music was worth taking seriously I'd better get good equipment. On January 4 I returned to the Art Nash Music Shop in Penge and rather wildly took on more debt: hire-purchase for £23 for a Watkins Westminster amplifier. That night I practiced with Steve, Cliff and another work-mate, Dennis Squires, who sang a little. We thought of calling ourselves "The Squires." A few days later we practiced at Len Holdaway's house and by January 15 Len had arranged an afternoon audition for us at the Starlight Ballroom, Penge.

At the audition, with Dennis on vocals and his brother Keith on drums, Steve Carroll and I also sang, while Steve and Cliff played guitars—all through one amp. Unbelievably I played guitar through my tape-recorder speaker set to record/pause. We were thrilled to be given a booking at the Starlight for January 21. By day, I was at Duponts working on the ledgers; by night, the rehearsals increased, with the same band and an Elvis-mad singer named Andy. We rehearsed the hits of the day.

When the big day came for our first public performance we were very nervous, but although our first set was bad, the second was very good. I broke a string and we had no spares; replacement was an expensive business, but our practice sessions continued and within a month we had played successfully at a wedding in Thornton Heath, Surrey.

There followed a series of the sort of gigs any semi-professional band looks for: parties at the houses of my parents, friends and a few youth clubs. Then Stewart Wealleans, who had his own group, borrowed my amplifier for a practice which Steve Carroll and I attended. We jammed with them and it was here that I met their lead guitarist, Brian Cade, who was to be an important cog in my musical wheel. Cliff finally found a singer for the band, Dave Harvey, who began to practice with us.

I continued to rehearse with Steve and Cliff, although finding somewhere for these practice sessions was a problem. We were offered the Freemasons Hall, Penge, for £1 a night, but that was far too expensive. Out of the blue, a phone call came from John A. Sparks, offering me my old job back as a clerk. I asked for £14 a week and accepted £13 5s.

The future of our group, still unnamed, was uncertain, as Keith Squires declined our offer to be the drummer. However, we recruited another local guy, Tony Chapman, and began rehearsals every Thursday night at the Lord Palmerston pub in Penge. It was time to kick the group into shape, decide on a name and get moving: we played for the first time as the newly named Cliftons at a wedding in Stockwell.

Diane said at this time: "I was never particularly interested in pop music before Bill took it up. I didn't mind him playing in a group. Even if I did, there was nothing I could have done. Once he started playing guitar, you couldn't get him to put it down."

The word was spreading among our friends that we'd formed a group but we had to turn down dates when Steve went on holiday for two weeks. On the day of his return, we were booked for the wedding reception of some friends at Anerley Town Hall. This was the first time we had ever played on an actual stage and we rose to the occasion, playing creditably. I felt the group was on its way.

One of the biggest turning points in my life came at the beginning of August 1961 when Diane and I went to Aylesbury to visit my sister Anne and her husband David. We went to a dance in an old converted cinema. On stage were the Barron Knights, who later became popular by brilliantly mimicking other people's hits. The sound of their bass guitar hit me straight in the balls. Staggered by its impact and the foundation it gave to the sound, I realized immediately what was missing in the Cliftons. From that moment, I wanted to play the bass.

It suited my personality. At twenty-four, I didn't see myself as an "upfront" musician, singing or playing at the head of a band. I was always more attuned to the overall sound, the need for internal dynamics and *precision*. I'm an orderly person; bass playing suits my outlook. I bought a set of bass strings and tried unsuccessfully to fit them on to my six-string instrument. Back in Beckenham, I told our new drummer, Tony Chapman, that the Cliftons needed a bassist and I intended to find an instrument. He found me a secondhand bass guitar for £8, which I couldn't really afford, but somehow I scraped the cash together.

I got to work on it immediately, reshaping it with the help of a neighbor's fretwork machine. I took all the frets out, intending to replace them with new ones, but it sounded so good that I kept it like that, making it the first fretless bass in England. I then realized I needed my own amplifier, so with the help of Tony Chapman and Stewart Wealleans I bought an eighteen-inch Goodman bass speaker. We had a huge cabinet built and put concrete in the bottom, as we'd heard this improved the sound. Unfortunately, it also made it really heavy to carry! We then sent off for a build-it-yourself Linear–Concorde 30-watt amplifier to run it through; this gave me electric shocks every time I plugged it in.

By January, our sound getting tighter, the Cliftons started playing occasional dances in Essex. We'd found someone to drive us around in a van and help with the gear. The two or three gigs a week didn't make us any profit, as we were all paying for our instruments and amplifiers by installments and there was petrol money to find, but Tony Chapman and I secured work outside the Cliftons, working with a pianist in a social club in Beckenham. We played hits like "Poetry in Motion" and were paid £2 a night each, plus drinks and sandwiches, in return for song requests. This was vital money, about 20 per cent of my "day job" take-home pay. It made all the difference when I faced that regular problem of buying spare strings. A set of bass guitar strings was £3 10s.—a load of money.

My brother Paul: "I used to go around with Bill as his great slave in the Cliftons days, carrying his amplifiers. I remember taking them from Beckenham to the Lord Palmerston pub in Penge, about four miles, and those things weighed a ton. We used to do that every week for practice sessions. I didn't want to be a burden—he was a grown-up and I was a kid—but I loved traipsing around and being with my big brother. Our parents went along OK with the Cliftons thing: our father had played the accordion in pubs for drinks and they simply felt Bill was doing the same, earning a little bit of extra cash. I don't think John, Judy or Anne had any interest because they didn't understand his music. They didn't know or understand his potential. To see people clap your brother on stage was a great feeling. He was very dedicated, very organized, long before he met the Stones."

Inside the Cliftons, Steve Carroll's guitar-work was starting to improve brilliantly. He could copy a Chuck Berry record note for note after only a couple of hearings, and his improvised runs were astonishing us. Brian Cade left Stewart Wealleans' group and joined us as second lead guitarist and the group was back with a fresh line-up and loads of enthusiasm.

All the Cliftons went to the Majestic Cinema in Mitcham, south London, to see a show by Jerry Lee Lewis. He was fantastic, and we yelled for encore after encore. When he didn't come out again we left and began walking down the road. Suddenly we heard that now-famous left-hand boogie rhythm pounding out. We rushed back into the theater and saw Jerry Lee, complete with towels around his shoulders, doing one more song. Fabulous!

We began playing regularly at a church youth club at St. Michael's Hall in Lower Sydenham, opposite the Wranglers, who were good. We bought matching jeans and black mohair jumpers, painted a sign with the band's name for display on stage and took photos at rehearsals. The gigs continued in Essex, Kent and southeast London, and our repertoire grew to include rock 'n' roll songs of the Coasters, Sam Cooke, Jerry Lee Lewis, Chuck Berry, Lloyd Price, Fats Domino, Larry Williams, Ray Charles and Little Richard. We were quite a long, progressive distance from the pop music of the day, from Cliff Richard, Brenda Lee, Kenny Ball, Helen Shapiro and Eden Kane. We liked music with more guts.

In June, unknown to the rest of the Cliftons, Tony Chapman answered a *Melody Maker* advertisement for a drummer by an unknown group called the Rollin' Stones. He went to rehearse with them at the Bricklayer's Arms in Soho.

One night in July, we played at Greenwich Town Hall opposite the Paramounts, a Southend group who played similar music to the Cliftons. We became friendly; they later became Procol Harum, and had an international hit with "Whiter Shade of Pale" in the mid-sixties.

A few days later our vocalist Dave Harvey left. We

decided to change our image and become more "white rock 'n' roll." Steve and I would do the singing. On July 26 I bought a new instrument to replace the second-hand model I'd been managing with. I returned to the Art Nash Music Shop to commit all the money I didn't have to buy an £84 Vox Phantom bass guitar. Shortly afterwards I bought a Vox AC30 amplifier from the same shop: this was the gear most of the sixties groups used. The Cliftons added a sax player and we started playing larger shows.

With the number of gigs increasing—a riverboat show up the Thames, an appearance at the London School of Economics that Michael Jagger might have seen and some exceptional shows at Chislehurst Caves, where one night we did several encores—my commitment to the bass guitar was now absolute.

All this was, of course, a year before the Beatles and the rest began the revolution. While I was being energized by rock 'n' roll, the country was gripped by a traditional jazz boom, with "The Three Bs," Acker Bilk, Chris Barber and Kenny Ball, taking their music to huge commercial success. There just wasn't any money in running a pop group, especially semi-professionally.

It was a bitter, but not unexpected, blow, therefore, when in September the Cliftons lost the saxophone player who gave us such a beefy sound. He returned to playing jazz for more money. Lack of cash, in fact, caused the bottom to fall out of our group: we were victims of rip-offs from promoters who failed to pay us for our appearances. Tony Chapman and I spent days in the office of one such promoter who owed us a lot of money. He wouldn't see us and we went home dejected and penniless. The band, with cash shortages and the loss of an important player just at the time its music was coming together, lost a lot of momentum that autumn of 1962.

At the beginning of December, Tony Chapman told me about the Rollin' Stones. He came to my flat and said they didn't have a bass player; he suggested I go with him to meet them. I asked what kind of stuff they played. "Blues music," he said, "very slow, easy to play." Tony had brought with him a tape-recorder with music by Jimmy Reed, the Stones' favorite, so that I could get the idea.

On December 5, 1962, Tony took me to the Red Lion pub in Sutton, Surrey, where a live band, the Presidents, led by Glyn Johns, was playing to a reasonable crowd of young people. In the interval I was introduced to Ian Stewart, the Stones' pianist, who was in the audience. Ian suggested I go to the Stones' rehearsal two days later, taking my equipment. Well, why not? What did I have to lose?

On Friday, December 7, it was snowing. After work about two inches of snow had collected on the ground and it was absolutely freezing as Tony Chapman and I went in his father's car to Chelsea for the audition. We entered the Wetherby Arms pub through a side door, directly into the back room where the Stones were rehearsing. I spoke to Ian Stewart again, who introduced me to Mike Jagger, who was quite friendly; I then met Brian Jones and Keith Richards, who were at the bar. For musicians, their appearance surprised me: they had hair down over their ears and looked very scruffy—Bohemian and arty. This was quite a shock: in the pop world I came from, smartness was automatic. I was neatly dressed, as for work, with a Tony Curtis hairstyle. My entire demeanor clashed with their unkempt look. People with casual, shabby jackets and trousers were not the sort of people I usually mixed with.

They were very cool and distant, showing little interest in knowing me. And the feeling was mutual. As Stu recalled: "They were in one of their funny moods and didn't even bother to talk to Bill. So he didn't know what was going on. Bill wasn't one bit impressed."

The big turning point came when I got my equipment in from the car and set it up. Their eyes opened wide on seeing my Vox AC30, my echo unit, plus the enormous wardrobe I'd built, which was about the size of a door, with my eighteen-inch speaker and amplifier that ran it. In those days, that was really big stuff. Keith remembers: "We all turned up for rehearsals, and in walks Bill with a huge speaker and a spare Vox AC30 amp, which was the biggest amp we'd seen in our lives! 'That's spare,' he said. 'You can put one of your guitars through there.' Whew! That put us up quite a few volts. He had the bass together already. He'd been playing in rock bands, knew how to play, but he didn't want to play with those shitty rock bands anymore." All *they* had to play through were two small amplifiers, about a foot square; all the speakers were distorted. My gear impressed them, and they acknowledged the fact that I had been playing successfully in a group. Stu said: "There's a certain amount of truth in the old story about Bill being taken on because he had a few amplifiers. But Bill was very good."

I bought a round of drinks and offered cigarettes. These were jumped on as if I were delivering famine relief. Still Brian and Keith hardly spoke. Mike asked me if I knew the music of any black blues players. I replied the only names I knew in that field were Chuck Berry and Fats Domino. I talked about the people who had inspired the Cliftons: the Coasters, Jerry Lee Lewis, Eddie Cochran, Johnny Burnette, Lloyd Price and Sam Cooke—but the looks I got from Mike, Brian and Keith showed their disdain.

We rehearsed some slow Jimmy Reed songs and other pretty authentic blues, with frequent breaks between songs. I was feeling my way; I was OK on the up-tempo stuff, when they played Chuck Berry songs, but I knew nothing about the more obscure Muddy Waters, Elmore James and Bo Diddley material that formed most of their repertoire. It seemed to me to be samey, monotonous music. I remarked on the format of the songs to them: "You can't play fucking twelve-bar blues *all* night!" They chatted a little but made it clear to me that I wasn't really in favor, even though they asked me to come to another rehearsal. I agreed and we went back to their flat in Edith Grove, Chelsea, to leave my equipment in the disaster zone—the front room. Tony Chapman and I drove back that night to south London. I wondered about the bizarre world I was entering. How on earth had this group of layabouts got together to play minority music with such conviction?

Brian Jones, the founder of the Stones, lived fast and died young. Long before the phrase "sex, drugs and rock 'n' roll" entered our dictionaries, he perfectly mirrored all three categories. Through his vision of music and his lifestyle, Brian was the inventor and inspiration of the Rolling Stones. The band would not have existed without him. He never received that proper credit during his life and I intend to ensure he gets it now. Many of the attitudes and sounds of the sixties were developed from Brian's style and determination, traceable to his own roots and frustrations. He was the archetypal middle-class kid screaming to break away from his background, bumming around in dead-end jobs before finally finding his niche. And when he found it, he hammered it across to the world, with idealism and commitment.

To understand the origins of the Rolling Stones it's essential to trace the wayward life of this man. In the sixties and seventies the Stones were considered the wild men of rock. Jagger, as lead singer, and Richards, who played his outlaw image to the hilt, were the front-runners to the public. But if ever a man genuinely lived the rock 'n' roll life and naturally characterized the Stones in every way—long before the five of us assumed a style—it was Brian Jones. I loved the guy. He pushed every friendship to the limit and way beyond, but he had great heart and was crucial to our existence.

He was a true child of the sixties, a philanderer, the father of five known illegitimate children, beginning on that trail at the early age of sixteen, when he was still at school. There, he was a typical grammar school student, academically very bright, but with a burning ambition to kick aside all the values of his comfortable life in the genteel town in which he was born: Cheltenham Spa, on the edge of the rolling green hills of the Cotswolds. The environment in which Brian grew up was best described by Keith Richards: "an old ladies' resting place . . . very pretty in its way. But dullsville."

Women and music were Brian's chief loves in his formative years. Drugs and drink came much, much later, with a vengeance typical of his addiction to excess. But the love of music that grew inside him was by far the most important force in the Stones' story. A rebel with a cause, he nursed an absolute fervor for true American blues. This obsession created the Stones, made them what they were—totally different from every other pop group. His knowledge of the origins of our music, and the translation of it into a British sound, was our blueprint.

His sex appeal, alongside that of Mick's, also made us different from every group on earth.

There was a hilarious rumor through the sixties that

Brian was gay. The word has never been more misapplied. He was a sexual athlete, and one of the most prodigious woman-chasers I have ever known. Maybe the homosexual rumor was fanned by the fact that he started a trend for men wearing jewelry.

Lewis Brian Hopkin-Jones was born on February 28, 1942, at the Park Nursing Home, Cheltenham. Brian was born into a comfortable family life at "Rosemead," Eldorado Road in Cheltenham. His Welsh-born father, Lewis Blount Jones, university-educated, was an aeronautical engineer. Dour, upright and conformist, Brian's father played piano and was the organist and secretary of the choral society at the local church. Brian's mother, Louisa Beatrice, was a piano teacher.

His sister Barbara was born the same year that Brian, not yet four, began infants school in Cheltenham. She became a skillful pianist and violinist. Brian's home life was stable and comparatively unaffected by wartime Britain. The main event in Brian's childhood was the croup he had when he was four, which left him with terrible asthma attacks; this would affect him for the rest of his life. His interest in music came early: at seven years old, as his parents moved him to the fee-paying Dean Close Junior Public School, he began piano lessons, augmenting his regular studies with piano theory and sight-reading, taught by his mother. He said later he had a natural "feel" for music. "I guess I knew that I was going to be interested only in music very early on." He studied piano until he was fourteen. At twelve he began clarinet lessons, joining the school orchestra. Within two years he was the lead clarinetist.

In September 1953 at the age of eleven he won a place to Cheltenham Grammar School. So far he seemed on course for a good education followed by a conventional career. At school he quickly excelled in music and in English. He invented a serialized space story, adding a new chapter weekly, with everyone eagerly awaiting new installments. The conservatism, stability and gentility of life in an English country town was partly accepted by Brian, but the creativity inside him began gnawing away with little release.

His mother recalls him as being very keen on sports at school, particularly cricket, table tennis and judo. He was a fine diver although he wasn't particularly interested in swimming. Later, however, Brian said he had found football and cricket "boring." "I just couldn't take games," he said. "All that running around for no real reason seemed a waste of time. I skived off whenever it was possible. I mean, what is the point of it all? The funny thing is that, almost despite my attitude, I wasn't bad at badminton. At least there was a bit of action there. Mostly, though, it was just that I couldn't stand being bored, or all the organization."

When Brian was listed for a football match he suddenly developed a nasty limp or coughed his way around school in an attempt to be excused. Later, as a Rolling Stone, he came on with the same symptoms, missing many rehearsals, recordings and live shows. The only difference was that in later life, the symptoms he grumbled about were for real, but people disbelieved him because of their frequency.

At fifteen Brian, who was nicknamed "Buster" at school, began playing washboard in a local skiffle group. Thousands of such groups sprang up around Britain, inspired by the song "Rock Island Line" by the Chris Barber band. Chris Rowe, a girl who sang in Brian's group, remembers how Brian played washboard and often lost his thimble as they practiced in the Community Center on the Rowanfield Estate: "We were just kids messing around; there was no long-term planning."

Academically, Brian was by far the most successful Rolling Stone when it came to exam successes. In July 1958, at the age of sixteen, he got nine O-level passes in the General Certificate of Education. His father pointed him towards science subjects for the next stage of his exams, although his heart was not really in it. Brian gained two A-levels in physics and chemistry, but failed biology. Brian recalled that as his behavior at school became more erratic, he was carpeted by the headmaster about once a week, and often caned: "I played the teachers up and skipped classes to go swimming."

"When I made the sixth form at age fifteen," Brian said, "I found myself accepted by the older boys, and suddenly I was *in*." In his first term in the sixth, during the autumn of 1957, Brian went to the local jazz club with some other boys, and from that first exposure to jazz sprang his addiction to experimental sounds. Friends remember him whistling along to traditional jazz tunes like "When the Saints Go Marching In" and "Muskrat Ramble." At a friend's house he heard old recordings of Charlie "Bird" Parker, on the alto-saxophone, and after hearing that innovative genius, Brian persuaded his parents to buy him an alto-sax. Jazz then became a religion to him; he borrowed records to listen to them repeatedly in his bedroom, trying to imitate Parker's improvisational runs.

A first mover and learner, he started his own band at sixteen. "We played in the interval at the local jazz club which met three or four times a week," he said. "Those nights I lost the habit of doing my homework but when it piled up I would work on it till three or four in the morning. I never neglected my work."

On his seventeenth birthday his parents gave him his first Spanish acoustic guitar, which cost £3. Brian was still a natural rebel. Rejecting discipline he was suspended from school twice. When the headmaster complained and his father asked him why he consistently disobeyed, Brian was, says Lewis Jones, "terribly logical about it all." Defending his and his friends' antics as simply the games of teenagers, Brian said to his father: "You want me to do the things you did. But I can't be like you. I have to live my own life."

Around the same time a fourteen-year-old schoolgirl named Valerie became pregnant by him. She refused his request to have an abortion and the baby boy was adopted at birth. Fatherhood at seventeen cast Brian as the rogue of his school and he quickly felt alienated from his classmates by the scandal. To add to his problems the girl refused to have anything further to do with him. He now felt marooned, a frustrated father and a reluctant scholar.

Leaving school at eighteen, Brian showed a passing interest in studying to be a dentist, but he quickly disappointed his father by refusing to go to university. He said he could not face even more years of study before becoming self-supporting in a job. Brian's decision was particularly distressing to his parents, who knew he had an IQ of 135.

Now began a period of aimless drifting. Nothing less than London would do for Brian. His father took him for

an interview with an optician in the capital. After that
Lewis Jones suggested hurrying for the five o'clock train.
"No, Dad, I want to go to some jazz clubs before we go
home. Would you like to come along?" His father said
no, after deducing that Brian knew his way around London from various hitchhiking trips. While his father returned home, Brian stayed and eventually got back to
Cheltenham at six o'clock the next morning.

The job with the optician came through in August 1959
and Brian moved to a spartan bed-sitter in London. But
boredom set in after a week. Music was now not an
interest but an addiction: "Quite honestly, I didn't feel
much of an urge to do anything else," he said, returning
to Cheltenham. He still rejected the thought of a regular
job: "I knew I'd be bored stiff." His father remembers:
"Brian was obsessed with music. He used to play modern
jazz records morning, noon and night. I saw it as a
positive evil in his life."

Back in Cheltenham, gossip and pressure from the
parents of the girl who bore his child once again forced
Brian to flee. Taking his guitar and saxophone, he went
to Scandinavia with friends, temporarily enjoying the life
of a busker among the fun-loving blondes he'd heard so
much about. Now away from the strictures of conventional life and the rigidity of school, Brian indulged himself. He almost starved, but he loved the freedom—and
the girls. Apart from music, sex dominated his life. "Those
few months were the most free and happy of my life," he
recalled. He limped back to Cheltenham in November
when he ran out of money. Vaguely planning his future
in music, he went to see a band at the Wooden Bridge
Hotel, Guildford, a venue which the Stones would later
play regularly. There he met a twenty-three-year-old married woman and enjoyed a one-night encounter that would
eventually produce his second illegitimate child.

The sedate town of Cheltenham, in these years long
before rock 'n' roll was part of growing up, was stifling
Brian. To relieve the boredom he became an habitué of
the local coffee bars. There his shaggy blond hair and
scruffy appearance attracted the eye of the local girls,
among whom he had quite a reputation. One, a sixteen-
year-old trainee beautician in a local chemist's shop, was
particularly drawn to him. Her name was Pat Andrews,

and she immediately recognized him as "different" from the other boys in the Aztec coffee bar. But they did not speak for over a month, until on January 10, 1960, she went to the cinema in the afternoon with two girlfriends. In the intermission they met and began chatting. After the film they all went to the Aztec for coffee. Brian took Pat home, beginning a romance that was to last intermittently for three years.

Pat mused on the deep-thinking, sensitive boy, who had the attraction of being the local Romeo. He was, after all, a father by one of her schoolfriends. He told her he was living in Cheltenham with his parents and working in the sports department of a local store.

Quickly, Brian introduced her to the music that he now loved, traditional jazz, and he took her to see a local group, the Chelton Six, rehearse.

Shortly after meeting Pat, Brian became a factory worker, catching the bus seven miles to Brockworth each day. The job ended abruptly when he got a lift one day in a work-mate's van. The vehicle overturned, Brian's leg was injured and a front tooth knocked out. From then on whenever he laughed he would cover his mouth with his hand, a habit he developed at this time.

Brian spent most days hanging out at the Aztec, Ken Smith's Patio Wine Bar on the Promenade, the Waikiki, the Bar-B-Q coffee bar and the El Flamenco (the El Flam) coffee bar. All were patronized by art students, local musicians and supporters of the Campaign for Nuclear Disarmament. At this stage his blond hair was short and his attire consisted of jeans, an open-neck shirt and sweater. He drifted around various parties and gained and discarded as many girlfriends as possible. Brian's sexual appetite, his continual desire for as many conquests as he could cram into each day, marked his life. His physical attractiveness to women, as a front-line member of the Stones, was to be very important to the band's success. But in these early years, back in Cheltenham, his association with girls spelled trouble.

In February 1960, as he celebrated his eighteenth birthday, the twenty-three-year-old woman he had met in Guildford found she was pregnant from her one-night union with Brian. Her husband stood by her and they decided to go ahead with the birth. The baby girl was born on August 4. When she was seven, the girl was temporarily paralyzed after what was revealed to be an epileptic fit. In 1981, at the age of twenty-one, she married but divorced three years later. By 1986, when she was living with her parents in southern England, the girl and I spoke about Brian. What she said seems to me to throw a revealing light on his demeanor and antics inside the Stones, behavior which puzzled us for so many years: his tantrums, illnesses, absences and general contrariness. Her theories about the father she never met also have an important bearing on the still-mysterious circumstances surrounding his death in the swimming pool of his home on July 3, 1969. "Death by misadventure . . . under the influence of drugs and alcohol," said the inquest verdict. This makes me wonder: did Brian hide a debility that affected his life, the Stones' career and even his death? More of that later, as the band's tale unfolds, because the early life of the Stones' founder is critical to our story, particularly the sounds he grew up to at the beginning of 1960.

Dixieland jazz was still enormously popular in Britain as a new decade dawned, for although Bill Haley had arrived with "Rock Around the Clock" five years earlier, nothing had happened so far to ignite British youth into do-it-yourself rock 'n' roll.

Brian had been playing acoustic guitar and saxophone with two local bands in Cheltenham: John Keen's trad band and Bill Nile's Delta Jazzband. At the clubs and pubs they played, girls hung around the band, flirting with him. Pat Andrews, then his regular girlfriend, became jealous of his popularity and they frequently argued. One night Brian punched her in the face and she ran home with a black eye, crying. A few hours later, Brian, the true romantic, arrived outside her home, throwing pebbles up at her window and shouting his apologies. They were quickly reunited.

The details of Brian's waywardness highlight the force that molded the early Stones. The nomadic lifestyle of some of the American musicians who played his beloved jazz and blues played a big part in shaping his attitude to life. Some might say Brian had a lot to answer for, since he boosted youth's confidence and independence by his example. The more I look at his story, the more I'm convinced that he was the prototype on which the attitudes of the Stones, and consequently a substantial slice of liberated sixties attitudes, were built.

All the time he rebelled against a structured life in the beautiful Cotswolds. His first work connected with music came in the month he became a father for the second time: Brian took a job as a sales assistant at Syd Tong's record shop in Cheltenham. It was hardly the professional route expected of a boy who had left grammar school with such solid academic achievements, but worse was to come as Brian fought orthodoxy and wondered how to make inroads into the music world.

The dramatic change in his life, and the true roots of the formation of the Rolling Stones, came in the autumn of that year, 1960. As a traditional jazz listener and occasional player, Brian went to a Cheltenham concert given by Chris Barber's Jazz Band.

Barber was a thirty-year-old trombonist leading a hugely popular band. More importantly for posterity, he was a studious musician who understood the roots of American blues. Having formed his band in 1954 as a breakaway unit from the Ken Colyer band, at whose London club the Stones would later nurture their sound, Barber launched "a band within a band." This featured what he considered to be "country blues," partly as a diversion on stage from the main band's repertoire of Dixieland music. "We called it skiffle music," recalls Chris, "from a record called 'Hometown Skiffle' made in 1928."

Tony Donegan, the Barber band's banjoist/guitarist, was the skiffle-group singer. Changing his name to Lonnie to honor his blues-singing hero Lonnie Johnson, Donegan sang on the Barber band's single "Rock Island Line," which became a Number One hit and million-seller in 1956, barely a year after the band's formation.

Barber was beginning a policy of importing little-known American giants of the blues into Britain to tour with him. On the bill that night was the harmonica-player Sonny Boy Williamson. The Barber band, too, was featuring songs like "I Got My Mojo Working" by the great Muddy Waters. Later that year Barber planned to bring Muddy to Britain.

Brian was entranced. He loved experimental, raw and genuine sounds, and the music struck a chord deep inside his soul. From that moment he investigated blues music played by American artists like Jimmy Reed, Howlin' Wolf and Robert Johnson, and they became his obsession. The future sound of the Rolling Stones was born inside Brian Jones's head.

While the seeds of a life in music had been planted inside him, Brian's working life was at a standstill. He became one of Cheltenham's best-known beatnik bums. The coffee-bar grapevine would tell him which parties were happening where. At the El Flamenco Brian became friendly with John Appleby, ten years his senior and something of a sage in the beat world. Collecting Brian from his home one night en route to a party, Appleby was hustled into the living room by Brian's mother, out of Brian's sight. She told of her worry about her son's party-going antics and his disorderly life. "He doesn't seem the least inclined to do any work. Please see what you can do about it."

As they drove away, John insisted to Brian that he get a job. Appleby had a somewhat freaky hobby, studying buses. He told Brian that the local bus company were very short of conductors. "I suggest you go down tomorrow and see about a temporary job. If you don't, I'm coming round tomorrow morning, and I'll drag you out of bed and push you into the manager's office." Next night Brian phoned Appleby: "You'll be interested to know that I'm starting the job on Monday."

There were at least two sides to Brian's personality. One Brian was introverted, shy, sensitive, deep-thinking. The other was a preening peacock, gregarious, artistic, desperately needing assurance from his peers. He enjoyed meeting people in his role as a conductor on Cheltenham's double-decker buses, but John Appleby sensed it would not last long. Indeed, after three weeks Brian quit. He was out of work again, and again his parents were nagging him to find a regular job.

On December 18, 1960, he began work as a coalman but, embarrassed by it, told his parents he had a more respectable job. He changed clothes and bathed at a friend's house before going home. He quit after three days, anyway, and on receiving his pay packet he bought two necklaces for Pat Andrews' birthday. A week later, on December 26, Pat and Brian called at the flat of a friend of his. Nobody was at home, but the door was open and the apartment empty. Brian and Pat went in and made love for the first time. Brian quickly became very possessive about Pat, feeling jealous and threatened by other boys she knew. He wanted her complete attention and loyalty, while insisting upon freedom for himself. This was the pattern of his life.

Like thousands of other beatniks at the start of 1961, who identified closely with the free-sounding music of jazz, Brian went to see the Kenny Ball Jazzmen at Cheltenham Rotunda, and he began talking to a young man named Dick Hattrell, whom he had seen at many local shows. He was glad to find a kindred spirit who loved blues music. Brian asked his help in finding obscure American import records by Sonny Boy Williamson and Muddy Waters, not exactly household names in those years.

He had another point of empathy with Dick: arguing with their parents, who grumbled about their late nights, partying and hanging around in coffee bars. Jones and Hattrell faced a simple ultimatum from their parents: if the loose living continued, they would have to live elsewhere. Dick left his Tewkesbury home and found digs at 38 Priory Street, Cheltenham. This was probably the push Brian needed. One night, returning home to Hatherley Road with Pat so that he could change clothes, Brian discovered the house locked. He had forgotten that his mother and father were away. Breaking a French window to gain entry, he collected his guitar and a few possessions and left, never to return.

He moved with Hattrell and two art students into a large bed-sitting-room in Parabola Road, Cheltenham for the next two months. There, he slept regularly with Pat, who soon fell pregnant. "Somehow," she recalled, "it came as no shock to me. It seemed right that I was to be the mother of Brian's child."

Just like the schoolgirl who had mothered his first illegitimate child, Pat refused Brian's request that she have an abortion. The imminence of a third baby scared Brian, and changed his attitude. There was no such phrase as "love child" in those years. Bastard children were a stigma on both parents. But Brian never used condoms—

and the birth-control pill was not in widespread use. Another child on the horizon was not good news; he was about to enjoy his new independence, living in a shared apartment away from home. And he'd been out of work since Christmas, supported by Pat's wages. Marriage was out of the question: Pat's parents, not surprisingly, didn't consider him stable enough to take their daughter's hand.

After another part-time job as a sales assistant in the electrical goods store Curry's, he gained a job as a junior architect, helping to design schools for Gloucestershire County Council.

One night in April, Brian had taken Pat to see James Dean in the film *Rebel Without a Cause.* The parallel between Dean and Brian was as obvious to them both as it is to me now.

By July he was seeing less of Pat. Her friends told her he was dating many other girls; being six months' pregnant, she tried to ignore this reality.

On September 1 Pat was asked to leave her job, but was promised she could return when the baby was born. A week later Brian moved with three boys to a flat in Pitfield Square, Cheltenham, where he could, as he recalled later, "kick around all over the place, doing nothing, going nowhere. I didn't really feel any great urge to work."

A glimmer of a change in his attitude occurred when, shortly after taking the new flat, Brian applied for a scholarship to Cheltenham Art College. He was overjoyed to be accepted. Two days after he received the offer his hopes crashed when a second letter arrived saying the authorities had reconsidered and withdrawn their acceptance. Brian heard from friends that someone had written to the college to say he was an irresponsible drifter and a potentially poor student.

Nobody who knew Brian well expected him to be loyal to any woman, but he wasn't a discreet two-timer. A heavily pregnant Pat visited him at his flat one Sunday morning in October to find him in bed with another girl. She was inconsolable for the week before being rushed to the Victoria Nursing Home, Cheltenham at midnight on October 22. Four hours later she gave birth to Brian's third illegitimate child, a boy weighing just under six pounds.

Pat did not expect to see Brian again, but she underestimated his sentimentality. On the day of the birth Brian sold his record collection, a fantastic gesture of self-deprivation, to buy a huge bouquet of red roses and carnations which he took to her in the nursing home. There was a musical end to this saga, for they decided to name the child Julian Mark, the first name chosen to reflect Brian's admiration for the jazz saxophonist Julian "Cannonball" Adderley. Brian visited Pat and his new son each day. On one visit he bumped into Pat's mother outside. After a terse exchange of words, she beat him with her umbrella.

Pat and baby Julian left the nursing home on November 2 to live with her parents, while Brian moved yet again, to a bed-sitter in Bath Road, Cheltenham. Pat visited him regularly but sexually he was still "playing the field."

In June 1961, Brian and Pat had gone regularly to the strangely named South London Jazz Club in Bishop's Cleeve, five miles north of Cheltenham. Hungry to catch the flavor of their music and tap their knowledge, Brian chatted to the musicians while Pat sulked in a corner, bored. At home Brian practiced on the acoustic guitar but found it difficult to make much progress.

The seeds of our approach to music were implanted into Brian's psyche by a French-born blues fan who was one of the pioneers of that music in Britain: Alexis Korner. Born in Paris on April 19, 1928 of an Austrian mother and Greek father, Korner was one of the great characters of the contemporary-music scene in Britain in the early 1960s.

Rather like Brian Jones, Alexis was a non-conforming reprobate as he grew up. Asked to leave St. Paul's School, Hammersmith, as well as the Boy Scouts and the Air Scouts, he then attended Finchden Manor, a school for extremely disturbed boys with high IQs. While there he built his first guitar from plywood and a shaved-down table leg. At the age of twelve he had stolen a Jimmy Yancey record from Shepherds Bush market and thus had begun an all-consuming interest in music. By 1953 his future as a musician was predictable as he began, at twenty-five, the rounds of the London pubs as a guitarist and singer.

In 1954 Alexis met a large, scruffy panel-beater named Cyril Davies, who played great harmonica and shared Alexis's passion for blues music. But it was a little early, and they had to pay some dues before they could make any impact. First came skiffle, which Korner initially played with a jazz band led by Ken Colyer, a British trumpeter whose re-creation of the New Orleans sounds of his black American idols was amazing.

In 1957 Korner met Cyril Davies again at the London Skiffle Club. Davies was also playing skiffle, but like so many inventive musicians he found the style restricting and unambitious. The two men joined forces and opened at the London Blues and Barrelhouse Club in Tottenham Court Road, playing what they called "folk-tinged blues." This was a truly radical move.

The first-night attendance totaled just three people, but they played on and eventually succeeded, running the club for three years and presenting many influential American performers, the first of which was the great Big Bill Broonzy, followed by charismatic blues figures Sonny Terry and Brownie McGhee, Jimmy Cotton, Little Brother Montgomery, Memphis Slim and Roosevelt Sykes.

Korner and Davies added more musicians to their band in 1958, including Geoff Bradord (guitar) and Keith Scott (piano). Two other names, destined to help shape British blues music, Long John Baldry (vocals) and Davy Graham (guitar), also played with them.

It's laughable now to report what caused Korner and Davies to move away from such modest beginnings to the center of the stage. Ejected from the London Blues and Barrelhouse Club in 1960 because they decided to use light amplification, they joined the Chris Barber Band, forming yet another blues unit within the main band.

Barber recalls: "Alexis, who was the only guy playing electric-guitar blues in England at that time, joined us along with Cyril Davies, who played harmonica. We did a thirty-minute rhythm-and-blues set at the end of every show and they played the blues break for eighteen months. We played once a week at the Marquee Club."

Barber was therefore a pivotal force in championing blues music in Britain. His importance in providing source material for Britain's emerging musicians has been criminally unrecognized. By providing a base first for skiffle and then for the blues, he was virtually a founding father of what came next: a British rock scene. "Playing the music here in England," an enthusiastic Barber said, explaining his adventurous acceptance of the Korner style, "we've always been cut off from what they're doing in America. So instead of playing the music of twenty or thirty years ago, I'd like to play this, the contemporary black music of today."

When Brian Jones and Dick Hattrell went to Cheltenham town hall in late 1961 to see a Barber band concert, the interval blues session by Korner blew their minds, and totally reshaped Brian's musical outlook. The sound was a synthesis of guitar-led vocals and free-flowing jazz rhythms, its roots definitely in the blues area with which Brian could identify. The sound touched a nerve deep inside him, he told us later. Because of his local status as an occasional jazz-band player, Brian had little trouble getting backstage after Korner's set, where he enthused about the night's music. Striking an immediate rapport, they adjourned to the Patio Wine Bar opposite. Korner, inviting Brian and Dick to visit him when they were in London, gave them his phone number and address.

Brian's lifestyle in Cheltenham contrasted with his application to music and intensity towards it. But he was constantly diverted by females. Now, as a nineteen-year-old unemployed father of three, Brian began dating a fourteen-year-old schoolgirl. He was soon to be seen openly walking arm in arm with her around the town—and she was dressed in her school uniform! Despite this Pat Andrews was reunited with him for a short time, but in December 1961, when he decided on a trip to London, he took his schoolgirl with him.

In London, Korner and Davies had now formed their own rhythm-and-blues band and called it Blues Incorporated. Alexis said: "We deliberately set out to destroy traditional jazz with its waistcoats, bowler hats and clarinets." After several phone conversations, Brian arrived on Korner's doorstep with his girl in tow and stayed with Korner and his wife for a few days. Inevitably a lot of time was spent playing Alexis's records. "I discovered

Elmore James," said Brian later, "and the earth seemed to shudder on its axis." So moved was he by James' ability to bare his soul through music that on returning to Cheltenham he went out and bought an electric guitar. He now became obsessed by the blues, sitting for hours practicing slide guitar, listening to any records he could find of Elmore James, Robert Johnson and Howlin' Wolf. He used a converted tape-recorder as an amplifier because he couldn't afford a proper one.

As Brian celebrated his twentieth birthday on February 28, 1962, the powerful forces that actually formed the Rolling Stones came into play. Brian, who had moved back to 23 Christchurch Road, met a young man named Paul Pond, later to become prominent under the name Paul Jones as a founder-member of Manfred Mann. Paul, who lived in Oxford, led a blues group called Thunder Odin's Big Secret. When his guitarist left he asked Brian to join him "because he was pretty good." Brian answered that he would join only on condition that he became the leader; Paul replied that the band already had a leader. Brian sat in with them a few times.

Paul quickly became aware of Brian's asthma: when he passed through Oxford, Brian would sleep on Paul's couch. One morning Paul awoke to hear wheezing and snorting, and Brian gasped that he was unable to breathe, having left his inhaler at a party they'd both attended the previous night. "I had to jump on my bike and dash off to get it for him."

Their enthusiasm for blues music inspired them to make a private tape together under the name of Elmo and Paul—Brian adapting the name of his hero of the hour, Elmore James.

Alexis Korner had persuaded Ealing Jazz Club to embark on its major contribution to changing the face of popular music by opening its doors to rhythm and blues. It became the first club in Britain to do so. An advertisement in the New Musical Express trumpeted:

Alexis Korner Blues Incorporated
The Most Exciting Event of the Year
Ealing Broadway station.
Turn left, cross the zebra and go down steps

between ABC Teashop and jewellers.
Saturday at 7.30 p.m.

Told of the vital breakthrough appearance by Korner, Brian and Dick Hattrell hitchhiked from Cheltenham to London for that important night, March 17, 1962.

Blues Incorporated comprised Korner (electric guitar), Charlie Watts (drums), Cyril Davies (harmonica), Dave Stevens (piano), Dick Heckstall-Smith (tenor sax) and a bass-playing friend of Charlie's named Andy Hoogenboom. Meeting up with Korner, Brian handed him the Elmo and Paul tape and asked for the chance to sit in with Blues Incorporated, a pretty brave request in view of Brian's inexperience.

On that first night a hundred people showed up, but within four weeks the attendance had doubled to the room's capacity of 200. The admission charge of five shillings included a year's membership. Korner had tapped a hidden following for true blues music in Britain and the club quickly had a membership of 800, with fans travelling down from as far away as Scotland. And all this sprang from small advertisements in a limited circulation paper, *Jazz News,* and in *New Musical Express*. This underground awareness of the blues was something Korner could never have predicted.

He recalled later: "The Ealing club, in the back room of the ABC bakery, was a drinking club. We drew most of our support every Saturday night from the folk area." Hattrell, remembering the exhausting journey with Brian from Cheltenham, said, "The hours and hours of hitch-hiking were well worth it. It was the first R & B club in Europe, a fantastic scene. We would get so wound up, it was incredible. We were literally spaced out with the music, it excited us so much. Brian was dying to play: he was a really good guitar player, even on that homemade amplifier of his. You could tell the sounds were there. He played a slide guitar before the average British guitarist had heard of it." Vitally for his future, Brian quickly developed a kinship with Korner and a core of blues players.

At the Ealing club's second session, on March 24, 1962, Brian sat in with Korner's Blues Incorporated. That night Brian spoke for the first time to the nineteen-year-old

drummer with Korner's band. By day, the drummer told
him, he worked as a graphic designer. Studious, shy and
quiet, Charlie Watts hasn't changed much. Being a Rolling Stone has almost passed him by. He has never courted
fame or sought pop stardom. Inside a band of powerful
personalities he remains a true British eccentric. Born
into a working-class family, at University College Hospital, Islington, on June 2, 1941, Charles Robert Watts was
the son of a British Railways lorry driver, Charles Richard Watts, and his wife Lillian Charlotte. As a child he
lived both with his parents at their Kingsbury home and
with his grandmother in King's Cross. Charlie recalled, "I
still can hear bombs exploding in the neighborhood. I
remember the mad rush from the house into the air-raid
shelters. War was something of a game to me and I don't
think I ever really and truly got frightened."

In 1948 Charlie's parents moved to Wembley when it
still had green fields and farms and in 1952 Charlie went
to Tylers Croft Secondary Modern School there. He
showed an early aptitude for art. "We had a choir but
nobody liked singing in it much; music consisted of a guy
lecturing, and nobody understood what he was saying." A
speedy right-winger who could have been a professional
footballer, he also loved cricket and had a trial for Middlesex. But he loathed physical training in the gymna-
sium: "I mean, it didn't get you anywhere."

His mother recalls him "rapping out tunes on the table
with pieces of wood or a knife and fork," but Charlie's
first instrument was a banjo, which he bought himself at
the age of fourteen. "I couldn't hit the dots on the frets
right, though. It drove me up the wall. After about four
weeks I took the thing apart. I made a stand for it out of
wood and played on the round skin part with brushes; it
was like a drum, anyway."

He adds: "I certainly can't claim I came from a musical
family. I reckon the only instrument any of them could
play at home was a gramophone." But it became obvious
that he wanted a drum kit, and for Christmas in 1955 his
parents bought him his first, for £12, convinced it would
be a nine-day wonder. "It was just a collection of bits and
pieces. I used to sell records to buy bigger cymbals," he
recalls. "I practiced at home to jazz records all the time.
The only rock 'n' roll I ever listened to was after the

Stones turned me on to it. I sort of picked up the technique by myself, by listening to other people's records and watching drummers. Of course, there were complaints from the neighbors but it was worth the odd argument. Gradually, I built up my confidence."

Leaving school in July 1957 at sixteen, he received two trophies for running plus three prizes and an O-level certificate for art. In September he began studying at Harrow School of Art. Then in the summer of 1960 he began work as a £2-a-week tea-boy at an advertising agency, Charles Hobson and Gray, and shortly afterwards he began to learn basics like lettering and poster design. His colleagues considered him the most stylish young man in the firm, wearing charcoal-colored trousers and good quality sweaters when he did not wear a suit. They also quickly learned that he was a walking encyclopaedia on jazz.

As his prowess at the drums increased, he sat in with various jazz bands in central London and gained the occasional gig at Jewish weddings "where I never knew what the hell was going on." He also played around coffee bars a couple of nights a week, acquiring a steady girlfriend, a blonde nineteen-year-old children's nurse. In 1961, at age twenty, he was so captivated by the sound of the great jazz saxophonist Charlie "Bird" Parker that he wrote a book based on him, *Ode to a High-flying Bird*. "It was a kid's book, with a bird character instead of Charlie Parker," says Charlie; the book was published in 1965, when the Stones had made it.

Alexis Korner met Charlie when he was working with a band at the Troubadour Club, Chelsea; Korner invited him to join his band in the late summer of 1961, but Charlie initially declined; instead he was sent to work in Denmark for a few months. There he played a few gigs with the prestigious American jazz saxophonist Don Byas.

Returning to London in January 1962, feeling unsettled, he soon met Alexis again, who this time persuaded him to join the band he had just formed with Cyril Davies: Blues Incorporated. "When I first played with Cyril Davies, I thought, 'What the fuck is happening here?' because I'd only ever heard a harmonica played by Larry Adler. Cyril was such a character; I loved him. But the rest of it—I didn't know what the hell was going on. Although I knew about playing a heavy backbeat, it wasn't like Chicago-style, which was what Cyril wanted. It was an amazing band, but a total cacophony of sound. On a good night it was amazing, a cross between R & B and Charlie Mingus, which was what Alexis wanted."

Around this time, Charlie first met Shirley Ann Shepherd, who would later become his wife. She was studying sculpture at the Royal College of Art and was one of the audience at a Korner gig when Charlie spotted her. "I liked her and asked her for a date. Except for a short break, we've been together ever since."

And so the graphic designer/drummer, one year older than Brian Jones, and possessing firm views on jazz, seemed a very unlikely candidate for a rock 'n' roll drum chair. Brian saw in Charlie, though, what *he* had in abundance and demanded from any musician: commitment and idealism.

There was an impudence, a purism about Brian, even in these early years, that pre-dated the thrusting reputation that later surrounded our group. In the British weekly music paper *Disc,* the top television producer Jack Good, who played such a big role in helping early pop by producing the TV series *Oh Boy!* and later *Shindig* in America, had raised the subject of R & B. Brian lost no chance to join the debate. Writing to the correspondence column of the paper, Brian said: "Rhythm and blues seems to be a term which needs defining, judging by Jack Good's column. It is a genuine blues style, evolved directly from the earlier, less sophisticated country blues. R & B in turn gave birth to a commercial offspring, universally known as rock 'n' roll. Billy Fury is a rock 'n' roll singer, not an R & B vocalist. Please will somebody play Jack Good a Muddy Waters or a Howlin' Wolf disc so that he can hear what R & B really is?"

On March 31 Brian sat in with Blues Incorporated at Ealing for the second successive Saturday. It was another milestone, the start of a melting pot for British music. Brian found that Korner had hired a bass player to replace Andy Hoogenboom: Jack Bruce, a Scotsman who would later go on to form Cream with Eric Clapton and Ginger Baker. A singer named Long John Baldry had joined Cyril Davies on the band vocals. On the underground after leaving the club, Brian and the others faced astonishing sights and sounds: dozens of people fresh from the Ealing club singing Muddy Waters' "Hoochie Coochie Man." The tube trains rocked to their rhythm. The sense of unity was almost tribal and Brian *belonged* to it. That night, Brian and Dick Hattrell did not return to Cheltenham but stayed the whole weekend with Korner, camping out on the floor of his Islington flat talking about music. But despite the comradeship that always exists in a band, Brian told nobody about his home life or his middle-class roots in Cheltenham. "He was very careful," recalled Alexis, "not to involve his music life with the past which he was escaping from."

Blues Incorporated quickly mushroomed into much more than just a little band of enthusiasts for a particular brand of music. It developed into an *attitude*. A friendship developed between Watts and Bruce, the new bassist, and within a month of Bruce joining the band the two began to share a flat together in Primrose Hill, northwest London. And a sure sign that something important was happening was the arrival at the Ealing club of Harold Pendleton, with Chris Barber, the co-proprietor of the Marquee Club in Oxford Street, fast becoming the most prestigious center for up-and-coming bands.

Charlie recalls: "We got the opportunity to do the off-nights through Chris Barber who owned the old Marquee, then on Oxford Street. We played Thursdays. It wasn't for money! You never made money, none of us did! I remember I told Alexis to turn his amp down. Ginger Baker used to sit in as well. After two weeks, Alexis held the record for people in attendance."

On April 7, 1962, Alexis Korner went to the microphone and told his audience: "We've got a guest to play some guitar . . . he's come all the way from Cheltenham just to play for you." Suddenly Brian, sitting hunched over his Hofner Committee electric guitar, and introduced as Elmo Lewis, lurched into slide guitar on the Elmore James classic "Dust My Broom." When he finished, to prolonged applause, a tall young man walked up to him to congratulate him and chat about music. His name was Mike Jagger, and he was visiting the club for the first time with three friends: Keith Richards, Dick Taylor and Allen Etherington.

Keith remembers: "Brian was really fantastic, the first

person I ever heard playing slide electric guitar. Mick and I both thought he was incredible. He mentioned he was forming a band. He could have easily joined another group but he wanted to form his own. The Rolling Stones was Brian's baby."

Michael Philip Jagger was born on July 26, 1943, at Livingstone Hospital, East Hill, Dartford, Kent. His father, Basil Fanshawe ("Joe") Jagger, a dour northerner, came from Greenfield, Lancashire, where his name is on a plaque in his old school hall as an outstanding sportsman. Later he met his future wife and Mick's mother, Eva Mary Scotts, who had been born in Australia and came to England as a teenager; she later worked as a hairdresser. They were married on December 7, 1940, at Holy Trinity Church, Dartford, Kent. After the war Joe became a physical education teacher at a local secondary school.

In September 1947 Mick started at Maypole Primary Infants School, Dartford. His mother said: "When he was about four he had a phase of hitting people for no reason. Once, on holiday, we were walking along a beach one day when Mick knocked down every single sandcastle we came across. Even ones that little boys were still building." His brother, Christopher Edward, was born in Dartford on December 19, 1947. And Mick recalls: "When Chris was only about two, as far as I was concerned he was nothing more than a punch bag . . . and I used to beat him up regularly."

Mick, aged seven in September 1950, started at Wentworth Junior County Primary School and in February 1951 Mick met Keith Richards for the first time at that school. Mick said: "Keith and I went to school together . . . We lived in the same block. We weren't great friends but we knew each other."

In the summer of 1954, the Jagger family moved to a spacious, white-pebbled detached house surrounded by trees in the village of Wilmington. Joe became director of physical education at a college.

Passing his scholarship exam, Mick went in September 1954 to Dartford Grammar School. He wasn't an ideal pupil, and his headmaster, a small bossy man known as "Lofty" Hudson, didn't take to him. But the boy loved music. Mick's mother Eva recalls: "Mick would sit for hours just listening to tunes on the radio, and then he'd sing them exactly as the original."

Joe: "I've never known a youngster with such an analytical approach to things. If he copied a song, he copied it slavishly, every note. He was able to capture the sound exactly, even when he was as young as eleven or twelve."

Eva: "In the summer of 1955 we and the boys toured the St. Tropez area on the French Riviera and camped on the famed Tahiti Beach. Mick acted as my interpreter. The boys have always loved outdoor activities such as rock climbing, camping and canoeing, and used to spend most of their time swimming while on holiday."

Chris Jagger remembers that his brother was never called Mick. "We called him Mike. He hated the name Mick. I only used it when I was teasing him.

"He bought his first guitar when we were all on holiday in Spain. It wasn't a very good guitar; still, he got a fairly good sound out of it."

His father later said: "He could have been a great athlete. He was excellent at basketball and cricket, but he didn't want to be tied down with all the practice. Playing for the school team every Saturday didn't interest him. He rebelled against that kind of prestige. He was a first-class camper, although I don't really think he would fancy bedding down in a tent these days."

Mick liked cricket and played for the first XI on several occasions. He also belonged to the history and—more importantly—the jazz societies at school. "There was traditional jazz and skiffle," Mick says. "People tend to forget how enormous that was. I was in loads of skiffle groups. I used to play with Dick Taylor, who was a folk guitarist and another friend who I went to college with. But these skiffle groups were also playing rock 'n' roll numbers. Nearly every guitarist was a folk-player, but they also played whatever was on the charts that week. English rock 'n' roll really started with skiffle groups."

Eva said: "Friends of Mick and Chris would be constantly in and out of the house. At times we used to tell them about their pop music being too loud, just as a generation earlier I was always being told off by my mother for not turning down the dance-music programs."

In July 1959, Mick obtained seven O-level passes in his GCE Examinations (history, English language, English literature, French, Latin, geography, mathematics), after a good ticking off by "Lofty." Unpopular with many of the masters, he was, however, liked by the French and history teachers.

In July 1960, at seventeen, he was earning money selling ice creams outside the public library in Dartford. Keith Richards bought one and they talked again briefly, after a five-year gap. Early in 1961 he also worked as a temporary porter at Bexley Mental Hospital for ninety shillings per week.

On July 26 he celebrated his eighteenth birthday and he got three A-level passes (history, English language, English literature) and won a scholarship to the London School of Economics. Signing a declaration to complete the course, he was aiming to be a lawyer, journalist or politician. He began studying economics and political science.

One morning in late October, on his way to the LSE, he met Keith (who was on his way to Sidcup Art College) at Dartford station.

Keith Richards was born on December 18, 1943, in Livingstone Hospital, East Hill, Dartford, where Mick Jagger had been born five months earlier. His father, Herbert William Richards, had come from a large working-class family in Walthamstow, northeast London. His mother, Doris Maud Lydia Dupree, met Bert during 1933 while sharing clerical jobs in a London office. Significantly perhaps, his grandfather, Theodore Augustus (Gus) Dupree, was a musician. He had a dance band in the 1930s, and played a variety of instruments, including guitar, fiddle, piano and saxophone.

Bert and Doris were married in London in 1936. In 1942 Bert left General Electric when he was called up into the army, where he served with the Bedfordshire & Hertfordshire Regiment as a clerk. In 1944, Bert, wounded in the leg, was sent to an orthopaedic hospital in Mansfield, Notts, the same town the Perks family had been evacuated to. Doris and Keith joined him there shortly afterwards. They remained there for the rest of the war and then returned to Dartford where Keith later attended Westhill Infants School at the end of the road. "With six aunts, he was a bit spoiled," his mother recalls.

But Keith comments: "It was great being an only child . . . didn't have to share my toys!"

He was very fond of animals; a loner; and he hated school. Doris says he was a "cry baby," often in tears. At school Keith met Mick Jagger for the first time. "I distinctly remember the first conversation I had with Keith," Mick says now. "I asked him what he wanted to do when he grew up. He said he wanted to be like Roy Rogers and play guitar."

Keith's family moved from Morland Avenue to the Temple Hill Estate on the other side of Dartford in 1955. Keith and his mother would often travel during that year to London to visit his grandfather. "Gus had this guitar standing in the corner," Doris Richards recalls, "and he was always afraid Keith would break it. He would go up and strum the strings; he loved the sound and admired Gus enormously." It was the first guitar Keith touched. "Before I could play an instrument," says Keith, "I used to sing. I was a choirboy soloist at school. The weirdest thing was that me and the three biggest hoods in school were singing like angels in Westminster Abbey at Christmas."

In September 1956, Keith, aged twelve, started at Dartford Technical College. "In cross-country," says Keith, "I would start off with the main bunch, and as the others raced off into the distance, I would hide myself behind a bush or tree and light up. A quick fag made me feel right as rain. Then it was just a matter of hanging around until the others came back, all exhausted. I'd tack myself on to the last few and accompany them back to school." During 1957 Keith joined the Boy Scouts briefly, but could not accept the discipline and quickly left.

That September, Keith was made to retake the third year studies with the younger kids. And that year also, Keith said, "The music from *Blackboard Jungle*—'Rock Around the Clock'—hit first. Not the movie, just the music. Everybody stood up for that music. I didn't think of playing it. I just wanted to go and listen to it. It took a year or so before anyone in England could make that music. We started listening to what was coming over the Atlantic. The ones that were hitting hard were Elvis Presley, Little Richard and Jerry Lee Lewis. Chuck Berry was never really that big in England. The movies he made, like *Go Johnny Go,* never got over because of distribution problems. Fats Domino was big. Freddie and the Bellboys too."

During 1958, as Keith enjoyed the quiet comfort of their neat council house in Dartford, Bert and Doris began to wonder if their son would ever break out. Doris Richards said: "Keith wanted a record-player, so we got one from the Dartford Co-op. By the time he got home he had nearly pulled his arm out of its socket, the record-player was so heavy."

Keith said: "That record-player was ridiculous. An old wind-up 78 gramophone. You had to change needles every six plays, and the needles were like nails. It was murder winding up the arm. The first record I bought was a bad Woolworth imitation of a Ricky Nelson song."

On his fifteenth birthday Keith's mother bought him his first acoustic guitar. He started to practice non-stop. Doris Richards said: "Keith was always worrying us for a guitar of his own. I told him I'd buy him one if he actually played it—but no mucking about. I didn't have any money, so I bought him a cheap acoustic guitar on hire-purchase for £7. From that day, playing the guitar has been the most important thing in his life. My father taught him a few chords, but the rest he has taught himself."

Keith said: "I had my own guitar when I was fifteen, and that's when I first started learning." He became hooked on rock 'n' roll and especially Elvis Presley.

He used to hang out at the snooker hall in Dartford, and became interested in motorbikes. When Keith was sixteen he was asked to leave Dartford Technical College because of truancy. The headmaster enrolled him into Sidcup Art School, where he took a course in advertising. Keith said: "I did graphic design and life-drawing for three years. But basically I played guitar. There were a lot of other guitar players at art school."

There he met Dick Taylor, who played guitar and was living in Bexleyheath, Kent. Dick recalls that Keith (then known as Ricky) always wore a purple shirt, jeans, pointed shoes and a jeans jacket, and was "always untidy." Keith sometimes stole from shops and got into fights. Taylor remembered him popping period pills, pain-killers such as Midol.

Dick asked Keith if he wanted to practice guitar with him. "Dick Taylor was the first guy I played with," says Keith. "We played together on acoustic guitars. Then I got an amplifier, like a little beat-up radio. Another guy at school, Michael Ross, decided to form a C & W band. The first time I got onstage was a sports dance at Eltham, near Sidcup, with this amateur C & W band."

Keith had started his final year at Sidcup Art College when the chance meeting that shaped the Stones occurred. When Keith and Mick met at Dartford station, under Mick's arm was a collection of imported R & B records he had received by mail from Chicago and New York. They included Chuck Berry's *One Dozen Berries*. Keith said: "I was going to art school, and it just so happened that the particular train I had to take was the same one as Mick caught to go to the LSE, although we didn't normally catch the same train. I noticed these records he had under his arm—otherwise, we may not have said more than hallo to each other. He had a particular Chuck Berry record I'd never seen before, so we got talking." Mick and Keith talked about Chuck Berry and other American singers until Keith got off at Sidcup. Mick had a fantastic collection of records. Before they parted they arranged to meet to listen to Mick's discs.

Doris remembers the episode well: "I remember the night Keith came in from art school and told me he'd met Mick at the station that morning. He was really excited about that meeting. He'd been playing guitar for ages, but always on his own. He was too shy to join in with anybody else, although Dick Taylor had often asked him."

Richards and Jagger got together and started to play regularly with guitarist Dick Taylor. They began rehearsing, locked away in an upstairs room at Mick's house.

Dick Taylor said: "About four or five boys used to rehearse around my place quite a bit. Keith asked me if I knew a guy named Mick Jagger. Although I'd been playing with some of the guys from school and playing with Keith, I'd never really cottoned on to the idea of doing anything together until Mick came on the scene. Keith knew me, and Mick knew me and we thought, 'Why not join forces?' "

Chris Jagger remembers: "It was a pretty terrible noise, but Mum and Dad were very patient. They never threw them out. When Keith and Dick came, Mick gave up the guitar and thought more about playing the harmonica and singing.''

Eva Jagger said: "I hardly knew they were there. Whenever I shoved my nose around the door they'd stop playing. I think Mick was a bit sensitive about his singing. He didn't like being watched or overheard. We loaned them the money for their early equipment, although money was tight. We had to, to keep Mick quiet."

During November 1961, Mick, Keith and Dick Taylor continued to practice together, and for the next few months at Dick's house they were joined by Bob Beckwith and Allen Etherington. Dick's parents were tolerant about rehearsals, although Dick admits: "Our music was pretty diabolical!"

At this time the band consisted of Mick (vocals), Dick Taylor (drums—which he'd inherited from his grandfather), Keith (guitar), Bob Beckwith (guitar—plugged into a primitive 6-watt amp no larger than a portable radio) and Allen Etherington (maracas). As far as they could, they tried to copy the sounds from Jimmy Reed and Chuck Berry records.

Dick's mother said: "Me and my friends used to sit in the next room and crease up with laughter. It was lovely, but so loud. I always heard more of Mick than I saw of him. I didn't dream that they were serious."

Mick, Keith and friends called their band Little Boy Blue and the Blue Boys.

It was in late March that they read about the Ealing club in *Jazz News*, and decided to investigate. On April 7 they visited the club for the first time. They drove in Allen's father's car, saw Brian play and chatted to him after the show. Unlike Brian, these two nineteen-year-olds had no plans to become full-time musicians.

Dick Taylor said: "We sent in the post to Alexis a tape that included the Blue Boys doing 'La Bamba,' 'Around and Around,' 'Reelin' and Rockin,' " and 'Bright Lights, Big City.' The one that's still very clear in my head is 'La Bamba,' a favorite record of Mick's. He got all the words off the record, pseudo-Spanish—words that sounded like Spanish, but weren't real words at all."

Alexis Korner said: "I thought, 'Whoo!' Cyril heard Mick and he liked him and the sound on the tape. I rang

Mick and invited him to come and visit me. Mick and Keith came up from Dartford and talked about Chuck Berry and Bo Diddley. I talked about Muddy Waters, Memphis Slim and Robert Johnson. We dug each other. Then Mick and Keith started to come down to gigs. They went everywhere together; you never got Mick without Keith."

When Keith and Mick visited the Ealing club, they jammed on stage with Blues Incorporated for the first time, doing "Around and Around." Long John Baldry said: "I can remember when Mick and Keith first came down to Ealing. Mick's repertoire then was all Chuck Berry things. The first thing I ever heard him sing was 'Beautiful Delilah.' Keith had some tatty old guitar, pretty primitive, but I don't think anybody had good guitars at that time."

For some time Brian had had the idea of putting a band together and before he left Cheltenham he went to see Gordon Harper, who had started playing in 1961 with his friend Alan Carter. Gordon Harper recalls: "One day Brian came to my home and played a Muddy Waters record. He said he was going to form a group that would play that type of music, and he asked me to join. I told him the group could never be successful and although he asked me a number of times, I turned down his offer."

The women in Brian Jones's world, meanwhile, gave him the real blues. He was getting tangled up in the kind of web that would always give him problems in his short life. His first permanent move to London was to a flat in Weech Road, west Hampstead; packing his suitcase in Cheltenham, he was joined briefly by his fourteen-year-old girlfriend. When Pat Andrews heard of this she decided to go to London herself.

With baby Julian, Pat planned to travel on Easter Saturday, April 21, 1962. She went to Cheltenham bus station with a mere 30 shillings and bought a 15-shilling ticket to London for the next day. Arriving at Victoria coach station at two in the morning, she had 2 shillings left. She took a bus to Kilburn and then walked with the pram and two suitcases. A man stopped her and paid for a taxi for her. When she arrived at his flat, Brian opened the door and almost fainted at the sight. Pat and Julian moved in.

But the relationship was quickly marred by Brian's restlessness. He had moved to London not just physically but psychologically, and he wanted liberation. As Keith recalls: "Brian knew about the problem of coming from a provincial town. He had to conquer London first." Dick Hattrell said: "Brian didn't want to be with Pat. He wanted the high-life, and beautiful girls who made eyes at him while he was performing. Pat was a very ordinary girl, and not at all artistic. She didn't really appreciate music. She was convenient, someone to clean the flat, cook his food and provide a sexual outlet."

A few days later, Brian and Pat were asked to leave Weech Road because of the baby. Brian took a job in the sports department at Whiteley's department store in Queensway and Pat went to work in a laundry. Julian was given to foster parents for a week until they found a flat in Powis Square, Notting Hill Gate. Brian continued to suffer from bouts of temper and jealousy. He made Pat give up her laundry job, after which she worked as a computer-tape operator. He left his job and began work at the Civil Service Stores in the Strand.

A major turning point came in May 1962 when Brian put an advertisement in *Jazz News* for people interested in forming an R & B band with him. Piano player Ian Stewart was the first person to answer it.

Stu had been born in Scotland into a middle-class family which had moved south to Cheam, Surrey, when he was a baby. In September 1956 he had been called up for National Service, but he was discharged for health reasons after a week or so and began working at ICI's head office as a clerk in their export sales department in London.

Stu said: "Brian wanted to form an R & B group. I went and saw him. He was a strange character, but was very knowledgeable. He'd done his homework and was a little like Ken Colyer, deadly serious about the whole thing. He wanted to play Muddy Waters, Blind Boy Fuller and stuff by Jimmy Reed—whom I'd never heard of. He couldn't find the people he wanted because not many people had heard that Chess and Vee Jay stuff. Then Howlin' Wolf's record 'You Can't be Beat' came out in London, and I think that was the style he was really trying to achieve.

"Brian was living in an unbelievably awful state, drinking spaghetti out of a cup. I thought it was a stunt, but they had no money whatsoever. We talked about music, and he said that he was going to have a rehearsal on Monday."

Brian started rehearsals at the White Bear pub in Leicester Square. The first rehearsal consisted of a friend of Charlie's called Andy Wren (Screaming Lord Sutch's piano player) who wanted to sing, another piano player who was playing like Count Basie and wasn't what Brian wanted and Brian on regular and slide guitar.

When Stu returned from a holiday in Scotland, he discovered that Brian had been rehearsing two or three times a week. He joined him for a few sessions—just before they were thrown out "because Brian used to climb over the bar and steal cigarettes." They continued rehearsing in the Bricklayer's Arms in Lisle Street, Soho. Alexis put Brian in touch with various guitarists and singers and he and Stu spent weeks experimenting with them until they saw a semblance of a group emerging.

Stu said: "Then Geoff Bradford came round. He'd worked with Cyril Davies and was into ethnic blues, the sounds of Muddy Waters, John Lee Hooker and Elmore James. Geoff was a really good guitar player, deadly serious, and he drew very distinct lines between what he'd play and what he wouldn't. His mate, Brian Knight, came round, too—a good harmonica player who later became quite a good guitarist." The idealism of Geoff Bradford was to be a key part in Brian's musical education, and in the policy of the Stones.

Brian then tried without success to persuade Paul Pond, who had been singing with Blues Incorporated, to join his rehearsal group, but Paul decided that his university studies came first.

By the end of the month Mick was singing three nights a week with Blues Incorporated, doing songs like Muddy Waters' "Got My Mojo Working," "Ride 'em on Down," Billy Boy Arnold's "Bad Boy" and "Don't Stay Out All Night." The British pop weekly *Disc* reported on May 19, 1962: "A nineteen-year-old Dartford rhythm and blues singer, Mick Jagger, has joined the Alexis Korner group, Blues Incorporated, and will sing with them regularly on their Saturday dates at Ealing and their Thursday sessions at the Marquee Jazz Club, London."

Mick remembers Long John Baldry and Paul Pond singing with him on "Got My Mojo Working": "They were much taller than me and I used to feel very small. Paul used to go up with shades on, trying to be ever so cool, with his donkey jacket, and he sang quite nicely. He was older than me—and much spottier. I'd never sung in public before and I was incredibly nervous and would get quite drunk. Alexis didn't use to pay us much bread, about 15 shillings. It used to just about pay my fares from where I lived in suburbia.

"The Ealing club was so wet that Cyril had to put a horrible sheet, revoltingly dirty, over the bandstand, so that the condensation didn't drip directly on you. But it just dripped through the sheet. It was very dangerous because of all the electricity and microphones. It was primitive, but I never got a shock. There was Alexis with his guitar with his big pick-up across it. We were all incredibly jealous of it because we didn't have the money for a down-payment on one."

By June 1962, however, Jagger quit Korner to join Brian and Ian Stewart's basic band. Jagger quickly brought in his Dartford friends Keith Richards and Dick Taylor, and Brian reshuffled the band to include them. They began rehearsing with Brian, Stu and Geoff every Wednesday and Friday.

Stu said: "Mick would only sing if Keith became a part of it. Keith liked the Muddy Waters thing, but he also liked Chuck Berry and Bo Diddley as well." Keith said: "Brian's version of blues was Muddy Waters, Elmore James, Sonny Boy Williamson, Howlin' Wolf and John Lee Hooker. Mick and I were much more into Chuck Berry, Jimmy Reed and Bo Diddley. Brian really got into Jimmy Reed. He would sit around for hours and hours, working out how Reed's sound was put together. He'd work at it and work at it. He'd really get it down. Brian didn't consider Berry to be in the same class, but when we proved to him that he was, he really started to dig him. He'd work with me on Berry things. We really got into that. We were working out the guitar parts and the rhythm, which was 4/4 swing beat, not a rock beat at all. It was jazz swing beat, except there would be another guitar playing. He was a good guitar player then. He had the touch and was just peaking. He was really working at it. He said that we were just amateurs, but we dug to play. That's where I met Stu. He was with Brian.

"Stu was unique from the first day I met him. He'd wear those ludicrous black leather shorts and always ride a bike. When we rehearsed, Stu would always be looking out the window to make sure his bike was still there. He'd keep one eye on the bike and one eye on the piano, and he'd always hit the right notes. At night the women of the street would appear, and Stu would always say something like: 'Whoa, I'd love to wrap myself around that,' and still he'd never miss a note."

Geoff Bradford was a good guitarist but he was a diehard blues purist, in whose eyes performers like Chuck Berry, Bo Diddley and Jimmy Reed were guilty of commercial opportunism. He found himself at odds with Keith, Mick and Brian, and soon departed.

Once, recalls Keith, Mick went round to Brian's pad, and "Brian wasn't there. He was a bit drunk and screwed Brian's old lady. Pat and the baby split, and Brian got thrown out of his flat." Pat and the baby returned to Cheltenham, and Brian moved into a cold-water basement flat in Brackley Road, Beckenham. He continued working in the Strand. Adds Keith: "Mick found Brian a place to stay in Beckenham. There was a big room built on to the house and it was quite groovy until he invited a girl down to cook for him one day and they burned half of it down. He continued living there, with a hole in the ceiling with a piece of canvas above it, trying to hide it from the landlord."

Brian tried to persuade Charlie Watts to leave Korner and join them but he was still loyal to Korner and preoccupied with his day job in graphic design. Brian then put an advertisement in *Melody Maker* for a drummer. A week later Tony Chapman went for an audition at the Bricklayers Arms. Stu said: "He really wasn't very good, and would get on to the on-beat and slow down, and finish the number in the middle of a chorus." Nevertheless, Tony started rehearsing regularly with the boys, and, with Brian, traveled home together on the train to New Beckenham station. Chapman said: "They liked me because I was the first drummer who liked to play the shuffle, which I learned in the Cliftons, doing Chuck Berry songs. We all met one time at Mick's house in Dartford, sat in his front room, and he played the album *Jimmy Reed at Carnegie Hall*. They asked me what I thought of it. I liked it and they said, 'Fine, because that's the sort of music we want to play.' "

Brian, meanwhile, had to try to earn some money. He began work in a record shop but was sacked for stealing from the till. He then worked briefly at W. H. Smith newsagents in Kingsway, until he was again fired for stealing. "Brian was totally dishonest," Stu said.

In July 1962, Korner's Blues Incorporated were causing enough of a stir among the cognoscenti to be offered a coveted radio spot on the BBC's *Jazz Club*. Unfortunately, it was on a Thursday. At the Marquee, their important residency, Harold Pendleton was adamant: "If you do that broadcast," he warned them, "I will not guarantee your gig back the Thursday after." A compromise with Pendleton was finally agreed: Jagger would hold down the Marquee with Brian, Keith and Stu plus whoever else there was; as it transpired they recruited Mick Avory on drums. (He later went on to success with the Kinks.)

But while Mick's personality had secured the Marquee date, it was still Brian's unit he was taking with him. For that gig, Brian decided to name the band the Rollin' Stones, from Muddy Waters' song, "Rollin' Stone Blues." Stu said it was a terrible name. It sounded, he argued, like the name of an Irish show band, "or something that ought to be playing at the Savoy."

Brian suddenly telephoned his parents, after months of silence, to say he wanted to talk to them about a band he was starting. A few days later he went to Cheltenham to see them. "He was full of ambition for the future," said Lewis Jones. "He appeared to have found what he was looking for, a chance to become a competent jazz musician. It was on this occasion that he first mentioned a group of people he called the Rollin' Stones. From that moment on there was a complete and lasting reconciliation."

On Tuesday, July 10, 1962, the first satellite pictures of Telstar-1 were shown on British television. Two nights later the move that would shake the earth for the Stones took place in London. On Wednesday, July 11 *Jazz News* stated:

Mick Jagger, R & B vocalist, is taking an R & B group into the Marquee tomorrow night while Blues Incorporated do their *Jazz Club* radio broadcast gig. Called the Rolling Stones, the line-up is: Mick Jagger (vocals), Keith Richards and Elmo Lewis (guitars), Dick Taylor (bass), Ian Stewart (piano) and Mick Avory (drums).

Before the gig Mick said: "I hope they don't think we're a rock 'n' roll outfit." The songs they played, recorded in Stu's diary, were: "Kansas City," "Honey What's Wrong," "Confessin' the Blues," "Bright Lights, Big City," "Dust My Broom," "Down the Road Apiece," "I Want to Love You," "Bad Boy," "I Ain't Got You." "Hush Hush," "Ride 'em on Down," "Back in the USA," "Up All Night," "Tell Me that You Love Me" and "Happy Home." From that list, it is obvious that they were psychologically a huge distance from the popular music of the day: the Number One record in Britain at the moment was Frank Ifield's "I Remember You," and the other hit names of the period were the Crickets, Pat Boone, Craig Douglas, Helen Shapiro, Billy Fury, Neil Sedaka and Bobby Darin.

Shortly after this, Keith completed his last term at Sidcup Art College, but took no formal examinations. He refused to get a job. Before the end of the month, the Stones did a gig at the Ealing Jazz Club, with Tony Chapman, who said: "I would sit there on this drum kit, on a metal stool, with all the plugs by my feet, and water lapping around them. It was very dangerous."

At this point, Brian and Keith became really tight friends. Keith left home and went to live off and on with Brian in the flat at Beckenham. Keith says they used to lie around listening to sounds and play all day. "There was a time when Brian and I had decided that this R & B thing was an absolute flop. We weren't gonna get away with it. Brian and I were gonna do an Everly Brothers thing, so we spent three or four days in the kitchen, rehearsing these terrible songs."

Mick then found a flat at 102 Edith Grove, Chelsea,

where the rent was £16 per week. He and Brian moved in in August 1962. Pat and the baby returned from Cheltenham to live with them; she said she would cook for everyone. The money Brian earned went on guitar strings and equipment, while Pat's money helped to support them all. A short time later, Keith moved into Edith Grove with them. Keith said: "I started to crash there sometimes, so as not to have to go home. Brian was in and out of work. He got caught stealing again and was very luckily let off. Mick went through his first camp period, and started wandering around in a blue linen housecoat. He was into that kick for about six months. Brian and I used to take the piss out of him. I never consciously thought about leaving Dartford, but the minute I got out I had pretty strong instincts that I'd never go back. There was no way I was gonna stay there."

Mick said: "Dartford isn't a bad place to come from, but it's not a very good place to go back to."

Once, the three of them were chatting to the background of a Muddy Waters album in Edith Grove and inevitably the talk drifted to their prospects of success. They wondered if they should get "proper jobs." Suppose, Brian said, they failed? Mick would have jeopardized a certain future in a legitimate profession, while Brian would have drifted even further down the path to nowhere. They decided to give it a year, in which they would have at least soaked up the music. "If we flop," Brian asked, "would it matter? At least we'd have tried." Once Keith looked for a job: "I took my portfolio around to one advertising agency in London, who gave me the usual la-di-da 'We'll let you know in a couple of days.' I just stuffed it in a corner and forgot about it."

Meanwhile an important development occurred in Brian's musical ambitions. He sometimes visited Cyril Davies at his home, where they would blow harmonicas together. Brian began to imitate Reed's lazy style and practice Davies' technique of bending and flattening the notes. This was the first step in Brian's departure from the guitar, searching for stimulation from more exotic sounds. Keith said: "I went out one morning and came back in the evening and Brian was blowing a harmonica. He got it together. Standing at the top of the stairs saying, 'Listen to this.' Whooooow. Whoooow. All these blues notes were coming out . . . 'I've learned how to do it. I've figured it out.' In *one day*. So then he started to really work on the harp. He dropped the guitar. He still dug to play it and was still into it and played very well but the harp became his thing. He'd walk around all the time playing his harp."

Battling against the club owners and promoters to get work, the early Rollin' Stones hit huge resistance. The traditional jazz boom was dying, leaving a vacuum, but there was an almost Mafia-like control of the bands hired by the clubs. They weren't going to invite a group of young upstarts who weren't very proficient on their instruments and who didn't play any form of jazz. The club owners played games with the Rollin' Stones, offering gigs and then canceling at the last minute. As Charlie remembers: "The Stones were so disliked inside the jazz world; nobody had a good word for them. They were complete outsiders, looked on as a gang of long-haired freaks."

During September 1962 they played only two gigs—both at the Ealing Jazz Club with Tony Chapman on drums—to small audiences. There was, though, a powerful rhythm-and-blues lobby building up in the clubs, which the jazzers would not be able to stop. By June 1962 Art Wood, brother of Ronnie, had joined Korner's Blues Incorporated* and a slow-moving but forceful, committed group of bands was playing rhythm and blues, the Mann-Hugg Blues Brothers, Blues By Six and Long John Baldry among them.

Stu kept his day job at ICI; he regarded their beatnik lifestyle as horrific, but as a good pianist with terrific jazz knowledge, he could hear some potential. The drum chair, however, was a perpetual problem, and always vacant. Charlie Watts, again asked by Brian to join, was too dedicated to a career in graphic design to throw in the towel. As Mick got the results in September 1962 of his first year examinations at the LSE (passing well),

---

*Art Wood went on to form a popular R & B band, the Artwoods, in 1964. This five-piece group lasted for three years and its members included keyboard player Jon Lord, who went on to form that quiet little band Deep Purple, and later Whitesnake, both with singer David Coverdale.

Dick Taylor left the band to pursue his studies. Taylor said: "I was a student at the Royal College of Art. I had to start concentrating on my exams. I think I was getting just a little bit done in by playing music and doing these things for college. We didn't have a row." Dick went on to play lead guitar with the Pretty Things.

Mick has recalled this time: "We'd get a group together —a drummer from Screaming Lord Sutch called Carlo [Little], and a bass player called Ricky [Fensen]—and play at Ealing on Saturdays occasionally. It got very crowded and incredibly hot, and we used to get Oiks coming down and demanding R & R numbers they thought we ought to play, like 'Ready, Teddy,' which they could have probably done better than me."

Tony Chapman remembers: "Stu had a big old pre-war Rover that he drove the gear about in, with the drums in the back seat and the amps in the boot. On the way home, he'd fall asleep at the traffic lights."

Stu said: "Once, in the Rover, I was driving Brian and Keith (who were both plastered) home from a party. We were half-way along the Thames Embankment. All of a sudden they started shouting at each other, arguing about clothes. Brian flung a punch at Keith, and Keith hit him back. I stopped the car and told them to get out and fight it out between them. They did!"

Pat and the baby left the Edith Grove flat in the autumn of 1962, saying that the strain of worrying for them all was too much. She had to put her baby first, as Brian did his music. After she left, Dick Hattrell moved in, but his relationship with Brian became more difficult as Brian, Mick and Keith drew closer.

Keith said: "Dick Hattrell supported Brian but instead of being incredibly nice to Dick as he usually was when there was nothing to interfere with the relationship, Brian was now hanging out with us. He didn't want us to think his association with Dick was too serious—too provincial a thing. He didn't want to be thought of as being part of some hick country scene. Dick was like a complete puppy toward him. Brian was incredible. Within two weeks Brian took him for every penny, and he conned Dick into buying him this new Harmony electric guitar, having his amp fixed and getting him a whole new set of harmonicas. Dick would do anything Brian said. It was freezing and the worst winter. Brian would say, 'Give me your overcoat,' and he gave Brian this army overcoat. 'Give Keith the sweater,' so I put the sweater on. 'Now you walk twenty yards behind us,' and off we'd walk to the local Wimpy Bar. 'Stay there. You can't come in. Give us £2.' Dick would stand outside this hamburger joint, freezing. Brian would invite Dick to lunch and the three of us would go to what we considered a really good restaurant, and have a hot meal, which nobody could afford, of course! Then we'd just walk out and leave Dick with the bill. Brian and I were so crazy at the time. One day Dick was asleep in Brian's bed and Brian went mad. He pulled this incredible stroke. He had these two absolutely harmless wires that were plugged into some inert piece of machinery. He threatened to electrocute Dick, chasing him around the room with these two wires. Dick was petrified. The poor guy completely freaked out. He charged out of the house and into the street wearing nothing but his underpants, and Brian left him there, in the snow, for hours. We eventually let him back in, by which time he'd turned blue."

Alexis Korner said: "Because of Brian's particular insecurities, he was very heavy on anyone else's insecurity. Obviously I dug Brian, but he could be very mean. Just plain evil, like twisting words and finding a way of saying something that would hurt, without it sounding like that at the time. He did it with Dick Hattrell, and he did it with anyone who would let him."

The biggest problem was coping with the hire-purchase payments for their instruments. Money to cover the repayments was stashed away in an old tin in the flat, and the cash often disappeared; Brian admitted he was usually guilty. It was too much of a temptation. He said: "There was I without a penny in my pocket and hidden away was all that money. A couple of quid seemed like a fortune to me so I kept dipping into it hoping the others wouldn't notice."

With Mick's education assuring him of a career, the motivation to make the band succeed fell more to Keith and Brian, who hung out together most days while Mick went to study. They clung to the Stones as their salvation, while Mick regarded music as a gamble he could afford to lose.

In October 1962, Keith's parents separated for good.* There were a few more engagements for the slightly ramshackle group still called the Rollin' Stones. They supported Alexis Korner at the Marquee, played the Ealing Jazz Club a few times and also played a show at the Woodstock Hotel, North Cheam in Surrey.

Ambitiously, they decided to forfeit some of the pay from these dates to enable them to pay for the recording of a "demo," in those days a lacquered acetate. On October 27, at the Curly Clayton Studio near Arsenal football ground in north London, Mick, Brian, Keith, Ian and Tony Chapman paid for an hour's studio time to record three songs: Bo Diddley's "You Can't Judge a Book by the Cover," Muddy Waters' "Soon Forgotten" and Jimmy Reed's "Close Together."†

The spartan studio facilities provided just one microphone in the middle of a small room; they had to balance the sound by moving the instruments around. Mick asked for the piano to be "turned up," but it could not be moved; it was nailed to the wall, and Stu's playing could hardly be heard.

They sent the acetate to Neville Skrimshire, a jazz guitarist who also worked at EMI Records, but it was rejected. Chapman then sent it to someone he knew at Decca, who responded: "It's a great band, but you'll never get anywhere with that singer."

Brian continued his evangelical work for R & B with another letter published in *Jazz News:*

It appears there exists in this country a growing confusion as to exactly what form of music the term R & B

---

*It was to be twenty years before Keith was to see his father again, and establish a close relationship that continues to the present day.
†The final record featured "Soon Forgotten" on one side, and "Close Together" and "You Can't Judge a Book" on the reverse. A well-worn acetate of this, originally belonging to Tony Chapman, was sold at Phillips Auctioneers' rock 'n' roll memorabilia sale in London on April 6, 1988, fetching £6,000.

applies to. There further appears to be a movement to promote what would be better termed "soul jazz" as R & B. Surely we must accept that R & B is the American city-Negro's pop music—nothing more, nothing less. R & B can hardly be considered a form of jazz. It is not based on improvisation, as is the latter. The impact is, and can only be, emotional. It would be ludicrous if the same type of pseudo-intellectual snobbery that one unfortunately finds contaminating the jazz scene were to be applied to anything as basic and vital as R & B. It must be apparent that R & R has a far greater affinity for R & B than the latter has for jazz, insofar as rock is a direct corruption of R & B, whereas jazz is Negro music on a different plane, intellectually higher, though emotionally less intense.

During November, the Rollin' Stones played Ealing Jazz Club, the Red Lion pub in Sutton and a few gigs at the Flamingo Jazz Club in London's Soho on a Sunday afternoon. Stu said: "It was *the* modern jazz club in town, with everybody in zoot suits. I said to Keith, 'You're not going to the Flamingo looking like *that*, are you?' Keith said: 'I've only got one pair of fucking jeans.' "

During that freezing winter of 1962 the lack of money hit them really hard. At Edith Grove Keith, Brian and Mick stole potatoes from local shops to boost the meager rations. Stu handed over the luncheon vouchers he got at the office. If there were even buns or margarine at the flat, it was a bonus.

In the downstairs flat lived a pharmacist named Judith Credland, who had a close friendship with Brian or Mick, or possibly both. She also provided them with groceries. Instant coffee was their staple diet. When they finished a jar, Judy would always help out. They would creep down to her kitchen at three or four in the morning for the odd jar, and leave scribbled IOUs on the draining board for when she woke up. Her great hobby was palm-reading. One night she took Mick's hand in hers and, as he opened his fingers, she gasped: "You've got the star of fame! *It's all there.*" Keith and Brian laughed, and though none of them took it seriously then, Mick has often referred to it since.

Brian said: "It was hard to concentrate on music when we were too hungry to think. We'd often go back to the apartment and think about silly things like tearing up the blankets and making sandwiches of them."

"That winter is ingrained in me," says Keith. "Luckily we had nothing else to do, and we were pretty determined. There was no other way to go, except up." Dick Hattrell suffered a burst appendix and moved back to Cheltenham, and on November 29 Keith, weak as a kitten, trundled back to Dartford, arriving at two in the morning. Mick and Brian had advised him to return home because he had a temperature and, they suspected, tonsilitis. He went straight to bed but insisted on getting up next day to play a date at the Piccadilly Jazz Club at 41 Great Windmill Street, Soho. They were third on the bill to Blues Incorporated and Dave Hunt's R & B Band.

After another night at Ealing Jazz Club, on December 4, 1962, the Rollin' Stones talked about their instrumental line-up. This was when Tony Chapman said, "I know a bass player who's got his own amp, huge speaker, plus a spare Vox AC30." And so this was the itinerant unit of starving, sullen, lapsed scholars and amateur music-makers whom I first encountered at the Wetherby Arms, World's End, Chelsea on December 7, 1962. Pop success was as remote a prospect as that of participating in a decade of profound cultural change. Fame and fortune were as distant as next week's pay check. The only question that concerned them was: *Can we get a band together and get some work?*

4

Birth of the Legend

The major difference between the Stones and me when we met mattered even more than music. I was a young family man with a wife, a nine-month-old child and a day job. After the early sexual problems with our marriage, Diane had become pregnant in February 1961. Excited at the prospect of a baby, I plastered bedroom walls, fixed curtains, rails and electric points and worked on the front garden. The flat needed a lot of improvement before a new-born baby could be taken there: it was so damp it was a health hazard. During the early months of my semi-pro work with the Cliftons, the prospect of being a father was both exciting and worrying. Where would the money come from? Then, after about a month, Diane suffered a miscarriage. The doctor advised us to try for another baby immediately, and by August Diane was pregnant again. Stephen Paul Wyman was born on March 29, 1962, in Stone (*sic*) Park Nursing Home, Beckenham. I was working at Sparks when the phone call brought the news that I was a father; my mates at work went out and bought cigars for a small celebration.

Charlie Watts had left Blues Incorporated at this time. Alexis Korner explained: "Charlie was working as a visualizer for an advertising agency, and was also quite a fair old drummer. When Blues Incorporated decided to go professional because there was too much work to cope with on a semi-pro basis, he wouldn't. He didn't think it was secure enough."

"The reason I left Blues Incorporated," says Charlie, "was because I really wasn't good enough. They were such fantastic musicians and I couldn't keep up with the pace. When I left, Ginger Baker took over, and I went around with a few different bands. I used to play with three bands at once."

It was mid-December when I made my proper entry into the Stones after my strange "audition" on December 7. I was still employed at Sparks, but the Cliftons had now disbanded. On December 12 Dick Taylor filled the bass guitar role at a gig by the Stones on their home ground, Sidcup Art College's Christmas dance. I would have been there, but I was working. They had also just played a show at south Oxhey, near Watford, where there were more band members on stage than fans in the audience. But on December 14, 1962, after work, I returned with Tony Chapman to meet them, this time at their Chelsea flat. It was freezing out. We picked up some fish and chips and took these to share with Brian, Mike and Keith. They were literally at starvation level, living mostly from Jagger's student grant of £7 a week.

Doris Richards says: "You should have seen the flat in Chelsea. It looked as though somebody had waged a war in there. There was so much stuff strewn about that it looked like a rubbish dump. I acted as their unpaid washerwoman. The shirts they used to send me to wash for them looked as though they'd been buried for a fortnight. I knew they were often desperate for money. I sent Keith cash whenever I could, and food parcels too, because I knew money would just go on cigarettes instead of on a good, solid meal."

Anyone visiting the flat was jumped on for food, cigarettes or money to feed the meter that fueled the single electric fire. That miserable winter the three Stones stayed in bed most days to keep warm. There was no flame of success on the horizon to cheer their spirits.

The place was an absolute pit which I shall never forget—it looked like it was bomb-damaged. The front room, overlooking the street, had a double bed with rubbish piled all round it. Keith and Brian shared that. The back room, much smaller, was Mick's.

I've never seen a kitchen like it—permanently piled high with dirty dishes, and filth everywhere. They took a strange delight in pointing out the various cultures that grew in about forty smelly milk bottles laying around in mold and on congealed eggs. The ceiling was covered with drawings they'd done from smoke with lighted candles. (The lighting system consisted of a single bare bulb.) Their habits were disgusting: they used to spit on the walls and then decide on names, which would be written alongside the sticking spit, depending on color: Yellow Humphrey, Green Gilbert, Scarlet Jenkins or Polka-dot Perkins. I never understood why they carried on like this. Although Keith came from a working-class background, Brian and Mick were from well-to-do families. It could not have been just the lack of money that caused them to sink. Bohemian Angst, more likely.

Their sick humor was typified by a crude trick they played in the lavatory. Anyone who went in there (not a decision to be made lightly) might have thought the wires entwined around the cistern were part of the Stones' primitive amplification system. The truth was more surreal. They had connected a microphone in the lavatory to a tape-recorder in another room, and recordings were played back to anyone who visited the flat.

Basically they were beatniks, but there was a something between them that I recognized, something that transcended the squalid conditions they were prepared to tolerate. Brian, Mick and Keith were very bright, highly motivated layabouts who hoped against all the prevailing odds that their devotion to a minority music would somehow "come together" and deliver them from obscurity.

Mick, the student of economics and political science, seemed the only one with an eye on the future if the Stones collapsed. He talked about becoming a lawyer, journalist or politician. Keith, a professional Teddy Boy, spat in his beer to ensure that nobody else drank it. He had no plans to work. Brian just felt that music was his vocation. They all had their hair down well over their ears and in those days that was rare.

The temperature in the flat was the same as in the street and we had to keep our coats on. There was nowhere to sit in the room except on the floor or on the double bed. One chair, with only three serviceable legs, was a death-trap. Brian, Mick and Keith reserved it for strangers and they laughed at the collapse that inevitably followed attempts to sit on it.

We carried our equipment round to the nearby Wetherby Arms for my second rehearsal. This time, perhaps loosened up by the fish and chips and the chat, everyone was more friendly. I took my old homemade bass and they seemed to prefer the sound and look of it to the sophisticated Vox Phantom. There was no formal offer of a job, but it seemed casually accepted that I was "in." They told me the first show for me was next night, Saturday, December 15, 1962, and to call for them at the flat.

From the flat Brian, Keith, Mick and I caught a bus to Putney, having a row with the conductor who didn't want to let us take our guitar cases and amplifiers on the bus. Eventually he relented, but we made it tough for him and he kept threatening to throw us off. The youth-club gig was a downer. We played two sets, doing authentic blues, Chuck Berry songs and a Fats Domino number. The audience was dead. Brian took whatever money was earned, saying it would be "donated" to living expenses at the flat. So much for my first gig with the Stones.

Keith said later: "It turned out that Bill really could play. At first he was very untogether, then slowly he started to play very natural, swinging bass lines. But Bill wasn't permanent. He played with us and came to rehearsals, but he couldn't make gigs sometimes because he had to work."

For an organized, methodical guy like me, joining such a ramshackle organization wasn't easy. Ian Stewart recalled later: "The Stones, then all unmarried, were sympathetic to Bill. We agreed that he would only play with us if the money was good. If it was bad, then he stayed at home." Bad? Very often there was no money at all! In the first weeks and months, money was a poor joke. My second gig, on December 21, was at the Piccadilly Jazz Club, for what we were told would be a three-hour show. There were Christmas decorations everywhere but no audience. Only about ten people turned up and we played for ourselves, using it as a rehearsal. Keith fell off the stage at one point—he must have been drunk. Whatever money was earned was again commandeered by Brian for "flat expenses." As Christmas neared, Keith marked his nineteenth birthday on December 18 by taking a job as a temporary postman.

"Mick, Keith and Brian were starving," recalled Ian Stewart. "Bill and I were buying them food with what little money was left out of our wages. I used to go there straight from work at about six, and they'd all still be in bed. When Bill and I arrived we would take them round to the Wimpy Bar for something to eat."

I went to the Edith Grove flat on December 22, 1962.
We all then took the tube to Ealing, and walked across to
the Ealing Jazz Club, a narrow and long room with a
small stage at one end, and a bar at the other. The
audience divided themselves equally between the two. I
remember Stu playing piano on the Muddy Waters' song
"I Put a Tiger in Your Tank" one minute and, before
we'd finished it, I saw him drinking at the bar with
friends!

Brian, Keith and Mick celebrated their Christmas in a
working-man's café. Pop music in 1962 offered no career
and the prospect of turning professional with them was
unthinkable. But something inside me told me to hang on
in, and despite all the sordid and chaotic circumstances, I
was strangely drawn to the Stones.

Gradually I became sucked into something that gathered its own momentum. Against the backdrop of generation gaps, social change, youth power, a fashion revolution
and the impact of new music created by the young, I
joined what people would later describe as the Greatest
Rock 'n' Roll Band in the World. In 1963 we changed
our name from the Rollin' Stones to the Rolling Stones,
and the beginning of this group was more like fable than
fact, for the bizarre events and components that would
deliver the Stones to the top could never be computed or
engineered.

Stu, who was totally devoted to the band, was given
some shares for the company he worked for—it was a
scheme to encourage workers to be shareholders—and he
promply sold them and used the money to buy a Volkswagen
van to drive the band around.

A guy called Jimmy Phelge moved into Edith Grove
with the boys. He worked in printing and advertising. His
domestic hygiene left a lot to be desired and got progres-
sively worse. Keith described him as "the most disgusting
person ever. You'd walk in, and he would be standing at
the top of the stairs, completely nude, with his filthy
underpants on the top of his head, and he'd spit at you."

Two vital moves clinched my arrival in the Stones as a
full-timer, although I was not to give up my day job for
another eight and a half months. First, I decided to
integrate myself into their "club" by growing my hair
longer and combing it forwards. A loud cheer from Mick,

Keith and Brian greeted my arrival at the ABC café, our meeting spot next door to the Ealing Jazz Club, just before our gig there on January 5. Jumping up when I walked in, they were pleased that I'd *visibly* joined. I immediately felt more at home in their company, now that they had generated a bit of warmth.

The second move was less pleasant, but even more important. We seemed all set for an uneventful gig at the Ricky Tick Club at Windsor the next week. It was a good night: the American servicemen in the audience understood the Chicago rhythm-and-blues music we were trying to emulate. But as we were packing up the equipment after the show, the boys told Tony Chapman he was fired. He was furious. Pulling me aside, he said, "Come on, Bill, let's go and start a new band." I replied that I was quite happy with the Stones. He left us there, red-faced and angry.

A few days earlier Brian, Mick and Keith had once again approached Charlie Watts, who was still living at home with his parents in a prefab in Neasden, and this time he had agreed to join the Stones permanently while continuing his day job in graphic design. "I was into modern jazz," Charlie recalled, "but I had a theory that R & B was going to be a big part of the scene and I wanted to be in it. The Stones were great, so I joined." Stu recalled that when it became obvious that things were going to happen with the band, "We said to Charlie: 'Look, you're in this band, that's it, end of story,' and Charlie said, 'Yeah, all right then, but I don't know what my dad's gonna say.' " Tony Chapman, musing later on his sacking, was painfully honest: "Charlie is an infinitely finer drummer. I'm moderately terrible."

Tony Chapman said: "When I left the Stones, I formed the original Preachers with Steve Carroll. Just before Steve was killed, we changed the name to the Herd, and Andy Bown joined. Then we got another guitar player called Taylor. Then Billy Gaff got involved and eased me out. Then I formed the 2nd Preachers, with Peter Frampton."

And so the Stones—Mick, Keith, Brian, Charlie, Stu and me—first played together on January 14, 1963, at the Flamingo, Soho.

*   *   *

The Rolling Stones that I joined was led by Brian Jones. To the millions who figured that it was Mick Jagger's band, it may come as a shock to record that in 1963 Mick was simply the singer. There was no doubt whatsoever who led the group in every way. Brian called the shots partly because he had pulled the musicians together, but mainly because what mattered most at that stage was music, and Brian was by far the most knowledgeable about what we were playing. He and Keith Richards worked out together on their guitars which songs would form our repertoire.

Brian was not merely the figurehead of the Stones. He was the business manager too in these formative days. He collected and controlled all the money at our gigs and divided it by five to pay us—sometimes. Before we received our cash he deducted what he said he needed to pay expenses: petrol, telephone, guitar strings, even offsetting the rent and food he shared with Mick and Keith. We'll never know where some of the money went. He conned us and we knew it, but he was such an energetic leader that nobody cared much about Brian's extra few pounds. He even wrote to the BBC radio program *Jazz Club*, an ambitious move in those years, and asked for an audition. We were much more concerned with getting the music right than arguing about income, and we all respected him as a leader.

The Stones took its musical stance entirely from Brian's passion for American rural blues music. His knowledge of the subject was impressive, and his genuine love for it couldn't fail to hit anyone. Brian's tastes were very earthy, unsophisticated, with no concessions to commercial popularity. Brian and Keith turned me on completely to a music I knew very little about: I had liked mostly American *pop*, the hits I'd heard on the radio—great stuff, but miles away from the esoteric work by obscure artists they were discussing.

When anyone entering the company of that group was not on their wavelength, like me in those early days, the "ride" was very uncomfortable. They were like a private club and you either joined it or steered well clear. Empathy with their music was essential; I didn't have it to begin with, but fortunately I was a fast learner. After working with Cyril Davies and his All-Stars one night I had a crack at copying the "walking bass" style of their bass player Ricky Brown (sometimes known as Ricky Fenson). I remember Brian looking round at me and saying: "Hey, *that's* good. Where did you get *that* from?" At that moment I joined the band on a new level.

Brian had a presence that was definitely electric. Mick did too, in a strange way, but I always felt Mick's personality was more self-consciously constructed: I don't remember him having the same sort of magical aura in those early days. When we were playing blues, I don't think anybody took much notice of Mick. Much more important was what *sound* Brian was making on the slide guitar and harmonica. Mick played harmonica too, but Brian was better, more imaginative.

Brian was an extraordinary mixture. He was the sincere, true blues purist, who wrote enthusiastic letters on behalf of the Stones to music papers and all sorts of people stating the case for our music. The other side of him craved the hedonistic world of the rich and famous pop star. In his short life, he achieved both ambitions, but his health couldn't keep pace. My research into his life has revealed to me what made Brian—and the Stones— tick. The events that drove us from near starvation to the top combined dedicated hard work with timing and good luck. And we also met the right people at the right time, people who needed the Stones as much as we needed them. For example at the Red Lion pub, Sutton, on January 9, 1963, we were again supported by the Presidents, and their singer, Glyn Johns. He worked as a recording engineer at IBC Studios, and he was to play an important part in our careers.

The first rumblings of a change in the established order of things, socially as well as musically, had begun the previous November, in 1962, when the Beatles crept into the charts with their debut single, "Love Me Do," eventually reaching number seventeen. Neither the Beatles nor the Stones realized the significance of what they were gradually achieving at the time: attracting teenagers out of the Dixieland jazz clubs and into the rock 'n' roll venues. Hundreds of pop groups around Britain were poised to threaten and eventually kill the stranglehold traditional jazz had exercised. What the Beatles did at

Liverpool's Cavern, we were doing on the Ricky Tick Club circuit and over at Ealing.

There were two jewels in the crown for the Stones to aspire to among the Soho jazz haunts. The Flamingo jazz club at 33 Wardour Street was the London hang-out for the "cool jazz" set, and we were presented by the promoters as "original R & B, starring the Rolling Stones and guest." Our gig on January 14, 1963, marked the debut of our "new" line-up: Jones, Richards, Jagger, Stewart, Wyman and Watts. But the jazz crowd received us coldly. We were too rock 'n' roll for the large contingent of blacks in the audience who had as their idol Georgie Fame, a regular performer. He was an incredibly good pianist and vocalist and reasonably friendly compared with most in the jazz fraternity. Later he told us that he would stand at the bar, so cool, watching us and thinking: "Who are these young upstarts?"

The other citadel was the Marquee, run by John Gee and Harold Pendleton. They never liked us, viewing us as a dangerous threat to the jazz status quo. The feeling was entirely mutual. We regarded them and kindred spirits as music snobs determined to sabotage our progress. What was odd about Pendleton's attitude to us was that his partner in the National Jazz Federation was Chris Barber, that true progressive in music and great champion of the blues music.

For our first Marquee gig, on January 10, 1963, I went on stage introduced as Lee Wyman. The name of my mate in the Royal Air Force had always impressed me; it sounded much more raunchy than Bill Perks, and since Brian Jones was still calling himself Elmo Lewis, I decided there and then that I wouldn't carry on being Bill Perks as a musician in a pop group.

We were second on the bill to the highly rated Cyril Davies All-Star R & B Group, a twelve-piece band that included the highly respected pianist, Nicky Hopkins, and a guitarist called Bernie Watson, who sat behind his amp with his back to the audience, a handkerchief over his head, playing great licks. All the Stones loved the Davies band; the way they interpreted Chuck Berry's "Deep Feeling" had to be heard to be believed. The second time we supported Cyril at the Marquee, he had added three black girls, the Velvettes, to his band to sing back-up vocals. Chris Jagger described Cyril as looking like a banker. "He used to wear a blue suit, and go ape-shit playing his harmonica, the way you'd expect a black man to do. It was devilishly exciting at the time."

These early days with the Stones were not profitable. Indeed, some of the gigs cost *me* money. After Brian's usual list of deductions for flat expenses, guitar strings, harmonicas, etc., some nights we were paid only 5 shillings each, and it cost me more than that to travel to the club from southeast London. But the band was beginning to gel. I found Charlie's drumming much easier to play along with than that of Tony Chapman. I also liked Charlie a lot. The rhythm section—Charlie, me and Stu—had an affinity beyond music: we had day jobs. Although Mick was still technically attending the LSE, his attendance was erratic, and on the whole the front-line trio was still clinging to a beatnik lifestyle and the notion that somehow the grind of club work might evolve into a career.

This mattered much more to Brian than to the other two. He sat for days at the flat, writing and rewriting letters to his parents. He wanted them to recognize that, after years of strife, he had at last got his act together, literally: he was *running a band!* But despite these frequent letters, and occasional visits to Cheltenham, he told Keith he could not communicate properly with them. "He was a lot more conscious of his background, and concerned about what his family thought than the rest of us were," Keith recalled.

On stage, with his shoulder-length hair and his aura of sad vulnerability, Brian was the magnet for the girls who were starting to hang around us after some of the shows. One night, after we'd played the Ricky Tick Club, Windsor, some of them began chatting to us as we packed away our equipment. This club at the Star and Garter Hotel was one of the first places where girls in the audience started making themselves available. Most of them looked very plain to me, with long straight hair and no make-up. Brian became very friendly with one sixteen-year-old, Linda Lawrence from Reading, Berkshire. It was the start of a tempestuous affair. Her memory of him contradicts some of the later stories about Brian. "What I liked about him at first," she said, "was that he treated me like a lady. He was so nice and polite. He was my first real relationship after leaving school and he looked after me."

The Stones played the Flamingo again on January 28, supporting the Graham Bond Trio, a good band. (Graham was to commit suicide on May 8, 1974, by throwing himself under a tube train in London.) This was our last gig there and when we left we stole three old metal stools which we carried around in the van and Brian, Mick and Keith used onstage everywhere we played. I would sit on my wardrobe bass cabinet, laid on its side most nights. We would perform like this, stopping between songs to light up cigarettes and drink beer and chat between ourselves. There was no stage presentation and we generally ignored the audience. It was a very different approach from other bands, and must have seemed quite bizarre to the audiences.

As we began the first of our Tuesday night residencies at the Ealing jazz club on February 5, 1963, it was snowing. Only about six people braved the weather, and it was so cold inside that we played with our coats on.

A few nights a week we still rehearsed at the Wetherby Arms and adjourned afterwards to the Wimpy Bar in Earls Court Road. The food wasn't up to much but the cabaret was fun, with lots of fights and plates being hurled about. One rehearsal night we invited two black girl singers with the idea of adding them as backing vocalists, inspired by Cyril Davies' black vocal trio.

We rehearsed with the two girls a few times, trying to do a version of "La Bamba," a song that would evolve into "Twist and Shout." But we soon lost patience. We thought they weren't very good and they were always giggling stupidly and disrupting what we regarded as important rehearsal time. Mick was dating one of them, Cleo Sylvester, but that made no difference—they had no future with us.

It was Brian who triggered our next vital connection. He had become friendly with a man named Giorgio Gomelski, an experimental film-maker who was full of enthusiasm for musical adventure and possessed a close affinity with jazz and the blues. Giorgio's father was a Russian doctor, and his mother was French. After hitch-hiking around the world, Giorgio had organized the first

Italian jazz festival, then had lived in Chicago for a while, where he discovered the blues. After producing a film of the Chris Barber Band in August 1961 at the first Richmond Jazz Festival, by early 1963 the excitable Giorgio was running his own club in the rear room at the Station Hotel, Richmond. This featured two future big names in music: jazz saxophonist Johnny Dankworth's band on Monday nights and, on Sundays, the Dave Hunt Band, featuring Ray Davies, later to lead the Kinks to international success.

Brian met Giorgio at a crucial time in the band's evolution. On January 31, after a great show, we asked Cyril Davies for more money—and were immediately fired. Harold Pendleton said later: "I came out of the Marquee with Cyril, and the Stones were packing their stuff into a van. I shouted goodnight to them, and they went 'Aaaa-aarag!' I said, 'What's the matter with them?' Cyril said, 'I've just fired them.' 'What for?' He said, 'They're not very authentic, and they're not very good.' " The truth was that we had been getting superb receptions at the Marquee and the audience had now swelled to an average of 600. I'd noticed that when we had a tremendous ovation and earned an encore, Cyril hadn't looked too happy at all. But it was a bad blow to us all the same.

So when Brian met a lively guy like Giorgio he immediately enthused to him: "You must come and hear this band of mine," he said. "Best band in London. We play *rhythm and blues.*" Few groups could claim that. Gomelski came to see us at the Red Lion on February 6 and liked what we were doing. As soon as one of his acts goofed, he said, he would bring us into one of his promotions.

Meanwhile, we felt that we were being ostracized by London jazz club promoters. For reasons we couldn't understand, the Stones had a bad name and we couldn't get bookings anywhere. It must have been jealousy and fear on the part of the jazz crowd: they thought that we constituted a threat to them—and they were right.

Giorgio, a great hustler, was just what the band needed at that time. He was to prove a catalyst, giving us confidence when the odds were mounting against us. Brian knew that Giorgio's regular band was not very reliable. He invited him back to Edith Grove for a chat. "Look, Giorgio," he said, "you can't run a club without knowing if your band's going to turn up! Give us a break. We'll do it for nothing!" And so Giorgio began to steer and stimulate us on a managerial level, searching for places where we could play. We played at the opening night of the Haringey jazz club at the Manor House pub on February 14, 1963. And then one day Giorgio had exciting news for us: the Dave Hunt R & B Band had given up their residency at Richmond. He said he would guarantee us £1 each per show, starting the following Sunday. We accepted with great enthusiasm. The break was crucial. We were getting dispirited by the whispering campaign around the jazz clubs, and attendances were poor. There were yet again only six people in the audience one snowy night at Ealing—and six on stage!

Things began to perk up in other ways: three days after Giorgio told us about the Richmond gigs, we met Glyn Johns again at the Red Lion pub. He suggested we get some songs together: he might be able to get a record company interested. It seemed a strange idea, but exciting.

On Thursday, February 21, 1963, Giorgio and some of the band went fly-sticking posters all over London, advertising the Richmond show that coming weekend. When they had finished, Mick and Keith asked Giorgio to give them the bucket of glue, rather than throw it away. "We'll find some use for it," Jagger said. Giorgio remembers: "I went round to their flat about two weeks later and the abominable smell met me as they opened the door. Mick and Keith had filled up this glue bucket with cigarette ends, old toilet paper, old socks, anything, it was terrible." That week's *Melody Maker* featured an advertisement by Giorgio that was fully in keeping with his zany promotional style: "R & B with the inimitable, incomparable, exhilarating Rolling Stones!"

The big day, Sunday, February 24, 1963, went fairly quietly. I met the band in town and we all drove in the van to Richmond and set up our own equipment. To an audience of about thirty, we played two forty-five-minute sets finishing with a Bo Diddley song called "Doing the Crawdaddy." We earned £7 10s. between us for this show, but the place was to mean much more to the band's future than money.

Promoter Vic Johnson remembers how he was "absolutely fascinated by the effect they had on the audience.

The kids, who seemed pretty blasé at first, were galvanized into action. I honestly didn't know whether to laugh at the Stones or send for an animal trainer—I'd never seen anything like them. It was a matter of atmosphere. They seemed in a world of their own as they played music that electrified the whole place. Kids watching had never sampled this sort of thing and didn't know what to make of it at first. But they'd heard a sound that knocked most of the other groups right off the scene."

As March began the Stones' work continued to grow and the spirit in the band was on the up. The only downer was the Ealing club, which had become quite boring to play. The Stones, with various line-ups, had been playing there for eight months and there was much grumbling about the fact that, because of Brian's accounting system, the gig never seemed to make us any money.

It was always difficult to separate the private life of Brian from the daily life and work of the group. His complex character meant that he was both the driving force and a liability. An early example of how the women in his life were indivisible from his work came at Ealing jazz club on March 2. Out of the blue, Pat Andrews arrived with Julian to see Brian, who was there with Linda Lawrence. When he needed to, Brian was capable of sweet-talking anyone, but in this situation he needed all the diplomacy he could muster. He managed to persuade Linda to go, and Pat and the baby joined Brian and all the other Stones on a trip to a Soho café. Brian walked around holding his son, the proud father.

Around this time a new breed of fans was congregating around the Stones. Young players just starting to learn their instruments would come up to us between sets, asking us questions about amps, chords, bass, strings, arrangements, songs and repertoire. At the Ricky Tick one boy introduced himself to me as Paul Samwell Smith. He came to all our gigs there and sat watching my every move. Pretty soon afterwards he helped to form the Yardbirds; they eventually replaced the Stones at all our gigs when we went out to the ballrooms and started touring.

On March 3, 1963, we played another gig arranged by Giorgio, this time an afternoon session at the Ken Colyer

Club, Studio 51, in Soho. It was ironic that we were given a great welcome by the ladies, Vi and Pat, who ran this stronghold of New Orleans-style jazz, whereas the jazz snobs at the Marquee and elsewhere saw us as upstarts who should not be encouraged. From the Colyer Club we drove straight to Richmond for our second gig at the Crawdaddy. Giorgio was getting into his stride as a publicist: this time he advertised in *Melody Maker* "the craziest new R & B sound of the unparalleled Rolling Stones." The crowd had doubled to sixty from the first gig, and our music was improving. We returned home feeling happy with our slow, sure progress.

The same pattern of gigs continued the next Sunday, but with two significant differences. The crowds were bigger at both places, and, at the Colyer Club, I noticed that there were faces from our other gigs, now following us from club to club. On to Richmond for the evening (for which Giorgio's advertisement trumpeted us as "the thrilling, exhilarating, galvanic, intoxicating, incomparable Rolling Stones'), where we were faced with an amazing *one hundred fans!* Hamish Grimes, an assistant of Giorgio's, said about us later: "They're barbaric. They love the music they play and don't let anything come in the way."

Next day, March 11, we finally went with Glyn Johns to the IBC recording studio in Portland Place. During a three-hour session on a two-track machine we recorded Bo Diddley's "Road-Runner" and "Diddley Daddy," Muddy Waters' "I Want to be Loved" and Jimmy Reed's "Honey What's Wrong?" When we found we had five minutes of paid-for time left, we did a first take of Jimmy Reed's "Bright Lights, Big City."

Glyn recalls: "The Stones were novel, because nobody had ever *heard* of Jimmy Reed and Bo Diddley in Britain, and that was basically what they were doing. Brian was pretty much the leader, certainly the spokesman for the group to me. He was very much concerned with the sounds that I would produce on tape. He wanted the Jimmy Reed-type sound.

"I was frightened to introduce them to George Clewson, the guy who owned the studio. The effect they had on people, with their appearance, their clothes, their hair—their whole attitude—was immediate. As soon as you saw them, they showed complete opposition to society, every-body, anything."

Brian was thrilled, filled with completely justifiable pride, at these tracks. They gave him more pleasure than anything else the Stones ever recorded. He played them repeatedly for visitors to Edith Grove. But our confidence was jolted by the news from Glyn: George Clewson had spent a week taking the tracks around six or seven record companies, only to have them rejected as not commercial enough for the pop charts, which were topped at this time by Cliff Richard's "Summer Holiday" film soundtrack. We were all very brought down by this, having run up a huge bill: £106 in recording costs.

Glyn Johns said: "The two guys who owned the studio knew absolutely nothing about the record business. They didn't realize what they had. They took it to all the wrong people and of course failed to sell it."

I went up to Edith Grove on March 17. Brian had borrowed a cheap record-player from a friend. He couldn't get it to work, and went to make coffee in the kitchen. Keith and I decided it was useless and disconnected the speaker leads. We then plugged them directly into the mains, the whole thing blew up in a cloud of smoke. Brian never did find out what really happened.

The sunshine continued, though, from Giorgio's infectious advertisements in *Melody Maker*, which raised a laugh and also built up the crowds at the Crawdaddy. "The unprecedented, incontestable, inexhaustible purveyors of spontaneous combustion" came next, followed by "untameable, wildfire explosion of impetuous R & B with the unsuppressibly storm-raising Rolling Stones."

Giorgio remembers: "Art students from Kingston College of Technology started coming to the club; it was really a *scene*. You had the feeling of being in a clan of people, sharing information and musical abilities, and everybody was into the blues. The lighting consisted of one red and one blue spot; we couldn't afford anything else. We started to teach people how to react to the Stones because at first they all stood there, immobile. It was ridiculous.

"It was hot and exciting: fans danced with their shirts off; and I encouraged people to dance on the table tops, so they could be seen and to encourage others to join in.

The beginning of that whole Stones thing was audience participation, where the audience went *Wow!* The last forty-five minutes of their show became a tribal ritual: the Stones would play Bo Diddley's 'Pretty Thing' or 'The Crawdaddy' for twenty minutes. It would be hypnotic. In the end people just went berserk. It was bigger than individual groups of people. I can't tell you the excitement at that place in those months. It was like, all of a sudden, you hit civilization right on the head. The energy was incredible and it gave everybody courage for years and years."

At work I began to get hassled about my appearance. My hair was getting longer and once I was rebuked for wearing a pink shirt, even though it was under a suit and a pullover, with only the collar visible. Charlie and Stu's hair was still quite short, but Mick, Keith and Brian all had very long hair by now.

The flat in Edith Grove where I met the band before we went to each gig had meanwhile become quite a mecca for people who had heard about the bizarre behavior of the layabouts who occupied the first floor. A trombone-playing journalist named Ian Gilchrist was told by the people he shared his flat with that three "really crazy" musicians lived on the floor above. They were called the Rolling Stones. "Bloody daft name. Won't get anywhere," Gilchrist commented. But intrigued, he went upstairs after a few days in residence. "I knocked on the door," he remembered, "and Mick appeared, naked and looking very angry. I asked if the landlord had been round lately. Mick didn't answer at first. He stood there looking at my feet and slowly moved his gaze upwards until it was level with my face. Then he spoke: 'Fuck off!' and slammed the door in my face."

Gilchrist's baptism into the weird world of the Stones had only just begun. "Strange things happened at Edith Grove," he recalled later. "At two o'clock one morning the lads suddenly and inexplicably hurled all their sheets and blankets out of the window into the yard and set fire to them. Two nights later we were fast asleep when there was a tremendous bang on the window. There, swinging away outside on the end of a rope, was a frying pan. They were trying to smash our window. The following night they came home at 3 a.m. and played a pop record through one of their stage speakers at a tremendous volume. By this time, the novelty of living under them was starting to wear thin."

A few nights later, Brian, Keith, and Mick returned home at 5 a.m. without their front-door key. "They kept hammering on the door until I got out of bed and let them in," says Gilchrist. "Without a word of thanks they went screaming past me, laughing their heads off." Next day, the Stones repeated their dawn chorus, hammering on the door. "Naturally we all stayed in bed." So Keith picked up his guitar case, smashed it through the door window, put his hand through and opened the door. "Strangely enough," Gilchrist says, "I decided to move. I was certain of one thing, though—I had definitely heard the last of a crummy group called the Rolling Stones."

A few days later, Brian Jones had a surprise visitor: Pat Andrews and Julian. She had heard that the group was making an impact in the clubs and decided to relocate to London. She took a flat in Ladbroke Grove Road, Notting Hill and began work in a pharmacy. She stayed with Brian a couple of days each week, and things appeared harmonious between them.

Back with the music, we sensed things were changing gear when, after a gig at Guildford on March 30 we were approached by a fan who introduced herself as Doreen Pettifer from Bagshot. She obviously had a crush on Brian and wanted to launch a fan club for us. It seemed unnecessary at that stage, with no records out and no real promise of fireworks, but we gave her the go-ahead. The next night, after the afternoon session at the Ken Colyer Club, we decided that Doreen might be on to something. The "Hyperheradox R & B voluptuousness from the tempestuously transporting Rolling Stones," as Giorgio now described us, attracted more than *300* fans to the Richmond club! "We got the message," remembers Keith, "and we knew we were on the right track—and we weren't even looking for it. That wasn't the reason the Stones were put together. We were sort of evangelists. It was a very pure, idealistic drive that did it. The money we needed to live on, we didn't give a damn about. That wasn't the point. The point was to spread the music. We were doing what we wanted. We had all these kids coming to clubs, and we were spreading the music and doing what we wanted to do. It wasn't to make money. The money was a secondary thing—and we didn't see any for a year or two."

A week later, at Richmond on April 7, "unrepressed R & B with the immitigating, ebullient Rolling Stones" brought in 320 fans. It was hot, sweaty and exciting. We talked to a reporter from the local paper, and his photographer took our pictures. We always used to finish our set with a Bo Diddley song called "Doing the Crawdaddy," and so the club was called the Crawdaddy from then on.

Giorgio remembered: "A local paper did a write-up on us, and asked us what we called the club. Up to then we'd never had a name. Without thinking almost, we said 'The Crawdaddy,' because this was a number the Stones played, and was very popular." Giorgio also recorded the fact that the Yardbirds, then featuring Eric Clapton, had just formed and wanted to play during the interval at this gig "but they never turned up."

Our very first press report, on April 13, 1963, appeared in the *Richmond and Twickenham Times*. A source of terrific pride and excitement, the report by Barry May read:

> A musical magnet is drawing the jazz beatniks to Richmond. The attraction is the Crawdaddy Club at the Station Hotel, the first of its kind in an area of flourishing modern and traditional jazz haunts. R & B is replacing traddy-pop. The deep earthy sound is typical of the best R & B, and gives all who hear it an irresistible urge to stand up and move. The four or five nights of jazz every week at Eel Pie Island have dwindled to only two at the weekend . . . Save from the swaying forms of the group on the spotlit stage, the room is in darkness. A patch of light from the entrance doors catches the sweating dancers and those who are slumped on the floor, the long hair, suede jackets, gaucho trousers and Chelsea boots. How sad and unfortunate that the Station Hotel is to be demolished. The Stones will go on Rolling.

Brian was ecstatic. For months he carried the newspaper cutting around, showing everyone—proof to all the cynics that we were moving.

It is interesting that this first observation of us in print made no mention of the "dirty, unkempt" appearance, an accusation that soon afterwards came from all parts of the press, radio and television. We'd noticed that in some pubs and shops we were being refused service because of our appearance, but we ascribed that more to the growing generation gap, the resentment by adults of teenage assertiveness, than to our looks. Brian and Mick particularly had long hair, but I didn't think we looked *grubby*.

We never dreamed that our appearance would play such a part in our rise to fame—but image was vitally important in the early sixties. However great our music, to make inroads into the charts was not going to be easy without powerful personalities. The Beatles had shown us this. When their second single, "Please Please Me," shot to the top of the charts on February 22, 1963, it signaled that the arrival of youth and pop music were indivisible. Before that, pop music meant songs made by adults.

Our link with the Beatles, which was always friendly, began on April 14, 1963, when Giorgio, this time wearing his film-making hat, went to Twickenham to see the TV show *Thank Your Lucky Stars* being recorded. While we were beginning our afternoon session at the Ken Colyer Club, Giorgio was talking to the Beatles about making a film. He told them about us and invited them to visit our show in Richmond, only three miles away, later that night.

The room was packed and we were in good form, driven on by the Crawdaddy regulars that now formed our core audience. Soon after we began our first set, we were staggered to see the four Beatles standing and watching us. They were dressed identically in long leather overcoats. I became very nervous, and said to myself: "Shit, that's the *Beatles!*"

George Harrison recalled later: "It was a real rave. The audience shouted and screamed and danced on tables. They were doing a dance that no one had seen up till then, but we now all know as the Shake. The beat the Stones laid down was so solid it shook off the walls and seemed to move right inside your head. A great sound."

We met them in the bar and chatted about our mutual ambitions and the problems of keeping going. They were one step ahead of us, just starting their recording career. We got on well enough for them to stay for the entire second set. They waited while we packed our equipment and came back to the Edith Grove flat where we sat chatting for hours about music.*

We played them our demonstration records, which still had not managed to interest any record companies, and our precious blues albums, including a rare, imported-from-America LP by Jimmy Reed. I remember that John, never a fan of raw blues music, was not very impressed by our beloved Jimmy Reed and made his views known in his usual forthright manner. Brian asked for, and got, an autographed photo of the Beatles and stuck it on the wall above the fireplace. "We talked about our hopes halfway through the night," Brian recalled later. "We could hardly believe that our kind of music would catch on."

They left at 4 a.m., inviting us to their show at the Royal Albert Hall the following Thursday, and promised to stay in touch. Stu ran George and Ringo back to the President Hotel in Russell Square; I returned home to Penge and Diane and Stephen after a memorable night in which a bond had been forged.

The Beatles, ahead of us career-wise, had the major advantage of a driving manager, Brian Epstein. What we could not realize was how crucial that was to any group's success. *Our* management was on the horizon, too, however.

Meanwhile, on April 18 Brian, Keith and Mick went to the Royal Albert Hall to see the Beatles top the bill over fifteen other artists. So they wouldn't have to buy tickets, the three Stones secured from the Beatles' party three guitars owned by John, Paul and George, which they proceeded to carry in through the back door of the hall. Mistaken for the Beatles they were mobbed by girls; it

---

*Recalling those heady days a quarter of a century later Mick Jagger, introducing two of the surviving Beatles at their induction into the Rock 'n' Roll Hall of Fame in New York on January 20, 1988, said: "When the Stones were first together we heard there was a group from Liverpool wth long hair, scruffy clothes and a record in the charts with a bluesy harmonica riff. And the combinaton of all this made me sick!"

was the first time they had experienced it, but they loved it. And Brian was ecstatic. "This is what we *like*," he kept saying, "being mobbed by people! This is what we *want!*"

Rubbing shoulders with the Beatles really whetted his appetite. He suddenly seemed desperate for success—quickly. It was obvious to all around him that he badly wanted to be a star, but a battle was going on inside him: he didn't want to compromise his musical integrity, or that of the band. And maybe, just maybe, he realized that it is usually the *singer* who gains the spotlight. Brian had only a grudging tolerance of singers. He did not consider them to be musicians. His philosophy was clear: "Somebody who plays an instrument is to be respected. *Anybody* can sing!" He had given Mick some tips about how to play the harmonica, but was superior to him on that instrument. The die was cast; as Mick inevitably began to capture the headlines, the two were destined for a partnership fraught with tension.

Meeting the Beatles acted as a spur to all of us. We were determined to work hard for the big break, but we still had no notion of how we could succeed. The odds seemed to be stacked against us, and we couldn't comprehend how a group that generated so much excitement in the clubs could not win the support of the record industry. Today, when armies of record men are out looking for new acts it's difficult to recapture the mood of our band that spring of 1963. We desperately wanted to make a record. And we were good. But the doors were firmly closed.

When Giorgio had no luck with his film idea with the Beatles, he phoned us all to say he wanted to shoot a twenty-minute documentary of us at the Crawdaddy Club. He asked us to rehearse the music and arrive there the following Sunday morning instead of simply for the evening performance.

We entered into the spirit of the thing, spending the Saturday afternoon before the big day at a recording studio in Morden, rehearsing and recording Bo Diddley's "Pretty Thing" especially for the project. Next day Giorgio filmed the afternoon session. As crowds began to queue for the evening, he filmed that too. Our feelings about Giorgio and his antics were ambivalent. His infectious enthusiasm was a great boost to the band, but Mick and

Brian felt he was "a kind of European madman who was very artistic and shouted and ranted": they didn't have much confidence in his ability.

However, his contribution to us and the young British blues/rock scene was to be significant, directly and indirectly. Although we could never have expected it, that sunny day, April 21, was a turning point. Before the Richmond gig Giorgio phoned Peter Jones, a writer with the *Record Mirror:* "Look, I'm filming a band and I would like you to come and see them." On a *Sunday?* Some British people are very conservative about the Sabbath. Jones was reluctant, but Gomelski was persuasive. Arriving in Richmond, Jones was surprised to see "people waiting on the pavement outside the club, and people having to step in the road to get by."

Giorgio said to him: "I'll get a couple of the boys to come out and talk to you." Jones said later: "We had a couple of pints of beer. Brian had the group wallet. There was no money in it, but there was a cutting from the local paper about the apparent success and controversy the band were creating and what they were about. They really bemoaned the fact that nobody was showing any interest in them in terms of a recording contract, or even taking any interest in them and coming to see them. I promised I would see what I could do."

Impressed with our act, Peter Jones was in no doubt that Brian was the leader, "the organizer, with this great memory; he could tell you how much material they had and exactly where it came from. It was he who laid down the guiding policies of the band. It was Brian who supervised every single move that they made. He talked about Muddy Waters, Jimmy Reed and people like that. But he was in no way super-optimistic."

At his office next day Peter Jones enthused to two colleagues—one a student of black music named Norman Jopling, who would later write about us. Then, leaving his office he connected with a young hustler known to *Record Mirror* staff. He was sharp in every sense, very quick-witted with an idea that he wanted to be a comedian; he was also acutely aware of teenage trends. His name was Andrew Loog Oldham. While this speedy guy's knowledge of music was limited, Jones registered that he had an uncanny "feel" for commercial pop. He had bumped into Beatles manager Brian Epstein in a TV studio and for a short period had worked as the Beatles' publicist, handling the press for "Please Please Me" and "I Want to Hold Your Hand."

At that stage we certainly needed a manager. The combined thrust of Gomelski and Peter Jones in pointing Oldham towards us was a stroke of luck at a critical moment. Things were looking bleak again: Giorgio had just taken the soundtrack of his seven-minute documentary to Decca, but they weren't interested. We were deflated by the record industry's negativity . . . and then, a mere six days after the tip-off from Jones, the bouncing Oldham arrived to see us at Richmond. With him, he brought the least likely person ever to set foot in a rock'n' roll club: "square" Eric Easton, a former cinema organist and a respectable show-business agent, who represented the staid guitarist Bert Weedon, BBC Establishment disc jockey Brian Matthew, ballad singer Julie Grant and honky-tonk pianist Mrs. Mills. Andrew, aged nineteen, was renting an office from thirty-five-year-old Eric in Regent Street. They were polar opposites: an irreverent young tiger blazing with energy, and a cautious, kindly adult who diligently balanced the books as well as the steady careers of his artists.

Andrew Oldham was painfully thin. He spoke in torrents of enthusiastic chat, leaving the listener breathless but convinced. Born out of wedlock in England on January 29, 1944, he received both parents' names. His father, a Dutch–American Air Force officer, was killed over Germany the same year. Andrew used to hang around the 2 Is coffee bar in Soho during his early teens. At the age of sixteen he was expelled from public school. He then moved to London and worked for fashion designer Mary Quant as odd-job boy, teamaker and messenger. In the evenings he worked as a waiter in the Flamingo jazz club and as a doorman at Ronnie Scott's jazz club. After an eight-month spell in the south of France, he handled publicity for singer Mark Wynter before trying to break into show business as a compère for pop shows, under the names "Sandy Beach" and "Chancery Lane," working for promoter Don Arden.

In April 1963 Andrew began to rent an office from Eric Easton.

Easton had been born in Rishton, near Preston, Lancashire in 1927 and was a very respected agent and manager. He was steeped in the show-business tradition that the Beatles were beginning to challenge. But if he, and others like him, thought the Beatles were revolutionary, what was he going to make of *us* on first sight?

Fortunately Oldham was, without exaggeration, spellbound by the sight of us. The jazz singer George Melly said later: "Andrew was dumbfounded. He looked at Mick like Sylvester looks at Tweetie Pie. Eric Easton was impressed but had certain reservations."

Oldham's recollections of that first night were typically animated, controversial and visionary: "They made an immediate impact on me and my reaction was: *This is it!* I felt they were magic. I saw that they had a unique style. The combination of music and sex was something I had never encountered in any other group and the surprising thing was that you could take them as they were, without asking them to change a thing in clothes, hairstyle or anything else." Sex? It seemed amazing to us. Brian and Mick had natural sex appeal, but on stage they were keen on projecting the *music*. Selling themselves as sexy pop stars had not crossed their minds. Although music certainly wasn't the only thing on Mick's mind at that time. Two days before Andrew and Eric came, he had met Chrissie Shrimpton, the nineteen-year-old younger sister of top British model Jean "the Shrimp" Shrimpton, who photographer David Bailey had helped to fame. They met at the Ricky Tick Club and were to date for three years. It was one of the headline-making affairs of the sixties, but the signal that it would be problematic came very early: at that Richmond gig Andrew saw the first set and then went outside in the interval. In an alley he saw Mick and Chrissie having a fight—forty-eight hours after their first meeting!

Easton's memories of the night were typical of the honesty of a man I came to like a lot. "I went along like an average character of my age, wearing a sports jacket and hoping the evening wasn't being wasted. Outside the Station Hotel was a queue of teenagers all dressed in the clothes of the day. We tagged on the end, feeling conspicuous.

"Every so often someone would have to come out for a

breath of fresh air and the box-office man would let someone else go in. Inside it was the first free Turkish bath I'd ever had, absolutely jammed with people, the most exciting atmosphere I'd ever experienced in a club or ballroom. The Stones were enjoying every minute of it. They were producing this fantastic sound which was obviously exactly right for the kids in the audience."

Andrew described that first evening: "I called him [Mick] over to meet Eric. Brian came over and joined us. We simply had a chat, sizing each other up. Brian put himself forward as leader of the group and the rest seemed to accept this."

The day after seeing us Oldham spoke to Easton about possibly linking up to form a management team for the Stones. Andrew realized Easton had experience of "leg work" in the music business, whereas he had none. "I felt that with my knowledge of the pop world and his business experience, we could provide a good service for them," recalled Andrew. Later that day Oldham phoned Brian, who arranged to meet at Easton's office to discuss management. Charlie, Stu and I were working during the day so we couldn't be there, while Mick was at the London School of Economics. After that meeting, Brian began making some inquiries about both Andrew and Eric within the music business.

Brian made three or four trips to Radnor House, the Regent Street offices, in the next few days to discuss management. Ian Stewart summed up the interaction. "The Stones liked Andrew. Like us, he was young, irreverent, full of enthusiasm and eager to make a fortune. He had little experience of the high-pressure world of pop music, but that was no handicap as far as the Stones were concerned." Stu didn't know what was shortly to be unleashed on him. The management contract between the Stones and Andrew Oldham and Eric Easton's new company, Impact Sound, was signed on behalf of the Stones by Brian Jones on May 1, 1963. It was to run for three years from May 6. Brian had spent a lot of time discussing its ramifications in Eric's office; he delayed the signing for two hours while he went with the contract to see Mick and Keith, who waited for him in the Lyons teashop round the corner. "Brian and Eric liked to think they were running the whole show," Andrew said later.

"My attitude was to let them get on with it. I wanted to get on with the music-making." The Stones also believed in Easton, he said, "but they weren't so close to him. They had less in common, because of the age gap." The group, Oldham says, "wanted our help but did not want to be ordered about."

Brian filled us in on all the details when we met at the Edith Grove flat that night before our next gig. There was tremendous excitement and anticipation about having a management deal. When we arrived at Eel Pie Island for the gig there was a reasonable crowd for a venue that had been dominated by traditional jazz bands: we went by van, parked by the River Thames, and carried our equipment over a narrow bridge to the island itself, paying a penny toll halfway across. The place, like a huge barn, held a maximum of 800 people and we drew about 300, many of them diehard fans who had followed us from Richmond, Ealing and Windsor. The feeling in the band around this time was great, an optimism that something good was about to happen.

At Eel Pie Island Andrew dropped his first bombshell. He insisted that our pianist, Stu, should step down from the band line-up on stage: his tidy image, he said, was "completely wrong" for the band. Stu was vital to the band's roots, musically and socially. But to Andrew, his looks—something the band had never cared about—were a major problem. Stu had a particularly prominent facial characteristic: an attack of measles at the age of eight had left him with a calcium deficiency that caused his jaw to grow very large. At eighteen he had an operation to correct it, but it remained very visible and he was highly conscious of the abnormality. Stu also felt that Andrew thought "my hair wasn't long enough. But there was a good reason for this. Bill and I were the only ones working and we just couldn't go around with long hair, or we would have got the sack." Stu's widow Cynthia says: "Whatever Stu or anybody else said, he *did* care about being relegated. He had enough to worry about because he was so painfully shy. But the bottom line for Andrew was that Stu's face didn't fit; Andrew loved the pretty, thin, long-haired boys. Stu felt bitter, not because he was not up there on stage, but about the savage way he was kicked to one side."

Andrew probably knew what a close unit we had become, and was aware of the shock waves his decree had caused, because he offered an olive branch: Stu should remain with the Stones, playing with us on recording sessions and also becoming our road manager. Fortunately for us, Stu accepted this new role, although reluctantly, and he became incredibly important to us. But here was the first indication that Andrew had a vision of the band as revolutionaries. We didn't realize at the time the extent of his thinking along these lines. Outwardly Stu took it well. Brian said to him: "Don't worry about it. You're part of the Stones. You'll always have a sixth of everything." Stu reflected later: "Brian told me all sorts of rubbish but I ignored it." His attitude to Brian, who had so willingly accepted Oldham's order, now became bitter and the tensions between group members began to increase. Brian's relationship with Mick blossomed temporarily, but there was an underlying feeling that ruthless determination was replacing idealism. I thought that the "sacking" was a strange way to repay Stu's incredible loyalty.

During the period of excitement and our union with Oldham and Easton, Giorgio had been in Switzerland for the funeral of his father. He knew nothing of the new deals Brian had signed. But to the Stones the relegation of the band's pianist seemed a small price to pay for a stepping-stone to stardom. And in elbowing aside Ian Stewart, the first act of surgery had been applied by Andrew Oldham.

As the success of the Stones increased I had to be available more often and my day job suffered. I arrived at Sparks each day exhausted, and my long hair contrasted with the "normal" looks of everyone else. My work-mate Jack Oliver covered for me while I took regular naps in the storeroom, and he would give me the nudge when the boss was about. This situation obviously could not be sustained for long: the day was fast approaching when I would have to make the decision about turning professional.

Andrew now began to move incredibly quickly. When Brian told our new managers about the recording session with Glyn Johns, Andrew and Eric decided to buy back the tapes on our behalf for the £106 it had cost us. On

May 9, only three days after signing a management agreement with Eric and Andrew, Brian signed a second deal with them, this time a three-year recording contract with Impact Sound. In the deal we were given a 6 per cent royalty between the five Stones.* A tape-lease agreement between Oldham/Easton and Decca, running for two years and giving Decca a first option on Stones' records, was signed. We were very green about the business, of course, just happy enough to see the ball rolling in our favor. To be fair to Oldham and Easton, owning our own tapes rather than signing ourselves away to a giant company (as the Beatles and hundreds of others had done) was in 1963 a very shrewd business move.

The pace was now rapid. The day after he had fired Stu from live performances, Andrew told us he'd booked a recording session for the following week—amazing news. Andrew had, very astutely, approached Dick Rowe, Decca's head of A & R (artists and repertoire), who was notorious as "The Man Who Turned Down the Beatles." This time Dick Rowe was receptive to the sound of new music from young people.

Coincidentally, Dick had been judging a beat-group contest in Liverpool along with George Harrison, who had suggested Rowe should "go and see the Stones and sign them up." This Rowe did on May 6, 1963, at Richmond. "As I had turned down the Beatles earlier," Rowe said later, "I didn't want to make the same mistake again. I was fascinated by the audience reaction and the dancing." Andrew, knowing Rowe's sore spot, exploited his position intelligently.

We had the nice problem of choosing which songs to record for our first single. Although we had a big repertoire of R & B songs for stage work, the pressure was on us to record a very commercial song. We went through our record collection at the Chelsea flat and Andrew came to see us rehearse a short-list of titles at the Wetherby Arms. After prolonged debate we eventually decided on Chuck Berry's "Come On" and Muddy Waters' "I Want to be Loved." We weren't sure about the first song.

---

*Needless to say, despite Brian's promises, Stu was not party to this contract.

There was something stilted about it and it didn't feel right, but it had a commercial edge.

I was working as usual all day in Streatham on May 10. That evening I met the band at the flat and we went to our first real recording session, at the old Olympic studios. The song was produced by Andrew, who was honest enough to admit: "Look, I'm the producer and this is the first session I've ever handled! I don't know a damned thing about recording—or music for that matter." Mick accurately described the session as "a bunch of bloody amateurs, ignorant as hell, making a hit single." Such was Andrew's naivety that when the engineer, Roger Savage, asked him if he wanted to mix the track, Andrew didn't know what he meant and told him just to do what was needed to finish off the single! After the session, Stu dropped me off at Victoria Station and I returned home by train. I opened that week's *Record Mirror* to the photo and article on the Stones and waited to be recognized. It didn't happen!

Backed up by the picture taken of us on stage at Richmond, the article by Norman Jopling stated: "Maybe you've never heard of them but, by gad, you will. They are probably destined to be the biggest group in the R & B scene. Unlike all other R & B groups the Stones have a definite visual appeal. They play and sing in a way one would expect more from a colored US R & B team. The group are mad about Bo Diddley . . . They have achieved the American sound better than any other group over here."

Inside the band, moods and attitudes were in flux. Brian's role as leader was inevitably changing, because the business reins had been picked up by our new managers. Inside Easton's office, Stu heard Brian say that Jagger had always had a weak voice and he had to be careful if he wanted to sing night after night. They'd just get rid of him if necessary. "I felt sure Brian would have done it," Stu remarked. "I told him not to be so bloody daft. I felt that Brian was now incapable of leadership. As soon as the group started to become in any way successful, Brian smelled money. He wanted to be a star. He was prepared to do anything that would make it happen and bring in money immediately, whereas Mick and Keith weren't into that."

When Giorgio heard the news of our liaison with Oldham and Easton, he felt well and truly burned. The group went round to his flat to see the film he had shot at Richmond. The last person to arrive was Brian, who had with him "a strange young man called Loog," as Giorgio put it. When Giorgio asked who the stranger was, Brian lied: an old school-friend from Cheltenham. Probably to spare Giorgio's blushes, nothing was said directly to him of Andrew's arrival inside the Stones team. He should have been told, straight. He found out soon enough anyway, and then he naturally believed he had been betrayed. "I thought we had a verbal understanding and felt tremendously let down when they left me," Giorgio said later. "Brian was so determined to be a star at any price."

The pop scene was in its infancy as far as hard dealing was concerned, but here was a fairly brutal example of how useful allies and kindred spirits were jettisoned when an act got a sniff of success. Giorgio was an enthusiast who had provided the Stones with an anchor when it was needed. Giorgio's contribution to our success has since been belittled. But while he may not have been right as our future manager, just chopping him out of the gang was insensitive, to put it mildly.

There's a theory that Andrew Oldham saw us from the start as wild rebels, hoping to get us publicized as snarling lions battling against traditional show-business values. This is not so. Our reputation and image as the Bad Boys came later, completely accidentally. Andrew never did engineer it. He simply exploited it exhaustively.

In fact, his first move was to smarten us up by making us wear *uniforms*. We went with him on the morning of Saturday, May 4, 1963, to Carnaby Street, where he bought us all tight black jeans, black roll-neck sweaters and highly fashionable Anello & Davide black Spanish boots with Cuban heels (later called Beatle boots). This was our new stage wear. That afternoon also marked the first gig Oldham and Easton had booked for us: the *News of the World* charity gala opening of Battersea Pleasure Gardens. Andrew expected us to wear the new uniforms, but Brian and Keith wore colored jackets over theirs, retaining the casual look, while Mick wore a brown suede jacket. I was the only one in Andrew's "uniform," not having a casual jacket to wear. It's obvious to me now that in trying to smarten us up, Andrew was attempting to make us look like the Beatles. From his association with them he was well aware of the power of marketing, and he was initially slotting us in as their natural successors rather than as counterparts.

It would have been a terrible mistake if we'd gone along with it. Personally I felt that being in show business always meant looking smart, so the issue didn't matter much to me. But it certainly wasn't all right to the others: Brian really hated the idea, Mick didn't like it and stopped wearing the boots after a while. Being the tallest of the group, he didn't want to exaggerate his height still further, so he usually wore flat shoes. Brian, Keith and I quite liked the Beatle boots. Charlie was always into clothes; he wore the boots occasionally, but not regularly. But the whole clothes thing was a statement: as a group, we could not be pushed around and manipulated.

At Battersea Pat Andrews arrived with Brian's baby, then aged two. There was a very soft and sensitive side to Brian, and he couldn't resist proudly parading the backstage area and around the boating pool with the child in his arms. He was immediately rebuked by Andrew, who instructed him that such a cozy sight was "bad for his image" as a tough rock 'n' roller. And he should not be seen by girl fans to be a father—he should be "available" to them. Brian wasn't used to getting orders, especially on his private life. But these were crucially important days, with a debut record on the way. He didn't want to rock any boats. He complied.

At a gig shortly after Battersea, at the Wooden Bridge Hotel, Guildford, Linda Lawrence arrived. Brian was still seeing Pat at the time, and tried to put Linda off. They had a blazing row outside in the pouring rain, with Linda reduced to tears. And yet nobody could accuse Brian of shortchanging the Stones. We were all mates and we genuinely admired the way he had set about getting us organized, and the fact that things were now happening.

Back in January, before he had met either Giorgio or Andrew and Eric, he had written to the BBC.

I am writing on behalf of the Rolling Stones R & B band. We have noticed recently in the musical press that you are seeking fresh talent for Jazz Club. We have West End residencies at the Flamingo Jazz Club on Mondays and at the Marquee Jazz Club on Thursdays, as well as several other suburban residencies.

We already have a large following in the London area and in view of the vast interest in R & B in Britain, an exceptionally good future has been predicted for us by many people. Our front line consists of vocal and harmonica (electric), and two guitars, supported by a rhythm section comprising bass, piano and drums. Our musical policy is simply to present an authentic Chicago R & B sound, using material of such R & B greats as Muddy Waters, Howlin' Wolf, Bo Diddley, Jimmy Reed and many others. We wonder if you could possibly arrange for us an audition. We look forward eagerly to hearing from you.

Yours faithfully,
Brian Jones

Because Charlie and I were working all day we missed the audition that the BBC eventually gave us four months later, on April 23: Carlo Little and Ricky Brown from the Cyril Davies All-Stars deputized for us in the test session with the BBC's Jimmy Grant. And by the time the BBC decided on the result, we had managers, a record deal, action and confidence. The polite rejection letter from David Dore, assistant light-entertainment booking manager, came on May 13: "We regret that the performance was not considered suitable for our purposes," the letter began. Adding that it "might be of help to you to know our opinions in a little more detail," Dore suggested contacting the BBC music organizer, Donald MacLean. One night at Edith Grove, Brian told us of the phone call he made to MacLean. It was hilarious. MacLean told him it was felt that "our singer sounded too black!" However, the BBC were "interested" in the group, perhaps to accompany visiting American recording stars on radio appearances!

But the early 1960s were halcyon days for young people, and we couldn't worry about a rejection that seemed to us an inverted compliment. The word "unemployment" wasn't in our dictionary: it was something our parents and grandparents reminisced over, a relic of the war. The exuberance of a youthful American president, John

Kennedy, wafted across to Britain, and the popularity surge of the Beatles ignited a confidence that was truly infectious. It was great to be young. But the notion that pop music might develop into such an art form, and provide a career for life, was too bizarre for us to contemplate.

Even so, Charlie, still living with his parents in Neasden, decided to give up his work as a graphic designer to become fully professional with the Rolling Stones.

Our star was certainly shining. With our debut single due for release on June 7, Andrew did his hustle and lined up interviews for us with some of the teenage magazines—*Rave, Fabulous, Boyfriend, Valentine, Jackie*— as well as the music papers.*

It was now that our appearance began to overtake our sound in people's perception of us. In the previous few weeks, we had been refused service in various cafés and pubs because of our long hair. We thougt little of it, assuming it was part of the usual aggravation adults give young people. But during one of our magazine interviews we were asked to leave a hotel lounge because of our "appearance." As we had arrived there, people stopped talking and stared. We went outside to an open café, where people giggled at us and nudged each other. We could not have cared less about this; we decided it was *their* problem.

Brian painted a picture of the Stones as five young guys willing to starve to get our musical message across. "We bite our fingernails because we're so hungry," he told a reporter. "We don't eat regularly. Sometimes when we're starving we go down the road and buy a ready-cooked chicken, bring it home, pull it to bits and eat it, but days go by and we forget to eat again." Not too far from the truth! Keith told one journalist: "The last time I had my hair cut was June last year." *Beat Monthly* described us as "five wild beatmen, Bill on his very own

---

*In one interview we were asked how we got the name the Rolling Stones and remembering that the Beatles were first thinking of calling themselves the Silver Beatles, we replied, tongue in cheek, that we were first known as the Silver Rolling Stones and later changed our name. This has since been stated as a fact in many books and articles on the Stones, much to our amusement.

homemade bass guitar, the Stones' wild haircuts or should I say hairnotcuts!''

But we had more pressing—musical—matters on our minds. As Mick later said, "I don't think 'Come On' was very good. In fact it was shit. We disliked it so much we didn't do it on any of our gigs." In fact, our first row with our managers developed because we *so* hated that first single that we refused to play it on live shows. We thought we'd compromised enough with Andrew to cut the bloody record; naive as we were, we thought it was his and Decca's job then to go out and sell it. We must have been the only artists in the world to refuse to play their all-important debut single.

To anyone who knew the group and its musical roots, the song was really a lie. Comparing it with the tapes we had recorded through Glyn Johns at IBC, it was obvious that Andrew was nudging us toward a hit at all costs. On stage, however, our blues repertoire remained intact.

Press reaction to "Come On" was lukewarm. *New Musical Express* was non-commital: "A song performance aimed straight at the current market for groups. Good chance of selling well." In *Melody Maker,* singer Craig Douglas reviewed the record, saying, "Very ordinary. I can't hear a word they're saying. I don't know what this is all about. If there were a Liverpool accent it might get somewhere." The paper also said: "One of the established R & B groups have suddenly turned up in Beatle haircuts and dark sweaters." This infuriated us. *Pop Weekly* insisted on the comparison: "Inspired by the Beatles-cum-Liverpool sound. A fast-moving, lively affair. The group has life and strength. This one just misses." Writing about the record later in the *New Musical Express,* Roy Carr said: "The Stones gave it a quick body job, stripped down the coachwork and totally rebuilt the chassis. Stuck in a new engine and tuned up the acceleration." That was just about right.

The most accurate and intelligent comments came in *Record Mirror* from Norman Jopling, whose paper had been the first to interview us at Richmond. "The disc doesn't sound like the Stones," he wrote, and he was right. "It's good, catchy, punchy and commercial, but it's not the fanatical R & B sound that the audiences wait hours to hear. It should make the charts in a smallish way."

But there was a shaft of sunlight from the pop weekly *Disc,* in which Don Nicholl wrote: "The Beatles, who recommended the Stones [to Decca], may well live to rue the day. This group could be challenging them for top places in the immediate future. The sturdy beat will drive you mad this summer."

My brother Paul: "The Stones created a niche just when it needed to be made. And it was their own niche; there was nobody around doing that music. And Bill saw its potential. He never boasted about the Stones' progress to the family. He was too modest for that. He didn't think the family was very interested, and he was right. My parents still thought he was nuts to be playing pop music."

I'd grown familiar with the habits and humor of Brian, Keith and Mick, so their categoric rejection of a song like "Come On" didn't surprise me. It was difficult for me not to "come on" as their older brother; I was, after all, six years older than Brian, who was twenty, and seven years older than Keith and Mick. At that stage in life it's a huge difference. And I was married, with a son! On some nights after a late finish, I'd sleep—carefully—in the chair at Edith Grove and wonder why they wanted to live in such squalor.

Then as Easton's office revved up the band's administration with the first single out, a real shock devastated the band. On Sunday, June 16, 1963, Giorgio greeted us at Richmond with the news that this would be our last night at the Crawdaddy Club. The brewers were worried about the intensity of the packed crowds and the fire regulations, and insisted that the club be closed. The trouble had come to a head three days earlier when Patrick Doncaster, the pop writer of the *Daily Mirror,* wrote: "In the half darkness, the guitars and drums twang and bang. Pulsating R & B. Shoulder to shoulder on the floor are 500 youngsters in black leather and sweaters. You could boil an egg in the atmosphere. Heads shake violently, and feet stamp in tribal style with hands above heads, clapped in rhythm. Shaking figures above the rest, held aloft by their colleagues, thrashing and yelling, like a revivalist meeting in America's deep south. It happens nowhere else in Britain. Nobody seems to care. They just do it."

Five hundred people was well over the club's legal limit and the end of the Station Hotel as our headquarters —the end of the "breaking in" of the Stones. We had been resident there for over three months of Sundays and the interaction between us and the crowd had done wonders for our confidence.

The Crawdaddy seemed irreplaceable but Giorgio came up with a solution. Though he was still smarting from "losing" us to Andrew and Eric, he loved the band and gave us much more loyalty than we deserved. He phoned to say that in two weeks he could re-establish the Crawdaddy at the Clubhouse at Richmond athletic ground, where a jazz festival was held every year. We debuted there on June 30; the crowd totaled 500 and we were paid a magnificent £50!

By now the single had been out a month and we agreed to mime to the record on the Saturday-night show *Thank Your Lucky Stars*. The fee was to be a massive £143 17s. 6d. The occasion was so crucial to us that Andrew decided we should have new uniforms. Meeting him in Carnaby Street, "the London group with the slightly wild look" was measured for black trousers and black and white dog-tooth jackets with black velvet collars. We bought blue shirts, black knitted ties and blue leather waistcoats and new boots.

The official Rolling Stones fan club, launched by Diane (Doreen Pettifer) Nelson, released our first biography to members. Personal ambitions were listed. Mick wanted to own his own business and to make a million-seller. Keith's interests were sports, boating and surfing. His personal ambition was to own a boat and his professional aim was to appear at the London Palladium. Brian's ambition was to live on a houseboat; Charlie's "to own a pink Cadillac." My favorite singers were listed as Chuck Berry and Jerry Lee Lewis, my favorite band was Stan Kenton. My personal ambition was to own a castle (which came true) and my professional ambition to appear in a film.

The big day came with a hundred-mile drive to a Birmingham TV studio. We were introduced by the disc jockey Pete Murray with a limp joke about a delegation from the hairdressers' union wanting to see us. This was unfunny but very mild compared with what was to be unleashed on us in the next few months. We mimed our first single on a set that looked like the veranda of a western-style saloon, and I played my homemade bass.

It was quite an evening. For one thing, Andrew told us we were going on a British tour with the Everly Brothers in the autumn! I was awe-struck at the prospect of meeting and playing alongside American stars who were so successful. For another a TV executive pulled Andrew aside during transmission and told him that if he had any ambitions for the Stones, then as their manager he would have to "get rid of the vile-looking singer with the tyre-tread lips." Oldham, not a guy who took advice or suggestions from *anyone*, liked to steer his own ship.

But during the week following our TV appearance, the papers were deluged with complaints from people who objected to our long hair and what they obviously regarded as our menacing sexuality. One critic said we "had gone way beyond the Beatles' acceptable boundaries. [The Beatles'] hair, unremarkable by today's standards, was merely shaggy and somewhat unkempt. [The Stones] came across as surly, sneering and deliberately provocative. The Beatles became the kids who charmed a nation. The Stones were the louts who kicked it in the bollocks."

While all the excitement was going on and our first single hovered around the bottom reaches of the chart interminably, we continued our round of bread-and-butter club work. Sunday afternoons at the Ken Colyer Club for £25; Sunday evenings at the new Crawdaddy Club for £50; the Ricky Tick for £35; Eel Pie Island for £55; and the Scene Club near Piccadilly Circus where the fee averaged only £25 but where we struck up a firm friendship with the owners, Ronan O'Rahilly and Lionel Blake. And we socialized after gigs at the Sous Sol restaurant in Earls Court Road. Open until 5 a.m., it was a haven for night travelers like us, and a considerable gastronomic step up from the Wimpy Bar.

Even a small hit gave Eric the chance to elevate our status. He told us he planned to send us around the country on ballroom appearances, to spread our reputation nationwide. We had been far too heavily concentrated on the London area until then.

In our attempts to reach wider audiences we went to the studio of Philip Gotlop, who did a photo session with us in our checked jackets. We then went on to Dezo Hoffman's studio where we did a session wearing our leather waistcoats.

Hoffman said: "When I began the session, Brian didn't have any cufflinks, so I lent him mine—they were gold, a wedding present from my wife. I never got them back, and later I heard that Brian had given a pair of gold cufflinks to Bo Diddley." I was reminded of an earlier instance with Long John Baldry. He said: "When I was living in west Hampstead, Jonesy came round with a girlfriend of his and borrowed some singles, which at that particular time were irreplaceable. American things like B. B. King. He never ever returned them. I think he lost them. I wouldn't speak to him for two years."

We were booked that evening for a debutante ball in Hastings for the coming out of Rosanna Lampson. On the journey Brian became really sick and it was clear that he would not be able to play. He stayed in the car while we went in and enjoyed the party. This was the first indication that Brian was vulnerable to illness. Stu said: "There were quite a few things wrong with Brian. He was allergic to a lot of things. He used to suffer very badly from asthma, had great breathing problems and always carried an inhaler and pills. He seemed allergic to a lot of the standard sort of pills you get for this. Once he had to go to hospital because somebody gave him some pills and his skin started literally to fall off his arms." It wasn't too important at this stage but it became an increasing problem.

The singer at the Hastings ball was Chris Andrews, who later had a big solo hit with "Yesterday Man." We became great friends. The evening was marked, according to Keith, by my getting drunk and being threatened by the organizers with ejection for trying to pull all the women there. I have no recollection of this and plead amnesia.

The ballroom gigs were patchy: our first, for an £18 fee at Wisbech Corn Exchange on July 20, was exciting for the sight of pictures and posters of ourselves outside as we arrived, but apart from a few enthusiastic girls at the front, the audience was dull. When we went into the ballrooms, we found we couldn't play slow Jimmy Reed numbers. We were expected to play music for them to dance to but everyone just stood there in front of us and gaped. So we started concentrating on more up-tempo songs: fast rhythm things, hard rockers, which seemed to work out quite well.

By the end of July 1963 our fan club had 300 members, with new ones joining every day. At the beginning of August, things were happening at such speed that I decided to turn professional. I'd been having terrible problems at work. I was always exhausted, grabbing a few hours of rest whenever I could. And my appearance was becoming an issue. I always wore a suit, but it was the hair that got them really angry: they insisted it be cut, because everyone else had a "short back and sides." As it got longer, they told me to make up my mind whether to stick by their rules or go. I said I was turning professional with the Rolling Stones and they begged me to stay: "You've got a permanent job and a pension, don't throw it away." Everybody, including Diane, advised me against playing bass guitar for a living. "Play safe, keep your job," said my parents, family and friends. They said I should ensure a regular income, since I had Diane and Stephen to support. But I'd made up my mind. We had managers with ambition, a sound that was improving all the time, and it was a chance that might not come again. I suppose I thought I could always return to an ordinary job if things didn't work out.

My brother Paul: "My father never had a steady job in his life, so Bill had what my father thought was the epitome of a real job: £12 per week, and retirement at sixty-five with a pension. Nobody in my father's or mother's family had ever had that before, and Bill was therefore, in their view, set up for life. He was looked up to as the most stable person in the family, someone we should all follow. It was *traumatic* for our mother and father to watch Bill chuck that in for pop music! They thought he was nuts. From where they stood they were right, but Bill was very calculating and knew exactly where he was going. And even if he'd screwed up with the Stones, if they'd flopped, he'd have found another band and been a lot better than the others around him."

There was some sadness about it, though: I lost touch

with my good mate at work, Jack Oliver, who had introduced me to photography, printing and developing.

The image of the Stones as dirty layabouts began to take over just as I joined them full-time. We hated the stage clothes and wore them only for important things like television. I remember arriving for one show and being rebuked by the promoter for being ten minutes late. He was agitated that we'd be very late on stage "by the time we'd changed." I assured him that as we didn't need to change, we were actually ten minutes early! Being from a no-nonsense part of south London, I was also ready with quick returns of service when I was mocked for my increasingly long hair. On the train home once a very straight-looking bloke in my carriage started muttering about "long-haired yobs who shouldn't be allowed in public places." I stared at him and said quietly: "I'm getting paid for looking like this. What's your excuse?"

If Andrew originally saw us as rivals to the Beatles, kitting us out with suits and ties, he quickly changed his stance when he realized that Brian, Mick and Keith were hard to control. He decided to capitalize on our appearance and attitudes instead. Running with this was an undercurrent of rivalry that gradually rose to the surface: as the Beatles and the Liverpool groups came south and overthrew the adult pop scene, there was a strong feeling of geographical competitiveness from London fans. The controversy was naturally fanned by the newspapers, but as far as the musicians were concerned it was false. We had become united, for in reality we had much more in common than we had differences. Whether you came from Manchester or Maidstone, if you played guitar in a group, you spoke the same language. As Brian put it, when discussing the north–south "divide": "The Liverpool–London controversy is all a load of rubbish invented by the newspapers. We are on very friendly terms with northern beat groups and there's mutual admiration between us. We obviously prefer American artists, but there's been nothing beatier in Britain for a long time."

One of our first adventures north was to a small club, the Alcove in Middlesbrough on July 13, 1963. We were support act to the Hollies, a top Manchester group that featured Graham Nash (later of course of the American supergroup Crosby, Stills, Nash and Young). We just set up our gear, I laid my homemade bass cabinet on its side at the back of the stage, and Brian, Keith and I sat on our three old metal stools, and played. We later found that the two groups had both been equally nervous of each other. From that day, the Hollies became one of our favorite groups and we subsequently worked with them on many occasions. Graham Nash said: "Coming from Manchester, we hadn't seen anything like that before. They didn't appear to be copying anybody and they seemed very free—they were obviously something different and didn't seem to give a fuck."

The jazz crowd remained elitist, but Giorgio had persuaded the organizers of the Third Richmond Jazz Festival to break with tradition and give us a spot on August 11 for a fee of £30. We were still bottom of the bill to such established jazz bands as Acker Bilk, Terry Lightfoot, Freddy Randall and Cyril Davies with Long John Baldry and the Velvettes. The organizer, Harold Pendleton, recalled: "When the festival opened there were a few thousand Stones fans waiting. When the gates opened they jammed the clubhouse to overflowing. The organizers had to move the group into the large marquee, where they eventually played to a crowd of 1,500. The Stones were an absolute sensation and the Jazz Festival was turned upside down by this, which stunned everyone. From then on it was called the Jazz *and Blues* Festival." What a moment! We'd beat the jazz boys on their own ground! Ronnie Wood remembers: "I saw you in the tent and the tent was rocking. I was the last one out. I was watching you pack up your gear, and I saw Jagger kissing this bird, and I fell over this great big tent peg and smashed my leg!"

Five days after that show, on August 16, we all met in Eric's office. He had by now taken over the role of paymaster and bookkeeper from Brian (thank God), and he gave us each £18. He told us that "Come On" had sold 40,000 copies so far; that week *New Musical Express* had placed it at number twenty-five. The record was having a terrific "life" as a small hit, but with the kind of crowds we were now attracting in the ballrooms—1,500 people had showed up the day before in

Margate*—the pressure was on for us to make a good second single.

For several weeks we had been planning this next single. There wasn't much time to rehearse, since we had a gig almost every night, but whenever we could we'd get back to Studio 51 to rehearse and try out a few songs. At Decca's west Hampstead studios, we recorded Benny Spellman's "Fortune-Teller" and the Clovers' "Poison Ivy." They sounded great, but we still weren't sure they were right for the single. The discussion continued.

The year 1963 was one of enormous change, and if any one day can be named as pivotal, it has to be August 9, when the independent television show, *Ready Steady Go!* began transmission from studios in Kingsway, London. It became the epicenter of Sixties music, fashion and attitudes.

On that same day Stu drove us to the factory of Jennings Music in Dartford, who made Vox amplification. In return for our endorsement of their gear they gave us a free set of equipment. Eric Easton, our much-maligned "straight" business manager, had arranged this.

It seemed that every day brought a milestone for the band's slow but sure progress. On August 19, after a photo session, we went to Eric and Andrew's office where we were played the first pressing of "Poison Ivy" and "Fortune-Teller." They sounded good. The single was all set to be released later in the month and Decca had already pressed some copies when, a week later, we decided to have it withdrawn. We were still not entirely satisfied that it was a strong enough follow-up. Our ego was being fed by some excellent publicity,† considering the fact that in those years the papers only recognized pop stars with hit records and we had just had a minor hit that had been in the chart for two months. We knew that our second single had to make a big impact.

We drove to Richmond to play a show at the athletic ground on August 18, 1963, to a record crowd of 800 (for

---

*At this show at the Dreamland, our support group, the Barron Knights, were the ones who two years before first inspired me to take up the bass guitar. Eric Easton later signed them.
†Even though one newpaper described the appearance of "five awesome apes who perpetrate fearful musical onslaughts"!

which Giorgio paid us £60). The production team of *Ready, Steady, Go!* were there looking for dancers for the show. After seeing us they promised to put us on the show as soon as possible, and this happened on August 26, the show's second broadcast. As we arrived at the studio in Kingsway, there were loads of girls outside and inside and we signed masses of autographs. The interviewer, Cathy McGowan, told us she was a regular visitor to our Monday evening shows at Soho's Ken Colyer Club. Our performance was live; the fans went crazy all the time we were on, and we were knocked out with the reception.

Cathy McGowan commented: "The Stones were fantastic, absolutely marvelous. Mick did all that jumping around that made the girls scream. We received literally thousands of letters asking to see them again. People who hadn't seen or heard of them before raved about them. Later older people started writing letters saying the Stones were disgusting, horrible and objectionable. We were even told it was a mistake to have put them on the show, but the reaction to that first performance was so great that within three months they were regulars."

When you're young and experiencing the sort of excitement we felt in August 1963, illness isn't expected to disrupt your life. Strong, enthusiastic and highly motivated, we coped easily with the hectic round of gigs, rehearsals, recording sessions and interviews. We had few worries: we had a record deal, two reliable managers, a growing battalion of fans and press support coupled with controversy, which helped. It was therefore amazing to us when Brian showed signs of weakness. This was his band, his early realization of a dream, yet he proved the most vulnerable.

At the height of our early thrust, on August 27, I went into town in the afternoon for rehearsals at Studio 51. Andrew and all the boys except Brian were there. He had apparently collapsed from nervous exhaustion. We canceled the rehearsal and went shopping with Andrew for clothes instead. We then drove to Windsor for the gig at the Ricky Tick Club, expecting Brian to be there. But he didn't show and we played without him for the first (but certainly not the last) time. Stu returned to the piano chair for this show and the night went well.

Next night, for our gig at Eel Pie Island, Brian was still ill, so we miked the piano and put it through an amplifier for Stu's sound to be improved. The place was full and the show went well. In the interval, I chatted to two pretty girls out on the grass by the River Thames. The one I fancied said she preferred Keith; the other was looking for an absent Brian. You win some and lose some.

The next gig was at the Oasis club, Manchester, where huge queues had formed and the excitement was great. Lots of friends had made the journey up from London to see us. After a great reception we all relaxed in a local club, the Twisted Wheel. Janie, a pretty blonde friend from London, stayed with me for the night in the hotel; she was a virgin, very sweet, and we had a lovely night together.

"A lot of the Stones' success depends on being seen," the *Northern Beat Scene* said after we'd made a tour up north. "One look is sufficient to arouse curiosity. When they need a trim, they tackle it themselves. Their stage gear is non-existent. They mount the stage wearing exactly what they please, be it jeans, bell-bottom trousers or leather jerkins. Individuality is their password. Their sound is so earthy you can almost taste it. It's alive with energy and wild solid beat. They're out of this world, but very much in it."

But despite that praise, I felt it was now time to harden up my sound. On September 2 I went back to my local music shop in Penge and bought myself a Framus Star bass guitar, deep red in color, with a wide body and very slim neck, which suited my small hands perfectly. At last I was able to pay cash, about £75. It was a good feeling. That night I played it, with a greatly improved sound, at the Ken Colyer Club at Studio 51. And the next day I sold my old bass cabinet and amplifier to Tony Chapman, who—I was glad to hear—had formed a new band after leaving the Stones.

By September 4 Brian was ill again. After our first set at Eel Pie Island he came out in blotches all over his face and said he felt awful. We sent him home and played the second set without him. He was still sick next day and stayed home, which was fortunate for him. We played a dump in Walmer, Kent called the Strand Palace Theater.

The audience comprised about 350 thugs. We were paid £55 and were glad to get away without any trouble—the promoter had failed to get a drinking license, which probably saved us. Gradually we were building quite a community of musicians, for on the bill with us were the Paramounts whom I'd known from my Cliftons period. Their leader, Gary Brooker, remains a firm friend. He played at my wedding in 1989.

The gig I shall always remember from this time was the one we played at Lowestoft, Suffolk on September 6, 1963. This was our first experience of teenage girls rushing the stage wanting our bodies. The day had begun as any normal gigging schedule, with Stu picking up first Mick and Keith from Edith Grove, then Charlie and me, before driving the 120 miles to the seaside town. Brian was still ill and this time it was his big loss. We stayed in great rooms at the Grand Hotel, where the show took place before 1,200 people. Half-way through the performance, girls attacked us on stage, tearing at our clothes. I thought to myself: "Well, there's nothing I can do. I must keep playing." I had half my shirt ripped away and buttons torn from my leather waistcoat. It happened to all four of us. The only sour note was that in the surge of the crowd to the stage one girl whipped a ring from my finger. It was of sentimental value and I told a group of fans to put the word about that I'd like it back. It was to turn up three weeks later. But otherwise what a great reception—particularly special because we stayed the night and all got fixed up with girls! We were paid £20 plus free accommodation.

We were now doing a journey nearly every day and a show every night. Strangely enough, we didn't register tiredness. The adrenalin must have kept us going. But the rock stars of today, who might manage an annual tour for their fans, would be horrified by the schedule we were keeping, the fees we were getting and the traveling across Britain that was involved—long before there was a network of motorways. Keith said: "We often slept in the back of the van, because of the most hard-hearted and callous roadie I've ever encountered: Stu! From one end of England to the other, in Stu's VW van, with all the equipment. Crafty Bill! For years we believed that he couldn't travel in the back of the van because he'd spew

Right: My mother and father in Margate, July 1935, the year before they married

Above: Me, aged five, 1942

Right: My parents with John, Judy, Anne and me, 1943

Above: Anne, John, Judy and me in our garden at Blenheim Road, in 1945

Left: My maternal grandmother in 1945. She helped to bring me up.

Left: Me in RAF uniform, summer 1955

Above: The Motor Transport football team at RAF Oldenburg, 1955. I am second from the left in the front row and my mate Lee Whyman is second from the right

Right: At work at John A. Sparks in Streatham, June 1959

Diane on our wedding day, October 24, 1959

Diane and me with my brother and a friend, 1962

The Cliftons in the summer of 1962: *(top to bottom)* Brian Cade, Tony Chapman, Steve Carroll, me, Cliff Starkey, Dave Harvey

1963 and one of our first publicity pictures—The Rolling Stones *(from left to right)* Brian Jones, Keith Richards, Mick Jagger, Charlie Watts and Bill Wyman

Left: Me and Charlie outside the Ken Colyer club, summer 1963

Above and left: Stu, Keith, Charlie and me at a gig at Eel Pie Island, June 1963

Right: Me with Dawn Malloy at Alexandra Palace, June 1964

Below: Eric Easton (center) with Mick at Alexandra Palace

Stu and Spike after the Alexandra Palace show

Stu with the van, September 1964

Murray the K and Brian at Carnegie Hall, June 1964

The five of us at Olympia, Paris, October 1964

Thank Your Lucky Stars presents the Rolling Stones, 1964

With Stephen, Kenilworth Court, 1965

Diane, Stephen and me on our first family trip to Paris, April 1965

Touring—Mick and Keith playing Monopoly in flight, 1965

Brian with Bob Bonis on our first US tour

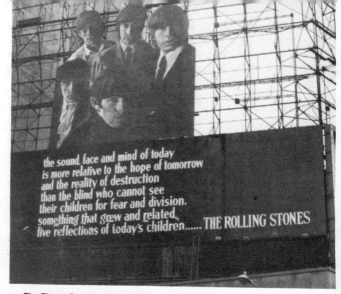

the sound, face and mind of today
is more relative to the hope of tomorrow
and the reality of destruction
than the blind who cannot see
their children for fear and division.
something that grew and related
five reflections of today's children...... THE ROLLING STONES

The Times Square billboard for *December's Children (and Everybody's)* with the David Bailey photo and Andrew's poem, October 1965

Stephen, 1965

all over us, so he was always allowed to sit in the only passenger seat. Years later, we found out he never gets travel sick at all!"

The journey from Lowestoft to Aberystwyth in Wales on Saturday, September 7, was horrendous. Stu drove us in the van without even a stop for food. We arrived in the evening for a three-hour performance which was to begin at 8:30 and we were immediately pounced upon by the Musicians Union, who threatened to stop the show if we didn't become members there and then. After a big row we reluctantly signed the forms. There was something strange about young pop players like us joining the Musicians Union: we had always felt it belonged exclusively to old dance-band musicians, a world apart from us.

Immediately after the show we drove straight through the night to Birmingham for another appearance on *Thank Your Lucky Stars*. None of us got any food or sleep. Arriving at the studios at six in the morning, we were (not surprisingly) told by the gate man that we were too early. We pleaded with him, promised to be quiet and go to sleep, and he allowed us to crash out in a small viewing room for three hours. Later Andrew and Brian arrived from London and we prepared for rehearsals at eleven o'clock.

We discovered that the singer Craig Douglas was also on the show. He had given our debut single a poor review three months previously. The Stones never forget anything: we also remembered that he'd been a milkman before becoming a somewhat wimpish ballad singer, so we went all round the studios gathering up empty milk bottles and put them outside his dressing-room door, with notes saying things like "Two pints, please" tucked in. Furious, he reported us to the producers, who sternly reprimanded us.

After the show, Stu drove Brian, Charlie and me back to London, all of us completely exhausted, while Mick and Keith went back in Andrew's car. Who could realize, at this early stage, that the splitting of the group in that way would mark our future? Stu said: "Keith and Mick were quite prepared to go along with anything Andrew said. They fed off each other. We had very little contact with them in those days. Edicts would just be issued from the Oldham office."

A turning point in the band's relationships came quickly. Edith Grove was finally evacuated at the start of September 1963. Mick and Keith moved into a flat in Mapesbury Road, west Hampstead, while Brian went to live with Linda Lawrence at her parents' house in Windsor. Shortly afterwards Andrew also moved into Mapesbury Road, and the Unholy Trinity, as Stu christened them, of Jagger–Richards–Oldham was born.

One rumor that hung around for some time, was that back in the Edith Grove days Mick and Brian had had some sort of gay relationship. There was never any basis for this from my observation. Brian was forever looking for his next woman while talking about his last; Mick was always obviously fully heterosexual. The origin of this rumor may have simply been that young guys looking like Mick and Brian did—and the long hair caused plenty of gibes that they were girlish—were living in the same house! In fact, Chrissie Shrimpton, eighteen years old and working at Decca after secretarial college, now moved in with Mick at Mapesbury Road.

"Come On" had not exactly been a smash-hit debut record, but it would not go away. It reached number twenty, its highest position, on August 23, and hovered in the national charts for four months, a long stay by any standards. By the autumn it had sold about 100,000 copies and we were still worrying about how to follow it up. We knew in our hearts that the song was false, not a true Stones track.

The problem facing us was that we idealistically wanted to "be ourselves" and put out a true rhythm-and-blues song as the second single, but our managers and our own common sense dictated that we had to find something totally commercial. Everywhere we were playing, the audiences were increasing, our reputation was getting better and our fees were going up. It made no sense to look success in the face and serve up minority music at that moment.

John Lennon and Paul McCartney solved our problem. By then they had truly arrived as hit songwriters and just as they headed for the top with the Beatles' fourth single, "She Loves You," they bumped into Andrew Oldham in Jermyn Street, Piccadilly, on their way home from a Variety Club lunch. Andrew told them we were mulling over what to record next; that as they chatted we were rehearsing at Studio 51 in Soho. John and Paul said they might have a song for us and accompanied Andrew to our rehearsal. They ran through it for us and Paul, being left-handed, amazed me by playing my bass backwards. When they left we started to change things around to suit our sound; Brian tried slide guitar on it, which sounded great. That's how "I Wanna Be Your Man," the Stones' second single, was born.

"The way Paul and John used to hustle tunes was great," Mick recalled. "We thought it sounded pretty commercial . . . But we were surprised that John and Paul would be prepared to give us one of their best numbers." Keith said how proud we were to do a Beatles number —"We just hope they'll like it."

And our link with the Beatles was to continue. On September 15 we had the unenviable task of opening a big concert that featured the Beatles at the top of the bill: the Great Pop Prom at London's Royal Albert Hall. The show was probably our biggest to date; we all wore dark trousers, pale-blue shirts, black ties and dark-blue leather waistcoats, a far cry from the garb we wore in the clubs. We tore into the show and tore the audience apart. The Beatles watched us and were, as they told us years later, very nervous about the reception we got. The cheering crowd gave us the best reception we'd had in our career thus far. We were swamped by fans and getting around the backstage area and out of the hall was difficult; we were paid only £35 for the show, which was in aid of the Printers' Pension Corporation. (This of course seemed rather ironic in view of the unkind things the papers were printing about us.) But the impact of the night proved a turning point for us. The reviews were terrific. *Boyfriend* magazine said: "Just one shake of their overgrown hair is enough to make every girl in the audience scream with tingling excitement. They stand in twos, facing each other, and live-wire their way through a performance, their heads shaking in time to the music, their hair flying out, their bodies executing a double-time rotation that has the girls in a frenzy . . . Their act is fast, wound-up, explosive . . . The Stones opened the show, the hardest thing in the world to do . . . the so-called cold audience nearly seared the seats out. The Royal

Albert Hall fairly shook on its foundations. Certainly it
had never, in its hundred or so years, ever heard anything to compare with the Stones."

The momentum was now really exciting. We were voted
into number six position by readers of the *Melody Maker*
in their annual popularity poll in that heady month of
September, and we were booked solidly for months ahead.
What it meant to me was that I'd converted a straight job
as a storekeeper's clerk into one that enabled me to pay
off those hire-purchase fees for instruments. It gave me
great pleasure to take Stephen, now eighteen months
old, back to meet my old work-mates at Sparks.

On September 12, we played a show at the Cellar
Club, Kingston-upon-Thames, which went great, but the
promoter Hugh O'Donnell put on a boxing-glove, kicked
us out and threatened us with his Alsatian dog! On top of
that he refused to pay us.

On September 22 we ended our residency at the Ken
Colyer Club at Studio 51 with incredible scenes. The
place was solid with people. You could not move inside;
kids were standing on others' shoulders and an estimated
400 jammed the street, listening through the iron grilles
in the pavement and dancing. We willingly did encores to
say farewell to a club that had been good to us. Afterwards we all went for a celebration drink to a local pub,
the Salisbury, which was popular with show-biz people—
Elizabeth Taylor and Richard Burton were regulars. But
any confidence we'd gained from recent events took an
immediate knock. The barman took one look at us with
our long hair and disheveled after-gig appearance and
asked us to get out. We argued in vain.

We drove the ten miles from Soho to Richmond that
same evening for another adieu, ending our residency at
the Crawdaddy Club. Fans had queued for hours, and by
7:15 the place was packed, and many were turned away.
They gave us a great send-off and again we had to do
encore after encore. The Yardbirds, whom Giorgio was
now managing, replaced us at the Crawdaddy. Later,
Giorgio observed: "The Stones audience got up and shook.
With the Yardbirds there was no hysteria." Two nights
later we played the last night of our residency at the
Ricky Tick Club. Again, it was the biggest crowd so far
and our best reception ever there.

We'd outgrown the clubs. There was a "buzz" around that meant we had to set our sights higher, aim for the concert halls and take the Rolling Stones right to the top, alongside the Beatles. Brian, very ambitious by now, loved the glamor, the girls and the prospect of being famous, even though the spotlight from the press fell mainly on Mick as the lead singer.

The real proof that we'd elevated the band from the clubs came when Brian, Charlie and I appeared on BBC radio's *Saturday Club,* backing Bo Diddley. There, we met him for the first time. He was extremely friendly, and we backed him on the program for live songs. Charlie kept playing that unique Diddley beat backwards but finally got it right and we came out such good friends that Diddley asked us to back him on his British tour. We were flattered but declined; we were popular in our own name and didn't want to assume a backing role at this stage.

Everywhere we looked and went, from the press to the public, from other musicians to the machinery of the record industry, there was evidence that we were on the crest of a wave. Even "Auntie," as the BBC was often called, gave in and agreed that our appearance on *Saturday Club* could be treated as an audition—and we had passed! It was a frantic time: photo sessions, rehearsals, a gig nearly every night and exhaustion as Stu drove us all round the country.

I remember playing a show at the Floral Hall in Morecambe, Lancashire. Stu had dropped everyone else off around 3 a.m., and was driving me home, but he kept pulling off the road and falling asleep for a few hours. I would wake up, cold and miserable, wondering where we were, wake Stu up and fall asleep again. He drove all around the suburbs of London, exhausted and lost. It was like a nightmare, and I recall waking up in Peckham once, waking Stu and getting him moving again, then waking in Sydenham and finding Stu asleep yet again. He finally arrived at my place at one o'clock the next afternoon. We had taken ten hours to drive from north London to south London. We had some lunch, crashed in the front room for two hours' sleep, and then left late that afternoon and drove to Walthamstow to play another show at the Assembly Hall.

On September 26, three weeks after our Lowestoft show, Brian drove Linda Lawrence down to Cheltenham to meet his parents. Linda said: "He thought I would please them. This quiet girl from the country. Our relationship was something to be proud of. We walked in the house and it was as if Brian weren't there. There was no word between them. We took them to a pub, hoping that getting them out of the house would loosen them up, but they were still really tight. His sister Barbara was a very straight normal person. Brian really wanted to contact them. He would play his music for them. His mother didn't really listen, but Lewis tried to. His father got excited and Brian would be happy about that, but then Lewis would pull back, and the atmosphere would return to its normal coldness."

Lewis Jones was proud of Brian's musical achievements but had trouble expressing it. He felt pressured by the standards of the community he was in. Brian was now—and looked like—a rock star, which was certainly not a very respectable thing to be. This was, remember, long before the mid-sixties hippy period when everyone wore hair down to their shoulders. In 1963 and 1964, when our reputation was being forged, appearances of people our age were pretty traditional. Hair over the ears, like the Beatles, was pretty unorthodox: hair down to the back of the neck, like ours, was really rebellious. It was much more than a fashion: it was a statement of opposition.

So when Andrew realized we were probably untameable, he took off on a very different tack and decided to *use* our natural appearance. Instead of being thrust forward as Beatles clones, we were projected as complete opposites. And we listened to Andrew because he had made things happen: he said he'd get us on radio and TV and concert tours, and he had. He was our age and we thought he was good news for the group.

Keith said: "On the first tour we wore the suits that Andrew wanted us to wear and said: 'All right, we'll do it. You know the game. We'll try it out.' But then the Stones thing started taking over; Charlie would leave his jacket in some dressing-room and I'd pull mine out and there'd be whisky stains all over it, or chocolate pudding. When we'd got rid of these dog-tooth jackets and the

Lord John shirts Andrew suddenly realized we were different and got fully behind it. After that, the press did all the work for us. We only needed to be refused permission to stay in a hotel to set the whole thing rolling again."

Andrew grasped the importance of contact with the fans, and with Eric providing the structure of his office it was time to knock the fan club into more aggressive shape. Back at the final night of the Ken Colyer Club residency, a sixteen-year-old duffle-coated girl named Shirley Arnold fainted in the heat of the place and was passed over the heads of everyone into the tea-room. When we finished the set we went to see her. She asked us if we had anyone to run the club—she had sent off her subscription of 5 shillings but had heard nothing. We immediately gave her the job of running the club, beginning a relationship with her that went right through until 1972.

"I was a starry-eyed fan working in the City," Shirley recalls. "You only had to see the Stones once and you were hooked on their music. I was earning £5 a week in my job, but they offered me £7 to run the club fulltime. I would have done it for nothing." Shirley inherited a club of 300 members and about 250 letters and postal orders.

The fan club was the barometer of our fast-rising popularity. When Brian said in an interview that he wore yellow socks, girls sent in hundreds of pairs for him. When Keith said he smoked Dunhill cigarettes, piles of packets were received.

Our biggest break in live shows came on September 29 when we began the British tour with the Everly Brothers at London's New Victoria Theatre. We went on midway through the first half and raced through "Poison Ivy," "Fortune-Teller," "Come On" and "Money" in ten minutes flat. "Before this," Keith said afterwards, "we'd rarely played a place much bigger than an apartment. When the curtains opened for the first time we thought we were in the Superdome. It seemed to stretch on forever. We were used to tripping over each other on stage in the clubs. Suddenly we had *all this room*!"

Bo Diddley, one of our heroes, followed us, and did a great show with a battery of amplifiers that left us open-mouthed; we loved his rousing version of "Road-Runner."

Don and Phil Everly closed the show. Joey Paige, their backing group's bass guitarist, recalled: "People said I wouldn't believe it, but nothing coud have possibly prepared me for that first sight of the Stones. When I saw them, I thought they just couldn't afford to buy clothes."

My whole family and all my friends came to this landmark show in the Stones' story. We were paid £42 10s. for each night of the tour, but it meant much more to us than money. As the tour gathered speed, it became clear that many R & B fans had only come to see Bo Diddley and the Stones; they left before the bill-toppers came on, much to the annoyance of the Everly Brothers' supporters.

The day after the tour opened was another milestone. During the previous six months Charlie, Stu and I had all taken the chance of leaving regular employment and turning professional with the Stones. Mick, always the last person in the band to take any risk, finally wrote a letter to the Kent Education Committee terminating his studies at the London School of Economics. "I have been offered a really excellent opportunity in the entertainment world," he wrote to them with his droll sense of humor. "My tutors were very decent about it," he said later. "They said I could return to my studies in a year if things didn't work out."

Musically as well as socially the Everlys/Bo Diddley tour was a nonstop *event*. We had a ball with the American guys on the road and after five nights Little Richard, the great rocker who had announced a year previously that he would never fly or sing rock 'n' roll again, flew in to join us. He closed the first half with "Long Tall Sally," "Rip it Up," "Tutti Frutti" and "Lucille." Halfway through his act he removed his jacket, tie, shirt and shoes, jumped into the audience and then stood on top of the piano as his finale. But secretly the group was a little disappointed: off-stage, he dressed very conventionally in a suit. But one of the great things about this tour was that we were all *learning*. I could have sat in the wings forever watching Little Richard, Don and Phil and Bo Diddley. We learned something new every night.

Our Volkswagen van now arrived, complete with windows in the back and seats for all of us. "Traveling is quite easy now," Keith remarked. "The old van was like motoring in the black hole of Calcutta. The only time we would come up for air was at transport cafés on the motorways."

At the Cardiff show some local Bo Diddley fans came backstage and we all chatted to them. One of the guys offered us some grass. The whole band freaked out and had him ejected. At that time, the only person I'd ever seen smoking grass had been Charlie. In a quiet moment at the Edith Grove flat about six months earlier, when only the two of us were in the front room, he took out some bright green grass that a jazz friend had given him, rolled a joint with some difficulty and then smoked it. Nothing seemed to happen.

It was now time to make our second single, and on Monday, October 7 we went into the De Lane Lea Studios in Holborn, London, to record the Lennon–McCartney song "I Wanna Be Your Man." Andrew was missing; nobody could find him. It later transpired that he had left for France, so Eric produced. Brian played bottleneck guitar, an entirely new sound, like nothing ever played before on a British disc. Brian really was a pioneer; even Keith, who later became a severe critic of Brian, admitted: "Brian *made* that record with that bottleneck." For all the aggravation he had begun to cause us, there's no doubt he was the musical brain of the group at this time. Even Bo Diddley commented that Brian's slide guitar was great; he described Brian as "a little dude that was trying to pull the group ahead. I saw him as the leader. He didn't take no mess. He was a fantastic cat; he handled the group beautifully."

By the time we had a good take of the A-side in the can there was little time left for recording the flip side, so we recorded a song we made up on the spot and called it "Stoned," with Stu on piano and everyone throwing in bits of lyrics for Mick to sing. As Keith said, the track was nothing more than just a nick off Booker T's "Green Onions." But both tracks were finished in a few hours and we were wildly excited at how good they sounded; we couldn't wait for the release date. Mick said we'd achieved an Elmore James sound with the A-side and we all predicted a hit. Keith said later how pleased he'd been with the sound Eric had achieved for us.

It's easy twenty-five years later to put a guy like Eric Easton down as a boring old-time agent who didn't understand what young tigers like the Stones were driving at, but he worked hard and well for us. He put his faith in us and was there when we needed support, and he had an office machine that ticked smoothly. It's crucial to any band to have good organization; it's no good having a brash ideas-man like Andrew Oldham if there's no support system. We were well served in those early days.

Pop music in the early sixties was young, spirited and innovative but not yet big business. Until Lennon and McCartney came along to start the fashion of writing original songs for their groups, artists aiming for successful records relied mainly on professional songwriters. At this stage of our career, with one small hit and another single just recorded we had no conception of which way we would shape ourselves, and no idea that songwriting would play such a major part in our lives. In fact our American blues repertoire meant that writing our own material was unnecessary. Nevertheless, Brian had a feeling that "Stoned" might be the start of something. After the session he suggested the songwriting royalties should be shared by all.

This marked the birth of an amusing part of Rolling Stones folklore. On September 11, a music publishing company, Nanker-Phelge Music Ltd., was incorporated (with Andrew and Mick signing as subscribers), for songs to which all members of the group would contribute. A Nanker was our description of the contorted faces we sometimes made for photographers, pulling down the skin under our eyes and pushing up the tips of our noses. Phelge was taken from Jimmy Phelge, the young printer Brian, Mick and Keith had known back in Edith Grove. His name had always intrigued them. Nanker-Phelge was a fine, cooperative concept.

I packed a suitcase on September 8 knowing that I'd be away on the Everly Brothers/Bo Diddley tour and other gigs of our own for a whole two weeks. I had never been away from Diane and Stephen for such a long period. We started off in Cheltenham where two shows at the Odeon weren't sold out, but the receptions were good. Pat Andrews came but to Brian's disappointment she did not come backstage. After the concert everyone went on the town with Brian and a bunch of his old friends, round the clubs and bars with the £15 we, as Stones, received as running expenses. I got together with one of the girls, who stayed the night with me. Next morning Brian bumped into Pat in the chemist shop where she used to work. They adjourned to a record shop, played a few records and chatted. Brian told her to get in touch with the Stones office if she needed anything for the baby. After lunch we drove to Worcester for two shows at the Gaumont. The first house was small and quiet, but the second was great. Even better news awaited me when we returned to the hotel back in Cheltenham: the same girl was waiting for me; we again spent the night together.

The screaming that greeted us when we took to the stage and when we ran for our van after the shows produced remarkably different attitudes at this stage. I loved it. Mick said that it had taken him some time to get used to it. Brian was as devoted as ever to the blues, but his comments on our gathering popularity exposed his love of stardom: "Girls, good food, sleep and money—great! But we'd pass all that up to be able to show the country that R & B is one of the most compelling and different styles of music." I'm not sure Brian's statement of priorities was to be believed.

Meanwhile our new van had been stripped by fans of every possible item, leaving us with a number plate with just the initials—OMM—on it.

At one show, between tour dates, at the Majestic Ballroom, in Kingston-upon-Hull, where Johnny Kidd and the Pirates supported us, fans broke into the dressing-room and stole our things and also one of each of Johnny Kidd's pairs of expensive pirate boots. He was well pissed off!

While we were staying at a hotel in Liverpool, news filtered through to us that Brian was collecting £5 more a week for being the leader of the band.

Stu remembered: "When we started playing outside London, Brian said, 'I'm the leader of the group and I think I'll stay at the best hotel. All the rest of you can stay in a cheaper hotel.' Of course, the rest of the Stones just laughed at him, and that was it from then on. It was all over for him as the leader. He started to isolate himself because of this attitude."

Keith said: "He had this arrangement with Easton,

that as leader of the band he was entitled to this extra payment. Everybody freaked out. That was the beginning of the decline of Brian. We said, 'Fuck you.' "

On October 16 we received our first weekly accounts from Eric and were paid £193 each, which seemed like a fortune. We were told that our second single, "I Wanna Be Your Man," would be released in a fortnight, on November 1, and that next January we had been booked to do a tour with the great American girl group the Ronettes. It was a period of anticipation, of barriers being crossed and dreams being realized.

Heading into Scotland for a show in Glasgow the next day Stu did a classic accent change in the van as we crossed the border. Arriving in Glasgow he stopped a cop directing traffic and, sticking his head out of the window, said: "Can ye nee tell mi thi way tee Odeon Cinema?" After getting directions he forgot his accent and answered in pure Cockney: "Fank ya very much."

As we criss-crossed Britain, friendships were established with so many people just on the verge of huge popularity. In Newcastle, for example, we went to the Club-A-Gogo after our show and saw the Alan Price Combo. We suggested they come to London and talk to Lionel Blake at the Scene Club, off Piccadilly. This they eventually did and, as the Animals, became successful very quickly.

Later that night in Newcastle we returned to the Station Hotel with various girls, but the night staff were incredibly strict and we couldn't get them into our rooms. Uncharacteristically, we had to give up and go to bed alone. Bradford next day was better. There were lots of Mods around, guys with Lambrettas and Vespa motor scooters, and we were very popular. Again we were mobbed at the theater and the hotel, where Brian and I chatted up two girls in the cocktail bar. They stayed the night with us. Brian was generally my partner in picking up girls after the shows. I suppose this was the real beginning of the "groupie" scene.

Moving south to Hanley, the mobbing continued. Stu managed to get us past the kids by driving the van up against the stage-door. We played two great shows but had the same crowd trouble when we tried to leave. Brian had picked up a girl inside the theater and invited her to return to London with him. He was all over her in the van all the way home. When we arrived in London we dropped Mick and Keith at their house then went to Brian's place. He leapt from the van, leaving the girl with us. He rushed into the house and barred the door. Charlie and I were left with the girl, who had no money and nowhere to stay. I suggested, rather dangerously, that she come home with me but, knowing that Diane would neither understand nor believe why I arrived with her, Charlie volunteered to come to Beckenham with me to verify the unlikely story of Brian's vanishing trick. He and the girl stayed the night with us. The next day we gave her some money and put her on a train back home and I went out and bought a present for Diane for our fourth wedding anniversary, due the following Thursday. Brian's unsettling behavior, if only we'd known, was a precursor of even more erratic behavior to come.

On October 22 in Sheffield after two quietish shows we went on the town and suddenly realized how vulnerable we had become. We began talking to two local lads in a coffee bar when out of nowhere a crowd formed outside the windows. The old guy who ran the café didn't know who we were, and didn't want any trouble so he threw us out. We survived a bit of a scramble back to the hotel, where Brian and I met two girls, later nicknamed the Pifco twins, and spent the night with them. While I was making love to one, at the last minute she produced an amyl nitrate "popper" and broke it under my nose!

Waking up in a Birmingham hotel on October 24 I celebrated my twenty-seventh birthday. The fans thought it was my twenty-second, since I'd knocked five years off my age in the interest of youthful popularity in all the fan-club publicity.

Through Bournemouth, Southampton and Taunton the tour continued. Little Richard got into his stride with a strip of his clothes, a ten-minute stroll through the audience and thirty or forty policemen to control the kids when he went into "Whole Lotta Shakin' Going On." By now the Everly Brothers, consistently good, were facing jeering from yobbos who didn't think they were dramatic enough for a rugged rock 'n' roll tour. "They had a job holding down the top spot after three weeks," Keith remembers. "By then our impudence had built up to a

point where we knew what was going to happen before
anybody . . . there was a new wind blowing."

We narrowly escaped death after a concert in Salisbury; we'd had a hectic time getting in and out of the
Gaumont Theatre and the van went out of control as Stu
drove under a railway bridge in an S–bend just as we
left the town. Our van bounced off the bridge wall but
fortunately managed to stay upright. "We nearly died,"
Stu said. "We should have all been dead."

The final night of the tour was on Sunday, November
3. Unlike everyone else on the show I was a family man,
so in the afternoon I took Stephen to see my parents.
Then in the evening at the Hammersmith Odeon we had
our best reception of the entire tour. The fans mobbed us
in and out of the hall, but cruelly they threw paper cups
at the Everlys. We said sad farewells to the entire cast at
a party backstage; it had been an important, eventful
baptism on the road for us, the tour that knocked the
band into shape and allowed us to reach out to our fans.
Even without a huge record success, things had changed.
And our bank balances were improving a little: we received £1,275 between us for the sixty shows in thirty
nights—it sounded great, but it was just £21 5s. per show
between us before expenses.

In the nineties, it is accepted that youth has a valid voice.
In the sixties, we were still fighting for it. The more we
grew our hair and attracted straight middle-class girls
with music that complemented our aggressive posture,
the more we alienated the adults. It wasn't deliberate on
our part; we were naturally impatient of older people
who couldn't be expected to know where we were coming from. In the early sixties a huge generation gap
became established and accepted, spurred on by films,
fashion, the media and especially by pop music.

It wasn't surprising that the Rolling Stones became
archetypal rebels. We were non-conformists from the
start, arriving via the jazz and blues clubs. In Britain that
wasn't the route for stardom. The clubs we'd come from
didn't breed many stars. The show-business Establishment had its well-oiled machine for finding singers like
Petula Clark, Cliff Richard, Adam Faith and Helen Shapiro pretty, melodic little songs and sending them out on

tour to entertain the mums and dads. It was all very safe, and didn't bring with it *attitude*. The rock 'n' roll we and hundreds of other groups delivered came as part of a new social fabric. Young people could no longer be "kept down"—they wanted a voice, and music was one of their methods of assertion.

The Beatles had arrived before us, of course. But they were safe compared with us. For example, they appeared on the Royal Variety Show. If we didn't exactly scowl, we certainly didn't appear friendly to adults, and as far as the Establishment was concerned we were anarchic.

One of the first media men to be confronted by our stance was Brian Matthew, the compère of the BBC light program's *Saturday Club*, the most important radio slot for pop music. By a strange coincidence, he was represented as an artist by Eric, but that made little difference to our meeting with him or his perception of us when we performed "Memphis Tennessee," "Come On" and "Roll Over Beethoven," and were interviewed by him on October 26.

He recalled later: "I was much older than they were and therefore not really into this rebellion thing which was their hallmark and continued to be so . . . I found their attitude in the studio, as apart from their music, extremely truculent. One can now look back and see what they were all about. Here was the big Establishment bit at the BBC and an ageing disc jockey; you can imagine what Jagger would have called it. In those days we used to have to interview the guys and this didn't go down at all well. One got a sort of 'No' and a 'Yeah'—and this is an interviewer's death. So I really didn't like them very much at all. It had nothing to do with their music, which was something apart. But it's a strange thing that many years later I had a letter from Brian Jones' mother where she said: 'I felt I could write to you and you would be sympathetic because Brian always used to say how much he liked you and how well you got on.' "

What was amazing, looking back now, was that we'd established ourselves so popularly "on the road" before we even had a second single released! "I Wanna Be Your Man," released on November 1, 1963, received mixed reviews from the pop press. "The backing is wild but too prominent," said disc jockey Pete Murray in *Melody Maker*.

"The vocals are lost, which may have been the intention but it wasn't a good one. Well, at least it's a different sound. This isn't as good as 'Come On.' " *Pop Weekly's* Peter Aldersley agreed: "Their fans who buy it will notice a sharp difference in sound from that which drives them into a frenzy at live performances. It's muzzy, undisciplined and technically gives the impression of complete chaos, which is a shame in these days of advanced recording techniques and facilities."

Not everyone reacted so negatively. Johnny Dean, in *Beat Monthly*, wrote that the single "could mean a Top Ten chart entry. All in all, a great double-side, well-produced by Eric Easton. The Stones are rolling again."

The reception strikes me as typical of the contrasts that surrounded us. It was becoming obvious now that you either liked or loathed the Stones. We weren't a group that allowed people to sit on the fence. Perhaps one of the best summaries of the difference between the Stones and other areas of show business came from a Preston journalist, Cynthia Bateman, after we'd appeared before an audience of a thousand at the town's Top Rank Ballroom on November 4: "Shut your eyes and the music was great. Open them and there were the Stones, eye-openers if ever there were any. For while the noise they make is tremendous, the appearance is stupefying. Even ballroom attendants, usually immune to the music, were foot tapping and shaking. On-stage they wear high-heel boots, tight pants, black leather waistcoats and even ties, except for Mick who wears his shirt with collar detached. Off-stage they wear a jumbled assortment of jeans, silk cardigans, camel jackets and sloppy sweaters. None of the slick suits sported by Billy J. Kramer or Gerry and the Pacemakers. Their sound isn't the only thing that's unique to the Stones. In Mick they must have the only vocalist who chews gum all the way through his numbers, a difficult feat admittedly but hardly one to be admired."

Brian and I believed that the northern fans were actually better at this stage than the southern ones. They were more intense and less reserved. Perhaps we had made more impact in the north because by the time we were on the road up there we'd switched from the clubs of London to ballrooms and concerts, with bigger crowds. (There was a bonus, too, of being away from home:

picking up girls was much easier, especially for me.) It was, however, a coincidence that on November 5, when Liverpool's greatest export the Beatles were in London making history by appearing before the Queen Mother on the Royal Variety Show, we were in Liverpool!

While some people were busy building a wall, metaphorically, dividing the north from the south in pop music, we found no barriers whatsoever from Merseyside fans. Walking around the city we were stopped and chatted to by friendly Liverpudlians, and back at our hotel we were visited by girls. In the evening our show at the Cavern, home of the Beatles, was fantastic, with a marvelous crowd. Two thousand fans queued for hours trying to get in. Twenty-five teenagers collapsed from the heat inside the dank, steaming cellar. Mick said afterwards: "Was it hot! We almost sweated away. They've had so many big groups at the Cavern that you've got to prove yourself . . . They asked us back, so they must have liked us."

The normal inclination of Britain's journalists is to "get a good row going," creating a false battleground between parties who aren't truthfully in combat. They were already warming up for a comparison between the Beatles and us, of good (them) versus bad (us), and clean (them) versus dirty (us). But at the end of 1963 the normally cynical British press had little alternative but to recognize the Stones' success, even if they hated our looks and attitudes. The *New Musical Express* was reporting that the Stones had "won the hearts of all northern fans" and *Beat Monthly* wrote: "The Stones, with long and strangely cut hair flowing in the blustery wind, managed to get inside the famous Cavern club. Outside, fantastic queues of fans; hundreds were later turned away because of the crush. These southern sensations have built up a huge wave of popularity all over the country. These five eccentrics show alarm only when confronted by a barber . . . they have garnered their following without a big hit record."

The last fact is the major difference between sixties pop groups and those in the seventies and eighties: we were lucky to have a club circuit, ballrooms and touring package-shows for the concert halls, in which we could cut our teeth and gradually build a following. These clubs were great "nurseries" where we built a repertoire and learned how to put on a show. When most of the clubs closed and ballrooms turned to discos in the seventies the industry changed. Bands with no experience of live work were signed to huge advances from record companies, put out their records and found that they had arrived at the top of the charts without the benefit of real performing experience. The reason groups like the Stones and the Beatles could cope was that we had paid our dues in clubs where the energy level has to be extremely high to hold a crowd's attention.

There was also, I think, more of a spirit of friendship on the scene: after the Liverpool show we went to the promoter Bob Wooler's house for a party where we met various musicians: the Escorts, Derry Wilkie and the Pressmen, Sonny Webb and the Cascades. Liverpool was really great; I returned to the hotel for the night with my local blonde.

And life on the road had its funny moments. We were booked to play a show at the Co-op Ballroom, Nuneaton on the evening of November 15, but before that we had to play an earlier show at 5:45, something they called their junior session. Here we faced a room full of kids aged from about six to ten, who were in the middle of their afternoon tea. They didn't appreciate R & B, and the little perishers proceeded to throw cream cakes at us throughout our set.

On Friday, November 8, our second single had entered the *New Musical Express* chart at number thirty. That night when we were appearing at Newcastle's Club-a-Gogo there were so many fans swarming around that we had to be smuggled into the dressing-room, then through the kitchen and through a serving hatch one by one, into the club-room and on to the stage. The room was solid with fans, who gave us a great reception. During the show a boy in the audience shouted, "Get your hair cut!" and was instantly jumped on, taken outside and beaten up. I broke my bass amp again—the second time in three days. The mornings after gigs seemed to be marked by my looking for instrument shops to get my amps repaired.

Returning to the hotel with a bunch of girls, we sat in the lobby having drinks. We spent the next three hours trying by every devious means possible to smuggle the girls into our rooms. Brian eventually managed it while we all diverted the attention of the night porter. But the manager was called and they proceeded to break into Brian's room and eject the girl. We finally gave up and went to bed alone.

It was the same picture next day at Whitley Bay's Club-a-Gogo: we were smuggled in through hundreds of fans, had another wildly successful show and afterwards went into the club cellars for a party with lots of girls. The place was furnished with large mattresses around the floors and very little lighting. We fooled around with the girls for a few hours before returning to the hotel with them and meeting the same management barrier we'd faced the night before, again failing to get the girls up to our rooms.

Back in London as our single rose nine positions to twenty-one in the charts we did a four-hour recording session at De Lane Lea Studios. This time we cut tracks for an EP, a format that was popular at the time and which usually featured four tracks. The songs were "Money," "Poison Ivy" (which featured me on backing vocal to Mick as well as playing bass) and "Talkin' 'Bout You." The idea behind the session was to capture in the studio the atmosphere of one of our dates, hence the concentration on strong, beaty numbers that might not have sufficient instant appeal for a single.

One fact which seems to have been overlooked about the Stones is that while people's attitude to us was intolerant, we became much more open-minded about music and people generally as we moved into the world of show business. The Everly Brothers tour had changed us perceptibly: their music was a million miles from ours but we admired their sound, the quality of their songs and their professionalism. We had the same views about an American singer who was to become a firm friend.

We were at Birmingham and after miming to "I Wanna Be Your Man" on *Thank Your Lucky Stars* we returned to our dressing-room to mess around with some songs. Gene Pitney, the American singer/songwriter recalls: "I was having a nap in my dressing-room. As soon as my eyes were closed, I heard guitars, harmonica, an out-of-tune piano and voices that seemed to get louder and louder. I investigated and two rooms away I saw them—and boy, did I get a shock. I didn't know if it was a gag, wigs or what. Their hair and appearance really surprised me. They were something that hadn't been sprung upon the world yet. I had a US senator with me and we took a picture of them. When he got home his wife asked him who the ugly women were. That's how uneducated the public were, especially the American public."

Later, Andrew took Mick and Keith to Pitney's room and Gene told them he was disappointed by his lack of success in Britain. His knowledge of the music business impressed them; this was at a time when Mick and Keith were being encouraged by Andrew to write songs together. Mick and Keith began loosely playing and singing one of their songs, called "My Only Girl." Pitney asked Andrew (who was soon to become his publicity officer) to arrange a recording session; he could not wait to cut that song. They drove back to London together, stopping at a "wayside inn," as Pitney called a pub. "I don't think we stopped talking about music once," Gene recalled. Later, he told the *Daily Mirror* of his early association with us: "If you can't beat 'em, join 'em. When I first saw them I didn't know whether to say hallo or bark! But then I got to know them. They're great!"

Only three days after we'd first met we were in the studios with Pitney to cut a demo version of the song. Gene converted it into more of a ballad for his style, rewrote the chorus with Mick and Keith and retitled it "That Girl Belongs to Yesterday." Everyone was having such a ball that we ended up recording demos for kicks.

Our next big concert was on November 19, just as we reached the sixth position in *Teenbeat* magazine's pop poll. We played to 1,200 fans at Kilburn's State Ballroom and police had to break up scuffles among hundreds of disappointed kids when the doors closed. Fans were all over us from start to finish, rushing on stage; there were police in the hall the entire time. It was a great show. When the spotlight went off at the end we rushed to the dressing-room with girls chasing us. Everyone made it safely except Charlie, who was pulled to the ground with girls all over him. Finally, the bouncers managed to free him and bundle him into the dressing-room. Poor Charlie was very proud of his new pink shirt but it had been torn to shreds. He was furious. It was here that I met a cute seventeen-year-old black girl, Virginia Romain, and I began seeing her whenever possible. I am still in touch with her.

It was some show. The local paper reported: "The Stones drew an even bigger crowd than the Beatles. Is this an omen that they are soon to be crushed by the Stones?" Well, we had a fair distance to travel to catch them up: they'd topped the album chart with their debut album, and their second album was released just as our second single had risen nine places, to number thirty-two.

The signs for us were good, but the truth is that our second single wasn't selling rapidly enough, although by December 7 it was at number sixteen in *New Record Mirror*. We were a hit in every place we played, and aroused terrific excitement at our live shows, but we were in the curious situation of not having a big hit record. It didn't worry us much but it was a reversal of the method by which pop fame was achieved. The accepted route was to make a hit record and then go on tour to consolidate it. In view of the perverse nature of the members of the Stones, it was not surprising perhaps that we stood the sequence on its head.

The intensity around the Stones at the end of 1963 was exciting: on November 23, while shopping in Penge I'd continually been stopped and asked for autographs by fans—it was becoming difficult to move around freely now. In the evening we played to 3,000 fans at Leyton Baths, and then drove on to Dalston's Chez Don Club, and broke a crowd record by attracting 850. Two shows per night were quite normal, the kind of schedule (and sheer enthusiasm to play and be successful) that rock bands in the seventies and eighties might find hard to comprehend.

We were now recording enthusiastically, and to the surprise of our friend the engineer Bill Farley, we adopted the tiny Regent Sound Studios in Denmark Street as our regular place. The studio was only thirty feet by twenty feet and its facilities would make most rock groups today laugh. There were nine microphones, Ampex recording units and Tiros mixers. Studio time was £5 an hour, which included the use of all equipment, acoustic piano, echo chamber and an experienced engineer. Demo discs cost 15 shillings for a single side and £1 2s. 6d. for a double-sided lacquer. We cut four demos here for Andrew on December 7 and were pleased with them. It was quite a typical day in the lives of a busy pop group in that period: after cutting the demo tracks, I went shopping for a leather jacket at Cecil Gee, we did a photo session and then drove by van to Croydon for two shows at Fairfield Halls. On the bill with us were Gerry and the Pacemakers, who insisted on topping the bill; so we closed the first half. Gerry suffered the dangerous consequences of following us: lots of fans left the show at the interval, not bothering to wait to see his show. The *Croydon Advertiser* reported that "hysterical girls howled successfully for an encore" from us. We celebrated a fine gig with a small party afterwards at my mum and dad's house in Penge.

Any thoughts that we were rivaling the Beatles were firmly dispelled when on December 12 we woke to the news that their third single, "I Want to Hold Your Hand," had gone straight to Number One in Britain, where it stayed for five weeks. By contrast, "I Wanna Be Your Man" rose five places to number twenty in the *New Musical Express*, and by one place to number fifteen in the *New Record Mirror*.

As our foothold strengthened, Brian's life continued to be disrupted by problems. In early December Linda Lawrence discovered she was pregnant. At the instigation of her parents, Brian and Linda decided to visit the Joneses to tell them about their expected grandchild. They drove down, but Brian and Linda did not feel the atmosphere was welcoming enough for them to break such news. Later, Brian told his mother and father by letter. "They thought I was terrible because I was pregnant," Linda recalled, "but they'd accepted me before. I had slept in their house. I felt very bad." Linda and Brian considered the possibility of an abortion. Shirley Shepherd, girlfriend of Charlie, took them to see a doctor who asked if they were in love. "Yes," Brian and Linda answered. The doctor said: "Go home, then. We're not going to do it."

I always fared much better than the others in the girl stakes. On December 11 after we'd played a show at the Arts Ball in Bradford we drove to Liverpool to stay at the Exchange Hotel for the night. My loyal little Liverpool blonde was awaiting my arrival.

The night's show increased our reputation in the Beatles' city, which ought to have been tough to crack. After our show at the Locarno, Paul Ryan, singer with Paul and the Streaks, said: "It was fantastic. Everyone lent a hand in carrying out girls who had fainted and eventually the safety barrier between the audience and the stage was pushed over. The folks in Liverpool said the Stones were better received there than the Beatles ever were." Back at the Exchange Hotel, Mick and I spent the night with two black girls: they would occasionally meet up with us on tours and stay with Mick and me.

The only thing we lacked during this heady period was sleep. At one point Mick said: "We've only had about four hours kip each night for most of this week. When we get back to London we'd like to do nothing but sleep until it's time to go on the road again. But there's always so much catching up to do on jobs which we can't look after on tour."

Tired though we were, we always took our pleasures seriously. On December 18, after a photo session for *Boyfriend* magazine and buying Keith a suitcase for his twentieth birthday, we left London by van, drove to Bristol for a superb sell-out show at the Corn Exchange and drove back to a party in London at the Mayfair flat of Tony Hall, who worked at Decca and was a good friend. I left the party in some style: the singer Dorothy Squires drove me home to Beckenham in her Thunderbird. It was a long but exhilarating day. Back to reality, the next day I fitted new curtains in the flat.

As our single rose five places to fifteen in the December 29 *New Musical Express*, the paper's pollwinners supplement named us sixth best British vocal group and fifth in the British small group section. Over in the *New Record Mirror*, we marked the imminence of Christmas with an advertisement featuring a photo of us and our message: "Best Wishes to All the Starving Hairdressers and their Families."

We had the usual problem getting past fans to honor a date at a ballroom in Baldock on December 21; after finally forcing a window at the rear and climbing in, we

found the room stacked floor to ceiling with chairs. Pushing our way through, we eventually got backstage and
played a good show to a record crowd. The response was
quiet compared with recent shows, but the money good
(£200) and there was brightness on the female front: here
I met a French girl named Doreen Samuels who became
one of my steady girlfriends over the next three years.*

Pete Townshend, later to lead The Who to glory, remembers seeing and supporting the Stones for the first
time at St. Mary's Hall, Putney, on December 22, 1963.
His band was then called the Detours.

Christmas loomed. On Christmas Eve I went for a
drink with the staff at the Art Nash music shop in Penge,
where they were fitting a new Baldwin pick-up on to my
old bass guitar. I then went uptown by train, met the rest
of the boys at Act One Scene One restaurant in Soho, a
regular rendezvous point, and drove to Leek, Staffordshire.
This seemed a bizarre place to have to visit on Christmas
Eve; we played a dance at the town hall. In the interval,
Stu went out and returned with meat pies. The show
went well but on the journey back to London Brian and I
were both ill with food poisoning from the pies and had
to stop frequently on the motorway to throw up. Happy
Christmas!

I arrived home shattered at 7 a.m. on Christmas Day,
slept for a few hours, then went to visit my parents; we
spent the day with them and some of the family. For all
the Stones it was a quiet Christmas after a turbulent year.
As Keith said: "This Christmas I'm going home to sleep.
And it's my turn to give presents this year. I've never had
the money before."

The Stones ended 1963 with a nod back to our roots: a
date at the Ken Colyer Club on December 30. We'd
spent the afternoon there rehearsing and learned Chuck
Berry's "Carol" and "I Can Tell" to add to our stretched
stage repertoire. Playing the next night, New Year's Eve,
at a dance at Lincoln, we saw the New Year in at a
beautiful beamed hotel, the White Hart. While I settled
in my room, Mick and Keith dressed Brian up in a sheet

---

*Doreen later became the girlfriend of folk-singer Donovan
before he met and eventually married Linda Lawrence, Brian
Jones's ex. Ah, the complications of women around the Stones!

and various bits and pieces to look like a ghost. They turned the hall lights out and came knocking on my door. I opened it, took one look at the ghostly apparition and said: "Go to bed, Brian, and stop messing about!" "You bastard!" he shouted. "It's taken us an hour to get this together!"

During the year there had been ninety million-selling records, including nine by the Beatles but none by us. The Rolling Stones had had a spectacular first year but we were yet to jump into the heavyweight ring.

5

The "Great Unwashed"

"Suggestions that the Stones should go and have short
back and sides are not just wrong but are beside the
point. You might as well suggest that Jackie Kennedy
should not dress elegantly, or that Fidel Castro should
shave his beard . . . The days of the glossy performer
are gone. This is why there's more than 1,000 beat
groups in Liverpool, why the majority of current artists are self-taught, and why musical instruments have
suddenly become big business. The Stones are popular
because they wear sweatshirts and cord trousers that
we can buy too. Long hair is a sign of protest against
the crop-headed discipline of the army during wartime. Bright, casual clothes for men are fashionable as
a reaction against wartime grey and drab demob suits.
When a concert turns into a riot, it's no more a riot
than the licensed hooliganism of the hunt, no noisier
or destructive than the average football crowd, no
more hysterical than some revival meetings."

A fan's letter, 1964

Brian, Mick, Keith and Charlie were not the sort of
blokes I'd have chosen as mates if I hadn't joined them in
a group. Not only was I much older than they were but
my entire background and outlook were different. It's
like with distant relatives—you don't want to see them
every day! Once or twice a year it's OK, but you're glad
they're not staying over in your house! They weren't the
kind of people I'd regard as close friends, that I'd confide
in or go to for help, although on the road that changed.
There we were responsible only to each other and there
were no people clinging on to Mick and Keith. We had a
good time and it was fun. Back in London they always
resented the fact that I had a steady—or rather unsteady—
marriage, and a young kid. I loved pop music but had no

deep commitment to the blues at this stage (although I was gradually building up my collection of John Lee Hooker, Jimmy Reed and Bo Diddley albums). I could never comprehend the shambles in which Brian, Mick and Keith were prepared to live; I had always liked structure in my life and preferred to keep myself highly organized. From a very young age, I'd always kept a note of things in diaries (which, unfortunately, my mother threw out when I went into military service). The other four Stones had not done National Service; it had been abolished by the time they would have been eligible.

The more we were on the road, though, the better our integration became. When you're thrown together in a van for hundreds of miles, sharing hotel rooms, stages and dressing-rooms, eating and drinking together and going through all that hysteria, you are like brothers in arms. Whatever the differences that made the five of us an unlikely alliance, a team spirit quickly became all-powerful. The Rolling Stones as an entity became the most important factor in our lives. Its progress, survival and commercial success were everything to us.

Nobody loved and believed in the Stones more than Brian. This was his true baby. The memory of his terribly messed-up pre-Stones life quickly evaporated as he tasted success and saw his musical convictions being recognized. And yet he was the most uneasy of all of us over the route to mass popularity we were being driven along by Andrew Oldham.

"When we left the club scene," said Brian as our success began, "we also left the diehard R & B fanatics and we temporarily made a compromise to cope with the pop fans we came across in dance halls and on tours. It's all very nice, I suppose, to know you're appreciated, but it's also rather frightening." Brian wanted fame and fortune but didn't want to sacrifice his musical integrity to get it. Other people were more prepared to make that final thrust which lifted the Stones into the top league. For Brian this could only mean disaster. In this and in other ways it could be said he engineered his own downfall, but the cold-hearted reaction to Brian's decline has troubled many people, like me, who loved the guy despite his many faults.

Three factors paved the way for Brian eventually being

tossed out in the cold. First, money and his own greed. Secondly, the Stones' need for a hit songwriting "machine," which basically didn't interest him. And thirdly, Andrew Oldham divided the band up very quickly once he moved into the same house as Mick and Keith: it immediately became those three on one side, Brian, Charlie and me on the other.

I must say that Brian planted the seeds of his own demise. There's nothing like money to start aggravation, and we had all suspected he was fiddling the books when he held back cash from the earliest shows, saying they were for band expenses. Nobody disputed his leadership but he always maintained that we were working cooperatively, that it was a five-way partnership in every sense. Yet right from the start we all had this nagging feeling that he was conning each of us out of several pounds at every gig. Being young and keen it didn't matter too much, except in principle. Perhaps Brian was motivated by fear. Perhaps, also, he saw the (song)writing on the wall.

Oldham knew he had to merge our appeal as rebels with unique, commercial songs that would pull us away from the gutsy, earthy music we'd filled the clubs with. He needed a songwriting team and he must have known that Brian would offer the most resistance to this. Brian was possibly too much of a musician to "think commercial" for the sake of a hit single—however essential.

Seeing that Brian was hung up on musical integrity, Andrew knew he had to bring Mick and Keith together. His problem here was in breaking Keith's natural musical partnership with Brian: from the beginning, as the two guitarists, they had interlinked their lines and worked really well together. Mick was the vital front man, blowing a bit of harmonica, but he wasn't a musical anchor.

Andrew's task was made easier by geography. When Mick, Keith and Andrew went to share in Mapesbury Road, we were a split band, which suited Andrew.

The stage was set. It was obvious, too, that Andrew began to encourage a whispering campaign about Brian. The atmosphere in the band began to change; the power-play and the subsequent decline of Brian Jones had begun.

You had to be strong to join the Stones. The faint-hearted or ultrasensitive would not have stood the gibes that poured from Mick and Keith. From the minute I joined I realized they had to have someone to poke fun at, not always in a humorous way, often spiteful and hurtful. They *had* to have a scapegoat or a guinea-pig and in the early days it was me, followed by Brian. This could range from the color socks I wore, which they went on about all the time, to the jackets I bought, the cigarettes I smoked, the drinks I drank. And they always made fun of me for liking rock 'n' roll. Jerry Lee Lewis, Eddie Cochran, Johnny Cash, Elvis Presley—I grew up loving the music of these people. The Stones won me over to the blues, but I didn't suddenly take a dislike to straight American pop. They laughed about it all the time, couldn't believe they had recruited a player who was right for the Stones but who liked "white" rock 'n' roll. (Slowly over the years they began to appreciate these people. Now if you ask Keith who his favorites are, Jerry Lee Lewis is at the top of his list. He hated Jerry Lee in the early days and ribbed me mercilessly about it!) They also persistently laughed at the fact that I was married with a child. They could never understand that I did not want to work at certain times—because of my son's birthday or later when he was having a holiday from school. They totally resented that. Even though I had a family, the band should come first in their view. They made no effort to help me or understand my needs. Their attitude changed only when *they* became married with children, suddenly realizing that anniversaries and birthdays are important to other people. It was pretty harmless stuff, but very irritating when it went on week after week.

Success came and confusion set in with Brian. Mick and Keith, egged on by Andrew, saw the golden chance to break through. Brian instinctively pulled back, yet at the same time—like the "power trio"—he was totally starstruck by the Beatles. All four idolized the Beatles and loved to be seen alongside them, socializing with them at the Ad Lib off Leicester Square after shows. Poor Brian's lust for this level of fame was always at odds with his conscience.

My own position was less vulnerable. I was made of stronger stuff, too. When I played that fast boogie bit all the way through the second single, "I Wanna Be Your

Man," it received a lot of praise. I was always able to do things faster than the rest of them: learn a song faster, memorize arrangements, remember lyrics. Mick and Keith forget even their own songs, what keys they are in, what chords they'd played, how the middle eight goes and how it ends. Right through the history of the Stones, it was always Wyman who told them. When Mick came sixth in the best vocalist section of the popularity polls, Brian fourth in the best guitarist section and Charlie eighth in the drummer category, I won the poll as the best bass player.

Charlie's great asset to the band was as a rock-solid drummer. He always viewed the pop scene with a bit of disdain and all his life has preferred jazz musicians for company. While the excitement of our breakthrough was consuming Mick, Keith, Andrew and Brian, Charlie went home most nights to his mother's home in Neasden, while I went to Penge and Diane and Stephen.

The first time I saw Brian I was struck by the deep-sunken bags under his eyes. "He carries a lot of luggage," we used to say. He always looked like he needed a long sleep. I regarded him as very intelligent, very articulate, well-spoken, shy, and highly sensitive. As the band's momentum gathered and he was cast aside by Andrew, Mick and Keith, it's obvious he was carrying a burden that we knew nothing about, a medical condition that may explain his often irrational behavior. Yet we didn't worry; he always walked around with an inhaler and we assumed he simply had occasional asthmatic bouts. He had gone sick and missed several gigs and we put that down to straight exhaustion and nothing very deep; he seemed a hypochondriac, and when you're young you haven't time for other people's illnesses. He was always taking medication for something: he had a sore back, his ear hurt, his legs ached, his teeth ached. Because he was always moaning, we got to ignore his symptoms, which changed daily. Instead Brian's illnesses became a band joke. He was always attending clinics and saying he'd been diagnosed as suffering from "nervous strain." Mick and Keith would say sarcastically: "Oh, Brian's ill again—did he send a doctor's certificate?" But I've now found evidence that suggests Brian's medical condition was more serious than we, and perhaps he, realized. It could easily have contributed to the behavioral patterns that caused such big problems in his attitude to the band and his relationships with all of us.

His activities with women were legendary and his total score-card of illegitimate children may never be known. But one illegitimate daughter, born on August 4, 1960, whom Brian never knew, whom I shall call Carol, has a medical condition causing behavior which is uncannily similar to the way Brian often behaved. She considers me a link with her father but wants to remain anonymous because the subject of Brian Jones is a taboo in the house where she lives with her family.

Carol told me: "I was about six years old when something clicked during an argument my parents were having over dinner. I realized from something that was said that the man across the table, whom I called Daddy, was not my father.

"My brother and I were not allowed to watch pop shows on television; Mum obviously recognized Brian. She had never told him she was pregnant and had carried guilt around with her from the one night they spent together after a dance in the south of England. She and my father had been going through a rough phase, not sleeping together, and suddenly she found she was pregnant.

"It came out into the open between Mother and me in 1975, when I was fifteen. My brother and I were standing in the hall, Mother was cooking dinner in the kitchen. He had bought a Rolling Stones record; I had never been a fan of the group, but I pointed at the photograph and said: 'Who's that?' He replied: 'That's Brian Jones. He's dead.' I felt as if I'd been hit in the stomach. Mother went berserk. She said: 'Never, ever bring anything like that home again.'

"Everything clicked in my head when I looked at the album cover and saw the little poem which Brian had written:

When this you see, remember me
and bear me in your mind
Let all the world say what they may
Speak of me as you find.

"When I read that I felt completely shattered.

"I then had a long conversation with Mother, who said how guilty she had felt since that one-night liaison. She dissolved into tears and there was much sobbing and cuddling. She said she felt so guilty that she had hurt her husband so much. With Daddy there has never been any discussion; if ever the Stones are mentioned he walks out of the room. Mother's marriage is now happy, so I don't want to upset them.

"But of course I began reading everything I could find about the Rolling Stone who was my father. I once read somebody saying that Brian didn't know whether he was here, there or anywhere, and that tallied exactly with one of the epileptic symptoms I suffer from. You really don't know if you're coming or going, whether you're in the past, present or future. It affects the memory; the brain is all over the place. You have no control whatsoever, and the only way to get rid of it is to go to sleep.

"I've since discovered that there were so many times when Brian went ill, didn't arrive for performances or canceled rehearsals; it's possible that the epileptic symptoms which I have, temporal-lobe epilepsy, is inherited from Brian. With my fits, I go straight into a collapse; I get no warning whatsoever. Often I have one in the middle of the night. My parents know about it but I don't know a thing because I've had it and gone straight to sleep; I just wake up in the morning feeling awful. It's possible, then, that Brian was having fits at night and not realizing it."

I said to Carol that Brian was permanently worried about his health but we were never aware that he had an epileptic condition. He *did* seem to suffer sudden depressions and swings of mood; the symptoms she described seemed to match certain behavior patterns by Brian. He *could* be OK one minute and then switch off from the conversation. She continued: "If he was having seizures and nobody around him was aware of his having them, it would be terrible. They can make you feel really ill; you don't know what's going on. It would mean he wouldn't be able to carry on a proper conversation with people. Your brain suddenly goes thud. You've had it.

"Maybe if he had told a doctor, he would have been treated. If you don't know, and you've come round and felt bloody awful, like sawdust, in the morning . . . then maybe Brian felt he had a hangover. There's no cure, but tablets or drugs can control it.

"I certainly feel for him. But if nobody knew what he was going through, nobody could help him."

Brian's physical weaknesses pose a big question. Did he know enough of his condition to realize that what seemed to me the quest for power by Andrew, Mick and Keith wasn't worth fighting? Had he been totally healthy, might he not have fought to keep control of the band he formed? He actively disliked the route the music was taking under Andrew Oldham. Why, other than for reasons we didn't know about, did Brian capitulate so easily to such a blatant overthrow of his leadership? He had a position of great strength if he wanted to use it. He had tremendous physical attraction to women. Considering Mick was the lead singer and in the spotlight every night, Brian, as a guitarist by his side, matched him for popularity to an amazing degree. He could easily have developed his songwriting, but he lacked confidence in his efforts. And in interviews, he was the most articulate and thoughtful Rolling Stone.

Instead of defending his corner he pulled back when confronted by two physically strong guys who made all the running. The schedule we kept was tough; you needed much more stamina than Brian showed to keep up. Even if you were fit, like Keith, Charlie, Mick and me, the traveling was exhausting. For Brian, with the debility of asthma and the strong possibility of epilepsy as described by his daughter, the pressures must have been much greater. Maybe, just maybe, he knew his problems better than we did. Maybe he chose not to battle with Mick and Keith, and just accepted the Good Life.

Brian was by far the most ambitious and progressive musician of the five of us, as he consistently proved, but he was never encouraged by them to tilt his talents in a more commercial way. That was one of Brian's many dilemmas: pressure from inside himself because he felt we'd sold out from the original blues band; then a fixation about stardom and a wallowing in the pleasures of the flesh; the problem of his health and his obsessions with all kinds of symptoms; and the push for control of the band, which must have knocked his large ego. "We felt like we had a wooden leg," Mick said after his death. That's not the way I prefer to remember Brian, but there is also a view that Charlie's and my passivity did not ease his problem.

Astrid Lundström, my girlfriend from 1967 to 1983, comments: "I think that Mick and Keith got away with murder because Bill and Charlie didn't create any waves. The more destructive characters in any situation are the people who *enable* other people to be sick. The worst criminals are the ones who don't stand up for themselves. Bill and Charlie *enabled* Mick and Keith to carry on being what I considered to be incredibly selfish. Bill started to change later, became more bitter and negative because he felt dumped on. But unfortunately he forgets his own part in allowing it to happen. I'm not blaming him because to be around those people leaves scars. He could never relax and was always aware of the vibes. It wasn't conducive to feeling relaxed and happy. It was tension, tension all the time."

The unity between Mick, Keith and Andrew, the isolation of Brian and the different personalities of Charlie and me inevitably caused a clear division. I became particularly close to Brian, while Charlie coolly positioned himself somewhere in the middle of the lot of us. He was able to be mates with everybody, flit from one to another and communicate with all of us quite naturally. Charlie's easy-going character is his strength.

Brian was not able to keep the peace like that. I'm not surprised. When he tried to write songs they were dismissed—not fairly, not "they're not good enough, let's try again," but with an out of hand: *"You* can't write *songs!"* Nobody except Mick and Keith got the opportunity or encouragement to write, apart from those songs to which we all contributed in the studio.

Brian didn't talk about his frustration much but I was aware of it all the time. As the years passed he showed more respect to musicians outside the Stones, friends like John Mayall, Steve Winwood, George Harrison, Keith Relf, Mick Fleetwood and members of the Animals, than he did to us, his colleagues. While the Stones functioned as a unit, Mick, Keith and Andrew were also busy with outside activities: songs for other acts and producing records for people like George Bean, Chris Farlowe, the Mighty Avengers, Marianne Faithfull and others.

And I felt there was injustice in the way some songs came to be written and credited solely to Mick and Keith. Experimenting in the studio, Brian or I often contributed a riff or a suggestion that was adopted and became a vital part of the song. To get them to accept the suggested "break" in the middle of one of their compositions, you had to convince them over a period of hours or even days that it was right, an improvement for the song. They knew what they wanted to do and if nobody liked it, they would still do it. On tour, Brian, Stu and I always traveled in the van and the others usually went in Andrew's or Mick's car. In hotels, if we shared a room it was the same split; and whenever I could I arranged for my room to be a fair distance from the others. I preferred switching off from much social contact with the band when we checked into a hotel.

Andrew undoubtedly pushed Keith against Brian for second place in the band behind Mick. When we began Brian and I did back-up singing, because Keith couldn't sing—he's still not a natural singer. Being the shy one who preferred not to sing if I could avoid it, I never pushed for vocal work, but Brian enjoyed it. He sang with Mick on "Walkin' the Dog," and did the whistling on that, and Brian and I did back-up vocals to Mick on "Time is on My Side" and lots of the early songs. But by 1965 Andrew was pushing Keith to sing in the studio so that he could project him with Mick as a coupling.

Brian knew he was a competent musician, more original than any of us, and his confidence in that held him for a while. But they whittled away at him and he left it too long to fight back. I was as close to Brian as anyone around the Stones, especially when he was made the outcast, and the methods used to wear him down were terrible to watch. Andrew would turn off his mike (without his knowledge) when we were recording; or on playbacks he would fade out his instrument. Brian would try to ingratiate himself with them by crawling first to Mick and then to Andrew, which didn't do any good. He should simply have been strong in himself. Then he would switch to Keith, with whom he *thought* he had most empathy of the three of them, but that didn't work; it was a closed shop. Brian was locked into a defensive position from which he could never return. When the manager of a group has pitted two strong, ambitious guys (who share his flat) against a sensitive guy with the personality complications of Brian Jones, only one team can win.

Yet the plan to align Mick and Keith didn't work in terms of popularity: it was Brian and Mick who were the most popular figures, and Brian was most popular with the girls. Not until the seventies was the Jagger–Richards partnership recognized and Keith came into his own—by which time Brian was dead.

Whatever grievances we had, however difficult the tensions in the band, once our bandwagon began to roll, we had one major belief in common: the band. We all loved the Rolling Stones much more than any individual in it. Irrespective of all the tensions, there was always a great spirit of the Show Must Go On. Whatever family or domestic problems we had, the band came first. We all took the same view: there are plenty of girlfriends out there; if you have a problem, change your girlfriend, but don't jeopardize the band, which is *not* replaceable. We were the cheap butt of comedians, adults, the Establishment and all strands of society, and partly because of that we were incredibly protective and supportive of each other. We intended the unit, the Stones, to survive, because we knew that it worked musically. That's why Brian stayed so long. He stayed for longer than anyone else would have.

The irony of Brian's situation was emphasized by Keith's admission at the end of 1963 that originally he had "never thought of songwriting . . . it just didn't occur to me. It was like being a novelist or a computer operator, for all I knew—a completely different field that I hadn't thought of. I just thought of myself as a guitar player. I remember sitting around with Brian a couple of times. We gave up in despair. It was Andrew who really forced Mick and me to sit down and try it and get us through that initial period where you write absolute rubbish, things you've heard, until you start coming up with songs of your own. Andrew made us persevere."

Mick, adding that the Beatles had encouraged them to write, said: "We got the feeling we were running out of standards, so we just had to start writing our own. We never wrote any blues numbers to start with. Original blues are very difficult to write. The tunes we wrote were more like ballads or pop songs." The first Jagger–Richards titles were "It Should be You" and "Will You be My Lover Tonight," and were recorded by an Oldham protégé, singer George Bean.

Glyn Johns, confirming that Andrew's pushing of Mick and Keith into songwriting "really caused Brian to be left behind," added: "Until that time Brian was pretty much the group's spokesman and had some very good musical ideas. A lot of Stones records were built of riffs, and Brian invariably played those riffs. Then Mick and Keith were encouraged to write and sell their songs and the whole balance of power shifted to them. They and Andrew took over directing the band."

1964 began promisingly. The *Daily Sketch* asked:

> Who would have thought a few months ago that half Britain's teenagers would end the year with heads like hairy pudding-basins? The Stones look straight out of the Stone Age. Already, with just one disc in the hit parade, they've reached fifth place in *Melody Maker's* ratings. Their success seems to lie in their off-handedness. "We just please ourselves," they say. But remember, millions of teenagers in 1964 may end up looking like them.

Mick managed to sound both assertive and cool, one of his notable talents of juxtaposition, when he declared: "This Mersey sound is no different from our River Thames sound. As for those Liverpool blokes proclaiming themselves better than anyone else, that's a load of rubbish. I've nothing against the Mersey sound. It's great. But it's not as new and exclusive as the groups make out. I can't say I blame them for jumping at this sort of publicity, though. If we came from Liverpool, we'd do the same. But we don't, and we're out to show the world."

He was still, incidentally, called Mike Jagger by members of the band, friends, family and some of the British media. This persisted right through to our first American tour in June, 1964.

As the plaudits came thick and fast we obviously had to move quickly on the record front, to capitalize on the reputation we were building in the press and in live shows. All this recognition was on the basis of our performances and our appearance. It was vital that 1964 became the year when we simultaneously cracked the record market.

After appearing on the first of the BBC's new *Top of the Pops* TV show we were all very hungry and stopped for a meal at a small Chinese restaurant on the outskirts of Manchester, where the show was recorded. The restaurant was practically empty. We sat down, ordered some drinks, and then made our choices for various items of food. After about half an hour the food hadn't arrived, and so we called the waiter over and ordered more drinks. He said the food was on its way. Another twenty minutes passed and no food arrived. By this time we were all impatient, and started moaning at the waiter. Nothing arrived, and we were getting nowhere, we decided to forget it. We put £10 on the table, shouted a few curses and left. Suddenly the chef burst out of the kitchen area with a meat cleaver, screaming at us, as we bolted for the door. We raced up the road to the van, to the sound of the chef screaming, "Come black, you flucking blastards!" We drove back to London hungry.

With a welcome payment of £125 from Eric for the previous two weeks' work, we went into Regent Sound studios on January 2. There we met Cleo Sylvester, now eighteen years old, one of the two black girls who had unsuccessfully rehearsed with us at the Wetherby Arms the February before. Now she was recording her first single for Andrew Oldham! We recorded "To Know Him is to Love Him," the classic 1958 hit by the American group the Teddy Bears (which had featured Phil Spector, who was now establishing himself as a major record producer). For the B-side we cut an instrumental called "There are but Five Rolling Stones." Next day, we did a Stones session, heading for our first album. Stu joined in on piano for our sessions, which were produced by Andrew. It was all fairly primitive but we were happy with the tracks.

"When they arrived," said Bill Farley, the engineer, "no one had any thought about arrangements. They just busked it until they got the feeling of the number. There was no dubbing. They just told me exactly what they wanted as soon as the number had been worked out. How it turned out so well in the end I never really knew."

The tracks were Chuck Berry's "Carol" and "Route 66," plus Bo Diddley's "Mona (I Need You Baby)." Brian's supremacy and instinctive musicianship was evident on the last track. Even Keith recalled later: "I've never heard anybody, before or since, get that Bo Diddley thing down. Diddley himself was astounded, saying that Brian was the only cat he knew who'd worked out the secret of it."

The record revolution led by the Beatles and the Stones was characterized by a crucial shift in emphasis: the musicians had gained control. Until British pop groups began coming in with their own ideas of sound, a backing track was often laid down by session players, and a record company A & R man was very much in charge. Performers were not expected to ask for their voice or guitar to be caught in a certain style or for any technical effects. The record company called most of the shots. Beginning with the Beatles and the Stones came that handing over of creative input to the players, changing forever the nature of pop music and the music industry. But, of course, the only way that could be maintained was through successful record sales. Had we and the acts that followed us failed to get hits, we'd quickly have been dictated to. The onus was therefore on us to use this new freedom commercially.

We continued our live work apace. The night of that recording session we drove to Forest Hill, London, for a hectic show at the Glenlyn Ballroom. Struggling through the crowd, we had a tough job getting in, only to be confronted by a temporary dressing-room made of wooden partitions at the side of the dance-floor. Fans were continually banging on the fragile structure, shaking the walls; some climbed on top; the door was torn off. Stu and his new assistant, Spike Palmer, took turns to hold it in place all evening. We took the stage with great difficulty and played well. Again our support group was the Detours, the chrysalis of The Who. The crowd went wild, almost rioting.

Our appearance now put us in the firing line. On January 4 we were driving to Oxford to play a show at the town hall when we stopped off at a service-station to eat breakfast. We sat down in a half-filled room and immediately started to hear sarcastic comments about our hair and dress. Then a few people shouted out. We sat quietly, eating our food. When we had finished we called the waiter over and asked him how many other people were in the restaurant. He said about forty. We ordered one fried egg to be served to everyone in the place. All the people who'd been abusing us suddenly got a single fried egg each put in front of them and were told that it was from us. Suddenly everyone started nodding at us, smiling, saying: "Oh—thanks very much." We paid our bill and walked out, splitting our sides with laughter.

Memories of the Everlys/Bo Diddley tour filled us with excitement at the prospect of our second "package" tour of Britain. These traveling shows, unique to the sixties, featured about eight acts on the road together; each had twenty minutes or so on stage. It was tremendous value for fans and the best way for any act to knock its stage work into shape. And it was competitive. This time we were paired with the Ronettes, a top American girl vocal group (Ronnie Ronette would later marry Phil Spector). We all loved their hit records like "Be My Baby" and "Baby I Love You," both destined to become classics. They were scheduled to head the bill, but a few days before the tour opened at the Granada, Harrow-on-the-Hill on January 6 we were promoted to the top spot. The first half of the show was: the Cheynes, Al Paige (compère), Dave Berry and the Cruisers and the Ronettes; and after the interval came Liverpool's Swinging Blue Jeans, Marty Wilde (the father of Kim) and the Wildcats and then the Stones.

After the gig at Slough Adelphi on January 7, Stu, Mick, Keith, Charlie and I went to London airport for food. It was about one in the morning. We were sitting in the cafeteria which was half empty, eating our meal, when a big American guy, with three or four other guys, about twenty feet away, started yelling insults at us. Mick got up, walked round and challenged him face to face. The guy suddenly swung a punch and hit Mick in the face, knocking him backwards. Keith then jumped up, walked round and challenged the same guy. The guy swung another punch and hit Keith in the face, knocking *him* back. Charlie and I took the hint. We all finished our meals, left, and returned home for the night, much the wiser.

There were plenty of drawbacks like this to touring, and the venues themselves weren't always that great—too big, and with lighting that was too strong. Sometimes I wished we could return to the clubs. But that day, though, there was a sad reminder of our club period with the death of one of the guys whose music at the Marquee Club had inspired the Stones. Cyril Davies, aged a mere thirty-two, died of leukemia. He left a widow and two children.

There was never direct competition in the band for pulling girls. Keith remembered: "The only time I remember Mick and me in any slight competition was with the Ronettes, when Mick wanted to pull Ronnie." We all became friendly. (Nedra, who now lives in Virginia Beach, came to see a 1989 Stones show in Washington, with three of her four children. We reminisced about old times. She had married my DJ friend Scott Ross around 1967 and they are still together.)

The attraction was musical as well as physical. Ronnie commented: "The Beatles were just four guys who stood there with their guitars. The Stones were always different. They were more of a threat. They did gutsy things on stage. The girls took to Mick. He was so sexy, provocative and gorgeous on stage." Mick returned the compliment: "Those Ronettes stopped us dead in our tracks. We were just knocked out by their looks, sense of humor and everything." Ronnie described Keith as "not so much shy as quiet. I could make him laugh but most of the time nothing was funny to him. He was very into himself, in his own room, in his own world; a bit of a softie." Keith joined in: "They do such a tremendous act. It's not just the singing. They twist around and shake like mad. They're all right little darlings. I think all the American groups have a similar styling but the Ronettes have that something extra that puts them above the rest of the crowd."

As always, Brian was the musical purist: "It was really

surprising to find the Ronettes were as good as their records. I don't mean that nastily but you often find there are acts that don't sound a bit like their records when you see them in person. The Ronettes sound so good in real life, Phil Spector must find them real pleasure to work with." Estelle predicted that the Stones could be "really big in the States," which was incredibly exciting news to us.

Although we were all basically attached to women, it was an open secret that there were affairs on the road, with the exception of Charlie, who was completely faithful. But at this time he and Shirley had broken up for a while. After a show at Wimbledon Palais on January 24, in which 3,000 fans gave us a fantastic reception, he and I met two nice models from London. It was foggy and I called Diane to say I couldn't get back that night. We then went back to the models' place in Chelsea and all spent the night in a large double-bed together.

It says a lot about the unsophisticated state of the record industry in 1964 that we seemed to be the last people to receive free copies of our own records. I had to place an order at my Penge record shop for the Stones' debut EP and the debut single by Cleo Sylvester. Entitled *The Rolling Stones,* our EP featured "Bye-Bye Johnny," "Money," "You Better Move On" and "Poison Ivy." It was produced by Impact Sound.* Cleo Sylvester's single, "To Know Him is to Love Him" and "There are but Five Rolling Stones," "was produced by Andrew Loog Oldham." We quickly went back to the studios at Regent Sound for an Andrew production of the Buddy Holly favorite, "Not Fade Away," which would become a hugely popular Stones track over the next twenty years. Andrew commented afterwards: "Although it was a Buddy Holly song, I consider it to be the first song Mick and Keith *wrote*. What made the record was that whole Bo Diddley thing to it. The way they arranged it was the beginning of the shaping of them as songwriters." This was an exag-

---

*This EP got to number fifteen in the singles charts and went to Number One in the EP charts on February 8, 1964. It stayed at Number One for thirteen weeks and remained in the EP charts for over a year.

gerated claim for Mick and Keith by Andrew. Any musician knows that Holly's version had been built on the Bo Diddley beat. I said at that time: "Keith played acoustic guitar, Brian harmonica. The rhythm was formed basically around the Buddy Holly song. We brought the rhythm up and emphasized it. Holly had used that Bo Diddley beat on his version but because he was using only bass, drums and guitar, the rhythm was sort of throw-away. Holly played it very lightly. We just got into it more and put the Bo Diddley beat up front."

Meanwhile life on the road continued. On January 21 we had a gig in Aylesbury and we all planned to meet first in town. Brian left in his car and drove to Cheltenham to see his parents, after we'd done a picture session and interview for the new magazine *Fabulous*, in which Keith Altham recalled his first experience of a Stones one-night stand:

I got aboard the Stones bandwagon bound for Aylesbury, and my illusions of the sweet life were shattered when I saw the inside of the van. They had a mountain of equipment piled at the back. Guitar cases, hold-alls and drums were piled on top of one another to the ceiling. After only fifteen minutes on the road, Keith keeled over in the front seat and slumped into Mick's lap. Bill said: "That often happens. Keith is the Rip Van Winkle in the group. You can't keep him awake, he just flakes clean out and dozes off for a couple of hours." At this point, Charlie turned on the radio and tuned into Luxembourg. Keith woke up in the front long enough to observe "here comes the fog," before he flaked out again. Our speed dropped to 15 m.p.h. and we crept along, following the cat's-eyes. Mick, who was navigating, yelled whenever he caught sight of a rear light in front. Then Mick and Charlie began talking about the old days, to kill time. It sounded quite a life, in snatches. "When we lived on fish and chips for a month . . . only sticks of furniture, a record player . . . we even flogged Stu's bike." Our one-hour trip by now had taken three hours and we were on the outskirts of Aylesbury when Mick shouted as Brian's car loomed out of the fog and began to pass us. Brian was obviously totally lost and heading in the opposite direction. We all yelled out of the windows, but were unheard and he disappeared into the fog.

Brian never reappeared from that foggy sighting but we arrived at Aylesbury and played two concerts without him. The Ronettes arrived five minutes before the end of the show.

A few days after, two fourteen-year-old fans wrote to the manager of the Granada Theatre asking if they could see the dressing-room we had used. Apparently they touched and kissed the door handle. All our parents were by now used to behavior like this from sightseers looking at our houses.

My father: "Fans used to come to our house pinching the milk bottles that Bill might have touched, or picking the grass he might have trodden on! They scraped the cement out of our brick wall as souvenirs of Bill Wyman's house! One girl brought an autograph book for him to sign and in the corner of a page was taped what looked like a small brown twig. When Bill asked what it was, she said it was a tooth from his comb which she'd found outside our house."

Eva Jagger recalled: "Many a young girl would knock at the door. They would come in all weathers and hitch from vast distances. I used to feel responsible, ask them in and make sure their mothers knew where they were. I still get letters not only from adoring fans but from their mothers, too. Mick's a very kind-hearted personality. In fact, all the Stones are. They are never rude to fans."

My mother: "The phone calls were the worst, the insults and the bad language. At three o'clock in the morning, when Bill was away on tour, they wouldn't believe he wasn't in to talk to them. Once, two girls aged about fifteen walked from Oxford to say they'd come to live with Bill! I gave them a meal, talked about Bill to them, then gave them their fares in return for a promise that they'd return to Oxford."

Brian's increasing alienation from the group was perfectly captured in a story which Stu remembered about one venue, Shrewsbury, on our Ronettes tour. "As our van drove into the town, Brian said he wanted to call at a chemist. As soon as he got out of the van Keith turned to us with a wicked grin and said: 'Come on, let's leave him to it.' We went to the theater and there were only a few fans. We got in through the stage door without any trouble. By the time Brian arrived the girls were out in force. They chased him through the streets, tearing the jacket from his back and ripping his shirt. We thought it was hilarious, but Brian didn't see the joke. Brian always felt a little left out of it, but he was left out because of bloody stupidity. He used to do such dumb things, anything to upset people. Then he would get all pathetic and say: 'Nobody loves me. Why is everybody against me?' "

As the van driver, Stu became irritated by fans who stole from the vehicle. At Leicester, everything that could be removed was stolen: number plates, wing mirrors, spotlights, door handles, windscreen wipers. Stu was furious, but we thought it funny; about this he proved just as touchy as Brian!

The fans were canny in working out how to block our exit from the shows. They began to know that the Stones dropped their guitars when the last number ended and ran for it. So the crowds from the first house would hang around until the second house had finished. It became quite a problem.

On January 13, I met everyone at London airport and we took a ninety-minute flight to Glasgow. This was the first time any of the others had flown, and they were all a little nervous. I felt like an old hand, having flown twice in the RAF. It was a great show, with 3,000 fans breaking the attendance record at the city's Barrowlands Ballroom.

Earlier that day we'd cut three demo tracks for Andrew Oldham. On these occasions he would give us a token £2 or £3 each for these sessions. We didn't mind this random payment at the time, since it was good fun and experience. But we were now hearing that Andrew and Eric Easton were beginning to fall out over money matters; this was to remain unresolved for some time. Theirs was a partnership almost certain to turn sour sooner or later, with the young half of the partnership living with Mick and Keith. As a launching pad, Andrew and Eric had been perfectly balanced. But now, as our star was shining and Andrew developed a strong kinship with the band, he began sowing seeds of disgruntlement with the staid older man. Eric was not "hip" or "cool," he would tell us. Mick and Keith may have accepted Andrew's put-down, but I didn't go along with it. Easton never was, nor did he pretend to be, young and trendy.

He had old-fashioned know-how of the music industry and the level we were reaching was possibly something of a surprise to him. However, I never had anything but respect for his fair dealing. He never tried to be "one of us" but got on with his agency work. As an example: a hotel near my home called the Bromley Court was *the* local place to play; they featured big name groups, and the Cliftons had never quite been in that league. But the Stones should have been different, and I always fancied playing there, for personal reasons. When the Stones first signed with Eric we asked him to book us there. Eric asked for £30. "I'm not paying £30 for an *unknown* band!" the booker replied. Three months later they called back, but Eric said the price was now £300. Amazed, Bromley Court said the jump in price was ridiculous, so again Eric didn't do the deal. About six months later the hotel phoned again and Eric said the price was now £800! We never played there. Eric always fought hard for our fees.

This was good old-fashioned agency dealing and Easton was experienced at it. Andrew was more immersed in self-projection, using the band as his alter ego. He was a terrific publicist for us at a time when we needed that drive and image-building. But as 1964 dawned it was obvious to me that things were going amiss between our management team. We'd heard of problems between them for some time but disregarded it. But now Andrew was busy building up other activities as well as co-managing the Stones. He began to see himself as a creative producer and modeled himself on Phil Spector. However, the problems just simmered for another year before finally boiling over.

The publicity about our so-called unkempt appearance made no impact on us privately. Life was too busy to debate it; we just flowed with the tide, traveling from concert to recording session to interview and photo session. There were, though, two aspects of our publicity that rankled with us. The first was that our looks somehow meant we were "unreliable"! As Keith remarked: "Promoters who saw pictures of us used to get the dead needle for no reason. They assumed we weren't capable of putting on a show because we didn't press our pants or comb our hair." This was infuriating since we were always highly professional. Only once, in the twenty-eight-year history of the Stones, did we fail to arrive for an engagement, and that was because we had been misled into thinking that a town called Amble was not far from Liverpool when it is actually twenty-five miles north of Newcastle, on the east coast! We phoned to say Brian was sick.

The second irritation was the theory that we were dirty. Most of us laughed it away, but Brian took it very badly. Long blond hair put him particularly in the hot seat and he wearily repeated to everyone, particularly the press, that he washed it at least once and often twice daily. As Keith verified: "Brian was so compulsive about his hair, we called him Mr. Shampoo. He was extremely sensitive about all that stuff about us having dirty hair. It really upset him."

At our next recording session, on February 4, with Andrew producing and Bill Farley engineering again, there were some surprise guests. We'd become friendly with Phil Spector and attended a star-studded party in his honor thrown by Decca a week earlier; so he continued the friendship by dropping in on our recording. Graham Nash and Allan Clark of the Hollies also came and later Gene Pitney arrived direct from the airport, with duty-free cognac. It was his birthday, and his family custom was that everyone had to drink a whole glass. Pitney played piano while Spector and the Hollies played tambourine and maracas and banged coins on empty bottles. We recorded three songs, "Little by Little," "Can I Get a Witness" and "Now I've Got a Witness," which we invented on the spot. The session then degenerated into silliness, but everybody had a great time cutting "Andrew's Blues" and "Spector and Pitney Came Too"—both of which were very rude.*

We had decided that our next single would be "Not Fade Away," with "Little by Little" on the B-side, to be released two weeks later. Meanwhile, as our EP rose to the top position in the *New Record Mirror* EP chart the

---

*It has always been said that we recorded "Not Fade Away" on this session, with Phil Spector playing maracas. Not true; it was in fact recorded on January 10. Andrew put the rumor around to generate publicity.

Beatles arrived in New York for their first American visit on February 7, to be greeted by 3,000 fans at the airport.

Our third major package tour of Britain began on February 8. The Australian impresario Robert Stigwoods acts dominated the cast: John Leyton, the actor-turned-singer who was to go on to great success in Hollywood films like *Von Ryan's Express, The Great Escape* and *Guns Of Batasi*; singers like Mike Sarne, Billie Davis and "ex-Shadow" Jet Harris. We were the hit of this tour, and the fan scenes around the country were really incredible. As we began, passing through Cheltenham for two shows, Brian's girl Pat Andrews was invited backstage by a friend of the group, but found Linda there with Brian. Once again he told Pat that if she ever needed anything for herself or Julian, she should get in touch with the office.

Later in the tour, as we moved to the blues heartland of Guildford in Surrey, Brian was apologetic in an interview, showing the discomfort under the surface of our stardom: "We are aware of the large R & B following here," he told a local reporter, "but unfortunately the band is moving away from our blues style and doing numbers like 'You Better Move On.' " Even the song title he chose to illustrate his point was prophetic for him. Sometimes Brian could be a pain when we were on the road and staying in provincial hotels where most of the guests went to bed at ten o'clock. Stu usually arranged for a cold meal and waiters to be there for our arrival in the early hours of the morning, but on the nights when he arrived without a girl, Brian often acted the fool. A typical scene was at the Scotch Corner Hotel after our show at Stockton on February 19. Brian walked around the corridors and halls in his underpants making silly noises, later throwing bread rolls around the room and demanding all sorts of food the waiters could not possibly provide at such a late hour. "Once he started," Stu recalled, "the others would join in. I used to get so bleeding embarrassed." It was childish behavior, for sure, but weighed against our image it was pretty harmless. And it certainly didn't compare with the savage stunts of some top rock bands who smashed up hotel rooms for fun in the seventies.

* * *

As the Bachelors' excruciating ballad "Diane" went to Number One in Britain, the Stones had their third British single released, "Not Fade Away" backed by "Little by Little," the writing of which was credited as "Phelge/Spector." Decca, presumably taking the title of the B-side literally, very generously sent us each a single copy of our own record. Reaction to the single was excellent. "A rip-roaring blues treatment with good raucous harmonica," said the *Daily Mail*. "A quivering, pounding, rhythmic opus . . . the backing beat is quite fantastic," said *New Musical Express*. The best response, which really delighted us, came from Jerry Lee Lewis, one of my all-time favorites: " 'Little by Little' sounds just like the Louisiana blues I've been hearing since I was a little kid. They sure do it real well."

In late February we drove to Weymouth to film our new single for *Top of the Pops*. They filmed us on a rocky beach miming away while dressed in hats, coats and scarves—it was freezing cold. They even rolled stones down the cliffs and filmed them. For all this we were paid £73 10s., a fee that we now regarded as small, but one that would have thrilled us only a year earlier, when we were on the breadline. We then drove on to Bournemouth for another stage of the package tour. As we fought our way through fans to get out of the theater, they tried to stop us by putting dustbins and boards around our van.

The incidents of that night were more like fiction than fact. Checking into the White Hart Hotel, Bournemouth, almost everyone had a girl. I asked mine how old she was. "Seventeen," she replied. We went to bed and at one o'clock I was woken up by the manager and the police demanding entry to my room. I asked the girl again how old she was. "Sixteen," she replied. When I finally let them into the room they dragged her out of bed and questioned us. They wanted the identity of the girl I was with. They phoned her parents and were told that she had celebrated her sixteenth birthday a week earlier. I breathed a mighty sigh of relief. After that the whole band met downstairs to hear that the police were looking for a thirteen-year-old who had been reported missing. The heat was off. The hotel manager and his staff were great, providing us all with sandwiches and tea to calm our obviously jangled nerves. There were many apologies and the police left. Just as we were returning to bed one of the blokes traveling with us appeared from the garden, having got rid of the girl who had been with him: the missing thirteen-year-old.

Next day driving to Birmingham the van broke down at Amesbury, Wiltshire: gearbox trouble. It was temporarily repaired in a garage from which we all had to push it out on to the road because the reverse gear could not be repaired. Charlie's dry humor gave us the quote of the day: "It's just as well we don't have to drive to Birmingham backwards!"

As the frequency of our recording sessions increased, Mick and Keith got into their stride as writers. On February 25 we returned to Regent Sound and cut three songs, one of which was Jagger–Richards composed and called "Good Times, Bad Times." By now Brian was definitely showing signs of an increased inferiority complex. Back home in Windsor with Linda, he tried to write songs. Linda remembers "the beam of light that flashed across his face when he wrote something he liked." Writing, she observed, was a comfort to him—"It was like talking to somebody. He was always writing poems and words for songs on little pieces of paper. Obviously, I loved them. They were romantic, sort of spiritual, like Donovan's . . . about his feelings."

But Brian, a victim of his own complexes, did not show his work to the Stones because he was insecure, believing his compositions were too sentimental. Linda added: "I would encourage him to do his own things but he would say, 'They're not finished.' That was his excuse all the time."

While Brian was losing his confidence, Mick's was increasing by the day. He took to stardom like a fish to water, while affecting an air of nonchalance with the press, whom he could disarm so effortlessly with his natural charm. With Brian, his chief threat in the popularity stakes, outflanked, Mick faced no competition. On stage, Mick handled his role as the front-man superbly. Once, at Romford Odeon on February 25, Mick was in the middle of a song when a hysterical teenager rushed toward him from the wings, sobbing, her arms outstretched. Mick ducked quickly, caught her in a fireman's lift and carried her back to the wings over his shoulder, where she was taken away by an attendant. Mick then carried on as if nothing had happened.

Offstage, Mick's clever method of dealing with the gathering publicity was to portray himself as indifferent, whereas in fact he cared very much what was happening to the Stones' popularity. "I still haven't grasped what all this talk of images is about," he told Ray Coleman of *Melody Maker,* who had joined us on tour. "I don't particularly care whether parents hate us or not. They might grow to like us one day. We don't set out to be grizzly. I can tell you this much—my parents like me. Success hasn't changed us; I'm not a chameleon."

The John Leyton tour rolled on and I noticed with amazement two facts about Jet Harris: he consumed a whole crate of light ale in his dressing room every night. And he mimed on stage while Billy Kyle of the Innocents played Jet's parts hidden behind curtains.

Around this time, a girlfriend of Brian's, Dawn Malloy, found herself pregnant by him; she had been Brian's girlfriend for about three months. However the mood in the band was very buoyant.

Wild enthusiasm awaited us at Bradford Gaumont on March 4. "The youngsters stamped, screeched and yelled before leaving their seats in dozens to surge toward the stage, where they remained crushed together like an ecstatic football crowd. From the start of the show until they appeared, there were cries of 'Bring on the Stones,' " a local paper reported. Scenes like this were now becoming the norm.

We were all becoming more fashion-conscious: Charlie, always dapper and noted for his formality (he usually wore a tie), bought a blue suede coat, which was quite daring. That month, too, Keith bought the cap that for some time was his trademark.

We also became quite sociable, contrary to the general theory that we were snubbing society to advance our image. After a show in Nottingham (in which the singer Eden Kane took to the stage in an astonishing white suit and white shoes), we all went to a party at the house of Albert Hand, who was president of the Elvis Presley fan club in England, and also editor of *Pop Weekly.* He'd written some tacky things about us when "Come On" was released, but that night he apologized. It was a good party in another respect: I met a pretty seventeen-year-old student named Helen who lived in Nottingham; she returned to the hotel in Manchester with me for the night and for the next two years she came to many shows and sometimes stayed with me when I was on the road. There were several girls who were more than one-night liaisons; some, like Helen, became good friends who traveled hundreds of miles to catch up with me.

On the last night of the tour at Morecambe on March 7 we all had a lot of fun playing tricks. Brian and I went onstage in overalls and swept the stage while the LeRoys were on. Andrew was outrageous, sticking his bare leg through the curtains and being generally rude to the audience. Jet Harris got drunk and, to a stunned audience, told dirty jokes throughout his set. Billie Davis's poodle walked onstage, peed on the spotlit vocal-mike stand and walked off while Jet was singing.

As "Not Fade Away" went to number five in the *Melody Maker* chart, the word was out that America was getting ready for a visit from us. On the *MM*'s front page, under the heading "Stones for States," Ray Coleman wrote: "They call them the ugliest pop group in Britain, the group parents detest. Their biggest hit, 'Not Fade Away,' has sparked off international interest in the five disheveled young men America wants, and they're off next month. France is bidding for them, and they're in line for a season at the Olympia. Britain's young fans have accepted them. They revel in their rebellious image because while adults hate their scruffiness, young people react predictably to the hate campaign by rallying round them. Three film companies have offered them screen debuts."

Next week, in its issue dated March 14, Coleman continued to discuss our Bad Boy image. Under the famous headline, "Would You Let Your Sister Go With a Rolling Stone?" he said: "They don't wear uniforms, don't need mirrors as they hardly bother with examining themselves before they wander on stage. Hair combing is rare, face make-up unheard of. And they are within striking distance of the big-time."

The message of the headline reverberated round the world as a clarion call to teenagers and a confirmation to adults. "Perfect!" thought Andrew Oldham. No manager could have hoped for such a marketing tool; he immediately set about promoting the Stones as *"Dangerous—It's Official!"* He said that *Melody Maker* had hit the nail on the head; that the Stones, as symbols of the generation gap, were staring them in the face and they should take the spotlight off those cuddly Beatles, so beloved by parents, if they wanted to fall in line with what teenagers *really* wanted!

Seizing on this opportunity to establish us firmly *opposite* the Beatles, Andrew declared: "If parents begin to like the Stones, the teenagers who made that group will begin to feel they're losing them to older people and discard the group. *I've made sure the Stones will not be liked too much by older people.* When they go to the US, if their records go well they'll be a sensation." This was from the guy who had first marched us up to Carnaby Street to put us in suits, tabbed-down shirts and knitted ties! We never sat down and said what we wanted to look like. It just happened: we wanted to dress individually, as we had done to play the clubs in the earliest days.

We were all annoyed when we weren't allowed in pubs, or shops to buy cigarettes, or restaurants told us they were closed—and then people following us would get tables. When we were tired and hungry, that was too much. But hoodlums? Delinquents? The reality for me was having the money at last to buy such things as a convector heater and light-fittings for our home and having firm friends like my old mate Steve Carroll from the Cliftons round for regular evenings. My image might have been shaped, and my life on tour was full of girls, but home life was pretty conventional.

My parents were hurt and my brothers and sisters reassured each other that the fastidious brother they knew was the same person now being propelled to notoriety as a "dirty layabout." I made them laugh at home with a tale of a man with a briefcase and rolled umbrella protesting to other passengers that a dirty urchin like me should be thrown out of a railway carriage.

My mother says: "When he grew his hair for the first time, I said: 'Bill, you look a disgrace.' He said: 'Mum, it's only for about three years, and I'll get a nice car and a nice house, fully furnished, out of it.' "

While three of the Stones at least began to embrace the trappings of stardom, in some ways my life continued much as before. At the end of our third UK tour, when the band split for a short holiday, Diane, Stephen and I went to the Brown Derby Hotel, Lyndhurst, in the New Forest, while Mick and Chrissie went to Paris; Brian drove to Scotland for a few days; and Charlie and Shirley, back together again, went to Gibraltar. While I was on holiday, when cashing a check at Barclays Bank I must have looked conspicuous in my black leather overcoat since I was recognized by a young clerk named Dave Burningham. He and I chatted for half an hour; he invited Diane and me to his house for a small party that night. He was a Stones supporter, and soon we were socializing, swapping records and tapes and exchanging visits. Our close friendship continues to this day.

One of the most extraordinary gigs we played that spring was without Charlie. He and Shirley were still on holiday in Gibraltar, unreachable, and we realized late in the day that for the Chatham show at the Invicta Ballroom on March 15 we would have to find a substitute drummer. Micky Waller,* then playing with Marty Wilde and his Wildcats, accepted the gig for a fee of £16.

It was a terrible night of sleet and pouring rain, but 1,000 fans had been queuing for hours when we arrived. The only way in for us was by sneaking through the back door, then passing across the back of the stage to our dressing-room while the support band were playing. This attempt at a private "prowl" by the Stones didn't go unnoticed by the audience, who went wild when they saw us. Jimmy Page† met us backstage and we chatted awhile, excited at the hot news that we were going to America in June.

---

*Formerly with Cyril Davies' band, Micky Waller had loads of experience, starting with the Fleerekkers, then with Joe Brown and the Bruvvers, before touring with Little Richard, Georgie Fame, Brian Auger's Trinity, John Mayall, the Walker Brothers, Cat Stevens and Jeff Beck.
†At that time, Jimmy Page, who would succeed Eric Clapton in the Yardbirds, was a session guitarist with a big reputation. This meeting was nearly five years before he formed Led Zeppelin.

It was a night of sheer madness. Girls jammed themselves twenty deep all around the stage and stewards struggled throughout the show to prevent them from pulling us down on to the dance-floor. As we played we were bombarded with letters, flowers and sweets. It was a great show; I blew my bass amp completely; and the ballroom manager described it as the wildest night he'd ever seen. Chairs and tables had collapsed in the dense mass of fans and at one time the stage curtains were used in a frenetic tug-of-war between security men and the fans. The local paper reported: "At the end of the deafening, thundering rhythm the fans were left limp, sweating and exhausted. Almost miraculously, no one was injured."

Considering he went on without a rehearsal, Micky played well. When he found out later that we'd been paid £300 for the show, he never stopped moaning about the £16 he'd been given. He was driven home by Brian in his car; he should have counted himself lucky he didn't have petrol money deducted!

A typical day during that year of intense Stones action was March 18. I left home mid-morning, met the boys in London and went to a studio to make tapes for four Radio Luxembourg programs to be broadcast a few weeks later. We cut fourteen tracks for a fee of £240. Being a hoarder, I kept the demonstration disc, and still have it. When we'd finished Stu drove us to Salisbury to play two shows at the city hall. Six students had planned to kidnap us in aid of Rag Week, but were unable to get past the guards around us. By 8:30 the hall was packed with 1,400 fans, but people were still trying to get in at ten. As we began playing, screaming girls massed at the front of the stage, twenty deep.

Our set at Salisbury was pretty well what we played regularly: "Talkin' 'Bout You," "Poison Ivy," "Walkin' the Dog," "Pretty Thing," "Cops and Robbers," "Jaguar and the Thunderbird," "Don't Lie to Me," "I Wanna Be Your Man," "Roll Over Beethoven," "You Better Move On," "Road-Runner," "Route 66" and "Bye-Bye Johnny." We had by now dropped "Come On."

After the first set we rushed off stage and ran for the dressing-room, followed by about thirty girls who had

managed to evade stewards and police. When we returned for the second set, police stood alongside us on
stage. While stewards were busy holding the main mass
of fans from us, a girl got through and leaped on to
Brian, kissing and hugging him until she was dragged
away. A dozen girls fainted and were carried out, and a
few more got through on to the stage. The manager said
we had created the most hysteria of any group at Salisbury, including the Beatles. In the next two years we
were to hear that statement regularly.

Quite an argument followed our appearance. After a
local paper published a front-page article unfavorably
reporting the mayhem, a fan named Susan Jackson wrote
a letter, with 254 signatures, to the paper. "Only a very
small minority of the audience misbehaved," she said. "It
was unbearably hot and this accounts for the number of
faintings."

With crazy scenes at our concerts and an American
visit on the horizon, as well as a British tour for the
autumn, spring of 1964 saw us making news everywhere:
on March 20 *New Musical Express* had our single up two
places to number three, the highest position it was to
reach, our EP fell one spot to twenty-seven, Gene Pitney's
single in which we had an interest, "That Girl Belongs to
Yesterday," rose three places to number ten and the same
song was at number twenty-four in the sheet-music chart,
which was another feature of those years that long since
passed into history. Mick's and Keith's names as songwriters went on to another debut record, this time by
Adrienne Posta.* Called "Shang A Doo Lang," it was
produced by Andrew.

It was gratifying that we had arrived at this level with
no compromise, whatever Brian's misgivings. As Mick
said quite proudly at that time: "We often announce a
song on stage with the name of its writer or performer.
Then the fans come up to us saying they've never heard
of him. Well, that's at least a few more educated people

---

*Adrienne Posta went to the Italia Conti school in Clapham
where she met Steve Marriott, later to find success with the
Small Faces ("Itchycoo Park") and Humble Pie. They formed a
group together called the Moments. Later Adrienne appeared
in such films as *Up the Junction* and *Here We Go Round the
Mulberry Bush*.

in the world." But recognition of our success didn't always extend to the pubs and clubs of my native southeast London. My father: "Bill, Diane, and my wife and I went to a firm's dance and when Bill came with me to the bar to order drinks, the bartender said to him, 'You ought to have this pint tipped over your head.' I was going to let fly but Bill stopped me. I don't know how he stayed calm against such insults, which happened everywhere, from the fish-and-chip shop to people on trains. And we saw only what they faced in Britain!"

Some of the press were hostile too. Maureen Cleave wrote a reactionary article in the London *Evening Standard* on March 21: "This horrible lot are not quite what they seem . . . they've done terrible things to the music scene, set it back, I would say, about eight years. Just when we'd got our pop singers looking all neat, tidy and cheerful, along come the Stones looking like beatniks. They've wrecked the image of the pop singer of the sixties . . . They're a horrible looking bunch, and Mick is indescribable."

Comments by Brian, Mick and Andrew in that same article showed how cleverly they rose to the image created for the Stones. In April 1964, when Brian moved from Linda's home in Windsor to 13 Chester Street, Belgravia, his neighbor was Lady Dartmouth. The move typified his flamboyant enjoyment of life as a pop star at the center of Swinging London.

The reverberations of the "unkempt" Stones reached all our families, often humorously. My father: "I went to the pub in Catford the night after the Stones had been on *Top of the Pops*. As I went to order my drink, one of the five men at the bar said: 'Did you see that dirty, rotten, filthy lot on television last night?' I asked if they'd met any of them. 'Wouldn't want to,' he replied. 'So how do you know they're dirty?' I said. 'They possibly have more baths in a week than you have in your life.' He didn't like this, so I went and sat down.

"A couple of weeks later I returned to the pub. Someone must have told them I was Bill Wyman's father. One of the crowd I'd exchanged words with came over and asked if this was true. When I said yes, he said: 'Would you get me their autographs?' I refused, adding: 'No! You wouldn't want the autographs of that dirty rotten, filthy lot . . .' "

Andrew was of course keen to exaggerate and play up the whole thing: "They don't wash too much and they aren't all that keen on clothes. They don't play nice-mannered music, but raw and masculine. People keep asking me if they're morons."

The stage was now set for a reasonably happy marriage with the media. They were proud of the fact that they'd cast us as yobs. The Stones, secure in the knowledge that we'd gained a career without changing our stance by a jot, went along with what seemed a smooth ride to fame. In 1964 we were too young and naive to realize there would be many bumps ahead.

Police involvement in our concerts was now essential. One of the most bizarre appearances of that spring was on March 21 on the weekend when, in America, the Beatles were paving the way for British pop there by hitting the Number One position with "She Loves You." The day began peacefully enough with Brian driving Charlie and me to a dance at the small Sussex town of East Grinstead. We stopped at a nice pub for lunch and, heading for a gig with about a thousand in the audience in the Whitehall, it should have been a reasonably straightforward night. But we arrived to find special police surrounding the hall and it became clear that it could develop into a big scene. As we pulled up, a few flustered girls crowded round our cars and we signed autographs. We were then hustled through a secret entrance (the fire exit!). So far everything was all right, but it fast developed into another crazy night. Twelve hundred kids jammed the hall and there was simply no room for dancing. Six bouncers fought a lost battle against a horde of screaming girls *on* the stage. There wasn't even room for us to hold our guitars properly and, amid hysterical scenes, Stu gave up trying to get us off the stage. We had originally planned two twenty-five-minute sets but as we found it impossible to leave the stage, we ended up playing one longer set.

The staff struggled to close the curtains, but it was too late: a girl was on stage shrieking, "I touched Brian's shoe!" and another was moaning, "Oh, I kissed him!" The bodies of forty-two girls who had fainted in the stifling heat were passed overhead. Fans had come great distances by special coaches, by cars and scooters. Many had arrived without any thought of how they would get home and either had to hire taxis, thumb lifts or walk. Even so, the police commented on the lack of really unruly behavior after one of the craziest nights of our career.

Next day, on the Isle of Wight, after a wonderful show at the Pavilion at Ryde, we checked into a lovely old-world hotel, discovering that girls had manned each of the hotel's six entrances to accost us on arrival. The hotel owner thought it would be a good idea to advertise in advance that the Stones were staying at her place but she didn't know what she was starting. We were invaded until 5 a.m. Outside his room, Mick turned a corridor and saw a posse of them waiting for him at the other end. Turning to run, he hurtled round the corner straight into a waitress carrying a tray of tea. We had a fine time here, overloaded with female company.

A few days later, as our shows gave us increasing confidence, Mick, Keith, Charlie and Andrew met Penny Valentine of the pop weekly *Disc* in Oldham's office to play the first test pressings of our new album. Her exclusive preview of it described it as "easily the most knockout thing the boys have ever done . . . the excitement in the room grew with each track we heard. Arrangements are fantastic, with tracks building up to a great crash of maraccas, harmonicas, shouting, clapping and whistling . . . this is probably the first time that something of the excitement that the Stones generate on stage has been captured on disc. LP of the month? All I know is that it will take some beating."

The shows continued every day. To Birmingham town hall, where Mick, Keith and Brian leapt around a stage pelted with fluffy toys, love letters, sweets and presents (and where Helen of Nottingham met me backstage). To Kidderminster for two shows which turned out great. Queues for tickets had been forming since 8:20 a.m.

The next evening we played Windsor Ex-Servicemen's Club. There were huge queues when we arrived and we broke the record, with 200 fans turned away.* Returning

---

*The promoter here was Leo Clark, who later became manager of the Birds, Ronnie Wood's first band.

to London we all went to the sixteenth birthday party of
Adrienne Posta, an event destined to shape Mick's future, symbolize the essence of the sixties' mood and also
mark the arrival of a successful girl singer. Here Mick
met Marianne Faithfull for the first time.

With her flowing blonde hair and waif-like personality,
seventeen-year-old Marianne attracted everybody, but she
was a tough catch. She had arrived at the party with her
boyfriend, John Dunbar, who was studying art at Churchill College, Cambridge. The eyes of Mick and Andrew
fell upon her immediately, for different reasons. Andrew
saw her charismatic potential as a pop star, without ever
hearing a note, and told her so during their opening
conversation. Mick vied for her attention for a more
obvious reason, but she was clearly attached to Dunbar.
So Mick "accidentally" spilled champagne down her dress
to make an impression: she would not forget that. Marianne was only at the party because Paul McCartney had
invited Dunbar, who was a friend of his at the time.* At
this stage, Mick was still attached to Chrissie Shrimpton;
his obvious enthusiasm for Marianne had to be put "on
ice."

There was also woman-trouble for Brian. His pre-Stones
problems resurfaced around this time. Pat Andrews and
her child moved back to London from Cheltenham. She
decided that Brian should contribute something toward
bringing up his son, since he could now afford to. Six
times she visited Andrew Oldham's and Eric Easton's
office, but each time she was refused his private address.
The office denied knowing about Brian's promises to
help her.

All the publicity we had been receiving—even the negative stuff—fanned the flames and our live shows built to a
crescendo: at a Club Noreik all-nighter in Tottenham,
London on March 28 (this followed a normal night's gig

---

*Born on December 29, 1946, Marianne Evelyn Faithfull was
the daughter of a university professor of Renaissance studies
and an Austrian former ballet dancer. Marianne met John Dunbar in February 1964. They became engaged at the beginning of
1965 and married in May at Cambridge Register Office. Their
son, Nicholas, was born in November 1965.

at Bletchley) we went onstage at 3 a.m. My friend Doreen Samuels was there and we spent some time together. It was the hottest we had ever known it here; Dave Burningham remembers the occasion because it was the first Stones gig he'd attended since meeting me in Lyndhurst. He wrote in his diary at that time: "We arrived at 2:30 a.m. and the scenes we witnessed were phenomenal. The Club Noreik had hundreds of people pouring out, many with hardly anything on, as the heat inside was unbearable. We pushed our way inside and near to the front. The Stones were performing and it was then that the atmosphere hit us—literally hundreds standing huddled together. The heat and throbbing music! It was more than heat, it was a hot, smelly, sticky, sweaty heat that clung and affected every one of us.

"Then there were the Stones. Mick, covered in sweat, had his shirt off. Bill looked his usual nonplussed self, and they were all playing brilliantly. Not even the heat could spoil that. They came off stage at 4 a.m. precisely. Girls then attached themselves to the band as they left the stage, only to be thrown off stage, into the crowd, by attendants. I left for home with the sound throbbing in my ears."

So much was happening to British pop and to our lives at that point. On Easter Sunday, March 29, Stephen celebrated his second birthday. I had the day off, slept till noon and in the evening Diane and I gave him a little birthday party.

That evening, Brian sat in with The Yardbirds, playing harmonica at the Crawdaddy Club, replacing their singer Keith Relf, who was ill.

That holiday weekend, too, Radio Caroline, Britain's first pirate radio station, began broadcasting from "somewhere in the North Sea." It was to be three years before the government banned the pirate radio ships that proliferated in the North Sea and broadcast illegally to enthusiastic British listeners. But by then they had helped generate a terrific anti-Establishment spirit for pop music, which the BBC could never hope to rival. There was superb music around, and the radio waves captured its vibrancy with that "outlaw" atmosphere that was essential.

On Easter Monday we made a triumphant return to

Guildford for a dance at the Plaza Ballroom. Fans had been queuing from seven in the morning! The crowd were slow and it was obvious they'd originally come to stand and watch rather than get into the atmosphere. Mick had other ideas. We didn't like the crowd much and Mick mocked them. "Now we'd like to do 'Roll Over Beethoven,' that famous number written by the Beatles," he said. The crowd said nothing. "You're thicker than I thought," Mick taunted. "Chuck Berry wrote the number."

As the front rows threw up their autograph books for us to sign, Mick announced the last number as "Bye-Bye Johnny." "I want you all to join in the 'Bye-Bye' chorus and wave your arms." At first, nobody joined in; we stopped playing. "Listen," said Mick, "if you don't join in, we walk off." Everybody joined in. Mods, not noted for getting excited, were jumping all over us and Keith was pulled offstage. He had to be dragged back on by bouncers. We moved out fast after a so-so show, en route to another gig that night at Reading's Olympia Ballroom, to a great reception. As we left Guildford, I noticed men selling big glossy pictures of the Stones—they were doing a roaring trade.

Things were less peaceful at the next day's packed show at Ramsgate's West Cliff Hall. The hall resembled a battlefield and we were glad to be distanced from it. Fortunately the high stage protected us, because more than forty girls and two boys fainted during the show and some fans were treated for cuts from bottles. Unfortunately, whenever there were casualties in an audience our reputation took another dive. "Jeers, Insults, Abuse. But Stones Couldn't Care Less," ran the headline in *Rave* magazine in April 1964. Beneath that, disc jockey Alan Freeman confirmed the mounting campaign against us when he wrote: "Dirty scruffy layabouts, long-haired thugs, that's the kind of talk you get when you mention that wonderful group the Rolling Stones."*

In conversation with Freeman, Brian was characteristically frank and perceptive. "We seem to arouse some sort of personal anxiety in people. They think we are getting away with things they never could. It's a sort of frustra-

---

*In 1988 I presented a framed original of this article to Alan Freeman when he was the subject of TV's *This is Your Life*.

tion. A lot of men would like to wear their hair long but they *daren't*. Mums and Dads say: 'We wouldn't let our kids watch that scruffy lot.' I am one of the few people who is doing what he wants. I took a gamble, forsaking study at university for R & B, and it paid off."

There was a lot of truth in this. Though the sixties was a time of liberation for youth, we jumped several fences very quickly in appearance, behavior and sexuality. It was obvious that we were having a good time and that fact must have irritated thousands of stuffy adults.

There was a letter in *New Musical Express* on April 3 by a girl named Esther Chamberlain, defending us: "The Rolling Stones corrupting teenagers? Ridiculous. I know them personally and they are well-mannered, appreciative of the things done for them. They should be held up as good examples for young people." She certainly did know us personally. Esther Chamberlain used to spend a lot of time writing letters to music papers and to us. She became a drag, pestering me in particular. Backstage at a concert one night there was a letter from her begging for a lock of my hair. I'd had enough of her as a nuisance, so with all the boys looking on I cut off some of my pubic hairs, which Keith and I tied together with cotton. I posted these to her and I never heard from her again.

At Lowestoft on April 6, we had a wild night at the Royal Hotel Ballroom for 1,200 fans, the biggest audience ever at this venue. Later, in the hotel, we had a big party in one of our rooms with lots of local girls and went to bed content. After a couple of hours Brian came to my room saying the girl he was with was a nymphomaniac and had exhausted him. My girl had already left so he sent her in to me and she stayed a couple of hours. She wore me out, too. Brian and I decided in the middle of the night to escape and drive back to town; we didn't want to risk the girl returning! We left for London, arriving back home, shattered, at around 5:30 a.m.

After our shows near London, Brian, Mick and Keith would adjourn to a club, often the Ad Lib in Soho, where pop stars led by the Beatles would hold court over drinks. They would often get to bed at dawn, feeling dead the next day. I had a comparatively sane existence, retiring to my home and family. Typically, on April 8 I was cooked lunch at home by Diane before going into town to meet the boys and driving to Wembley for a show at the Empire Pool that night: the important *Ready Steady Go!* Mod Ball. Organized by the Variety Club of Great Britain, it was televised live. The afternoon was devoted to rehearsals along with all the other acts: Cilla Black, the Fourmost, Freddie and the Dreamers, Kathy Kirby, Billy J. Kramer with the Dakotas, Kenny Lynch, Manfred Mann, the Merseybeats, the Searchers and Sounds Incorporated. The Stones, the Dakotas and the Fourmost had to use the same set of drums because there would be no time to switch them during the show. When we discovered that we had to play on a huge revolving rostrum, Mick stared mournfully at it and said: "They're going to pull us round on that thing? Thousands will be killed and I'll fall off!"

We were instructed to mime to our first song as we walked from backstage through a corridor of security men to the moveable stage which was in the center of the audience of 8,000 fans. The moment we were announced we ran forward into the security corridor. This immediately collapsed. We then had to fight our way to the stage as best we could—while our song played to an empty rostrum! Finally on stage, Keith, pulled off-balance by some girls, disappeared head-first into the crowd; the only parts of him that could be seen in the confusion were his feet waving about. Charlie scrambled on stage with fans clinging on to each of his legs. Mick gave up miming as he was too busy playing tug-of-war with fans. During the rest of our set we were regularly pulled off the stage into the crowd. We had a great time. When we finished playing "High-Heel Sneakers" we were unable to leave the moving rostrum for thirty minutes. Finally we fought our way backstage with the help of a stronger security force. Outside, police fought with Rockers on motorbikes; they were demonstrating against the event, which was billed as a Mod Ball. Thirty people were arrested. None of the other acts had reactions anything like this. Reporting in *Melody Maker*, Ray Coleman wrote: "In mass popularity the Stones are second only to the Beatles. The [Mod Ball] line-up was strong, yet it was the Stones who caused a near-riot."

Yet still our income was only around £200 a week each; our big money from records had not begun. My life as a family man meant I was more frugal than the others in the band with my cash.

A single by the Andrew Oldham Orchestra was released on Decca on April 10—"365 Rolling Stones (One for Every Day of the Year)" backed with "Oh, I Do Like to See Me" on the B-Side. Charlie and I played on both sides of this single. Unfortunately, Andrew failed to realize that this was a leap-year, and that there were 366 days in 1964!

As the Beatles went to the top in both Britain and America with "Can't Buy Me Love," my life and John Lennon's suddenly seemed similar. He had been revealed as the married one of the group, a fact that their manager Brian Epstein had tried to keep secret but had to admit when they left Liverpool and the press caught sight of John's wife Cynthia with their baby son. On April 11 my marriage was revealed, so both top groups were seen to have one family man each. The London *Evening Standard*'s Maureen Cleave wrote: "The married Rolling Stone is Bill Wyman, the one who resembles Charles I. The secret has been miraculously kept since the Stones, who have very long, floppy hair and dress eccentrically to the point of messiness, became known." Miraculously kept secret? We didn't go round telling anyone, but then, nobody asked. There had been no "master plan" to hush it up. If anybody had followed me home each night to Beckenham, they'd have found out quickly of Diane's and Stephen's existence; it was well known throughout the area we lived in. Lennon's marriage made no difference to the Beatles' rising popularity and mine was not going to affect us either.

On April 16, after the mundane act of buying a pair of specially tailored trousers for seven guineas near my home, Stu picked me and then Brian up, and drove by van to Rochdale, Lancashire, for what turned out to be a dramatic opening night of the Cubi-Klub. We were greeted by more than 1,500 rioting fans outside and by about sixty policemen surrounding the place. Inside there were another 1,000 fans waiting. Paddy Jones, the joint owner of the club, said: "We just could not move the crowd from the stage." He added that we'd have been "torn apart" if we'd gone on, and police canceled the show, meeting the car carrying Mick, Keith and Charlie and diverting them to Manchester where we met them once Brian and I had been freed by police after several hours in our dressing-room.

Queues had been forming at the club since 5 p.m., kids coming from all over the northwest. Inside the club, condensation streaming from the walls, excitement was feverish. A thirteen-year-old girl could not be revived and had to be taken to hospital; outside, Rochdale police with dogs struggled to hold back disappointed fans. Scuffles broke out and four youths were arrested. Eggs were thrown and a screwdriver narrowly missed a policeman. The crowd was ten deep outside and children at the front had to be rescued from being trampled. Eventually we reunited in a Manchester hotel and took comfort from the fact that, though we didn't play a note, we were paid our fee of £332 10s.

"The Rolling Stones aren't just a group; they're a way of life." Andrew Oldham's brilliant quote, which encapsulated the philosophy of the band so succinctly, was absolutely true by now, whichever side of the fence you sat. Andrew used that sentence on the sleeve of our debut album, released on March 17, 1964. With no title and no words on the cover (the first time this had been done), it featured a color picture by Nicholas Wright.*

Despite all the hysteria of live performances, we were all tremendously excited by its release. In 1964 the pop scene was dominated by singles; an album was an *event*. The reception for our debut was generally very good, with a few predictable dissidents. Richard Green in the *New Musical Express* called it "fantastic, excellent, the Stones are back with R & B." There were many similar reviews, but some critics had a go. In *Melody Maker* Bob Dawbarn, who disliked us intensely, insisted that the first

---

*The album went straight to Number One in the week of its release and stayed there for twelve weeks. Altogether it remained in the charts for sixty-seven. "Tell Me" was the first Jagger–Richards song released by the Stones. Stu played piano on this and on "Can I Get a Witness," and organ on "Now I've Got a Witness."

Jagger–Richards composition, "Tell Me" showed "the Negroid mask slipping away . . . both tune and lyric are secondhand Liverpool." And Mike Nevard in the *Daily Herald* wrote: "Their singles have a strange appeal but the LP is a stinker." Describing it as "probably the finest first album ever to have been produced by a rock band," Roy Carr, one of the most intense students of the Stones, wrote that Mick and Keith would forever disagree on the making of the record. "Keith insists it was unfinished, some of the tracks being nothing more than demos; Mick argues to the contrary." Carr added that "from the opening high-octane power surge of 'Route 66' right through to the very last cymbal crash on 'Walkin' the Dog,' this album exudes a frenetic primal magnificence and a total commitment to the music that only a band of enthusiastic young activists, dedicated to spreading the word, could ever hope to create." Along with the Beatles, Carr added, we were just about the only group trying seriously to produce an album's worth of potential singles.

Interviewed by music and national press, we realized the album was an important milestone. Andrew called us "five great talents with a great understanding and appreciation of music. Not long-haired members of just another beat group, as some of the public still like to think, even if they're terribly unpunctual for rehearsals or recording sessions."* I told a reporter: "On our first album we cut everything in mono; the band had to record more or less live in the studio, so what was on the record was basically our act, which we played on the ballroom and club circuits. It was really just the show we did onstage, recorded in one take—as it should be!"

Keith said: "We did our early records in a room insulated with little egg cartons. It was a little demo studio, a tiny little back room and it was all done on a two-track Revox. Under these primitive conditions it was easy to make the kind of sound we got on our first album and the early singles, but hard to make a much better one."

---

*I wasn't, although I'd become used to all the other Stones being unreliable in their timekeeping. I was always early for a rehearsal, a recording, a photo session or a meeting. The others could be up to an hour late; but at least in this they were consistent and predictable.

And the touring continued. A show at the Royalty, Chester on April 18 was one of the most bizarre we ever did. It was almost like music hall. At the beginning of the show a Miss Olivia Dunn, seated at a piano on the dance-floor in front of the stage, played a selection of songs. She was followed by a group of sailors who proceeded to announce every song with a small, supposedly funny comment. The one that sticks in my mind is: "And now! The Fish-Fryer's delight! 'Mashed Potatoes' " (a song popular in America at the time). While all this was going on and we were watching in fits of laughter, Olivia remained seated at her piano. In the interval she played again. Then we went onstage and started the first song and the crowd went crazy. They all rushed down the front, trampling poor Miss Dunn and her piano, who disappeared under a mass of bodies, never to be seen again. Once again we were rescued by police and driven away in one of their Land Rovers. When we met up with Stu later, he informed us that to top it all off, the sailor group had nicked one of our amps! (This was recovered by Stu a few days later.)

Stu drove Brian and me back to London. Keith, Charlie and Mick drove back in Mick's car. At 12:30 a.m., while driving through Wolverhampton, Mick was reported to the police by indignant motorists for dangerous driving. Mick was eventually charged with driving his car with no insurance, with no name or address in the registration book and without a license, but the police didn't proceed with the dangerous driving allegations. As we were going to Montreux the next day, I stayed the night at Brian's flat at Chester Street with Doreen Samuels, an arrangement I'd made earlier.

We were disappointed that "Not Fade Away" had only got to number three, and had mixed feelings when we were told that in America, the Crickets' version of the song had been re-released to compete with our version, which had been released there a month earlier than in Britain. At this stage, though we fancied a visit to the States, it was just a pipe-dream. The Beatles had proved that you needed record success before taking your music to American kids. And a politician speaking in Rochdale said: "Our relations with America are bound to deteriorate considerably as soon as the Rolling Stones get there. What sort of picture of British youth will they create across the Atlantic? I'll tell you. A very, very bad one. The Americans will assume that British youth had reached a new low in degradation and it will be thought that this country of ours has finally, irrevocably, gone to the dogs."

Our first visit outside Britain, less dramatic, was nevertheless romantic and eventful. On April 19 Brian and I met up with the boys plus Andrew and Eric at London airport. Joined by singer Kenny Lynch, Patrick Kerr, Cathy McGowan, Michael Aldred and forty *Ready Steady Go!* dancers, we were surrounded by hundreds of fans who eventually waved goodbye from the airport roof as we took off for Geneva on a charter flight. Bernie Winters, the comedian, and his wife were also on the plane; he reminded me later that we threw bread rolls around during the bumpy flight. When we arrived a few girls screamed and tried to get autographs and Mick and Brian talked briefly to the waiting press.

When we boarded a steamer for a five-hour trip down Lake Geneva to Montreux, we all stayed on deck, dumbfounded by the incredible mountain scenery and the mist on the lake. (Andrew ostentatiously played his portable record-player all the way.) Stopping in Lausanne, we went to a café but a curious crowd gathered so we returned to the boat. After we arrived and checked into the Palace Hotel, Patrick, Cathy, Michael, some of the dancers and I went to a small club with soft lights, awful old-fashioned music and people dancing the fox-trot and tango. We requested a Beatles record but they shrugged their shoulders quizzically at our English, so we gave up.

Next day I got up early and looked out at the amazing view of snow-capped mountains, the lake, blossom and sunshine. We then went to the casino where we rehearsed. Trouble came when we arrived back at the casino, ready for the actual filming. The gendarmes calmly told us that we couldn't go in. Hundreds of Swiss teenagers filled the streets around, making it impossible for them to open the doors. We frantically explained that we were *on* the show, but the gendarmes laughed. At last we managed to sneak inside through a back door.

In the evening we did the show, which was the British entry for the International Golden Rose TV Awards. We played live on stage to an audience of about 1,000 Swiss teenagers, but they were *so* square—we were in shock! They had no idea how to react. The Swiss kids were dumbfounded by the English dancers, because the Swiss dance together in lines, not individually, or at least they did then. Everyone said Switzerland would never be the same again.

We returned to the hotel, changed and met downstairs in the cocktail bar. There we celebrated with the dancers and friends. Kenny Lynch went on piano, Brian on guitar and me on double-bass. We played old standards and after a while Eric took over on piano. At around 2:30 a.m. we all went out to a few clubs. When I tried to get into a taxi with a crowd, the driver said: "Non, mademoiselle." Next day, out shopping to buy gifts for Diane and Stephen, I was called mademoiselle several times.

At the airport en route home, Swiss fans asked for our autographs—quite a breakthrough! Charlie, sick with food poisoning, couldn't leave, so Eric and Andrew stayed back with him. We flew from Geneva to London and Keith slept all the way. We were greeted on arrival by the rain, lots of photographers and about 200 screaming fans. Passengers at Heathrow were pushed aside as fans dashed from one customs exit to another trying to get at us. Airport security finally smuggled us out through a side door into waiting cars. Back at Geneva, there was a bonus for the ailing Charlie, who met the great jazz bass-player Charles Mingus at the airport. Shortly after I returned I asked Diane to cut my hair a bit shorter; perhaps I'd been subconsciously affected by being called mademoiselle!

Back in Britain our debut album had replaced the Beatles at the top spot in the LP charts, a position they had held for eleven months. The Beatles' first two albums had sold 1,450,000 in eleven months; the Stones' first album had sold 110,000 in its first week of release. This was our biggest moment since our first real single success with "Not Fade Away."

The social status of the band began to increase too. We

were in the curious position of being admired by "Top People" for our success and disliked by middle-class parents for our appearance (which had contributed to that success). The president of the National Federation of Hairdressers, Mr. Wallace Snowcroft, announced that "A free haircut awaits the next artist or group to be top of the pops. The Rolling Stones are the worst. One of them looks as if he's got a feather duster on his head." What they didn't understand was that all these swipes helped us. Mick and Keith were invited to 11 Downing Street by Caroline Maudling to a cocktail party following Reginald Maudling's Budget. So while Patrick Doncaster in the *Daily Mirror* suggested that "everything seems to be against the Stones . . . [they] are not looked on very kindly by most parents or adults," we were actually watching our career blossom.

When we next met the Beatles, in their dressing-room at Wembley's Empire Pool on April 26 for the *New Musical Express* Pollwinners' Concert, John Lennon congratulated us on our album success. The Beatles and Stones starred in a huge line-up that now reads like a *Who's Who* of sixties pop: Swinging Blue Jeans, Joe Brown and the Bruvvers, Dave Clark Five, Big Dee Irwin, the Shadows, Cliff Richard, Manfred Mann, Brian Poole and the Tremeloes, Billy J. Kramer with the Dakotas, Gerry and the Pacemakers, the Searchers, the Merseybeats and American disc jockey Murray the K. Actor Roger Moore presented the awards.*

The Stones had a wonderful reception from the 10,000 crowd and the Beatles admitted later that the response to our show "freaked them out." Nevertheless, they closed the show to a tremendous ovation. Murray the K taped the concert for his radio show in New York, which helped boost our name in the States. Later that night we did a second performance, with a different all-star bill.

We were saddened to hear of an accident related to our next concert, in Birkenhead. Two fans who had bought tickets for our show had been badly injured in a car accident and had lost limbs. We decided to go to the town early and visit the hospital to cheer them up. Trav-

---

*In 1988 Roger Moore recalled that when the police directed his car away after the concert, he ran over the foot of a fan.

eling to the hospital in Mick's car, he was stopped for speeding; he was now in trouble after the incident earlier that month in Wolverhampton. It was only now that he realized that his new insurance policy was out of order; it had been taken out by his father and did not cover Mick.

But we met the kids and chatted to them and others for some time before driving on to the Majestic Ballroom, packed with 900 fans. Immediately we went on the crowd went crazy. When we played the opening chords of "Not Fade Away," before Mick even began to sing, fans were already on stage. We all dropped our instruments, vaulted Charlie's drums and ran for dear life. Fortunately the police were ready, and herded us into one of their vehicles. Stu was left to retrieve our equipment as best he could. In the charging of the stage Mick had been dragged to the floor, a girl had been taken to hospital with a broken leg and many others were carried out after fainting. The place was teeming with police.

Fame was now hemming all of us in considerably. It was impossible to walk anywhere without being jumped on by fans or pointed at and, because of our reputation as long-haired louts, made fun of. At a London press conference at this time I said: "I used to go out with my friends. Now, if they come round, I'm very seldom there or I'm too tired to go out. In fact, it's very difficult to go out now. My wife has to get things for me and I stay home with my baby son . . . We had a dog once, but we couldn't keep it because I was never at home and he used to bite me when I turned up!"

Because of his asthma, Brian found stage work hard and though he loved fame, the pressure got to him. The unpredictability of his attacks meant he always carried his inhaler with him. The emotional drain of a performance sometimes got him so worked up that he looked dangerously exhausted at the end. Perhaps because of that inner tension and fear of an attack while he played, he promoted the most unsmiling, insolent image of all five of us. This made him even more attractive to the girls.

In May, Keith started going out with Linda Keith, a British model.

Charlie, still bewildered by his success, was busy amassing clothes. His role as the true eccentric of the group was secured. His mother was given fourteen shirts a week to wash. Understandably, Lillian Watts was bemused by her son's involvement in a group with such a dubious reputation. "He's always been a good boy. Never had any police knocking on the door or anything like that. And he's always been terribly kind to old people. He was always a neat dresser. That's why I get perturbed when they're called ugly and dirty. When he's home you can't get him out of the bathroom. People think he's moody. But he's not really. He's just quiet. He hates fuss and gossip."

What endeared Charlie to everyone was his imperturbable, laid-back, non pop-star, friendly approach. "Drums fascinate me," he said. "Don't ask me why I took up drums; I suppose it's just that I like the noise they make." Many people observe that on stage he seems detached from us; that's because music is a form of religion to him and he is totally immersed in it. We are lucky to have him, for the drums are the foundation of our great sound.

Charlie's parents had by 1964 moved to a new house on a Kingsbury council estate. He was never a "show-biz" person: "I don't particularly want to drive, but if I were a millionaire, I'd buy vintage cars just to look at them, because they're beautiful." (Charlie never learnt how to drive, but in 1983 he did buy a very expensive 1930s Lagonda, which he sits in and looks at.)

My own stance was also talked about. I scarcely moved when playing on stage; the static rhythm section of Charlie and me contrasted with the cavorting of Mick, Brian and Keith. I never considered myself in the "performance" league and was content to get the music right. That seems to me to be the true role of a bassist. When people commented, I said simply: "When Charlie moves, I'll move."

Over in America, as our debut album was released under the title *England's Newest Hitmakers—The Rolling Stones*, plans were afoot for our first tour. Impresario Norman Weiss asked a friend, Bob Bonis, to act as our tour manager to take care of these "wise guys with terrible reputations," coming from England. Bonis recalled later: "I said: Come *on*, I wasn't interested in going on

the road anymore." But Weiss persisted, showing Bonis
the famous article from the *Melody Maker*—"Would You
Let Your Sister Marry a Rolling Stone?" Bonis responded:
"That's a great sales pitch," and he agreed to tour with us.

I realized we were well on the way to true international
success when the American tour came on the horizon. At
last, it seemed, we were going to play for people who
really knew our kind of music. Keith said: "We knew it
would be a hard struggle, like starting all over again," and
Brian said that the first night the Stones spent talking
about the trip was like a repetition of when we met
Andrew and realized we had the chance to make something of ourselves. For a pop group in the mid-sixties,
cracking America was the crucial business break; fame at
home in Britain was connected more with personal pride.

The publicity machine now swung into action for the
early build-up in the USA. *Vogue* magazine, with a full-
page photo of Mick by his friend David Bailey, ran an
article saying: "To the inner group in London the new
spectacular is a solemn young man, Mick Jagger, one of
the five Rolling Stones, those singers who will set out to
cross America by bandwagon in June. For the British,
the Stones have a perverse, unsettling sex appeal, with
Jagger out in front of his team-mates. To women, Jagger
looks fascinating, to men, a scare. The Rolling Stones
pushed ahead of the Beatles, perhaps because their message and their music is a shade more gutsy. They are
quite different from the Beatles, and more terrifying.
The effect is sex . . ." Andrew was quoted as saying:
"Pop music is sex and you have to hit them in the face
with it."

As people around us talked about a possible Stones
film, with a script by Lionel Bart, *New Musical Express*
began a series called "1964 Stone Age," with me as the
first subject. Richard Green wrote on May 5: "While
Mick shuffle-shakes about on stage, and Brian thumps a
tambourine for all he's worth, and Keith runs backwards
with his guitar, Bill just stands there and grins through it
all. Holding his guitar so erect that it is almost always
parallel to his body, Bill seems oblivious to the pandemonium breaking out all round him. Even when a gift hurled
by an ecstatic fan hits him on the head, he shows no sign

of noticing it. But that's just the way Bill is. He takes his work as seriously as being a Stone allows. Yet he has a sense of humor that at times breaks out and sends people into fits of laughter. Perhaps the most unexpected thing he ever did was to join the Stones in the first place. If he had told his employers that he would one day be a member of the group whose album would shift the Beatles from the number one spot, they would have laughed at him."

Around the same time I told a reporter that "the screams are all part of it but we really want the fans to listen to the music." This was wishful thinking, really: the riots at our shows continued, the sobbings and the faintings increased. The noise drowning our music got louder. At Bridlington's Spa Royal, called the northeast's finest ballroom, we played to an audience which had been restricted to 3,000 fans, but many more tried to get in. The show was from 8 to 11:45 p.m., and tickets were 6s. 6d., although they were being sold on the black market for £5 10s. It was a complete sell-out. Long after all the tickets had been sold, applications were still flooding in at 450 a day. We did two thirty-minute spots and the crowd was very appreciative.

The *Yorkshire Post* reported that as "the Stones finished their first session, a little blonde girl, lifted on the stage, half fainted, screamed, tears streaming down her face, her body shaking with sobs. She collapsed on me. I shook her and said: 'What's wrong?' She moaned and said: *'I touched him, I touched him.'* The dance finished just before midnight. The relics were still there next morning: the shelters around the harbor full of youngsters, unable to get back home."

One girl was found walking backstage, almost bent double, and confessed she'd been hiding for a long time under a table in a dressing-room. A girl said: "They weren't half as scruffy as I expected, and I enjoyed meeting them. I felt sorry for them, so popular, but they seemed so lonely, shut up in their dressing-room." A boy said: "It was awful in there. No wonder girls fainted. I found I could take my feet off the ground without falling, as we were pressed so tightly together." We rushed from the stage afterward, racing away to Manchester to stay the night at the Queens Hotel.

Mob hysteria had now become a feature of all our concerts. From Bournemouth to Newcastle, from Bradford to Stoke, from Nelson to Folkestone, from Leicester to East Ham, the scenes reached such degrees of madness that it was difficult to get in and out of the venues without being mauled. Anything that had been touched by a Stone was stolen by eager fans seeking mementoes: reporters' pencils, car number plates, door handles, cups. After one particular concert at Bradford, Brian was attacked. The moment we finished our first set at St. George's Hall on May 14, after the maddest reception for some time, we rushed from the stage as usual while the national anthem was being played (it was incongruous that while the audience always stood somberly at this moment, we were fleeing the theater). We all tried to dash the fifteen yards across the road into the hotel, but a large crowd of fans were waiting. Mick and Keith, first out, made it safely, but Charlie and I got stuck and had to return to the dressing-rooms for the interval. Brian, last, was separated from the others and found his way blocked, in front and behind. Girls were leaping on him, one on top of another, and his only choice was to run down the road. He ran in fear of his life, chased by hordes of girls who tore off his jacket, waistcoat, then half his shirt before he managed to return and rush in the hotel door. He patched his wounds, relaxed and had as big a laugh about what happened as we all had. But he was shaken.

The sixties was a great period for impromptu jam sessions as well as mass-hysteria concerts. Stu and I went on May 6 to Eel Pie Island and got onstage and had a jam session, with Jimmy Page and Jeff Beck on guitars, Stu on piano, myself on bass, Stu's friends Wint on drums and Knocker on harmonica. As we had no singer, everyone had a go at singing. I sang three or four songs. Stu said: "Nobody knew we were going, and we had a marvelous evening, just playing the sort of music we all like."

On May 9 we drove to the Astoria, Finsbury Park (later the Rainbow) where the Chuck Berry, Carl Perkins, Nashville Teens package show was playing. We went backstage in the hopes of meeting Chuck Berry but although we passed messages to him he refused to come out and see us. Instead, we watched Carl Perkins do his show backed by the Nashville Teens, which was very good. They had a wonderful piano player. We eventually got in to see Berry briefly, and found he'd been cooking his dinner in there on a portable stove. His attitude toward us was weird, uncommunicative.

This made us very late for that night's show and we roared over to Catford, south London, to play to 1,800 fans. When we arrived chaos surrounded the Savoy Ballroom and it was impossible to get in. The promoters finally made some arrangements and we were led through a private house of an old woman next door, then out into the garden, over the fence and in the back. When we arrived backstage we were greeted by the sight of dozens of girls who had fainted, laid out on the stairs, in the corridors and in all the rooms.

Stu recalled the scenes later: "You couldn't see the bloody ballroom for ambulances. They were carrying girls out one after another. The promoter had let far more people into the hall than it would hold and they were passing out left, right and center. There was this vast great stairway on one side of the building and when we left it was covered in bodies. Just gone. Flaked out. They carried hundreds out that night. It was awful. All fucking Chuck Berry's fault."

My brother Paul: "After the Stones show in Catford I realized how tiring it was for them to perform. I'd been backstage listening to the whole performance. Then we all ran out, got into the van and I began telling them all what a great time I'd had. Suddenly, Bill just went— boom. He was out, with his chin on his chest. Is he dead, I wondered? A heart attack? Someone said I should leave him alone. I was shocked, but half an hour later he woke up and answered the question I had asked before he'd keeled over. *I* didn't even remember the question he was answering. He'd just completely passed out, utterly exhausted."

Bristol was the center of a whole load of problems, for here began the saga of the Hotel Ban. The Establishment had a tough enough job with our long hair and irrever-

ence. At that time hotels let people like us know that
while we might have fame and money, we didn't have
any authority to flout their rules. Bristol, our first major
trouble-spot in the confrontation, was plagued from the
start for our concert at the Colston Hall on May 10.

We were scheduled to play two shows, at 5:30 and
7:45. After lunch at home I was collected by Stu and
Spike. We checked in at the Grand Hotel, waiting for
Mick, Keith and Charlie, who all came in Mick's car
which had been delayed by a puncture. Brian, driving
himself, hadn't arrived by the time we had to leave for
the venue, so we played the first show without him.

It later transpired that he had been held up just outside
Reading by a car crash, which had blocked the road.
When he finally reached the center of Bristol at 7:15 he
had no way of getting safely into the hall, so he headed
for the traffic department of Bristol's central police station. He had some trouble identifying himself, but luckily
he carried a press cutting with his picture on it. He was
taken by police car to the hall, but all the backstage
doors were locked and six attempts to get him through
the front failed. Fans followed the police car, throwing
themselves on to the bonnet. He was eventually more or
less carried in, arriving just before the start of the second
show.

In the second show a girl managed to get on stage and
leap on Mick before attendants dragged her away. As we
played our last song, "I Wanna Be Your Man," two girls
jumped down from seats behind the stage and hurled
themselves at Charlie, whose trousers were torn before
the girls were rugby-tackled by officials and dragged off.
The audience completely drowned our performance.
Brian's father stood backstage smiling with pride and
said: "The idea of the Rolling Stones took a bit of getting
used to. I wanted Brian to go to Cambridge. But now I'm
proud that he stuck to music. These boys are fantastic.
Their musicianship is incredible." The national anthem
was almost drowned by screams as we rushed off stage
straight into the van, which was waiting with the engine
running.* We swept through a mass of fans gathered

---

*Although it now seems hard to believe, at this time the na-
tional anthem was still played after all live performances.

behind the hall. A boy jumping up and down excitedly on the roof of a car was charged by the police.

Brian went back to Cheltenham with his parents, and we stayed the night at the Grand Hotel. Fans mobbed the hotel until 2 a.m., singing, screaming, shouting, scrawling lipstick messages on our van. Some fans were still waiting at breakfast time. At lunchtime the next day we invited several girls to have a drink in the cocktail bar. We then went for lunch in the hotel restaurant but the tail-coated headwaiter refused us permission to eat in there as we had no ties or jackets. He offered to lend us some, but we walked out. This incident was reported extensively in the national press for the next few weeks; the same thing had happened to American singer Chubby Checker there in 1962. Mick explained: "I'm not going to dress up in their clothes. We dress like this, and that's that. I don't see why we were turned out. I have no intention of wearing borrowed clothes to eat in my hotel." Keith said: "We intended to buy lunch for some of our regular fans who always turn up when we're in the west country. We've stayed in plusher hotels than this and there's never been any question of not allowing us into the dining rooms." The headwaiter replied: "I realize the gentleman is a celebrity, but that does not change the position. I would feel compelled to refuse service to anyone, even a king, if he did not dress correctly. It is a strict rule of the hotel." The *Daily Mail* reported: "The final blow came when, after paying their bill, they were refused a drink at the hotel before they left for Bournemouth. They were told that the bar was closed and as they had booked out they were no longer guests and not entitled to drink out of licensing hours."

Finally we ended up in the Bali restaurant in Park Street, where we had a nice lunch of curried prawns and Cokes. It was the first real meal we'd had for twenty-four hours! We created quite a sensation when we arrived at the Bali. There were girls hanging out of windows all the way up the street. But in the *Daily Sketch* a reader wrote: "The criterion for good manners—when in Rome do as the Romans do—seems to have been forgotten by this group of young men. If they did not wish to wear ties on this occasion, they should not have attempted to eat in a restaurant where the majority of people genuinely prefer to dress in a certain way." The outraged writer, Mr. K. E. Fearson, turned out to be Chairman of the Tie Manufacturers Association.

While Eric Easton was in New York organizing our coming tour and signing an eighteen-month agency agreement with the huge General Artists Corporation, we were in the thick of our British popularity. Yet there were still pockets of Britain left to conquer. Scotland came next, and it was wild. We flew to Glasgow on May 18 for a show in the ballroom at the Chantinghall Hotel, Hamilton. Two thousand tickets had been sold a fortnight earlier and the police and the promoter, Ronnie Kirkwood, spoke of special, secret security arrangements. "Luckily," said Kirkwood, "the hotel is surrounded by a wall, which should help police control the crowds." But we arrived at the hotel to find the usual riot going on, caused by hundreds of fans with forged tickets. Extra police were called in from Motherwell and Wishaw and more than 300 kids were treated by ambulancemen. Fire escapes were opened; billowing clouds of steam escaped from the hall as exhausted girls escaped into the fresh air.

Police tried unsuccessfully to keep control. The stage was surrounded by wire fencing, ten feet high. We went on stage at 11:15 to do our fifty-minute spot and ended up playing stripped to the waist, drenched in sweat. The fans tried continually to climb the wire throughout the show. There were fantastic scenes. Dozens of police and bouncers were swept aside as fights broke out inside. Black-market operators had forged at least a thousand tickets. The promoter ordered everyone with real or forged tickets to be allowed in but before long it was so packed that it was impossible to squeeze any more in. Dancers began to faint in the pushing, frantic mass of bodies. Attendants pulled these fans over the wires to safety and carried them to side rooms, then out into the fresh air. After the show there was a traffic jam and bus windows were shattered by bottles and stones. There were fifty policemen and CID officers still standing by at one in the morning.

The *Scottish Daily Mail* reported that "throughout the entire four-hour show police, many of whom had been on duty since the afternoon, patrolled the hotel grounds. Ambulancemen treated cases until after midnight. Several girls were taken to hospital. On the way to and from the dance, fans smashed windows, ripped cords from the roofs of buses and stoned parked cars." Commandant of the ambulances, Gavin Lang, said: "In all my thirty years as an ambulanceman, I have never experienced anything like this. The scenes were incredible." Exhausted promoter Ronnie Kirkwood said: "Pop shows? Never again! The trouble over the Rolling Stones is enough for me. Even if it had not cost me money I would have nothing more to do with beat shows. From now on I'm sticking to jazz. The fans' behavior was indescribable. Some were just like animals. The girls were the worst."

Next day in Hamilton the local organizer announced that the planned visit of the Hollies the following month was canceled. Hamilton magistrates imposed a ban on beat groups a few weeks later.

We then drove to Aberdeen to do two shows at the Capitol Theatre. Theater manager Les Lovell said: "I am not particularly perturbed about the news from Hamilton. We will have adequate staff on duty in Aberdeen to meet any developments." Both houses were sold out. We played to 4,000 fans, but backstage we had a big row with the promoters about our billing. We were the more popular group, but Freddie and the Dreamers insisted on closing the six-act show. We were asked to close the first half, which we finally agreed to do for the sake of peace.

Freddie told reporters: "The Dreamers and I aren't at all happy with these concerts, especially the way they've been advertised in the press. It looks like 'The Rolling Stones and supporting cast.' This isn't the case at all. We are the stars."

We were asked by the management to return on stage for a bow after Freddie's finale. We told them to get lost. After our second show, fans got so frenzied that police advised us to leave for our own safety. When Freddie closed the second house over 300 angry fans staged a sit-down strike, yelling, "We want the Rolling Stones," and it took attendants and police almost an hour to clear them from the theater. We had left earlier and were smuggled out of town in a closed van, transferred to our own transport and driven to a Dundee hotel for the night.

There were similar frenzied scenes when we played at Dundee and Edinburgh. By now Keith, Brian and Charlie were feeling the effects from smallpox vaccinations we'd had on the 12th for the American trip, and they were running high temperatures. A doctor came to the dressing-room and advised them to take things easy. Some chance! We gave him a present of the haggis that had been given to us on our arrival in Edinburgh.

Both Edinburgh shows went well considering the boys were ill. We played to 2,700 fans at each house. Once again, we closed the first half and Freddie closed the second, with fans chanting "We want the Stones."

Our relationships with the originators of blues and rock 'n' roll music should have been excellent. As genuine lovers of their art, we had substantially helped its recognition. Mick said as our popularity zoomed: "I believe that the acceptance of music like ours, the Yardbirds and other R & B groups, has done tremendous good for people like Bo Diddley, Muddy Waters and others like them." It seemed odd to us, therefore, that Chuck Berry continued to treat us with such disdain. As his great record, "No Particular Place to Go," raced up the British charts and he toured the UK, Mick and Charlie had a strange encounter with him—or, rather, a non-encounter. They were in a hotel elevator; the door opened and there stood Chuck Berry. He stepped in, saw the two Stones, turned his back and, when the doors opened again walked out without saying a word.

By contrast, Muddy Waters was as enthusiastic about us as he was about his great protégé and friend Eric Clapton. "They're my boys," Muddy told *Melody Maker* in May 1964. "I like their version of 'I Just Wanna Make Love to You.' "

It was therefore an odd feeling, akin to taking coals to Newcastle, for us to contemplate our American visit. The media there were beginning to whip up advance excitement. "A British singing aggregation which makes the

Beatles look like Bond Street dandies will be on American TV June 13 via the *Hollywood Palace Show*," wrote one New York journalist. "Shaggier, shabbier and uglier than the Beatles, the group recently rolled Ringo and his mates out of the Number One position on the English charts."

Other American writers used the Beatles connection, too: Frank Farrell said: "If you think the Beatles were way out, wait till you gander the Stones, newest and hottest singing group from Britain. They recently topped the Beatles for Number One position on English disc lists. Seedier and shaggier than the Beatles, the Stones have signed for staid London Records, and ABC won out the spirited bidding for their American TV debut, via Hollywood Palace, June 13."

The Toronto *Telegram* wrote on May 26: "Those who think the Beatles caused too much of an uproar when they arrived here had better take to the bomb shelters when the Rolling Stones arrive. They are hard to describe. They don't believe in bathing (it's bad for your health); they wear dirty old clothes, their hair is twice as long as the Beatles' and they never comb it. London Records has invested $85,000 in this quintet."

We were all ready to go!

6

The Selling of a Rebellion

Standing in the wings, waiting for the curtains to part, you get your first real glimpse of all the excitement. Stagehands frantically beat off girls who are trying to wrench back the drapes. The atmosphere is more than electric by now—it's something tangible, like a vast elastic band, ready to snap at any moment. And then we're off. The curtains slowly part. Keith roars into "Talkin' 'Bout You." As our music gains momentum, the kids sway like palm trees in a hurricane. A huge roar swamps our amplifiers. We feel as if we're really in there with the fans. As the excitement mounts, the girls surge down to the footlights and start showering us with gifts—sweets, peanuts and cuddly toys. We're feeling very good. Suddenly it's all over. The curtains close quickly, shutting off the faces behind that ear-splitting roar. Back in the dressing-room, we swallow Cokes to get the sandpaper taste out of our throats. We start to unwind as we wait for the police to arrange our getaway. We always feel a little sad, driving away through the surging throng.

Brian Jones, 1964

We'd walk into some of those places and it was like they had the Battle of the Crimea going on, people gasping, tits hanging out, chicks choking, nurses running around with ambulances. We couldn't hear ourselves. It was impossible to play as a band onstage.

Keith Richards

The anticipation of a trip to America was tremendous for the Stones. With the world now so small, it's hard to recapture the excitement felt by young people in the sixties, when jet travel was new and the States seemed an unreachable goal. The transatlantic visits of pop stars to America and Britain were just beginning.

And we felt we were leaving behind a healthy polarization between adults and kids. The headmaster of a secondary modern school announced: "When most of the boys started sporting Stones' hair-dos, I sent them straight home. I announced that unduly long hair was untidy and likely to be unhygienic. Most of them did get their hair cut but there were six or seven I sent home with a request that their parents get it cut. No parent has protested." Generally, though, it was a time when kids learned to assert themselves and make up their own minds about attitudes and appearances—partly because pop people like us gained notoriety and therefore the right to speak.

Brian, the target of everyone, became the most vociferous on the whole subject. "I know the image of us is that we are hooligans and unwashed layabouts," he said, "but we're all very interested in clothes. I would love to be a fashion designer, but I never will be, of course. On stage we dress like we do because we feel more comfortable. They say we're dirty and scruffy because we've long hair. We've become a figurehead for all the kinds who would like to rebel against authority. We're expressing something they cannot say or do. We have been accused of antagonizing parents. Of course we feel the criticism personally, but we don't worry too much."

While critics were constantly analyzing our appearance, we looked ahead to the US trip. Brian said: "It's people I want to see, not so much the places. I want to meet up with people who have the same ideas on music as we do. I like Bo Diddley and the great Muddy Waters. Muddy's said some really great things about us and has been an idol of ours for a long time. The Ronettes too, lovely girls. At this stage, we don't want to say too much about what we hope for in the Stones. I don't believe in anything good until it happens. Don't forget, we had a lot of disappointment in the early days and it's made me rather cautious. Obviously, we hope we're a success."

Mick: "I'd like to go to the deep south and see some of the blues singers there, but we won't be able to on this trip. On a tour like this, you don't get time. I'll chase up some musicians I've heard about and whose records I collect. To see and hear them work in person will be a big thing for me."

We took particular pride when John Lee Hooker, an

early Stones' hero and influence, appeared on *Ready Steady Go!* Without our success, he and others might not have this kind of recognition. Despite all the controversy surrounding us, we did feel, almost evangelically, that we'd done "our bit" toward educating the British public.

"British pop music is not very original," Brian said. "American pop music is largely the music of the Negroes. They get it first- and secondhand while we get it third or fourth. I don't think British music will have any lasting effect on America because, quite honestly, British pop music is itself a sort of mongrel." Mick agreed with this: "British music has nearly all been inspired by America, though it does have some originality. I think the Beatles have influenced American music, but it's really only American music going over to the Beatles and the Beatles bringing it back to America."

Now we were earning good money in Britain, the thought of making a fortune in America was very attractive. Keith put it baldly, though no doubt with a degree of irony: "All I'm interested in is staying in the business and getting rich."

What counted most, for an unknown act in America, was hype. By the time we boarded the jet for New York the media had ensured that many thousands of citizens were intrigued about what we looked like, what we sounded like and the circumstances of our private lives. On our arrival, there was a special publication called *The Crazy World of England's Rolling Stones.* It reported that the Stones' girlfriends were Chrissie Shrimpton, Linda Keith, Linda Lawrence and Shirley Shepherd, with no mention of Diane.

On July 1, 1964, I went by car to London airport, accompanied that far by Diane and Stephen, en route to America on the Stones' first USA tour. Eric reckoned it would earn us over $100,000. We arrived first, and there were about a hundred screaming girls charging about everywhere. Stephen looked a little alarmed when he saw this. The police did their best to guard and protect us as girls swarmed around. The plan had been to drive us around the back as we arrived, but we got there separately and all of us except Brian were spotted by the fans. Screaming girls surrounded Mick and a policeman tried to guard him. Keith was pulled away from his police guard by girls; finally they got us into a private lounge where we could relax. Mick and I sat on the floor and played toy cars with Stephen.

Stu said: "To get the Stones rolling is simply a matter of bullying, threatening, pleading and bribing. Then getting down on your knees and praying that they'll turn up in time. It was like that throughout the first US tour. It started at London airport, where I died every time our flight number was called, until about five minutes before take-off when the Stones ambled in without a care in the world. All except Charlie, who always managed to arrive on cue, sixty seconds after my nervous breakdown."

We eventually said our goodbyes and flew BOAC flight 505 (Mick and Keith wrote a song two years later unknowingly using this title) direct to New York. Brian, Charlie and I sat together, and Brian and I spent a lot of time in the cockpit. As we landed in New York Brian, asked what he thought of his first glimpse of the city, replied: "It looks like a bigger version of Balham." Arriving at 3:30, we were shocked to find the temperature in the high 80s and 500 screaming fans waiting. What they lacked in numbers they more than made up for in noise, which drowned the jet engines! I was amazed, having thought we were practically unknown in the US, with no hit record.* Fifty policemen tried to hold the screamers back, but they broke through and two fans presented us with carnations from their gardens. One of the boys said: "The natives appear to be friendly. We don't need the beads and trinkets after all."

We were a long time getting through immigration, where we had a health check—something that no other English group had been subjected to. There was also a protracted search for some of our luggage, which seemed to be missing. When it was found we proceeded through customs. Airport workers and passengers obviously couldn't believe their eyes, and there were many cries of "Get your hair cut"; "Where are the razors?" and "Are you the Beatles?" In a large lounge we held our first American conference, presided over by disc jockey Murray the K; the audience included two English sheepdogs, many

---

*Our single "Not Fade Away" was only eighty-eight in the *Cashbox* chart.

high-school-girl magazine editors and fan-clubs presidents. We were presented with bouquets of flowers and presents, and Charlie was given a cake with twenty-two candles for his birthday the following day (although it was in fact his twenty-third birthday). After a series of questions we were finally talked into having photos taken with one of the Old English sheepdogs—pretty corny.

Then we were escorted to five separate limousines; the idea was that we were going to be interviewed by reporters en route to the hotel. Hundreds of fans behind wooden barriers outside screamed and waved signs, then several of the girls broke loose and stampeded through the police cordon and barriers. As the cars slowly moved off police fought to hold the fans back and one girl was almost struck by the leading car. The convoy with police escorts raced across the airfield. Dozens of cars and cabs followed us into the city and some drove alongside, bombarding us with roses, love notes and stuffed animals.

At the Astor Hotel in Times Square there were only four policemen guarding the entrance. They had no hope of controlling the crowd, who swarmed over the cars as we pulled up. Police started pulling us out, saying: "Run! It's every man for himself." In seconds the hotel reception area became an insane asylum. Mick and I made a dash into the lobby, and Hilda Skarfe of *Song Hits* magazine raced after us, followed by about seventy screaming girls, with police close behind. Bellboys dropped their bundles and guests ran for cover as all hell broke loose. We ran into a laundry closet by mistake and were trapped. It was like a scene from a movie! Photographers and police tried to keep the door open for air. Finally the police dragged us through to a waiting, heavily guarded elevator, and we were thrown to the floor, safe. Mick turned to Hilda and solemnly said: "By the way, I don't think we've been formally introduced."

We finally found our four rooms on the third floor. Each room had twin beds and we were sharing: Brian and I in one, Mick and Keith, Stu and Eric, Charlie and Andrew the others. We settled in, had a good laugh about the airport and hotel arrival and relaxed at last. Every time we looked out of our windows into the street there would be screams from the 200 or so fans down below. The hotel then organized security guards who patrolled our corridor day and night.

A little later, we gave a press conference in the hotel, then radio interviews and photo sessions. Brian fooled around, taking photos of the photographers. We tolerated a lot of silly questions again, then fought our way through fans, jumped into cars and were driven to do a radio show hosted by Murray the K. We were on the air live for three hours, talking, joking, asking each other for fags (which freaked everyone out) and reading commercials.

After the show Murray played us a single by the Valentinos (Bobby Womack) called "It's All Over Now," and suggested that we cover it for our next single. We liked it, later recorded it, and it became our first Number One single. After the show Murray the K took us to a New York club called the Peppermint Lounge (where Joey Dee and the Starlighters had made their name around 1961 with "The Peppermint Twist"). We had drinks and watched a very good trio called the Younger Brothers, who did great musical impersonations. They joined us after their set and we chatted for a while. We finally left there, feeling jet-lagged and tired, and returned to our hotel for the night, getting to bed at 1:30.

Next day we experienced our first American breakfast, which included English muffins (uniquely American!).

During these first two days we did a series of press receptions, photo calls and radio and TV shows. By the evening of the second day I was feeling out of sorts and had practically lost my voice. A Dr. Gilbert arrived, diagnosed laryngitis, gave me a painful penicillin injection and a throat spray and charged $25. I stayed back at the hotel on his advice while the rest of the boys went out sightseeing, fighting their way through fans wherever they went.

On Day Three, rising early, we did our packing and checked out of the hotel. Keith discovered he'd lost his passport, which became a problem later. We got through some fans and were taken by limousines to Kennedy Airport for the five-hour flight to Los Angeles. On arrival we again found fans waiting to give us a great welcome. Limousines took us to the Beverly Hilton Hotel where we checked into our four double rooms and settled in. This was the high-life!

In the afternoon we went to the TV studios for rehearsals for the important *Hollywood Palace Show*, with Dean Martin as compère; his kids came over for our autographs. It was odd; we sensed an almost hostile attitude by everyone and we felt we were being treated like a comedy act. In *Teenbeat* magazine Jackie Kallen wrote: "NBC, CBS and Ed Sullivan turned the Stones down. They could appear on the *Hollywood Palace Show* on condition that they would not perform on another TV show for twenty-one days before or after their appearance. Consequently their appearance on a show headed by an alcoholic who takes pride in mentioning how he can drink and hold his liquor, was anything but helpful for their popular image. Besides terrible treatment at the hands of Dean Martin, who vilified and degraded them in a vindictive manner for some reason, their hit record 'Not Fade Away' was cut out completely."

We performed "Not Fade Away," "I Just Want to Make Love to You" and "Tell Me," playing live. Unluckily, Keith broke a string halfway through "Not Fade Away" and had to play the rest of our set like that. The only act on the show that we'd heard of was the Kaye Sisters. Other acts included performing elephants and a trampolinist. It quickly transpired we'd been set up for ritual slaughter by Dean Martin, who seemed inebriated throughout the show. He persistently insulted us on the air to grab cheap laughs, and between songs and commercial breaks he made such jibes as: "Their hair is not long, it's just smaller foreheads and higher eyebrows," and, "Now don't go away, anybody, you wouldn't want to leave me with those Rolling Stones, would you?" Introducing a trampoline artist he said: "That's the father of the Rolling Stones; he's been trying to kill himself ever since."*

Before the show the producer had given us money to "go out and buy uniforms." We said: "We don't wear uniforms." The whole atmosphere was just awful. Dean Martin and our tour manager Bob Bonis began arguing, and Keith was about to pop Martin one with his guitar.

---

*Bob Dylan referred to these comments on the liner notes of one of his early LPs, criticizing Dean Martin for treating us badly.

Stu said at the time: "Unless you've been with the Stones, you would never believe the insults they have to face from prejudiced people just because they have long hair and dress unorthodox. Everybody seems to expect the worst."

Very dejected, we returned to our hotel where we found Joey Paige, the Everly Brothers' bass-player, waiting to show us some of the local clubs on Sunset Strip. I got chatting to a pretty twenty-five-year-old waitress at one of them, and when she got off work she joined me. We got back to the hotel and off to bed late. After the misery of Dean Martin, the night had at least ended well.

Soaking up Hollywood for the first time was a magical experience. Joey Paige and his friend Marshall Lieb (who sang with Phil Spector in the Teddy Bears' song "To Know Him is to Love Him') took us to Malibu Beach for a sunny afternoon, and in the evening we went with Andrew to the RCA recording studios and met Jack Nitzsche, Phil Spector's arranger. Jackie De Shannon and Darlene Love were doing backing vocals on a new record. After dinner and a tour of the clubs on the Strip I met my waitress friend again and she returned to the hotel with me for the night.

On Friday the 5th, back in England the *New Musical Express* still had our album *The Rolling Stones* at Number One. We were on top of the world.

When we tried to leave the hotel the next day we found fans waiting for us at the elevators and in the lobby. This access to the hotel lobby by fans is something American hotels allowed but was not allowed in Europe. Battling past them into a coach, we set off for our first show of the tour, sixty-two miles away at the Swing Auditorium in San Bernardino. On arrival we were cheered by lots of screaming girls running up to the bus; they were tanned and mostly dressed in tight shorts, some with bare feet and bare midriffs. We played eleven songs to an audience of 4,400 who went wild, chucking jelly-babies, autograph books and love letters on stage, and waving banners saying: "We Love the Stones." Local police, with revolvers at their hips, couldn't hold them when they started the inevitable rush forward. Cops climbed up on stage brandishing their night-sticks. The odd girl managed to get through and eventually some got on stage, one grabbing Mick around the waist and pulling him bodily across the stage before three large policemen ripped her off. Keith had a girl hanging around his neck, but managed to keep playing, while Brian almost had his harmonica pushed down his throat. I kept well wide of all this. Mick stormed around the stage with his four maracas, leaping into the air doing his dancing tricks. Police threatened to stop the concert unless the girls stopped storming the stage, which subdued them a bit.

As Keith said, the first gig in San Bernardino was "a gas." They all knew the songs and were all bopping. It was like being back home. "Route 66" mentioned San Bernardino, so everybody was into it. Bob Bonis remembers: "The Stones were very exciting, but at that time they had no monitors. Bill had a Vox bass amp that had two speakers, with one on each side so he could be heard and the boys could lean on him, and Charlie was solid. The whole band moved, except for Bill, a really fine bass player who was like the local lamp post. They were a raw, vibrant, very entertaining group."

After the concert a crowd of about 2,000 surrounded our bus parked at the stage door. The sheriff's office, anticipating what was to follow, had taken the precaution of barricading the area. The riot squad stood behind the wooden barriers and after about fifteen minutes we made a dash for the bus. Then in just a split second I thought, "Oh no, a riot." The barricades splintered under the crush of fans, the cops were swept up in the wave: pandemonium! But somehow they scrambled us on the bus, struggling past tearing hands and screaming girls. The coach was pursued by fans in cars while others ran alongside. We left at high speed for Los Angeles, feeling much happier and like we belonged in America at last.

Woken early on June 6, we left for the airport in limos at 7 a.m. On arrival, we were again greeted by a police cordon holding back the fans. We flew to San Antonio, Texas, stopping off twice on the way. We arrived at lunchtime to find it incredibly hot and only a handful of fans waiting. Our first worries about the American trip had come soon after we arrived. When we heard about some of the shows we were to do, they didn't sound quite the right sort of venues, not being the places where teenage audiences could be expected. Now this worry seemed justified. We drove directly from the airport to play an afternoon show at the state fair in San Antonio. When we arrived most people were watching a rodeo going on nearby.

On the bill with us were George Jones, the great country singer, and singer Bobby Vee. Here we first met Bobby Keys, who was playing sax with Vee's band. Keys was born in Lubbock, Texas (the same town as Buddy Holly) on the same day as Keith, which practically made them bloodbrothers. During the 1970s and 1980s, he played on many tours and sessions with the Stones and other bands. Bobby remembers the period: "The whole Bobby Vee band were dressed in mohair suits, high-rolled collar shirts, silk ties and handmade shoes. At this point in time everybody was dressed alike and we did these little steps. Bobby Vee was *big* then. What was the deal with these English bad boys? They came onstage and they weren't dressed alike! That impressed me more than anything I had seen, apart from the fact that they were singing one of Buddy Holly's songs, 'Not Fade Away.' "

The concert was in the open air and everyone got a poor reception from a mixed crowd of cowboys and kids. We had to go on after some performing monkeys. What the *hell* were we doing here? People didn't know whether to take us seriously or as a joke! We fared only slightly better than the rest. Cowboys jeered at us and Mick told them to go and jump on their horses. We left there feeling very low. Jack Hutton reported in the *Daily Mirror*: "The Stones are being treated as freaks in America. People gasp in amazement when they appear at airports, in hotel lobbies and in the streets. Men have whistled and girls ask, 'Do they wear lipstick and eye make-up and carry purses?' No one takes them seriously."

We returned for the evening show at the San Antonio State Fair, chatting backstage with George Jones and Bobby Vee before doing our set. Bobby Keys: "In the dressing-room I remember saying that all the American groups changed clothes before going onstage. Brian said, 'Well, we can do that.' So, not to be un-American, they switched clothes with each other, which immediately won my heart."

That show was not much better than the afternoon one

as far as the reaction was concerned. We returned to the hotel and got to bed. What had we let ourselves in for? Crowds were great to us at airports and hotels but these two shows set us back years! There was no solace from the press. We were described, fairly typically, by the *Omaha World Herald* as "scruffy, undisciplined, skinny, ugly, and a menace." The next day while we were sunbathing around the hotel pool in a temperature of 95° a young waiter who was serving us drinks said that a guest had complained to the hotel that girls were at the pool, swimming and sunbathing topless—that was us! A little later we were joined by about six *real* girls who were very friendly but extremely naive. One got very excited and tried to pull Brian's hair off, saying she thought it was a wig. A few of us tried pulling them. I took one to our room for a while and fooled around a bit, but gave up when I came up against those American "passion-killers" —tight one-piece clinging elastic knickers, high in the waist and half-way to the knees—almost like corsets. There was no getting them off.

Instead duty called and, full of apprehension, we went to play the afternoon show at the state fair again. Here, Bobby Vee amazed us by going onstage in Bermuda shorts, looking really ridiculous. Bobby Keys: "He could do that—he was the lead vocalist. So I said 'OK, man, if they can do it, shit! So can I.' It was like a show of allegiance. I damn near got fired over that."

On the Monday we all went shopping and sightseeing downtown and asked to be driven through the black quarter of San Antonio, but the drivers said they wouldn't take us—"too dangerous." We visited the Alamo, but didn't go in because of queues of tourists waiting. There seemed to be a lot of bad feeling against the Mexicans here, to put it mildly. We heard on the radio that fifteen Mexicans had been involved in shooting incidents the previous day—mostly on the receiving end; we were amazed to hear that you could just go into a shop and buy any gun you wanted. We didn't believe it, so we went and tried. It was perfectly true, to our astonishment, and I bought a Browning Automatic for $35, but no ammunition. All we had to do was fill in our names and give our addresses as the hotel!

In the evening two local guys took me out to some bars

which all had swing doors and jukeboxes with Sam Cooke and Jimmy Reed records blaring. This was a good taste of the America we'd heard of. Next day, following my example, Charlie and Stu (who had shaved his beard off that day) went out with some local guys in a jeep right into the heart of the country. They drove along a dried-up river bed, looking for rattlesnakes, hoping to use their new weapons. Charlie, a gun enthusiast, was later found wandering in a dazed fashion around a huge armory in a local gunsmith's.

Late in the afternoon we flew first to Dallas and then on to Chicago, arriving at eleven. We stayed at the Water Tower Inn and Brian, always the sentimentalist, quickly sent Linda a postcard of the lake and town.

Next day's first stop in Chicago were interviews on the *Jack Eigen Radio Show*: another series of stupid questions. Afterwards we heard Eigen on the car radio, talking to later guests on his show, making fun of us. A music paper said: "Eigen is one of those humble Americans who self-effacingly plugs himself and his knowledge of the world throughout his entire show, while pretending to do anything but. The Stones didn't play ball with him and, when they'd gone, he couldn't wait to let the prejudice loose. A woman accused the Stones of being dirty and of not combing their hair. Eigen laughed and said that they may have more in their group than they think." (Presumably a reference to fleas.) America, we decided, was going to be just as prejudiced as Britain. The Land of the Free?

Our next move seemed historic to us. We went to a recording session at 2120 South Michigan Avenue, home of the legendary Chess Studios. We set our equipment up and my bass guitar *lead* was plugged into a wall socket, of all things! The engineer there was Ron Malo (who did the recording for most of our idols) and Andrew was producing. It was a milestone event for us to be in an American studio, recording on 4-track. We knew the sound we were getting live in clubs and concerts was not what came across on the records we had cut in England. People were not used to that kind of roughness; a really good, funky American feel was what we were after. We'd known that our best move was to get to America as quickly as possible and record there. The big trouble in

England was that for a rock group the studio acoustics were bad, because you couldn't play loud. When we recorded at Chess, Ron Malo knew exactly what we wanted and got it almost immediately. We felt we were taking part in a little bit of history there. We knew pretty well what numbers we wanted to get in the can and the atmosphere was so marvelous that we got through them in double-quick time. In four hours we cut four tracks: the Valentinos' "It's All Over Now," Muddy Waters' "I Can't be Satisfied" and a jam that we called "Stewed and Keefed" and "Time is on My Side." During the session we were thrilled to be visited by blues guitarist Buddy Guy and songwriter Willie Dixon (who tried to sell us some of his songs).

Thoroughly pleased with ourselves, we went on to do a TV appearance in Chicago, and then a radio show. After that we wanted to visit some of the black music clubs on the south side, but were advised against it because of recent troubles.

Next morning we went to a traffic island in the center of Michigan Avenue, where we proceeded to hold a press conference. This was one of Andrew's brilliant publicity stunts and it worked like a dream. A bunch of shrieking girls and many onlookers caused quite a stir, and traffic began piling up. Soon we were forced to move on by police. We did, however, achieve what we set out to do, and that was to hit the TV news and papers. We moved to the sidewalk just north of the bridge, where we did TV, radio, photos and interviews.

Elated, we then headed for our second recording session at the Chess Studios. On arrival we were helping Stu unload the equipment and instruments from the van when we were flabbergasted to see the great Muddy Waters himself. We were even more shaken when he proceeded to help us carry in our guitars. Stunned, we recorded all afternoon and evening and finished at midnight.

We first cut two tracks: Chuck Berry's "Confessing the Blues" and "Around and Around." Berry himself walked in and stayed a long while, chatting to us about amps and things. "Swing on, gentlemen!" he told us. "You are sounding most well, if I may say so." This was the nicest I can remember him ever being, but then, we were making money for him! I do remember feeling pleased when, while we were recording "Down the Road Apiece," he said to us: "Wow, you guys are really getting it on!"

We then cut another seven tracks: Solomon Burke's "If You Need Me," Tommy Tucker's "High-Heel Sneakers," Howlin' Wolf's "Down in the Bottom," Mick's and Keith's "Empty Heart" and "Tell Me Baby," and a song I started with a bass riff, later called "2120 South Michigan Avenue," which was credited to the band.

Our next concert, the following evening at a ballroom at the Excelsior Fair in Minneapolis, had only been booked a few days earlier, so we faced a tiny audience of about 400. Very few people seemed to have heard of us. Their reaction was very similar to our first ballroom dates in England—curiosity and disbelief. They did, however, warm to us towards the end of our set. We left feeling low again. It was that kind of tour—full of ups and downs.

Keith remembered the difficulties later: "Sometimes there were 600 people in a 15,000-seat hall. That's what stopped us from turning into pop stars then. We had to *work* America and it really got the band together. Some towns you went to on that first tour, they'd look at you with a look that could kill. You could just tell they wanted to beat the shit out of you."

Brian continued to send cards to Linda, the next one of the First National Building in Minneapolis, reading: "How's Pip [the poodle he had bought for her]? Hope he's OK. America's really a gas! I'll soon be home to see you. Love, Brian."

Backstage in the dressing-room we watched the *Hollywood Palace Show,* confirming our fears that Dean Martin's remarks about us were disgusting. They'd cut "Not Fade Away" completely, and only showed forty-five seconds of "I Just Want to Make Love to You," which really disappointed us.* Mick was furious, and immediately phoned Eric Easton, now back in London, and screamed at him for making the booking.

But "Not Fade Away" was up ten spots to sixty-six in *Cashbox* and we had our second single released in the

---

*When we became more popular in America, they re-ran our complete spot many times, cunningly substituting different compères saying favorable things instead. Later Brian became friendly with one of Dean Martin's daughters.

States on Saturday the 13th. It had a color sleeve, something unheard of in England, where color was reserved for EP covers. The tracks were: "Tell Me" (Jagger–Richards) and "I Just Want to Make Love to You" (Dixon).* *Record World* said of it: "This looks like the big one this week. It starts with a slow beat that builds, shifts and then builds again. The singing and off-beat instrumentation will captivate teen listeners."

We flew to Omaha, Nebraska with Andrew. A crowd of about 200 fans greeted us and police escorted us to the press conference. Keith said: "We really felt like a sore pimple in Omaha." We did a local TV show before our concert at the Music Hall in the City Auditorium.

There we ran into problems: these were the days of Scotch and Coke as the pop stars' favorite drink. A cop who looked in the dressing-room and saw a whisky bottle made us pour it, together with all our other drinks, down a sink. We were livid. Keith said: "The thing was, I was only drinking Coca-Cola. I refused to pour mine away thinking, why the fuck was an American cop telling me to pour the national drink down the bog? The cop pulled a gun on me. A very strange scene, a cop ordering me at gunpoint to pour a Coke down the john."

We played to about 1,500 fans, who gave us quite a good reception. Robert McMorris of the *Omaha World Herald* said: "When the Rolling Stones cut loose at their show, many of the audience lost their inhibitions. The sparse but vocal audience was composed mainly of teenage girls who turned into a screaming, jumping mob as they clamored for a closer look at their idols. To us older folks the first Rolling Stone who poked his shaggy head through the curtain was a sight that belonged to a science-fiction movie. The guitar player came out in a kind of crouch. He maintained this stance throughout the concert. He stared at the crowd with furtive, almost hostile eyes. Was this the creature from the black lagoon? He was followed on stage by four seedy, unlikely-looking heroes and the screaming soared to new heights of delirium."

*"Tell Me" got into the twenties in the singles charts in August, and in 1973 was featured in the soundtrack of Martin Scorsese's film, *Mean Streets*.

Brian, the old romantic, sent Linda a postcard of the town at night which said: "I really miss Texas. The weather was so hot and everything was great. I killed a rattlesnake too! *(sic)*. I've got this rattler for you! I'm looking forward to seeing you. Bye, Brian." Another said: "Life is so happy here. I don't want to come back to England ever— except to get you and Pip and Billy. Love, Brian." He also sent his parents a postcard: "Dear Mum and Dad, America's just about the greatest place I've ever seen. We've just been to Atlanta *(sic)*, New York and Chicago. I'm having a fantastic time. If you want to come over I've just got to send you some tickets and you can come over. Really great, sorry I didn't write sooner. Love, Brian."

By Sunday, June 14, en route to Detroit, we were all fed up with the continual sarcastic and rude comments everywhere we went. Maybe as a result we went through a truly bizarre trip in the Chicago airport lounge. Andrew found an airport wheelchair, sat in it with his legs folded under him and was pushed around the lounges. Finally, after asking a man the way to the toilets, Andrew just stood up and walked away.

Detroit's Olympia Stadium seated 13,000, but our audience numbered less than a thousand. The small number was understandable as the show had been promoted for only three days. However, the fans were very enthusiastic, jumping about, and there were quite a few black kids, which was very encouraging. Our set included "Not Fade Away," "I Wanna Be Your Man," "High-Heel Sneakers," and "I'm Alright." It went off very well for us and we were reasonably happy.

A Detroit paper said: "The Stones, often described as scruffy and dirty, will return and predict they'll really be big next time. They haven't quite made it in this city. Their records aren't selling well and DJs only play them occasionally. They said, 'We'll be back and when we come, the people will know about it.' "

We were driven from the stadium to the Holiday Inn where we found dozens of fans. We got in safely and relaxed. A little later Mick, Brian, Keith and Andrew went off to a local party, to which they had been invited by a local journalist. She wrote: "The party was a lively one and the four foreigners fitted in perfectly. The only

difference was the length of their hair and their notice-
ably British accents." Later we all ended up in one of the
rooms with a local DJ called Terry Knight (who later
became the manager of the successful group Grand Funk
Railroad), the journalist, Jackie Kallen, and her friend
Pat Powell (with whom I've kept contact to the present
day). After interviews the hotel staff finally cleared the
hotel of fans at 5 a.m. The hotel manager said: "There
are eleven entrances and we've never had a night like it."
Next day, we had a day off and decided to go over the
Canadian border to Windsor to do some essential promotion. We were stopped by immigration because Keith still
had no passport. We returned, disappointed, to the hotel, only to find it completely swamped by fans. Fighting
our way in, we decided to move to a quieter hotel,
hoping for peace and quiet. Naturally, the fans followed
us.

Jackie Kallen recalled: "My girlfriend and I, with Mick
and Brian, set out the next morning in my '64 Mustang
and headed straight for Belle Isle, where they took turns
trying to drive on the other side of the road. Next we
stopped at Hudsons downtown to shop, and then back to
my house for a home-cooked meal. Everything American
was new and fascinating to them."

Mo Schulman of London Records took Stu, Charlie
and me to a local record store, where we were allowed to
help ourselves to whatever we wanted. I got myself eight
albums; Stu took fifty! It was "like a dream come true,"
he said.

We checked out of the Detroit hotel and traveled by
coach to Pittsburgh, where fantastic news came at the
Carlton Hotel. Eric phoned us from London with the
news that the Stones had been voted the number one
group in England in the *New Musical Express* pop poll.
We were over the moon! On to two TV shows in Pittsburgh, followed by a radio show and a concert at Westview
Park, where 1,300 fans gave us a great reception. Things
were improving. We drove through the night to Cleveland, arrived and had to look around for a motel at which
to stay, as there were no reservations made for us. Finally at 5 a.m., exhausted, we checked into a local hotel
and got to bed.

We were up at 9:30 the next day for a TV show, where

crowds of girl fans were waiting, then on to do two radio shows. At one we were interviewed by Mike Douglas (before he found fame on TV). The studio was swamped by about 200 girls. Staff had to call for police reinforcements to get us out and on to a coach to head for Hershey. We arrived at midnight and checked into a local hotel, where we found complimentary Hershey bars everywhere we looked.

The previous day we'd driven 300 miles to reach Cleveland; we now had a *fifteen-mile flight* to Harrisburg! The reason for this insanity was that there was a big airport reception laid on for us. A small banquet in our honor was held inside the airport buildings. After the show we left by coach and drove directly to New York, arriving at 2:30 a.m.

Back in England on June 19 Marianne Faithfull's debut single, "As Tears Go By," was released. The songwriting was credited to Jagger–Richards–Oldham and marked the start of a link between Marianne and Mick that nobody could then have predicted. Our first album remained top of the *NME* album chart and in the *Record Mirror* pop awards the Stones were Number One male vocal group (British section), and Number Two (world section); Mick was Number One individual group member, and "Not Fade Away" was Number Two best disc.

In New York, after appearing on the *Clay Cole Saturday Show* on TV we played two shows at Carnegie Hall, a matinee and an evening performance. The promoter was Sid Bernstein, famous for first promoting the Beatles in America. The temperature was 92° and nobody, including the police, thought the fans would come early, but when we arrived we were confronted by dozens outside. We were eventually dragged into the stage entrance by the police. The compère, Murray the K, introduced us individually to the audience, which went crazy. Stu said: "I have never heard screaming like it. Girls got up on their seats, and bedlam broke out." Fans rushed forward and many got on stage before being caught. Brian was elated: "I've never seen anything quite like this. It's marvelous, but it scares me a bit at the same time."

After the show the police searched the theater and found fans hiding in phone booths, closets, hallways and rest-rooms. We were kept prisoners in our dressing-room.

During the interval, the Hall management and police met and tried to persuade us to cancel the evening show. We refused, but agreed to go on earlier than originally planned. Extra police were drafted in.

As we were being escorted to the stage a door burst open in a passageway and about fifteen fans leapt out and jumped on us. Police finally pulled them off us.

We got on stage, opening the second show, and had another crazy audience, who poured all over the stage. Fortunately after the show we got out easily and returned to the hotel for the night. It had been a great way of ending what was frankly a very disappointing tour: we all felt just a little bit better, though Mick still said: "We feel we've been given the business here. We would never get involved in this kind of tour again."

The problem with the US visit was that it was premature and ill-conceived. We did not have a big hit to capitalize on. Nor had we been marketed towards teenagers or booked into the right venues, with the exception of San Bernardino and Carnegie Hall. Mick said: "It was really like being a new group trying to break through." And there were the usual aggravations: "Hair questions drove me potty in America. I suppose they've got to start from scratch in a new country where they don't know us, but I got cheesed off with the whole thing." Our tour manager Bob Bonis summed up: "It was a strange tour . . . We'd show up at one place and it would be packed and we couldn't move. Then we'd show up at another and there were only 300 kids there. Everywhere they went, people would say, 'Oh, there go the Beatles.' "

Lillian Roxon, the Queen of American rock writers, put it beautifully later: "Even at the early, early stage they did their own thing. And their thing was the full slummy English lout barrow-boy gutter-rat routine. Mean, moody and magnificent. While the Beatles looked as if they had been personally scrubbed down by Brian Epstein himself, the Rolling Stones looked as if they had been sent to bed every night for a week with the same clothes on and no supper. The Beatles' songs had been rinsed and hung out to dry. The Stones had never seen soap and water. And where the adorable little wind-up Beatle mop-tops wanted no more than to hold a hand, the hateful rasping Stones were bent on rape, pillage and plunder. No one had ever seen a white man move on stage the way Jagger moved. Later, like Elvis, whom he completely overshadowed, he was to become the prototype for stage sexuality, the most imitated singer in rock."

We spent our final day in New York in the Park Sheraton Hotel, with fans everywhere. The phones never stopped ringing. We finally left the hotel and flew overnight to London.

We landed at London airport at 7:30 a.m. on June 22. The aircrew said we had to leave the plane last because of waiting fans. We saw hundreds of screaming fans lining barriers, the police holding them back. In the customs hall, police cleared a passageway for the other passengers and, while they were fighting off dozens of girls, we slipped out of a side door into a conference room. Within seconds, fifty fans had got wind of us slipping away, and went screaming off in all directions. Police helmets were rolling all over the place.

We then did a press conference with a TV crew and lots of photographs and reporters after which, with the protection of the iron fences, we left for home in a variety of cars. Andrew's driver and Chrissie Shrimpton—having taken the day off from her job at Radio Caroline where she now worked—arrived in Andrew's new Chevrolet. I got home and relaxed for the rest of the day, but there was no real rest-time. In the evening, for the Commemoration Ball at Magdalen College, Oxford, Stones fans had started to gather outside the college lodge about three hours before we arrived. By 9:30 there were about a hundred waiting. People going to the ball had to force their way through the girls chanting, "We want the Stones." Police moved in and they started chanting, "We love you, policemen." We slipped in in odd cars. When fans saw Mick after he'd got inside, they climbed up the railings and screamed their heads off. They expected us to play three sets of forty-five minutes each but, exhausted, we settled on two sets. My friend Doreen Samuels was there to see me and we spent a lot of time together walking in the grounds.

We had the next day off, thank God, and I was so tired that I stayed in bed until late afternoon. Diane told me that we could get a modern flat in Penge for £7 per week, which was expensive for that area. However, we went to view it, at 9 Kenilworth Court, over a garage and opposite Beckenham Grammar School. With two bedrooms, bathroom, lounge and kitchen, it was appealing and we decided to go for it. Meanwhile, Mick and Keith had decided to leave the flat in Mapesbury Road (where Andrew was still living) and move into 10a Holly Hill, in Hampstead. It was a period of change.

On June 24 I went to the Waldorf Hotel for lunch with Eric, Andrew, the rest of the boys and a solicitor, where we discussed making the Rolling Stones a limited company as soon as possible. I also spoke to the solicitor about changing my name to Wyman by deed poll. I formalized the name the world was now using less than two weeks later.

On the morning of June 25, we heard that we definitely had the new flat. It was no palace, but a major jump forward. It was the first place I ever lived in that had a bathroom, hot running water and a toilet inside.

As Roy Orbison's "It's Over" went to the top in Britain that weekend, the Stones had their fourth single released in the UK. The titles, recorded earlier in the month in Chicago, coupled the Womacks', "It's All Over Now" with Mick and Keith's "Good Times, Bad Times."* Response to this record, which has since become one of our most lasting hits, was puzzlement in some quarters. In *New Musical Express* Roy Carr said: " 'It's All Over Now' by the Valentinos is an extremely difficult record to try and cover, let alone surpass. To their credit, the Stones chose to approach it from an entirely different angle and, by doing so, revealed they had the kind of charismatic style their competitors sadly lacked." But Robert Bickford in the *Daily Mail* thought we had gone country: " 'It's All Over Now' is a happy canter in the country style, which is going to cause some soul-searching among the fans. Whatever happened to that rough raucous R & B?"

Mick explained: "We never thought about it, we just played. I suppose it is a bit hicky. We certainly haven't gone off R & B. We play the way we feel. If it comes out country-sounding, well it comes out that way." I agreed

---

*Two weeks after its release it became our first Number One single in Europe.

with him: "We like the sound of it. We didn't think it
sounded C & W until we read it somewhere. I think it's
the twelve-string guitar and harmonizing that do it. The
style is not a sudden change. Every one of our records
has been different. We don't want to do the same old
thing every time, or people would get fed up with it."

But the first chink of Brian's dissatisfaction with our
musical route came when he said: "I'm not too keen on
the record. It's all right, but I just don't know. There's
just *something . . .*" He was obviously feeling restless
after the US visit: "I'm keen to get back to America, and
I plan to fly to New York this week, when we begin our
holiday. I have friends in the music-publishing business. I
might even do some demo discs if I get the chance. I
know we didn't go well everywhere we appeared, but
that was because we played a lot of the smaller places
where nobody had heard of us. America was terrific
though. I'd love to live there. It's just the place for me,
particularly New York."

One of the most important pop shows on TV in the
sixties was *Juke Box Jury*, featuring four personality
panelists listening to new record releases and giving their
opinions, predicting "hit" or "miss" for each single. The
chairman was David Jacobs. The Stones were among the
few groups booked to occupy the whole panel; we went
to Shepherds Bush to "take over" and pre-record the
show on June 27.

We arrived in a security van. A mass of fans smashed
their way through the police cordons and ran forward,
but we got in safely. The BBC had planned to film our
arrival, but this went haywire when the van went in the
wrong entrance. Fans had started queuing at 10 a.m. and
by 7 p.m., when we arrived, there were hundreds outside. Nearly 10,000 applications for studio-audience tickets were received! We met David Jacobs in the dressing-room area, but he reacted very coolly, a bit snobby
and rather conceited, and not really very friendly—a
typical BBC type, and rather insulting as the BBC was
expecting a record 20 million viewers for this show, instead of the usual 12 million.

On the show it was very hard to give five different
opinions on new records, as our tastes in music were very

similar. Once one of us had expressed an opinion there was very little else for the others to add so there was too much confirmation of what had already been said. We enjoyed it, but there were to be a lot of repercussions later in the media. Our fee was £157 10s.

After the show, half the audience wouldn't leave and stayed behind in the studio, hoping to grab us. Waiting in a private room for the moment to escape, we were besieged for over an hour before we could get out. Eventually we were driven out to tele-record *Top of the Pops*. When we arrived, with fans everywhere, we all burrowed down in the bottom of the Chevrolet as best we could.

Since returning from America it had been an exhausting, exhilarating period. We were all drained and, as Mick put it, "Home is where you finish up between tours." Now, it was holiday time. Mick and Charlie were off to Ibiza together with Chrissie and Shirley, but when they all arrived at London airport Charlie discovered he had forgotten his passport. He and Mick rushed back to Kingsbury for it, but they missed the flight. The girls flew out alone, and Mick and Charlie caught the next flight. As soon as they touched down they were recognized by scores of fans as they made their way to the Palmyra Hotel. Keith had been planning to go, but his girlfriend Linda Keith had had a car accident, and they had to cancel.

It was a time for some of us to get our private lives organized after being so frantic. Brian had just moved out of his £42-a-week flat at 13 Chester Street* and I was concerned with the trivia of domestic life: getting the carpets and linoleum fitted, and gas put into our new home. On July 7 we finally moved in. A few weeks later I went round to the old flat and cleared up. I was burning rubbish in the fireplace and accidentally set the chimney on fire. In no time, the fire-engines and police were round. When the fire was out, two policemen came with me to the new flat to take a statement. Ever since I'd moved, I'd had the gun that I'd bought in America just lying on the sideboard. There was no ammunition, so it was harmless—in fact, I'd forgotten it was there, but a

---

*Another pop group, the Pretty Things, with Dick Taylor on bass guitar, moved in.

policeman noticed it and asked me if I had a gun license.
I explained how I came to have it and they asked how I'd
got it into the country. I said that I'd just packed it in my
suitcase. They said that it was a prison offense to have a
gun without a license, but if I decided to let them hand it
in at the local police station, nothing more would be said
about the incident. I agreed.

A week later Charlie also moved, leaving his parents'
council house in Kingsbury and moving into 143 Ivor
Court, Gloucester Place (the same block as Andrew's
office). He and I played a game around this time, testing
out the plush hotels that were supposed to frown on us as
dirty layabouts. I sat in the lounge of the Hilton for ten
minutes waiting for him, and nobody ejected me.

Meanwhile, as our company Rolling Stones Limited
was incorporated on July 1, reports were coming back
from the States that showed things swinging in our favor
after the disappointing tour. "Well," said a writer, "the
Rolling Stones have left America and I don't blame them
if they hate this country. Their first TV performance
lasted not more than a minute and five seconds, after
which Dean Martin was rude to them." The writer urged
us to return to our many fans there. A record dealer in
Birmingham, Alabama sent us the news that our tour had
worked commercially:"We'd been aware," he said, "that
the Stones were the hottest property next to the Beatles.
But the demand for their debut album is exceptional. It
looks as if nothing can stand in the way of the biggest
smash in music history. There hasn't been so much action
since Elvis." But London Records, our American label,
was disappointed with the slow sales of "Not Fade Away,"
and was pinning great hopes on our new single release,
"Tell Me," instead.

There was however, also a small Establishment backlash: Carnegie Hall banned all rock 'n' roll from its
aristocratic stage as a direct result of riots by Stones fans.

By now there were also repercussions from our *Juke
Box Jury* appearance. It was a family-entertainment show,
and if a national television show can be said to have been
the first to polarize the nation on the "loutishness" of the
Stones, this was it. I did not think we had been great, but
the records chosen for us didn't inspire much debate. But
a week later, when it aired, the press blasted us. In the

Daily Sketch, Fergus Cashin wrote: "I report with no regret the death of a sacred cow on TV. A group of neanderthal young men who call themselves the Rolling Stones sat in judgement as the jury men. It was a mockery of a trial as the gum-chewing, ill-mannered, ill-humored, illiberal and illogical jurors indicated their pleasure or displeasure by catarrhal grunts that an ear, trained in the illiterate school of young people, could sometimes distinguish as, 'Well, yeah er, I, er, mean, like, well it's, ha-ha, awful then. Naw, definitely not, in'it?' " The *Daily Mail* put it more succinctly: "The Rolling Stones scandalized millions of parents by their *Juke Box Jury* appearance." Even the music papers went for us. *New Musical Express* said: "The Rolling Stones' appearance on *Juke Box Jury* was an utter disgrace," and a fan in the same paper wrote: "Never in the course of human history has so much drivel been spouted by so few in front of so many." Another fan responded: "Never in the course of *Juke Box Jury* has so much drivel been played to the panel in front of so many."

"All right," said Keith later, "so it wasn't a knockout! I think the whole program's very limited. We weren't great, and that's a fact, but the records they played us—horrible! It was an experience I personally would rather forget." I said to a reporter at the time: "People knew what to expect when they invited us on to the show. They didn't want a sophisticated panel and they didn't get one. They got what they wanted. If some of the viewers didn't like it, they should have switched off."

Fortunately the show's producer, Barry Langford, came to our defense: "I feel that more than a little of the criticism which has been leveled against the Rolling Stones' *Juke Box Jury* appearance is unjust. It has been suggested that they slated everything, but before they went on I gave them instructions to be completely honest and frank. They said, for instance, that they acknowledged Elvis is the greatest ever but that they didn't like his present choice of material. Valid comment, surely. And it's significant that all their votes, hits and misses, have subsequently been proved right."

We received an avalanche of letters, most supporting our outspoken verdicts on the records and taking our side in what was now developing into a war with national journalists. What happened is that the people who hated us were given evidence of our slightly sullen posture in their living rooms, where we hadn't been invited! We didn't act a part, but we were ourselves. Slightly cocky with success, maybe, but honest, too. For Andrew Oldham all this was another card falling into place. He revelled in the publicity against us, knowing that it could only line up the young fans on our side. While this controversy built up money was still not exactly pouring in: our pay for this week of glory was £90 19s. 4d! Andrew sent me a congratulations telegram for our single reaching the top; on the night of the big news I wrote back to eight fans; a hobby which was to continue.

Over in Ibiza Mick had been "discovered" by journalists. "We are wondering whether to abandon our holiday," he said. "We wish we hadn't come. We've been forced to spend most of our time trapped in our hotel. We planned a holiday away from it all, where we could have some peace and quiet and continental food. The first meal they gave us here was roast beef and veg." Shirley Shepherd, who was particularly keen to be unrecognized throughout the holiday, said: "I expect I'll be expelled from art college when I get home. There are still a few weeks of school left, but I had hoped nobody would know I was here."

On hearing the news of our first chart-topper, Mick said: "I don't care a damn if our new record has reached Number One. I reckon it will do half a million in this country and others. What's it matter anyway? Now it's reached the top it's great, but none of us have been worried about it." Mick was just being modest. With our single and album at Number One in most charts, and *Fabulous* magazine devoting twenty pages to us in a special Stones edition, it was impossible to walk away from the newly commercial status of the group.

But *still* the controversy about our appearance surrounded nearly every concert. One of the strangest events was at Bridlington on July 11. The town's entertainment authorities decreed that a ticket alone would not get people inside the hall for our show. The management of the Spa Royal Hall made a statement: "The management reserve the right to refuse permission to anyone not wearing orthodox dress. Jeans and leather jackets will be barred." Fans would have to be clean, too. Those who arrived looking grubby would first be shown to the hall's washroom; if they still failed the test after a clean-up, they would be banned! "The Rolling Stones are very clean, intelligent lads," Bridlington's deputy entertainments manager Ron Smith told the *Daily Mirror*. "But some of the fans who like to dress in the same fashion seem to think they have to be dirty, too." The rules applied to girls as well as boys, he said. The "clean-fans-only" show began with fifty being turned away from the door. Some girls tried it on, by wearing jeans and carrying skirts in their bags. They were taken to the cloakroom to change. Once inside a hundred girls took up positions at the front of the stage and remained there all night. The place was full, with a crowd of 3,000, and when we took the stage there was mass hysteria. Fans rushed on to the dance floor with chairs, which they stood on to get a better view. There were worries that they would be injured in the crush; appeals were made to no avail. Some girls climbed on to boys' shoulders. It was almost impossible for us to hear the music through their screaming. We were a bit stiff after our lay-off, but soon got back into it, playing for thirty-five minutes to a great reception. Brian used his pear-shaped Vox guitar for the first time.

Next night at Leeds' Queens Hall, we were due to play two thirty-minute shows on a revolving stage in the middle of the audience. This was a petrifying prospect. About forty police were on duty and a mass of strong-armed attendants tried to make a way through for us, but fans gave us a rough passage. We had a great reception; our concert repertoire at this juncture was: "Walking the Dog," "High-Heel Sneakers," "You Can Make it If You Try," "Not Fade Away," "Can I Get a Witness," "I Just Wanna Make Love to You" and "It's All Over Now."

Mick had his shirt torn and I had a waistcoat split by fans grabbing at us as we left the stage; in the dressing-room afterwards there was a scene typical of some of the girls who managed to break through the security and reach us. They wanted to have pictures taken of themselves with us, so Keith and I broke off from playing snooker to stand in a huddle with everybody for the photo to be taken. Mick told them about his new flat; he described it as having fitted carpets, a kitchen with a fridge, a cocktail cabinet, a phone and a maid, plus two bedrooms with two double-beds. One of the girls asked: "Is it rude to ask why?" Mick answered: "For the birds, but you're good girls, aren't you?" She said: "Good at what?" Mick: "You wouldn't get into a double-bed, would you?" She didn't reply. The girls asked our address and Keith gave Andrew's office, saying we'd receive mail there, "because nobody writes to Andrew." "Send a stamped, addressed envelope and we'll reply," he added.

At the end of the second show we again had to run the gamut of the fans to our dressing-room. As Stu recalled: "We had it all worked out, with a gang of bouncers all around the four of them. Brian was fucking about on stage half asleep, and me picking up instruments. Then Brian realized the other four had gone, panicked and said: '*Do* something.' Within seconds the kids realized he was still there and ka-pow! Brian was destroyed again." Finally, he caught us up and Stu drove him and me to London, arriving at dawn, while Mick, Keith and Charlie went in Mick's Ford Zephyr—in which, by day, Keith was having driving lessons.

The events of mid-1964 combined a spiraling career pattern with changes that affected our lifestyle. It sounds contradictory, but because we hadn't been working regularly, I wasn't sleeping! I wasn't used to doing nothing and preferred getting to bed in the early hours. Now, I kept waking at 3 a.m. One day, rising at 5:40, I went for a long walk around the streets. Diane could not understand this; she was used to my lying in until noon. But I was looking forward to the national tour which was planned.

Everywhere we turned, the news was promising. Stu arrived one day in a flash Jaguar, the first band member to have a new car, and drove Stephen and me uptown. We went to the Dallas factory and exchanged my old Framus Star bass for a new one before moving on to the office. There Eric Easton gave us the wonderful news that we were topping the bill at the fourth National Jazz and Blues Festival at Richmond on August 7. They'd even changed the name, adding "and Blues' because of our reception the previous year and to enable them to book more popular groups, for commercial reasons. We were to get 50 per cent of the receipts, which could be as much as £2,500, said Eric, compared with the £30 we received in 1963, and we'd be billed as "A triumphant return for the conquering heroes."

Elsewhere, there was plenty of activity. At the London première of the Beatles' film *A Hard Day's Night*, there were scuffles between Beatles and Stones fans; at one stage there was an open fight between girls scratching and pulling each other's hair. After, the Beatles had a celebration party at the Dorchester Hotel, which Brian and Keith attended, uninvited and casually dressed. They were welcomed with champagne by the Beatles. The Stones and Beatles were receiving an average of 300 fan letters a day at this time.

"When fans really start raving, they seem almost like enemies," Brian said. "You know in your heart that all they're trying to do is to make contact, to touch you or talk to you. But what it seems is that thousands of kids are trying to tear you apart, to throw things at you, to knock you over. This drives us into ourselves, so that the only people we talk to properly are the other people in the group."

No sooner had Brian said this than big trouble began surrounding our concerts. On July 18 hundreds of fans jammed the streets around the West End of London and there were police everywhere when we played the Beat City Club in Oxford Street. Inside, the heat was terrible. Tom Jones and his band, relatively unknown at that time, were our support group; he later reminded me that the temperature was so high that stewards were throwing buckets of water over both him and us during our respective performances. We played a forty-five minute spot to an audience of 600; sixty fainting girls had to be carried out—10 per cent of the audience! We left the stage utterly soaked in sweat. This remarkable gig was co-promoted by our old friend Alexis Korner, and our fee was excellent: £500.

Blackpool was something else. It was a Scots holiday weekend. The sweltering ballroom was packed with sweating Glaswegians, many of them drunk. Despite a heavy force of security men and policemen—who were not allowed inside the hall and stayed backstage out of sight—there was an atmosphere of impending violence from the moment we took the stage. We began with our usual show, but Brian seemed to enjoy teasing the more demonstrative members of the crowd near the stage. Roy Carr, a musician who preceded us on stage and who later wrote for *New Musical Express,* asserts that Brian had been attempting to upstage Mick's theatricality. "Someone at the very front of the stage suddenly took exception to Brian's effete posturing," says Roy. "So did his cronies. As Brian nervously bounced closer to the edge of the stage, this gang of sodden louts began a contest to see which one of them could spit on the Stone. Not one of them missed their target."

Keith was livid. He moved over to where Brian was being abused and gave the ringleader a warning between songs. Minutes later, Keith was spat on. Outraged, he retaliated by jamming the heel of his boot down on the knuckles of the spitting troublemaker who had been leaning with his hands and chin resting on the lip of the stage. Nor did he end it there; after taking one step backwards, he plunged the toe of his boot into the lout's nose.

In the ensuing riot, we would have been slaughtered if the stage hadn't been about six feet high. Stu recalled later: "It was very nearly the date on my gravestone. There were no cops, no bouncers, just a couple of old retainers in uniform at each corner of the stage. They had only one final number to do at the end of the second set and I thought: 'They'll be off, if they're lucky.' Then one guy in the front spat at Keith, and Keith kicked him in the head. And that was it. Good night. The whole place erupted. Keith still thought he was God and that he could kick one of these guys and get away with it. The rest of the band had already turned, realizing they'd got to get off the stage. I pushed Keith and said: 'For fuck's sake get out of here while you're still alive.' And I went off as well."

We were smuggled out of the building over a roof and guided to a back door, where a police van was waiting and they drove us away quickly to the station, where our own car picked us up. But for the police, one of us would almost certainly have been killed. There was a lull in the ballroom for a few seconds when it was thought we would return, then the riot started in earnest. The angry mob of teenagers began breaking up the place. Hundreds

of youths stormed the stage. Some were thrown bodily
back into the crowd. Amplifiers, drum kits and other
equipment worth about £2,000 were kicked off the stage
and smashed. Pieces were hurled at policemen and attendants. Red-and-gold curtains had been ripped down, chairs
and heavy plush ten-feet-long seating forms wrenched
apart, with pieces crashing against stage lighting. Clocks
were smashed and a bottle was hurled through the huge
chandelier. There was a hail of shoes, bottles, coins and
other missiles. Before police and staff could restore order, running fights broke out all over the ballroom. Cymbals went through the air and people thumped each other
as all the amplifiers were smashed up. Then there was
the most glorious crash of all time: a Steinway grand
piano was pushed off stage, smashing into pieces. Charlie
hadn't been using his drums that night; he'd borrowed a
kit from a guy who was sitting there crying over his lovely
Ludwig kit. He got one cymbal back. They didn't steal
the drums, they just smashed them. Of the amps, only
bits of wood were left and I think we got one loud-
speaker chassis without any cone in it. That was all.
Everything else was totally mangled. One mob, chanting
"Scotland, Scotland!" challenged the police to a fight.
During the riot scores of police reinforcements were called
in. Wielding batons, they charged straight into the mob
and eventually broke up the riot. Two policemen and
about thirty members of the audience had their injuries
treated at Blackpool's Victoria Hospital, which resembled a casualty clearing center. One had been hit by a
microphone. A number of arrests were made and several
youths were hustled into a police van outside. At eleven
o'clock the recorded pop music, which had been played
throughout the riot, was switched off as police escorted
the last dancers outside.

This was the only time we'd had to face a crowd so
aggressively anti-Stones. We'd booked in at a hotel in
Preston, twenty miles away, but took the precaution of
first visiting the police station there. The cops walked
around and around the hotel, the Bull and Royal, all
night. At 3 a.m. Stu arrived and filled us in on what had
happened after we left. He then produced pieces of shred-
ded equipment, saying, "This is your amp, and here's
your guitar . . ."

Deputy Chief Constable Ronald Gregory said: "We shall advise the Winter Gardens authorities that they must not have the Rolling Stones again. Such scenes cannot be tolerated." As Brian said: "Why should the crowd want to do that? We went out there to entertain them and everyone was enjoying it except for a few groups of rowdies who started all the trouble." Keith, now being criticized for kicking the guy who spat, said: "It went too far. I just lost my temper. But isn't it a strange thing that so many fans like us and get a kick out of our music, yet we get more abuse than any half-dozen other acts put together?"

After Blackpool, things could never be the same. Before, our concerts had been healthy fun for eager fans and usually there was sensible security. Suddenly it had turned violent and the Stones were in the firing line. Next day, we awoke to every newspaper full of the riot story and television and radio news announcing we were banned from returning to Blackpool. At home in Penge, my phone rang all the time and we had to change the number; outside the hotel there were 400 fans all day long. We went to the home of a friend for lunch, but 200 fans collected outside there too.

An immediate problem was our need for equipment for the show that night at the Imperial Ballroom, Nelson. Eric Easton arrived direct from the Jennings (Vox) factory in Dartford with a new £700-set of amplifiers, microphones and speakers. We left Preston and checked in at Nelson police station, from where a Black Maria took us to the ballroom. The word was now out that a Stones show could bring violent trouble. But the show went off successfully. Next day, four youths appeared in court in Blackpool charged with assault and with carrying offensive weapons.

Our third American single was released, coupling "It's All Over Now" with "Good Times, Bad Times" in another colored sleeve,* and there was more trouble: the words "half-assed game" on the A-side got it banned by some radio stations before the disc jockeys chopped those words out! How times have changed. "Not Fade Away" was at Number One in Greece, and "It's All Over Now"

*The single reached number twenty-seven in the US charts.

was top in Germany and Holland, while it was knocked
into second place by the Beatles in Britain.

Still more controversy surrounded our name. Our
compère friend Tony Marsh appeared in court after being
literally caught with his trousers down at the side of the
stage when he had compèred our show in Slough. People
in the front row saw him wagging his naked bum in time
to our music as he stood in the wings. Seven angry
mothers surrounded him after the show. He was fined £5
with 10 guineas costs. More headlines for the trouble-
making Stones, adding to *our* image as Bad Boys.

We were now beset with internal problems. First we
found that insurance companies would refuse to cover
any member of the band for anything more powerful
than a family saloon; so Mick could not progress from a
Ford Zephyr to a sports car! Then Andrew "went missing"
for a few days after his chauffeur took him home from a
recording session. He "did not appear too well," and next
day his bed had not been slept in. He emerged later, but
by the end of the month he was talking of retiring from
show business. This was news to us. Andrew told everybody he had sold his consultancy agency, Image, to a guy
named Tony Calder. "I don't enjoy it anymore," he told
Melody Maker, while a national newspaper reported that
he earned £500 a week as co-manager of the Stones.
"There are a lot of talented people of my age in this
country," he said. "You start out wanting to earn loot
and when you get it there's nothing else left."

Retirement at the age of twenty, with the Stones only
just begun, struck me as unbelievable. We knew Oldham
had "communication problems" with Easton, but we didn't
expect him to depart at this stage. He didn't, either. But
our relationship with him was not to last forever.

His association with Mick was clearly much warmer
than with the rest of us and he made no secret about it.
"The most important thing about Mick is that he is such a
distinct personality," Andrew said at this time. "A very
intelligent and creative one. He has strong ideas about
music . . . to get the best from him and the other Stones
at a recording session, I aim at the right atmosphere. A
relaxed and informal one. Plenty of tea, Cokes and gags.
I also hold the session in the evening if I can. That's the
time when Mick is in the right mood, when his feel for

his music is at peak." With comments like that, it was hardly surprising that there was resentment among the rest of us towards Andrew.

And the more he aligned himself with Mick and the more Mick became the media's focus, the more ostracized and embittered Brian became. His personal problems mounted on July 23, 1964, when his resident girlfriend, Linda Lawrence, gave birth to his fourth illegitimate child. To complicate matters, they named him Julian Mark, the same first names as Pat Andrews' child. For a while there was talk that they should marry.

All this was at a period when daily life—hedged in between a hostile public and overly adoring fans—was becoming more and more difficult. So it was hardly surprising that we slipped easily into the roles into which society had cast us. Once, when I rang a theater and asked for tickets, giving my name, the woman in the box office slammed the phone down on me. In pubs, barmen just ignored us when it was our turn to order drinks. We tried to laugh it off, but it wasn't really a laughing matter, being cut off from the human race just because we had got long hair. On tour, we sometimes arranged for an all-night bowling alley to be opened for us. It was expensive, but worth it to be able to get out of the hotel. And yet "the prison life of hotel bedrooms and dressing-rooms," as Brian called it, brought some benefits: we could relax more on tour than we could at home. As Brian said: "You don't know you're marooned until you want something like toothpaste. Then you have to remind yourself that if you go outside, you'll get your clothes torn and lose a few handfuls of hair."

Charlie, on a shopping expedition in Portobello Road, was accosted by an old lady who asked him what he was doing there. "She was quite angry because she thought I should do all my shopping in the expensive stores!"

Home life for me, Diane and Stephen was disrupted by fame. Our new address was soon discovered by kids who came round and pestered me, or Diane and Stephen when I was away. We seemed to be becoming a national obsession. In Scotland a fourteen-year-old boy was turned away from his secondary school four times in a week because he had a "Stones haircut." His headmaster gave him an ultimatum: Get your hair cut or go into a girls' class! When the threat was carried out, the boy retorted: "Being with a crowd of girls doesn't bother me a bit. I quite enjoy it. I don't think I'll fancy sewing, but I don't mind having a bash at cookery." The girls said: "He's smashing. It's nice to have a man around the place."

By the end of July 1964 our fan club had 8,126 members, but the cynicism that surrounded the mere mention of our name was best summed up in a statement by Lennie Hastings, drummer with the Alex Welsh Dixieland jazz band: "I predict that whatever the Rolling Stones get called now is nothing to what they will be called in twenty-five years' time, when they appear in 'All Our Yesterdays,' " he said. "By that time, the kids who now buy their records will have matured enough to know they were taken in." How wrong he was! I saw his comments as those of a musician whose scene had been not just threatened by rock 'n' roll at that time, but was in the midst of being overthrown by groups like ours. The beat revolution was in full swing, and the jazz scene was suffering, while our stars were shining. In *Beat Monthly* magazine's popularity poll we were number one jointly with the Beatles in August 1964, and the individual voting put Brian at three, me at six, Mick at seven, Keith at nine and Charlie at thirty-two. "Hair is the most controversial subject of the beat era," the magazine said. It sure was: a reader wrote to say she "hated to think how many little creatures must be running around in Brian's hair." Ray Coleman wrote in *Melody Maker*: "Five young men have caused international uproar, and started a fashion that could result in starving hairdressers . . . All the Stones have to do to achieve fame is behave normally. When it was discovered that Mick and Chrissie were friendly, the *News of the World* could hardly contain itself."

That month, everything surrounding the Stones was revving up to full throttle. Sometimes, it seemed that the only people keeping their heads were the Stones: Andrew had announced his retirement as our manager (which he didn't follow through), and every time we were due to play a concert the local paper whipped up an atmosphere of an impending riot.

On July 31 the *Northern Daily Mail* reported:

Ulster police are taking special precautions against possible beat-fan riots today when the Rolling Stones visit the province. Extra police are being dragged in to the center of the city to control the thousands expected to welcome the group. Crash barriers will be used by police to control the crowd . . . this morning a special conference between police chiefs and forty civilian supervisors hired by the promoters will be held. Extra first-aid men will be on duty.

Riots for the Stones were becoming rituals.

Four of us made the BEA flight to Belfast on August 1. Keith missed it. At Aldergrove airport, only twenty fans greeted us but they made up in noise what they lacked in number. We were driven in two cars on a very long, devious route into the city by two garrulous Irishmen who talked non-stop about the need for security.

Arriving at the television studios we did an interview for the evening *6:10* show. Larry Nixon, writing in the *Belfast Newsletter,* said: "I went to sneer and I stayed to cheer. There is a certain endearing amateurish quality about this shaggy, ungroomed group which is more effective than the most professional polish."

Keith joined us at our hotel later. He had overslept and caught the next flight. We heard that fans had started queuing at the Ulster Hall for the night's show at 7 a.m. and plate-glass windows near the hall had been boarded up. The signs were ominous, and the signs proved right.

We arrived at the hall at 10 p.m. in a black Daimler. People broke loose immediately and the crash barriers were of no use. It took us forty-five minutes to get inside the hall. There was pandemonium as we took the stage. A policeman jumped on stage to urge the crowd to stay well back. We hesitated in our playing but then kept the music going. Police, who couldn't defend the stage as we became surrounded by fans, tried to stop the show after the first song. We carried on, but they finally stopped the show after twelve minutes. The problem was that they'd allowed seating behind us and more and more kids joined the stage until we could hardly breathe, let alone play. "Bloody horrifying," said Stu. We raced through "I Wanna Be Your Man," "It's All Over Now" and "I Just Want to Make Love to You," but ambulancemen were talking about hundreds of fainting cases; the total in the end was about 400, with twenty-five taken to hospital and six detained. The 5,000 crowd was so dense that those who fainted could only be got out by dragging them onstage in front of us and then out through the stage door. Mick and Charlie argued with the police, when they tried to stop the show after the first song, but several girls were so hysterical that ambulancemen had to strap them to stretchers. After the show's premature end, fighting broke out between fans and police.

Amid the hysteria, we were nearly knocked to the ground as we tried to leave the stage. Fans were carried out, screaming and fighting, in straitjackets. Others were lifted bodily from the ballroom, to lie at our feet as we played and sang. Some casualties were laid out in the wings. It was more like a war scene than a pop concert.

Belfast councilor William Kennedy declared: "I ordered the doors to be closed at 9 p.m. By that time I believe there were 3,000 in the hall, although the maximum number permitted is 1,200." A police spokesman said: "We were not expecting anything out of the ordinary. Certainly nothing approaching the Beatles' visit." When the dust had settled, he admitted: "I've never seen anything like it nor ever want to again." Stu summed it up best: "Quite a night. Never been nearer. We should have got mangled." The fee for this fiasco was £500. I thought we deserved five times that amount in danger money.

We left Belfast at 11 p.m., quite shaken, and drove straight to Ballymena for a show at the Flamingo ballroom. Here, whole streets were closed off and plate-glass windows near the ballroom were boarded up. Despite the lateness of the hour the whole town seemed to be out on the streets behind crash barriers, waving Union Jacks and greetings messages. It was like a royal visit. The show was much better organized and although there were twenty fainting cases from the crowd of 1,500, we had a good show, quite a recovery from the earlier débâcle.

The pace was fast. We left Belfast at one the next afternoon, flew back to London and went by van to Hastings. Meeting up with the police, we changed from our van to an ambulance as a decoy. Accompanied by a police van we were escorted through fantastic crowds with a wailing siren blocking the promenade awaiting us. We'd driven through them before they realized it was us. Then screaming girls chased our vehicle the whole length of the pier until it stopped in the actual foyer of the Pier Ballroom.

Every concert from now on was a grand, if dangerous, *event*. We were on a tidal wave of publicity; getting in and out of every show had to be carefully orchestrated. Our dodgy image was a great advantage, because the press liked nothing better than the theme of "kids against authority." Throw in a bit of violence, which marked some of our shows, and we were hardly off the front pages for months. We learned fast that to have a strong image was a terrific advantage. Lots of talented musicians generally went unnoticed only because they didn't stand out from the crowd.

It suddenly seemed to become OK for the upper classes or high society to be seen to court the Stones. We were invited to perform an open-air concert on August 2 at Longleat House, the seat of the fifty-nine-year-old, pop-conscious Marquess of Bath. With pictures by Rembrandt and Reynolds, and the first book ever printed in English, Longleat usually attracted 24,000 visitors a year. We were to equal that figure in just one day! It was an unlikely place for Mick to be driving me, but on arrival we were treated warmly, drinking in the garden and chatting with the marquess. He told us fans had begun arriving at 10 p.m. the previous night.

We were then shown around some of the house, ending up in the Green Room; this was to be our dressing-room. The rest of the group arrived and, like me, were astounded at the beauty of this venue on a gloriously sunny day.

At 6:15 there was a reception for the press and local dignitaries. We signed a few autographs and supped from the dwindling supply of drinks which had been guzzled by about thirty reporters and photographers from the national newspapers. Television cameramen were there, too, expecting action. Brian was staring open-mouthed at the huge paintings. Mick wandered into the room and ordered a beer from the makeshift bar. The rest of us arranged ourselves around the room and relaxed in huge leather armchairs.

Outside the tension was rising as more and more people crowded towards the crash barrier separating them from the steps where we were to appear. Several girls had already succumbed to the sun and the relentless pressure of the restless crowd. One luckless female was grabbed by some youths and swung into one of the ornate pools near the house. Police were busy shepherding the last of the sightseers from the house and closing the gates in the crash-barrier.

There was a 25,000 crowd; tickets were 2s. 6d. Around seven the Marquess of Bath, in a long black wig, tried to say a few words, but was drowned out, and with a flourish of his arms he introduced us to the audience and we played a forty-minute spot on the front steps of the house. The audience was held back by a high wire fence. During "High-Heel Sneakers" no fewer than twenty-two girls were carried away on stretchers. Mick moved off the platform to a lower step, and the crowd surged again. "Not Fade Away" followed, and the ambulancemen ran out of stretchers. Mick pleaded with the people at the back to move back and ease the crush at the front, but it was hopeless. At the side of the stage Eric Easton signaled two more numbers. Then the crowd went mad as Keith and Brian led the way into "It's All Over Now," and it was. Our fee from the Marquess was £1,000.

The Marquess of Bath commented that it had been "A delightful day; it was the best controlled large crowd we have had at Longleat." But the police were worried by the crowds. A spokesman was quoted as saying that "If they keep on at this rate, there'll be a disaster." And another said, "We could have easily have some dead on our hands, if things go on as they are."

We were upset when we were told to cut short our show. We reckoned that thousands of fans had paid a lot of money to see and hear us, and had queued for hours. After Belfast and Blackpool, we were now getting tetchy and opinionated on the subject. While a minority caused trouble at some of our performances, and others fainted, the majority, we felt, should not lose out.

Lord Bath seemed to agree with us: "I can't see eye to eye with police about this although I appreciate that parents should forbid children of seven or eight coming to such shows, which are what teenagers want today. It's not my fault if people get hurt. They come here knowing fully what to expect."

Not even an apparently harmless event like a television show's birthday party could come and go without trouble for us. On August 7 we appeared at the first anniversary show of *Ready Steady Go!* Our dressing-room was crammed to breaking point with fans, instruments, friends, cases, road managers and hangers-on. On the show we gained more screams than the rest of the cast put together. Brian and I did the "amateur disc jockey" spot. Afterwards, we had a small drinks party, joining Brian Poole and the Tremeloes, Gerry and the Pacemakers, Cilla Black, Kenny Lynch, the Nashville Teens, Billy J. Kramer and the Dakotas, Elkie Brooks, Paul McCartney, Marianne Faithfull and Brian Epstein.

Leaving the studios we fought our way through the crowds of fans with the help of police. We jumped into a Daimler limousine but as it pulled away the back door, which was open, knocked a policeman down, slammed against a tree and was wrenched from its hinges. We drove to Bow Street police station, minus the door, and were transferred to an *Evening Standard* delivery van. Brian missed all this—in the rush he was left standing on the pavement and got a lift with Eric Easton, lying on the floor of his car. Twenty police, plus some on motorbikes, tried to control this escape.

In the newspaper van we arrived unnoticed by 7,000 fans at the athletic association grounds at Richmond, where we topped the bill at the Fourth National Jazz and Blues Festival. Our old friend Giorgio Gomelski was the compère; we were hurried through the rain, into a tent marked "Lady Artists Only," which would have amused our enemies.

Our next confrontation took place the following night in Holland. We'd flown to The Hague for a thirty-five-minute spot in a beautiful old opera house at Scheveninghen. The moment the curtains opened and we began to play, the crowd (mostly boys) went completely berserk. In no time, dozens of police stormed the stage, fighting the fans who were trying to get up there with us. After our first two songs the microphone leads (which ran along the front of the stage) were torn out. We tried to continue playing minus vocals, but police cut the power. Stu, standing at the side of the stage, was hit on the head by a bottle thrown from the crowd. We carried on for five more minutes with drums, tambourine and maracas but then had to give up.

Stu was amazed by the uncompromising Dutch police: "They formed a chain like firefighters and as soon as a teenager came forward he was passed along the line, thumped as he went past and then thrown out of the door, down some steps, where there were more policemen waiting to help him on his way. I have never seen policemen so vicious." Later we heard that half the seats in the theater had been ruined. Chairs were hanging from chandeliers; tapestries were torn off the walls.

Behind the scenes, Andrew Oldham still seemed to be playing cat and mouse, and we were as unsure as the press about his future relationship with us. "I'd be a fool to give up all that loot," he told Maureen Cleave in the *Evening Standard*.

On September 16 he married Sheila Klein in Glasgow, having spent two weeks with her in Scotland to qualify for the marriage license. Andrew was twenty at the time. "We had to do it this way. Her parents don't like me," he explained. Sheila sent her father, a psychoanalyst, a telegram from Glasgow to say she had married Andrew; her father had thought she was abroad.

Police escorts were the safest accompaniment for us to move around. A police van met us at Manchester airport on August 9; we were taken to Belle Vue's New Elizabethan Ballroom for a concert—but on arrival we were told that Stu, traveling back from Holland by boat with our equipment, was stuck in customs. We delayed our spot as long as possible in the hope that he would make it in time. Eventually, after prolonged arguments, we agreed (or were forced!) to go on stage by Jimmy Savile, the compère, and the management, borrowing equipment from our support group, the Mysteries.

But there had been a half-hour delay, and the kids had heard on the grapevine about our instrument problems. Three and a half thousand impatient fans surged towards the stage, chanting "We want the Stones." In the crush, about twelve girls fainted and seventy had to have first-aid treatment. Two policewomen were injured, and throughout the pandemonium, with police helmets flying and clothing ripped as police mounted the stage, Jimmy Savile played records to try to calm the crowd. Eventually, after police broke up fights and restored order, we went on.

The next day, Mick was in court in Liverpool to answer a summons. He pleaded guilty to three charges: having no insurance, failing to produce a driving license, and driving his Ford Consul at 48–50 m.p.h. in a 30 m.p.h. zone. Mick had not been able to produce his driving license because it had been stolen from his car by fans three days earlier. He was fined a total of £32 with two license endorsements.

That night we played at New Brighton's Tower Ballroom. The compère and promoter was Bob Wooler of the Cavern Club and on the bill with us were twelve finalists in a beat contest. Elaborate plans had been made to get us into the venue by means of a chair-lift, but it was finally decided that it would be too dangerous if fans got out of hand. The crowd of 5,000 got out of hand anyway. We waited five hours to go on stage and, despite some laughs backstage with Jimmy Savile, one of the contest judges, we were already tired. Fighting began when we struck up the music; it was Mods versus Rockers, with the Tower Ballroom's spotlights picking out the fights! The battle lasted forty-five minutes and fifty youths had been ejected from the hall, two with knives. We had orders to carry on as normal, and so we played a set of fourteen songs and there was no arrests.

It was the same pattern we'd experienced so often: girls being pushed by those at the back, and the result a terrible crush at the stage. How could such hysteria be contained? Bob Wooler said: "The answer is to give the kids plenty of space to let off steam, but see you have complete control from start to finish. The bouncers did a fine job. They may have seemed ruthless, but you could see they had to be, for the kids' own sakes, and the kids knew it."

This might have been true. I saw a girl with a ripped pink dress being dragged away by her hair. Later I asked her what sort of time she had had. "Fab," she replied.

The problems weren't our fault but again we were held responsible. The *Daily Mirror* described us as "a menace to law and order," and added that as a result of our "vocal laryngitis, cranial fur and sex, the police are diverted from bank robberies, murders and other forms of mayhem to quell the mob violence that they generate."

They put a police dog on stage to guard us during our show at the Palace Ballroom, Douglas, Isle of Man, on August 13. Rex stuck his job for twenty minutes before fidgeting. "When it was obvious he was getting uneasy," a police superintendent said, "we decided that the beat music and the screaming were getting him excited. But by that time he'd done his job, acting as a deterrent."* Then 7,000 screaming teenagers tried to rush the stage. Soon seventy girls had fainted as the crowd hurled itself against a specially built timber-and-wire-netting barrier that cracked under the strain. Fifty police had been called in from all over the island and together with forty attendants formed one of the biggest forces ever mustered there. Youths fought with police and three of them were frog-marched outside. Ambulancemen worked flat out, treating streams of girls for fainting, hysteria, cuts and scratches. Girls were laid out in blankets in the foyer. The final rush to the stage came as we ended our fifty-minute spot with "It's All Over Now."

Our second EP record to be issued in Britain was released by Decca on August 14. Titled *Five by Five,* it was the result of our session two months earlier in Chicago, and joined Chuck Berry's "Around and Around" and two other established songs, "If You Need Me" and "Confessin' the Blues," with two Nanker-Phelge compositions: an all-instrumental "2120 South Michigan Avenue," a dedication to the inspirational home where we recorded, and "Empty Heart." It's a great shame that the EP format became obsolete. The advantage was that it was not aimed at the charts and so could focus tightly on a theme, in this case a pilgrimage to our musical, spiritual inspiration. The record was warmly received, described by *New Musical Express* as "full of vitality, appeal and authority." It got to the top of the EP charts on September 26, 1964, and stayed there for nine weeks, remaining in the EP charts for fifty-six weeks.

*Rex was the only police dog on the island; I wonder if he ever recovered.

For our show at Wimbledon Palais in southwest London on August 14, the management forecast no trouble. Before we went on stage, Charlie was asked by a reporter: "How do you describe your music?" With his famous deadpan face, Charlie answered: "I don't like your question," and walked away. We did a forty-five minute set and more than a hundred girls had to be treated. Brian and I were jumped on by shrieking girls who tried to drag us from the stage. But this was fairly mild stuff compared with what we'd experienced.

From one island to another. We flew to Guernsey on August 18 to start a tour of the Channel Islands. On arrival we were driven to a private house, where we were to stay to avoid fans. They had installed food, drinks and even a few girls to keep us company. Brian and I made friends with two of them, who took care of us until we left. (At this stage Brian was living with Linda in Reading, where there was a picture of him hanging above the front door. Linda had put this up; her entire family was very "star-struck.")

Next morning we all went go-kart racing on a track they closed for us. Once we were all used to driving, they organized a knock-out competition between the band and a few friends. I eventually met Mick in the final, beat him and was presented with a small silver cup as a memento. We went again the following day but Keith had a nasty accident, coming down the bank upside down with the machine on top of him, taking all the skin off his back and side. In the afternoon we went sightseeing around the island, visiting the old underground bunkers that the Germans used during World War II.

When we returned to the house later by car we found fans waiting outside; Stu pulled up on to the pavement so that we could run straight into the entrance. The local police promptly booked him for driving on the pavement.

The more we gained credibility as musicians, the more difficult relations with the inescapable Man in the Street became. On Jersey we went to a jewelry shop to buy gifts and within minutes, while I was buying a gold bracelet for Diane, a crowd had gathered outside, making faces and standing on window ledges, trying to get in. The manager locked the shop for us but they wouldn't give up. He called a taxi and we escaped by the back door, returning to our hotel. At the concert that night at the Springfield Hall in St. Helier, Jersey tomatoes and eggs were thrown at us, but the culprit was found and thrown out.

Later we adjourned to a private party where they had lots of girls and some dull blue films. Brian and I went to a late club with the local promoter, who got involved in a row with a huge guy. They eventually went outside to settle the argument—we couldn't see ourselves getting out of the place alive. But after terrible noises and crashes and yells our promoter, nicknamed Jack the Dog, returned, triumphant.

The flight next morning was no less eventful. We flew direct to Bournemouth on Channel Airways; the stewardess was obnoxiously rude from the moment we climbed the steps to the plane: "Well, boys, have you washed today?" She could see we were all angry, but wouldn't let it go. "When did you last have a haircut?" she asked as we sat down. We christened her Hilary Hedgehopper and decided to keep her running throughout the flight, continuously asking her for drinks, coffee and cigarettes. By the time we landed, she was in tears. Naturally, the authorities assumed that she was right and we were wrong. We were told we could never fly on the airline again, which was no big problem for us. Brian commented that we should have bought the airline.

In Bournemouth, we were greeted by a new assistant, Mike Dorsey, who was employed by Eric Easton. His first remark to us became his trademark: "Hallo, chaps!" We got on well with him from the start. After an uneventful concert in Bournemouth that evening which earned us a poor review for "a sloppy stage act devoid of showmanship" (Bournemouth and Dorset Times), we returned to the hotel. There waiting for me was my girlfriend Helen from Nottingham, who traveled with me throughout the next week of concerts in the West Country. During this stretch of one-nighters, Mick and Keith's flat in Hampstead was ransacked and all their clothes stolen.

September was a month of high activity. Mick sang on a demonstration record for Andrew called "Da Doo Ron Ron," which was to be released on an album Andrew was planning for his own orchestra. Surrounded by tumult, we must have seemed like the Untouchables to our fans.

But the reality was different. I was still finding time to watch a few football matches at Crystal Palace. And as sales for *Five by Five* passed a quarter of a million within two weeks of its release, gaining us a Silver Disc award, my personal bank account showed a credit of a measly £129.

Back in London on September 2 we returned to a recording session at Regent Sound. Bill Farley was the engineer and Andrew the producer for a full day's session cutting four tracks for the next album, including "Little Red Rooster" and "Off the Hook." Our friend "Scottish" Dave Thomson was there and helped a little with lyrics for "Off the Hook," and also took some pictures. Mick's brother Chris, another guest at the session, was impressed with "Little Red Rooster"; so was Charlie, so much so that when it ended, he exclaimed: "Well—could be a single." It was a bold statement that nobody except the five Rolling Stones thought could possibly be right. A slow, intense blues song as a single? It might be true to our roots, but it was, argued Andrew Oldham, totally uncommercial and wrong for our new-found fame. He wanted a more direct, poppier song for our next hit. But it felt right to us and, amid much disagreement, we won the day: "Little Red Rooster" would be our next defiant aim for the top of the singles chart. We were optimistic as rules were being broken every day anyway.

"POLICE RIOT SQUADS READY FOR ACTION" announced the front page of *Melody Maker* on September 5, 1964. Our third British tour, about to begin, merited a "military operation to shield the Stones from fearless fans . . . they will travel in a secret form of transportation, locked inside a windowless vehicle," reported the paper. Profits from the tour were agreed at 40 per cent to the promoter, Robert Stigwood, 40 per cent to the Stones and 20 per cent to Eric Easton Ltd. The start of a tour was now hitting me quite strongly as a father. Whenever Stu arrived to collect me and Stephen saw me with a case in my hand, he would howl the house down. Stu recalled later that I seemed at my happiest "crawling across the carpet, playing games with Stephen," and he felt unwelcome in the house because he'd "come to take his father away."

This tour was musically very strong; our reputation was

now secure and we had American singers Inez and Charlie Foxx on the package with us. We opened with "Not Fade Away" and then went into "I Just Wanna Make Love to You," "Walking the Dog," "If You Need Me," "Around and Around" and "I'm a King Bee," followed by "I'm Alright," which sent every crowd wild. Brian and Mick generated a great visual show, with Brian hammering away on tambourine and Mick pushing the crowd to the limit, risking his own safety on the very edge of the stage. We finished with "It's All Over Now," the words and the music totally drowned by the screams.

Andrew regarded himself as the sixth Stone, much closer to the group than a traditional manager, a role now increasingly filled by Eric. "The Stones are now their own publicists," Andrew stated. Who needed a publicity man when male students were refused enrollment at Peterborough Technical College because their hair was considered too long, and a young engineer in Gateshead-on-Tyne was not allowed to start work because he had not obeyed an instruction to cut his "Stones-style" hair?

In Leicester for two concerts at the Odeon, there was a backstage scuffle. Brian tore a fan's coat as he made a frantic exit. She later successfully sued him for £62 in damages! But there was bright news from London: we had topped the Beatles by winning *Melody Maker* readers' popularity poll. Number One in the British section, we were second to the Beatles in the international division, with Mick third in the British male singers' section. Our single "Not Fade Away" was voted top disc of the year, which was strange considering that it reached only three in the charts. The *Los Angeles Times* was quick with the news and a headline: "Beatles No Longer Number One in British Polls." Eric Easton commemorated our prestigious awards by buying us each a watch.

The star-studded lunch celebrating these awards was at the Savoy Hotel on September 10. The media focused on our casual dress: Mick set the tone with a green shirt with stiff white collar and a white cardigan, Brian and Charlie wore ties. Leaving there amid flashing bulbs from press photographers, we drove to Cheltenham with our own 8mm Russian movie cameras, which we'd just received for endorsing them. When we arrived at the venue, we had to fight our way through a large crowd of fans.

Cheltenham was always special. Brian's parents came to the first house of our concert and also backstage during shows. There was no sign of the rift between them that people talked about; they seemed very proud of him. A big party had been arranged for us in a hotel after the shows but news leaked out and fans arrived; it was impossible for us to attend. Changing from the police vehicle to our own car, we then had to drive forty miles to a transport café before we could find something to eat. We drove on to Monmouth, arriving at nine the next morning to find a big crowd awaiting us at the Beaufort Arms Hotel. We got through and collapsed into bed at ten, exhausted.

Against all the publicity, we behaved quite normally when given the chance of freedom! After some sleep, we left the hotel for a sightseeing tour of the Wye Valley. We visited ancient monuments and buildings, and found an old house where antiques were sold. Brian bought an eighteenth-century washstand, Mick and Keith an old Spanish chest and some daggers and I bought antique brass bellows. We relaxed in the grounds and played around with the dogs there, and filmed the visit with our new movie cameras.

On to Cardiff for two concerts at the Capitol on the Inez and Charlie Foxx tour. We had to fight our way in and the crowds went mad from the start. The danger we were exposed to literally hit Charlie in the face: he was hit by an airgun pellet. There was blood, and he shrieked with pain, but was able to carry on. The police Black Maria exit was now normal after the show, whisking us to our own car several miles away. I arrived home at 4 a.m.

A similar incident occurred at Chester, where an idiot shot an air-rifle slug through one of the dressing-room windows. Fortunately nobody was hurt. We escaped by climbing over a ten-foot wall with the aid of the ladder, dropping into the empty backyard of the Swan Hotel where a police van was awaiting us.

At Manchester on September 15, after recording a couple of great shows, we went to Liverpool's Adelphi Hotel for the night and with the spirit of camaraderie that marked the sixties so well we went to the Blue Angel club with Inez and Charlie Foxx and the Mojos. We met and jammed with several local bands for a couple of hours, finally leaving the club at about 5:30 a.m. Mick remarked afterwards: "These days it's just impossible to do what we really enjoy like this, getting together for a real good blow without having to fight off the fans. We enjoyed it. We hope to be able to do it again."

No such chance at Carlisle two nights later. Six girls broke security and got on stage, leaping all over Mick, Brian and Keith, which left just Charlie and me playing the music. Police brought in dogs to help control the crowd. A cluster of attendants finally chased the girls off the stage; later, smuggled out by the police and driven to our car, we drove sixty miles to Melrose, near Edinburgh, checking into a lovely quiet hotel set in beautiful countryside. It was so good to relax in peaceful surroundings after all the commotion of touring. In every dressing-room there were dozens of letters from fans which needed replies and I enjoyed unwinding by replying to them before turning in for the night. It was a kind of therapy for me, a return to normality from the madness of life on the road.

The tour continued at Edinburgh on September 19, with the 2,500-seater Usher Hall crammed for both houses. We had to be "liberated" by police in an armored payroll van after the show. Back in Melrose, the grapevine had leaked our hotel: a hundred of them were waiting for us at one in the morning as we arrived.

At a press conference before the first live shows ever held in Kingston-upon-Hull, we enjoyed being interviewed by two pretty girls, Clare Walton and Gail Buckingham, from Oxford University's magazine *Cherwell*. We then went on stage for the first show. This was madness. Two dozen tough rugby players from Hull's Kingston Rovers team formed a crash barrier in front of the orchestra pit to protect us, but one screaming girl defeated them. As Mick started to tight-rope his way along the balustrade of the orchestra pit, the girl grabbed hold of his legs and he lost his balance, falling three feet into the pit, flat on his back. He jumped up quickly and climbed on stage. Later, the fif-teen-year-old who achieved the impossible sighed: "I touched him!" Next day, the *Hull Daily Mail* reported: "Even the fantastic scenes which marked the Beatles visit did not match those in and around the ABC Theatre. A twenty-strong team of stewards could hardly hold the crowds."

Mick attempted to repeat his intrepid walk in the second house but the stewards turned him back as he neared the edge of the stage. At the end, during "It's All Over Now," a teenage girl jumped over the balustrade into the orchestra pit but, before she could vault on stage, attendants grabbed her and carried her, struggling, away from the stage. Many girls were carried, crying hysterically, to a medical station set up in the theater restaurant.

That extraordinary night was also filmed by ABC–Pathé and edited into a six-minute Pathé Pictorial film, shown in cinemas under the title *The Rolling Stones Gather Moss, 1964*. They had filmed fans queuing, us in the dressing-rooms and also miming to "Around and Around" on stage.

At Doncaster, the logistical problem of getting into the theater was enormous: local police said they had a bigger headache than for any royal visit for the St. Leger race. The chanting, swaying crowd awaiting our arrival had grown to 500, completely jamming the narrow alley to the stage door of the Gaumont Theatre. Girls sat atop each other's shoulders to peer into the dressing-room windows.

Sixty men formed the security in front of the stage. The show was riotous. Two thousand screaming, hysterical fans went out of control and a solid line of uniformed police inside the orchestra pit could not hold back the wave surging forward as soon as the curtain went up on "Not Fade Away." Cinema officials, ambulancemen and detectives joined in the struggle. Our music was totally drowned by the uproar. Firemen arrived to help the authorities battle against the teenagers. Two girls scrambled over the barrier, but before they could reach us they were lifted bodily and hurled back into the audience. Sobbing girls rolled about the aisles. Serious cases were carried out to the foyer but were soon back, screaming for more.

We waited for a long time before we could safely leave the theater and drive to Manchester, checking into the Queens Hotel for three nights. To unwind, we adjourned to the local ten-pin bowling alley and played until 7 a.m. before returning to bed. When the adrenalin of a show has been racing, it's impossible simply to switch off.

* * *

At the end of September we released our fourth single in the States: "Time is on My Side," coupled with a Mick and Keith song, "Congratulations." It reached number six in the charts. Our future in the States looked bright: American Stones fan-club secretary Annette Florence sent a petition with 8,000 signatures asking us to return there to tour.

And by the last week in that month we were all over the charts. Our EP *Five by Five* was at Number One and we received our third Silver Disc for it; as there was only one award I got it. Our EP *The Rolling Stones* was at number four and in the album chart *The Rolling Stones* LP was number two. Marianne Faithfull's single "As Tears Go By" was number nine in the single chart. And in America we received our first gold record for our single "It's All Over Now." Meanwhile the national papers had lots to get their teeth into, with pandemonium always accurately predicted in each city we played.

Bradford, September 26, was no exception. Picked up by a police van on the edge of the town, we were smuggled with difficulty into the Odeon Theatre. Before the curtains parted hundreds of teenage girls scrambled from their seats and rushed the stage. The line of fifteen policemen held them back. As the music began the air was thick with flying objects: autograph books, scarves, sweets and home-made toys. Policemen lost their helmets, thirty girls fainted and a wall panel near the stage was crushed by the weight of bodies.

Backstage between shows we met a boy who was suffering from a muscular disease. His mother wrote to a Bradford paper about us: "The Stones were kindness itself. They were so interested in him and how he was getting on. It was a joy to see it. They were so nice and well mannered, completely different to what you might think when you read about them. They complained they couldn't get out for a meal. They were in a state of siege, without a morsel to eat."

The diary was packed, but we thrived on it. On September 28 after lunch we recorded tracks for our second album in London before heading out to Romford, Essex, to continue the Foxx tour with two performances. Next day, it was the same routine: recording, followed by two shows at Guildford. "We won't last forever," Mick was saying now. "We're having a ball but what will be happening in one, five, ten, even twenty years' time?" But if we wanted proof that things had changed from mere music-making to pop stardom, it came when we took delivery of thousands of wallet-sized publicity photos of ourselves we'd had printed. We planned to throw them to the fans while we were on the road.

Confidence stretched even to Keith, probably the most stage-shy of all of us in the beginning. "I used to wish I could have a screen between me and the audience," he told *Beat Instrumental*. "I just wanted to play, not put on any showmanship. I guess I'm more confident now. I realize people like to watch something as well as listen."

We thought we'd come up against enough in our spring to the top, but our appearance at Bristol Colston Hall on October 1 was exceptional judged even by the crazy pattern of our lives. After meeting the police between the two shows to discuss methods of exit, we went on stage for the second house. Girls rushed the stage to be rammed back by staff, but two fans leaped the eight feet down from the seats behind the stage and flung themselves at Charlie. He was knocked to the floor with his drum kit crashing around him and the two girls on top. Stewards sprang across the stage and dragged the girls away and Charlie, grinning, returned to his kit and played on as if nothing had happened.

The hall manager accused Mick and Brian of provocative behavior. "It was a near thing; the Stones could have stopped it," he said. "In the last-but-one number, when things were getting pretty tense, Mick and Brian deliberately provoked the girls to try to rush the stage. They came forward right to the edge and Mick dangled a foot forward. It was virtually an invitation to trouble." Actually there was never any need for us to "egg the girls on"—ask the hall managers and promoters around the country.

A fine one for "egging the girls on," Brian was awaiting the arrival of his fifth illegitimate child. An occasional girlfriend of his named Dawn Malloy announced to Brian and to the band's management that she was pregnant. Brian must have felt panic-stricken, because he would do nothing to help the girl in any way. Andrew and Mick took it upon themselves to get her to sign the following letter:

I have received a cheque for £700 from Andrew Loog Oldham Ltd, paid to me by the said company on behalf of Brian Jones, in full settlement of any claims arising, damages and inconveniences caused, by me, by the birth of my son and I understand completely that the matter is now closed and that I will make no statement about Brian Jones or the child to any member of the press or public.

It was signed by Dawn and witnessed by Mick, but not dated.

The letter was executed without Brian's knowledge, and the £700 deducted later from his earnings without his realizing it. Brian must have wondered how he'd managed to escape this problem so easily. But he was so caught up in enjoying life that he may have forgotten about the episode and even about his fatherhood on this occasion. He was still leaving a trail of problems behind him.

My friend Dave Burningham could hardly get through the traffic to see us at the Gaumont, Southampton on October 4. "There were police everywhere and even a small contingent of army brought in from the Salisbury camp," he wrote in his diary. The scenes, he said, were like a siege.

It was always special to be playing my home area of Lewisham, and as the long tour neared its end we were set for two shows at the Odeon Theatre on October 8. But I now faced some domestic problems of my own and it was all my fault. Doreen Samuels was on one side of the stage, my girlfriend from Liverpool on the other, and Helen was in the dressing-room. Then Diane came backstage to the dressing-room for an hour between shows. The boys helped me juggle the girls around. What was amazing to me was that none of them seemed aware of the others being there. The Number One record in the chart had an appropriate title at that time: Roy Orbison's "Oh, Pretty Woman."

The tour ended with great shows at Southend (notable for the fact that girls and police were fighting with each other until nurses were called in), and Brighton. We had farewell drinks backstage with the whole bill: Kevin Scott and the Kinsmen, compère Don Spencer, singer Julie

Grant, the Wildcats, Marty Wilde, the Echoes, Kenny Lynch; Inez and Charlie Foxx said they had never heard screaming or receptions like we received.

It had been a remarkable, important tour for us, a massive breakthrough in popularity. We were now in the top league—and it had happened in just one year. But the tour ended on a sour note. Money, as usual, was the root of it. The Stones and Eric Easton decided to bring an action in the High Court claiming our share of the profits for the seventy-two-show tour. Robert Stigwood Associates were the defendants, and we felt the September 3 letter of agreement between Easton and Stigwood, dividing the profits, had not been honored.

Eric said: "We have made every effort to settle this amicably, unfortunately without success. The Stones were paid their basic salaries as agreed. This action is over profits." At this time, my bank account showed a credit of £39. In the end we did not pursue the case; nor did we ever retrieve any money. We felt we were owed in the region of £12,000, a veritable fortune at the time.* When working on this book, every time I typed the name Robert Stigwood, my finger jumped one letter on the typewriter and his name appeared as "Robery" Stigwood.

Earlier we had struck up a friendship with Dave Thomson, a student of textile design at Glasgow Art School. He'd bluffed his way into our coterie by posing as a press photographer. Because Dave was heading towards the Royal College of Art in London, his first friendship was with Charlie, since Shirley was already there. Dave joined the touring entourage, sometimes sharing hotel rooms with Brian when we all "doubled-up"; they became so close that when he moved to London, he went to live in Brian's flat. Dave was probably the first person outside the Stones to observe the isolation of Brian.

He recalled: "Brian was paranoid because he had every reason to be: it was a paranoia based on reality. In a hotel, I saw Brian standing outside a room with his ear to

*In the 1970s when we were looking for a new recording deal, Stigwood approached us with an offer. Over dinner with the five of us and Rupert Lowenstein, we said—pay us the twelve grand and we'll talk. Not only did negotiations collapse but we were left with the bill for dinner!

the door. When he saw me he said: 'They're talking about me. Go in and find out what they're saying'—and when I went in, I found out he was right. Brian was definitely being excluded. He thought Mick was at the root of it."

The powerful trio of Mick, Keith and Andrew always had to have a foil within the Stones and being married with a young son, I had so far been their convenient "outsider." The emphasis should have switched from me to Charlie when, on October 14, 1964, he married Shirley. But shrewd Charlie did not tell the rest of us of the big event. They married at Bradford Register Office, with their Dutch friends Jeanette and Andy Hoogenboom as witnesses. He wore a suit and tie and she a mustard-colored dress, both fairly conventional.

After their wedding they celebrated with a beer, champagne and chicken lunch at a country inn near Ripon before visiting Bolton Abbey, a Yorkshire beauty spot. They returned to London by train. "I liked him at first sight," Shirley declared when the news leaked out a month later. "He was an unknown in those days but I knew he was the only boy for me. We decided on the secret wedding at Bradford a few days beforehand. We had to get a three-day special license; if Charlie was given a last-minute recording job all our plans would have been ruined. I don't remember much about the actual ceremony, it was all so quick. We slipped into the side door to get married without anyone seeing."

Andy Hoogenboom recalled: "Charlie and Shirley were so much in love they wanted to get married as soon as possible. The only way out seemed to be to tell no one, not even his manager or the group." Charlie had tried to get a license in Fulham but was spotted by fans. The Bradford registrar, Mr. J. R. Hinkins, was so determined to keep the marriage secret that he didn't even tell his thirteen-year-old daughter, a Stones fan.

Steve Hiett, a friend of mine who is now a fashion photographer in Paris, dated Shirley while they were both at the Royal College of Art. "She was very pretty, very much a girl of the sixties, with long blonde hair and a center parting. Incredible, penetrating, pale blue eyes. She seemed to talk about nothing but horses. She was obsessed with them! [Shirley's interest in horses has con-

tinued to this day.] I was studying graphic design and met
her in the college library. Later, we had a terrible altercation at the college dance. She was a girl with a temper
and we split up. About two weeks later, she came down
the Cromwell Road towards me and said: 'This is my new
boyfriend, Charlie.' And that was that."

Despite their initial opposition to the marriage, Shirley
was accepted more readily by the Stones circle than my
wife Diane ever was. As a student she merged more
comfortably with the outlook of Mick and Keith. She had
lived in Muswell Hill, north London, too, a district artier
than Beckenham or Penge. Mick, Keith, Brian and Andrew didn't like Diane much: they were reasonably polite
to her but made disparaging remarks about her behind
her back, which I caught. I was glad Charlie and Shirley
had married. Now the rhythm section was truly different
from the front line.

With a sense of achievement in Britain and new passports
arranged for us by Eric Easton, we went into the autumn
of 1964 with confidence that we could be successful round
the globe. Our records were selling well in France; tickets for our Paris Olympia shows sold out in thirty-six
hours—disappointed fans tore the box office to pieces.
Our debut album was scheduled for German release.

The Musicians Union stopped us from accepting a tour
of South Africa, but on October 17 Diane and Stephen
flew to Johannesburg en route to Durban for a holiday
with some of her relatives who lived there.

Next day marked the start of an eventful European
tour. At Brussels airport we were surprised to be greeted
by 5,000 fans—the largest ever for visiting pop artists.
Brian said: "I don't think the Stones are more popular
than Shakespeare, but he has been going longer." From
Brussels airport a police motorcade took us, after a first
press conference, to another in the city; a publicity stunt
had been arranged there, and an aircraft flew over, releasing 500 miniature parachutes carrying our records
and photos. Then at lunch at a posh restaurant the chef
had created a sophisticated menu for the palates of five
guys whose tastes were pretty basic: tomato soup, tomatoes stuffed with shrimps, roast pork with a special sauce
and all the accompaniments. We asked for chips and a

bottle of HP sauce. "I feel like committing suicide or murder," the chef said. "I worked hours of overtime preparing a special sauce for them." His research was really bad: he obviously knew nothing of Mick's lifelong hatred of tomatoes.

At the Amerikaans Theatre the Minister of the Interior refused to allow us to perform, fearing trouble, but he was persuaded by the producer. Half the audience joined us on stage for the televised show; it was remarkable for a strong stand taken by Mick. He stopped the session midway, instructing the cameramen to put equal focus on the other four Stones. "Kids don't want to look at me all the time," he told them. "This is a team, not a one-man show." (How times change!)

Next day Stu and Spike drove the van to Paris while we flew. At Brussels airport, Andrew again pretended to be a cripple, showing difficulty in walking down a staircase. In Paris, 2,000 fans awaited our press conference at the Club Locomotive, expecting us to play; we adjourned to a café round the corner and decided to overcome the problem by inviting the fans as well as the journalists to ask questions.

Moving on to do a Paris TV show, we had no equipment. All our instruments had been detained at French customs. This was to become a regular problem. We had no option but to borrow guitars; they were terrible cheap ones, and there was no bass at all. Fortunately, the show was a mime; we sailed through some songs, including "Carol," very popular in France. Stu finally arrived at 10 p.m. with our gear, hungry and harassed.

We went for an evening on the town and hit trouble. In one bar we were having a quiet drink when a bunch of men started making fun of us. Eventually one of them turned to us and said in English: "Are you the Supremes?" Before the smile had time to fade Keith leaped across the tables and punched him in the face. Nobody retaliated. Fortunately the idiots left soon afterwards and we returned to the Hotel de Paris for the night.

There was a hilarious press conference next day. A bewildered young disc jockey caught us in the right mood. "You are the silent Stone, Charlie," he began. "Yes," said Charlie. "Why do they call you the silent Stone, Charlie?" "Because I don't talk much."

The perplexed Frenchman turned his attention to me. "You are married, yes?" "Yes." "Are you taking your wife a present home from France?" "No." "Why not?" he asked, astounded. "Because she's not there."

The interviewer then sought confirmation from Mick that he played harmonica as well as sang with the Stones. "No," Mick said, deadpan. "I sort of blow and suck it."

Next he asked Brian what he did in the early days, pre-Stones. "Nothing."

We left a puzzled radio station for a small restaurant on the Île St. Louis. We were served baskets of fresh vegetables and salad, together with hams, sausage and various meats. We stuffed ourselves, only to find that this was just the first course. They then offered us huge steaks, cooked on an open fire, which we forced ourselves to eat. We'd never seen food like this. The wine was also superb. Mick and Keith ended the meal by playing "La Marseillaise" on their wine glasses with spoons. This ended dramatically; to a huge round of applause, Keith's glass cracked, spurting a jet of red wine into his lap. Andrew then stood up and proposed toasts to Napoleon, General de Gaulle, *Fabulous* magazine and many others. Our French guests did not latch on to all of the toasts, but nevertheless entered into the spirit with great enthusiasm. One suggested Rudolph Valentino, and he was saluted with great ceremony by all.

On leaving the restaurant Andrew ran joyfully up to a patrolling gendarme and shook his hand enthusiastically. "Je suis James Bond from England," explained Andrew. The gendarme took a good look at Andrew's tinted green glasses, his long black scarf flapping in the breeze and hair curling around his neck. "How do you do, 007?" he replied in perfect English, and left an astounded Oldham staring after him.

We roamed around Paris, Charlie thumbing through Picasso and Buffet prints; Brian visited a bookshop to buy *Fanny Hill,* banned in Britain at that time.

The atmosphere was truly electric for our concert at the Paris Olympia. Hustled by police through fans into a police "riot van," we found bars on the windows and sub-machine guns strapped to the inside walls. "I began to wonder what sort of trouble they were expecting,"

Mick reflected later. At least we felt well protected on
the journey to the theater.

The security system was necessary. As the van swung
into the side street of the theater, hundreds of fans ran
screaming from the pavements after us. Police cut off
their pursuit by lowering barriers. Backstage to meet us
were many French stars including singers Johnny Hallyday
and Françoise Hardy.

Plainclothes police sat among the fans as a tremendous
2,000-crowd roar welcomed us. Whenever an over-
enthusiastic teenager stood up, a torch picked him out; if
he didn't sit down immediately, he was thrown out. Around
fifty bouncers were constantly kicking out illegal photographers and hysterical fans. We got an amazing reception
as we ran through eight songs (including "Time is on My
Side") and three encores. As police drove us around
Paris for ninety minutes to let the crowds subside, Mick
got fed up, opened the back door of the police van and
disappeared into the crowds. He got back to the hotel
safely by cab. Meanwhile, back at the Olympia, stampeding fans rampaged through the foyer. Police reinforcements arrived as windows were smashed, a stage manager
was injured by flying glass and scores of youths were
bundled into police vans. On the boulevard, kids tore
down posters, broke windows and slashed the fronts of
newspaper kiosks. At a café they overturned tables and
threw customers on to the pavements. About £1,400 damage was done to the Olympia and 150 youths were arrested.

The legendary promoter of the Olympia show, Bruno
Coquatrix, one of Europe's most experienced impresa-
rios, said the Stones had had the best reception of any
British group, making more impact than the Beatles. The
French magazine *Best* reported that "The Rolling Stones
hurricane came by and in one night they succeeded in
filling the Parisians with enthusiasm."

After returning to the hotel Charlie left to spend the
night playing jazz records at the flat of Vince Taylor,
whose band had opened for us at the Olympia. Brian and
Keith began a lifelong friendship here with Taylor's tambourine player Stash. Keith, Mick, Brian and I went to
dinner and then on a bar crawl, including New Jimmy's. I
met a girl there and adjourned to her flat for the night;
the other three got back to the hotel at 4 a.m. Brian was

really in love with Paris, saying he wanted flats in Brussels, Paris and New York.

Reality hit me when we flew back to London the following day. Fame, travel, girls, hit records and adulation were all around, but there was still little money. My bank account had a credit of £210 at this time. We had no real cash at this stage of our career. But we were so high on adrenalin and enjoying ourselves that it only bothered me intermittently.

We got a kick out of something that happened up north: the vicar of the parish church at Slaithwaite, in Yorkshire, could hardly believe his ears when instead of bell peals, our hit "I Wanna Be Your Man" rang out from a gramophone in the church porch. Three girls, believed to be the culprits, were seen hurrying away.

A mere forty-eight hours after returning from Paris, we were off to the States on October 23 for a long concert tour. The huge interest in British pop that was building up over there meant we anticipated much greater success than our first mediocre trip, which we now realized had been premature. On our last trip people were curious. This time there was excitement: we were knocked sideways with the news that our American fan club had grown to 52,000-strong.

Charlie insisted on taking his own drum kit on this tour and Brian took his Pear drop Vox guitar. We hired Fender amps to play through. Everyone read and slept through the hours on the flight over and we were all rather tense when we landed at Kennedy Airport. Police had banned any reception committees but about 500 fans did get by the barricades.

At a press conference a reporter asked: "How long have you been growing your hair?" Brian: "Just about as long as you have been growing yours."

Cadillacs—very impressive—took us to Manhattan, where hundreds of fans were storming the hotel lobby. Police and security guards eventually got us in and accompanied us to our rooms. June Harris reported in *Disc*, the British pop weekly: "There were riots and pandemonium when the Rolling Stones finally got into Manhattan. The scene outside the hotel was positively frightening. Hundreds of enthusiastic fans were storming the street and hotel lobby. Inside, it was even worse.

Several people were injured in the fracas. Even tough security didn't stop screaming fans throwing themselves on the boys in the lobby."

It was impossible to get to the press conference in the normal way. We finally used the hotel service elevator to the basement, then walked through cellars and the kitchen and up to the room where the press were waiting. Armed guards from Pinkerton's detective agency had kept corridors clear.

The conference was a shambles. Dozens of girls, masquerading as high school press representatives, created a storm. Windows were smashed and genuine reporters were mobbed by shrieking girls. We sat at a long table with five mikes. The room was packed. Cameras flashed and everyone talked at once. As Keith said: "It's a bit different this time, isn't it?"

After settling in and then attending a rehearsal for the important coast-to-coast *Ed Sullivan Show,* it was time for a look around town. We went to the Peppermint Lounge for a few hours, but had trouble with fans wherever we went. Back at the hotel, the management demanded that the detectives be doubled.

Two milestones marked October 24, 1964. Our second album, entitled *12 × 5* was released in America, with a cover photo by David Bailey,* who had struck up a close friendship with Mick (Bailey took the breakthrough fashion pictures of top model Jean Shrimpton, Chrissie's sister). And on that day I celebrated my twenty-eighth birthday. I was still considered by fans to be twenty-three.

New York in 1964 was an exhilarating experience for young British pop stars. The sheer size, speed and vitality of America made an important impact on us. In the home of popular music, we could hardly wait to grapple with the culture that was our inspiration. We were hypnotized by the range of choice, and the speedy styles, of the programs on television and radio in our hotel rooms. Nobody summed up the pace of that pop era better than the disc jockey Murray the K. A great champion of British pop, he rapped away at terrific speed, a great interviewer and raconteur who had the knack of identifying with both the fans and the artists he wel-

---

*This album just made the US top twenty.

comed on to his shows. When we went down to see him at the start of our visit, a weird thing happened. It seemed that half the people listening decided to leave their radio sets and come over to the radio station to besiege us. So when the show ended we couldn't get out. The cops finally arrived and decided that the only method was muscle. A whole gang of them forced their way to our two limousines. However I ran into trouble, finding myself on the wrong side of the police guards—alone in the midst of thousands of fans. I managed to shove my way back into the radio station before I was torn to shreds. Later, I was given a special squad of private detectives who formed an archway out on the street to ensure that my next exit was smoother.

I "escaped" in time to join the band for the *Clay Cole Show,* where we mimed six songs. Then it was on to the first of two shows at the Academy of Music promoted by Sid Bernstein. Originally he'd set us for one show, but tickets sold so quickly that he added a matinee. Fans stood up throughout our set, which opened with "Tell Me"; the reception was wild and some girls managed to get on stage.

"They look divine," one writer, Jane Holzer reported. "You know what Mick said to me? He said: 'Come on love, give us a kiss' . . . How can one express it? Look at Mick at the center of the stage, a short thin boy with a sweatshirt on, the neck of his shirt almost falling over his shoulders they are so narrow. All this surmounted by this enormous head with hair puffing down over the forehead and ears. This boy has exceptional lips, particularly gross and extraordinary red lips. They hang off his face like giblets. Slowly his eyes pore over the horde and then close. Then the lips start spreading into the most languid, confidential, wettest, most labial, concupiscent grin imaginable. Nirvana!"

In the interval between shows, I received dozens of birthday presents, including several cakes, and a girl gave me a small black kitten which I gave away to a fan later. We then played our second show in the evening, a little quieter but also great. At night, a party in our honor was thrown by Nicky Haslam, the art director of *Show* magazine in a loft studio overlooking Central Park, at the home of photographer Jerry Schatzberg. There were 350 guests and it ran until 5 a.m. Amongst the guests were Jane Holzer, also celebrating her birthday, Jean Shrimpton and the Ronettes. Mick, Keith and Brian went off with them later, continuing their friendship. I chatted to DJ Scott Ross for a while and he introduced me to a very pretty blonde, Francesca Overman. I took her phone number and said I'd call her the next day, after the *Ed Sullivan Show*. Francesca remembers me telling her she was much prettier than Jean Shrimpton, "which stuck in my mind because I thought that she was *the* biggest fashion model going at the time. Bill was very romantic."

Romantic maybe, but broke too! Back in England my bank account showed a debit of £133 on this day!

Once inside the TV studios for the *Ed Sullivan Show* on Sunday, October 25, we were prisoners for the whole day. Police guarded the doors and refused to let us leave because of the hundreds of fans that stayed outside the whole time, hoping for a glimpse.

The afternoon rehearsal was very good and then in the evening, we did the show live. This was even better. We played "Around and Around" on the first part, then returned with "Time is on My Side" to continual screams throughout the show. Sullivan told us that it was the wildest, most enthusiastic audience he'd seen any artist get in the history of his show. We got a message from him a few days later, saying, "Received hundreds of letters from parents complaining about you, but thousands from teenagers saying how much they enjoyed your performance."

Not everyone was impressed. Nat Hentoff, a critic steeped in jazz and no friend of ours, reported in the *New Musical Express*: "They did not impress this reviewer. Mick lacked fire and depth, and was otherwise unconvincing. Looked very unkempt."

Sullivan's reaction is a bit of a mystery in view of an article by Dennis Braithwaite in the *Toronto Globe and Mail:* "Ed Sullivan wrote to say that he agreed with my description of the Rolling Stones as a grubby lot, and to pledge that he won't have them back. But he denied that the screaming teenagers who made his show a bedlam were a deliberate part of the act. He wrote, 'We tried in every way to prevent our audience being dominated by these screaming girls. We asked the CBS ticket division to guard against it in every way possible, but what happened is that the parents of these kids applied for the tickets, and then turned them over to the children.' I am bucked by Ed's promise that 'So help me, the untidy Rolling Stones will never again darken our portals.' "

All this did not reach our ears—we left New York confident that Sullivan was happy. The switchboard of his TV station was jammed for hours with calls from irate parents complaining about us, and from the kids asking for us to be booked again. So the same polarization that Andrew loved in England, and which worked so well, was happening here!

Later on, when we were in the Midwest, the mystery deepened. Ed Sullivan announced: "I had not met the Stones until the day before they were due to appear. They were recommended to me by my agents in England. I was shocked when I saw them; *I promise you they'll never be back on the show.*" Actually we did appear on his show several times after this!

"Now the Dave Clark Five are nice fellows. They are gentlemen and they perform well. It took me seventeen years to build up this show and I'm not going to have it destroyed in a matter of weeks," Sullivan added. This attitude differed greatly from Sullivan's face-to-face response to us when we met.

That evening I called Francesca and invited her over. She arrived shortly afterwards and stayed the night. We had a very nice time together. I later found out that I was only the second man she'd been with.

California beckoned. On October 26 we flew from New York to Sacramento, unsure whether our name had stretched this far across the continent. We needn't have worried: there were 4,500 at that night's concert at the Memorial Auditorium. Police threatened to stop the concert when parts of the crowd had to be prevented from bodily throwing themselves on stage.

There was just time enough for Charlie, a student of the American Civil War, to go gun-hunting (he bought six Civil War pistols and hats) before moving on to Los Angeles. Meanwhile back in New York, Eric Easton went down with pneumonia and instead of joining us in California went back to London. Recovered, there he announced plans for us to visit Australia and New Zealand and told colleagues we would perhaps "try to fit in

Hong Kong, Singapore and Tokyo on the way back, plus a visit to New York for a major TV show, maybe Ed Sullivan."

We left the Hollywood hotel next day for the Santa Monica Civic Auditorium to rehearse and film the *Tami (Teen-Age Music International) Show*. This was recorded using a technique called Electronovision. The film was fairly incidental to the importance of the occasion. What was important was that we met a whole string of artists and other people here who would figure in our career. Jack Nitzsche, Phil Spector's arranger on his records, was conducting the big band that accompanied all the other acts. This band included Leon Russell (piano); Sonny Bono (percussion and later prominent as half of Sonny and Cher); Nino Tempo (sax—remember "Deep Purple" by Nino Tempo and April Stevens?); and Glen Campbell (guitar). We were booked as top of the bill, and though the Supremes came and said hallo to us, hardly any other performers spoke to us during a strange day: clearly they were put off by our appearance.

The full power of the bill for the *Tami* film hit us next day. We'd heard that James Brown had wanted to close the show but the producers insisted on us. Brown then said he was going to "make the Rolling Stones wish they'd never come to America" and, watching the other acts do their spots, we had a feeling he could be right. They included Chuck Berry, Smokey Robinson and the Miracles, Marvin Gaye with the Marvelettes, Gerry and the Pacemakers, Billy J. Kramer with the Dakotas and Jan and Dean and the Supremes. As each act went on, we watched with the other artists backstage in a big viewing room, yelling encouragement and cheering. During an incredible set from James Brown and his Famous Flames, all the acts went as crazy as the audience out front. We now knew what James Brown meant and were petrified at the prospect of following him. But in our dressing-room Chuck Berry and Marvin Gaye, who shared with us, were very encouraging. Marvin told us: "People love you because of what you do on stage, so just go out there and do your thing—that's what I do."

Still apprehensive, we went on. Even the sight of us contrasted vividly with the acts that preceded us. All the Motown artists had been backed by the big band and

James Brown had also had his own band playing with him. There we were with two guitars, bass, drums and a lead singer! We played "Around and Around," "Off the Hook," "Time is on My Side," "It's All Over Now" and "I'm Alright." In a grand finale, with all the acts on stage, everybody ad-libbed with "I'm Alright"/"Get Together," with the big band behind us. Fortunately, we received a fantastic reception from the 5,000 teenagers. And the crowning moment for me came as we left the stage. James Brown walked up to us, shook our hands, and congratulated us. We became good friends, seeing him often on this and future US tours. Visiting the States was critically important to our musical education. Pop stars we might have been, but the people who formed the roots of our music were still our teachers.

In fact, we made a firm impression on all the artists. Marvin Gaye told Britain's *Rave* magazine: "They say that the music comes first and all the trimmings come way down the list. For their biting music they're sure right. They communicate more by the violence of their music. See that guy Jagger stand suddenly still, then whirl around with those maracas. He doesn't plan it but it's sure exciting."

Dennis Wilson, drummer with the Beach Boys, said: "They're tough, kinda uncompromising, no pandering to an audience. The Stones are rough, musically—sort of musical gangsters, and that's a compliment."

The film, released originally with the title *The Tami Show*, was released in America and shown at a few theaters in England. It was renamed with the corny title of *Gather no Moss*. The Beach Boys filmed their part but were not on the finished film, although they were seen on stage during the grand finale. Bo Diddley and Ike and Tina Turner were filmed at a later date. But they were not included in the finished film either.

Our impact in America was so far bigger than our achievement. Through word of mouth and our stage appearances, plus the cachet of being British, we were building fast, yet we still hadn't had a hit single. "Time is on My Side" rose to number thirty-five in America's *Music Business* chart and our album *The Rolling Stones* rose only one place that week, to number eighty-three. It was no great shakes.

But as our friend Joey Paige said, people had wised up to the fact that our appearance was not a gimmick and our influence was gaining ground: "Experienced musicians respect them." He noted that we were happier, dressed better and had neater hair than on our first trip, when indeed we were slightly green.

The young girl reporters, great fans, who attached themselves to us like limpets, were totally different from the cooler journalists we'd experienced in Britain. The critical difference we noted was that while America had many fan magazines, there was no national weekly music paper like *New Musical Express, Melody Maker, Record Mirror* or *Disc*. These UK papers were a powerful channel to British fans. And they helped make the music scene a parish, a community, spreading information and opinions every single week. Their combined sale in Britain was half a million. No such paper existed nationally in America: *Rolling Stone* magazine was not launched until 1966, when the rock scene was well under way.

What we found, in abundance, were young regional writers from magazines like *Keen Teen* and *16* magazine. They usually latched on to their particular pin-up Stone and were unable to conduct a proper interview.

From Los Angeles to San Bernardino, we knew we were slowly but positively on the way to "happening" in the USA. "The Stones is Coming," proclaimed posters outside the Swing Auditorium. Inside, a writer named Becki Hughes, from *Keen Teen*, was circling us backstage. She wrote with that wide-eyed innocence of the teenage American journalist: "I was nearest to Brian, who is cute and real handsome . . . He asked for my name, and I told him. I also told him I was reporting for *Keen Teen*, and he questioned: 'Rather young, aren't you?' to which I replied, 'Sixteen isn't too young, is it?' He laughed and so did I. He took me to a table and we had Cokes as we talked. He didn't talk very much, but was smiling and laughing so much. Sometimes he has such a melancholy look on his face, that you think he's about to cry . . ." And so on.

Later on the tour we found the other extreme. It was hard to believe the low standard of questioning from some reporters from "straight" newspapers. They didn't have to like us, but every pop musician in the sixties was bored and irritated by the sheer laziness of journalists who came unprepared to ask questions of even moderate intelligence.

There was a typical episode in Milwaukee. Reporters began our press conference by virtually interviewing each other to glean some information about us. Then a press agent invited the newsmen to fire questions at us. There was silence. The agent repeated: "Any questions for the Rolling Stones?" One reporter wanted to know what our names were.

But in San Bernardino 5,000 fans went crazy when we went on. Our set included "Not Fade Away," "Time is on My Side," "I'm Alright," "It's All Over Now," "If You Need Me," "Carol" and "I'm a King Bee." Now our records started to move in the States: radio station KRLA's chart put us top of their singles and album charts with "Time is on My Side" and *12 x 5*.

While such fresh-faced enthusiasm surrounded us in the States, the typical cynicism of Britain continued. The *News of the World*, later to become a sworn enemy of the Stones, wrote on November 1, 1964: "The Rolling Stones leer rather than smile. They don't wear natty clothes. They glower. Nobody would accuse them of radiating charm. The extraordinary thing is that more and more youngsters are turning towards them. How true is this carefully nourished picture of five indolent morons? They give the feeling that they really enjoy wallowing in a swill-tub of their own repulsiveness."

While Britain awoke to that kind of Sunday paper summary of the Stones, we were visiting Long Beach Arena, California, to an ecstatic crowd of 13,000. The reception was wild, the place so heavily surrounded by fans we couldn't get inside, so they brought a coach to the front entrance and took us in lifts, along passages and downstairs to the backstage area. When we left after a great show the coach came to the stage door as a decoy; we exited in a car another way. There were a few faintings here, and girls stripped the luggage rack from our record company's car. That was in the afternoon. Flying, tired, straight to San Diego in a charter plane, we went to the Balboa Park Bowl for an evening show. This was the kind of schedule we were on.

We flew back to Los Angeles for the night. There was

now so much confidence in our commercial prospects that next day at 11 a.m. we headed for RCA Studios in Hollywood, which was 4-track, to cut six songs, with Andrew producing. We cut Marvin Gaye's "Hitch-Hike," Solomon Burke's "Everybody Needs Somebody to Love," Otis Redding's "Pain in My Heart," Alvin Robinson's "Down-Home Girl," Mick and Keith's "Heart of Stone" and "Oh Baby." I played six-string bass on two of the songs.

Mick, Keith and Andrew stayed until 2 a.m. doing over-dubs, and Andrew enthused: "The whole set-up was terrific. We completely insulated ourselves from the outside. The boys recorded for fifteen hours non-stop, from 11 a.m. to 4 a.m., and I spent another three hours in the studio overdubbing and editing the masters. This session has produced a new Rolling Stones sound, and certainly brought out the best of Keith, whose guitar playing was magnificent. The only outsider was Jack Nitzsche, who played a toy piano and was able to make it sound like any instrument you like; on some tracks, it even sounds like a trombone."

Keith said: "The atmosphere and studio, plus the fact that we knew we had good material, made the session a good one. We didn't think it would work out at first, as the studio is so gigantic we were terrified. Then Andrew hit on the idea of putting us in one corner, shutting off the main lights and just using a spotlight, to make it more cosy. The control room was also in darkness. A bit mad, but it did the trick. Me and the boys really let ourselves go. Bill should be mentioned. He really did a great job on one number, double-tracking on bass and six-string bass."

Jack Nitzsche commented: "They were the first rock 'n' roll band I met that were intelligent. They could all talk, which was the most impressive thing about them. They were all really bright. They could make conversation with anyone, which must have freaked people out. Up until then, all the rock and rollers I met seemed to be assholes. The Stones were the first ones I saw say 'Fuck you' to everybody. There was no guidance at all on those records, and very little need for it. This was the first time a band got together and just played. They changed my whole idea of recording. Before, I'd just been doing sessions, three hours to get the tunes down. Working with the Stones made sense right away. The great new thing about them was they'd record a song the way they had written it. If it didn't work, nobody thought twice about making it a tango! They tried every way possible. Nobody had the big ego thing about keeping a song a certain way. That changed me. That was the first really free feeling I had in the studio."

We left the hotel on the morning of November 3 and had great difficulty getting through fans to the cars. This made us miss our flight, so we flew direct to Cleveland, arriving five hours late. The Mayor of Cleveland had earlier said on local radio that our performances were immoral and that no teenagers should be allowed to see them. Promoter Ed Padzur demanded a retraction. On arrival, we were welcomed and attacked by hundreds of fans. London's *Daily Telegraph* reported: "Britain's Rolling Stones will have the distinction of being the last beat group to appear at the Public Hall in Cleveland, Ohio. A ban on rock 'n' roll and beat groups goes into effect after their performance. The Mayor of Cleveland, Mr. Ralph Locher, said, 'Such groups do not add to the community's culture or entertainment.' "

The attendance and reception was disappointing, partly because of the radio broadcast, partly because it was election night (Lyndon B. Johnson was elected President of the United States this night). There were quite a few empty seats. Amusingly, though, Cambridge University students back in Britain showed they approved of us: a motion that "popular culture is debased and debasing" was defeated by 274 to 82 at the Cambridge Union. Proposing the motion, twenty-one-year-old John Costello burned a photograph of Mick Jagger to a tape-recording of "I Wanna Be Your Man"!

From Cleveland we went on to Providence, Rhode Island, where a big crowd greeted us at the airport. Here was another city in which the Stones were to be responsible for causing a ban on future pop shows—and again, it was not our fault. An audience of 3,400 gave us a fantastic reception, and during the second number girls charged the stage. The flimsy wooden cover over the orchestra pit quickly broke under their weight. After four songs the show was stopped and the audience was asked to return to its seats. Most did, but they were up again as soor as

the show restarted. More and more girls raced on to the
stage. The pit was completely demolished. The show was
stopped again, because the theater personnel were afraid
someone would be hurt, and after only five songs, we left
the stage.

We took a train to New York immediately afterwards
arriving at Grand Central Station at 4 a.m. Here we
faced a lot of abuse from black porters and cleaners on
the platform, yelling things like "Are you the Beatles,
are you girls?" I turned round and shouted back "Are
you the Harlem Globetrotters?" which seemed to leave
them totally confused. So much for American humor. We
were met by our friend Scott Ross. All the boys went to
check in at the hotel while I went back to Scott's flat. His
girlfriend was there with my friend Francesca, who stayed
the night with me.

Next day, which we had off, I spent the whole day at
Scott's flat relaxing with Francesca and got an early night.
In the evening, Mick, Keith and Andrew went to the
Apollo Theater in Harlem and saw James Brown perform. They were the only white people in the theater and
when Brown discovered they were in the audience he
called them on stage amid much screaming to take a
bow. Mick was tremendously impressed by Brown's act:
"He did an hour and a half act, non-stop and some
fantastic footwork. I asked a choreographer later if it
could be learned but he said he moves so fast it's almost
impossible to see what he does. I do a bit of James
Brown now, but a very watered-down version." In his
dressing-room afterwards, he served Mick and Keith champagne from a tub in the corner of the room, then sat like
a lord, telephone in his hand, while someone combed his
hair. He certainly made an impression on Mick.

On days off like this, we mostly just lazed around in
our hotel rooms. It was anyway quite difficult to get out
because of the crowds. Charlie, however, tended to find
the jazz spots. His big thrill was driving around New
York at 3 a.m. talking to the likes of trumpeter Clark
Terry and trombonist Bob Brookmeyer. He saw the Sonny
Rollins Quartet at Birdland, Mary Lou Williams, drum
star Jake Hanna, Billy Taylor, the Charlie Mingus big
band, Dizzy Gillespie and Max Roach. For Charlie, still
a jazz fan at heart and sometimes faintly embarrassed by

playing in a pop group, this was heaven. "What a gas!" he exclaimed at the time. "It's a wonderful scene in New York. I was offered a job backing a singer at Birdland, but I said no."

While I enjoyed New York, and Diane and Stephen were still in South Africa, thieves broke into our flat in Penge. My mother, whom I called from the States, said the place had been ransacked, and that the burglars had taken a television, radiogram, guitar, tape-recorders and jewelry belonging to Diane. The biggest loss, though, was my collection of records—irreplaceable because they had sentimental value as being my first musical purchases—and our silver disc for the *Five by Five* EP. By lucky chance, Mo Schulman called me at this time and when I explained that all my records in England had been stolen, he said I could choose some from his office. A little later, he arrived at the hotel, picked up Francesca and me and took us over to London Records, where I was invited to select as many albums as I wanted, to make up for my losses with the burglary. I finished up with about thirty!

That evening, Brian, Scott Ross, Francesca and I went down to Greenwich Village and bumped into the great blues artist, Lonnie Johnson, on the street. We then went to the Village Gate to see Dizzy Gillespie, missed his show, but saw a white blues artist singing and playing alone onstage, who was great. His name was John Hammond. We met him after the show and chatted for a while. Later, we went back to his place for drinks. There were quite a few people there, all drinking and smoking grass.

Francesca remembers how I became angry with her for smoking grass: "You didn't approve and you left me there. John took you back to the hotel on the back of his motorbike. I was pretty pissed off and I took a taxi and followed you back to the hotel, because it was your last night there. When I got up to the room, you were all right. In fact, you were quite sweet."

Nothing could stop our creative juices from flowing. A midnight flight out of New York took us to Chicago for another recording session at Chess Studios on November 8. The atmosphere wasn't as electric as last time because, as Mick commented, "Sunday in Chicago is like Sunday in Scotland—dead." However with Andrew producing we recorded all day and cut five or six tracks of strong material, including Don Covay's "Mercy Mercy," Little Walter's "Key to the Highway," Mick and Keith's "What a Shame" and my own composition, "Goodbye Girl" (which was never released).

The guitar wizard whose great record "The World is Waiting for the Sunrise" had been my first purchase suddenly appeared before me in the lobby of our hotel. To my surprise Les Paul told me he was appearing in the hotel; Stu came with me to see a performance that was impressively unconventional. He had a small black box fitted to his guitar, enabling him to play something and then double-track it and continue to multi-track from then on. After the show Stu and I chatted to him, then went back to his room to continue the conversaton for a couple of hours; we found him charming.

During this US tour, Brian definitely had the edge over Mick in popularity. Back in Britain, our fan-club secretary Shirley Arnold had sensed early friction between Jagger and Jones—"but it wasn't that ugly; Mick didn't feel threatened by Brian at that stage. Mick was a complete professional, moving on musically. Later, Brian held him back. Mick was ambitious and creative while Brian's attitude became: 'Oh let's have another drink and smoke another joint . . .' Brian couldn't cope with it all and he freaked out," she says.

Although the big problems of Brian's personality and debility were not to affect us severely for another year, he was becoming intoxicated by fame more than the rest of us. As the best-looking guy in the group, and the least stable, a big change in him was predictable. Brian's rebellion, sexual appetite and identity crisis had been forged way back in Cheltenham; now in America we thought that it was pure adrenalin—which we all suffered—that caused him to go over the top occasionally.

But it ran deeper. At seven o'clock on the morning of November 10 Brian phoned Mike Dorsey, Eric's representative in the room next to him in the Sherman House Hotel, and said he felt very grim. For a couple of days he'd complained to Mick of feeling lousy, and he certainly looked even paler than usual. But he kept up with our work: the press calls, the rehearsals, the socializing and the concerts. Dorsey called the house doctor who gave him a sedative and found his temperature was 105°.

Unless Brian was admitted to hospital immediately, the doctor said, he would not be responsible for the consequences. At the Passavant Hospital doctors said Brian was suffering from bronchitis and extreme exhaustion; he became delirious and had to be fed intravenously. There was clearly no way he could appear on stage in Milwaukee next night.

As it turned out, he didn't miss much. A campaign against us had been launched by the mayor of Milwaukee, who went on the radio before we arrived in the town, saying it would be a sign of immorality for teenagers to attend a Stones concert. His broadside had the desired effect. Out of a capacity of 6,266 seats at Milwaukee Auditorium, only 1,274 were sold. Considering the empty seats and Brian's absence, we did quite well. We were very choked about his illness, and Keith and I worked particularly hard to fill for him.

Weighing in against us next day, Michael Drew in the *Milwaukee Journal* wrote: "Unless someone teaches guitar chords to chimpanzees, the visual ultimate has been reached with the Rolling Stones. Screams from a thousand throats drowned out all but the most insistent electronic cacophony, and the two-fisted smashes of drummer Charlie. With shoulder-length hair and high-heeled boots, they seemed more feminine than their fans."

The Midwest tour continued by car to Fort Wayne, Indiana, still without Brian. Police cars, sirens wailing, escorted us into town and to a TV studio for a live interview. This was chaotic, with fans swarming, and it took quite a while for the producer to get the audience to calm down. The concert that night passed off successfully, though I well remember an awful set by the Shangri-Las. Their final song was their hit, "Leader of the Pack" —which they *mimed* to. Their encore was a repetition of the song, again *mimed*. At the time we thought this was unbelievably shoddy.

Rumors that Brian's ill-health was serious began to spread, together with a suggestion that he was leaving the group since he could not stand our hectic lifestyle. Brian was hurt by all this. Later he made a public statement: "I'm not on my last legs and I'm not leaving the Stones. I felt ill during our American tour and I wasn't enjoying very good health when we arrived back in Britain. That's

why I have to take things easy for a while. The thought
of leaving the Stones has never entered my head." The
predictions of Brian's departure were, as it turned out,
five years premature.

A loud moan went through the audience at Dayton,
Ohio, at the announcement that Brian was ill and would
not be on stage. But it soon turned to screaming and
shouting as we ran through half a dozen songs. A 400-mile
drive took us to our next town, Louisville, Kentucky,
swapping jokes with the redneck owner of a coffee house
en route. This was real Bluegrass country but the reception was wild for the two thirty-five minute sets we played.
The crowd was small, 1,700 only, probably because James
Brown was in town too; Mick and I went to see him
backstage and he took us on stage for a bow.

For the final night of the tour, back in our Midwest
base of Chicago, we did a long autograph session for
hundreds of fans backstage. We sat at long trestle-tables
while they filed past, each bearing a gift for us; we
collected four tables of items from chewing gum to gonks,
a fantastic sight. Keith was given a puppy. Brian was
released from the hospital and was fit enough to play.
We got by far the best reception of the entire tour; the
stage rose up out of the ground until it was level with the
audience, and the 5,500 crowd in the Arie Crown Theatre went berserk. When it ended, we flew to New York,
Keith clutching his puppy. The New York news was
exciting for us: *Cashbox* magazine said our album was
the fastest seller and King Karol, the biggest distributor
of records in the New York area, said our records were
out-selling the Beatles by 3–1.

Mick, Charlie and Brian immediately returned to Lon-
don; on arrival, Brian went to a specialist, Mr. J.
Musgrove, whose six-guinea fee he eventually paid on
October 4, 1965, nearly a year later.

Back in New York I was having a good time. I met a
pretty black girl called Emeretta in the corridor outside
my hotel room. She spent the afternoon with me and we
made love. She left in the early evening and I arranged to
see her next day. At about 11 p.m., Francesca arrived
with her mother, and later spent the night of her birthday
with me. Francesca left in the morning and Emeretta
then came over!

We returned to a stunning achievement. On November 20 "Little Red Rooster" had shot straight to the top of the British charts on its first entry, pushing the Supremes' "Baby Love" into second place. Our gamble in putting out a slow blues as a single had paid off. It was a dangerous move after only seventeen months of making records. Only a year earlier, we didn't think we were capable of selling blues records. But our instincts were working well for us. The British beat boom had now exploded over the world and we wanted to retain our musical identity. As Keith said: "Singles were all-important. You put yourself on the line every three months and distinctiveness was the only way we could set ourselves apart from everything else." Written by US blues singer Willie Dixon, the song had been recorded on an album by the great Howlin' Wolf and later by Sam Cooke. Brian played slide guitar and the tempo made the track virtually undanceable. Its success was a victory for our popularity. This was the only successful blues single ever released—and we had released it on Friday November 13. The B-side was the Nanker-Phelge composition, "Off the Hook."

Mick explained it to Penny Valentine in *Disc:* "The reason we recorded 'Little Red Rooster' isn't because we want to bring blues to the masses. We've been going on and on about blues, so we thought it was about time we stopped talking and did something about it. We liked that particular song, so we released it. We're not on the blues kick as far as recording goes. The next record will be entirely different, just as all the others have been."

The media's reaction to "Rooster" was mixed. Brian Matthew criticized it on BBC radio's *Saturday Club;* my friend Dave Burningham phoned him to complain, telling Matthew he was "furious at such immature criticism of an outstanding number." (Matthew apologized.)

I believe "Rooster" provided Brian Jones with one of his finest hours. It realized a cherished ambition to put blues music at the top of the charts, and meant his guilt of having "sold out" completely to pop fame was diminished. Mick had an amusing view of the slow tempo of the record: "It's suitable for dancing. It just depends who you're dancing *with!*"

While "Rooster" was hitting Britain, and our album was number two in the *Melody Maker* chart, "Time is on

My Side" was top of the American radio station WMCA's list and Marianne's "As Tears Go By" was sixty-nine in *Cashbox*.

On November 19 I flew with Andrew and Keith from New York to London. I got up early next day and went to the airport to meet Diane and Stephen, who had flown back from South Africa. After lunch I went uptown, met the boys again and we did *Ready Steady Go!* Keith collapsed at the end of the show, but was OK later; he hadn't slept for five nights, and was thoroughly exhausted.

Cheered by the public's vote of confidence against the cynicism of most of the media, we were in buoyant mood as 1964 neared its end. Neatly summing up our American tour, Mick told the *Melody Maker:* "It's like starting all over again. I enjoyed the trip, but the pressure and pace is so great. Everything's a great big deal. Every town you go to, you have got to face a whole big scene, TV people, pressmen, and DJs at the airport. That's before the concert, of course. When you have to face this, night after night, it's a bit much. Then there was the hotel rubbish. You're pretty tired after a show, and then you find girls hiding in the corridors, and even in your rooms. You have to fight your way out of theaters and fight your way into hotels. Sometimes I just wanted to scream the place down, because we couldn't get much peace."

Before the Beatles and the Stones blew the pop scene wide open, there hadn't been a great interest in the private lives of the stars in the "hit parade," as the charts used to be called. I don't remember anyone caring much whether Petula Clark or Russ Conway was married, or what they were wearing. But now, through the Beatles' sharpness and the Stones' abrasiveness, the public eye was focused on everything we did.

There were no serious drugs in pop music at this stage. It's true that "purple hearts"—pep pills—were abundant, but marijuana was used mostly by the jazz crowd. Drink was the chief vice of pop people and the Stones had never been a hard-drinking band. So the press had nothing meatier to get their teeth into than our private lives.

I tried hard to maintain a fairly normal kind of life through all this. For example, I maintained strong friendships with old mates back in Penge, people like Brian

Cade and Stewart Wealleans, who had been part of my formative years in the Cliftons. On November 24 Stewart took me to Wallington Public Hall, where he worked as a disc jockey. Jimmy Reed, whose songs we'd covered in the early days, was playing; I met him for a chat backstage before his set; his performance was excellent. The British group called the Herd were also there and I joined them on stage for two songs.*

Charlie, the least visible Stone, was bemused by the hubbub around our stardom, and his method of handling it was to pretend it wasn't happening. He was jolted into reality when news of his "secret" marriage leaked out at the end of November, two months after his wedding. He knew Andrew was worried (without justification) about our losing popularity if our girl fans saw two married Stones. So when a journalist confronted him with the "leak," Charlie stated: "I emphatically deny I am married. These reports are completely untrue." But when we all asked Charlie if it was true, he admitted it was. Then Andrew, Mick and Keith cold-shouldered him for a short time, treating him as unacceptable; it was quite childish and ridiculous.

The press finally extracted the truth from the Bradford registrar who had married Charlie and Shirley. He said: "I haven't spoken about this wedding until now but it seems it is no longer a secret. The couple are charming. I had to promise to keep the wedding secret for obvious reasons."

Charlie, confessing all, said after a few hours of denials: "Yes, I am married. I kept it a secret from the boys. I thought that if the news leaked out it would have a bad effect on them. I intended keeping it a secret as long as I could." Shirley added: "We have wanted to marry for about a year and just didn't dare. We thought it would harm Charlie's career. The months went on and we decided we could not live separately any longer. Now the secret's out I suppose I'll be in hot water at college. You're supposed to tell them when you marry because it

---

*The Herd starred my young guitarist friend Peter Frampton, later to be named "The Face of '68." Peter was among many guitarists considered in 1975 on the departure of Mick Taylor, but we signed Ronnie Wood instead.

changes your grant. I'm terribly happy being Charlie's wife. It's just wonderful."

Eric Easton, told the news by the *Daily Express*, made the most sensible remark: "Charlie didn't tell me he was getting married. I suppose now I will have to buy him a wedding present."

But generally everything seemed too quiet. It was high time we were involved in another furor. The simmering problems between Eric Easton and Andrew Oldham provided the next controversy. Without consulting the band, and while we were in America, Eric had booked us on three radio shows for the week of November 23: *Saturday Club*, *Top Gear* and *The Joe Loss Show*. Andrew canceled these on our behalf. When we didn't arrive for a *Saturday Club* recording, the BBC was angry; on November 28 hundreds of fans jammed the BBC switchboard demanding to know why the Stones hadn't appeared as advertised. The BBC said no more contracts would be made with the Stones until they had considered the position. The matter went to lawyers. Mick said: "It is not true to say we intentionally miss engagements. We have never done a stupid thing like that. The BBC contract, if there was one, must have been signed while we were touring America. We were never told about it." This battle with the BBC, unhealthy for us, was to smolder for several months.

While many parts of the Establishment saw us as a dire threat to the moral fiber of the western world, some were more tolerant and supportive. And measuring our "rebellion" in the sixties against the excesses of others in the seventies and eighties, we were tame. When Mick appeared in the magistrates' court at Tettenhall, Staffordshire on November 26, 1964, to plead guilty to three motoring offenses, his solicitor Dale Parkinson made a theatrical speech in his defense. Jagger had long hair but that did not make him an idiot, he said. Others who were far from stupid had worn long hair. "The Duke of Marlborough had much longer hair than my client, and he won some famous battles. He powdered his, too, because of the fleas. My client has no fleas. The Emperor Caesar Augustus also had rather long hair. He won many great victories. Barristers, too, wear long hair in the shape of wigs with curled-up ends. A lost license will seriously affect Jagger's mobility and that of the whole Rolling Stones group. Britain needs every dollar she can earn, and the Rolling Stones earn more dollars than many professional exporters ... Put out of your minds the nonsense talked about these young men, the Rolling Stones. They are not long-haired idiots, but highly intelligent university men."*

Mick was fined £10 for the insurance offense, and £3 on each of the other two summonses. "You are very lucky. We will treat the Liverpool endorsements as one, so that at this stage you are in a position where, if you are involved in any other incident, you will be on the road to losing your license," the magistrates' chairman told him.

And while our contract argument with the BBC simmered, we ran into another controversy. At the Birmingham studio of *Thank Your Lucky Stars,* where we mimed to "Little Red Rooster" for the show transmitted on December 5, the police wanted to get us out of the building quickly afterwards to circumvent fans, but the TV people wanted us to attend a backstage reception and pose for pictures with the other stars on the show: Petula Clark, Sandie Shaw, Clinton Ford and Mark Wynter. ABC TV said they'd given us several days' notice of the party: here was another appointment made on our behalf that we knew nothing about in advance. These mix-ups caused our reputation as troublemakers to escalate. Promoters and producers considered us completely professional, and we always worked with them cooperatively.

Worse was to come. Despite its enormous success, "Little Red Rooster," which was at Number One, was not featured on *Top of the Pops* on December 3; the BBC said this was "not a policy matter," but everyone linked it with our running dispute with the Corporation over the radio shows. Replying to a hue and cry from our fans about this snub, the BBC stated: "There is no battle between the BBC and the Rolling Stones. The BBC doesn't ban artists, nor does it ban records."

Well, it sure looked that way to us. On December 6, Andrew arrived at Broadcasting House to be interviewed

---

*Not true, of course. Only Mick had been to university—and he hadn't stayed long!

on *Teen Scene*, but was told ten miutes before he was due to go on that he could not appear. As he said: "I find it very amusing, but it is very unethical for the BBC to make a statement to the music press one week that there is no feud with the Rolling Stones, then to carry out this under-the-table ban on me." An order had gone from the director of sound broadcasting that neither the Stones nor anyone connected with us could appear on any radio shows.

Finally, the BBC owned up. "As there has been some misunderstanding with the Rolling Stones," they announced, "it was thought inadvisable for their manager to appear in an unscripted interview. Following the Stones' non-appearance at a recording session, the contractual situation is being considered."

Saturday Club, a key program, now said: "We are not going to book them. I doubt if they will appear on *Saturday Club* again, at least as far as producer Brian Willey is concerned. Nobody is booking them until the dispute is cleared up and how long that will take is anybody's guess."

Mick and Brian meanwhile went to Paris for the weekend. While they were there Brian went to a party given by the Animals after their show at the Olympia. There the actor Dennis Hopper met Brian. He later introduced him to art-gallery owner Robert Fraser, who would loom large in the Stones' story. Brian was now taking all sorts of amphetamines, which made him really paranoid. Friends advised him to smoke dope rather than pop so many pills—at least that might calm him rather than feed his paranoia. Although Brian knew the dangers, he persuaded himself that pills and booze were good for him and that he needed them just to cope.

As 1964 neared its end, Brian and Linda finally broke up. Their baby was now four months old and Brian still refused to marry her. Brian, who had been living at her parents' house in Reading, was thrown out. He went flat-hunting in London, leaving behind the girl many believed to be the only true love of his life.

Elsewhere, there was buoyancy. Rolling Stones jigsaw puzzles, greetings cards, tea towels, pillow cases, bubblegum and plastic reproduction guitars were planned in Britain within the next few months. Since my bank account showed a credit of just £14, this could only be good news. On December 10 the first Rolling Stones Ltd. board meeting was held and was attended by everyone except me, as Diane was ill. We were given figures for most of the year, and later Eric called me at home to give me a rundown on how we were doing. Next day I went to his office to inspect the company business and check the figures.

The gibes continued. On television's *Juke Box Jury* Lonnie Donegan (of all people!) insulted us and spat on the floor, complaining that we were exploiting blues artists and making money out of them. There was a flood of protests, but none more forcibly and accurately expressed than in a letter to *Record Mirror* by John Berry: "Although not interested in the recent beat boom I was glad the Stones made it. I've been a blues fan since before the skiffle days. The Stones are very serious about the blues and have done it and its exponents a lot of good—more than can be said for the skiffle craze. As for saying that the Stones are exploiting blues artists and making money out of it, Mr. Donegan has got things the wrong way round. When the Stones record a number by a blues artist, the credit is given to him and he gets the royalties. They also seize every chance to make these artists more known here. In Mr. Donegan's day, the idea was to take a song of an obscure artist, adapt it to skiffle and record it as 'Trad., arr. Donegan' or whatever name was involved. Surely, that's nearer 'exploitation.' " Ouch!

It was round about now that Mick and Keith wrote "The Last Time" at their flat in Hampstead. They thought the title was weak and tried for a long period to improve on it, but finally decided to go with their first idea.

Intuition told me that the Stones was going to be a hard barrier to crack with my own compositions, since the "Unholy Trinity" controlled what was recorded. So I was making plans to get other outlets for my songwriting ambitions. Another interest of mine was record production, even at this early stage. After seeing a group called the Cheynes with Mick Fleetwood on drums (the forerunners of Fleetwood Mac), I arranged to produce them with Glyn Johns.

With Brian Cade, I'd written the B-side to the new single by the Cheynes, and played bass on it, too: "Stop Running Around." I then registered a new production

company for myself called Temeraire Ltd. and talked to
Dave Berry, the singer ("The Crying Game") and Julie
Grant about possible songs which I had for them. Symbolically, at the same time Andrew, Mick and Keith
formed a music publishing company outside the Stones
called Mirage Music Ltd. The division in the band had
begun to show.

As Keith celebrated his twenty-first birthday on December 18, 1964, news came from America that "Little Red
Rooster" was banned from record release because of its
"sexual connotations." This was astonishing when one
considered the blatant sex in some of the lyrics of the
blues and even pop songs; but they probably reckoned
that a Stones disc would be listened to more than most.
So as an answer on December 19, London Records released as our fifth US single, "Heart of Stone" backed by
"What a Shame," on which Stu played piano. Both sides
had been recorded at the Chess Studios in Chicago.* As
it was released, "Time is on My Side" stayed at sixth
position in the American charts and in Britain the summary of the Stones year in *Record Mirror* said the Stones
were "the stars who made the most progress in 1964.
They can outdraw any other act in the country."

So despite a slow-burning undercurrent of problems
and personality clashes in the group, there was much to
celebrate at Christmas. Specially pleasing for Diane and
me was a £270 insurance award for my home being bur-
gled. Since I had virtually nothing in the bank (£20 to be
precise), the money was very welcome. I was immersed
in family life at this time, going home to lay out and test
Stephen's car track, his Christmas present.

The Beatles went to the top of the American charts
with "I Feel Fine," but the song's sentiments were ours,
too: it had been a year when we were more prolific than
we would ever be again, releasing some fifty different
songs (two UK EPs, three UK singles, five US singles, one
UK album, two US albums) and we broke the record for
British bands for most gigs in a year. We also received
our second gold record, for the single "Time is on My Side."

*It finally got to number fifteen in the American singles charts
in mid-February 1965.

This was a vintage year for pop music generally: there were a hundred million-selling records, including eleven by the Beatles, five by the Dave Clark Five, three each by Elvis Presley and the Supremes and two each by the Bachelors, Beach Boys, Cilla Black, Manfred Mann, Roger Miller, Roy Orbison, Peter and Gordon, Jim Reeves, the Shangri-Las—and by the Rolling Stones, the singles "It's All Over Now" and "Time is on My Side."

In the *New Musical Express* charts summary of 1964, we were third in the overall points table; and we carried off the number one position in the best-selling album of the year category, with our LP *The Rolling Stones*.

7

The Unholy Trinity

With position comes responsibility. It is a thought we recommend to the Rolling Stones. We would urge pop stars everywhere to give at least passing consideration to the financial straits in which the manufacturers are likely to find themselves if the next generation goes eternally open-necked.

The Tailor and Cutter, London, March 1965

The trouble with a tie is that it dangles in the soup. It is also something extra on to which fans can hang when you are trying to get in and out of the theater. We are really sorry for the tie industry but we won't change our ways.

Mick Jagger

Modern youth, the Rolling Stones and such, are something one has to live with and understand.

Dr. Ramsey, Archbishop of Canterbury, March 1965

Our Irish tour had begun comfortably enough in Belfast on January 6. We laughed away mistakes by reporters who asked questions like: "Are you Mick Jones?" Between shows, we drank champagne with the British athlete Mary Peters.* Irish fans proved very excitable, chucking all manner of things at us as we played the shows: an ashtray missed my face by inches, an iron bolt,

---

*Mary Peters recalled in 1982: "The Stones weren't very nice to me at all. They were not really switched on to the occasion and kept sticking their heads out of the window to the screaming groupies outside. I remember it vividly and was really thrilled to meet them, but they didn't know who I was and were not interested."

of all things, hit Mick on the thigh, and a girl's patent-leather shoe swirled towards Brian, who smiled and ducked elegantly.

En route from Belfast to Dublin, our train's corridors were jammed by autograph-hunting fans. A railway guard stood sentry over our carriage while we ate. We played two very successful sell-out shows in the city to almost 5,000 fans. In December 1982 Bob Geldof told me that his sister had taken him to the first show. They had sneaked in during our sound check. Geldof remembers Andrew Oldham sitting halfway back in the stalls, and Mick balancing on the footlights. When Andrew said, "Get on with it," Mick turned round and said, "Fuck off!" "This was exactly what we expected him to say," said Geldof. I asked what his strongest memory was of the actual concert, and he replied, "The overpowering smell, and the sight of urine covering the floors!"

Driving from Dublin to Cork in the pouring rain, I took movie film throughout, shooting scenes of incredible beauty. Rural Ireland made a big impression on me: I have pictures of old women in black shawls and capes with hoods that make them look like something from the Middle Ages. It seemed like medieval times: a young guy in black walked down the street with a dead turkey under his arm.

We stopped at a small shop in a village and were refused service by the proprietor, who muttered provocatively: "I don't want to serve you. You're English—we haven't forgotten Oliver Cromwell." We thought it was hilarious at first, but he meant it, so we gave a few well-chosen insults and walked out; then Andrew had a pee against his shop front. The shop owner chased us to our cars, jumped up on the bonnet of my car, and began kicking the windscreen wipers off. He was lucky not to have been hurt—and we'd been lucky not to have been beheaded.

In Cork we got great receptions from the two packed shows at the Savoy theater. Later, at the local hotel set on a hillside overlooking the town and the river that runs to the sea, we all sat talking, drinking coffee and playing guitars in my room until 5 a.m. when a clock struck on the hillside and a howling wind broke the silence. We talked of ghosts as dawn broke, and Brian said: "Ghosts of the morning can be seen on the skyline, if you watch intently enough . . ."

Advance orders of 210,000 greeted the release of our second album in Britain, *The Rolling Stones No. 2,* on January 15, 1965. The album photo was taken by David Bailey. Musically, it occupied the middle ground for us, combining favorites like "Time is on My Side" and "You Can't Catch Me" with near-standards "Down the Road Apiece" and "Under the Boardwalk." Only two compositions by Jagger and Richards were featured, "What a Shame" and "Grown Up Wrong," while one Nanker-Phelge group contribution went on the record. I was particularly pleased with the six-string bass effect I gained on "Down-Home Girl" and "Pain in My Heart," and although the album was a milestone for us, there were mixed feelings from some. John Lennon, noted for his impatience, commented: "The album's great but I don't like five-minute numbers." While one writer commended the album as "tight, intense, fat and fiery," a correspondent wrote angrily to *Melody Maker:* "How far will Andrew Oldham's obsession with Phil Spector take him? The new LP seems to be a testing ground to discover how many weird sounds he can produce on each track." Yet the album was Number One for thirteen weeks in Britain, remaining in the album charts for thirty-seven weeks.

In the mid-sixties, pop stars occupied center stage. The music, important and often innovative, propelled us into a role for which we were often ill-equipped: arbiters of the morality of the country, experts on everything from nuclear war to sex, from religion to materialism.

We had such a rough ride with the press that to be treated seriously and asked fair questions was stimulating. While Andrew enjoyed putting joke ads in the music papers such as: "Mick Jagger lips. Order now. Be with the in-crowd. Full details from your local lip dealers," occasionally we were able to say some serious things.

Talking about teenage rebellion, Brian said, "Every generation brings a fresh wave of ideas, and if this were to be stifled, society and culture would be doomed. Our children will be rebelling against us in twenty years' time, in just the same way." Asked what he wanted in world progress, he replied intriguingly: "I'd like lots of money spent on neuro-research, to find out what causes mental illness. When man can understand the human brain, he'll understand everything."

Mick denied any moral responsibility towards the fans: "Stars and celebrities should not try to set any levels in morals. Who are we to say what is right and what is wrong?"

Keith, asked by a reporter about religion, replied: "You won't find any of the Stones going around praying, see us in church or reading the Bible. We're atheists and not ashamed to admit it. When you get to know us, we're pretty good guys at heart. People who go to church just for the sake of it, to keep up appearances and smile at the vicar, are idiots. Those who go because they believe in God's faith, that's fine. We'll leave religion to the dedicated."

I mostly talked about my role in the group: "I would never work for anyone else now. I would like to stay in the business, and I'm making plans to do just that. I've got to be ready for when the Stones die, as ultimately they must. Over the past two years, life has taken on new horizons. My whole approach has widened." Indeed, life without the Stones was looking promising: Dick Rowe of Decca accepted the single I produced for Bobbie Miller. But meanwhile life with the Stones continued, with a visit to Australia and New Zealand.

Later that month, while we were in Melbourne, my "solo" career was consolidated with the release of Bobbie Miller's "What a Guy," backed by the Wyman–Brian Cade composition "You Went Away"; I had produced this Decca single. And the Cheynes' single "Down and Out," with Brian and my own song "Stop Running Around" also came out at this time on Columbia. This was a joint production by Glyn Johns and me.

Charlie too had something going for him while we were away; his book on the life of jazz saxophonist Charlie "Bird" Parker was finally published: *Ode to a High-Flying Bird*.

I was put in charge of the petty cash for the tour, which began on January 17 with a flight to Los Angeles, and I was quickly busy at London airport, where we incurred a $230 excess-baggage charge for guitars, amplifiers and other items.

Our twenty-four-hour stopover in Los Angeles was productive and enjoyable. I signed a contract with Irving Music for "Cause I'm in Love with You," my composition with Brian Cade, which Joey Paige planned to record for a single in the US soon. The rest of the Stones went shopping, blowing $2,000 on clothes before we all met at RCA Studios in Hollywood to record two Mick and Keith songs, "The Last Time" and "A Mess of Fire" (later renamed "Play with Fire"), plus three old blues numbers. Exhausted, I returned to the Beverly Hilton Hotel, took a hot bath and went to bed. Mick and Keith carried on working in the studio with Andrew until 3 a.m., finishing the single. At 4 a.m. Brian phoned England to hear that our new album had entered the *singles* chart at number twenty-four in its first week.

Next morning we flew to Hawaii, on to Fiji where I bought stamps at the airport for my son, and then to Sydney, with dawn breaking as the plane came in. We lost January 20 because we crossed the international dateline; so while we were on the plane Brian wrote to Eric Easton:

Dear Eric,
    We left Los Angeles at 8 p.m. on Tuesday, January 19. It is now 6 a.m. on Thursday January 21. You are currently enjoying Wednesday, January 20, your time now being 10 p.m. It has, as I understand it, always been our policy to work together in a spirit of harmony and understanding, so where is our Wednesday? I trust you will rectify this matter as early as possible and won't steal another day from us.
    Sincerely, Brian

Three thousand fans greeted us in Sydney. Three hundred of them lining a thirty-foot wire barricade were buried when the barricade collapsed. Screaming, weeping youngsters fell, and bodies piled up six deep in one spot. When our plane landed, five girls who had been hiding behind a tarmac mobile staircase rushed across to the plane door. Three reached Mick, Charlie and me but were dragged away by police, kicking and screaming. Amazingly, although scores of kids were bruised and scratched, nobody was seriously hurt.

Describing the scene as "yet another historical event in the cultural development of this nation," Australia's *TV Times* reported a policeman as saying: "You know, ten or fifteen years ago we'd have lumbered those blokes on a vagrancy charge for impersonating females." The magazine also quoted someone as saying: "I am unable to believe that five young men would make themselves look this way for real . . . it is all, I believe, a gigantic hoax on us, their elders."

We took a whole floor at the Chevron Hilton, which had fantastic views over Sydney Harbour. Huge crowds were outside all the time. The scene in our hotel room was excellently captured by Judy Wade, reporting back to *New Musical Express:* "They were taking their first look at the Sydney skyline from the terrace . . . Keith was busy dropping whisky glasses from the balcony into the empty car park five stories below, to see if he could hear them tinkle on the concrete. Charlie was gazing at the half-finished Sydney Opera House nearby and his knowledgeable remarks about its far-out design earned respectful looks. While Mick burst into a few choruses of 'Baby I Need Your Loving,' in the background, Brian borrowed my pen to take down an attractive girl's phone number."

Mick went to visit his aunt, his mother's sister, who had seen him when she visited England a year earlier. He also met some cousins for the first time. Mick's mother had written to her sister saying: "I solemnly advise you to take earplugs, because after the last concert I saw my doctor had to treat me for perforated eardrums."

Early signs that the Australian visit would be eventful came when Brian, Keith, Charlie and Andrew went to a private beach and became involved in a skirmish when they took a rowing boat out into the harbor. Three schoolboys in a fishing boat began heckling: "Go home Rolling Stones," and "Look at the white suntans!" Keith shouted: "Come over here and say that," and as the boats drew closer the two sides began splashing each other with oars. Then one schoolboy dived into the water, grabbed the Stones' boat and began rocking it, trying to turn it over. "The attack was quite unprovoked," said Andrew. "We didn't want to fight but we were forced into it."

Our debut Australian concerts, five shows over two days at the Agricultural Hall, Sydney, with audiences of 5,200, were terrific, with girls swarming towards the stage, toppling chairs and anything in their way, nearly scrambling on stage. We were joint top of the bill with the great Roy Orbison,* but while he was praised for his family-type image, we were predictably caned by the press. "A blatantly sexual act which the chaste Beatles had not prepared our tender teens for," wrote one. "They're shockers. Ugly Looks, Ugly Speech, Ugly Manners," said the *Sydney Morning Herald*.

The hedonistic side of Brian surfaced very quickly. Every country we saw or played, he enthused about in roughly the same way: "I like this place," he said of Sydney. "I'd like to have a flat here." (He had said the same of Paris, Brussels and New York!) The Aussie press tried to whip up a scandal saying we were having wild, all-night parties and orgies. As Andrew commented: "I wish we were!"

On the day Winston Churchill died in London, we were in a plane flying the 500 miles from Sydney to Brisbane where we were greeted by 1,500 fans. Checking into the city's Lennon's Hotel (which gave us a laugh), we discovered that the Kinks, Manfred Mann and the Honeycombs were there too, on another tour. After a press conference, we did balcony appearances for the fans gathered outside. I had thought only royalty did that! Next morning some of the guys went water-skiing, with Brian driving the speedboat.

Our two sell-out shows at City Hall were nearly marred by riots. Police had to act fast to hold back the crowds; two teenage girls managed to jump on stage and hug Mick and the show faced the prospect of premature closure.

The day after our two sell-out shows I slept, and then the girl who had stayed with me arranged with her girlfriend to drive me and Paul Jones of Manfred Mann into the country, so I could shoot some film. We were amazed to see animal bones and skulls lying around. The temperature was 95°, then suddenly, on the drive back, two inches of rain fell in thirty minutes.

*His backing guitarist was Bobby Goldsboro, who later had a successful solo career.

Mick, Brian, Keith and Charlie, meanwhile, had hired a couple of cars and drove fifty miles up the coast to Paradise Island, a holiday resort also known as Surfers Paradise, on the coast near Brisbane. Here they spent the day sunbathing and surfing. Returning to the hotel, on a particularly fast stretch of road, they were involved in a small accident with a car driven by a local surfer. Keith walloped his head on the windscreen and got a nasty headache, but otherwise they were very lucky.

The abrasive Aussie press could not prevent our popularity. Within two days we'd played before 25,000 people and Sydney asked for two extra concerts to be slotted in. "Little Red Rooster"—announced on stage by Charlie— was the most popular song; after the encore Sydney shows, the promoter Harry Miller organized a party at his home. It was very snooty, so we didn't stay long.

On January 28 we were up early and flew to Melbourne to be greeted by a crowd of 2,000 fans waiting in a temperature of 80°. Our records were breaking out all over the Australian charts, and we could hardly switch on the hotel radio without hearing ourselves; we had a load of singles released that were not out in that format anywhere else, including "Walking the Dog."

There were masses of girls to take our pick from in Australia. Keith swears that the international rock musician's word "groupie" was invented by me during this tour. I remember better the two code words that we used. "Laundry" was one. We were flanked by security men all the time and didn't want to ask our road managers about girls in front of the bodyguards, so we dropped into the habit of saying to road crew like Mike Dorsey: "Did you arrange the laundry for tonight?"

We had fairly elaborate ways of choosing the girls we fancied—and for getting rid of them quickly. A typical example: on February 9, 1965, in Melbourne, we stayed at a three-story modern hotel with wide grass verges at the front. Between fifty and a hundred girls camped outside day and night and we could see them clearly from our room. Brian and I each had a double bedroom with a shared sitting-room between us. We brought a couple of girls back after the show, and the four of us had drinks before splitting to our bedrooms for an hour and a half. Brian and I had prearranged to meet in the sitting-room.

If Brian was first, he'd shout to me to hurry, and vice versa. We had a drink, said goodbye to the girls and looked out of the window, spying a couple down by a tree, waving frantically up to us.

We called the porter at reception, saying: "There are two girls outside . . ."

"There are *lots* of girls outside," he replied.

"No," I said. "There's one in a red top and another in a blue-and-white striped jumper. Could you send them up to the room for a drink?"

He went out and invited them to come up, and we followed the same drinks-and-bedroom routine as before. This went on the whole time we were in Melbourne.

We used the code words "room service" to get rid of the girls. Brian and I would say to each other: "Shall we order something from room service?" "Yes, let's." Then we'd say to them: "OK, girls, you've got to go. We want to get something up from room service."

Despite the good times like these, we weren't sorry to leave Australia. The fans loved us, but the air of hostility from the media was very unsettling. Statistically, the tour was great: we did seven shows before 35,000 people in Sydney and another seven in Melbourne for 21,000. "Under the Boardwalk" went to the top as a single, with great success too for "Heart of Stone" and "Little Red Rooster."

After a four-hour flight on January 31 to Christchurch, New Zealand, we arrived in a downpour to be greeted by about 3,000 fans, who had been waiting for two hours. We were very impressed by this reception; here we were joined by six security guards who accompanied us throughout the trip, one for each member of the group. We thought the hotel we used, the United Service Hotel in Cathedral Square, Christchurch, was a dump, though supposedly the best in town. It was so lacking in amenities that we had to wash our own socks and shirts; we complained that there were too few bathrooms, and Mick commented that in view of the place, "You can't blame us if we smell."

When told that in New Zealand little emphasis was placed on hit parades, in contrast with Australia, we decided to check out the local shops ourselves. Talking to the retailers we discovered we were outselling everybody else, including the Beatles—very satisfying!

We got ourselves together for the night's two shows at the Theatre Royal, Christchurch, continuing the tour with Roy Orbison. The first house was quiet, the second much more like it, with kids rushing the stage. Later, we adjourned to a club and cheered ourselves up with some girls who returned to the hotel with us for the night.

After a bumpy flight to the old-fashioned town of Invercargill next day, the audiences at both of our shows were dead, so we cut our sets short; I even noticed forty-year-olds scattered throughout the audience. Mick described the town as "the arsehole of the world. There are twenty-eight rooms in the hotel and only two baths. The last meal ends at 7 p.m." There was some consolation for me: the girl I'd left in Christchurch flew in and stayed with me again. But Invercargill was one of the most boring places we encountered and we vowed never to return.

Dunedin was better. The girl had come in again, so I was fine. In the hotel, Roy Orbison kept us awake by telling us of the early days of Elvis Presley, when they toured together, and he and Bobby Goldsboro amused us with the sickest jokes we'd ever heard.

Next day the boys took a dip in the hot springs and went horse-back riding. I also visited the famous volcanic area of Rotarua and Maori village where I used two reels of home movie film and bought souvenirs (including a real sheepskin which I shipped back to London direct).

When I awoke on the morning of February 8 after our concerts in Auckland I could hardly open my left eye. The infection gave me pain all day on the flight to Wellington. For the next week I saw doctors at various stops on the tour until finally, in Perth, an eye specialist said I should wear dark glasses until it cleared up. People thought this was part of the "look," but it simply provided a little relief.

"Don't stand up or you'll get arrested," Mick shouted to the fans at the Wellington concert. They were far too heavily policed for Mick's liking; one girl got within inches of the stage but was firmly ejected. After seeing so many police in front of him on so many concerts, Mick could stand no more, so between shows he formally

protested to the inspector in charge of crowd control, but
to no avail.

Before the show I'd been driven by Stu and my minder
(nicknamed Yorkie), to Titahi Bay to visit a friend who
lived there with his family. George Smith from Penge
had semi-managed my old group the Cliftons before emi-
grating; they all came to the second show. For me, it was
a great reunion and another excuse for home movies.

New Zealand was a much quieter experience than Australia, partly because radio featured little pop and the
Stones' sound had not saturated the country. Demand for
tickets back in Australia had been so great that they
asked us to go back after New Zealand; we flew from
Wellington to Christchurch and then on to Melbourne to
do two extra shows, checking in back at a motel where
the owners had organized a welcoming barbecue for us.
This went on for hours before we retired, exhausted,
with various girls. Mick told us later that he slept with
the woman owner *and* her daughter!

Adelaide was notable for an excellent press conference
at which I met and dated a really pretty girl reporter who
took me sightseeing to a lovely valley and beach. During
the conference two teenage girls who had been hiding in
a cupboard in an adjoining room for two hours burst out
and attempted to reach us; they were removed by security guards. Shame. My eye was still giving me trouble,
but the shows in the Centennial Hall, both sold out, went
well.

Back at the hotel we relaxed at a party for the Newbeats,
the American group ("Bread and Butter") who shared
our bill. They were returning to the States next day.
During the party, Brian disappeared with the girl journalist I'd been seeing. I went to his room to investigate
but he wouldn't open the door or answer. I decided to
wreak my revenge. Returning to my room, I took all her
possessions (handbag, coat and other items) and dropped
them out of the window into a goldfish pond three floors
below. I went to bed much happier.

There were riotous scenes from a thousand fans as we
flew into Perth on February 13. Police had a wild time,
darting around to stop them reaching us, but twenty fans
got through and girls flung themselves at us. Police lifted
them bodily off the ground, arms and legs waving, and

dumped them back over the barrier. A few hostile youths jeered us, so Brian squirted suntan cream at them from our bus window.

After a matinee show at Perth's Capitol Theatre, back at the hotel I found my great-aunt (the sister of Grandmother Perks), Kate London, and some of her family waiting to meet me. They stayed an hour drinking and chatting before I needed to see my third doctor and eye-specialist; they couldn't help much and told me to continue wearing dark glasses at all times. The evening crowd at the first of two shows was mad. Hundreds of screaming, hysterical girls fought with security guards, who linked arms as fans were trampled to the ground trying to get on stage.

Waikiki Beach proved a bit of a respite from fans, and after a rendezvous with some girls back at the hotel, it was Singapore next stop.* We arrived to a welcome from a crowd of 1,000 European, Chinese and Malaysian fans in incredible heat and humidity: as we walked down the steps of the plane we were instantly drenched in sweat. It was like walking fully clothed into a shower. Security was astonishing. Fifty men of the reserve unit of the British Military Police and naval shore patrol sealed the fans in the "waving gallery" of the terminal; they had a clear view of us and the authorities had total control. At the Singapura Hotel I took a shower, changed into fresh clothes, walked out on to the balcony and was immediately just as sticky and sweaty as before.

Since we were ostracized by so many authorities around the world, it was refreshing to be driven next day to Government House for lunch with the British Deputy High Commissioner, Philip Moore, and his family. After a spectacular meal we were shown the beautiful grounds; at night, concerts for two audiences of 10,000 took place at Badminton Stadium. Again, there was incredible security.

Driving back to the hotel amidst bangs from fire-crackers going off throughout the city to celebrate the Chinese New Year, we could not anticipate what was in store. At a drinks party later at the apartment of the concert pro-

---

*On the day we arrived in Singapore, February 15, 1965, the great singer Nat "King" Cole died in America, aged forty-five.

moter Freddie Yu, we met a dozen "ladies of the night" invited for our benefit. We were invited to choose one each and retire to one of the rooms provided. We were all very shy about this public display; eventually, Andrew got the ball rolling and chose first, then Mick and then me. I don't know what happened with the others but when I was alone with my girl, I found it impossible to perform. I'd never been with a paid girl before. After she'd tried everything, I suggested we forget it. But she persevered, went into the bathroom, put some mentholated toothpaste in her mouth, returned to me, and presto—I learned the "Toothpaste Trick!"

As our global activities continued—with an exceptionally good press welcome for our third album in the USA, *The Rolling Stones, Now!**— our records were tearing up the charts in Europe, Australia and Singapore. From there we flew to Hong Kong for a stopover and some brief shopping and then to Tokyo, where we did an airport press conference before flying to Los Angeles.

All the way over, Charlie was worrying himself silly about Shirley, who had traveled to Los Angeles from England. When we touched down she was not at the barrier, so he phoned the hotel. She wasn't there either. That was it! He stormed through the customs barrier without even waiting to be cleared, grabbed a record-company executive by the scruff of his jacket and whisked him over to the nearest taxi. "Where's Shirl?" he panted. "We've booked her into another hotel," said the executive. Charlie rushed him into the taxi and off they sped. They met up eventually and a few hours later flew off to Miami for a short holiday with relatives.

We checked into the Ambassador Hotel; there were soon lots of girls hanging around the foyer and we took our pick. The band then began to disperse: Mick, Keith and Andrew went to RCA Studios to re-do the vocals on "The Last Time"; Brian and I returned to London, after a day in Hollywood, which Mick described as "quite a pleasant town, very picturesque, but it houses a terrible lot of phonies. Even the waitresses want to become film stars."

*This eventually reached number five and stayed in the American charts for fifty-one weeks.

"The Last Time," our sixth single in Britain, was released on February 26, 1965, to a mixed reception. "You can remember the tune after one spin," said *Record Mirror*. "Quite good, but it does go on a bit," said *Melody Maker*. "Andrew Oldham should stop pontificating so much about the pop scene in general and do more editing on the Stones discs in particular."* "Best thing they've released," said *Disc*. "Without doubt their best number ever," opined the *Daily Mail*. Interestingly, there was almost as much enthusiasm for the B-side, the folky Nanker-Phelge composition "Play with Fire."

Decca sent us no copies so I could not give my verdict on "The Last Time" to reporters who asked me that day. "I'm going out to buy the record as soon as it's in the shops," I told some writers, truthfully. I added that we'd cut it in Los Angeles "because you get a much better sound there."

"The Queen of the Mods," Cathy McGowan, was the epitome of swinging London in the mid-sixties. Miniskirted and thigh-booted, she held court every Friday tea-time as compère of *Ready Steady Go!* We hated the phoneyness of miming but the show was too important to miss. On the release day of "The Last Time" Cathy interviewed Mick on the show; the conversation vividly demonstrated her deficiencies as an interviewer:

Cathy: "How did you enjoy the tour?"

Mick: "Very much, actually."

"You know, when you're going to come on, we get hundreds of letters from girls and the kind of things they want to know is: how many times a week you wash your hair."

"About twice a week," Mick answered.

"And who cuts it for you?"

"Usually Keith, but sometimes other people," Mick said.

"And who cuts Keith's?"

"Keith cuts his with a mirror," said Mick, patiently.

---

*There was no holding back Andrew by now; immune to criticism, he was a self-appointed guru of pop, busy with all kinds of deals. He also released yet another single produced by him and written by Mick and Keith: the Mighty Avengers' "Blue Turns to Grey."

"Mums write in to me and say: how many times do you take a bath?"

Mick: "If it's a hot country, every day."

Cathy: "That's a super answer, Mick, and do you think if you got married it would affect you as a person, and your popularity?"

"It might do. I only fancy unmarried people, so why should anyone fancy a married me?"

"That's quite true anyway," Cathy said. "Anyway, let's hear the A-side of your new record."

We mimed to "The Last Time." As the show ended, screaming girls in the TV studio audience broke through a safety barrier, dragged Mick from the rostrum; he suffered a twisted ankle. Millions of viewers saw the scuffle on their screens.

For our *Ready Steady Go!* appearance we were paid the statutory fee of £42 10s. There was better news from America about money: a statement arrived at this time from London Records in New York showing that from January 1, 1964, to February 28, 1965, shared royalties due to us from Nanker-Phelge Music totaled $79,984.55, just under $16,000 each—not that we received it at that time! My bank account showed a credit now of a mere £136!

But while we had some cash to look forward to, the rollercoaster of trouble gathered speed, making us headline news. And it was totally unrelated to music. Without any planning by us, a series of incidents increased our reputation as "loutish dangers to society."

The first broadside came because Andrew had written provocative notes on the cover of our second album. We knew nothing about it until we saw the finished record; but Andrew's doodlings in the bath one night pitched us into a major controversy, causing questions to be asked in the House of Lords. He wrote: "Cast deep in your pocket for loot to buy this disc of groovies and fancy words. If you don't have bread, see that blind man, knock him on the head, steal his wallet and lo, you have the loot. If you put in the boot, good, another one sold."

"Sheer damned bad taste," declared the National Association for the Blind. "It is extraordinary that a company like Decca should print anything like this." Decca's chairman, Sir Edward Lewis, responded: "I am told that this inscription was intended to be humorous, but I am afraid this jargon does not make sense to me."

Mick told a newspaper: "The stuff about the blind man has nothing to do with us; we didn't write it," while Keith commented: "It is just a sick joke. I'm sorry if the blind people are upset but you can see a lot sicker things on TV." Andrew said he composed the words for fun: "I'm fed up with reading the usual blurbs on sleeves."

Many people, though, continued to find the remarks offensive. On March 16 Lord Conesford asked in the House of Lords what government action was planned and if the attention of the Director of Public Prosecutions had been drawn to the "offensive" album cover. The Home Office Joint Parliamentary under-secretary replied that the director was aware of the matter but in his view there was "no evidence that these words have been published in circumstances constituting a criminal offense." The heat of the controversy was reduced when Sir Edward Lewis instructed that the offending words be deleted from future pressings of the LP. We had survived another round.

As the American magazine *Sixteen* announced that Prince Charles and Princess Anne were keen fans of the Stones and the Beatles, we began another two-shows-a-night package tour at the Regal Edmonton on March 5, 1965. The Hollies, Dave Berry and the Cruisers, the Original Checkmates and an American girl group called Goldie and the Gingerbreads shared the bill. Graham Nash of the Hollies remarked: "It was absolutely insane. There was an incredible difference between the depth of emotion expressed for the Stones and for us. We could certainly drive them crazy, but it went to a brand new level when the Stones came on—it was somehow deeper and darker than Beatlemania."

Our set was "Everybody Needs Somebody to Love," "Pain in My Heart," "Down the Road Apiece," "Time is on My Side," "I'm Alright," "Little Red Rooster," "Route 66" and "The Last Time," and our show was recorded live by Glyn Johns, as were future shows at Liverpool and Manchester. We had plans to release a "live" LP. Mick pointed to Charlie before "Little Red Rooster"; the crowd went wild as he went forward to Mick's microphone to introduce the song. But not a word could be heard above the roar from the fans. In the interval we checked with Charlie what he'd said onstage. "I thought about it for a long time," he said drolly, "and then I eventually decided to say: 'Hallo, Edmonton.' I shall obviously have to rehearse something more punchy, for future shows." Brian complained furiously that the lighting was so bad that he couldn't see to ensure his guitar-fingering was right on the newer songs.

We'd returned from our international travels more mature and professional. The key to our new presentation was simplicity: no gimmicks, no smart uniforms and no phoney antics. Brian remarked: "I don't do anything. I just stand there and earn my money." The Rolling Stones had become much more consciously commercial as a unit. This was confirmed when all the major record companies started bidding for us, since the contract between Impact Sound and Decca was to expire in May. Eric Easton said: "There have been approaches from every other record company, and of course Decca; the Stones are a very attractive proposition to anybody." CBS stated they were ready to top any offer from other companies.

As "The Last Time" went to the top of the charts, Eric Easton revealed that he had rejected an offer of a million-dollar minimum for our records over the next five years. He maintained that we should earn that much in a year, but I must say nobody had told me or my bank manager this. Eric was still receiving offers from various record companies; he said that Impact Sound could probably demand royalties of sixpence a single, which would bring in £25,000 for every million sold. About half of this would go to the group.

But on the road, the same dispiriting hotel problems continued. After a show in Liverpool we drove to Manchester, where we had hoped to stay at the Grand Hotel for two nights, but they refused our booking with no explanation. There was a recurrence of yet another old problem at the hotel that did take us on March 6, the Midland. When Mick strolled into the grill room for lunch wearing a gray crew-necked sweater and stripped trousers, he was refused entry. The headwaiter told him: "No ties, no meals, the usual condition one can expect at a first-class hotel." By now we'd stopped fighting this rule; Mick retired to his room and we all lunched there.

Outside the hotel that night three girls camped in the hope of meeting us: Pam Johnson, aged fourteen, Pam McClore, fifteen and Kathy Healey, seventeen, all from Manchester; we knew nothing of them at this stage but their ardor was to cause us problems later.

The show at Manchester Palace Theatre next night was another round of mayhem. While Mick was singing "Pain in My Heart," two girls were hanging round his neck, while Brian was lost from sight under a scrum of squealing kids. After fifty seconds of the show, the curtain came down and the house lights went on while police dragged the kids away; when it went up again police stood shoulder to shoulder across the front row. The reception was so good that the live recording of an excellent show had far too much applause and screaming, and therefore was impossible to use. Many remarked at the fact that Mick held on to his microphone despite being mauled by girls. "Well, I was recording, wasn't I?" he said stoically.

For the second successive night, the three teenage girls spent the night camped outside the Midland Hotel.

On March 8 Mick and Keith left Manchester early in Mick's car; they headed for Scarborough, stopping off en route to pursue a hobby they had developed, interviewing local country people, in Rievaulx Abbey and Chop Gate. The rest of the group went straight to the Futurist Theatre where we met up for two excellent shows, adjourning to the Scotch Corner Hotel for the night. Those three Manchester girl fans had followed us again, hitchhiking 125 miles. All they'd had to eat was a shared bar of chocolate, they told us. It was now becoming a worry and a responsibility, since next morning we discovered the three asleep in a phone box outside the hotel. Brian, Mick and I spent thirty minutes on the hotel steps, lecturing them and trying to persuade them to return home. We sent them off with money for a meal and promised that if they returned home we would arrange a later meeting with them and all the Stones. It really was taking fan-fever too far; we were concerned about their parents.

After the next night's show, in Sunderland, we returned to the hotel to find the girls there again. They were tired and frozen and we had to act. We lectured them again and arranged hotel accommodation for them. Mick phoned the mother of Pam Johnson to say the girls were all right, and next day we paid for their train tickets and put them on the train to Huddersfield to be collected by their parents.

That done, we behaved stupidly. We checked out of our individual rooms but kept one room booked where we passed the afternoon. We got bored and went silly, writing all over the wallpaper, throwing cakes around and treading biscuits into the carpet. The staff eventually threw us out. It was just childish and although we paid for the damage, the receptionist complained that we used bad language. The Stones?

On March 12, as "The Last Time" went to the top of the British singles chart and our album *The Rolling Stones No. 2* remained at the top of the album chart, "The Last Time" was released in America, our sixth single there.* After our concert at the Granada, Rugby, on March 13, all the Stones left immediately after the final curtain except me since I had planned to travel back with Stu in the van. Seeing a girl in a state of collapse near the stage door, I asked that she be allowed in. She caught hold of me, and in a flood of tears cried, "Mick, Mick bring me Mick." I thought to myself, "Well, that's *fine*, that is. That's just *great*."

But the incident that would irrevocably cast us as villains, the famous Garage Wall Event, started with a move by me on the night of March 18, 1965. On that day we were voted most popular recording artists in France by radio Europe Number One, quite an accolade. It was also the final night of our tour with the Hollies, at Romford Odeon.

It was a perfect concert, a fitting end to a very strong tour. We were all in a great mood. At 11:10, with excellent police security, we rushed straight off stage, jumped into a car before the fans could leave the theater and headed back to town. Twenty minutes later I needed to use a toilet, so we pulled into the Francis Service Station in east London. I asked the attendant if I could use their

*This reached number eight in the USA. In June 1965 we were awarded our third gold record for this single.

toilet. He said, "There isn't a toilet." I replied: "This is a big garage, and there are service bays and showrooms, so there *must* be one." He said, "There isn't, so get off my forecourt."

Absolutely bursting to go, I returned to the car, where I explained what had happened. Mick took my hand and said, "Come on, Bill, we'll find you a toilet." Then Mick, myself, Joey Paige and Brian returned to the attendant and asked him once more if we could use the toilet. He started screaming at us, "Get off my forecourt! Get off my forecourt!"

Brian suddenly started dancing around pulling a "Nanker" face and singing, "Get off my foreskin!" The attendant once more told us to leave. We walked across the forecourt into the adjoining side road, went about ten yards up this road and proceeded to pee against the wall. We returned through the forecourt, yelled a few insults at the attendant, got back in the car and continued our journey.

We considered the incident closed, but two days later the *Daily Express* ran a story which surprised us. Mr. Eric Lavender, a customer who had been at the service station, said there was an "incident which led to him and a mechanic reporting two members of the pop group to the police. Mr. Charles Keely, on duty at the garage as night breakdown-mechanic, said it was about 11:30 p.m. on Thursday when the big black car pulled up and a long-haired type wearing dark glasses got out. After an incident, he told the people with the car to move off. 'Mr. Lavender told them their behavior was disgusting,' he said, 'and they started shouting and screaming. They went back to the car and I took a note of the number.' Mr. Lavender was quoted as saying that if the police did not prosecute, he would press for a private prosecution. Later a Metropolitan Police spokesman, confirming that an incident was reported, added: 'It is believed members of the Rolling Stones were involved. Inquiries are in hand.' "

Three months later the case reached East Ham Magistrates' Court, London. Fifty policemen were on duty outside, where a crowd of nearly 300 surrounded the gate leading to the court and waited behind a police cordon on the pavement across the road. Inside, the spectators' gallery was packed with about sixty teenage fans, three policemen standing either side of the gallery.

Mick, Brian and I were summoned for insulting behavior. I was further charged with using obscene language. We were allowed to write down our addresses, to keep them secret from the fans. We denied using insulting behavior by urinating against a wall and pleaded not guilty. Charlie and Keith, who had come for moral support, listened from the back of the court.

Prosecuting, Kenneth Richardson said: "If the magistrates were satisfied that disgusting behavior had taken place, it was no great crime, but it was regrettable behavior, and the three might themselves agree in time. They are well known to a certain section of the public, and it is wrong that they should show such disregard for the feelings and morals of others."

Magistrates' Chairman A. C. Morey asked Keely: "You have talked about long-haired monsters. Did that influence you in bringing the charge?"

Keely: "The conception of long-haired monsters did not influence my decision to complain, although it might have started the ball rolling. It made me determined not to let them go to the staff toilet."

I told the court: "We finished two shows at the Romford Odeon at 10:45. We didn't have time to go to the dressing-room after the show because as soon as the curtain fell, we had to leave the stage and rush to the car to avoid fans."

Brian, giving evidence, said: "We drank only Coca-Cola and tea. We were very happy because we had had a great night. I was not aggressive. We were laughing a lot because Mr. Keely's behavior was so comical. We are rather more mature than that."

Mick said: "I think we were top of the hit parade at the time and we were discussing our forthcoming American tour. We had every reason to be happy. I've never been in a bad enough mood to want to hit anyone. We have played in many places from Texas to Miami, to Helsinki* and this is the first time we have been in any trouble with the police." Keith also gave evidence and said he saw no incident at the service station.

Our defending counsel, Dale Parkinson, said: "This is a trivial case, and you are making a mountain out of a molehill."

*We hadn't played Helsinki *or* Miami yet!

We were all found guilty of using insulting behavior whereby a breach of the peace may have occurred. We were each fined £5, and ordered to pay 15 guineas costs. We all gave notice to appeal.

I was also found not guilty on the other charge, of using obscene language.

The magistrates' chairman said: "Whether it is the Rolling Stones, the Beatles or anyone else, we will not tolerate conduct of this character. Because you have reached the exalted heights in your profession, it does not mean you have the right to act like this. On the contrary, you should set a standard of behavior which should be a moral pattern for your large number of supporters. You have been found guilty of behavior not becoming young gentlemen."

Brian said later: "We've always had a wild image. We built ourselves on that fact. Groups like the Hollies envy our image a little. The garage incident was grossly exaggerated. The kids in court were amused by an incident blown up out of all perspective. It may do us some harm, but I doubt it. There's always America."

Charlie said: "I kept out of trouble. I was asleep in the back seat of the car, man."

After the hearing, we were smuggled out of the court, and driven back to town. The episode did us no damage with our fans and might even have persuaded a few people that we were human!

But we all had our reputations within the Stones, and mine returned on March 21 during our drive back from Birmingham where we'd mimed "The Last Time" on *Thank Your Lucky Stars*. On the outskirts of the city I needed to visit a toilet again, much to the amusement of the boys. We stopped in a deserted area and I peed up against a fence. Halfway through, a policeman came up and shone his torch on me, inquiring what I was doing, which I thought should have been pretty obvious. He warned me not to do it again. I was relieved in more ways than one.

Brian, however, had more serious problems. In the spring of 1965 he moved into a new house, 7 Elm Park Lane, Chelsea, which he rented for £272 a month. In this fashionable mews cottage—which Brian believed to be haunted

adding to its appeal—Brian enjoyed living out his fantasy
life as a rich pop star. He often greeted visitors clad in a
white polo-necked sweater and gray slacks, a cigar in one
hand, a glass of Scotch and Coke in another. But the
classy Regency-styled furniture and velvet curtains could
not conceal the Edith Grove side of Brian: the kitchen
was usually a disaster zone with opened, dirty tins, old,
encrusted milk bottles—in fact, the entire five-roomed
cottage was totally disorganized. His huge bedroom wardrobes were empty while his suitcases were bursting with
clothes. Newly laundered shirts and underclothes were
left in their packets all over the bed and on the floor. The
only possessions that appeared to merit careful handling
were a record player and a twelve-string guitar. Whatever trappings Brian accumulated, he could never eradi-
cate the beatnik lingering inside him, even though when
he dressed up he was the dandiest Stone by far. Brian
always wanted more of everything: he dreamed of a big
Hollywood house with a pool and planned to buy one on
our next visit. This hunger was exacerbated by his insecurities and alienation from Mick, Keith and Andrew.

Dave Thomson was witness to what was happening
behind Brian's back that March: "Andrew was slagging
off Brian. 'We've got to get rid of him . . . how are we
gonna get rid of him?' They mocked Brian, saying: 'Did
you *see* what he was trying to *do?*' " Later, Thomson,
who didn't hit it off with Oldham, challenged Mick and
Keith about the plan to dump Brian. "I said: 'You can't
seriously consider chucking Brian out of the group.' Keith
said no. Mick just shrugged. Andrew was the one who
was always doing the slagging. It was jealousy."

All this was building up against an increasingly hectic
schedule. We flew into Copenhagen on March 25 and
had a great reception from about 2,000 fans and hundreds of photographers. But next day during rehearsals
at Odense Mick and I received some severe electric shocks.
I was trying my bass and amplifier while Mick was testing
the microphones. He suddenly started dancing about frantically around the stage. We thought he was playing
about, but then I realized it was serious. Brian pulled the
plug, as I was shocked too. Mick, who got the full force,
suffered slight burns to his hands. We were fit enough by
the evening to carry on with the concert for 4,000 fans.

For the visit to Stockholm on March 27, we were turned away by the manager of the Hotel Foresta on the Island of Lidingoe, who said:"We don't want trouble. We want to know in advance who is going to be responsible for the security of the group, as well as of our other guests. The Beatles stayed here last year. We remember how it was when they were here."

It was time for fun after two great shows at the Tivoli Gardens, Copenhagen, on March 28. We went to the Monmartre Club, La Cunana Club and Le Carousel, where I met a pretty blonde Danish girl who stayed the night and whom I saw frequently. Mick and Keith were refused entry to one of the clubs because they were not wearing ties, and Brian got drunk and woke next morning to find himself looking well and truly "out of it" in newspaper pictures.

There was a load of fun on this tour: Mick telephoned the *New Musical Express* in London and said: "Everything's swinging up here; can you tell me who is Number One this week? We are? That's half-a-crown I've lost!" Eric Easton had to fly back to London when news came that Decca were trying to outbid American CBS for the Stones' contract renewal. And after two great shows at Gothenburg's Masshallen, we were all invited to a party. Mick and I were the only two who felt like going; on arrival, we found there were thirteen girls and only one other guy.

Mick and I were tossing up for the girls, and Mick immediately went for two little blonde twins, aged about seventeen. So instead of two of us looking at thirteen girls, I was now looking at eleven! And I had to figure out which one was going to go to bed with me, because in those days some of them didn't.

I finally chose one girl I really fancied and started talking to her—and the others realized it and faded away. I said to her, "Do you want to come back to the hotel with me and spend the night?" She said no, she couldn't, she had to go to work in the morning. I thought I'd picked the wrong one, then she said I could go home with her if I liked.

Now I was back "up" again. We took a taxi to her house and I thought I was laughing until I came face to face with her mum and dad sitting in the kitchen. Again I thought I'd blown it. They got out coffee and biscuits and snacks; we sat around talking and the girl asked: "Do you want to meet my little brother? He's got posters of you all round his bedroom." I said we shouldn't wake him up. "Yeah, but he'd never forgive me." I thought, this is a real downer . . . I can't wait to get back to the hotel! But I went upstairs, they woke him, a nice kid of about eleven, really excited, showing me all his Stones records, then I thought: "This is a good deed done, now can I *please* get back to the hotel?"

Instead I went back downstairs, sat with the parents at the table, and then the girl said: "Shall we go to bed then?" I didn't quite understand what she meant, thinking she wanted me to leave. She repeated: "Shall we go to bed? Or don't you want to go to bed with me?" My answer was clear. She said: "Well, come on then. Good night, Mum, good night, Dad," and up to bed we went.

Next morning, Mum and Dad cooked breakfast, the boy said goodbye on his way to school, and she dropped me at the hotel on the way to work! I never heard from or saw her again. Now I knew what Brian was looking for when he had gone on a trek around Scandinavia from Cheltenham years before.

Flying into Paris at Easter for our second visit there, the major difference between the fans of the various countries struck us: French *men* besieged us, whereas in every other country, it was the girls who screamed. Our fans in France therefore had no hang-up about our attachment to ladies, and a male writer in *France Soir* recorded my arrival favorably: "Bill Wyman, the most romantic of the Stones, is also an excellent father. He arrived in France with his wife Diane and son Stephen, aged three, whose hair is cut much shorter than his Daddy's." Another writer described Stephen as "the sixth Rolling Stone, who bewitched Parisians." If I'd been seen with my wife and child in another country, there would have been a public outcry. "It's not very professional to bring over a family," I said rather defensively, "but this is the first opportunity we've had of being together for some time."

The three-day trip developed into a Main Event. The viciousness of the gendarmes in dealing with our mostly male audience at the Olympia was unbelievable: they shone flashlights throughout the show in fans' faces, and if one youngster excitedly stood up they pounced, and frog-marched him out of the theater. The victim was helped on his unwilling journey by some stick-prodding and wrestling holds. *France Soir* reported: "In order to avoid any kind of incident at the end of the concert, the police chief of the 9th Arrondissement had sent several dozen policemen orders. They were precise: 'Those who yell—you take away.' Two young boys were put into the Black Maria under these conditions."

There was police protection at our hotel even when we weren't inside. We played an excellent show with particularly good response from the blues-loving French fans for "Time is on My Side" and "Little Red Rooster"; the great Françoise Hardy, one of our staunchest fans, was at this concert and came backstage to congratulate us.

At the second night's concert, the crowd was even wilder. We needed a police van to enter the Olympia and the fans were agitated before we went on, but we pacified them with encore after encore.

The backstage organization was a shambles: there seemed no logic in the decision of the authorities to allow young kids back at random, but deny access to friends and British journalists who had traveled in specially. Tickets for our three Paris shows had been sold within hours of going on sale, so an extra midnight show was planned. But this was banned by the police, who said they could not allow 2,000 "over-excited" young people to be let loose in the Paris streets at 2 a.m.—by then the Métro would have stopped, and they wouldn't be able to get home.

When we checked out of the Hôtel de Paris on Easter Monday I noticed that the charges to Mick's and Keith's suites were more than those to the rest of the Stones: Mick's bill was a huge 1,973 francs, compared with the average 500. Yet the whole thing was debited to the group's account, which meant we all paid equally. This imbalance in spending recurred in many ways and always irritated me, since apart from extra for songwriting by Mick and Keith, the money coming *in* to the Stones was split five ways.

Only four Stones returned to London. Brian, who loved Paris, considered that although there weren't as many

luscious women there as in Britain, he still wanted to
have a short break and look around the city; he stayed
with Françoise Hardy and her fiancé, Jean-Marie Perier.

Back in London, Mick and Keith had to quit their flat
in Hampstead. "It was getting beyond a joke," Mick
explained. "We had the ground-floor flat, so as well as
sneaking in through the front door, fans used to climb in
through the windows. At weekends there would be about
fifty of them. We didn't mind signing autographs but
when it came to having the place ransacked and having
our clothes taken, it got a bit much."

But they wouldn't be able to look for a new home for a
while, as we were off out of the country almost immediately. Within three days of returning from Paris we were
away to our first visit to Canada, followed by our third
North American concert tour. At Heathrow on April 22
a swarm of teenage girls, part of a crowd of some 300
who came to see us off, invaded the tarmac, flinging their
arms around Mick and Brian. Police finally shepherded
them back to the airport buildings and we took off for
Montreal. For our Canadian debut at Montreal's Maurice
Richard Arena on April 23, the tour program, which
we had designed, named Mick as "Mick the Magic Jagger" for the first time. There were terrific security problems, with 6,000 fans insisting on standing up throughout
the show; but there were also pluses. The local girls were
pretty and a new friend, a disc jockey named Lord Jim
(who gave me my first Aretha Franklin album) took me
out to a local club with some models.

Next day we drove for two hours to Ottawa, checking
into the Château Laurier Hotel where the 200 fans who
greeted us were somewhat warmer than the manager,
who declared: "The Rolling Stones would never have
been booked here if we'd known ahead of time who they
were. They were booked under individual names and we
didn't know until too late."

At the concert at the YMCA Auditorium, thirty policemen were on stage throughout the show. They cut the
power six times, spoiling the show for everyone. Promoter Harvey Glatt commented later: "All we needed
between the stage and the audience was a ten-foot moat
with alligators!"

Later at the hotel, a doorman required four stitches to

close a cut above his eye after he was struck by a teenager trying to reach us. Canada was proving just as
raucous as other countries.

Hotel trouble had preceded our arrival, again by car,
next day in Toronto. The Westbury Hotel had refused to
accept us only days before because they were frightened
of fan hysteria, but the quiet hotel we finally found was
pleasant enough. A police motorcycle escort guided the
Stones in two station-wagons into the Maple Leaf Gardens for our concert on April 25; about ten warm-up
groups were midway through their acts as we entered the
venue via the rear door on a large ramp. We attracted
12,000 fans in this 15,000-seat arena. At a press conference while the support groups played, Brian was particularly articulate, explaining patiently that both the Beatles
and the Stones borrowed their styles from the blues of
the American Negro, "but the Stones have kept closer to
the model."

While acknowledging the success of the concert, the
Toronto Star said we "left many of our fans feeling
cheated" by "being on stage a mere twenty-five minutes,
during which time they mixed obscene gestures with in-
audible singing." The crowd, though, had drowned us
out. It was a really wild audience, with inadequate security and the usual panic resulting: the police were extremely rough with the fans. One girl fell and had a deep
gash in her leg, requiring a stretcher to take her to
hospital. During the last song, "I'm Alright," four teenage girls ran out of the mass and confronted the policemen hard, the first of several waves of fans roaring
towards the stage. We were accused of encouraging them
by beckoning them. With the whole audience in disarray,
we exited through the curtains at the back of the stage
into a station-wagon while the crowd continued its screaming. Two dozen girls were being treated by first-aid staff
as our stupid and panicky driver charged full tilt into the
crowd, throwing several fans up on to the hood.

Brian's growing discontent surfaced again in Toronto
when he called our disc jockey friend Scott Ross in New
York. Deeply upset after an altercation with Mick, Keith
and Andrew, Brian sought refuge by asking Scott if he
could go and stay with him rather than continue with the
Stones tour. "He said he didn't want to go on to the

recording sessions in Chicago, either," Scott remembers. "I tried to talk him out of it, and at least realize that it was a pretty big decision with big implications if he didn't show up at the sessions. But he didn't care. He just said he couldn't do it, wasn't in the frame of mind to record. He was angry, despondent, so he came to New York and stayed with me for about three days. He talked about it a lot, how he was on his own, and felt like he was being cut out." Needless to say, he never missed a gig or a recording session.

At our next stop, in London, Ontario, the crowd, said Mick later, was wilder than most. "The police, without any warning at all, turned the power off. The ensuing riot wasn't our fault. We're always the ones to get the blame." Brian said: "Some kids came from as far away as Detroit, and all they got was four numbers." It was a sad way to leave Canada.

We flew to New York next day, and within a few hours of our arrival Scott Ross took us to the apartment of Bob Crewe, manager of the Four Seasons, for a small party. This was a fantastic place: a running stream and a fountain in every room, huge green plants and marble statues everywhere plus bear-skin rugs and paintings from floor to ceiling. Our eyes popped out. The British-born jazz pianist George Shearing was a guest and I found my conversation with this charming man most enlightening.

On April 28 we were driven to a rehearsal room to prepare for the *Ed Sullivan Show*— despite all the earlier protests and statements by Sullivan, we were due back on the most powerful show in America. Conversely, in Britain, we had turned down the biggest family-entertainment show, *Sunday Night at the London Palladium, five times*. Whereas the Sullivan show had all kinds of performers, the Palladium show struck us as too middle-aged, wrong for our audience. We didn't need it.

Switching hotels in New York we met the singer Big Dee Irwin, who leaped out of his car and ran over to say hallo. The pop music community of Britain and America had become a thriving club by mid-1965, and all the groups must have accounted for a huge profit by the airlines as we criss-crossed the Atlantic. Irwin told us that the Hollies had just left town but that Wayne Fontana and the Mindbenders, who had just enjoyed a Number

One with "Groovy Kind of Love," were still in town; we met them in the hotel later for drinks.

That night, Mick, Keith and Brian went to the Apollo to see an impressive Wilson Pickett; they were equally bowled over by the fact that James Brown had left them messages saying he was trying to catch up with us.

Two shows next day at Albany, a 150-mile drive from New York City, passed successfully, with police exerting an iron grip on 2,000 fans at each show. Brian's amplifier blew up during our first show and he had to borrow a small one from a support group. The PA system was terrible, something that plagued all our shows at this time, but the squeals from the crowd were so overpowering that they could hardly have noticed. The same combination of fatuous questions faced us at a press conference afterwards, and we were driven to our now-customary habit of facetious replies: Reporter: "Which one are you?" Brian: "Me."

As Eric Easton and Andrew flew into New York to join the tour, the London magazine *Rave* was having a crack at summarizing the changing personalities in the group. People were always surprised by my conscientiousness in replying to fan mail; during this American tour I continued to answer batches, often in my hotel rooms. *Rave* reported: "Bill probably holds the world record for answering fan mail. Plods away hour after hour at it. Obviously a person who appreciates interest being shown. He may try to send you up with the straightest poker face you ever saw and, of course, in the kindest possible way. If you know a good song he's not heard, you need hum it through but once and he has the melody for keeps. You can talk to him about symphonies, cool jazz, R & B, C & W—and practically any kind of music. His disc library is as varied as anyone could make it.* Charlie doesn't easily get worked up about anything but he has quiet zeal for modern jazz, Sammy Davis and Buddy Greco. In other fields he has a thing about Picasso and antique guns in particular."†

Before the show at New York's Academy of Music on

---

*My record collection at this stage totaled 150 albums.
†Charlie has not changed a scrap and his interest in and knowledge of jazz, art and guns is formidable.

May 1 we held a fan club get-together backstage, and received a load of presents. Our buddy Scott Ross, who compèred, had a beautiful leather jacket torn to shreds by fans who leaped on stage, but on the whole it was a smooth show which began at 1 p.m.; for the evening we were driven to the Convention Hall, Philadelphia for an eight o'clock start to a famous Dick Clark package show. There was a huge bill, but we had been added because tickets were not selling too well. The cast featured Herman's Hermits, Little Anthony and the Imperials, Bobby Vee, Freddy Cannon, Reparata and the Delrons, Brenda Holloway, the Hondells, the Ikettes and others.

The problem here was that the promoter hadn't bothered to settle in advance who would headline the bill. A long hassle developed, resolved only when Andrew Oldham met Harvey Lisberg, manager of Herman's Hermits. They agreed that Herman would top the Dick Clark show, with the Stones following him after a forty-five-minute break, making it appear like a totally different show. But Herman overran, and with a midnight curfew on the performances it seemed that Herman was lengthening his show to make it difficult for us to go on at all. We moaned in the wings, finally going on to an ecstatic audience of 13,000, and Herman became rather jealous and moody. Later, he said that though he liked our show, we didn't appear to like his: "They never came over to say hallo to me, except Mick. You'd think that when you're 3,500 miles away from home and on the same show, they might at least say hallo." Mick told a reporter: "Herman's a great guy but we don't really go for his music. I wish people would stop asking us what we think of Herman's Hermits. We don't think of them at all. We think their music is wet and watery and not very significant."

That week, though, Herman went to the top in America with "Mrs. Brown, You've Got a Lovely Daughter." On May 2 we returned to the *Ed Sullivan Show*, which also featured Tom Jones and Morecambe and Wise; and a film of Dusty Springfield. We performed "The Last Time," "Little Red Rooster," "Everybody Needs Somebody to Love" and the show faded out on "2120 South Michigan Avenue."

The British groups' success in the States was supported

heavily by the very artists we'd drawn inspiration from: Solomon Burke went on record with: "The Rolling Stones are the soul of British beat music. I was driving along in my car, where I have a TV installed, and suddenly on my screen came the Stones singing my song, 'Everybody Needs Somebody to Love.' What a knockout!"

But our hotel security was dangerously erratic in the States; leaving the Sullivan show, we fought our way back to the hotel with no security outside at all. Our fans seemed to have a built-in homing device. We went to our rooms to find them hiding in the wardrobes, under beds, in the bathroom. They'd climbed fire escapes and drainpipes, and clambered over glass roofs to reach us.

Later we battled our way out again to attend a press reception and special dinner in honor of us and Tom Jones, arranged by London Records at the Playboy Club. Driving through Central Park, trying to get away from some people who were following, we encountered four or five men in a convertible who screamed things about "faggots." When we arrived, Brian yelled: "Let's get the colonists." So Mick, Keith and Brian jumped into their convertible and started fighting with them. Charlie, Scott and I went into the club and they stayed outside and continued their fight. Francesca, whom I'd spent time with on the last visit here, had come by the hotel and vividly remembers Keith booting one of them in the mouth. Inside the Playboy and surrounded by bunnies, we were presented with record players and records—I was particularly pleased with Bob Dylan's new album which had some tracks very much like ours. Roy Orbison came by to see us for a grand reunion.

After filming for the highly rated *Clay Cole Show* on Monday, May 3, we had our first free time to absorb a little of New York. Charlie, Stu, Mike Dorsey and I went to a record shop where I bought $100 worth of albums (quite an investment considering my bank account that week showed a credit of only £66).

We just caught the plane to Atlanta, Georgia next morning, together with Stu and our equipment. However, our luggage didn't make it and Bob Bonis and Mike Dorsey stayed back to bring it on a later flight. At Atlanta we had a bad landing when the hydraulic brakes failed. As we touched down smoke came from the landing-gear, and fire engines and other emergency vehicles chased us down the runway. The plane finally stopped and then it had to be towed into a parking area. We then changed planes and flew to Savannah where the temperature was 80° and the vegetation quite fantastic. We rushed straight off and drove fifty miles to Statesboro. Our luggage didn't arrive, so we weren't able to change for the show. We faced a packed audience with a diabolical PA system that spoiled the show for us, although it went over well with the fans.

Gered Mankowitz, photographer: "Bill was always stone-faced on stage and didn't *give* very much. He told me why he held the guitar up vertically, like he did. It was to shadow his face from the spotlight so he could see the girls in the front row. I watched him *pulling from the stage!* He held the guitar almost upright against himself . . . everybody thought it was very moody and it looked great. But he was pulling the girls at the front—and mouthing his room number at them!"

After all this rush we lazed around the motel pool the next day, swimming and sunbathing in 90° temperatures. Then Charlie went to the local fort to see some Civil War relics and I went into Savannah, sightseeing with one of the local DJs. I loved the docks, the pirate's house and all the wonderful wood houses with front porches and rocking chairs. The whole place was quite beautiful and atmospheric, with long gray moss hanging from the trees.

That night we flew to Tampa, Florida, stopping at Jacksonville, Daytona and Orlando. On arrival we were driven to Clearwater where we checked into the Gulf Motel. Although it was supposed to be a secret, there were still about thirty fans there. After a meal we returned for drinks in the bar. Brian and I met two very nice models, who stayed with us until we left town.

As fame and the pressure of life on the road hit us, Brian's behavior became a liability.

At Clearwater I slept late on May 6 then joined the others at the poolside along with my girl. Then my girl's friend, who had slept with Brian, arrived, looking battered and bruised, and said Brian had beaten her up. We were disgusted by this. Mike Dorsey promptly disappeared into the hotel in search of Brian. When they met, blows were exchanged and Brian suffered two cracked ribs, to the satisfaction of everyone.

Within a couple of days, news of the punch-up had trickled out to the press. We concocted a story. I gave an interview to *New Musical Express* by phone, saying: "We had a gorgeous pool here in Clearwater and we were doing karate beside it. Brian fell heavily and the next day a lump came up on his chest. The doctor told him he had cracked two ribs. He wears an elastic belt, which we call his 'corset.' He's recovering rapidly, I'm glad to say." Lies!

Gered Mankowitz said: "Brian was a curious person, a very, very strange guy who would do some weird things. One day, he was playing so badly, so loosely, that Stu grabbed him in the wings, lifted him up and said: 'Why do you want to beat everybody down, you little bag of shit? *Why?* WHY?' "

Wanting the spotlight, he became jealous, envious, frustrated that it wasn't always naturally on him . . . although he was enormously popular with audiences on the road.

It was at Clearwater, also, that Keith first played to Mick the tune that would become our biggest single hit internationally: "(I Can't Get No) Satisfaction." Keith originally conceived it as a folk song, probably a good filler track for our next album. Neither Mick nor Keith saw it as a potential single, and certainly not a hit. But Keith's instinct must have told him it was worth some effort, because he kept working on it.

After that and with the Brian incident fresh in our thoughts, it had to be business as usual: we faced 4,000 unruly fans at the Jack Russell Baseball Stadium, Clearwater. Before we appeared, rolls of toilet tissue and crumpled cups were being hurled at the police; the show's compère and the police chief warned that our performance would be canceled unless order was restored. This announcement brought loud jeers and an increase in the bombardment. But it turned out to be no idle threat. After only four songs, hordes of screaming teenagers rushed forward, taunting the ring of police stationed around the performers' platform rather than rushing at us. Police immediately ordered us to stop and return to our hotel. As our car drove off, scores of shouting fans chased it, some falling dangerously close to the moving vehicle. Condemning the riots, the police chief said that his men had been there "for the mutual protection of all, and were harassed and vilified." Both he and the director of the city recreation department said there would never be another rock show in Clearwater again.

The chopping of our concerts after only a few songs was getting tiresome. Usually, a minority of kids spoiled it for the thousands of genuine fans, but it seemed to us that the police always acted too hastily, and were unable to maintain adequate security. We lamented these bum concerts: in the end it reflected badly on us in the eyes of thousands of real Stones' fans who had ended up paying good money for a mere fifteen minutes of performance.

We hired three small planes for the three-hour flight on May 7 to Birmingham, Alabama. Driving through the black area of the town we were appalled by the poverty, the worst we'd seen in America. We drove straight to the Legion Fields Stadium to top a bill that included such famous names as the Beach Boys, the Righteous Brothers and country singers Marty Robbins and Skeeter Davis; unfortunately they were all pretty dire on stage. But we received a great reception from the 20,000 crowd and it was a relief to have a show that wasn't marred by problems. Immediately afterwards we flew to Jacksonville, Florida. Arriving at 3:30 in the morning we found our hotel to be a dump, with sailors, drunks and fans all over the place. We finally checked in two hours later at the Thunderbird Hotel on the beach and I phoned Diane before going to bed. The news from London was that my bank account was now showing a debit of £2!

Before our next show in Chicago a press conference had been organized at the Sheraton Hotel by promoter Ed Pazdur. When we arrived, we found the place surrounded by hundreds of fans. We tried repeatedly to get into the hotel through the crowds, but were unsuccessful. We finally made it after ninety minutes and four attempts. Inside there were another 500 fans wanting photos and autographs but we were furious to hear later that the promoter had charged $10 per person for entrance. Our American agent, Norman Weiss, wrote to Pazdur on July 19: "I just received a letter from the Rolling Stones manager who had received a letter from a fan in Chicago where she outlines your policy of the teen parties and the press conference for which you charge a $10 fee. On any future dates you may promote on the Rolling Stones they are not to be included in this arrangement because the Stones feel that you are running the press conferences as a commercial venture."

Chicago always had our affection, though, since it was a blues city; we had fond memories of our recording sessions there a year earlier. On May 10 we drove to Chess Studios for what became a nine-hour recording session, cutting several songs, including "Try Me," "That's How Strong My Love Is," "The Under-Assistant West Coast Promotion Man,"* "Mercy, Mercy" and the first version of "Satisfaction," which wasn't very good. "I didn't think much of it," Keith said. "We considered it a good B-side or maybe an LP track." But Scott Ross heard a demo of the original track and said: "It had a harmonica track on it—Brian on harmonica. I bet Mick, Keith and Brian that it was going to be the biggest record the Stones had ever had, and that was *before* the fuzz-tone was put on. Mick disagreed with me, and the bet was for a pair of boots from Anello & Davide. And I did get them!"

Moving to Los Angeles on May 11 we prepared for the next two days to immerse ourselves in recording at the RCA Studios in Hollywood. These became our most gruelling but productive sessions; we recorded on May 12 from 10 a.m. until 2:15 the following morning. Attempting "Satisfaction" again, we found it suddenly went right with Keith using a fuzz-box and Charlie laying down a different tempo: the song just gelled. Keith and Mick were still not completely happy about it, though. After we listened to the master, we discussed whether it should be the next single, as Andrew and Dave Hassinger, our patient recording engineer, were so positive about it. We put it to the vote. Andrew, Dave, Stu, Brian, Charlie and I voted yes, while Mick and Keith voted no. The majority carried the day: it would be our next single. In later years, Mick always said that only Keith was doubtful about it.

---

*This Nanker-Phelge composition was a dig at George Sherlock, the London Records promotion man who had accompanied us on our first US tour.

We also cut the Temptations song "My Girl," which gave me problems. It took me a while to twig exactly what I was supposed to do. The notes and musical content were straightforward enough but the timing had me stumped; I seemed to be playing on the wrong beat. As it transpired, I was doing it right all along, but I had to wait for the playback to hear that my work was fitting in well.

Next afternoon we returned to the studio and to Dave Hassinger, working for eight hours from one o'clock. We cut another half-dozen tracks, including "Good Times," "Cry to Me," "I've Been Loving You Too Long," "The Spider and the Fly" and "One More Try." Mick, Keith and Andrew worked incredibly hard, staying behind when we left at nine to work on overdubs and the vocals; they finally got away twelve hours later.

We marked our concert return to California with two successful concerts: in San Francisco on May 14 before 5,000 at the New Civic Auditorium, with twenty police on stage with us at the end of the show to protect us from the fans; and, fittingly, in San Bernardino, scene of our very first successful concert in the US a year earlier: 4,500 fans roared their approval there.

When we returned to our Los Angeles hotel there was an amusing reminder of our security problems. Bob Bonis had stopped by for Keith in his room, and before letting him in Keith had hidden two girls on the balcony. Bonis, who was very security-conscious, carefully locked the balcony door as was his custom. Not wanting to let Bonis know what he'd done, Keith said nothing, figuring the girls would climb down—forgetting they were five floors up; when we returned after the show at 1 a.m., the girls were still trapped on the balcony.

The Rolling Stones came within an ace of being crushed to death on May 16. A fantastic afternoon concert in every way, with perfect acoustics in the egg-shaped arena at Long Beach civic auditorium, degenerated into the most dangerous hour of our lives. The concert for about 8,000 fans was as near perfect as we could have expected and we were on good form. Our set began with "Everybody Needs Somebody to Love" followed by "Around and Around," "Off the Hook," featuring Mick's famous dancing, and then the words: "This, my friends, is Charlie Watts." Charlie then made his economical speech—

"And we're now going to do 'Little Red Rooster' "—and the crowd went wild.

However, many fans had noticed that we had simply driven in through them to reach the stage, and they realized there was no other exit. Throughout our final song, "The Last Time," they were trickling out of the arena to take up positions along our exit route. Hundreds of girls refused to budge when Stu requested they move to let us out. So he got in the car and started driving backwards slowly towards them. Immediately, a big police sergeant with two guns hanging from his belt stormed over to Stu and said: "You just stop that, boy. You try any more of that and I'll have you straight in jail."

The result was that when we got in the car and Stu started driving us out, fans rushed it, jumped on top of the roof and the car with us inside was totally submerged by a sea of bodies. We lay on the floor of the car, holding up the roof with our feet to prevent it caving in. We were pushing for our lives; outside girls were terrified, fighting for breath as they were pushed up against the windows. I thought we'd had it, that there was nothing we could do to save ourselves. Our arms and legs ached as we pushed for several minutes to hold the roof up. The kids outside, trapped, kept jumping up to the roof for air and "safety." Stu said later: "The police panicked and rushed in with sticks, belting everybody they saw. There was blood everywhere and several people had to be taken to hospital." Without the police intervention, though, we'd have been sunk. It took us forty-five minutes, with them ahead of us, to drive a hundred yards, and we were very shaken by the experience. Brian, particularly, was wide-eyed with fear. The car finally made it to a heliport. Looking down as we flew, we saw the battered and severely dented sedan; we felt lucky to have escaped from it.

It took thirty policemen another hour to disperse the mob after we left. One motorcycle cop was bruised when he was knocked from his bike and several had their uniforms ripped. Back in Los Angeles, unbelievably, we went straight to work in the evening, probably good therapy. We filmed four songs for a television show, and Brian and I later felt fresh enough to go out to the Action Club, where Brian eventually got up on stage and sat in with the band, playing harmonica.

Brian's behavior was bizarre that night and Kathy (West) Townsend, a girlfriend of mine at the time, recalls that he had been "dropping acid, running all over the Ambassador Hotel, jumping over snakes." I, too, remember Brian walking from the car to the entrance of the Action Club, saying the ground was covered with snakes; he proceeded to jump over the imaginary reptiles.

The riots, and the shows which were shortened by police, plus all the aggravation of touring, disappeared with a virtual shrug of our shoulders: there was no alternative but to keep going.

Next night, continuing our sequence of California shows up in San Diego, our car broke down, making us thirty minutes late arriving at the theater. The Byrds, that popular group who hit with Dylan's "Mr. Tambourine Man," had preceded us on several concerts, and now they had to stay on stage to keep the audience entertained until we arrived. We were amused to see that by the time we got to the stage, they had run through their entire repertoire and were playing Rolling Stones songs!

That May both Charlie and Brian were hit by affiliation orders in Britain. Christine White, the nineteen-year-old daughter of a Stepney taxi-driver, alleged Charlie was the father of her fourteen-month-old child, but this case was dropped in July. Linda Lawrence began her proceedings seeking affiliation with Brian over Julian Mark. Linda's solicitors wrote to Eric Easton saying she would be prepared to accept a lump sum "in full and final settlement of your client's liability." After we had also returned to London, on June 3 he received notice that Pat Andrews also had begun proceedings against him, alleging "breach of promise of marriage, enticement and for affiliation for child Julian Mark." Brian instructed the Stones lawyer for domestic issues, Dale Parkinson, to represent him, but the case was to drag on for some considerable time.

The première of the song which was now named "(I Can't Get No) Satisfaction" was on TV's *Shindig,* produced in Los Angeles by the expatriate British pop guru Jack Good. Keith played a new Gibson Firebird on this show on May 20; we had requested that blues artists Howlin' Wolf (who had recorded "Little Red Rooster") and Son House should be on the show with us. We were in hysterics when Jack Good persistently referred to him, in his "proper" English, as "Mr. Howlin.' " The backing group here consisted of Leon Russell, who later worked with me on my solo albums, James Burton, the guitar ace, and Delaney; Sonny and Cher and Jimmie Rodgers were also on the show.

During our Los Angeles trip, there was an attempt to put together a film project for the band. These meetings, arranged by Norman Weiss of GAC (who fixed our tours), involved Bill Tennant, Irving Salkow and science-fiction writer Harlan Ellison, whom we all liked and with whom I became friends.

After a good show in San Jose there was an afternoon show at Fresno the next day where, as a local reporter wrote, a peaceful show at Ratcliffe Stadium "turned into a full-scale demand for puberty rights." The bandstand was ringed by seventy-five police but after twenty-eight minutes we had to end the show in the middle of "The Last Time." (A fan had earlier asked Charlie for a souvenir, and in his inimitable way he offered her a chair.)

The tour neared its end with a date in Sacramento on May 22. We were astonished by the news that the promoter, Buck Herring, had a deal going: in order to buy a ticket for our show, fans also had to buy a ticket to see the forthcoming Dick Clark Caravan of Stars package. As Norman Weiss protested on our behalf, if the Stones were needed to sell tickets to the Dick Clark show, we should at least have got a percentage of the profit.

The tour ended and we received a statement showing that we had sold 11,427 programs, which seemed rather low.

Charlie planned a visit to Gettysburg, Pennsylvania, to study American history. While Mick and Keith took a motoring holiday through the Arizona desert, Brian and I stayed in Los Angeles, where he spent a fortune at stores like DeVoss and Beau Gentry. I met a small, very pretty dark-haired girl and we became great mates. She stayed with me there. But I heard from some friends that she might have been dabbling in drugs.

I introduced her to Harlan Ellison, who frequently welcomed us to his tree house during our many get-togethers. When I left town, Harlan began dating her and a few months later they were married and, shortly afterwards, divorced. I think she left him the goldfish!

The Stones met up in New York on May 29 for three shows at the Academy of Music. Later Geist Ely threw a bon voyage party in our honor at the Ondine Club. Scott Ross recalls: "At this time, everybody was smoking dope. Mick and Keith went into some room and were smoking in there. We didn't have anything outside. I started kicking on the door. Mick opened it and said, 'What do you want?' I said, 'What have you got in there? Can we have some?' and he said, 'Oh, we can't do that.' I said 'Oh! You're a big star now then?' and started pushing on the door. We were yelling at each other, and I remember grabbing him and pushing him up against the wall."

Back in London we received our third gold record—for "The Last Time" in the USA—but the five Stones whose records littered the international charts and whose audiences around the world ran into millions were still not financially stable. I returned from California to find a bank statement showing my weekly £50 from the office had resulted in a credit balance of £14. Eric had been putting money into separate accounts for us with the Bradford & Bingley Building Society towards our eventual tax bill; Brian's showed £635 and Mick and Keith each had £942 at this time. Though a lot of our expenses were paid by Rolling Stones Ltd, we felt a long way from the millionaire pop stars the newspapers described.

Even so, our credit was good. Mick gave Chrissie Shrimpton a "return home" present of a white Austin Mini (probably not knowing she had been dating the singer P. J. Proby during his absence). Keith's mother Doris passed her driving test and he bought her an Austin 1100. I was more interested in a new eight-roomed house I had seen, with more space for Diane, Stephen and me; I wanted to purchase The Oaks, Forest Drive, Keston, in Kent, for £12,000, and the Stones agreed to loan me half the money.

Since returning from the States, Mick and Keith had stayed at the Hilton Hotel, London while they were looking for a new place, but soon found it too expensive. For a short time, Mick moved into the big Regent's Park house of his friend David Bailey.* During his stay, he

*David Bailey, the top fashion photographer in London in the sixties, took our pictures for six album covers: *The Rolling Stones No. 2, 12 x 5, The Rolling Stones Now!, Out of Our Heads* (US), *Get Yer Ya Ya's Out* and *Goats Head Soup*.

briefly met actress Jacqueline Bisset, who had had a day's unsuccessful posing with Bailey. As Mick walked in, Bailey said to him: "Put her on your back and let's try it again." It worked: the resulting picture of Mick carrying Jacqueline was seen by millions and she was launched.

"If it hadn't been for David Bailey I'd have been homeless," Mick said at the time. "Staying with him was like living in a hotel; his pad is quite big with three bathrooms and as we were never in at the same time we rarely crossed paths."

Keith rented a flat in St. John's Wood, northwest London. Mick soon moved into a flat at 13a Bryanston Mews East, Marble Arch, saying: "Just because Keith and I aren't sharing this flat, everyone thinks we've had a bust-up. There's absolutely no truth in that. We simply couldn't find a flat suitable for the both of us." He was actively looking for a permanent home, "something to suit my own personal taste, not what someone else has thrown together. The decor should be very warm and homely, because it's always so cold in England."

Charlie, who had begun married life with Shirley at a flat in Regent's Park, invested wisely: in July 1965 for £8,850 he bought a sixteenth-century country house from Lord Shawcross, former British attorney-general in the Labor Government. The Old Brewery House in Lewes, Sussex, had once belonged to the Archbishop of Canterbury and, importantly, since Shirley loved horses, had stables. Here, Charlie settled in with his massive collections of military artifacts and art. He was the first of the Stones to head for the countryside, but we were all to follow suit.

Maybe it was time for us to move too, because too many unwelcome visitors were turning up on our doorstep. One evening after Diane had gone to bed I answered a ring on the door. A large drunken man stood there, asking for Diane. I asked him what he wanted and he became very aggressive. I told him to leave and slammed the door in his face. Diane, who had heard the commotion, came down to the lounge crying and explained that she'd been having an affair with him while I'd been away. I asked her why she hadn't told me before and she admitted that she had been scared of the consequences. I told her to get in touch with him and tell him not to come round again, and the incident was forgotten.

* * *

Our recording career continued to blossom. In America our seventh single, "(I Can't Get No) Satisfaction,"* was released on June 5, backed by "The Under-Assistant West Coast Promotion Man" and it was released in a color sleeve. "Satisfaction's" lyrics consolidated our reputation in the States as "bad boys"; while in Britain, five days after that release, our third EP came out. *Got Live If You Want It!* also featured a color sleeve and comprised five songs recorded live in London, Manchester and Liverpool, together with an opening track, called "We Want the Stones", consisting entirely of an audience chanting those four words. (We claimed the publishing royalties on this for the group as Nanker-Phelge, by listing it as a separate track!)†

Keith and his girlfriend Linda Keith, a model, returned from a Greek holiday on June 15 just in time to fly the same day to Scotland where we began another tour that was to be marked by screaming hysterical audiences. After flight delays at London, we had to be whisked by police escort straight to the Glasgow Odeon Theater for two concerts; more than 240 police on foot, twenty mounted police and twelve patrol cars were on duty, with the most elaborate plans ever made to meet teenage trouble, local authorities told us. The 3,000 fans who arrived for the first show were "quick-marched" into the theater and, although there were twenty-five arrests for various clashes with police, and 145 fans treated for fainting, it was lightweight stuff compared with the riots in America. At least here we could complete our show without worrying that the police would cut the power. But as one writer said in reporting the volume of screaming: "I felt sorry for those who actually wanted to hear as well as see the Stones." Mick described his voice as

---

*"Satisfaction," which was Number One for four weeks in America, is one of only two songs—the other is "White Christmas"—to have been a hit in five different years, with charted cover versions by Otis Redding (1966), Aretha Franklin (1967), Bubblerock (a pseudonym for Jonathan King) (1974) and Devo (1976).
†This reached the top of the EP charts and number six in the British singles charts.

"rotten"; he had not sung for a fortnight and needed to "break it in" again.

After two mad shows at the Usher Hall in Edinburgh on June 16, we set off by road for Aberdeen. A memorable moment came when we stopped off for a fry-up at a country pub in Laurencekirk and a seventy-five-year-old character named Tom Carney sang Scots folksongs to us. In a broad accent he told us: "You look awfly like lassies, but I like ye!"

There were the same sort of scenes at Edinburgh, Aberdeen and Dundee as there had been at Glasgow, and the trail of debris left by the tour provoked an inquest in national papers. "The sad and inevitable result of this behavior is that it always reflects upon the artist in the center of it," stated the *New Musical Express*. Mick was defensive: "The fans don't mean to break the seats," he said. "In many cases they just stand on them to see better and in some of the older theaters the seats can't take it. Sure, you get a couple of fellows who come along to throw tomatoes, but nobody turns up with the idea of wrecking the joint." Mick was severely affected by the tour, though: as the rest of us flew back to London, he said he was suffering from exhaustion and he stayed behind at the Gleneagles Hotel for a night; Charlie remained to keep an eye on him.

Back in Kent Eva Jagger, worrying about her son, commented: "I know he hates touring. I just wish I could see more of him now. I miss the times when, after being out late, he came to my bedroom and chatted to me. He doesn't show his feelings much but I know he loves his family. If he takes after his father he'll be bald before he's thirty."

"Screaming girls with tears running down their cheeks fainted; one climbed on to the stage, embraced Charlie and fainted afterwards with a happy smile on her face . . ." (*Daily Mirror*) The pattern was now familiar. But this was neither America nor Britain but Oslo, Norway on June 24, at the start of our second Scandinavian tour. Thousands greeted us at the airport and fire-engines used water cannons to keep the kids back.

"Satisfaction," by now up to four in the *Billboard* American chart, but released nowhere else, had been played on Finnish radio because the underground network of disc jockeys was formidable. We met several of them when we sailed out to visit some pirate radio stations between Copenhagen and Sweden. One was Radio Syd, the world's first pirate radio station. My firmest memory of Copenhagen is of a record shop where Charlie and I were astounded by the amount of obscure blues albums in stock. I bought nineteen and Charlie thirteen, a treasure trove of material which kept me listening for years.

On to Helsinki, Finland, and a comical press conference at the Hotel Turku, where writers commented on our apparent shyness, not a word I'd use to describe the Stones. Mick reprimanded the journalists: "Hey, guys, the Rolling Stones are *here*—that's the bar," he shouted to some writers who were busy getting drinks at the other end of the room. Later at Yyteri Beach we played an open-air show to 15,000. It was only dark between about 12:30 and 2 a.m. at that time of year. We had had to get to the beach by driving over the sand-dunes in a jeep. What a ride! All the people who came slept on the beach in tents.

But we returned to the hotel in Turku, and later went for dinner and drinks in the hotel restaurant. They had a dance-floor in the middle of the restaurant and the local people were doing the Twist and the Cha-cha. We ordered and Keith asked for soup. When the food arrived, Keith's soup didn't come. Angry, he asked for it again, pointing to the menu. He still didn't get it, and he showed the waiter the menu again. When the waiter arrived with a meal on a plate, Keith went mad, stood up, flung it on to the dance floor and stormed out. Only then did we realize that the soup he had been pointing to on the menu was really the word "supper!"

The next episode in our continuing battle with authority brought us a mention in the House of Commons after a stipendiary magistrate in Glasgow had attacked us on June 30. Dealing with a boy who admitted breaking a shop window near the Odeon Cinema during our concert there a fortnight earlier, Mr. James Langmuir told him: "I am surprised you go along and mix with the long-haired gentlemen called the Rolling Stones. What is the attraction for you? Complete morons like that. They wear their hair down to their shoulders, wear filthy clothes and act like clowns. You buy a ticket to see animals like that? You think if people come here with their *banjos* and hair down to their waist you can smash windows?"

Two days later in the House of Commons Tom Driberg, the Labor MP for Barking, tabled a motion saying: "That this House deplores the action of a Glasgow magistrate, James Langmuir, in using his privileged position to make irrelevant, snobbish and insulting personal comment on the appearance and performance of the Rolling Stones, who are making a substantial contribution to public entertainment and the export drive."

Andrew summed up our views on the magistrate's attitude when he told the *Daily Mirror*: "I was staggered to hear of this man's comments. Trouble is that he is a member of the dead generation that just is not with it."

On July 10 "(I Can't Get No) Satisfaction" jumped to the top position in both American Top Hundred charts published by *Billboard* and *Cashbox;* we were awarded our fourth gold disc for it. Rolling Stones records appeared in virtually every international chart with albums, singles and EPs. Yet my bank account showed a credit of £82, and the weekly pay from the Rolling Stones' office was still £50. Something seemed wrong. We'd been performing successfully, touring extensively in Britain, Europe and America for two full years, reached the heights, and still had no actual cash in the bank. Accounts for the group showed that I had drawn £4,155 in the year ended June 30, 1965, including the weekly £50.

More significantly, a statement (prepared at a later date) from London Records produced a royalty statement for Nanker-Phelge Music Ltd showing a profit from March 1, 1965, to June 30, 1965 (a mere four months), of $61,317 for the entire band. By the end of July 1965 this figure had risen to $69,964. Accounts for the year ended June 30, 1965, stated that from performances (concerts, television, radio, merchandising, etc.) we had earned £82,605 gross, and that Rolling Stones Limited made a profit of £9,922.

Interestingly, Mick was correctly credited with 3/12ths of all Jagger–Richards songs (i.e. half the writers' share), and for Nanker-Phelge songs he received 1/10th of "Empty Heart," 2/15ths of "It's All Right," 1/12th of "Little by

Little," "Now I've Got a Witness" and "Stoned," 4/12ths of "Play with Fire" (probably because he wrote the lyric) and 6/12ths of "2120 South Michigan Avenue," a track he didn't even sing on!

These figures were unknown to me, and possibly the other Stones, at that time. While we asked no questions and believed that the money would come in eventually, others close to us obviously believed it was coming too slowly.

As we scored more points than the Beatles to win a Radio Luxembourg listener-voting competition called Battle of the Bands,* Eric Easton wrote to Norman Weiss, our American concert agent, on June 23: "I agree that this tour looks as though it is going to be much better financially, but I always have to reckon with the fact that the boys have a permanent picture in mind of the Beatles' $1 million, ten-day stint. Their idea is: if Eppy [Brian Epstein] can get this sort of deal for the Beatles, why can't you get it for the Stones? While I realize that miracles take a little longer to perform, I have at least got to kid myself that I am making the effort to actually perform miracles."

The man who held out the possibility of those miracles coming true was Allen Klein. A tigerish New York accountant who developed a big appetite for British pop acts, he was brought into the Rolling Stones' life by Andrew Oldham, who met him in mid-July 1965 at the Columbia Records convention in Miami. There, Andrew also met Klein's lawyer, Marty Machat, and hired him to act on his behalf; hitherto Andrew's lawyer was David Jacobs in London, who represented a wide range of show-business personalities. Convinced that Klein was essential to confront record companies aggressively to secure the Stones and himself much better deals, Andrew

---

*The presentation took place on July 15, 1965, aboard the Thames pleasure-cruiser *Kingswood*. Anita Harris presented it to Keith, Charlie and Brian on the chilly top deck. They dutifully posed for photographers when the award was made, but when she kissed each of them, Charlie remained grim-faced, bringing a shout of laughter from reveling journalists, who had emerged briefly from the bar.

moved decisively and unilaterally to appoint him, writing to him while he was still in America on July 12:

> You are hereby authorized to negotiate in my behalf as the producer of the Rolling Stones and the co-manager of said group for a new phonographic recording agreement. I will inform the other manager, Eric Easton and the artists who comprise the Rolling Stones that you have been exclusively retained by me for such purposes. Inquiries from record companies will be directed to you and all negotiations and submissions of negotiations will be submitted to me and my solicitor in England, David Jacobs. For your services, we agree to pay you Twenty Per Cent (20%) of the gross compensation paid pursuant to the agreement we enter into, that is either guaranteed, paid or earned under the agreements you negotiate. It is understood that your appointment hereunder is exclusive and can be revoked by you or myself by giving each other prior written notice of no less than 90 days.
>
> Yours truly,
> Andrew Oldham

With that letter he sent Klein a letter of authority, which said:

> To whom it may concern:
> Please be advised that the undersigned, as producer and co-manager of the artists known as the Rolling Stones, has retained Allen Klein and Company, Inc. to exclusively negotiate and be the exclusive business manager and representative for the Rolling Stones for the phonograph record industry. You are hereby authorized to conduct all negotiations and inquiries directly with Mr. Klein.
>
> Very truly yours,
> Andrew Oldham

Additionally, Andrew appointed Klein as his personal business manager and adviser "for myself and all artists I represent in the phonograph record industry." His letter of agreement to Klein on this matter read:

. . . You agree to represent me in such capacity and to negotiate on my behalf all phonograph record agreements for myself as a producer and for any artists that are presently or may be signed to me in the future . . . you are to receive a fee equal to 20% (Twenty Per Cent) of all sums guaranteed or earned from agreements made in my behalf from this date forward or which are negotiated during the term of this agreement even though payment may be received subsequent to the term of this agreement. The term of this agreement shall be for *three years* and shall be exclusive. We each shall have the right to terminate this agreement upon 90 days prior written notice of each other. In the event of such termination, you will continue to receive your 20% (Twenty Per Cent) of all sums either guaranteed or received or earned based on agreements or negotiations entered into prior to the termination of this agreement. *This agreement is limited to the United States and Canada* . . .

Andrew returned to London on July 24 and met Mick and Keith to discuss getting together with Klein. It was obvious by now that the days of Oldham and Easton's partnership were numbered. It was ironic that two days later, July 26, I incorporated my own company, Freeway Music, to handle my personal record production and songwriting activities outside the Stones. That day, on Mick's twenty-second birthday, the whole band congregated at Andrew's office at 138 Ivor Court en route to the Hilton Hotel to meet Klein in his suite. Andrew filled us in on his ideas for the future of the band. I felt very uneasy. I said to the other four that before we talked business with Klein we should have our own lawyer present, checking over all the documents before we signed anything. I was immediately shouted down by everybody. Keith jumped up and said: "Don't be so fucking mercenary. We've got to trust *someone*."

I maintained that we should not be unprotected in a potential business agreement, but what I didn't realize at the Hilton Hotel was that it was a *fait accompli:* Andrew had already signed those letters of agreement that Klein had prepared for him. I was also unaware that Mick and Keith had met him two days earlier.

I was never comfortable with Allen Klein. I didn't trust

him and he knew it. "Why don't you like me, Bill?" he would say on many occasions. "Because I don't trust you, Allen," I would reply. This feeling has never changed, and my initial instincts and worries were borne out by events.

We left that meeting to drive to Birmingham to record *Thank Your Lucky Stars,* so our minds were temporarily diverted from Klein. But the plot thickened quickly. Next day, we all gathered again at Andrew's office for a second meeting, and then on to Decca House on Albert Embankment, together with Marty Machat. It was at this meeting that we first realized that since May 1963 Impact Sound (Andrew and Eric Easton) had been receiving a 14 per cent royalty from Decca on our records, but were paying us only 6 per cent of that amount to share between us. Of that 6 per cent, Andrew and Eric were also taking a 25 per cent management fee (i.e., leaving us with 4.5 per cent as against their 9.5 per cent). We were told this would be changed on the new contract. Of course, these figures had never been mentioned to us before. This blatantly unfair arrangement caused some of the group to believe that the arrival of Klein would correct *all* injustices.

However, I was still unsure of Klein, and Brian, too, was beginning to feel anxious about the prospect of his working for us. It had all happened too quickly and these bulldozing tactics worried us. Klein told us that when he met the Decca executives, we were to "just to be there as a show of strength, and say nothing" while he discussed a new record deal with the "powers-that-be."

The men now running our affairs knew how to oil the wheels to secure our immediate smiles. Two days later, on July 29, we were all summoned to meet Oldham and Klein at Decca House. In the boardroom with the chairman, Sir Edward Lewis, and his colleagues, we signed a new record contract. We were then each presented with a check for £2,500, our first year's guarantee on the deal with Klein; we were also each guaranteed ten annual payments of $7,000 from Decca Records (UK) from July 30, 1965, to July 1, 1974. We were then given two letters of agreement from Andrew Oldham (but really from Klein) to the Rolling Stones, dated that day, July 29:

Gentlemen,

Because of your phenomenal success in the record-ing business, which we gratefully appreciate, we have decided to increase your royalty on all record sales so that all royalties received on gramophone record sales from inception will be divided equally—fifty per cent (50%) for the Rolling Stones and fifty per cent (50%) on behalf of the producer.

Very truly yours,

Andrew Loog Oldham, on behalf of Andrew Loog Oldham and Eric Easton

Gentlemen,

Reference is made to an Agreement dated 5/9/63 between Eric Easton, Andrew Loog Oldham and Brian Jones on behalf of the Rolling tones. Specific refer-ence is made to Paragraph 6 on Page 2 of said agree-ment regarding commission of twenty-five per cent (25%) on all gramophone record royalties. Please be advised that as we are receiving producing royalty on the same gramophone record sales it would not be ethical or fair for us to receive the twenty-five per cent (25%) commission on your share of the royalties. We therefore consider that portion of the Agreement eliminated.

Very truly yours,

Andrew Loog Oldham, on behalf of Andrew Loog Oldham and Eric Easton

While he was named as a signatory to those letters, Eric Easton had been conspicuously absent from all dis-cussions about Klein.

A fat check had allayed any fears I had and I re-turned elated to Beckenham, showing Diane the biggest payout I'd ever had. We celebrated quietly at home that night. I was in high spirits—things were finally looking up. My bank account, which had been in the red, sud-denly went into credit to the tune of £2,469, a small fortune in 1965. We were walking on air, but within five years we would again be engulfed by financial problems.*

---

*Allen Klein was to loom large in the final years of the Beatles' story, too. During their rift in the chaotic period of their Apple

The touring schedule, meanwhile, rolled on: to Exeter, Portsmouth, Bournemouth and Great Yarmouth with a large cast: the Walker Brothers, the Steam Packet (with Long John Baldry, Brian Auger, Rod Stewart and Julie Driscoll) and Elkie Brooks. We were still top of the US singles charts with "Satisfaction."

The energy of the sixties was something special, as pop, fashion and attitudes merged into a lively scene that was not fueled purely by money. Class barriers were being eroded: Mick and Chrissie went to a coming-out party for the three Ormsby Gore daughters, staged by their mother, Lady Harlech and attended by Princess Margaret, Princess Alexandra and Lord Snowdon. Brian was jetting around the European capitals, to Paris, to Stockholm and other cities, as often as he could, and becoming very popular at the "in" spots; and at home he was frequenting Soho's sods club with friends like Eric Clapton, Georgie Fame and Dave Davies of the Kinks.

In London Chrissie Shrimpton got involved in a fight with Beatles fans who were awaiting Ringo's arrival at his home near Mick's in Bryanston Mews East. Mick arrived and saw Chrissie and a fifteen-year-old girl in combat. "I got really annoyed," Mick said. "The fans had had an argument with Chrissie the previous evening and she was very upset. I pulled the girl off and gave her a kick in the bottom. I was only wearing plimsolls so I didn't hurt her much. In fact I got the worst of it, because she gave me a few clouts." The girl, Ann Richards, remarked: "Chrissie was knocking the Beatles and I won't let anyone get away with that." Mick retorted: "She was laying into my girl and using filthy language. Sure I kicked her."

Our fourth American album release, *Out of Our Heads*, on July 30, 1965, featured a cover photograph of our unsmiling faces in tight focus. We were projected as

organization in 1969, Mick had suggested that Lennon get Klein to sort out the Beatles' affairs, and John Lennon hired Klein as his personal manager. The other three Beatles would not sign. His entry marked the start of the deepening crisis between Lennon and McCartney, who wanted his father-in-law, New York lawyer Lee Eastman, to represent him. Within five years, Lennon was describing the period as the Beatles' *"de-Klein."*

almost sullen, and the evolution of our music was now seen as the antithesis of American teenage pop. These were the tracks recorded at Chess Studios, Chicago, and RCA Studios, Hollywood, with Ron Malo and Dave Hassinger as engineers and Andrew as producer. The music, particularly diverse, drew from inspired sources: our own monster hits "Satisfaction" and "The Last Time" contrasted with Marvin Gaye's "Hitch-Hike," Sam Cooke's "Good Times" and what was often described as Mick's best-ever pure soul vocal on "That's How Strong My Love Is." America's most respected critic, Lillian Roxon, said that with the album the Stones were truly finding their niche.*

A kind of milestone occurred in London when we hired the Palladium for two concerts promoted by Eric Easton on August 1. I used my new red, pear-shaped "Wyman bass" which Vox built for me, with especially small frets and finger-board to accommodate my small hands. Brian, dressed all in white, was the visual attraction of this show and made sure he was heard, too: everyone commented on his volume, which drowned Mick's vocals completely throughout the show. The crowd, almost American in its wildness, rushed the stage and the show was marred by the strong-arm methods employed by police and ushers. "Teenage girls trying to get near the stage were roughly manhandled in the gangways by officials using Gestapo-like methods," reported Keith Altham in *New Musical Express*. Leaving the theater, police guarded us as fans battered away at the doors and windows of our car.

Fortunately, on August 3 we began a three-week holiday. We needed it. There was a great deal to contemplate as Keith and Linda Keith went to the south of France and Diane and I planned a visit to Düsseldorf to visit my married brother John, who was in the RAF there. Mick and Chrissie went to Tangiers with Brian and Linda Lawrence. This was an incongruous quartet, particularly because at the time they flew off, Linda was seeking a court affiliation order, claiming that Brian was the father of her baby Julian.

---

*This was our first chart-dropping album in America, staying there for three weeks; it was actually in the charts for sixty-five weeks.

By the time they had returned from what Linda called "the most marvelous holiday," she decided that court action was unnecessary. "We are not going to be married, but Brian has done the next-best thing and paid me a lump sum for Julian, agreed to become a sleeping partner in a boutique business and promised to meet all family expenses in the future," Linda said in a statement. "I realize what a lucky girl I am, having such a famous boyfriend . . . Brian has done my career no end of good. I used to be a hairdresser, now I design mod gear for other girls and soon I'll be opening a boutique in Windsor. I'd marry Brian if he wanted to settle down. Maybe in a year or two he might do that, but for the time being we remain very good friends."

Brian was typically complicated about the affair: "Linda is absolutely wrong if she thinks that we have any sort of friendly arrangement. I certainly have no business relationship with her. I have cut off all association with her. Linda and I came to a financial arrangement before we went to Tangier. I settled a lump sum on the child a long time ago, not because of some sudden friendship that sprung up in Tangier."

Not surprisingly, they finally broke up and went their separate ways. Shortly afterwards Linda started stepping out with Donovan (Leitch), who had finished his relationship with Doreen Samuels, my ex-girlfriend. In 1968, she went to America with her son, and opened a boutique. But in 1970, she returned to live with her parents in Windsor, and on October 2 of that year she married Donovan at Windsor Register Office. Donovan wrote his smash hit "Sunshine Superman" about Linda.

Brian was quite proud of the fact that he was footloose and fancy-free, despite his many relationships. "I haven't tied myself down with a girl yet. After all, how many girls could I find who would make me tea, cook me meals, tidy my house and talk intelligently to me while I sit and watch with my feet up? I'm very lazy. I like girls who phone me up to ask how I am, and come round the house to help me. I love all that, being pampered. I keep my relationships with girls casual. I'm very wary because I've been hurt and disillusioned a few times. Even when they've loved me, girls have schemed against me."

Mick also insisted to the press that he had no plans to

marry Chrissie, who was busy herself, to Mick's embarrassment, with a column for the American teen magazine *Tiger Beat* called "From London With Love." But his mate David Bailey did marry, in typical sixties style, French actress Catherine Deneuve that August. Mick, the best man, wore a blue denim shirt with no tie.

Britain now prepared for the release of the single "Satisfaction,"* which had been such a colossal Number One in America, selling 1½ million copies. We decided the B-side over there, "The Under-Assistant West Coast Promotion Man," wouldn't make much sense to British ears, so we chose "The Spider and the Fly" instead. Release date was set for August 20, but three weeks earlier Decca had begun pressing the American coupling when Andrew phoned to tell them of our decision. Decca director Bill Townsley, who said Andrew had "let us know rather too late," said 25,000 copies had been pressed with the USA B-side, and though they would be exported, the waste to Decca would be a few thousand pounds, as they had printed 200,000 record labels with the "wrong" titles. The impact of the single was reduced because many British radio stations had been playing imported versions for weeks before the official release date.

It didn't take long for the grip by Allen Klein on our financial structure to be sealed. On August 4 Andrew was quoted by the *Daily Express* as saying: "Under the terms of a deal concluded by our American business manager, Mr. Allen Klein, the Stones are guaranteed $3 million over the next five years." The contracts that mentioned such a figure, involving Nanker-Phelge Ltd, Andrew, Klein, Decca Records UK and London Records USA were many and various. (They are printed in Appendix 1, pp. 645–52.)

While Andrew, Mick and Keith had been romancing Klein, they had attacked Easton. During Andrew's visit to see Allen in New York on August 13 Eric sent the three of them a letter care of Klein's New York office which dealt with a list of requests and complaints the trio had supposedly made about a German tour, money due and a concert tour of Britain, as well as a projected concert at the Isle of Man on September 8:

*This was Number One for three weeks in Britain.

Dear Andrew,

I have received this morning the following cables:

(1) In order to secure the written consent of the Rolling Stones required for contracts on the proposed English tour please forward forthwith all contracts and pertinent details to Allen Klein (New York address). The Rolling Stones will not be the promoters. Mick, Keith and Andy.

(2) In order to secure the written consent of the Rolling Stones required for contracts on the proposed German tour please forward forthwith all contracts and pertinent details to Allen Klein (New York address). Keith, Andy and Mick.

(3) We direct that you desist from holding our money at the GAC [General Artists Corporation]. It is our money isn't it. Keith and Mick.

(4) It is impossible to do Isle of Man on 8th. We need record. Must record between 5th and 10th, cancel date. Mick, Keith and Andy.

I cannot understand how the cables were supposed to have been sent by Mick since I have spoken to him on the telephone this morning at his flat in London. He told me that he has only just returned from Tangier and was very surprised to hear that cables had been sent to me bearing his name. He told me that he had no idea of what is going on in New York. Neither have I for that matter. [My italics]

As to cable No. 1. As you and the Stones well know, the position with regard to the forthcoming English tour is as follows: 24 theaters have been booked by Rolling Stones Ltd, and contracts to confirm the hiring of these theaters have been signed by Mick as director for and on behalf of Rolling Stones Ltd. In order to refresh your memory the dates and theaters are shown on the attached list. I also confirm that this tour is being promoted by the Stones themselves through their company. This is what they all wanted to do and with which you agreed. The cost of the basic rentals in respect of the hire of the 24 theaters amounts to approximately £8,500. As the tour is to start on 9/24/65 I have made all the arrangements for advertising, printing, etc., and most of the supporting acts for the tour have been booked by Rolling Stones Ltd, after discussions with you and the Stones. If you really do want to have copies of the hiring agreements with Rank, ABC, Moss Empires, Newcastle Corporation and Leicester Corporation I can let you have them but I think I have just given you sufficient information with regard to the tour. I do not understand the reference in the cable to the Rolling Stones not being the promoters. They are the promoters in fact because of the Agreements for the hire of the theaters.

As to cable No. 2. The German tour was briefly discussed with the Stones at the meeting of directors on 8/2/65. A day or so later the actual contract and its terms and conditions were discussed in detail with Mick. He was happy about it and he thereupon signed the contract as director for and on behalf of Rolling Stones Ltd. I enclose a copy of the contract.

As to cable No. 3. As you and the Stones know and by arrangement with you all, contracts in respect of the American personal appearances in the past have always been entered into by Eric Easton Ltd, to present the Rolling Stones. I enclose a copy of the statement (which you and the Stones have all previously seen) prepared by us following the completion of the first American tour so that you can see exactly how the monies received have been dealt with. Details of income and expenditure, along with photostats of all invoices and hotel bills paid by GAC on behalf of the Stones were received in May in respect of the second American tour. Work is well advanced in analyzing the figures of that particular tour but the work is somewhat involved since we have to debit yourself and each of the Stones with your and their own individual items of expenditure. The job is made doubly difficult as some of the photostats are quite illegible and we shall eventually have to ask GAC to supply more distinct copies of certain accounts in order that a true picture can be arrived at. We have still to receive an account from GAC in respect of the third and last American tour. I have asked them about this on a number of occasions, the last time being in my letter to them dated 7/23/65. You will understand that as Eric Easton Ltd is liable to account to you and each of the Stones for the final balance due to each one of you and we are unable to do this until we have completed our analysis of the figures since you and each of the Stones have incurred various amounts in personal items of expenditure. For instance, I had a letter from GAC dated 7/14/65, telling me that you had dropped in for some money, but I have no idea as to the amount they paid you. You and each of the Stones will be presented with a statement and will be paid out the appropriate amounts due the moment our statements for the second and third tours have been completed. I would add that the position with regard to the American tour money was explained to the Stones at the directors' meeting on 8/2/65.

As to cable No. 4. I think that you should tell Mick and Keith that the Stones must appear in the Isle of Man on 9/8/65. The contract for this engagement was signed by Mick Jagger for and on behalf of Rolling Stones Ltd last week. The management will certainly have some strong things to say if the Stones do not appear as contracted. I have dealt at length with the various points raised in the cables. You and I, as the joint managers of the Stones, have a joint responsibility to advise our Artists as to their contractual obligations. It seems to me to be quite clear that one thing we must do is to advise them to fulfill their contracts and I feel sure that on reflection you will agree with me on this.

Yours sincerely,
Eric Easton

Mick and Keith flew to New York on August 14, 1965, checking into the Drake Hotel and meeting up with Andrew; the next night the trio went to see the Beatles at Shea Stadium, accompanied by Scott Ross, one of the compères for the show. With the rest of the Stones knowing nothing of such a meeting, Mick, Keith and Andrew met Marty Machat and the Decca Records and London Records lawyers on August 16 before flying back to London that night. Next day there was another "private" meeting at Andrew's London office, attended by Mick, Keith and Charlie, followed by a letter signed by those three, asking Klein's accountants, Goodman Myers, to take over from H. T. Chenhall and Co. as our representatives.

Their behavior was furtive to say the least: on the very night they sent that letter, and a mere day after returning from New York, Brian flew back from Morocco and I from Germany to attend a full band meeting with promoter Helmut Voss to discuss our coming German tour. Nothing was mentioned to Brian or me about the meetings they had conducted supposedly on the band's behalf.

By now the schism that had been apparent in the band was confirmed as Andrew, with Mick and Keith, decided our destiny. The hiring of Klein had come as stealthily as the erosion of Brian's role as an equal front-liner, and the imminent, inevitable departure of Eric Easton. Naturally, as they had sealed the Klein deal, they did all the interviews about his arrival and Easton's departure. Early in September Keith was to tell *Music Echo:* "Eric Easton was just too tired. We couldn't get anything done. He's not all that young, and after the strain of our last two US tours, he couldn't make the third one.* In fact, he was ill. It's been a very happy relationship. Klein is young and knows what's happening. We'll keep in touch by phone." He told *New Musical Express:* "We decided on an American as our new business manager because, let's face it, when you are handling worldwide transactions America is the only place to work from, and we do so much business there it's very useful to have a man on the spot." But this is to jump ahead.

On August 24 and 25 we all congregated, along with Marty Machat, in Klein's suite at the London Hilton, where Klein sat behind an antique desk wearing a red T-shirt and basketball boots. Klein later gave an interview to *New Musical Express* with the masterly prediction: "I believe the whole group scene is going to disappear in six months, with the exception of entertainers like the Beatles, the Stones and the Animals." On the 27th we discussed our future before Eric arrived and we had a confrontation with him. Klein made various accusations against Easton and the atmosphere became bitterly acrimonious. Eric remained calm throughout. On Saturday, August 28 we met again and all signed the contracts between ourselves, Decca Records, Andrew and Allen Klein. That week, Bob Dylan entered the British top ten with his song "Like a Rolling Stone." The song seemed

---

*This was untrue and a camouflage. Easton functioned efficiently as our agent. Furthermore, Klein was not succeeding him in that role; we hired Tito Burns as our agent in Britain.

to be uncannily prophetic of the big changes that the group was experiencing.

Another salvo had clearly been sent by Mick, Keith and Andrew to GAC, because on August 26, GAC sent a cable to the Stones at Klein's office: "Shocked by tour wire. All monies on first 2 tours have been fully paid out as per contract to corporation authorized by you and your manager. Balance monies of 3rd Tour being held pending joint written instructions from each of you and from the corporate entity in whose name the tour contracts were signed. Therefore we vigorously deny that this serves as any basis for your attempted repudiation of forthcoming American tour which we have booked on specific instructions first from Eric Easton Ltd., whom you previously authorized."

While all these machinations were going on Andrew was launching his own record label. He had grown disenchanted with big-corporation thinking and though a group of our size needed that sort of support, he saw the need for a small label that could move quickly, nurturing promising artists and providing the family-like atmosphere that was missing in the giant companies. In this at least he showed great foresight. When he launched Immediate Records in August 1965 it was a forerunner for the independent labels that would proliferate in the seventies. He chose as his partner a hard-headed young businessman named Tony Calder* and distributed through Philips Records. Oldham said: "Immediate will operate in the same way as any good, small independent label in America. We will be bringing in new producers, while our main hope lies with the top session guitarist who's turned producer Jimmy Page† and my two friends, Stones Mick and Keith."

Immediate's launch party on August 20, attended by Mick, Eric Clapton, Mike Clark of the Byrds and Nico, later to be a much-respected singer with the Velvet Underground, was marked by its first single release, "Hang on Sloopy" by the McCoys. This went to Number One,

---

*Calder later launched Ice Records with Eddy Grant, the hugely successful leader of the group the Equals.
†The same Jimmy Page who formed Led Zeppelin, the biggest rock band of the seventies.

and the label became the starting point for many excellent acts, including the Small Faces (from which sprang Rod Stewart and Humble Pie) and the Nice (from which came Emerson, Lake and Palmer).

The same day, our "Satisfaction" was released to excellent reviews in Britain and within forty-eight hours of release had jumped to third place in the national chart. Things were changing all around us: Mike Dorsey, Eric's representative, wrote to explain that he had to leave for personal reasons, obviously because of the split with Eric.* This was a big loss of a good friend.

My own production activities were also building up by now. On September 3, as "Satisfaction" went to the top with 250,000 British sales, a record I produced by the Preachers was released. Finances continued to be mysterious. We were told that in America Allen Klein had opened personal accounts for all five Stones at the Chemical Bank in New York. By September 8 I received a puzzling statement of a "loan" from Nanker-Phelge, New York, putting $47,326 into the account!

The fans remained constant. On August 23, when we went to Manchester to appear on *Scene at 6:30,* a fireman turned a hosepipe on 200 screaming girls as they rushed through the gates of the TV studio. The fans thought we were being smuggled in with a furniture van; a gate was broken as the girls swarmed forward. The fireman's cold jet stopped the rush but some of the girls danced in the water singing "We shall not be moved" and "We shall overcome." Police eventually moved them on.

We flew to Dublin on September 3 with a film crew of three hired by Andrew to shoot a documentary on the Stones. The idea was partly to promote our next single on television. Many years before the video explosion, we felt there was something static about such programs as *Top of the Pops.* There was always much talk of a major Stones movie, with a budget of £1,700,000 bandied about by Klein and Oldham, but this never happened. No doubt the Beatles' 1964 success with *A Hard Day's Night* enthused people. Our quickly made fifty-minute film, later

---

*Mike Dorsey moved to Australia and had a very successful film and TV career. At present he runs large finance and business companies there.

entitled *Charlie Is My Darling,* was mostly interviews with us and fans; shots of us traveling in limousines to and from theaters and hotels; footage of our concert showed us performing "The Last Time" and "It's Alright"; and we are also seen jamming backstage on the old music-hall song "Maybe it's Because I'm a Londoner." The soundtrack included "Satisfaction," "Get Off of My Cloud," "Heart of Stone" and "Goin' Home," and the film gathered dust.

We did two shows at the Dublin Adelphi that night.

Between concerts we were relaxing in our dressing-room when we were suddenly disturbed by two boys who, having climbed three stories outside the building, popped their hands through the open window and calmly asked us for autographs. We duly signed and they returned to the ground the same way.

The second show was riotous. As we finished playing "Satisfaction" fierce fighting broke out between fans and theater attendants, stopping the show. I was knocked to the floor against a piano, sustaining a badly sprained arm as screaming teenagers stormed the stage. Mick was lifted off his feet and pushed through a door at the side of the stage, his jacket torn to shreds. Andrew cracked his head as he fought to clear the kids from the stage and Brian wrestled with three teenagers. Keith and Brian ran out of a stage door into a waiting car and Charlie was turned over on his back with his drums on top of him. Mick, Charlie and I raced to join them as the dressing-room windows were shattered.

We were all shaken, but I was the worst affected with that arm; Andrew described it as one of the most frightening scenes he had seen at a "beat show" (the generic word "rock" had not yet arrived). My own vivid memory of the mêlée was one of the marauding young guys trying to imitate Mick at the microphone until police hauled him away. Still, the gross takings here were £2,678, of which we were to receive 42 per cent.

After playing two nights in Belfast, we flew to London on Sunday, September 5, and then on to Los Angeles for recording sessions throughout that night for our new album. We cut "Get Off of My Cloud" and returned to the hotel jet-lagged and exhausted. Recording throughout the next night until 6:30 a.m., with Jack Nitzsche and

Stu on keyboards, we cut "I'm Free" and "Looking
Tired." I almost collapsed from exhaustion and a doctor
was called to the studio, but the prescription was rest—
which was not available.

Catching an 8 a.m. flight from Los Angeles on September 7, we slept most of the way, arriving in London at 6
a.m. A car delivered us all to our homes to freshen up,
but by 1 p.m. we were back at Heathrow, to catch a
plane to Douglas, Isle of Man for a show that night. This
controversial engagement, the subject of Mick, Keith and
Andrew's cable, was our final dance-hall date anywhere.
The security was poor enough in some cinemas, where
the stage was high above the crowd; in the dance halls
there was no way of holding the fans at bay. We had to
end our days in those vulnerable places. Though we were
all exhausted the show passed off well, and we adjourned
into the Casino for dinner and gambled on the roulette
wheels before getting to bed. Next morning, Mick was
given a check for £946 15s., our fee, which was 70 per
cent of the box-office gross. He lost it and eventually we
had to ask the promoter to re-issue it.

The plan to jettison Eric Easton had still to be resolved. There was talk of him being paid a lump-sum
"golden handshake," but on September 10 he declared:
"My contract as agent and co-manager of the Rolling
Stones still has nine months to run. Legally I have to
refute these reports until a settlement is made. Meanwhile, I am continuing in my capacity as the group's
co-manager, and am currently making arrangements for
the Stones' one-nighter tour which starts later this month."
Easton's lawyers added: "Eric Easton wishes it to be
known that, contrary to recent reports, overtures have
been made to him to acquire his interest in the management of the Rolling Stones, but no arrangements to that
effect have yet been made by Mr. Easton with Mr. Klein
who, it is reported, claims to be the group's new business
manager. The matter is in the hands of Mr. Easton's
solicitors."

We escaped to Germany on September 11, where two
excellent concerts in Münster marked our debut in what
turned out to be a never-to-be-forgotten tour. At Essen,
mounted police charged 2,000 yelling teenagers, who stood
on seats, unbolted the tubular chairs to wave in the air

and threw toilet rolls. A German policeman told the *Daily Mail:* "I have seen nothing like this since the old days of a Nazi or Communist rally."

Hamburg, next night, was worse. During two great shows for a total audience of 14,000, there were riots outside by kids who hadn't been able to get seats. Baton-wielding police on horses charged the fans. Between shows we watched these riots from the dressing-room windows. Later police announced that forty-seven had been arrested and thirty-seven injured in the street fighting. We could not believe the level of police brutality; backstage, too, the cops were wandering around armed to the teeth, trying to scrounge drinks from everyone. Keith took a half-filled whisky bottle, peed in it, shook it and passed it to the cops standing outside our dressing-room. They proceeded to pass it around to each other, taking swigs, toasting our health.

After the shows, at Hamburg's Hotel Lilienhof, where we all met for dinner after freshening up in our rooms, the night ended with a bizarre experience. I was sitting between Mick and Keith with Brian directly opposite me. Charlie sat next to him. Everyone else was evenly dispersed around the large oak banquet table, which held about fourteen people. There were large metal candlesticks at intervals along the table. In the middle of the meal, while we were chatting and joking, the candlestick that was between Brian and me suddenly leaned over at a 45-degree angle, the flames acting as if they were in a strong draught! The candlestick then went back to its original position as if nothing had happened. The conversation stopped. Brian and I thought someone was playing a joke and started checking under the table and asking who did it. After a while we continued with our meal. Then it happened again. We all moved our chairs away from the table and watched it return to normal. Shaken, we called the headwaiter over. He told us that the hotel was haunted, which made for some very interesting conversation before we retired to bed.

Between our two concerts on September 14 in Munich, Brian met Anita Pallenberg for the first time.* This was a

---

*Born in Italy on January 25, 1943, Anita Pallenberg came from an artistic family based in Rome, with family contacts in Germany, Spain and France. Educated in Germany, she grew up fluent in four languages and as a teenager studied picture restoration, medicine and graphic design.

romance which would dramatically affect his, and our, future. Anita, a model in town on a fashion job, went to the first show and saw us perform. After the show she persuaded a Swedish photographer to smuggle her backstage. She returned to the hotel for the night with a tearful Brian, who was reeling from a verbal hammering we'd all given him about his Pat Andrews problem.

For the police, promoters and fans, Munich proved a hazardous visit, but all that paled into insignificance against our next stop, West Berlin next day. We had an early inkling of problems: the Berlin Hilton had refused our reservations for fifteen first-class rooms, saying the security of its other guests had priority. So reservations were made at the Hotel Garhus instead.

On arrival in the city we were met by a huge police escort and a fleet of cars. The journey into town was amazing. Police lined the entire route and every road junction was blocked off by more police. We tore through the streets at 70 m.p.h. with nothing in our way. Later, we were told that the same security arrangements had been used for the Queen's visit a year earlier. Stepping out of the hotel to look around the town a little, we were driven to the Berlin Wall, where we went inside a tall building that overlooked East Berlin. I remember that all the streets were gray and empty there, apart from one car. But we could see soldiers stationed in every building, looking out of the windows. It was a depressing sight.

In the evening, we were driven to the Waldbühne Halle to play an open-air show in the stadium where Hitler Youth rallies had been held before the war. Our dressing-rooms were in the old military bunkers underground and we had to walk through a hundred yards of tunnels to get to the stage area. Backstage there were police with dogs everywhere. We started playing and the stage was immediately swamped by fans. I received a nice bump over my left eye from something that was thrown at the stage. We had to come off and return to our dressing-room. The police took fifteen minutes to settle the crowd, and then we went back on and continued with the show. One fan got on stage and tore off Mick's jacket, which fans ripped to shreds in seconds. Mick admitted he was "pretty scared. There was a great roar like a cup final between each number. There were so many casualities, they started a temporary hospital behind the stage. I think over sixty went to a real hospital in the end." Afterwards, we ran from the stage, escaping through the bunkers to our cars and the hotel for the night.

The crowd, meanwhile, rioted. Then they went on into town and smashed up the East Berlin train, amongst other things. The London *Evening News* was one of many papers to report the incident: "East Germany has claimed damages of almost 200,000 marks (about £18,000) for Berlin overhead coaches wrecked by teenagers going home from the Rolling Stones concert. In a letter to the West Berlin Senate, Herr Erwin Kramer, East German transport minister, demanded that 17,198 marks be paid for the damaged carriages of the railway, which is run by East Germany."

And the official East German Communist Party newspaper said: "This scandalous conduct shows anew the dangerous extent of crime in West Berlin."

News of a bomb threat made us jittery as we drove into Vienna on September 17 for a concert for 12,500 at the Wiener Stadthalle. The police said that they had had a call that a bomb would explode before we appeared on stage, but they thought it was a hoax. Exploding pellets were thrown at us as we played and one boy needed medical treatment when a pellet exploded in his hand. But there was no riot thanks to 800 police who arrested some of the pellet-throwers, and Mick remarked that the city of waltz lovers had done us proud.

We returned to news of our successes in *Melody Maker* 1965 readers' poll results. Among other listings, Mick was number three British singer and the Rolling Stones were number two British group and international group.

My activities outside the group fueled rumors in the autumn of 1965 that I was to leave the Stones, but this I flatly denied. Despite my discomfort at the arrival of Allen Klein, and what I thought of as the power axis of Mick–Keith–Andrew, I still felt loyal to the group and whatever the problems and the criticism, what still mattered was the music and our commitment to it. There was never any internal resentment of my record production and songwriting for other acts and there was no interest in it either; this attitude of non-encouragement by the others continues to this day. On September 20 I signed contracts for my new house in Keston, borrowing £5,150 from Rolling Stones Ltd. That same day, I produced four tracks with a new group called Moon's Train with Glyn Johns. The next day the new house was the scene of photo sessions for a new group I managed from Guildford, called the End.

Life was busy. That afternoon the grinding business affairs of the Stones went off at a new tangent when the five of us convened at Andrew's office to discuss the Oldham–Klein situation. (See Appendix 1, p. 645.) Mick then wrote on our behalf to Moss Empires and to the Rank Organization regarding the coming UK tour. This four-week tour came against the backdrop of our third album release in the UK on September 24. *Out of Our Heads*, with a cover picture by Gered Mankowitz, had different tracks on it from the American version, because US record-buyers liked to have hit singles on albums, whereas in Britain that was considered a con, and buyers demanded new tracks that hadn't been released previously. It went to Number One. Critical response was excellent. The next day in America our eighth single there was released, only three weeks after we had recorded it in Hollywood.*

When "Get Off of My Cloud" was played by US radio stations, disc jockeys decided with horror that the song was about a marijuana dream, the hippy antidote to the threatening tones of the Number One hit in America at that time, Barry McGuire's song about nuclear war, "Eve of Destruction."

The tour, our sixth in Britain, opened at the Astoria, Finsbury Park, on the day of the album's release. It was estimated that within the four-week trek, 100,000 people would see us and 90,000 souvenir programs would be sold! A new chauffeur, Tom Keylock, who was to be a key figure in the unfolding drama of life within the Stones, arrived to drive us in the Austin Princess; supporting acts included the group I managed, the End, plus such leading names as Unit Four Plus Two and the Spencer Davis Group. On some dates, the Moody Blues played.

*It reached number two for two weeks and earned us our sixth gold record.

We dressed much more sharply for this tour: Mick in a lightweight blue jacket with two vents, checked shirt and gray hipsters; Keith with a snow-white jacket on top of a brown polo-neck sweater; Brian immaculate in an all-white rig-out: white trousers, white shoes and a V-necked woolen jumper; Charlie with a dark-gray sports jacket, blue shirt and a long, pointed button-down collar and a tie; and me in a brown corduroy jacket over a red-striped shirt with a stiff white collar.

There was a subtle change to our act. With more confidence from American and European tours, the front-line trio even managed some smiles and waves to the crowds to replace the aloof look that had characterized our act until now. Some critics remarked that if we weren't careful, parents would begin to enjoy us and then we would be finished! Musically we offered a repertoire that consciously avoided the old favorites: new material from our album, which audiences had not heard, included "Mercy Mercy"; "Cry to Me"; "That's How Strong My Love Is" (with Brian on electric organ) and "Oh Baby." We also featured "I'm Moving On" and "The Last Time" before closing with "Satisfaction." I was reported as "grinning solidly throughout the performance" and Mick cheerfully accepted being pelted with peanuts, managing regular "thank yous" to the crowd.

The tour trundled on: Southampton, Cheltenham, Cardiff, Shrewsbury, Hanley, Chester. In Bristol on September 27 during the last number, "Satisfaction," two girls launched themselves over the six-foot balcony behind the stage and rushed Charlie, one hurling herself at him with such fervor that she knocked him from his stool, sending his drums tumbling across the stage. We kept playing while the girls were dragged away.

Our wardrobe was now changing frequently: Brian in a white sheepskin lining from a car coat he'd bought in Sweden, Charlie in a three-piece suit of gray tweed with a button-down waistcoat, me in an olive-green corduroy jacket and Keith in a black jacket with yellow corduroy slacks. We were expected to set a sartorial style, the only rule being unpredictability. Fans loved our evolution: Mick now swung the microphone like a drum major, augmenting his dance movements imaginatively, and there was thunderous applause when Brian moved over to the organ.

In Manchester on October 3 an elaborate plan to foil the hundreds of fans waiting outside the Piccadilly Hotel and the Odeon Cinema went into operation. Mick remarked that the scheme must have been masterminded by Field-Marshal Montgomery, it was so military in conception. We were smuggled down a back stairway in the hotel and through a fire exit to a van in the underground car park. Then, near the cinema, the van stopped. An identical decoy van, a policeman beside the driver, drove up to the side entrance at the cinema and the teenagers rushed this, rocked it and nearly tore open the doors. Then we were driven to an office block behind the cinema and led to our dressing-rooms through a connecting door.

In Bradford next night, there was a delightful surprise in our dressing-room, where we found a table sagging under the weight of cooked chicken, bunches of grapes and a load of fruit, together with bottles of Scotch. The banquet had been prepared by Joan Wild, whose invalid son we had met a year earlier. She told us she wanted to return our kindness to Paul.

Although merchandising had not yet gripped rock, we had endorsed several products, including Vox amplifiers in 1963. By 1964 the Stones were recognized as being a useful commercial property: I was invited to the Dallas musical instrument company in London when my bass became damaged. They invited me to sign a three-year sponsorship deal endorsing the Framus bass and gave me a new instrument, two sets of strings and a new lead. And in autumn 1965 a statement came in showing sales of 8,399 guitars with our name, 2,563 six-string guitars, 4,706 cutaway junior guitars and 8,743 harmonicas. From all these sales we received a 5 per cent royalty. I also had a personal deal at this time with Jennings Musical Industries, makers of Vox guitars: I signed an agreement to endorse the Wyman bass for a three-year period with a royalty of 5 per cent of the factory price coming to me. I negotiated with them to give me a Thomas organ as an advance on my royalties.

There was occasionally an amusing side to these sponsorship deals. Andrew received a letter from a shampoo manufacturer, Cynamid, saying: "We have recently learned from an article in a Danish magazine that Brian Jones uses Breck shampoo. As you may know, this is one of our products and we will be happy to send Brian and the other Stones a free supply of shampoo if you would kindly let us know the hair-type of each of the boys. Perhaps they would also like to have some hairspray, if they use it."

But shampoo aside, Andrew was busy with his newly formed label and on October 8 Immediate Records released a single by comedian Jimmy Tarbuck called "Someday You'll Want Me to Want You." Keeping the royalties from songwriting in "the family," Mick and Keith had written the B-side, "We're Wasting Time"; Andrew was the producer.

In Glasgow more than seventy teenage girls were treated by ambulance attendants for hysteria and fainting. It was during these two shows that we met Joan Baez for the first time backstage. The missiles chucked by British fans were not always as harmless as the toilet rolls favored by American audiences. At Stockton-on-Tees on October 8 a coin struck Mick over the right eye and he finished the peformance dabbing at the cut. He appeared on stage next night at Leeds with a large piece of sticking-plaster and a big bruise. Most alarming of all, a fan carrying a double-barreled shotgun tried to get into the Liverpool concert on October 10. Twenty teenagers fainted, thirteen were treated for bruises, and eight were taken to hospital with wounds caused by stiletto heels; stampeding girls climbed over the orchestra pit, and the management lowered the curtain on the last number.

It was Keith's turn to be hit when we reached North-ampton on October 16. During the opening song a hail of sweets, cigarettes and other objects hit the stage and something caught Keith in the face. He spun round, staggered for a moment, crashed on an amplifier and slid down to the stage, face downwards and motionless. Mick, in mid-gesture, dropped the mike and ran to him. Brian waved for the curtains to be closed while I switched off the electrical equipment. The curtains closed to the odd shout of "fake" and a few boos, but mostly silence as the compère Ray Cameron told jokes. After a few minutes, Keith recovered, regained his nerve and we continued the show.

*   *   *

The autumn of 1965 found the Rolling Stones strengthening its social (some would say anti-social) grip that was to become all-powerful in the psychedelic era. And, curiously, that grip had no foundation in Brian's or Mick's sex-appeal or the polarization with adults; that battle had been fought and won. And with the Beatles invested with MBEs by the Queen on October 26 the alternative voice of youth had finally been recognized.

The reshaping of the Stones' role came directly from the songwriting posture of Mick and Keith. Hit singles like "The Last Time" had been just that: solid commercial records that hadn't strayed too far from the popular music path and were vehicles that allowed us to get our act together.

From our formation, the group was the Rolling Stones with a five-way split in money. It was never Mick Jagger and the Rolling Stones. But the extra money they made from songwriting and publishing effectively made Mick and Keith more the leaders than Brian, Charlie and me—their names carried the weight. They'd bring a song in, suggest a style and what the bass line and drums might do, and then we'd play around with it, perhaps, and throw in our own ideas. And they'd say: "Yeah, that's better, let's do that"—but that input by me or Brian or Charlie was never recognized financially.

With "(I Can't Get No) Satisfaction" and "Get Off of My Cloud" (our eighth single, released in Britain on October 22),* our songwriters articulated sexual desire and independence. Their inspiration came from being "on the road," that lifeblood of a rock 'n' roll band which we all loved. Attitudes were struck, life observed and, with the maniacal experiences we encountered—from brutal policemen to the groupie scene in its infancy, from riots we couldn't control to the monotony of hotel and aeroplane life—we grew up quickly. Mick's and Keith's crucial repositioning of the Stones in the autumn of 1965 drew from their experiences and observations. I don't believe their gradual shift was consciously contrived. It happened naturally, and Mick confirmed that in several conversations: "We just don't know the direction we're moving in. I don't think anyone knows. Who can ever

*This stayed at Number One in Britain for three weeks.

say how they're progressing? We've evolved a policy of letting things happen to us. We don't plan the future or try to mold the group in patterns. We always try to progress and improve, but it's never a planned campaign."

The band was changing in every way as I celebrated my twenty-ninth birthday (and fans wished me a happy twenty-fourth). Brian bought a Rolls-Royce, the epitome of the Establishment we were supposed to be fighting.* Charlie moved that autumn to the Tudor house in Lewes rumored to be haunted; and we gained "cover" versions of our hits that somehow acted as a seal of approval. In America, the great Otis Redding and Quincy Jones recorded "Satisfaction," and there were three versions in Japanese, while in Britain, the unthinkable happened: on the radio, "The Last Time," "Satisfaction" and "Get Off of My Cloud" were actually performed by the Joe Loss orchestra, that bastion of the dance-band era. There were still pockets of resistance from the Old Guard: disc jockey David Jacobs said on *Juke Box Jury* that he couldn't hear the lyrics of "Get Off of My Cloud," and Keith remarked: "Perhaps he's a bit deaf." I figured Jacobs still hated us from our infamous appearance on *Juke Box Jury.* "I don't know all the words myself," I admitted at the time, "but it makes no difference to the overall sound."

On the same day that our single was released, the End's debut single, produced by Glyn Johns and me for my company Freeway, was released. Two of the band, Colin Giffin and Dave Brown, wrote the two songs, "I Can't Get Any Joy" and "Hey Little Girl," achieving a jazz-based Detroit sound. It was very well received.

Mick and Keith, meanwhile, formed an independent record-production company with Andrew called We Three

---

*I don't know whether he bought it for its eerie registration plate, which was DD 666. DD could stand for the Devil's Disciple, and the three sixes are the mark of the beast in Revelations. Brian must have been aware of it, because he was intrigued by demonology and magic; even if he acquired the number plate by pure chance, it seemed to mark a turning point, for the rest of his life was mostly tragic.

Producers. The plot thickened. But Andrew had his loyal supporters and his admirers.

Cynthia Stewart, Andrew Oldham's personal assistant for five years, considers his role crucial: "He was the *enfant terrible,* but a staggeringly inventive young man, nineteen when I met him. A frustrated performer and immense spender, he walked around in dark glasses, stretching himself out in a Rolls-Royce with black windows. He had a big ego, but also a great 'feel' for the Stones, and in all the circumstances in which we found ourselves he never showed me discourtesy or rudeness. I saw him quite vicious to others but I could not fault Andrew's behavior to me. Stu, however, was contemptuous of Andrew—understandably as he kicked him out of the band."

Gered Mankowitz said: "The Beatles were very clean, family-orientated. The Stones didn't give a shit and were encouraged not to give a shit by Andrew. And it showed. Andrew was absolutely crucial to everything that was going on, an incredibly important force in the image-making, the look, the style and the feel. The actual personal choice was left with the individual Stones, but Andrew guided them all the time. Andrew even taught Mick and Keith how to shop—not what to buy, but how to shop."

A hundred-foot-high illuminated billboard dominated Times Square on our arrival in New York on October 27, 1965. As we began our fourth US tour, our fifth American album, *December's Children (and Everbody's*) was promoted on the Manhattan skyline with a David Bailey photograph.*

It took us about fifteen minutes to battle through fans and finally get inside the City Squire Hotel. (The Warwick Hotel had turned us down "because the penthouse suites had only just been redecorated!") Gered Mankowitz remembers the chaotic scene well: "When we pulled up outside all hell broke loose—there was an enormous crowd

---

*And *Newsweek* later referred sarcastically to the "portentous prose" of "Andrew Loog Oldham, the group's twenty-one-year-old 'creative manager.' "

of little girls blocking the road. The cops were trying to hold them back, but at the same time trying not to injure them—they were banging on the sides of the car and climbing on the roof. I think our driver was terrified in case anybody accidentally got injured. I'd certainly never seen anything like it, but the band took it all in their stride. In fact, even when the weight of the girls on the top of the car was causing the roof to buckle, so that Mick, Keith and I were literally holding the roof up with our hands, Bill was still trying to chat up the prettiest girls through the window."

Next morning we had the weird experience of riding up to our press conference in the Hilton while still in our limousine: the car was lifted by a freight elevator. Apart from President Kennedy in 1963, we were the only personalities to be taken inside the hotel in a car.

I was sure this would be our toughest American tour, and I said so. Because of heavy traveling throughout the six weeks, we had chartered our own plane and were looking ahead to the end of the trail when we could unwind in sunny California. The imminent hard work was cushioned by the news from Andrew that the tour would gross an unprecedented $1½ million. "Cloud" went to Number One as we flew in.

Happy at the news, we went on a shopping spree straight from the Hilton. I bought four jackets but Charlie claimed the record with a purchase of eight suits and two jackets. We also bought a supply of records and players to pass the time in the hotels on the road. Charlie, who bought a new drum kit at the percussion specialists Manny's and had it shipped back to England, then sent flowers to Shirley back in Sussex, a habit Mick was to adopt regularly for Chrissie during this tour. On October 29, Mick began a weekly arrangement for a £20 allowance to be paid to Chrissie, who was spending many evenings in his absence at the London discothèque the Scotch of St. James, and later Sybilla's, a club owned by George Harrison.

On our first night in New York, Klein, looking for ideas for a film for us, had arranged for a private showing of the film *The Wild Ones,* starring Marlon Brando. Back at the City Squire later, Bob Dylan visited Brian in his room, beginning a lasting friendship.*

The opening night of our tour at Montreal's Forum was accurately described by the police as "the wildest show Canada has ever seen—and we don't want another like it." We had flown into the city with some pride—our first privately hired plane, a Martin twin-prop. With us were the Vibrations (a black male vocal group who carried their own supply of chili sauce so they could convert standard airplane fare into soul food), Patti LaBelle and the Bluebells, a white American group called the Rockin' Ramrods (who opened the show and also provided the backing for the Vibrations and Patti LaBelle), Patti's manager, Ronnie Schneider (the tour accountant, who was Allen Klein's nephew and was responsible for collecting the money from the promoters), Ian Stewart, photographer Gered Mankowitz, tour manager Bob Bonis, Jerry Brandt (from the William Morris Agency, newly appointed by Klein as our US agents) and his partner Mike Gruber (the advance man, who usually traveled a day ahead of us).

Keith discovered during the flight that he had once again lost his passport. On arrival in Montreal we smuggled him through immigration by crowding the area, continually moving around to confuse the officials.

At the show, 8,000 fans went crazy and our security people had terrible trouble stopping them from storming the stage. Thirty teenagers were injured, eight needing hospital treatment, and in the skirmishes on stage Charlie's bass drum was battered to pulp. We'd never been so exposed at a concert, and the high fee of $15,000 was no compensation. We were mightily relieved to be on our plane that night bound for Syracuse; Mick, Keith and I began the in-flight game of poker that usually took place. Also in the party was a character named Pete Bennett,

---

*That same year, 1965, Dylan told a Carnegie Hall audience that his song "Like a Rolling Stone" was written for Brian, who later claimed that Dylan asked him to join his band. Brian might have told him of his simmering discontent within the Stones at that time. Another Dylan song, "Ballad of a Thin Man," caused a paranoid Brian to decide that the put-down of a "Mr. Jones" in the lyric was a tilt at him.

Allen Klein's promotion man, whom we nicknamed our Mafia Promo Man.

The tour continued more peacefully through Cornell University in Ithaca and Syracuse, but flying to Toronto for our concert there on October 31, we encountered headwinds of fifty knots, the bumpiest flight we'd ever had. Drinks flew everywhere and we left the plane soaked. Patti LaBelle and the Bluebells and Stu were terribly sick and we felt very shaken at the press conference. Here Andrew demanded that one radio interviewer destroy his tape "because he was asking stupid questions," and a photographer was asked to hand over a roll of film with a picture of a blonde journalist sitting next to Brian. "We've had trouble before," Andrew explained to the journalists. "Next thing you know, they'll say she's his wife."

At the Maple Leaf Gardens, where six months earlier the police had shut down the power when they feared a riot, only one fan managed to break through massive security. It was a great show with Brian, looking dandy in scarlet corduroy trousers, playing electric organ on "That's How Strong My Love Is" and "Play With Fire." I blew the first of many speakers on this tour and had to have replacements flown over from England. The Toronto show, for 13,000 fans, earned us $18,744.

8

Riots and Romances

Everything in the Rolling Stones' garden is very nice at present. But despite their heights of appeal, they haven't got the staying power of the Beatles. Because of changes in taste in popular music, the Stones cannot hope for lasting popularity. The very nature of their music precludes drastic change . . . It is difficult to see or discover which direction they are travelling in. Where do they go from here?

Melody Maker, January 1966

A neighbor in Penge, out shopping, saw my wife and child and asked: "And where's your daddy, Stephen?" to which the boy promptly replied: "Oh! My daddy lives in an aeroplane."

We woke in a hotel in Rochester, New York on November 1, 1965, to the news that "Get Off of My Cloud" was top of the charts in both America and Britain—and that we had won our sixth gold record. With this the Stones had achieved five consecutive chart-topping records, a total previously held only by Elvis Presley and the Beatles.

Back in London, two extra fan-club secretaries were hired to cope with our mounting mail: Margaret Murwald was paid £4 a week to deal with Mick's and Charlie's mail, while Brian's, Keith's and my own fan matters were dealt with by Pauline Stead, recruited at £5 a week. One of their first moves was to enter the T-shirt business, ordering a thousand to sell to club members, followed by 10,000 picture postcards distributed free.

Also from England we were shocked by news that there had been another group who had called themselves the Rolling Stones for the last eight years. Brian Stone told the *Daily Mail*: "We are the *original* Rolling Stones. We registered the name The Rolling Stones under the

Companies Act in November 1957. We live in Bristol and
do a cabaret turn at dances. When we appear, the public
think we have been misleading them. Who can blame
them? After all, we are family men. We're not teenagers.
We have our hair cut regularly, and we don't even play
the same type of music." We checked and found that the
three Stone brothers from Bristol had indeed registered
the name. We decided just to leave things as they stood.

After a brutal concert in Rochester, very badly handled by the police, who eventually stopped it after only
six songs, we headed for New York City. The fee from
Rochester was $10,000, but we felt bad about the kids
getting short-changed.

Manhattan was better: we all went to a party at an
exclusive discothèque called Ondine's, where I met my
new friend Barbara again, and she stayed with me while I
was in New York. A week earlier, I had finished my
relationship with Francesca Overman. She later recalled
the circumstances: "I saw Barbara in the hall as I was
going to your room and she said she was going out with
you. She was married, very thin, had dark hair, was a
good singer in the Cake, a three-girl group. You said you
didn't want to see me anymore because I was smoking
cannabis and that I was going to get into trouble—which
you were right about. I do understand how you felt at the
time."

Two concerts in different cities on one day were not
infrequent on our American tours. After a show at midday at the New York Academy of Music on November 6,
we drove to Philadelphia for another in the evening; we
returned to Manhattan for the night and later met Bob
Dylan at a club called the Phone Booth, where I met up
with Barbara, who came back to the hotel and stayed the
night with me. Brian had become particularly tight with
Dylan, who took him around Greenwich Village clubs
until the early hours. Later they were to go into a recording studio with Wilson Pickett, work on lyrics and then
cut a disc together. Charlie, meanwhile, was soaking up
the jazz from such greats as Earl Hines and Wes Montgomery in Greenwich Village. Andrew had managed to
talk him out of making a one-day trip back to London to
see Shirley.

On November 9 I was in my room with Barbara and a

few other friends sitting around chatting. The girls were telling us that the only way they could get up to our rooms here was by giving head to the security guards downstairs! Suddenly around 5 p.m., all the power went off, and stayed off for the next twelve hours. The hotel supplied us with candles, one of which we accidentally knocked over, setting fire to Gered's bed. Gered recalls: "There was a party underway. Naturally, there were girls, booze and dope in abundance, and by one in the morning, we were totally wrecked. It was a great party, bouncing around from room to room by candle-light. What nobody realized was that the wax got so hot that it caused the glass ashtray it was standing in to shatter, sending a shower of wax on to my bed and setting it on fire. Ronnie Schneider and I ran into Bill's room for shelter, to be followed minutes later by a couple of smoke-begrimed girls, who'd put the fire out with water from ice buckets. When the lights came back on at five in the morning, there were grubby, half-dressed people everywhere, on beds and under them."

The biggest disappointment was that we were to have attended a big party at Ondine's, but this was canceled: none of the elevators was working. We eventually retired to bed early the next morning. Scott Ross says of that evening: "The first time I dropped pills was with Brian. I think I knew even then that one day he was going to kill himself with an overdose. He went at it in a crazy way, mixing ups and downs, red pills, yellow pills, pills with stripes on them. 'You ought to try this,' Brian said, handing me a fistful of multi-colored capsules. I don't think even he knew what they were. Somebody had given them to him and Brian was the kind to try anything . . . a party was going on, had been going on for four days. Brian popped four of the pills into his mouth. 'Groovy,' he said. I took two of them and they were groovy all right! When we walked back into the party a little later, I felt like I was the tallest one in the room. 'Let's go over to my hotel,' Brian said. 'I've got some of the good stuff, straight from Mexico.' I had never smoked marijuana, but the mood I was in, anything sounded good. As Brian's chauffeur-driven Cadillac was heading crosstown the streetlights began to look brown to me. I figured it was the pills. But then they went out altogether. The lights in the stores were out too. I rolled down the window. Women were screaming. 'Maybe the world is coming to an end,' Brian said. The traffic lights weren't working and the limousine slowed to a crawl. Automobile headlights were the only illumination on the streets. At last our driver weaved his way through the snarl to the hotel. I wouldn't have believed it. In spite of the weird, blacked-out city, there was a group of teeny-boppers in front of the main entrance waiting for Brian to come back. 'There he is!' they shouted. 'Quick!' said Brian. He pushed me through the service door and waved to the man on duty. Obviously the guy had been through this before, because he had the door locked behind us almost before we were through it. He handed us a candle and showed us how to get up to the lobby since the elevators weren't working. The lobby, too, was candle-lit. We climbed a lot of flights to Brian's suite. We were taking our coats off when there was a knock on the door. Brian took the candle and opened it. It was Bob Dylan with a bunch of people. 'It's an invasion from Mars,' said Bob. They all came in and we stood at Brian's windows looking out over the dark city. It was wild, like Glasgow in the war. 'Let's turn on,' said Bob. 'What better time? The little green men have landed.' Brian rolled me my first marijuana cigarette. Neither he nor Bob could believe that I had never smoked pot. By now they were saying on the transistor radio that the blackout was probably nothing more than a massive power failure. But we knew better. It was the end of the world and we were going out on cloud nine."

That night Brian took part in a jam session with Dylan, Robbie Robertson and Bobby Neuwirth in his room. They played acoustic guitars by candle-light, but there was no power to record the music: this session was always referred to later as "The Lost Jam."

We checked out of the hotel on November 10, the day promoter Bill Graham put on his first historic concert at the Fillmore in San Francisco. As usual we left behind a trail of devastation and damage. Scott says: "We all trashed the City Squire Hotel, going to every floor, turning over everything in the halls." Later we were told that in the days we'd stayed there, over-enthusiastic fans had done about $50,000 worth of damage, causing the Loews hotel group to ban pop artists from its New York hotels.

The tour continued through Greensboro, and then on to Washington. I always shared a hotel suite with Brian. Mick and Keith were together, Charlie usually shared with Stu or Andrew. Brian and I liked to share because we were always after the girls more than the others. We were on the prowl all day long and every night, chatting up girls in shops, girls backstage, reporters interviewing us, fan-club secretaries. In 1965 we sat down one evening in a hotel and worked out that since the band had started two years earlier, I'd had 278 girls, Brian 130, Mick about thirty, Keith six and Charlie none. People always assume that Mick, particularly, was very active sexually, but that wasn't so in the sixties. Mick and Keith usually stayed in their room writing songs, and back in London they had steady girlfriends, to whom they were vaguely faithful. Charlie was a hundred per cent faithful to Shirley. Brian and I were not faithful at all.

This tour clinched our arrival in the top league, with fees in the region of $15,000 for each show and our records flying all over the charts.* The tour continued successfully through Baltimore, Knoxville and Charlotte, where Gered Mankowitz and Charlie were beaten up in the hotel coffee bar by a little old lady with an umbrella, who looked exactly like Granny Clampett of *The Beverly Hillbillies*. She'd taken a dislike to them because of the length of their hair. The manager finally led her away.

We then flew to Nashville and had a good show. Back at the hotel I was introduced to Luther Perkins, Johnny Cash's guitarist, who took me to some local clubs where I saw many performers, including the Steadman Family. It was great to hear country music in its homeland. Here and in Memphis, the deep south, the crowds seemed more intent on enjoying our shows than in causing riots, although a few days later, before the show in Shreveport, Louisiana, when the promoter asked how he could protect us, Bob Bonis casually suggested they put a moat

---

*That was the good news. The bad was that $72,252 of ours was being held by the Irving Trust Co., by order of the Supreme Court pending a court case which came about because Allen Klein had signed us into the William Morris Agency although we were committed, via Eric Easton, to GAC. We ended up footing the bill for Allen's decision.

between us and the crowd—and they did. It was fifteen feet wide and was filled with water—and nobody got on stage for a change.

From Memphis we flew to Miami for a day off, to relax in the sun. Anita Pallenberg flew in from Paris to join Brian for a week on the tour, and rumors began circulating in Europe that the two would soon be married. At a celebration party in Paris for French singer Johnny Halliday, the talk between the singer, Sylvie Vartan, Françoise Hardy and her fiancé Jean-Marie Perier was about Brian's and Anita's natural togetherness and the strong chance that they would wed. As a couple they seemed perfectly matched, with people even commenting on the similarity of their features.

Brian and Anita spent most of the time in their room, but when they emerged, the first thing he wanted to do was go on a motor boat. He got into one, pointed it out to sea and just kept going till he ran out of gas. The guy who ran the boat-hire had to go after him and tow him back in. Brian thought it was terribly funny and, apart from the fact that we had to pay a huge deposit for hiring boats after that, no harm was done. But if it hadn't been a calm day, he could easily have drowned.

After a few days with Brian, Anita flew from Detroit back to Paris and went to a party where reporters confronted her with questions about her romance with Brian. She replied: "We are going steady. If we are going to get married it will be soon. Otherwise, it won't be at all."

But Brian denied the mating calls—sort of. "I've been going out with Anita for about three months, but there are no plans. Anita is the first girl I've met that I've been serious about. We're very fond of each other and obviously it's more than a casual acquaintanceship."

Brian's bizarre behavior surfaced again en route from Fort Worth to Dallas on November 22, when we stopped at a roadside burger place. Brian said he wasn't hungry and sat in the car as we all went in. Just as we were leaving, Brian decided he wanted food. Despite our protests that we were running late, he was obviously determined to relax over a large meal. Finally Andrew told Pete Bennett to "go get him." We all sat in the car looking into the glass-fronted restaurant as Pete marched in, picked Brian up by the scruff of his neck and frog-marched him back to the car, complete with half-eaten hamburger. Brian was speechless. The humiliation probably added to his paranoia, but the incident was typical of the way he focused attention on himself and infuriated those around him, even over small things.

Later from his hotel room Brian summoned Gered and invited him to "share a trip." When Gered, who never touched acid, said no, Brian had a counter-proposal: would Gered stay with him and write down everything he said? Gered demurred, saying this was too weird a situation for him to be involved in. Brian often behaved like that, forcing a friend or colleague to deny him something, to be hard on him.

When shopping in Dallas, I bought various goods, paying by check from the huge presentation folder that Klein had given us each; there was a balance of more than $47,000 in my account at the Chemical Bank in New York, so these small purchases should have been trouble-free. I could not then have guessed the consequences, although I was still very uneasy about Klein's involvement, and the bad feelings that had sprung up between Easton and the band.

These worries were quickly forgotten in Sacramento on December 3 when Keith was lucky to escape with his life when we played the Memorial Hall to a crowd of 4,500. Throughout six songs Mick jumped, got down on his knees, did his splits act. Generally we were doing a great show. Girls were screaming, hands clapping enthusiastically —then, three sentences into the first verse of "The Last Time," Keith ran to the mike to sing back-up vocals on the chorus and found it was facing the wrong way. He gave it a sharp knock with his guitar to turn it towards him. There was a blinding flash and he fell flat on his back, out cold. I raced across and snatched out his guitar lead. The promoters closed the curtains, police and medical attendants swarmed all over the stage. From the audience the screaming continued and then, as the realization of what had happened hit them, there was absolute silence; then some fans screamed, while others prayed. Others sat, too shocked to move. After a few minutes, with Brian, Mick, Charlie and me standing around helplessly, Keith came round and seemed OK. We looked at his guitar and found three of his guitar strings had been burned apart, just like fuse wire. He was taken to hospital where doctors claimed that the thick rubber soles of his Hush-Puppie shoes had cushioned the jolt of electric power and saved his life by preventing the electrical surge from grounding. Keith was returned by hospital ambulance to our hotel and another doctor examined him.

He was subdued but after a night's rest he was fit to fly on with us next day, December 4, to San Jose for our next show. That day too, our fifth album was officially released in the US. *December's Children (and Everybody's)* received great reviews, particularly the ballad "Blue Turns to Grey" sung by Mick, which because of its strings was compared with the Beatles' "Yesterday." Although the album continued Mick and Keith's evolution as writers, we regarded it as a bit of a hotch-potch, accurately summarized by Brian as "a mixture of very old and new tracks, an album of rejects." However, it reached number four and stayed in the American charts for thirty-three weeks.·

After the San Jose show, which earned us a cool $18,000, Mick, Chrissie, Brian and Anita flew to San Diego. The rest of us returned to the San Jose hotel before going to a party. We rejoined Mick and Brian in San Diego next day and after a successful afternoon concert continued to Los Angeles, checking into the Beverly Wilshire Hotel before the final concert of the tour.

We were later presented with the breakdown of monies for the thirty-five-city US tour which had been so successful in reaching our fans. The figures showed that on this tour we had grossed $542,589.87; other acts cost $30,028.53; the William Morris Agency received $53,695.95; Andrew's and Klein's management fees were $46,097.15 each. The Rolling Stones themselves made a profit of $214,152.65 after all expenses. Each Stone earned $50,418.62, less our advances (Mick $10,749.10; Keith $8,082.20; Charlie $7,062.65; Bill $3,297.63; Brian $8,748.88). This money did not go into our own accounts in Britain, but was held by Klein in New York.

We were still wide-eyed at some aspects of American lifestyle. After the show some of the group went with Jack Nitzsche to visit the top session drummer Hal Blaine, who recalled: "We went up the hill to my house and as I approached the garage I pushed the button on my dashboard. The door opened and I pushed the button again and it closed behind us. They couldn't figure it out. I said: 'Oh, this garage knows my car whenever it pulls up.' Charlie was knocked out by the garage-door button and fiddled with it interminably." It was that night, also, that Keith and Brian took LSD at a party given by the writer Ken Kesey and his followers. Gered Mankowitz observed on this, his only tour with the Stones: "In a lot of cases the band were treated like absolute shit, so of course they took it out on their surroundings. They'd piss in the sinks and so on. An endless stream of notes would be thrown onstage, often pinned to bras and underpants, with telephone numbers, quite lurid love poems and very explicit sexual offers. The name of the hotel would often get leaked and somebody would have to go into each room and flush out the fans. It wasn't at all rare to pull back the shower curtain and find two giggling fourteen-year-old girls."

The visit to Los Angeles was unique because we all chose different hotels: Brian and Anita went to stay at the house of a friend; Mick and Chrissie went to the Bel-Air Hotel; and Keith, Gered and Ronnie Schneider left Los Angeles, flew to Phoenix and went on an overnight horse-ride into the McDowell Mountains. We arranged to meet next night at the RCA Studios for the first of three nights of sessions. We loved this studio because it was custom-built: with no windows, we neither knew nor cared whether it was night or day but just kept playing on. As I arrived two girls we had met in Phoenix were hanging around outside. I got them into the studio quietly and told them to strip and walk in on the boys to shock them, which they did. Andrew grabbed one and pulled her into the control room for "action" in front of everyone.

During these three sessions we cut ten tracks, including "Mother's Little Helper," "Sitting on the Fence" and "Goin' Home," this last track running to twelve minutes. While we were playing it, we awaited a signal to stop but no one signaled. There is a gap in the drumming at one point when Keith picked up his coat and threw it at Charlie, but that didn't stop him for long. On this session, Charlie played bongos, congas, timpani and a giant bass drum, while Brian experimented with a harpsichord. The piano and organ were played by Stu and Jack Nitzsche.

Before leaving California next day, we sent a cable to *New Musical Express* to thank their readers for voting for us in their annual poll: we were named top British group and "Satisfaction" was best new disc of the year. Mick and Chrissie then flew to Jamaica for a holiday at Coral Sea. Brian and Anita went to the Virgin Islands and then on to New York. There, they met Bob Dylan at the Chelsea Hotel. When Dylan saw Brian he said, "Hallo, Brian, how's your paranoia?" Anita remembers: "He started putting us down because Brian had a limousine to take us to a club. He kept saying, 'What, a *limousine?* There goes a pop star in a *limousine*.' "

Charlie and I returned to London where, going through customs at Heathrow, he was searched for more than an hour and eventually charged £60 duty on clothes. "I can only think they were looking for guns," said Charlie. "Previously I've brought guns into this country after tours abroad, but I have never had any trouble with customs. The kind of guns I collect aren't subject to duty. They're mostly antiques."

At the start of the tour, there had been a strange twist to our financial status as we all fondly enjoyed what we believed was our growing affluence. Allen Klein had made a big production out of giving us those huge, foldersized office-type checkbooks in stiff covers for our New York dollar accounts, emphasizing that the accounts were our private ones. Brian and I had used these American checks for fairly small purchases. When Klein discovered that we had used checks, he erupted, saying we "couldn't cash checks or pay for things on these accounts." This was too strange to be believed. In London, however, my bank account showed a healthy credit of £1,905.

On December 18 our ninth single, "As Tears Go By," was released in USA. This reached number three. Brian flew in with Anita from New York on December 27 feeling rather ill, having picked up a tropical virus. And the year ended with eight gold records by the Beatles and six by the Stones: "The Last Time," "(I Can't Get No) Satisfaction," "Get Off of My Cloud" and "As Tears Go

By," and for our albums, *Out of Our Heads* and *December's Children*. Rolling Stones Ltd showed a credit balance of £14,588 and merchandising sales bearing our name totaled 5,906 guitars, 1,871 twelve-string guitars, 1,281 cutaway junior guitars and 5,598 harmonicas. This sounded like a lot but our 5 per cent royalty on these sales came to a meager £314. In January 1966, the magazine *Beat Instrumental* gave its Gold Star Awards for the previous twelve months. I won the bass guitar section, the Stones won the best stage group category, and in the songwriting section, Keith and Mick were second to Lennon and McCartney.

As we became more accepted, Andrew could be relied upon still to stoke the fire of our rebel image. He floated to some journalist friends the news that the title of our next album would be: "Could YOU Walk on the Water?" The sleeve picture was planned as a reservoir with the Stones' heads protruding just above the water-line. When Decca heard of this, they issued a statement, saying "We would not issue it with that title at any price."

Over in Geneva the city council, labeling the Stones as "undesirable," banned us from a planned concert at an ice rink. They said it could lead to rioting and damage, adding that we could perform in a circus marquee on a public square, on condition we gave a quarter of our receipts to the city's poor and to the council.

Public perception of us as monsters would have been shaken in 1966 if they knew that we could behave quite normally, especially in our treatment of fans. We replied to their letters and I enjoyed being the Stones' representative to an American visitor, Amy Goodman, who was put in touch with me by Andrew's office. Later she wrote to *Fabulous* magazine: "When the phone rang, I didn't know whether or not to believe the voice that told me it was Bill Wyman. Finally he convinced us, and invited us to his home to spend the day with him, Diane and Stephen. When we arrived Bill greeted us at the door with an armload of toys, and asked me to carry in his milk bottles for him. We went inside to the living room and had tea with them. Bill showed us scrapbooks and clippings he kept, and played several records for us that had never come to the States. Then he invited us for dinner and to watch the Stones, televised from the night before.

When the Stones were on, Stephen ran up to the set, put his finger on Mick's face and shouted, 'It's Uncle Micky!' They couldn't have been warmer. When I got back to the States I wrote Bill a letter and sent him a record, and he wrote back right away to thank me."

And also on the social side I was still seeing Doreen Samuels regularly. I hung out at the Scotch of St. James Club with Keith Moon of the Who, Paul McCartney, singer Kenny Lynch and his mate, the actor Harry Fowler, Barry Reeves of the Checkmates and Chas Chandler and Dave Rowberry of the Animals, among others. The sixties pop groups bred a terrific spirit of togetherness, and at the Scotch I struck up friendships with many visiting Americans—even the great Otis Redding. I also felt it important to lead a full life outside the Stones. I developed interests in astronomy, archaeology and early civilizations. We finally moved into the Keston house and loved the new, rural setting of our lives.

I was preoccupied with domestic matters like buying new carpets and furniture for the house, and I lent £1,000 to Uncle Jack to invest in a chicken farm (the last I saw of the money). Also in January 1966 I began driving lessons, having confidently bought a Morris Minor 1000 Traveller for £648. Later, when I'd passed my test, I bought an MGB sports car, and then a Mercedes 250 saloon.

My brother Paul said: "Our parents couldn't accept the fact that from pop music, he'd bought a big house in Keston and eventually was driving around in a Mercedes Benz. The family wouldn't even have been able to afford the insurance on such a car when we were growing up! But Father couldn't shake the feeling that it would end pretty quickly: 'Put your money in the bank. Don't spend it.' "

Although Keith couldn't drive at this time, he bought a dark blue Bentley S3 Continental four-door saloon, and started employing a chauffeur. Six weeks later, Keith took his driving test and failed, the day before I passed mine.

While we were all settling down, Brian's life continued to be more problematical. In answer to Pat Andrews' proceedings against him for affiliation for their child, Brian (not in court) was found guilty. Hilariously described as a millionaire, he was ordered to pay £2 10s. per week, £60 costs and £18 towards Pat's confinement expenses. Condemning the absent Brian's behavior, the magistrates' chairman said it was "deplorable that the four-year-old boy should not have been recognized and helped by his father till the present date. I find it impossible to understand his attitude. If we could make a larger order we would do so."

With the release of our ninth British single, "19th Nervous Breakdown," on February 4, 1966, Mick and Keith moved into top gear as acerbic counterparts to the burgeoning hippy movement. Mick, particularly, had been moving on the fringes of high society. Denying the regular comments that he and Keith were adopting a Bob Dylan style, Mick said "19th Nervous Breakdown" alluded to "a neurotic bird." The song in fact was a condemnation of the spoiled debutantes who, cushioned by material comfort, became self-indulgent.

But apart from the title, few people detected the wordplay and even a reference to drugs in the third verse passed the radio producers who would probably have banned it had they known. The track was especially important for me: one reviewer wrote of "those unforgettable, thundering, dive-bombing bass runs from Bill."

The B-side, featuring Mick singing solo on the Marianne Faithfull hit "As Tears Go By," was alternately received as "pretentious" or "Mick doing his Paul McCartney bit, with chamber-music-type strings." The record tore to the top of the charts and stayed there for three weeks, most people preferring it to our previous single, "Get Off of My Cloud."

The rising profile of Mick was boosted by an appearance on the famous Eamonn Andrews TV show on February 6, 1966; we all played our new single, receiving a fee of £200, and Mick got the same amount again as one of the show's chat guests. It was an important break as the Andrews show attracted a family audience. At this time, in an interview, I described Mick as more difficult to get on with than when I'd first met him three years earlier. "He's automatically on guard now with people he's not sure about," I said. "But he's always been very close to the rest of the group. At no time have we been

scared that he was going to quit and turn solo . . . he gets
depressed sometimes and we have to bear with it. He's a
bit careful with money, not extravagant like Keith. I also
think Mick's a romantic, very much so."

My remarks on Mick were part of a series in *Disc* in
which each Stone described another. Brian, commenting
on me as "always the Rolling Stone that nobody ever
knew," said: "I'm very fond of Bill. In fact I often feel
very paternal towards him. He gets drunk more easily
than the rest of us. He's more difficult for us to understand because he's married and until recently lived a very
reserved home life. But now he and his wife are coming
out more. I'm considered the mad raver of the group and
he's the opposite. He's older than the rest of us and more
stable. Rather matter-of-fact. He's a very likeable guy
and an excellent musician. He picks things up more easily
than the rest of us. We take the mickey out of Bill a lot
but he takes it well. He's pretty well organized . . . Bill is
very concerned with money and he's very precise with
things."

In an illuminating analysis, Mick described Keith: "I've
known him longer than anyone else in the group. I went
to school with him. I still don't know what he's thinking
at any time and he really is one of my closest friends.
From time to time, we've had little arguments . . . we
disagree quite a lot but we usually come to a compromise. There's never any hard feeling. He's forgetful and
so he doesn't remember to bear a grudge. He's very good
at his songwriting now and we've got a relatively efficient
way of going about it. He's very good about the group.
Very optimistic. This cheers me up when I'm feeling low.
I think people find it difficult to know Keith. Sometimes
he's shy and other times he can't be bothered to take an
interest in people."

Charlie said of Brian: "The first time I met Brian he
had a guitar in his hand. My first impression of him was
just of a very good guitar player. He's basically a very
quiet bloke. He likes being left alone—not on his own
though. He's really a very soft person. His biggest fault is
the same as mine—people don't know him. I know him
really only as someone I play with. He can be very funny
though—when he feels like it. He's one of these people
who, if he's feeling a bit ill or tired, likes to be left alone.

He gets annoyed at people putting themselves on him when he doesn't want to know. He's fairly quick-tempered but he gets over it. Like all of us, he's a bit moody. I think he's generous to people he wants to be generous to. He's very wary of people he doesn't know. This business makes people that way. At the start in particular he worked very hard with great determination for the success of the group. When the only place he could learn and rehearse was from records, he used to sit there for hours listening to LPs."

Keith was most interesting in his assessment of Charlie: "He hasn't changed much since I met him first except that he's a lot happier since he got married. Charlie's a very deep thinker. It's hard to tell if he's listening to a conversation or thinking about something else. Then, when you think he hasn't heard a thing you've been talking about, he'll start discussing the subject a couple of hours later. But he's not that deep that we don't know him—although he still surprises us. We asked him over to join us when we were earning £2 a night each. I'm glad he came—he's a good bloke."

Twenty-four years after those descriptions, their accuracy and perceptiveness are remarkable.

It seemed, also, a period for Brian to indulge in some self-examination. Reflecting on his past and the fact that his whole life had been shaped by escapism, he declared: "I can identify myself with the group but I'm not sure about the image. This rebel thing has gone, now; life is a paradox for me. I'm so contradictory. I have this need for expression but I'm not certain what it is I want to do. I'm not personally *insecure*, just *unsure*." It's interesting that at this point in 1966, as Mick and Keith were really breaking through as writers, Brian said: "I would like to write but I lack confidence and need encouragement."

Life with the Stones was so frenziedly busy at this point, and we were all so consumed with success and ourselves, that we paid no heed to Brian's soul-searching. Although Brian enjoyed stardom himself, he could never face the simple truth that Mick, as the lead singer, would always attract a vast amount of attention. Brian wanted to view the band as a cooperative; when people remarked that on "19th Nervous Breakdown" Mick's voice was half-hidden by the backing, which was described as too loud, Brian answered: "We're the *Rolling Stones,* not Mick Jagger! He might have done 'As Tears Go By' on his own, but he doesn't usually set out to be the only one on record. Mick sings, and we play the instruments. It's *us!* It's an integrated group thing and no one's trying to drown Mick out."

Dave Thomson, who moved into Elm Park Lane with Brian, said: "Brian's main worry was that they were laughing at him, not taking him seriously, and therefore he couldn't take himself seriously. Once, we were going to write a song together and he chopped it, saying: 'If I take it into the studio, they'll just mock it, won't use it.' Brian was incredibly gifted. He had only to look at an instrument to figure out how to play it, but he rarely took the guitar out at home. There was no impetus for him to pick up a guitar because he was frightened to write anything because he would be laughed at. Yet Brian was a superb, natural musician. I saw George Harrison once put a sitar—an incredibly difficult instrument to play—in Brian's hand, and within minutes Brian knew his way around it.

"When I first met Brian, if they were on tour he was drinking maybe a bottle and a half of whisky a day. When they came back from America, Charlie came to see me and asked if I could help get Brian off the booze. The doctor had said if he carried on drinking like that he had only two years to live. Then, after 1965 he started really getting into smoking dope and he seemed to be able to handle that, but it definitely diminished his perception." A guy who was known as the "Junkie Doctor of Chelsea"* was supplying Brian with drugs at that time, and Brian got into amyl nitrate ("poppers").

The straight-talking Stu was tough on Brian: "Brian actually set out to be as stupid as he could be," he declared. "It's a shame, really. As soon as he got any real taste of money and success, he just went mad."

There's a theory that Brian's downward slope began when he left the clan of musicians to befriend people in other areas of art who influenced him. "There's a group

---

*He is the "Dr. Robert" in John Lennon's song on the Beatles' *Revolver* album.

of people in France trying to get at me," Brian said mysteriously to Dave Thomson.

But while Brian's introversion deepened, the rest of us were busy looking outwards. "19th Nervous Breakdown" went to Number One in Britain on Friday February 11, 1966, the same day that we flew to New York en route to an Australian tour. The next day it was released as our tenth single in America, reaching Number One for one week.

A middle-aged mother stated in the women's magazine *McCalls* that the single carried "sardonic references to alienation, parental over-protection, inability to relate, even a reference to the mind-bending drug LSD." So what else was new?

We were booked yet again for the *Ed Sullivan Show*. After rehearsals we were forced to stay inside the studio for nine hours because fans had massed outside and we couldn't leave. We played the show live, the first color broadcast on US television. After the group did "Satisfaction" and "19th Nervous Breakdown," Mick and Keith performed "As Tears Go By." As in Britain, the older generation of Americans now were forced to recognize our success, even if they didn't admire our music or appearance. Helen Eustic, in *McCalls*, said: "Tears began to roll by on quite a few faces in the audience around me. When it was all over we were exhausted by emotion, by sheer exposure to sound. We left the hall listlessly, in a kind of torpor. This music is not for the ears alone. You must listen to it with the marrow of your bones."

While we were in New York, our dispute with the GAC agency, precipitated by the arrival of Allen Klein and his switch of our agency work to William Morris, came to a head. It was agreed to pay GAC $37,500 plus costs of $10,247 in an out-of-court settlement. At this time the Stones number one account showed a credit of £4,631 6s. 9d.

We flew to Los Angeles, then via Honolulu and Fiji to Sydney, arriving on February 16 with our seventy-two pieces of luggage and 110 pieces of instruments and amplification equipment. At the airport press conference there was good news from the tour promoter Harry Miller: it was the biggest box-office attraction he had ever had, with concerts in all the states' capitals sold out for days and extra matinees planned to accommodate demand. And things lived up to their promise: in five shows in Sydney we played to 25,000 people. Despite unexpected rain which marked our arrival and lasted five days, Sydney was welcoming: we checked into the Chevron Hilton, where I met a very pretty Chinese girl with whom I spent all my time in the city.

The first of two shows on February 18 before 6,000 fans at Sydney Commemorative Auditorium in the Showgrounds was our first performance for two months; the Searchers, who were our support band on this tour, opened well, and we began "The Last Time" to a deafening roar. And yet I felt that there was something happening within the band, an almost chemical change. Brian's aura seemed to have dimmed, and Mick and Keith were running the show. On Sunday, February 20, a day off, we were staggered to hear that the Searchers had all gone to church that morning, a most unusual move for a rock 'n' roll band.

Brisbane, our next stop, had more rain for two shows but the next day brought sunshine and we made for the beach where we were filmed for *Top of the Pops*. A waiter dressed in tails and looking ultra-English arrived with champagne and glasses to serve us all; on the spur of the moment I walked into the sea fully dressed to join the rest of the band, who were swimming. I never saw the program.

Brisbane and Adelaide proved good concerts. In Adelaide we sat around the small deserted hotel swimming-pool. After a short while, we were joined by two local girls. One said she had a tattoo. We all wanted a see, so she promptly took off her bikini bottom and showed us. Her tattoo from a short distance looked like a flower-patterned bikini bottom. Looking closer, we were amazed to see a little red devil sitting on her pubic mound. It gave us something to talk about for weeks later!

I then had a strange experience when we met up with a crowd of girls we'd hung out with in the city a year earlier. The girl I'd been with was missing and I asked her friend where she was. She replied that after our last encounter she had become pregnant by me, and, not wanting to cause any problems, had moved to New Zealand where she'd given birth to a baby girl and was living happily. I heard nothing from her when we visited New Zealand and to this day have never heard from her again.

Out of the blue we heard that we had won the Carl-Alan award as the most outstanding group of 1965 for the second successive year.

Over three nights we played six terrific concerts at the Palais Theatre in St. Kilda, a suburb of Melbourne, best summarized by the local paper *The Age:* "Whatever the Stones have, and it's an indefinable quality, the audience loved it. The sheer animal throb of the group was sufficient to spark off a torrent of streamers, screams, gasps, sighs, tears and handclaps . . . their cultivated arrogance makes them a force the younger generation seems unable to resist."

Before we left Australia for New Zealand, Mick bought something that lingers in my memory: a kangaroo jacket. It smelled really bad.

On our arrival at Wellington airport in New Zealand, about 400 fans crammed the vantage points to welcome us; some climbed along the roof and tried unsuccessfully to climb down a fifteen-foot wall and rush the plane.

Our impression of New Zealand was summed up by Mick: "A bit quiet, like my Dad told me England was during the war." Our boredom can be judged by the hotel phone bills during our one-night stay in Wellington: I spent $56.29, Brian spent $219.06, Charlie $106.54 and Mick $83.93.

One of my calls to our new Keston home brought news of a fire. Stephen had been playing with matches in my music room, trying to discover which types of wood burned. He managed to set alight one of the curtains, which burned out an acoustic guitar and damaged my new Thomas organ. The fire brigade was called and damage was estimated at £205.

Just before our show at Wellington's Town Hall on February 28 (Brian's twenty-fourth birthday), four teenagers were found hiding in cupboards in our dressing-rooms. Security men found three more hiding in big rubbish bins in the garage, expecting to get a view of our arrival. The concert was predictably hysterical: police helmets flew as they forced more than a hundred teenagers back down the aisles. One girl jumped from the rear balcony to throw her arms around Mick, who kept on singing as they tried to drag her away; the girl, still clinging to him, pulled him with her for several yards. The comments from the town hall caretakers echoed the kind of reaction we'd heard around the world: "The police should have stopped the show . . . this was worse than the Beatles . . ."

When we returned to the hotel, fans were everywhere and I got chatting to three girls, and invited them to my room. We eventually all went to bed together. Suddenly, there was a knock on the door from the rest of the boys, who had heard about my three girls and wanted to come in. I told them to go away, but they persisted. They lay on the floor in the hall, looking under a large gap at the bottom of my door, yelling at me to let them in. Eventually they got the hotel porter to open the door and burst in. Laughing and pulling the clothes off the bed, they spoiled what might have been something special; the girls dressed and left.

After concerts in Auckland and Perth, Brian, Bob Bonis and I flew back to Los Angeles. At the Ambassador Hotel we checked into three chalets. By the evening, girls had found out we were there, and had started to hang around outside. In the nine days that Brian and I were there, our bungalows were staked out by about fifty girls who stayed outside on the grass, day and night, the whole time. We would take our pick of them, and I finished up sleeping with thirteen girls here.

I was continuing to monitor expenditure on several fronts, because "where the money went" fascinated me. On the business side the Australia–New Zealand tour grossed receipts of $59,136. After tour expenses were paid our agent Tito Burns received $5,913.60; Allen Klein and Andrew Oldham $5,321.97 each; and the Stones earned, after expenses, $7,063.54 each.

In the spring of 1966 Keith bought Redlands, a large Tudor farmhouse six miles south of Chichester, West Sussex, for £17,750. Completely encircled by a Saxon moat, it was reputedly once owned by the Bishop of Chichester. Keith moved in on April 16, 1966. Redlands was to become part of Rolling Stones folklore, with one of the most famous drug busts in rock history taking place there; but back then, in early 1966, it just represented a successful pop musician's imaginative investment.

While Redlands was being bought, we received our tenth gold record in the US for our single "19th Nervous Breakdown." And on February 6 we entered the RCA Studios in Hollywood, with Dave Hassinger as engineer and Andrew producing, for one of our most fruitful sessions. During four days we recorded about twenty Mick and Keith compositions, usually beginning in the afternoon and going right through until the early hours. Mick said: "We were thinking of moving our beds into the studio at one stage."* It was now that Andrew made a remarkable tribute to Brian's work: "His contribution can be heard on every track, and what he didn't know how to play he went out and learned. You can hear his color all over 'Lady Jane' and 'Paint It Black'. It was more than a decorative effect. Sometimes Brian pulled the whole record together." Yet while Andrew paid lip-service to Brian, and Mick and Keith knew that Brian's flexibility and prowess as a musician helped give many tracks a touch of magic, there seemed an unwritten rule that he was kept down, made to feel simply a contributor. Nobody wanted to deny the vital roles of Mick and Keith. But Brian was psychologically worn away, and felt inferior.

Another episode in Andrew's campaign to boost Keith's and Mick's leadership came with the release on March 11 of an album called *Today's Pop Symphony*, featuring the Aranbee Pop Orchestra. Released on Andrew's Immediate label, it featured our "Play With Fire," "Mother's Little Helper," "Take It or Leave It" and "Sitting on the Fence." The sleeve said: "Directed and Produced: Keith Richards."

Keith told the *New Musical Express* that an orchestral version of our songs was "something I'd always wanted

---

*We often invited Stu to play piano on tracks, but if he didn't like the music he wouldn't do it. His wife, Cynthia, tried to persuade him to play occasionally, pointing out to him that unless he gave the band something extra, he could only be expected to be paid as a road manager. But if he did not admire a song, he could not be persuaded to go to the piano. Stu did guest on some tracks in the studio, but never on stage until he and Charlie formed an occasional jazz group, Rocket 88, in the late seventies.

to do," and Mick spoke for him: "He's trying to prove he's a musician and not just a rock'n' roll guitarist." And *Record Mirror* commented: "Anyone who thinks Keith's talents are limited will be forced to think again from this . . . he takes ten quality pop songs and under his direction they perform them in near-classical style . . . his way of blending pop and classical together has worked out well."

I have always doubted that Keith had anything to do with its production or instigation. I think it was probably Andrew's idea and execution, purely an Oldham projection of Keith to promote the album and to boost his public image, yet another round in Andrew's campaign to increase Keith's profile.

But Keith's elevation couldn't stop the media favoring Brian, in particular. Mick might have held the aces as the lead singer but Brian's image of vulnerability and sensitivity made him at least Mick's equal in popularity: on March 12 the powerful front-page color picture of *Fabulous* magazine featured Brian.

On February 11 a single I produced by the singer Bobbie Miller, with a B-side that I co-wrote, had me on bass, Keith on guitar, Stu on piano and Tony Meehan (ex-Shadows) on drums. It had good reviews. But typically with this and my other independent work, nobody within the group or around us would advise, encourage or help me in my record production or songwriting activities. It was virtually ignored, and treated as a part-time hobby, whereas Mick and Keith were given royal treatment whatever they did in or out of the group.

Mick, Keith, Charlie, Shirley and I flew to London from Los Angeles on March 12, while Brian and Andrew went to New York for a few days. The day I arrived home I took Stephen (now almost four) out for a drive in my new MGB. It was great to see him again and we enjoyed the afternoon together walking around Richmond Park, where we photographed a herd of deer.

Two days later, having dealt with an important financial transaction—opening a deposit account for Stephen, with a first payment of £2—I decided that I would take stock of my own finances and confront Allen Klein about the American dollar account which, for all practical purposes, was "frozen." I had returned to find a recent deposit in my bank account had brought the balance to £1,465 11s. 4d.—not a lot for a supposedly millionaire pop star. My credit rating was good, of course, but despite the soothing words of Klein and Oldham, I could not see the cash coming in and I felt uneasy.

I phoned Klein. He suggested I draw a $40,000 check and deposit it with my local bank in Penge to "see what would happen." I didn't realize it at the time, but now I think that he was using me as a guinea-pig. So I did what he said.

On March 18 Barclays received my American check and applied to the Bank of England for permission to regard these funds as available for investment. Four days later I called Klein again in New York and we spoke for forty-five minutes about the money I'd placed in my British bank; this call cost me £44, an absolute fortune, and all I emerged with was his statement that he was "dealing with it." But not successfully, as subsequent events proved.

Barclays in Penge wrote to me on March 30:

> As you are aware, we have endeavored to obtain a preferential rate for the conversion of your dollar check which we sent for collection. The Bank of England can find no record of the authority for opening USA accounts or for the sale of Nankerphelge Ltd and advise us that they require the authority number for the opening of the account and for the sale of Nankerphelge Ltd. We regret troubling you in this matter, but this request has come from the Bank of England. You told us that the Bank of England authority was obtained, so presumably the authority number is known.

The plot thickened on April 4 when the British accountants for Klein and the Stones, Goodman, Myers, wrote to Barclays: "We have written to America in order to ascertain the circumstances of the transactions referred to therein, and we will inform you as soon as we receive a reply. In the meantime we should be pleased to know whether the funds that have been transferred to Mr. Wyman's Account are available for his use at this moment."

While my American dollar account appeared to be

frozen by the Bank of England "stalemate," Klein found a way of alleviating the situation elsewhere. On April 9 Klein's assistant Joel Silver wrote to Keith: "I am enclosing a letter to Mr. Robert F. Peyser of the Chemical Bank New York Trust Company authorizing him to wire $45,000 (£16,090 6s. 7d.) to your account at the Lloyds Bank in London.* Kindly sign the letter and mail in the enclosed return addressed envelope. Mr. Peyser has already wired the money to your account."

Andrew Oldham's assistant Janice Legg replied to Klein: "Attached please find Keith's check in favor of yourself for $45,000 to reimburse you for the money transferred to his London bank in respect of his house."

Klein had clearly decided to get our money to us from our Chemical Bank, New York, accounts in a method different from the one he had tried for me. Now he was loaning us our own money while mine was tied up with the Bank of England! It seemed to me all too weird. We'd got the fame and the glory and were having a ball. But the real cash was all tied up with Klein in New York. On April 14 the bass guitarist with the Rolling Stones had exactly £567 in his bank account; Rolling Stones Ltd's number one account showed a debit of £2,827, with outstanding bills for £11,495.

Brian arrived back at his flat from New York on March 17 to discover he had mislaid his keys: he gained entry by smashing a first-floor window. He then proceeded to hold court in the company of friends Steve Winwood and Spencer Davis, demonstrating the dulcimer he'd featured on our Hollywood recording sessions. "I think we've reached a peak in Britain," Brian said, "but things are still opening up for us in the States. We've built up an intellectual following among the hippies. The Greenwich Village crowd all dig us."

Whatever problems he faced inside the Stones, and no matter how great Mick's power-base became, Brian epitomized to many thousands of people the essence of the Swinging Sixties. He became quite a social butterfly, and

*This money was for the purchase of Redlands.

developed a notable friendship with Tara Browne of the Guinness family.*

Meanwhile, the same silly old stuff about being refused entrance to restaurants continued: on March 25 Mick and Andrew had arranged to meet the disc jockey Alan Freeman in Mayfair but the headwaiter said they could not enter without ties. "On a roll-neck sweater?" asked Mick. "To put on my swollen glands?" asked Andrew. They adjourned to the friendlier Trattoria Terraza in Soho, the forerunner of the craze for Italian restaurants in London and "home" to the aristocracy of pop.

This was the calm before the storm of yet another European tour, which opened on March 26 in The Hague in the beautiful old opera house, Braband Hall, Den Bosche. The audience ripped the place apart. Half of them ended up with black eyes and broken noses. It turned out to be a mass riot. Police stopped the show and pushed us through a side door into waiting police vans, back to the safety of the hotel.

There was a similar spectacle next night in Brussels: fist fights broke out when police moved in to try to calm the 2,000 fans. The sound was appalling, since the hall we played in used to be an indoor cycle track. "I hope I never hear the Stones sound like that again," I told a friend. Keith said mischievously: "Good concert! All the kids leaping about and screaming, with the police giving them plenty of truncheon!"

The whole tour seemed to attract trouble and near-disaster. We flew to Paris on March 28 and checked into the George V Hotel, where Anita was waiting for Brian. Later the whole group went out together for a shopping spree. Our cars were waiting outside but en route to mine I signed autographs "on the run" for a cluster of fans. Breaking away to rejoin the other four Stones on the other side of the road, I looked the "wrong" way,

---

*Tara was going out with a model named Suki Potier. It was a huge and tragic irony that all three would die young. Tara died in a car crash on December 18, 1966, after some confusion at a traffic light. This inspired John Lennon's famous line in the Beatles' song "Day in the Life," featured on the *Sergeant Pepper* album: "He blew his mind out in a car, he didn't notice that the lights had changed."

being English, and suddenly heard a screech of brakes. A Cadillac was inches away from me; as the bumper touched my legs I slapped one hand down on the bonnet and vaulted over the front of the car to safety.

That wasn't the end of our motor madness. As our car accelerated away, a persistent youth attached himself to its tail fin. "Accelerate now! I want to see him bounce!" said Brian. When we stopped at a traffic light, the boy jumped off, pursued by Mike Gruber, our American road manager. As we moved off again, Mike returned to the car and the fan renewed his position. In this bizarre style, like something from a movie, we drove through Paris followed by a motorcade of fans and photographers in cars and taxis. Finally we called a halt to the lunacy simply by stopping and walking to a café for a lager.

There was, predictably, a riot at the Olympia during our Paris show on March 29. Ten policemen were injured when the 2,500 fans rioted. It was a typical French rock 'n' roll show in which the audience believes it is a bigger attraction than the act on stage! Our set was "The Last Time," "Mercy Mercy," "She Said Yeah," "Play With Fire," "Not Fade Away," "The Spider and the Fly," "Time is on My Side," "19th Nervous Breakdown," "Get Off of My Cloud," "I'm Alright" and "Satisfaction."

Back at our hotel later a phone message said that Brigitte Bardot and her friends were popping in to see us. We were breathless with anticipation, and when she arrived with about six young men we were all, particularly Brian, totally captivated. She told us how much she'd enjoyed the show and only when she left were we able to relax. She later asked the Stones to appear in her film *Two Weeks in September* but this was turned down by our management because we were "doing our own film"; this project never made it, so we lost out on the Bardot offer for no good reason. Shame.

At our Marseilles concert before 1,200 fans next night, Mick was badly hurt. As he sang "Satisfaction" as our finale, a fan threw a piece of wood from a chair back, hitting him over the right eye. The crowd were going really crazy, but he bravely finished the song before being rushed to hospital, needing six stitches. "It took us about thirty minutes to find the emergency ward," Mick complained later. "Then I saw an incredible thing: running down the corridor of this hospital was a huge rat! An incredible size!" His eye stayed closed for a few days and he was shaken, but we pressed on with two shows for a total of 4,000 fans the following day in Lyons.

Weary after this first leg of our European tour, Mick, Keith and Charlie flew back to London on a charter plane while Brian and I took the sleeper train to Paris, where Doreen Samuels and Anita Pallenberg were awaiting us in the George V. Paris always seemed to bring problems for the Stones. This time an innocent visit by Brian and me to a TV show caused Andrew to erupt. A *New Musical Express* writer, Keith Altham, was in Paris and phoned me at the hotel to say that *Ready Steady Go!*, featuring The Who and the Yardbirds, was being filmed at La Locomotive Club. That evening, Brian and I visited, hung around with the musicians and appeared on the show as part of the audience, which included Brigitte Bardot's sister. Altham reported: "Minor riots broke out at the arrival of Bill and Brian, sufficient to bring half the audience screaming down towards the stage for autographs. Brian was practically buried under a bevy of birds."

After this I received a "headmaster's letter" from Andrew Oldham:

Although I am quite sure your motives were innocent and were done without knowledge of anything I might be doing on your behalf, I would be grateful if in future you could refrain from appearing on television shows without consulting me. As it happens, I was put in an embarrassing position as I had spent the last month with *Ready Steady Go!* trying to get you to do a show from Paris following the Olympia venue. I had explained that this was impossible because you would either be on holiday or travelling. The real reason was I did not want you to do *RSG* as I have been negotiating with Rediffusion for us to do our own "special" in place of a *RSG*, which I consider undesirable for you at the moment. To have you turn up on their TV show rather made a mockery of my plans. The fact is, you are supposed to be the No. 2 group in the world although that status is at times difficult to maintain, and I do not want you just dropping in on TV shows. If you consider the point unimportant and not worth bothering about then we really have nothing to talk about. P.S. *If you feel that your personal points of view are not put across properly to the public, I would be quite happy to arrange for you to be interviewed.* [My italics]

As our sixth album in the States went on release on April 2, *Big Hits (High Tide and Green Grass)** the Stones' number one account bank statement from March 29 to April 1 showed a debit of £4,121, with £5,965 in outstanding bills. How could it be that five guys who had been working consistently and successfully for three years in a high-income role should "run" a poor company? Mick was talking of buying a country house, but for the moment remained in his Marble Arch flat; Keith was waiting to move into Redlands but was still in St. John's Wood; Brian lived fairly modestly (for a pop star) in his Chelsea mews house; I had a suburban home out at Keston; while Charlie and Shirley were in their house in Lewes. Massive crowds, world tours and international hits were not reflected in our bank balances or homes.

Mick and Jack Nitzsche went to a Larry Page session of the Troggs (mentioned in the famous Trogg Tape). Next day, together with Charlie and Keith, he flew to Stockholm to continue the European tour, where Brian and I joined them from Paris for two afternoon concerts. The final night of the European tour passed off peacefully and successfully with two shows at the K.B. Hallen, Copenhagen. On this tour each Stone earned $6,212.31 after expenses. This did not go into our personal accounts, but went to Klein's office in New York.

Our fourth British album, released on April 15, was the first to be written entirely by Mick and Keith. *Aftermath,* regarded by many as the Stones' finest work, was certainly a watershed.† Gathering ecstatic reviews, the fourteen tracks were the result of our long hours at the RCA Studios and featured Stu on piano, organ and harpsichord, Brian on dulcimer, sitar, marimbas and bells

---

*This reached number three in America and stayed in the album charts for ninety-two weeks.
†This reached Number One in Britain and stayed there for eleven weeks.

and Jack Nitzsche on percussion, piano, organ and harp-sichord. *Aftermath* was critical to the Stones' evolution on so many fronts. Instrumentally, Brian showed his versatility once again; one track, "Goin' Home," was 11 minutes, 35 seconds long, the longest rock song ever on an album up to that time, uncut because the improvising was so powerful that everyone agreed we should break with tradition. Sexist and chauvinistic as well as musicianly, *Aftermath* was accurately described by Andrew as "the consequences of the Stones' growth, an expression of the things around them. In the early days, audiences and fans saw themselves as a mirror of the Stones. It's still the same today except that everyone's grown older and become more mature. Mick and Keith write about everyday things that are happening and their songs reflect the world around them."

Roy Carr wrote: *"Aftermath* is an on-the-road album. It reflects life in a goldfish-bowl, being fawned over, having every whim pandered to and thrust into a position to order anything on room service that will temporarily sate any pleasure or perversion." Tracks like "Mother's Little Helper," "Stupid Girl," "Lady Jane," "Under My Thumb," "Doncha Bother Me," "Out of Time," "Take It or Leave It" and "What to Do" branded Mick and Keith as anti-feminist writers making no bones of their taste for male dominance and female submission.

The album had a cover design by "Sandy Beach" (Andrew's old pseudonym when he had tried to be a compère); Brian disliked the cover, but at this time he was far more generous to Mick than Mick was to him, stating publicly that Mick was the "best pop performer Britain's ever had" and he was proud of the progress the album made for the group.*

---

*Like many other gold-album winners, we'd always fondly believed that it was our music on the vinyl covered in gold—but Tom Keylock, Brian's driver, had a £5 bet with film director Michael Lindsay-Hogg that the music would not be ours, if it played music at all. Lo and behold, the sounds that boomed out from some of our golds were Buddy Holly, country singer Ferlin Husky and Mantovani's orchestra! We were diverted to find that the gold disc for *Aftermath* played the "Tales of Hypotenuse Turtle," the Walt Disney music from the film *Bambi!*

Aftermath attracted many cover versions; the Searchers recorded "Take It or Leave It"; "Out of Time" was a Number One for Chris Farlowe; the Zombies, David Garrick and Tony Merrick issued "Lady Jane"; "Under My Thumb" was covered by Wayne Gibson.

While Keith moved into Redlands on April 16 I went with my parents to view a new house for them at 16a Crescent Road, Beckenham. Soon after I purchased it for them for £7,750, and they happily moved in.

On April 20 Klein's office arranged for $15,000 to be wired from Mick's New York Chemical Bank account to his London account with the Westminster Bank. This time Klein had managed to get Mick money in that way while mine was still locked into the dispute over the Bank of England issue. With his cash, Mick bought a navy-blue Aston Martin DB6 with electric windows, record-player and radio.

The saga over my "frozen" dollars continued with a letter to me from Barclays in Penge:

May we refer to the above mentioned transaction for which we submitted an application to the Bank of England on 3/18/66 for permission to regard these funds as available for investment, and to our subsequent conversations when we advised you that the Bank of England required you to know the following information in respect of this application:

(1) Full details of the music publishing company Nanker-Phelge Ltd.

(2) Whether permission was obtained for the sale of this British registered company to a non-resident of the UK and Scheduled Territories, and if so, the Bank of England reference.

(3) Whether you were given permission to maintain a dollar account in the USA and if so, the Bank of England reference under which such permission was given.

In view of the length of time which has elapsed since this transaction commenced and the amount involved, we shall be grateful if you will endeavour to obtain as soon as possible the answers to the questions posed by the Bank of England, as pending receipt of this information you will appreciate our Chief Foreign Branch are holding the sum of US $40,000 at your exchange risk. There is also always the possibility that the forth-coming Budget may alter the position with regard to transactions of this nature.

I was further aggravated on May 2 when Klein this time got Charlie $9,886.91 from the Chemical Bank.* Around this time, Klein bought a slice of MGM Records for about £1 million. I decided to lash out with a deposit of £1,000 on my new Mercedes 250S.

I was trying not to let the money situation get me down, and spent a lot of time hanging out with Tara Browne, Keith Moon of The Who and their road manager John "Wiggy" Wolfe. One night after Keith went home, the three of us met two pretty Danish girls and went back to their flat. Tara left, and Wiggy and I stayed the night with them, being particularly quiet because of the landlady upstairs. In the morning the girls cooked us breakfast and then we crept to the front door. Just as we were going out of it, Wiggy shouted at the top of his voice: "And who else lives in this fuckin' slum?" slammed the door and ran away.

At the beginning of May, Brian properly cemented his relationship with Anita. His French girlfriend Zou-Zou returned to Paris and Anita, in London on a modeling assignment, phoned Brian at his home. "It was then that we started going out seriously," Brian said. "I realized I was getting very fond of her." He asked her out and she moved in with him.

Our records were dominating the airwaves and this seemed our most prolific period: as *Aftermath* stayed at the top of the album charts, the advance orders in Britain for our tenth single, "Paint It Black" reached 300,000 a week before its release on May 13. The song featured Brian on sitar and acoustic guitar, and me on bass and organ pedals—I had played normal bass and then, on listening to the playback, I suggested Hammond organ pedals. I

---

*At Klein's suggestion I wrote a check on May 11 for most of the balance of my American dollar account to Rolling Stones Ltd for $7,424.15 and four days later I received a check from Klein for the equivalent in sterling (£2,598).

lay on the floor under the organ and played a second bass riff on the pedals, with my fists, at double-time.

The single, released during a period when the pop world was becoming very sitar-conscious, struck a chord with all our fans. Asked what the title meant, Mick replied: "It means paint it black. I can't get no satisfaction means I can't get no satisfaction." "Pow! What a stormer!" wrote the conservative Derek Johnson in *New Musical Express*. "The fascinating oriental flavour will haunt you. Great!"

Allen Klein arrived in London with ideas for developing our careers. Before leaving New York he'd bought a hundred copies of *Only Lovers Left Alive*, a book by British writer David Wallis that dealt with an imaginary conquest of England by its violent and rebellious youth. In it, the adults commit suicide and teenagers turn Britain into a Fascist jungle. Andrew and Klein eventually bought the film rights for us, Andrew declaring that the theme "could have been written for the Stones." We were said to be getting a million dollars for our debut in this film, although figures varied: other reports said our income would be £300,000, with filming due to begin in August. This prospect suited Mick, who stated on June 4, 1966: "In ten years I hope I'll be an actor and still make the occasional record. It's very unlikely that the Stones will still be going in ten years' time. I've worked out that I'd be fifty in 1984.* Horrible, isn't it? Halfway to a hundred. Ugh! I can see myself coming on stage in my invalid carriage with a stick. Then I turn around, wiggle my bottom at the audience and say something like: 'Now here's an old song you might remember called "Satisfaction"!"

There was another fascinating quote from Keith, with which I only wished I could agree: "I suppose you can say we're rich. We've certainly reached the stage where we can go out and just buy anything we want. We don't have to worry about money anymore." Mick moved into 52 Harley House, Regent's Park, enjoying the limousine life by hiring a Daimler to go to Harrods and buy a cooker, refrigerator and dishwasher. Keith was being chauffeured around London in his Bentley. I was always

*And this was from an LSE student! Mick was forty-one in 1984.

more frugal, part-exchanging my tape-recorder for a new one.

As "Paint It Black" soared effortlessly to the top of the charts on April 28 and *Aftermath* remained at Number One, I was more concerned with the family dog. Lucky was run over and had to be put down: a few days later I went to Battersea Dogs' Home and bought a mongrel that Stephen named Noddy. It was completely wild, tearing up carpets, lino, chairs, curtains. Whenever Stephen came into the house the dog jumped and knocked him over. He finally did us all a favor and ran away, never to be seen again. His successor was a golden retriever puppy, bought from Dulwich Village; Stephen called him Big Ears.

Most of us were settling down to domesticity after a frantic period of travel and record-making. Brian seemed the only one floating freely around the clubs of London. He visited Marbella twice, for less than a week each visit, to stay with friends. Despite his closeness to Anita he seemed strangely rootless and restless. I got a taste of the stress he must have faced with the Linda Lawrence paternity suit when, at the end of May 1966, a girl who had stayed with me when we were on tour in Denmark in June 1965 contacted the Stones office in London, saying she had just given birth to my child. I consulted my diaries and found that she was two months out with her calculations and her arithmetic was politely corrected. Nothing further was ever heard from her!

On June 3 Mick was examined in Harley Street by Dr. Samuel Weinstock, who pronounced him to be suffering from nervous exhaustion and unfit for work. Fortunately, we were neither touring nor in the studio; time away from both activities to "take stock" was essential. Ten days later Mick went into what our office described to the press as "isolation, having been ordered to take a total rest."

All the Stones and our ladies shared a box at the Royal Albert Hall on June 1 for a Bob Dylan concert that helped to unite the great rock audience and alienate a lot of purists. After playing acoustic guitar in the first half of the show (true to his folk-music roots), Dylan was booed when he returned after the interval supported by The Band; they played an all-electric set, historically shaping the course of folk-rock. We all enjoyed it and adjourned to the Scotch of St. James Club for food and drinks. This was the epicenter of rock musicians in the mid-sixties, a basement off Masons Yard, not far from Fortnum and Mason. "The Scotch" was the acknowledged refuge after a concert or for plain socializing. I favored the Scotch, while Brian sometimes also went to Blaises; Keith usually ate at La Terrazza, the trendy Soho trattoria, and Brian's favorite restaurant was Alvaro in King's Road, not far from his home. Mick usually ate at the Casserole in Chelsea.

Sometimes I met Doreen Samuels at the Scotch and after one such night in June 1966 I drove her to her home near Hatfield, Hertfordshire. On arrival we tried to find somewhere private to finish off the night, but ended up in the car in a deserted parking lot. We eventually succeeded, despite the cramped conditions of my MGB with a solid roof. So much for the glamorous life of a rock star!

More glamor: "I'm rich and so are the Stones. Put it this way: we need never work again." Andrew Oldham said that to *Disc* on June 4 as we received our twelfth gold record for "Paint It Black" in the USA. As he spoke, the group's number one account showed a debit of £2,026, with outstanding bills for £2,751. My account at Barclays showed a credit of £8,311 and my account at the Chemical Bank had a credit of $365. From a financial viewpoint, I was glad our fifth American tour was looming, especially with "Paint It Black" top of the *Billboard* charts.

But there was the usual hassle with hotels to be gone through. Fourteen of New York's top hotels turned us down and, while Allen Klein protested strongly to New York's attorney-general, we filed a damages suit for $5 million, claiming that the refusals had injured our reputaton and subjected us to humiliation, ridicule and shame. We claimed that the refusal of bookings amounted to discrimination on account of our national origin, violating New York's civil rights. Each Stone claimed $1 million in damages. We did not need to pursue this claim, but it made a lot of noise for us.

Back in London, Keith had a more domestic problem: a letter from his landlord at the place he was staying in

St. John's Wood. Several tenants had complained about
Stones fans who gathered outside and, ". . . while we are
aware of the obvious difficulties in keeping these people
away, we must ask you in fairness to the other tenants to
take all possible steps to ensure that the disturbances
cease to arise." Coincidentally on June 8 Keith bought
Staff Cottage at Redlands for £5,600 at an auction in
Chichester.

Brian was by now quite a dandy dresser, so it wasn't
surprising that he turned up at London airport on June
23 in a blazer colored lemon and blue with pink stripes.

Flying into New York, we checked into the Holiday
Inn, the only decent hotel that would have us. A short
time later I had a phone call from John Hammond, the
blues musician, who was at a studio recording, asking me
if I'd like to play bass. I agreed, told Brian, who wanted
to come, and a short time later, Stu took us over. I
played bass alongside guitarist Robbie Robertson (of The
Band), and various others, cutting three tracks. During
the session Bob Dylan popped in. At the end John Hammond asked me where to send the session fee and how I
wanted my album-credit worded. I said I'd check back
with him tomorrow, after talking to my people.

He then invited everyone back to his flat for drinks.
We left, and walked back to his flat, stopping off at a
couple of delis and small shops. In amazement I watched
someone being served while some of the others shop-
lifted various small items in each place. When we arrived
at the flat there were already a bunch of people there,
drinking and smoking pot. I was introduced to a pretty
girl called Suzanne, and we hit it off right away. When I
left she returned to the hotel with me and stayed the
night.

Next morning I phoned Klein and told him about the
session with John Hammond. He was pretty mad about
me doing it and insisted that I must not be paid for it as it
could cause certain tax, work permit and contractual
problems. He agreed that John could give me a credit on
the album, but stressed that I shouldn't do anything like
this again. This was crazy, as "sitting in" was, and remains, an important and enjoyable part of a rock musician's life.

We then moved on to the familiar routine next day of a

charter plane for the grueling tour. The destination was Lynn, Massachusetts and we didn't have to wait long for fireworks to start at an open-air concert for 15,000. The concert had gone well despite pouring rain, when we hit our final song, "Satisfaction." Hordes of teenagers broke through cordons of about seventy-five police with such force that they could not be restrained. The sight of the police being overwhelmed, and the use of tear-gas, was enough; we stopped playing and scrambled over the stage, flinging ourselves into two waiting cars.

On to Cleveland, Pittsburgh, then Washington, where I was very surprised to find Suzanne waiting for me. We had some food, went to bed and were making love when the connecting door to the next room opened, and in crept Andrew, Mick and Keith. They laughed, made a few snide comments and left. I was furious.

The concerts rolled on comparatively peacefully before we reached Hartford, Connecticut, where there was absolute chaos. Canada too was wild: the Maple Leaf Gardens concert at Toronto on June 29 attracted 11,000 fans and pandemonium as a girl climbed over the net strung along the seats above the stage. After clinging to the ledge for what seemed minutes she fell into the arms of an officer who was climbing up to get her. "It was a stupid and dangerous stunt she pulled," reported the *Daily Star,* "but in its pure impetuosity, beautiful."

At the Montreal Forum we had to run off stage in fear of our lives when the wrestlers whom we were booing in support of the fans they'd been manhandling jumped on stage to come at us. We were scared but made it back to our cars and then the plane for a flight back to the sanctuary of New York. Keith and Charlie went for a wander around Greenwich Village, returning at 4 a.m. to a stern admonishment from Andrew about the dangers of being "on the street" alone at such an hour. Keith answered that he was old enough to do whatever he pleased.

"This album does the best job yet of alienating the over-20s. The reason—they attempt to *sing.*" So ran one critic's reaction to *Aftermath,* the seventh Stones album released in the US, on July 2.* That same day we released a single, "Mother's Little Helper" backed by "Lady

*This reached number two in America.

Jane,"* but it was the album that American observers detected as marking a shift in our emphasis and approach. "Some of the brute force (in the early Stones) had gone," wrote Lillian Roxon. ". . . [and was] replaced by more than a touch of the sardonic."

To coincide with the record releases we held a press conference at New York's West 79th Street Marina, on the Hudson River, on the SS *Sea Panther,* which Klein had rented. Here, we first met Linda Eastman (later to marry Paul McCartney) who was taking photos of us. Mick spent a night with her, and she wrote about it in an American teen magazine.

There were 9,400 fans and 375 police at Forest Hills Tennis Stadium in Queens, New York, when we helicoptered in from Manhattan for our concert on the night of *Aftermath*'s release. Many of the expensive $5 and $10 seats were unsold and the stadium was only three-quarters full. After our usual set, we began the usual finale, "Satisfaction." On cue, a rush of fans from the stands broke through a deep police cordon and for five minutes there was pandemonium. That was the signal: the house lights were up and our helicopter whisked us into the New York sky. Our fee was $25,000. That night in Manhattan, as the kids of Forest Hills disappeared, we adjourned to a club to see the little-known Jimi Hendrix (then called Jimmy James).

The confusion that always punctuated our American tours was epitomized by an event at Syracuse, New York on July 6. To get on stage at the War Memorial Auditorium we were sent under the building, through a basement which contained all the heating and air-conditioning systems. After the show, returning to our dressing-room by the same route, Brian noticed a dirty, tattered American flag lying over an old boiler pipe. He grabbed it, saying he fancied it as a souvenir, and tucked it under his arm. Police escorting us immediately set upon us, pushing us around and finally bundling us into a backstage office where uniformed and plain clothes police snatched the flag from Brian and gave us all a hard time, accusing us of insulting the American flag. They threatened to throw us all in jail. We protested that Brian was behaving

*This reached number four in America. Both earned gold records.

innocently, but anything we said was ignored. Finally we calmed them down and they let us go.

Next day at Chicago, Mick commented: "Chicago is a great place for people chucking chair legs at you!"

A week later in Vancouver, hundreds tried to smash through police lines to reach us on stage and, within five minutes of the start of the show, a police inspector pulled the plug on our power. When this happened, Mick turned and pointed his finger at the police officer, then thumbed his nose. The audience screamed its approval. The police insisted the kids returned to their seats before the show continued, but the moment the music started the standing, screaming, jostling and rushing began again. The city police inspector said: "This was the most prolonged demand of physical endurance I have ever seen police confronted with during my thirty-three years of service." He added: "As soon as the R & R hits its tempo, the fans are 'gone.' The bumps and grinds are really what you would expect only an adult to be watching in a burlesque show. It is not only vulgar, it is disgusting. It's a tribal dance."

Plane trouble hit us a few days later, when a window cracked. We all suffered pains in our ears from the decompression, but landed safely. We finally arrived for the big one: an evening performance at the famous Hollywood Bowl on July 25 before 17,500 fans. Tickets had sold out within hours of going on sale. Acclaiming the "earthy, physical vitality" of our music, which "rated the royal acclaim," Charles Champlin wrote in the *Los Angeles Times:* "Their onstage performance is permeated by the legend of their off-stage cavorting. As reigning symbols of sex as opposed to romance, they have long since dethroned the Beatles. They are talented, inventive musicians." Everyone was particularly impressed with Mick's performance of "Lady Jane" and Brian's accompaniment on dulcimer.

Mick celebrated his twenty-third birthday on July 26 uneventfully, in flight from Los Angeles to San Francisco, and after a fine concert we returned to LA's Century Plaza Hotel for the night. Next day we flew to Honolulu. Relaxing in the Kahala Hilton Hotel and watching the sunset, we all decided to go out to dinner and look for girls. I was the lucky one: a pretty little local eighteen-year-old came back to the hotel with me.

As we settled into Honululu for a concert and a few days' rest, a car collected Shirley Watts and Chrissie Shrimpton to take them for a plane from London to Hawaii to join Charlie and Mick. This was just as well, because a couple of nights later, on our last night in Hawaii, I met another girl who stayed with me. After making love she told me that her younger sister was the girl who'd stayed with me a few nights earlier. As none of the group had been able to pick up any girls on this visit, they were well-choked with me for having had two.

Our concert had gone very well and Charlie, Shirley and I later went to a stables in the hills. We all went pony-trekking and Charlie and I took some lasso lessons; I took many color slides.

In Los Angeles, our next stop on August 3, Brian and I went to all the clubs before returning to our hotel, the Beverly Wilshire, at about 3 a.m. In the coffee shop I met a very pretty girl, who was dressed very "flower-power," and after a long chat she stayed the night with me. In the morning, as she left me, Keith picked her up in the corridor and she spent the morning in his room.

By the time Diane arrived in Los Angeles a few days later for a two-week holiday, and we'd moved to a rented house in the Hollywood Hills, I discovered I had a dose from the flower-power girl. This was the first and only time in my life a date had gone sour like this. A local doctor gave me and Diane penicillin injections. The source of this problem was never in doubt: Keith got a dose, too, proving conclusively to me that cheats never prosper.

This period was marked by historic events that would appear even more dramatic and significant when compared with the humdrum seventies and eighties. On August 3, 1966, the great satirical comedian Lenny Bruce died of a drugs overdose in New York, aged forty. That week, too, John Lennon made his famous statement that the Beatles were "more popular than Jesus," causing a furor in America. "Paint It Black" went to the top, incongruously, in South Africa. In America, Bob Dylan had a motorcycle accident in which he broke his neck; after this his voice was never the same. As the psyche-delic movement gained ground, drugs became a central part of the fabric of rock, irrevocably changing its course.

Mick, Keith and Brian were all dabbling in drugs, but Charlie and I, the married ones, stayed out of that scene. We were later described as "the straightest rhythm section in rock 'n' roll." I was having a great time and never felt the need for stimulants to mess with my mind or body. All around me I saw the casualties in other bands, and pretty soon I was to see it adversely affect the Stones too.

In Los Angeles, winding up our holiday, Diane and I shopped and went sightseeing while some of the boys bought military clothes and effects (mostly Nazi) from a shop called Hollywood Military Hobbies. Then, as Diane and I went to the doctors for final injections, clearing ourselves of infection, everyone else departed for London. It was at this point, upon our return from a heady American tour, that a serious change seemed to occur in Brian. Unwittingly, it was reflected in a two-page article on him in the British teen magazine *Rave*, where Stones-watcher Dawn James wrote: "Brian Jones seems to have disappeared from the public eye! He doesn't feature very much in the Stones' present image. Once, the rather weird, long-haired, almost mystical Brian was the most talked-of and popular Stone, but nowadays people don't discuss him so much."

Dawn had been flatly refused an interview with Brian by Andrew: "You cannot see him or phone him and he cannot give you any quotes."* From fan-club headquarters, Shirley Arnold sprang to Brian's defense: "Popularity-wise, he's doing better than ever. He gets as many fan letters as Mick and Keith. He seems to bring out the motherly instinct in the fans." But Brian's changing behavior and growing reclusiveness were confirmed by Rod Harrod at the Scotch of St. James Club: "Last year, before Brian met Anita, he was in here every other night. Nowadays he hardly ever comes in."

The changes in the Stones had finally got to Brian. His status as a star was not in doubt but the evidence that the group would be controlled by Mick and Keith stared at him. While Brian could understand Jagger's position by virtue of his role as a singer, he was less inclined to

---

*For some time Andrew had been arranging interviews for Mick and Keith only, strengthening their position.

concede any superiority of position to Keith, who was certainly less popular with the fans and who contributed less musical inventiveness than Brian to our sound.

The proof of the Jagger–Richards partnership was all around: on August 6 our single "Mother's Little Helper" rose two places, to number five in America's *Cashbox* magazine and stayed at number nine in *Billboard;* "Lady Jane" was forty-six and thirty-nine respectively in the same magazines. *Aftermath*—gold in the US—was number three in the *Melody Maker* and *Record Mirror* charts and four in the *Disc* chart. Our albums *Out of Our Heads* and *Big Hits* (*High Tide and Green Grass*) were 126 and eighteen in the American *Billboard* chart, while *Aftermath* remained at number three in the same publication. And other Mick and Keith songs were in the charts in Britain: Chris Farlowe's "Out of Time" and Twice as Much's "Sitting on the Fence."

Brian's ego was severely dented and his bank balance too contrasted with Mick's and Keith's, whose future fortunes from songwriting were guaranteed. On returning from America my bank balance had dropped to £269, and Brian's can't have been much more. The state of the three Stones promotions accounts was parlous. All of them showed debits of several hundred pounds. A significant letter from Klein to Stan Blackbourn at the London office of Rolling Stones Promotions on August 8 said that he understood Blackbourn's points about the financial situation in Britain, but his aim was to ensure that we kept our money: "If there is too much money readily available, I feel it will only be squandered."

While Charlie and Shirley were on holiday in Greece, Brian made plans to take a holiday in Morocco, a country that fascinated him, with Anita and antique dealer Christopher Gibbs, a friend of his as well as of Mick and Keith. The party flew to Tangier on August 28, but the trip was quickly marred by tensions between Brian and Anita. This couple, so magnetically drawn together, began squabbling about almost everything—both in the privacy of their room and publicly in restaurants. There were stories of fights and after seven days Brian returned to London with a broken left wrist in a plaster cast. Various reasons were given. First Brian said he broke it while climbing; Christopher Gibbs declared that Brian tried to hit Anita, missed, and hit the metal frame of a window; and finally Brian stated: "I fell on a slippery bathroom floor and trapped my hand under my hip and the bath. That's the real story." Nobody who knew Brian's record of fisticuffs with women doubted that the broken wrist was traceable to an altercation with Anita. The battle had begun, and in September Brian slept with Marianne Faithfull (who also had a short fling with Keith before starting to see Mick secretly).

Keith was meanwhile busy getting himself settled into Redlands, shipping a copper garden fountain from the States and installing in the beautiful house such items as two lioness-skin rugs, a specially made wildebeest-skin mat, a rabbit-skin rug and a gray wolf-skin rug—and all the time I had thought Keith was fond of animals!

An injury less dramatic than Brian's afflicted me when I was working in the garden of my Keston home on September 4: a screwdriver slipped and only just missed my right eye. I still have the scar on my eyebrow. The same day that Brian and Anita returned from Tangier, Mick, Andrew and Sheila Oldham, Keith and Stu flew to Los Angeles. In the evening at RCA studios they worked on finishing our eleventh British and thirteenth American single, "Have You Seen Your Mother Baby." It was released, after our return to London, on September 23 to terrific reviews.* In *New Musical Express,* Derek Johnson praised the new single's "complexity of startling sounds that leave you breathless. Raw, earthy, invigorating, it's enhanced by punchy brass in the background." Penny Valentine wrote in *Disc:* "I don't know what this is all about but it doesn't really matter since it's probably one of the most exciting records the Stones have made . . . the Stones sound as if they are an entire army on the march. The most certain Number One they've ever had."

*This reached number two in Britain and four in America. Backed by "Who's Driving Your Plane," this track was written by Mick and Keith during our last American tour. The horn arrangements were by Mike Leander; Keith always maintained that the incorrectly mixed version was released as the single. The track was featured in *Superstars in Film Concert* (1971), a Peter Clifton film that also had footage of Tina Turner, John and Yoko, the Animals, Donovan, Ten Years After, Arthur Brown and others.

And Jonathan King wrote in *Record Mirror:* "The most fantastic, best-ever Stones disc. Atmosphere, sound, intensity: a barrier of wailing, beaty, crashing, rumbling, thumping tideways."

The next day Brian (plaster now removed), Charlie and I flew to New York to join the others there to film our slot for the *Ed Sullivan Show.* Since Brian could not play because of his not-yet-healed wrist, we mimed to pre-recorded backing tracks, playing "Paint It Black," "Lady Jane" and "Have You Seen Your Mother Baby." This song provided another milestone in our image-making. Photographer Jerry Schatzberg put us into drag and took us into a back street off Park Avenue. I became "Penelope," seated in a wheelchair; "Molly" Richards and "Sarah" Jagger looked like a couple of aunties; "Millicent" Watts looked like an ageing transvestite, while "Flossie" Jones camped it up under a blonde wig. After this legendary picture session, we went into a nearby bar, ordered a round of beers and watched television. Nobody fluttered an eyelid—or made a pass!

Back in London it was announced that the Stones had helped to add £231,000 to the profits of Decca in the past year. It seemed a meaningless figure to me, since accounts for the Rolling Stones Partnership from August 23 to September 12, 1966, showed a debit of £1,308 and outstanding bills of £11,305. For a group with hits round the world and packed stadiums on tours, we still seemed financially all at sea. I could not figure out why so little money was coming into our individual bank accounts.

My life away from the Stones was busy: I sent flowers to Diane and visited her on August 12 when she went into Harley Street Clinic for an operation and I remember taking Stephen, in his Batman outfit, to Kelsey Park, Beckenham, to feed the ducks and swans.

Brian was no sooner back in England than he was changing course again. Within a couple of days of returning, he and Anita had vacated 7 Elm Park Lane and moved to a new flat at 1 Courtfield Road, South Kensington. Brian took to his new home, with its cavernous lounge and minstrel gallery in heavy oak, and huge Moroccan tapestries to drape around the vast rooms, which he kept very dimly lit. The inventory check at the flat they left showed masses of cigarette burns throughout—

window sills, carpets and furniture—plus many break-ages. The wonder was that they departed from it without having had the place burn down.

In three years of mayhem with the media, we had never had a press agent, but with Andrew concentrating more on the business and music production, it seemed right that we should now appoint one. There was little choice: it was clear that the best operator in London was Leslie Perrin, who wore a suit, seemed some distance from rock 'n' roll and numbered Frank Sinatra among his many clients. Softly spoken and shy, but with brilliant tactics, he became an ally of many a British pop act in the sixties. His appointment came only just in time, as problems away from music that we could not have forecast began to envelop the Stones.

The same day our new single was released we started our next—extraordinary—tour at the Royal Albert Hall in London. Jonathan King, Keith Moon and John Entwistle of The Who were among the audience, as were Brigitte Bardot and James Mason. On the bill were Ike and Tina Turner, whom we'd brought over from the States. (They had an entourage of nineteen people.) The rest of the bill featured the Yardbirds with Jeff Beck and Jimmy Page.

When Long John Baldry announced us, we took the stage to a deafening wall of screams. As we plugged in our guitars and turned to face the audience with "Paint It Black," a huge tidal wave of young girls engulfed us and hijacked the show. Fans who had pushed the commis-sionaires aside to scale the stage pulled me to the floor. One by one the other four were also grabbed and yanked down. Stu and the stagehands flung themselves into the battle and after a few minutes we were free to race back to the safety of the dressing-room. The stage was a seeth-ing, screaming mass; never, in all the riots in America and Britain in three years, had all five Stones been pulled to the floor of the stage during an opening song! Atten-dants finally cleared the stage and Long John Baldry told the audience that the police had warned the show would end immediately unless order was restored. He appealed to them all to sit down and we reappeared some ten minutes later. The Albert Hall, with its reputation for decorum even with pop acts, had never seen anything so wild.

Afterwards, at a party at the Kensington Palace Hotel, there was a presentation: we each received four gold discs for our American sales. The riotous Albert Hall show had given us plenty to contemplate and I was in no mood to go home or end the night early, so some of us adjourned to the Scotch of St. James. Then in Leeds the next night we began the familiar routine of two concerts after a day of traveling. But it was great to watch Ike and Tina Turner most nights from the wings.

Backstage at Manchester we heard that in New York Allen Klein had announced his estimate that we would have overseas earnings of *$20 million* in the next year! This was made up from income from discs, personal appearances and two films. I'm still waiting!

The "millionaire" talk traveled with us to Scotland. There the police decided to clear totally three streets around the Odeon theater to ensure that we arrived and departed without incident. Even then, a few arrests were made. After our press conference, Mick confirmed that the figure of millionaire status had been "calculated by Allen Klein, our American business manager." We grossed £3,316 before expenses from the Glasgow shows.

The film part of Klein's announcement was of particular interest to Brian. Because of his individuality and attractiveness to women, he was predicted by many to be the potential film star inside the Stones. As he regularly ate at the Alvaro, films were delivered to him there from Soho so that he could view them at home: *The Bedford Incident, Goldwhiskers, Springtime for Samantha, Polygamous Polonius, House Of Wax, Repulsion* and many more. He pored over them in the studio of his flat. He said he was "more excited than ever" at this extension of the Stones' abilities, and was confident that we could prove ourselves in what would be the biggest test. For Brian, there always had to be artistic adventure.

But while Klein had formed a company specially for the making of *Only Lovers Left Alive,* people in the business were cynically describing it as "the most expensive film never made." It had first been announced in July 1965 and now, in the autumn of 1966, it was no closer. Andrew announced a starting date for filming in November or December, but this seemed doubtful. I did not begin drama lessons until October 14: acting was quite a journey from rock 'n' roll. Mick began piano lessons but the other three were not actively learning. The film seemed a great idea but still remote. We were still on the road with the Ike and Tina Turner package. Through Newcastle, Ipswich, Birmingham, Bristol and Cardiff, with Glyn Johns sometimes recording us, we whipped up hysteria that continued to amaze the media. From Mick came the admission that it seemed the entire western world had been waiting for. He stated that his act was based on sexual attraction: "I entice the audience. I do it in every way I can think of."

Charlie, however, kept up his laconic responses throughout this year of turbulence for the Stones. Asked what he thought of life as a pop star, he answered: "You live, you die. Even at weekends."

The tour finally ended at Southampton on October 9, grossing £27,586. The Yardbirds received £2,300 and Ike and Tina Turner £6,183, which after all the expenses had been paid left Rolling Stones Promotions with a staggering profit of £615. The Stones' company account at this time had outstanding bills for £9,179. And the Rolling Stones Partnership showed a debit of £2,640.

Yet the tour was artistically important for us. Our contemporaries on the music scene, some of whom had been guarded about our ability when we began, were now aware that our roots in music were different and that the very strong rhythm-and-blues movement in Britain could be traced partly to our pioneering work. "The Stones opened a new field with R&B," Eric Clapton stated, "and gave everyone else an opportunity. They are a criterion of English pop music." Chris Farlowe talked about our "big influence on other groups," and Alan Price of the Animals, whose sources were similar to ours, declared: "The Stones helped R&B get off the ground with the Bo Diddley and Chuck Berry sound."

We took a small but serious knock when we failed to reach the top of the British chart with "Have You Seen Your Mother Baby." It only got to number two. Bobby Elliott of the Hollies had a view taken by many: "The record was basically above the fans' heads. It was too hip and those photographs showing the Stones in drag put the youngsters off a bit." There was more controversy when Brian went with Anita to Munich, where she was filming *A Degree of Murder*. There he posed in a Nazi uniform.

The British release on November 4 of our compendium, *Big Hits (High Tide and Green Grass)** was heralded as "a delight for every fan, to replace all those worn-out scratchy singles." The collection did indeed herald the end of an era in rock 'n' roll. Mick and Keith's songwriting now became more introspective and inspired; on November 16, at the Olympic Studios in Barnes, we cut "Title 8," which later became "Ruby Tuesday." On this I over-dubbed double-bass, with me selecting the notes and Keith bowing the strings. This was a month of adventure in the studio and Jack Nitzsche flew in from Los Angeles to play keyboards on some tracks.†

These sessions were attended by a mass of Mick's, Keith's and Brian's friends and hangers-on, including Marianne, Anita, Prince Stanislaus Klossowski de Rola, Spanish Tony Sanchez (the guy who scored for Keith), photographer Michael Cooper, art-gallery owner Robert Fraser, guitarist Jimi Hendrix and comedians Peter Cook and Dudley Moore. These sessions were notable more for the dopey camaraderie than for the music they produced.

Meanwhile, on December 10, we had our eighth album released in the USA, *Got Live If You Want It*. This reached number six in the US charts. In Britain's *New Musical Express*, we were voted number two British vocal group, number two British R&B group and number four world vocal group.

But the dominant themes within the Stones at year's end 1966 were personal rather than musical. When Anita quit the film set in Munich and flew back to London, with Brian meeting her at the airport, German and British sources predicted an early marriage. Brian squashed

---

*This reached number three in Britain.
†We also cut Mick and Keith compositions "If You Let Me" (unreleased), "Looking Tired" (written in Ireland), "Sitting on the Fence" (Mick and Keith wrote this in Sweden) and the traditional "Trouble in Mind." There was a funny pressing of it featuring the backchat in the studio.

these rumors: "We do not consider marriage is necessarily the most logical step in our relationship at this time," he told reporters.

The death in a London car crash on December 18 of his friend Tara Browne had thrown Brian into despondency. He valued relationships deeply and he was never to come to terms with the loss of this friend.

Keith flew with Brian to Los Angeles on December 6 for a ten-day holiday with Jack Nitzsche. This was hardly the most likely of partnerships, but Keith saw that Brian needed a break and some support. And Mick met Marianne at the airport and took her shopping in Harrods where they bought a child's cycle, a Christmas present for her son Nicholas. For more than a month, Mick had been scheduled to go on holiday with Chrissie; the flight tickets had been bought and hotel reservations made. But some time during November, Chrissie's facility of sending her bills to the Stones office, to be charged to Mick's account, was halted. And on Thursday, December 15, the day of their intended flight from London to Jamaica, Mick canceled their holiday and was seen lunching with Marianne in Knightsbridge.

The huge row that finally ended the three-year relationship of Mick and Chrissie occurred at Mick's Harley House flat on Sunday, December 18. "We had loads of rows and it reached the point where a split was the only wise thing left," Mick said. Afterwards Chrissie was reported to have attempted suicide and was admitted to the Greenway Nursing Home, Hampstead, for treatment. The bill for her stay was sent to Mick, who returned it to Greenway, asking them to send bills direct to Chrissie; on Christmas Eve Mick hired a van to collect all Chrissie's personal belongings from his flat and return them to her. She went on to date Steve Marriott of the Faces, but that partnership lasted only four months. Mick could now "step out" publicly with Marianne, with whom he had been carrying on a clandestine relationship for some two months. Pretty soon Marianne moved in to Harley House with him. Their liaison became yet another symbol of Swinging London as the psychedelic era continued, with Marianne a strong advocate of the hippie philosophy. To the world of pop, here was the Stones' perfect complement to the romances of George Harrison and model Pattie Boyd and Paul McCartney and actress Jane Asher.

Fate decreed that my life was going to change dramatically, too. On December 8 I went into town alone to the Scotch of St. James. A pretty young girl introduced herself to me as Astrid. I didn't think much of the incident, adjourned to the Bag o' Nails club and then went home.

Ten nights later I met Astrid again, this time at the Bag o' Nails. We began chatting, together with Chas Chandler, bass-player with the Animals, and his girlfriend. It was Chas's birthday and he invited us to his flat in Kensington for drinks. There were about twenty people there, many of whom were smoking joints. This was neither my scene nor Astrid's but we drank a lot, and when she wanted to leave we returned to my car. She got in. I suddenly felt very ill and vanished, spending a very long time throwing up nearby. I returned to the car after about twenty minutes and found her sitting there quite calmly, totally unaware of the time-lapse. I drove her to Bayswater Road where she was staying with friends, and then went home for the night.

We met at the Bag o' Nails for the next two nights. She was in London studying English, she said, and she planned to return to her family in Sweden for Christmas.* She would get in touch with me on her return in January. On December 21 she took the ferry from Hull to Gothenberg. I had no idea that this was the person who would be an important part of my life for the next sixteen years.

It was Christmas: Keith and Linda went to Paris to be joined by Brian and Anita. In London on New Year's Eve I went to the Bag o' Nails club to celebrate. Here I was approached by a very dressed-up, good-looking woman who came on to me like crazy, inviting me back to her place. Quite drunk, I went—and we went straight to bed. She insisted on having all the lights on. We made love on this huge bed, with mirrors everywhere. Just as we had finished, a guy walked into the room—her husband, or boyfriend—who'd been watching the whole thing, obvi-

---

*Astrid Margareta Lundström, born in Farila, Sweden on December 27, 1947, was the eldest of five children of a middle-class couple.

ously getting off on it. I made a polite exit and returned home for the night. Happy new year!

1966 had ended magnificently for the Stones: out of the ninety-eight million-selling records, we had six, with five by the Beatles and four by Elvis. We received gold records for our singles "19th Nervous Breakdown," "Paint It Black," "Have You Seen Your Mother Baby," "Mother's Little Helper," and for the albums *Aftermath* and *Big Hits* (*High Tide and Green Grass*). We had also sold more records in America than any other act. We were number one in all three album polls, and number two in all three singles categories.

After a rumor that I was leaving the band (denied by all), another more serious tale shot across the Atlantic—that Mick was dead. News agencies and radio stations in both the States and Britain were swamped with calls from journalists and sobbing fans. "Mr. Jagger wishes to deny that he is dead and says that the rumors have been grossly exaggerated," announced Leslie Perrin. Nothing more deadly than a bill for £121 faced Mick, who had crashed his Aston Martin into the Countess of Carlisle's car. His photographer mate David Bailey had wanted to make a film with the curious title of *The Assassination of Mick Jagger*, but the idea remained just that.

9

Addictions and Frictions

Never, ever would I say that the atmosphere of the Stones was relaxed and happy. These five incredibly strong personalities were definitely guarded, controlling their emotions. They weren't very open with *each other*, so they certainly couldn't have appeared relaxed to outsiders! There was rarely any outburst. It was just this tension, a moodiness, a sulking. You could never call them hypocrites. They're all very real, whether their nastiness or niceness is showing. But they exercised what I'd describe as controlling silences. They took themselves a bit too seriously sometimes—yet I believe their tension helped the music.

Nothing about them could be changed, then or now. They are five addictive personalities; and Bill has his own addiction away from drugs, the personal, emotional side of life. So they were all terribly manipulative.

They're not demonstrative. It's a loose-sounding band but they're not loose people! I've never in my life experienced five such uptight people. On the other hand, if somebody's sick or in a crisis, they have always been very good and loyal.

As for Bill—well, his passivity was manipulative, too. He had total emotional control at all times; didn't show whether he liked somebody or didn't. A person with passivity is incapable of an interchange of feelings, so there's no introduction of aggravation from him.

There was never talk of them splitting up. Other bands argued in the open, or even had fist fights. The Stones never did anything like that. They couldn't express their anger any more than they could express their caring feelings.

—Astrid Lundström, who came on
every Stones tour with me during
our sixteen years together,
1967–83

The beat group revolution had now been in full swing for nearly four years. Like so many groups (The Who, the Moody Blues and Cream, for example), our early determination and need for quick success was replaced by a profound change in the psychological approach to music. "We've got time to look at ourselves," Mick said now, "at our relationships with other people, and everything that concerns us." He believed our forthcoming new album, an advance on *Aftermath,* would indicate the future of the Stones. Dissecting himself, he added that he had grown up and was "not as nasty as I used to be . . . I'm not worried about trivialities any longer. I used to worry about everything, however small."

Our stars were shining in *Beat Instrumental* magazine's 1966 gold star awards: Keith was number six lead guitarist; Brian was number four rhythm guitarist; I was number three bass guitarist; Andrew Oldham was number five recording manager; Mick was number ten recording vocalist; The Rolling Stones were number four group on stage.

The period was reflected by the emergence of Jimi Hendrix as a superstar. I saw one of his first shows in England, on January 5, 1967. At the end of his set he set fire to his guitar on stage. A few days later I saw him again—at the Bag o' Nails, where the audience read like a *Who's Who* of rock. Paul McCartney, Ringo Starr; Pete Townshend and John Entwistle of The Who; Brian Epstein; Allan Clark and Bobby Elliott of the Hollies; Eric Clapton, the Small Faces, the Animals, Donovan, Georgie Fame, Denny Laine and Lulu all marveled at the inspired guitar work of a guy who had been discovered in the States by my friend Chas Chandler of the Animals. Hendrix's music and wild appearance personified the changing, adventurous sounds.

Brian was deeper and more contemplative on what he saw as the chemical changes in society. And his outlook showed his sensibilities: "I have a code by which I lead my life and I'm trying to develop this. I'm learning about a lot of weird things. Now I'm much more interested in developing coordination between the brain and the body and the health scene than making money. I haven't shown much of these things because the pop world is full of entrepreneurs and agents and I can't get on with them.

I'm not particularly interested in making bread all the time.

"I got my first offer to write film music, within the last few days."*

It was the beginning of the drugs sub-culture, and there were traces of the dream-world in Mick's and Brian's attitudes; the effect of marijuana and LSD brought about a sea-change in the outlooks, attitudes and aspirations of thousands of musicians around the world, and their audiences. Dope had been smoked for many years by jazz musicians as a means of relaxation. Now that, together with LSD and other hallucinogenic, "mind-expanding" drugs, entered the world of rock 'n' roll. And the label "pop," which still represented the disposable sounds of artists like Bobby Vee and Nancy Sinatra, gave way to the more meaningful term "rock" for bands like ours, the Beatles, Pink Floyd and dozens of influential "hippie" bands from America's west coast. We were all in *bands* making *albums,* no longer *groups* making *singles.*

Rock 'n' roll headquarters in London were the night-clubs in which all the musicians gathered and held court, traded stories, drank and debated the desirability of the latest dope. The Speakeasy, in Margaret Street, London, opened on January 4, 1967, and Glyn Johns and I went to the opening: it was an important center for all the gossip.

Dope never attracted me. My great "high" in the drug-laden year of 1967 came from the pleasure of being in a successful band, which in turn gave me freedom to do some songwriting and production elsewhere. I was always active with the various bands I enjoyed producing. The End were particularly successful with one single I produced, rising to number four in Spain.

Stu, our trusty road manager, pianist and, above all, mate from the earliest days, was married on January 2, 1967, to Cynthia, Andrew Oldham's secretary. After the service which some of the Stones attended at St. Andrew's Church, Cheam, Surrey, there was a wedding

---

*This was for *A Degree of Murder*. He composed and produced the soundtrack, which featured pianist Nicky Hopkins and guitarist Jimmy Page; it was another example of Brian's versatility, for he played sitar, organ, dulcimer, clarinet, harmonica and harpsichord.

breakfast for twenty-six guests. At the reception in the evening, Cynthia recalls her father, a professor of pediatrics, walking past some of the Stones and Marianne who were sitting on a long sofa smoking pot. "Someone's got a bonfire," he said innocently. "It was a bitterly cold January day and nobody could possibly have had a bonfire, but he identified this 'strong odor, a garden fragrance,' " she remembers.

At this time my own marriage was disintegrating. The decision by Diane and me to separate was not sudden; we had been drifting apart for a considerable time. We no longer had a lot in common: she was never particularly interested in my world of music, though she enjoyed the material comforts and fame as the wife of a Stone. I'm sure her criticism of me was that I was far too absorbed with life as a musician to help make the marriage work.

My sister Judy, who did not like Diane from the first, says: "I never thought the marriage would last. I never did think they were right for each other." She feels the reason the marriage survived so long was "because Bill is the sort of person who doesn't like arguments, bad feeling or confrontation." Certainly this was never a strong marriage. We'd stayed together mostly because of Stephen, and I was away so much that being married, even unhappily, was no irritant to my life.

The night after Stu's wedding Diane decided to go to South Africa for a while to visit relatives, leaving Stephen with me and his nanny. Three nights later, I went as usual to the Bag o'' Nails club, where I met Doreen Samuels. We stayed the night at the Hyde Park Towers Hotel.

By Monday, January 9, Diane had arranged everything with her relatives, and Stephen and I saw her off at London airport. Stephen, at four too young to be told of the serious implications of her trip, returned home to Keston with me under the impression his mother had simply gone away temporarily. Coincidentally, as Diane flew into Durban, Astrid left Gothenberg for London.

Astrid remembers: "We had started to talk at Chas Chandler's birthday party and I said I was going home to Sweden for Christmas. Bill said: 'Call me when you get back,' and I said of course I would. But I had no intention of doing so, because it wasn't done. I thought: Well, you mustn't call *men!* My knowledge of the pop scene was nil. I was trying very hard to be grown up. My sister, Ulla, four years younger, had pop posters round her room and I thought it was childish. I wanted very much to be older. I had heard of the Stones, obviously, but I didn't particularly like them. I preferred the Beatles and jazz."

Next day, Brian, Charlie, Keith and I flew to New York for another appearance on the *Ed Sullivan Show.* We had a hair-raising moment at Kennedy airport: the motorcade of limousines that met us was crossing a runway when one almost collided with a taxiing jet. As we settled into a few days in Manhattan, Friday the 13th in Britain heralded yet another chapter of controversy as our twelfth British single, "Let's Spend the Night Together," backed by "Ruby Tuesday," was released to a chorus of criticism.* Recorded on November 16, 1966, at the Olympic Studios, with Glyn Johns as engineer and Andrew producing, this was one of our most ambitious cuts, with Keith on bass on "Night" and Brian playing piano and recorder on the plaintive ballad "Ruby Tuesday," which also featured Keith and me on bowed double-bass.

Unambiguous, blatantly sexual, "Let's Spend the Night Together" plunged us into trouble from all sides of the media. Cleverly defusing the problem and the ban on the title that could result, Andrew decided to name the record as a double A-side—a regular ploy in those years, inviting disc jockeys and reviewers to choose whichever title they fancied.

We were accused of corrupting the young with "Let's Spend the Night Together" and the critics again had a field day: suggestive, a bad influence on innocent kids and bordering on the obscene, said some, though we had our supporters. Malcolm Morris, producer of the Eamonn Andrews TV show, said: "What's wrong with it? If Cole Porter's 'Love For Sale' was all right, then there's nothing wrong with this"; and disc jocky Alan Freeman said: "Of course it doesn't matter. It's a bit of a giggle. If I had

---

*This reached number two in Britain but went to Number One in America for two weeks.

children I wouldn't stop them listening to it. Frankly I don't care who Mick spends the night with."

But as Mick flew to New York to join the rest of us on January 13, the single, our fourteenth in America, was being played on the radio with a "bleep" over the word "night." Some stations banned the song, playing "Ruby Tuesday" as the A-side.

We had great problems getting into the CBS Theatre in Manhattan for a rehearsal for the Sullivan show. After trying several entrances and facing a gathering crowd of fans, we finally had to rush the glass doors with kids all around us. The doorman refused to open a door so we smashed one down and forced our way in. Mick cut his hand. Keith screamed at the doorman and punched him.

A different battle awaited us inside. Ed Sullivan told us bluntly that he would not allow the lyrics of our controversial song to be sung. "I've hundreds of thousands of kids watching my show. I won't stand for anything like that with a double meaning. Either the song goes, or the Stones go." The value of that program was too great to jeopardize for the promotion of the single. And it was the only reason we'd flown to New York. So we compromised, agreeing that the song would be introduced as "Let's Spend Some Time Together." On the show we first performed "Ruby Tuesday" and then the controversial song. As Mick sang the amended words, his eyes turned skywards, making the change obvious to the audience.

While we were described as part of pop's royalty, and people swallowed Klein's prediction that we'd be millionaires within a year, the finances around us were still being handled in a bizarre fashion. On January 18 Stan Blackbourn, bookkeeper at Rolling Stones Promotions, sent a telex to Klein: "Andrew needs £763 13s. for house agreement tomorrow at 11 a.m. our time. Bank has refused further credit. Laurence Myers said shall we borrow money temporarily from Stones." Klein telexed back the same day. "OK to borrow the £763 13s. from the Stones."

A further telex that day, from Ronnie Schneider in the Klein office in New York to Myers, asked for £2,500 to be transferred from Essex Music to my account. "A letter to Essex will follow," the telex added. I had no idea why my money should come from Essex Music, the music-publisher in England. Our payments were still erratic, but Klein was still switching money around whenever we asked for it. A great many small charges were being absorbed by the Stones (like Mick paying for a regular chauffeur-driven car from Marianne's home in Lennox Gardens to the West End). There was still blind faith that Klein would be our financial salvation, and that he was a great business manager. Everyone believed that. Everyone except me. And even if I had had any support, our lives were so busy professionally and personally that to embark on any kind of confrontation with him would have been unthinkable at this stage. We had work to do.

Between the Buttons, our sixth British album, released on January 20, 1967, was the result of the first studio session at which we concentrated on an album as a finished product, and it eventually reached number two both in Britain and in America. With our usual nonchalance epitomized on the front cover picture by Gered Mankowitz, the back of the jacket carried six cartoon drawings by Charlie, characterizing our popularity but making the graphic point that we had been rejected by the music-industry authorities. Charlie designed the cover and wrote the following poem to add to the back sleeve:

> *To understand this little rhyme*
> *You must tap your foot in time*
> *Then the buttons come much nearer*
> *And the Stones you see more clearer.*

Gered Mankowitz said: "Most of the photographic compositions were mine, with a certain amount of input from Andrew and a great deal of help from the group. We endlessly found ourselves working in spite of Brian. During the *Between the Buttons* session he continuously tried to screw the pictures up: he was hiding behind his collar; he'd bought himself a newspaper and buried himself in it; he was just not cooperating. I wouldn't say Brian was trying to ruin the session, but he was so often being difficult. The whole point of the *Between the Buttons* pictures is that we were consciously trying to get an image of a band that had a vagueness to it, where you didn't have to be presented with everything in detail. And I was experimenting by putting Vaseline on the lens and using strange, distorted colors. The front cover didn't actually have words on it except for the words *Between the Buttons* on Charlie's buttons on his jacket. We were trying to break away from tradition."

Nicky Hopkins, later to become the most sought-after keyboard session-man in rock, played piano, and Brian played saxophone on one track, "Something Happened to Me Yesterday," which was a parody of the popular British TV personality of the sixties, Police-Constable Dixon of Dock Green.

However this cohesive album faced much criticism. Described by longtime Stones critic Roy Carr as "a turkey," the twelve tracks were said to have found us "temporarily drained of all positive inspiration, enthusiasm and direction." Carr went on to say that much of the blame for the failure of *Between the Buttons* could be laid at the door of Andrew, who now autocratically saw the Stones as a projection of his own inflated ego. There was a grain of truth in this: as Keith once said, Andrew was so influenced by Phil Spector that he wanted the Stones' records to turn out like the Righteous Brothers or the Ronettes; "Andrew used to think," Keith added, "that anything was possible if you put enough echo on it." However, America was already hailing the album as a masterpiece.

On the evening of January 21, 1967, the young Peter Frampton called me and I offered to take him up to town for the evening. I showed him around a few clubs, ending up at the Scotch of St. James, where we bumped into Astrid and her girlfriend. They'd just got back from Sweden, but Astrid hadn't called me. Later Peter and I took the girls back to their flat, where he disappeared with Astrid's friend. A little later, we drove Peter to Victoria Station and I got him on the last train home, as I had promised his mother. A couple of weeks later I received a strange phone call from him; he'd been trying to reach me while I was away in Spain. Some days after his liaison with Astrid's girlfriend, he'd found "strange creatures" on his body. He'd got scared and finally had to tell his mum. She'd taken him to the doctor, who diagnosed crabs. It had been Peter's first experience with a girl.

To some, a further chink in our armor came with our decision to appear on the TV show *Sunday Night at the London Palladium* on January 22, the bastion of all-round entertainers—ballad singers, jugglers, comedians and double-acts. Its huge audience was mostly adult, the opposite of what we were expected to attract: but Andrew felt we could no longer restrict our audience to teenagers, and that we ought to widen our net.

For a fee of £1,500 we were booked to sing an uncensored version of "Let's Spend the Night Together," plus "Ruby Tuesday"; we mimed to a pre-recorded tape, with Mick singing live. "It's not as if we can't play live," said Keith. "But we couldn't rely on them to get the sound we wanted." We were seen in nine and a quarter million homes, the highest audience figure in more than a year, pushing the Palladium show to the top of the weekly list of the twenty most popular programs.

But, as always, we sparked off an outcry for something unrelated to our music or performance. A traditional aspect of the Palladium show was the finale, in which all participants stood on a revolving roundabout to wave farewell to the audience and viewers. We hated this, considering it too show-bizzy—everything we'd been fighting for the past four years. We became embroiled in a mighty row with the television producer Albert Locke and his colleagues when we announced that we would not go on the roundabout at the end.

Andrew maintained we should, Mick angrily refused; Tito Burns, our agent, steeped in show-business tradition as a former dance-band leader, said it could do no harm. As Albert Locke stomped off to devise an alternative finale, Andrew left in a huff, having faced a band he could not persuade. How strange that Oldham, who had been credited with molding our anti-Establishment image, should have wanted us to toe the line on such an issue. Charlie was vituperative in his condemnation of the Palladium show: "I didn't want to do the show in the first place, and I'm not sure why we did," he grumbled. "Nobody ever does any good on that show except Sammy Davis Jr., and he can perform on a pavement." Amid all the arguments, which persisted in the papers for weeks, there were some amusing views. An example of the level of the argument: "Surely anyone having the privilege of starring on the Palladium would have the decency to dress respectably," said an Essex reader to the *Daily Mirror*. "The Rolling Stones have truly let Britain down."

Afterwards Mick and Keith met up with Paul McCartney. "I thought it was a very funny show, with strange people making pathetic remarks about pop stars," Mick said. Brian and friends went for dinner at the Hungry Horse in Fulham Road, while I made for the Bag o' Nails, as I often did, to meet Astrid. Mick joined us later. The consolation for all the aggravation came with the chart positions: in one week we rose ten places to number four in *Melody Maker*. In America we entered the *Cashbox* chart at forty-six, while our live album, *Got Live If You Want It*, remained at six in the *Billboard* lists.

I kept in touch with Diane in South Africa, but was keen to develop my relationship with Astrid. I went to the Bag o' Nails on January 25 and met her again. A little later that night Paul McCartney, Beatles aide Neil Aspinall and Paul's uncle joined us at the table. After a while, I realized that Paul was playing "footsie" with Astrid; she confirmed it as I was driving her home. As we sat talking in the car near her flat we saw Paul arrive. He saw us and drove around and around her flat until he finally gave up and drove away. We continued talking, had an argument and I became very upset, before telling her: "I don't care how much we argue, because I *know* that we will be together for a very long time." She thought this statement quite weird.

A week later, I went to the club and met her again. The place was pretty crowded and we were sitting with David Rowberry and friends when the boss told me Paul McCartney had just arrived and asked whether he could join our table. *No!* I replied angrily. (Despite this we continued to be mates!)

On January 28 I arranged for a car to collect her and bring her to my house for the first time. I packed a case and we checked into separate rooms at the Mayfair Hotel for the night, before flying to Madrid with Glyn Johns. Glyn and I had appointments with Sonoplay Records to discuss releases of his solo records and our joint productions. But the romantic aspect of my first proper outing with Astrid was truly bizarre. When it was time to go to bed, Astrid, uncertain of her feelings towards me, really didn't want us to sleep together—but there was only one double-bed in the room. She spent hours in the bathroom, hoping I'd fall asleep. Finally she came to bed, wrapped up in layers of clothing. She slept on one edge of the bed, while I stayed on the other. There was no contact. Next day, after Glyn and I had our meetings, he met a girl he knew and the four of us went to dinner. Back in the hotel room later, Astrid and I went through the same performance again. The next day Glyn and I had contracts to draft with Sonoplay so we decided to stay an extra day. That night I had a showdown with Astrid and stomped out. Relaxing in Glyn's room, I told him about the problem and decided to play a trick on Astrid. Glyn phoned her to ask where I was and she began to panic. We left her wondering about my whereabouts for a few hours, during which time she kept calling Glyn. Eventually I returned to the room and we made up and made love for the first time. Happier, we stayed on in Madrid for another couple of nights while Glyn returned to London.

Back in town, Astrid was still unhappy about seeing me regularly because I was married. She was suddenly thrown out of her flat, so I had the Stones office reserve her a room at the Mayfair Hotel for a while. We continued to meet often at the Bag o' Nails, but our relationship went "on hold."

Astrid says: "I first met the Stones together in a club. Then Bill asked me to go to a recording session, adding that they didn't like women around but he had told them he was bringing me and they'd better behave because he liked me. So I arrived terrified; I was so painfully shy in those days I could barely speak. I found out a couple of years later that they interpreted this as my being incredibly snobbish. Mick I didn't take to in a big way at the start. I got on with Brian. But the person I felt most at ease with, who made me feel comfortable, was Keith. I thought Charlie was rude but that was because I couldn't understand him at the beginning."

While Brian was still firmly attached to Anita, sending her flowers while she was away filming in Munich, Mick was consolidating life with Marianne. When she went to sing at the San Remo song festival on January 28 he followed two days later, and their romance was revealed to the media. The jet-set image was completed when Mick and Marianne rented a yacht in San Remo and sailed to Cannes to meet up with her baby, Nicholas, and his nanny.

On February 5 London's *News of the World* ran the second of a five-part series on the drugs habits of pop stars. In it, Mick was alleged to have taken LSD at the Roehampton home of the Moody Blues. Mick reacted angrily and issued a statement: "I am shocked that a responsible newspaper like the *News of the World* can publish such a defamatory article about me. I want to make it quite clear that this picture of me is misleading and untrue, and therefore the only way left for me to prevent this libel being repeated is for me to ask my lawyer to take legal action in the High Court immediately."

That night we appeared on the Eamonn Andrews show. We arrived, expecting to mime "Let's Spend the Night Together," But the Musicians Union prevented this, insisting we play live. After much wrangling we substituted "She Smiled Sweetly" from our new album. Our fee was £200.

Mick earned a further £150 by appearing on the discussion panel during the show, alongside singer Susan Maughan ("Bobby's Girl") and comic Terry Scott. Asked by Eamonn Andrews if he felt any responsibility to his teenage fans for what he did outside the sphere of show business, Mick answered: "I don't believe I have any real moral responsibility to them at all. They will work out their own moral values for themselves."

At this a barrage of criticism was hurled by Terry Scott and Susan Maughan, but Mick stood his ground with dignity while his critics became overheated. His contempt showed later: "They weren't big show-biz names. C'mon— *Susan Maughan!* Who's she? She's had about one hit record in five years. She's kept up by an occasional picture in the *Daily Sketch*. As for Terry Scott—when I was very small and had an infantile sense of humor, he used to amuse me."

While we were on the Eamonn Andrews show, across town at *Sunday Night at the London Palladium,* Peter Cook and Dudley Moore, now good friends of ours, were performing. They achieved what the authorities couldn't, and put "us" on the farewell roundabout—with "larger than life" paper dummies made by cartoonist Gerald Scarfe.

The Stones had never been great party-goers or hosts. Social meetings with the music business and with people on the fringe of it usually ran to foursomes or casual meetings at clubs like the Bag o' Nails, the Scotch or the Cromwellian. We rarely visited each other's homes; with Keith settled out at West Wittering, Charlie at Lewes and me at Keston, we were quite scattered. Only Mick and Brian remained in London.

Astrid recalls that she was "immediately aware of the split in the band: Mick and Keith together, and Brian, Bill and Charlie on the other side. I found it frustrating to be with somebody who was able to be that passive. I felt Bill should be more outspoken, not put up with as much as he did, and I told him so. He said he tried but didn't get very far. To me, this was an alien way of thinking.

"It was kind of obvious that they thought he was far too straight. They thought of themselves as having some sort of power or right, and they'd basically decided to be in charge. And then I suppose Bill and Charlie accepted that. I don't think Brian did, but he was quite unstable and not in a position to make much of a dent. He was very sensitive but he was also unwell. Had he not got so heavily into drugs I don't think he would have stayed so long with the Stones. He would have cracked."

Looking back, the friendship that appeared to exist between Brian and Keith was in reality superficial. Brian reluctantly came to accept his reduced role within the Stones. The genesis of the switch by Anita from Brian to Keith's side began when Keith split from his girlfriend Linda and went to stay awhile with Brian in his Courtfield Road apartment. Brian had sensed that Keith and Anita were getting "warm," but initially ascribed this to her powerful personality, which bewitched everyone. The three of them flew to Munich together on February 8 so that they could see Anita filming.

On Saturday February 11 we all met at the Olympic studios for an evening recording session. Using only four-track, we cut two versions of a song called "Blues 1" before Astrid and I went first to the Cromwellian, then the Bag o' Nails and finally returned to the Mayfair Hotel for the night. Keith in his chauffeured Bentley, Mick and Marianne in Mick's new Mini-Cooper "S," and a bunch of friends drove down to Redlands immediately after the session in a convoy of cars. There were nine in the party: Mick, Marianne, Keith, Robert Fraser, Fraser's Moroccan servant Ali Mohammed, photographer Michael Cooper, Christopher Gibbs, Nicky Kramer, a Chelsea hippie, and a twenty-seven-year-old Canadian, David Schneiderman, known as "Acid-King David." They arrived at about eleven o'clock and were joined by a couple whose identity Keith protected, describing them later as "a married couple, fairly old friends of mine, in the same line of business"—George and Pattie Harrison.

Bacon and eggs were served to the hungry party by Ali Mohammed, while an exhausted Keith retired to an armchair to read a book. The others were chatting and listening to records by Bob Dylan and The Who. Keith eventually went to sleep in the armchair and the party broke up at about 5 a.m., George and Pattie Harrison leaving, luckily for them, and the other guests retiring to bed.

While the party had been in full swing, an informant, who had earlier telephoned the *News of the World,* arrived at the newspaper's offices. In that first phone call at 10 p.m. on Saturday, he told a reporter that he had some information about a party some of the Rolling Stones were holding in West Sussex.

The informant rejected the paper's suggestion that he should go to the police, saying: "I want to remain anonymous, but I think the police should know what is going on." Giving the Redlands address, he said a weekend party would continue throughout Sunday. It was obviously an insider: who else would know that only "some" of the Stones would be there? The editor, convinced of the informant's "sincerity," decided he had a duty to pass such information to the police. A senior newspaper executive, advised by Scotland Yard that the police force directly concerned should be notified, then gave the information to drug-squad officers connected with West Sussex police.

David Schneiderman's contribution to the weekend had been a briefcase packed with sophisticated narcotics. He woke up most of the guests on Sunday morning with cups of tea and offered some of them "white lightning," a hallucinogenic drug that had the effect of LSD but was slightly less powerful. While Mick, Marianne and the other guests went back to sleep, Detective-Sergeant Stanley Scudmore obtained from the local magistrates warrants to carry out a raid on Redlands.

Keith recalled: "I woke up around 11 a.m. Schneiderman, who had followed my car to Redlands, was up and dressed when I woke, and a few people were walking about. Mohammed was in the kitchen. The weather was nice and I went into the garden for an hour or so. I had no idea what the rest of the guests were doing indoors, but went back in because I heard talk of a beach party being planned. We all went, except for two guests, and were on the beach for twenty minutes or half an hour. We traveled in Schneiderman's Mini-van. On the way back I got out at a village a mile and a half from my house with two other guests and walked back home. In the afternoon, everybody went on a Mini-bus Mystery Tour around West Sussex."

Michael Cooper photographed Keith, in sunglasses and Afghan fur coat, on the beach, and there was an abortive expedition to the house of Edward James, the father of English surrealist art, at West Dean, before everyone returned in the evening to Redlands. They sat around talking, playing records, watching television. "Everything was perfectly respectable," Christopher Gibbs said.

The nine guests all sat down to dinner cooked by Ali Mohammed and then began to watch TV in the drawing-room. Some were smoking joints. Marianne, who had had a bath, did not want to put on her muddy jeans again, so she wrapped herself in a big fur rug.

At 7:55 p.m., Chief-Inspector Gordon Dineley, with eighteen other police officers (including three police-women), drove up the narrow lane leading to Redlands. After knocking on the door they were kept waiting for a few minutes, because when Keith looked up and saw what he thought was a "little old lady" outside (a police-woman peering through the drawing-room window), he thought it was an autograph-seeking fan.

Police knocks on the door increased and, after they had announced themselves, Keith opened the door and after the police had explained the purpose of their visit, he immediately phoned his solicitor Timothy Hardacre in London, who hired a car from our travel agent and went to Redlands with Leslie Perrin. Keith was shown the warrant, issued under the Dangerous Drugs Act of 1965. Police then interviewed all the people at the party and searched their possessions.

In one bedroom, Detective-Constable John Challon found a green jacket on the back of a chair. In a pocket was a plastic phial containing four tablets, with an Italian label saying Stenamina. Mick admitted the coat belonged to him. Asked about the tablets, he replied: "Yes, my doctor prescribed them." Asked who the doctor was, he said: "I think it is Dr. Dixon Firth but I can't remember." Mick said he was not sure but he thought the doctor lived in Wilton Crescent, Knightsbridge. Mick was said to have told the police he used the tablets "to stay awake and work." Mick later claimed that he had purchased the pills from a vending machine at the airport in Italy during his trip to San Remo.

A police officer found a dark-colored jacket behind the drawing-room door. Eight green capsules were in the right-hand jacket pocket, and Robert Fraser said: "I have trouble with my stomach. I got them on prescription, from a doctor in London." Asked which doctor, he said it was one of three but he did not know the addresses of their surgeries. When he was searched, a small box containing twenty-four white tablets was found in his trouser pocket. Robert said: "I am a diabetic. These are prescribed by my doctor." Asked if he had any card to show he was diabetic, he said he thought it might be upstairs, but a search failed to find it. He was told by a senior police officer that the tablets looked like heroin and he replied: "Definitely not." The officer returned them to Fraser but then said: "I'd better keep just one back for analysis." At that moment, Fraser knew the game was up for him. The twenty-four heroin "jacks" had been supplied to him by Spanish Tony Sanchez.

On Schneiderman, police found a tin containing pieces of a brown substance, a decorated wooden pipe containing cannabis resin, an envelope containing small particles of a brown substance and a ball of a brown substance.

Police took possession of a briar pipe-bowl without a stem from a drawing-room table and found in it traces of cannabis resin, which was also found on a drawing-room table. They found a pudding basin beside a bedside table containing ash. They also found a tin containing what appeared to be incense, and elsewhere they found sticks of incense. They even opened airline mustard sample packs and miniature bars of soap from hotels, which Keith always collected. In all, they took away twenty-nine items, including cigarettes, four candlesticks, soap and the butt ends of cigarettes. Before they left, police told Keith that if dangerous drugs were found to have been used and they had no relation to an individual, he would be held responsible. "I see," Keith replied. "They pin it all on me."

As the police prepared to leave Redlands, someone with bitter insouciance put a record on the turntable: Bob Dylan singing "Rainy-Day Women," featuring the classic chorus line: "Everybody must get stoned!"

For Mick, the timing of all this was ironic. Being in the process of suing the *News of the World* for an allegation in a drugs story, he was now center stage in a massive drugs bust.

Just as the police left, Brian phoned from London. He had been prevented from joining the party because he'd been working on the music for *A Degree of Murder*. He and Anita had completed their work, he said, and would be at West Wittering in a couple of hours. "Don't bother," Keith told him. "We've been busted."

The party began to split up. As Keith, Mick and Marianne conferred with Hardacre and Perrin, Robert Fraser, Ali Mohammed and David Schneiderman returned to London. That night, Schneiderman left the country, never to be seen or heard from again.

The focus then shifted to Spanish Tony Sanchez, Keith's "friend." Alerted that there had been an enormous Stones bust, he suggested it was worth trying to bribe the police analysts. After offering to "sound out" various policemen he knew in the West End division who might be receptive to a pay-off, he returned to Keith, Mick and Robert Fraser. A bribe of £7,000 would ensure that the substances taken from Redlands could be "lost," he assured them. Mick and Keith coughed up £5,000, Fraser gave £2,000 and Spanish Tony handed over the money in a pub. Alas, this costly operation had absolutely no effect on the outcome of the case. All it did was buy Mick and Keith some temporary peace of mind as the police machinery moved inexorably into position for a trial, and Timothy Hardacre brought in Victor Durand, QC, to be briefed by Mick and Keith.

It was somehow typical of life with the Stones that our recording session at the Olympic continued on schedule, twenty-four hours after the Redlands bust. It was, in fact, just another normal working day for us: Charlie coming in from Lewes, me at Keston before going to the Mayfair Hotel and helping Astrid check out and move into a shared Bayswater flat before making for the studios and then to the Bag o' Nails, where we met Brian and Keith as if nothing had happened. A unique diversion for Brian and Anita was joining the model agency English Boys Ltd, where they would be paid 100 guineas an hour for special work. Brian could probably use that money at this stage! Though Mick and Keith had their songwriting royalties, I can't imagine that Brian could have been any better placed than me financially, and I certainly wasn't rich: on February 18 my bank balance showed a credit of £26. A cleaner employed by Brian for six weeks to the end of March 1967 at £6 week was still unpaid one year later.

An atmosphere of tetchiness was now growing towards Klein's handling of our financial affairs. Laurence Myers cabled Klein as follows on February 16: "Dear Allen: (1) There was only £5,000 left at Essex which we have taken for tax. This is adequate. (2) Are you sending Bill £2,000 as requested in previous telex. He is pressing me for news of this. (3) Andrew wants to know urgently how much he has borrowed from US companies, especially Rolling Stones Ltd. (4) Tito Burns wants to know address of Chemical Bank to which we can arrange to have payments made re. forthcoming European tour. Please advise."

Next day, Mick cabled Klein: "Please cable by Saturday morning (18th) £5,000 and credit Rolling Stones Number 3 account at Westminster Bank.* Also please send and credit my personal account with £2,000 loaned to Marianne and please debit her account. Any query, kindly get in touch."

Klein's office (via Ruth, his secretary) responded with the news that "Allen Klein and entourage arriving TWA 700 on 18th and will be at the Hilton hotel at 10:30 a.m. Also, no money has been received in USA in respect of Marianne Faithfull, Mighty Avengers and Poets' (two groups who had covered Jagger–Richards songs).

Soothing words followed that cable in a telex from Klein to Mick the same day: "Have received your telex and am taking care of the money situation." Referring to the drugs bust at Redlands, Klein added rather furtively: "In respect of the other matter under no circumstances do anything at all until I see you. Repeat do nothing until I arrive."

And the money did indeed start to move in Mick's direction as he requested. $13,975.55 was loaned to the Stones number three account from Nanker-Phelge Music while Mick received his £5,000 cash from the Rolling Stones Partnership.†

The Stones bust was now a major topic in the fraternity of musicians, and with the use of dope widespread there was a shudder at the news that aggressive counter-drugs action was planned by police with particular attention to pop artists and pop parties. New drug squads were being formed and more raids expected after busts considerably smaller than the Redlands affair had discovered purple hearts, LSD and Indian hemp. The British police were said to be cooperating with Interpol, presumably in an attempt to root out the sources. This kind of

*This was the bribe money for Tony Sanchez.
†All sorts of extra expenses were incurred. Typical of the psychedelic era and the free-and-easy spirit of "hanging out" which it engendered, was the attendance at the Olympic studios of Marianne's estranged husband, John Dunbar, and his Greek friend, Alexis Mardas Smith. They convinced Mick and Keith that they could create amazing visual effects using colored lights and magnetic fields, for our imminent European tour. They managed to get various sums from the hard-pressed Stones account to fund these projects but there always seemed to be problems when we asked to see examples of their work.

news didn't affect Charlie or me, but Brian, Mick and Keith were wide open.

While Brian was immersed in writing and producing his film music, the planning for the drugs trial occupied Mick and Keith. They went to the Hilton Hotel, London, on February 20 to confer with Timothy Hardacre, Victor Durand and Allen Klein. The pressure was heavy: this was rock's first major drugs bust, and the climate was charged by the clash of the new rock and youth culture and the Establishment. They faced a real danger of imprisonment after the May 10 trial.

To get away from the heat of it, and from media attention, a short holiday was planned. Keith arranged car insurance for a motoring visit to France and Spain, and commandeered Brian's chauffeur, Tom Keylock, whom Keith insured as his second driver. By now there was much camaraderie between Keith and Brian, and with Mick preoccupied with Marianne, and Charlie and me married, they were uniquely "independent" and, as far as attitudes to the Stones went, they were brothers-in-arms.

Their plan was to motor from France through Spain and down to Morocco. Keith joined Tom Keylock in Paris at the George V hotel on February 25, to be followed later by Brian and Anita. They were joined by Deborah Dixon, the American girlfriend of director Donald Cammell.

With Keylock at the wheel they all began the long drive down to North Africa. The intention was to meet Mick, Marianne, Michael Cooper, Robert Fraser and Christopher Gibbs at the El Minzah Hotel in Tangier. But before they reached the Spanish border Brian was taken so ill—with either asthma or pneumonia or a drugs overdose, or a combination of these—that they had to get him medical treatment.

At the Centre Hospitalier d'Albi in Tarn, near Toulouse, Brian was told he'd have to be admitted for several days. He insisted that the rest of the party, who had checked into a local hotel for the night, should continue their journey in the morning without him.

I sent him a telegram for his twenty-fifth birthday the next day, February 28, which he spent in hospital while the rest of the party drove across the border and along the east coast of Spain, stopping off at Barcelona. There it was Keith's turn to face a problem, albeit smaller than Brian's: he got into a bitter row with waiters, who refused to accept his Diners Club card without his passport. Keith, Anita and Deborah were taken to police headquarters and questioned for several hours about their identity, destination and general unruliness before being released.

When they returned to their hotel at dawn a telegram from Brian asked Anita to return to Toulouse to meet him as he left hospital. He was blissfully unaware of the relationship that in his absence had built up between Keith and Anita in the back of the Bentley, one that, many people believe, depressed him so much that it contributed to his death.

Anita ignored the telegram. Deborah flew back to Paris as Tom Keylock drove Keith and Anita from Barcelona to Marbella, where they stayed overnight. It was here that the serious liaison between Keith and Anita began. Unaware of that, or even of the whereabouts of Keith, Anita and Tom, Brian sent another telegram on March 2, this time to the Stones office: "Feeling almost fully recovered. Must leave here as soon as possible for Tangier assuming no complications. Very very unlikely. Please book flights first class Toulouse/Paris/Tangier early next week and mail tickets immediately. Also notify others of arrival and ask them to wait for me. Will recuperate fully in sun. Love, Brian."

After four nights with Keith in Marbella, Anita joined Brian in Toulouse on Sunday, March 5. Tom Keylock drove Keith to Gibraltar where they crossed over to North Africa and on to Tangier, meeting up with Christopher Gibbs, Robert Fraser, Michael Cooper and friends. Two days later Brian was fit enough to fly back to London with her so that he could have some tests. At the Harley Street Nursing Home Brian had a chest X-ray; later, Klein phoned, and Brian, Anita and some friends had lunch before Brian entered the West London Hospital for what was described as an overnight post-pneumonia check-up.

By Saturday Brian had left hospital after treatment and he and Anita immediately flew from London to Tangier via Madrid and Gibraltar. Mick also flew there, separately, and the party was united at the El Minzah. There, they met a man named Achmed, who ran a store at the back of the hotel. Achmed exported fancy Moroccan leather shoes, which had thick leather soles and looked like clogs: a cover for bringing in hashish. Shortly after arriving, everyone also met an eccentric called Brion Gysin, who was to figure heavily in Brian's escapades in Morocco.

This should have been the idyllic break Brian needed after his illness: the sunshine, his lady and friends, and the backdrop of eastern culture which so intrigued him. But when the party drove down to Marrakesh to continue their holiday, things degenerated quickly. Brian had a penchant for prostitutes and group sex. When Anita refused to have sex with him and some women he had met in town, his violent streak emerged: she was beaten up so severely that she said later she was in fear of her life.

During the evening of March 14 the party met Sir Cecil Beaton in the hotel lobby and adjourned to a Moroccan restaurant. Mick, expounding the benefits of LSD to him, said it would be beneficial to an artist. It should preferably be taken in the country, surrounded by flowers, he continued: "You'd have no bad effects. It's only people who hate themselves who suffer . . . they can't stamp it out. It's like the atom bomb. Once it's been discovered it can never be forgotten, and it's too easy to make." Next day Mick emerged at the hotel pool to discover an atmosphere of indefinable but unmistakable passion developing between Keith, who was swimming, and Anita, who stared motionless and endlessly at him from her poolside chair. Beaton then took Mick through the trees to photograph him in the midday sun. But the next crucial chapter in our story shattered the serenity of the "holiday."

That afternoon, Brion Gysin had taken Brian around Marrakesh to absorb Moroccan music. After Brian had left the hotel, Keith decided to leave with Anita. Brian was proving to be so difficult that Tom Keylock helped them escape. Returning from the Atlas Mountains where he had been smoking dope and absorbing the magical pipe sounds of the musicians of JouJouka, Brian was staggered. Everybody had left: Anita, Keith, Tom Keylock

. . . he was alone. He phoned Brion, sobbing: "Come quickly! They've all gone and left me. Cleared out—I don't know where they've gone. No message—The hotel won't tell me. I'm here all alone. Help me." To compound what Brian saw as an unforgivable defection, Keylock had helped them—from that moment he became Keith's chauffeur.

Brian immediately left Morocco and flew to Paris where he stayed with Donald Cammell. Cammell describes the dramatic arrival of Brian: "He called me from the airport. I had absolutely no idea what was going on. Brian was always so fastidious about his clothes, but when he came up to my place he was filthy; he hadn't changed his shirt and was wearing bedraggled lace and tattered velvet. He was alone, a figure of great pathos, totally distraught and out of it." Two days later Brian flew into London, went to the Alvaro for dinner, and licked his wounds. He could not and would not accept that Anita would not return to him.

Mick, sensing the tension in the air in Morocco, flew home, to be met at London airport by Marianne in a chauffeured Daimler. That left Keith and Anita still together in Marrakesh. Finally, Anita returned to London alone on March 22. Brian met her at the airport. The split was inevitable but Brian found it impossible to accept his loss as permanent.

"I think the loss of Anita *destroyed* Brian," Dave Thomson says. "He was totally in love with her. It finished him. At that time, Brian had no direction. He said: 'They took my music; they took my band; and now they've taken my love.' "

His father confirmed that "nothing was the same for him after that." But while Brian was visibly broken, Keith was much more dismissive of his mourning: "Just because a chick leaves somebody to go with somebody else is no reason to feel guilty. It could have been someone 12,000 miles away but it *happened* to be the guy who stood on the other side of Mick onstage. And that was that."*

*Anita and Keith were together from 1967 to 1980, and they had two children, Marlon and Dandelion (whose name was later changed to Angela). On December 18, 1983, Keith married

Anita's switch was a major landmark in the Rolling Stones story. Brian, who had been distanced from the nerve-center of the group for four years, was now completely isolated and—even worse—humiliated. However badly he treated Anita, he loved her and her embrace of a man he had thought was a mate was heartbreaking. He leaned increasingly on drink, LSD and marijuana to help him through; he was obviously shattered.

Compared with the fireworks of Brian, Anita and Keith, the decision by Diane and me to split was processed like a well-oiled machine. By the end of February, Diane had returned from South Africa and was staying with her father in Sydenham. She came over to the Keston house during the days to sort out her belongings while making plans to return to live in South Africa.

Through solicitors I agreed to pay her £50 a week for ten years with a three-year advance payment of £7,800. It was all pretty friendly: I bought her a trunk for her possessions and delivered this to her at her father's home, giving her £500 and asking my accountant to get Klein to transfer a further £7,300 to Barclays Bank in Natal, South Africa, to await Diane's arrival.

While Diane prepared for her flight on March 10 and I lived with Stephen at Keston, having assumed custody, Astrid moved in with me. We left for a driving holiday in the West Country on March 11, stopping off at Stonehenge en route to Devon and Cornwall, taking color slides. We drove along the coast of Cornwall, returning after four days via Exeter and the New Forest (beautiful country for photography). My parents were at Keston to meet Astrid for the first time; Stephen and his nanny were back, too, from a holiday in Blackpool. Astrid and I went out to a local restaurant, the Fantail, for dinner that night—and from then we were together for sixteen years.

Astonishingly, during this period of high drama in Brian's life, he was at his most prolific as a musician. He began taking guitar lessons in March 1967, feeling the need to improve his technique. And the new dimension to his

Patti Hansen—with Mick as best man. They have two daughters, Theodora, born on March 18, 1985, and Alexandra, born on July 28, 1986.

career that the film soundtrack provided was widely praised. The German director Volker Schlondorff declared: "Brian's music has worked out marvelously. It fits in wonderfully with the story." The film was chosen as Germany's entry to the 1967 Cannes Film Festival. The thought that this could begin a new interest for him, outside the Stones, crossed our minds. He certainly needed a strong diversion from standing on stage alongside Keith during these dark days.

When Astrid says she thinks the Stones are "the most uptight band in the world," she has a point. With my marriage breaking up, bitterness between Brian and Anita, plus the looming drugs trial for Mick, Keith, Marianne and their friends, the spring of 1967 found us cast as the world's baddest band. Everywhere we turned and everything we touched became controversial. It seemed the worst possible time to hit the road, because touring needs unity. But a European tour is precisely what we embarked on.

On March 24, as Astrid went to stay with my parents in Beckenham, the Stones flew to Copenhagen en route to Malmö where the hard reality of our reputation as "druggies" was rammed home by the customs officers. Our seventeen pieces of luggage were ruthlessly searched by a mobile unit known in Sweden as the Black Gang, famous for finding smuggled goods, particularly narcotics. They even ordered Mick to unscrew the back of a heavy chest when we found that its key had been lost. Mick and I were taken into separate rooms for body searches. They went through every bit of clothing we had, even our underclothes. They only stopped when Mick insisted on having an independent witness in the private room with him. They found nothing, of course. The head of the search unit said: "We didn't know this group was coming to Sweden. This was a *routine* raid [*his* word!] and they were not delayed long considering the amount of baggage they had." This annoying, time-wasting episode was evidence that the Redlands bust had stigmatized the Stones for ever.

When the European tour began next night in Malmö, riots were avoided, but only just: police charged the stage at one point to prevent us continuing, and Mick nearly got beaten up when he shouted at them in protest at their brutal handling of kids. Police retorted by turning off the electricity. Worse scenes occurred two nights later in Örebro, where five teenagers and a policeman ended up in hospital.

Mick sent flowers to Marianne in London, Charlie sent some to Shirley in Lewes and I phoned Stephen and his nanny to ensure everything was fine before we moved from Sweden to Germany. Here, Keith met a German model, Uschi Obermeier, and had a brief affair during our concerts in Bremen, Cologne, Dortmund and Hamburg.

These were successful shows but fairly tame. When we moved on to Austria, arriving in Vienna in April 2 for two shows, each before 14,000 fans each at the Stadthalle, things changed. Here, where we were known as "The Mushroom Heads," smoke bombs were thrown, chairs broken and paint and eggs chucked at the stage as police tried to restore order. The cops were well prepared for all this. They had a scale of penalties for any disturbances. Special corrugated iron cells had been put up in the hall and they were soon overcrowded as 154 fans were held. On-the-spot penalties were imposed: approximately 15s. for being rowdy, £14 for smashing a chair!

Keith flew to Paris next day and checked into the George V while Mick, Brian, Charlie and I went back to London. Brian, putting on a brave face, went shopping for clothes in Chelsea Antique Market, and spent almost £500. Then in the evening he went to the Bag o' Nails: an expensive twenty-four hours!

Strange things were happening to the bookkeeping at this time. Brian hired a chauffeured car from Ealing to London airport to the West End and to Ealing, which was charged to me; Anita flew from Munich to Paris to join Keith, which was (ironically) charged to Brian; and when Marianne was driven to London airport en route to Mick in Milan, the bill for her car was charged to Keith.

After two shows in Bologna, we drove to Rome on April 6. Here our friend Stash arrived and took us all to his palatial family house, more like a castle, where we sat around chatting and drinking. A blonde Italian model and I hit it off right away; sadly she was flying to Milan a little later, but we arranged to meet there next day.

At the two concerts that night at the Palazzo Dello Sport, the audience included Brigitte Bardot, Gina Lollobrigida and Jane Fonda. Mick commented afterwards: "All the people in the front rows were over twenty-five, a lot of them over forty! So we had to give a proper concert and play really well."

Back at the hotel, another girl whom I'd met at Stash's house took me out in her car, showing me the sights of Rome. After being out all night we finished with breakfast in town, returning to the hotel at eight o'clock, just in time to prepare for the flight to Milan, where my blonde model friend had arrived. We spent the next three days together there.

After two shows each in Milan and Genoa, Mick and Marianne flew back to London, the rest of us to Zurich where we changed planes and flew on to Paris. There, we went through a really heavy trip with customs officials. They looked carefully at aspirin tablets and Beecham powders we were carrying, and we told them to keep them. There was better news for me at the George V Hotel, where Doreen Samuels had arrived to join me.

The drugs witch-hunt seemed to finally get to Mick when he flew into Orly airport the next day. Pacing around his hotel suite at the George V in a purple velvet smoking jacket, floral shirt and gray slacks, Mick told a journalist: "We were searched at Orly airport because I am on the customs international 'red list.' Of course there is a list. And of course they are after me." A customs official in London said: "As far as I'm aware there is no official list of suspects circulating round the member countries of the Customs Cooperation Council. It is possible, however, that customs officials at various ports keep unofficial lists of their own. Anyone engaged in detecting crime would have to build up a list of suspects."

Paris was always a stronghold for us and the first of two shows at the Olympia on April 11 was great. Mick wore a floor-length satin gown, and at the end of the concert he threw tulips into the audience who, as *France Soir* reported, tried to make more noise than we did. The only injury was to Charlie who was accidentally hit on the nose by an overeager fan with a camera, just as we were leaving for the hotel.

While we were performing, all our hotel rooms were ransacked and money, clothes, cameras and radios were stolen. We strongly suspected young waiters at the hotel, but the management refused to accept responsibility. The Stones never stayed at the George V again as a group.

The now-traditional airport hassle awaited us next morning as we arrived at Le Bourget. We looked colorful and there was no mistaking the sight of a pop group on the move: I wore a velvet jacket, flowered shirt, scarf and sunglasses; Keith had on a black hat and a sheepskin coat draped over his shoulders, plus sunglasses; Brian also wore a large, conspicuous hat.

We handed our passports to Tom Keylock who gave them in together, thinking this would save time. One of the five immigration men confronting us began shouting, and Mick told him to "calm down," which he understood. He appeared to go berserk, and a punch caught Keith; then the guy aimed a punch at Mick, who was still trying to calm him. Keith was grabbed by his lapels and a fist was brandished in his face, while all the time the official spoke rapidly in French. One punch hit Keith in the chest, another was fended off by Keylock. It transpired that all they wanted was the presentation of each passport by the individual holder, intead of collectively! More airport frayed nerves, and we were totally blameless, but we were all over the British papers next morning. A cartoon by Osbert Lancaster caught the mood.

Our plane took off ninety minutes late and we flew to Vienna, where we changed and flew to Warsaw. In 1967, with the Iron Curtain firmly in position, a decadent western pop group going into Poland was unheard of. It was our idea, rather than any promoter's. There was no money in it: the fee was a pittance. But we'd heard that kids in the Eastern bloc got records from the west on the black market, and that they could hear us on the radio. Long before *glasnost* became a fashionable word we were keen to break down the barriers that existed between east and west.

On arrival, we found that the airport buildings looked like army Nissen huts. There were about a hundred fans waiting there to greet us. In customs, a tin hut, the tables for luggage inspection were just slatted wood. We were met by a party of Polish security men and Madame Katarska, the local promoter who was to act as our guide/translator. We were driven into a depressingly gray and dismal Warsaw, to the best hotel in town, the Orbis-Europejski, another cold, gray building.

"If you ask me, it won't be the Daily Express or General de Gaulle who'll keep us out of Europe, but the Rolling Stones!"

My room was triangular in shape with a huge concrete pillar in the center. Everybody was in and out of each other's rooms, comparing them to see who had the "best." There were no TVs but there were radios. However, when we tried to tune them in, we found that all but the local stations were being jammed. In the evening we all met in the hotel restaurant, accompanied by our Polish guides, for a fairly basic dinner which cost a fortune.

Next day, April 13, a few of us walked around the hotel, noticing plainclothes security men watching us everywhere and stepping into doorways when we looked back at them. When we stepped out of the front doors of the hotel, intending to wander around Warsaw, we were stopped by security men and asked to remain in the hotel, where I did manage to take a few photos from the hotel doorway.

Our press conference that afternoon in the hotel nearly became a fiasco from the start: the organizers forgot to inform the hotel about it and when newsmen and photographers gathered, a hotel official asked everyone to leave.

Trouble was averted by our urbane press agent, Leslie Perrin, who simply took out his British checkbook, wrote the enraged hotel official the required sum, and the press conference began.

As we left later by minibus for two concerts, big crowds of youngsters who gathered in front of the hotel were held back by police. They waved handkerchiefs and shouted: "Long live the Stones." As we arrived at the venue, thousands of people were demonstrating in the streets. We quickly learned why: all the tickets for our shows had been distributed to Communist party members, and none had been available to the real fans.

Both shows went very well but the audiences were very reserved, probably because the police and military were standing in the aisles and all round the theater. Every time people stood up to applaud or cheer, officials would force their way through to the offenders and reprimand them. On stage we were powerless; it was terrible to watch such repression of people's feelings.

Towards the end of our set the crowd began chanting: "*Icantgetno! Icantgetno!*" but it took a while for us to realize that they wanted "(I Can't Get No) Satisfaction."

Les Perrin and a host of British reporters witnessed big riots outside the theater. In the interval they told us that the fans outside were fighting in the streets with the police and military, and being charged by police on horses and chased away by armored cars with machine-guns on top. Reporting it graphically in *New Musical Express*, Perrin wrote:

Behind the Iron Curtain the Stones have triggered off something that western politics could never incite—riots! Outside the Palace of Culture in Warsaw I witnessed 10,000 fan-crazy Polish teenagers locked out. Others were marching in bodies of 2,000, chanting "Why Can't We See the Stones" and then spelling out the group's name, led by a cheerleader. The square, lined with literally hundreds of police, became a battleground . . . Came the 8 p.m. show and the unrest in the square outside reached a new peak. Two or 3,000 teenagers charged the massive iron gates, trying to get into the hall. I saw the authorities order two large armored cars into position, backed by a brace of water-cannon, to hose-pipe the marchers. A company of steel-helmeted soldiers with sub-machine guns and guard dogs added force. The police and troops shot tear-gas into the crowd.

After the shows we returned to the hotel and were so incensed about what had taken place outside the concert hall that we arranged for a van, took boxes of our singles and EPs and drove back into the city. Whenever we saw groups of kids in the streets, we would slow down and throw records out to them. We did this until all the hundred records were gone, and then returned to the hotel for the night—much happier.

Checking out next morning, April 14, we found that, by an incredible coincidence, our bill came to *exactly* the same amount as our proceeds from the previous night's two concerts! Leaving Poland, we reflected on an adventure that was a cultural success, but we hated the way the kids' enthusiasm was squashed. Sadly, twelve years after our visit Eric Clapton went to the same hall, encountered precisely the same problems, and was scarcely able to play because the brutality in front of the stage sickened him.

We flew to Zurich into a good, old-fashioned western airport riot! Hustled by police into two black Mercedes with no customs or passport checks, we were driven away at top speed as fans on the airport roof 300 yards away yelled in anger at our getaway. They swarmed on to the airfield as we drove off. As police fought to push them back, three airport fire-engines raced up and turned hoses on them. The drenched fans scattered and fled.

At the Dolder Grand Hotel, my blonde model girlfriend from Italy met me, and after lunch we went shopping. I bought myself a new Braun Nizo movie camera. Sydney Brent of the Carnaby Street Shop flew in from London to open a boutique, bringing with him a replacement pair of trousers for me. All very gentle stuff, bearing no relation to the concert that night at Zurich's Hallen Stadium. During a really fantastic reception the 12,000 crowd got out of control. Mick was knocked to the floor by a youth who broke through a cordon of 300 police. I don't know how the guy got up the thirteen-foot high stage, but when he did he rushed Mick from behind. To our amazement, he grabbed Mick by the lapels of his jacket, flung him to the floor and then began jumping on him. Police rushed to Mick's rescue but it all happened so quickly, the damage had been done. Tom Keylock, standing in the wings, yelled at the police to stand aside. He waded in with an uppercut to the guy's jaw, and broke his hand. This was one of our wildest concerts ever, and locals confirmed it as Zurich's worst display of mass vandalism.

As we endured that brawl, Marianne was venturing out as an actress, at London's Royal Court Theatre, playing Irina in a production of Chekhov's *Three Sisters*. Mick had sent flowers to her dressing-room. He could have used some himself after the concert.

After a concert in The Hague, in the Netherlands, mild compared with the Zurich débâcle, we returned to London en route to Greece for the finale of this tour. I phoned Diane in South Africa for permission to take Stephen out of the country; she agreed and Astrid, Stephen and I flew to Athens on April 16, where airport press photographers took the first pictures of the three of us together. At the Athens Hilton we met up with the rest of the lads—all except Brian, who stayed back in London for a doctor's appointment, lunch at the Alvaro and a night at the Speakeasy before flying in to join us next day. In our hotel suite Stephen played on the balcony with his toy cars and I took many photos of him and the view of the city.

The stage for our show on April 17 was set up in the center of the pitch at the Panathinaikos football stadium; the crowd, who were in the regular seating and not allowed on to the pitch itself, were consequently a long way from the stage. Cordons of police were stationed around the stage and everywhere else: here were shades of Poland, as police restrained their enthusiasm, often with the unnecessary use of batons. Towards the end of the show Mick had planned to distribute red carnations among the fans, but the police would not allow him to leave the stage. Instead, we got Tom Keylock to run across the field to do the honors. He was immediately pounced on by half a dozen police who dragged him back to the stage area. Furious, we stopped playing and the show ended. When the Greek promoter announced the show was over, there was pandemonium. We returned to the hotel in an angry mood yet again over brutality, but the reasons for this became apparent to us a few days later when, in a military coup, the royal family of Greece was overthrown. At the airport next day the boys were hassled by customs, who thought they were trying to take out of the country money we earned from the concert. They explained that our agent always took care of that: Charlie had £1, Mick had £10, Brian had nothing. Keith, whom they suspected most, was held up for an hour, missed the plane and had to take the next one home.

Astrid, Stephen, Glyn Johns and I stayed in Athens for a short holiday.

When Glyn returned to London, Astrid, Stephen and I checked out of the hotel and were driven out to Glyfada, where we settled into our own beach-house at the Astir Beach Hotel.

Our idyll was shattered two days later by the sound of gunfire coming from across the bay in Athens. I called the Greek promoter's office to be told that troops had occupied government buildings. I was warned that a 6 p.m. curfew had been imposed for tonight and that under no circumstances should we leave the beach-house after that time. All contact with the outside world had been cut and we could make no contact with the Stones office by phone, telegram or letter. We just had to wait until the situation was resolved and try to continue to enjoy the short holiday until the airport was reopened for commercial flights.

Meanwhile, in Britain, Brian decided on a break. With Linda Keith he was driven by his new chauffeur Brian Palastanga to the Lygon Arms Hotel in Broadway, near Worcester. Brian and Linda checked in, awaiting the arrival of Robert Fraser.

For four nights, Brian and Linda continually reserved rooms for their expected guest, who never showed (an indication of Brian's isolation around this time). Finally, a telegram from Brian to Stephanie Bluestone in our accountant's office said: "A thousand apologies. Had trouble with car. Cannot possibly get back in time. This is quite genuine and not a product of my ingenuity. Love, Brian." The Rolls-Royce was under repair in Cheltenham and Brian was stranded again, the story of his life.

In Greece we were finally "cleared for departure" by the promoter, who told us on Sunday, April 23, that the military coup had been resolved. Astrid, Stephen and I went straight to the reopened airport to find it swarming with military personnel. Before we reached immigration I was approached by British newsreel crews who begged me to take reels of film back to London for the BBC. It was lucky I refused: immigration searched us thoroughly and we had to declare every penny we had: which was only £30 between us. All our Greek money was confiscated.

After the troubles in Warsaw, Zurich and Athens, we were glad to settle back into Britain, even with the big court case on the horizon. In an interview with *Melody Maker* on our return, Mick was heavily "down" on touring generally, and declared that we would "never tour America again!"

10

(Drug) Trials and
Tribulations

An incredible four-way tug-of-love now enveloped the
Stones. Brian attempted to harmonize and repair his relationship with the guy who had stolen his woman. Keith
had retained his London flat at St. John's Wood, but
Redlands was, as a home, the great love of his life and
remains so today. Brian frequently visited him there shortly
after his traumatic loss of Anita, romantically believing
that she would return to him. But then, Brian was a dreamer.

Keith, too, now strove to encourage an atmosphere of
co-existence with Brian, whatever the difficulties. They
went shopping together for velvet suits at the Hung On
You boutique. Nobody was under any illusion that Linda
Keith, though temporarily with Brian, was not sore at
her loss of Keith. She tried to get him back and failed.

At the beginning of May, Keith and Anita flew to
France, first to Paris then on to Cannes. While Astrid
and I set off on a driving holiday around East Anglia
(with only £40 in my bank account), Brian went back to
Harley Street for a consultation, tests and a cardiograph.
He was not in the best shape but nothing would prevent
him from going to Cannes to see *A Degree of Murder*,
launched as Germany's entry in the film festival.

Checking into the same hotel as Keith and Anita,
Brian decided on a final attempt at a reconciliation with
Anita. Keith stayed in his room, deciding to let them
fight it out. Brian failed to get her to change her mind
and after the film première flew back to London alone,
while Keith and Anita remained for a few days longer.

Back in London, resuming the rounds of the Alvaro,
the Bag o' Nails and the Speakeasy, Brian played the
field with women. Two girls named Nikki and Tina moved
into his Courtfield Road home and he introduced an-

other friend, Nico, to the American cult group Velvet Underground; she became their singer. Interestingly, Brian often chose girls who looked like himself: first Anita, then Nico, bore uncanny facial similarities to his own often doleful expression.

Brian was a "very screwed-up boy with a major personality problem," according to Gered Mankowitz. And yet, despite frequently being completely stoned, Brian could still often stun everyone with his instrumental prowess. "Once," recalled Mankowitz, "he was in such an awful state in the Olympic studio, falling into his food. He had to play a little recorder part. In a little side booth where they did the vocals, he was propped up with chairs so that he couldn't fall over. But he played, and did so very well. He was a natural musician who could play almost anything."

And so, with Brian cast aside first by the Stones he created and then by Anita, and with his health a continual worry, his slide was unstoppable. Keith remarked that he had always been wary of taking Anita because bad vibes were bound to ensure—but that both he and Anita believed she needed "rescuing" rather than stealing, since Brian was such a threat to her. One thing is certain: Anita's "defection," as Brian always saw it after her final decision in Cannes, had a cataclysmic effect on Brian and, by consequence, on the band's future.

Whatever noises of superficial comfort and friendship Keith extended towards Brian, their rapport from the Edith Grove days had long disappeared, and Keith's fundamental antipathy towards him is *not* a figment of my imagination; nor does my memory play tricks. As recently as October 1988, Keith stated in an interview with London's *Q* magazine: "I don't think honestly that you'll find anyone who liked Brian. He had so many hang-ups, he was unreliable, he wanted to be a star. I admired his grit and determination . . . listen, I'm being honest, right? I could say: Oh yeah, Brian, lovely guy. But I'm being honest and he had so many hang-ups he didn't know where to hang himself. So he drowned himself.

"There was extra hassles between Brian and me because I took his old lady. You know, he enjoyed beating chicks up. Not a likeable guy. And we all tried at certain times to get on with him but then he'd shit on you."

Brian certainly had other critics, like Kathy Etchingham (who lived with Jimi Hendrix for two years): "Brian did some bloody evil things to me. We went to this party together and he told me the drinks were in the garage. He didn't tell me there was a big hole in the floor. I went marching in there and went straight into it. I had no skin on my knees and elbows. He was behind me and had brought a few friends to watch. He thought it was very, very funny.

"Anytime he wanted to get rid of a chick, he just called me up and said: 'Come over, and we'll have a laugh.' I would go upstairs with him and we would sit in his bedroom and talk for thirty minutes, and leave them downstairs alone. He would walk back downstairs and say: 'It's about time you left, isn't it?' One time I went over there after he called, and he was in bed with two chicks. He just threw their clothes on the bed and said: 'Do you mind leaving?' "

My life and Charlie's continued to be well structured, compared with the turbulence surrounding those of Mick, Keith and Brian. We'd long realized that our lives had to go on beyond the Stones if we wanted to retain our sanity. With Peter Gosling of the group Moon's Train, I formed Merlin Music for our joint songwriting efforts, while Charlie had on April 4, 1967, bought a new house for £26,000. Peckhams, at Halland, near Lewes, not far from his first house, was a beautiful six-bedroom property with a staff flat and cottage plus a swimming-pool, farm buildings and thirty-four acres of land.

Preparation for the Redlands bust trial was, by Stones standards, well organized. Keith returned from the South of France on May 9, while Anita flew off to Germany. He met up with Mick for lunch at that quintessentially English restaurant, Simpsons, where they discussed the next day's court hearing before going to Redlands to stay the night.

In the morning Leslie Perrin, who was being paid 50 guineas a week to achieve the impossible—get the Stones a good press—arrived at Redlands to discuss a day that promised a massive focus of public attention. Extra police had been called to the court-house at Chichester, West Sussex, to cope with the two coachloads of Stones fans expected from London. Police used walkie-talkies and guarded the back of the building. The doors to the first-floor forty-two-seat public gallery were closed half-an-hour before the case began.

When Mick and Keith arrived at the court in a red minicab, there was only a small crowd waiting. Mick was wearing a green jacket, white shirt and dark gray floral tie; Keith, a navy-blue jacket and pink tie; Robert Fraser, a light gray suit. It was a warm sunny morning and outside some long-haired youths, carrying a card inscribed "Legalize marijuana," squatted on the court-house steps.

The three then attended the court hearing with Mr. Basil Shippam as chairman. Mick, Keith and Robert Fraser stood in the front row of what was normally the jury box. Keith was accused of permitting Redlands to be used for the purpose of smoking cannabis resin. Mick faced a summons of being in unauthorized possession of four tablets of amphetamine sulphate and methyl amphetamine hydrochloride. Robert Fraser was accused of being in unauthorized possession of a dangerous drug— heroin—contrary to the Dangerous Drugs Act, 1965, and of a second summons accusing him of having in his possession eight capsules of methyl amphetamine hydrochloride contrary to the Drugs (Prevention of Misuse) Act, 1964.

When the court adjourned for lunch, Mick and Keith came out of court to a crowd of about 600 youngsters and housewives. There were screams, cheers and even boos. Miniskirted girls grabbed at Mick's hair and coat. Half a dozen policemen helped them to reach their car amid outbursts of cheering and abortive attempts to obtain autographs. They then all went to a Chichester hotel for lunch.

The court hearing reconvened after lunch. Mr. Anthony McCowan (prosecuting) said that a pharmaceutical chemist would say that the two substances in the tablets in the phial belonging to Mick were not available in Britain. The only question was whether the drug was obtained on a prescription from a qualified medical practitioner.

Mr. McCowan then said there was the clearest indication that somebody had been smoking Indian hemp in Keith's house. It was suggested that incense might have been used to mask the smell of smoke. On a drawing-room table was a deposit found to contain cannabis resin. Analysis showed that ash found beside a bedside table in a pudding basin with three cigarette ends also contained that substance.

He went on to say that the white tablets found in Robert's trouser pocket were found to be a preparation containing heroin, and the capsules methyl amphetamine hydrochloride.

Of the substances found in the possession of David Schneiderman (not named at this time) the ball contained 150 grains of cannabis resin, the envelope some 13 grains, and the tin 66 grains.

All three were sent for trial at West Sussex Quarter Sessions on June 22, after electing for trial by jury, and were released on £100 bail.

When the hearing ended, Mick and Keith had to dodge a hundred waiting fans by being smuggled out of the back door of the court and driven back to Redlands.

In the evening, Keith was driven to London airport, and then flew to Paris for a week. "There is nothing to stop me traveling around," he said. "I'll probably be going in and out of the country about ten times before the court case on June 22."

Was Brian simply jinxed or did he live the kind of life that would always attract trouble? Between the period of the Redlands bust and the first court hearing, Brian had been warned that he could be next, that the police were out to "get" the Stones. As the Beatles had become part of the Establishment, they were considered safe from police harassment. The Stones were, however, still bad news. To bust a Beatle would be to squash the dreams of millions of adults as well as their children. But to bust a Rolling Stone was OK—most parents hated us anyway.

While Mick, Keith and Robert awaited their fate, Brian was busted at 4 p.m. that same day, May 10, at his Courtfield Road flat, along with twenty-four-year-old Prince Stanislaus Klossowski de Rola—"Stash"—who frequently stayed with him. The police had already got Mick and Keith and they wanted to bust another one and dispatch the Stones for good—that's what the lawyers seemed to indicate.

Stash recalls that they were asleep when the police arrived: "We had been up late the night before. The doorbell kept buzzing and finally there was a man saying: 'Open the door.' We hung up the intercom-phone, thinking they were reporters wanting to interview Brian over the Chichester trial. It was a million miles from our thoughts that it could be the police. But it was.

" 'I'm afraid,' they said very politely, 'we have a warrant to search these premises for drugs.' About twelve detectives entered the flat and for forty minutes searched the place thoroughly.

"Brian came to see what all the commotion was about. In the next minute, they'd flipped Brian's mattress on the floor and with a smile of triumph produced a purple leather wallet. Inside was this ridiculous grass. My first thought was: 'Who is the stupid chick who's left this here?' There were always girls in and out and I felt we were getting busted for some girl. But none of us ever knew how it got there."

Brian, asked if he had any drugs, on prescription or otherwise, said: "I suffer from asthma. The only drugs I have are for that." But the police found eleven objects, including two metal canisters, two pipes, two cigarette ends and a chair castor obviously used as an ashtray. The total number of grains, whether of cannabis or cannabis resin, would have made between seven and ten cigarettes. Brian was shown the items by detectives, and a phial bearing traces of cocaine.

Brian said: "Yes, it is hash. We do smoke. But not the cocaine, man. That is not my scene. No man, no man. I am not a junkie. That is not mine at all."

Brian then left the house with detectives either side of him. The rest of the squad followed. Brian and Stash sat in the back of a police car to be driven to Kensington police station. Stash says: "There, where the TV news cameramen were already in position, amid autograph signing and joking with the cops, we were told to stand up and shut up and listen to the charges." Brian and Stash were charged under the Dangerous Drugs Act with unlawful possession of approximately 50 grains of cannabis resin. They were released on bail, both to appear at West London Magistrates' Court next day.

"The reporters had got Brian's chauffeur to take his Rolls right outside the door, but we slipped out of the back into a taxi and went to the Hilton Hotel," says

Stash. "There, in Allen Klein's suite, we saw ourselves on the news. When the Hilton Hotel management found out who we were they wanted to kick us out, but Klein insisted we stay, saying he spent a fantastic sum at the hotel and he would make a stink if we were ejected!"

Brian did not return to his flat. Instead, typically, he joined four friends and went to the Odeon Cinema, Marble Arch. "We never returned to Courtfield Road, except to collect some things," Stash says. "Brian and I stayed together for two or three nights before the lawyers insisted we split up. Until then, the bust was an amusing game for Brian but it then turned sour when he was deprived of his friends. The lawyers and the police gave Brian the horrors, as he called it; they worried him, and he became very depressed. 'Look, they're too strong for us,' he said, defeatedly."

Brian and Stash were driven to West London Magistrates' Court the next day in Brian's silver-gray Rolls-Royce. Outside the courtroom a crowd of a hundred including several shopgirls and girls in school blazers waited. Police guarded the entrance to the court as the crowd surged round the car. They were smuggled into court via a back door an hour before the hearing, Brian as dandy as ever in a navy-blue mod suit with bell-bottom trousers and flared jacket, large, floppy blue-and-white-spotted tie and Cuban-heeled shoes.

The hearing took three minutes, during which time neither Brian nor Stash spoke. Detective-Sergeant Norman Pilcher of Scotland Yard's drugs squad said: "There is a large amount of property taken away from these premises, all of which has to be analyzed by a laboratory. I ask for as long a remand as possible."

Brian and Stash were remanded on £250 bail each, and the case was adjourned until June 2; they elected to go for trial by jury. Brian immediately sent a telegram to his parents in Cheltenham: "Please don't worry. Don't jump to nasty conclusions, and don't judge me too harshly. All my love."

By the time Brian and Stash left the court, a crowd of 150 had collected outside, and police had to force a way for them to get to their car.

There followed a period when Brian could not bring himself to speak to Keith. Such was the aura of trouble around all of us at this time that the Brian–Keith coldness became strangely "official." Brian's lawyers told him not to have contact with any of the Stones during this period.

It would be six months before Brian's fate was decided by the courts, an interminable and intolerable stretch for such a worrier. Brian might have survived this black period with the comfort and love of his new girlfriend, Suki Potier, and his other friends, but the worry of the bust and another major factor combined to accelerate his descent. Stash believes the bust and the drug-taking which—ironically—it induced in Brian, caused his decline, rather than the loss of Anita.

"An American guy latched on to Brian and introduced him to Mandrax, which are downers, and he became a pill-head and there was an utter transformation in his behavior. And Brian's decline began as a result of that court case, because he wouldn't have been under such amazing stress, and wouldn't have taken these tranquillizers if he had not been made paranoid and alienated from his friends.

"The lawyers drove us all apart. I remember Mick asking where Brian was, and I said he'd been told not to hang out with us. He began to hang around with a horrible group of people who leeched off him and he decayed, physically, mentally and musically. Then Brian would turn to me and ask: 'What are the *Stones* doing?' He almost didn't consider himself a Stone anymore. I saw him in the studio, incapable of playing. Then I knew the end had come. Because normally Brian's musicianship in the studio was such that he would know if a note was a quarter-tone out of true . . .

"Brian was haunted by the fear of going to jail. They dropped the charge against me and Brian was persuaded to plead guilty to a lesser charge—plea-bargaining. I said, 'Please, Brian, forget the plea-bargain, plead Not Guilty, because you're *not* guilty.' But it was impossible to talk him out of pleading guilty."

Twelve days after his arrest, twelve drug squad detectives with a dog raided Dandie Fashions, a boutique used by us and the Beatles. A coincidence, or just police routine? Girls were told to empty their handbags and men their pockets. Dandie Fashions had been half owned by Tara Browne, Brian's friend who had died in December 1966.

The pressures mounting around us might have been easier to endure if our business affairs had been more straightforwardly managed. We were always described as millionaires, a word still irritatingly inaccurate. A telex on May 23 from Laurence Myers to Klein said: "You must deal with Bill's exchange-control problem as a matter of utmost urgency." Money was harder and harder to get from his office in New York. Apart from our yearly guarantees from the record companies, there were no regular payments to us. Most bills going into the Stones office were left unpaid for three months or more. I found this embarrassing and wrote my own checks from home. The rest of the boys didn't seem to care, and bills like their rents for houses and flats, plus service payments for such items as dry cleaning, chauffeurs and flowers, went unpaid for long periods. For a band at our level, it was chaotic.

It infuriated me that many personal expenses of all kinds incurred by Brian, Keith, Mick and Charlie were being paid by petty-cash from the office. Such things as medicine, taxis, cash payments of amounts of around £50, theater tickets, domestic house items and things for their relatives were charged as Stones expenses but were nothing whatsoever to do with the group collectively.

Annoyance over money even got to the normally unflappable Charlie who telexed Klein tersely on June 5: "What has happened to the money for my house?" Our accountant Laurence Myers followed this up with a reminder that Charlie had still not received money, adding: "Please confirm that it has been sent. I would like to talk to you and would be grateful if you could phone me." Three days later, Myers again telexed Klein: "I telephoned you last night but you were not available. Joynson-Hicks have pressed me for signed copies of the pledge-holders' agreement. As I have not heard from you in connection with this I am today sending them off. If you are not agreeable please let me know immediately."

On June 1 we all received our £2,500 yearly guarantee payment from Decca Records and more money arrived for me with a convivial note from Klein on June 6, enclosing two checks totaling $11,250, two of my record-guarantee payments. He pointed out that when we delivered the soundtrack of *Only Lovers Left Alive* the guarantee would nearly double, to $2 million. He closed by confirming that my next record-guarantee payment was due in less than two months.

It was all too weird and haphazard to be believed. Allen Klein made a statement to *Melody Maker* at this time that work on *Only Lovers Left Alive* was due to start "pretty soon." He said Mick and Keith would write all the music for the film and refused to comment on the rumor that Mick, rather than the whole group, would star in it. Nor would he say where the film would be made—hardly surprising since it had lain dormant for a year.

The Stones and Anita may have slipped away from Brian but it couldn't be said that he went down without asserting himself. Our sharpest dresser, he had an eye for current fashion (essential in the hippie period) and spent a small fortune at boutiques. Collecting clothes might have been his kind of therapy, as he shopped more frequently during times of stress: the day after his court case was adjourned he went to Chelsea Antique Market for a spree typical in its list of exotic purchases: a mandarin coat, a pink fringed coat, pink velvet cape, a flannel-and-lace jacket, embroidered and velvet jackets, two velvet scarves, four pairs of trousers, two kimonos and two scarves, two strings of bells, a blouse and a pink beaded belt. In New York, too, Brian had indulged himself in expeditions to the ladies jewelry departments of such stores as Saks Fifth Avenue and Bergdorf Goodman. A New York journalist friend commented: "If he gave nothing else to the world, Brian was the first heterosexual male to start wearing costume jewelry from Saks Fifth Avenue."

In the run-up to the court trials, we virtually dispersed, apart from recording one song: Mick, Keith and Brian had been warmed by the sympathetic messages from fans anxious about the crackdown on them and Mick and Keith wrote a song by way of thanks. Before the trials we went into the Olympic studios on June 12 and 13 to record "We Love You," produced by Andrew. In July John Lennon and Paul McCartney overdubbed back-up vocals as a gesture of support, and another sound-effect was added after the trial: the sound of a prison door being slammed. The record was released after the out-come of the Redlands case.*

On an impulse, Brian went to the historic Monterey Festival in California, looking dazzling as he mingled with the hippies in a gold lamé coat festooned with beads, a crystal swastika and lace. With the actor Dennis Hopper he took LSD there and when he returned, enthusing about the performance of Jimi Hendrix, the adventurer in him was bubbling. He visited a property called Aston Somerville Hall, near Broadway in Worcestershire. Ten miles north of his home town of Cheltenham, the £12,500 house attracted Brian because, he explained, "I was born and bred in the Cotswolds and would like to live there again." But nothing came of this.

It was holiday time in mid-June: Keith and Anita flew to Paris, while Mick, Marianne, son Nicholas and nanny flew to Tangier. Astrid and I went on a driving holiday in the West Country, Wales and Snowdonia during this period when the Stones activity went on hold as we all braced ourselves for the court cases.

Ruby Tuesday, June 27, 1967: Mick, Keith and Robert

---

*The interaction between the Stones and the Beatles was always friendly, particularly since Mick and Keith and John and Paul had all embraced a hippie philosophy. In mid-June Brian played tenor sax on a Beatles recording session of the song "You Know My Name (Look Up the Number)." Beatles experts have for twenty years been uncertain of whether it was the Stones' Brian or another Brian Jones (of the Liverpool group the Undertakers) on the record. I can confirm categorically that it was our Brian: he said so. Paul McCartney remembers asking Brian to a Beatles session at Abbey Road in June, 1967: "To our surprise he brought along a sax. I remember him turning up in this big Afghan coat at Abbey Road and he opened up a sax case and we said, 'We've got a little track here,' and so he played sax on it. It was a crazy record, a sort of B-side . . . it's a funny sax solo—it isn't amazingly well played but it happened to be ex-actly what we wanted, a ropey sax, kind of shaky. Brian was very good like that."

On the same day they returned from a break in Tangier, Mick and Marianne joined Brian in appearing on the Beatles "All You Need Is Love" live satellite-TV telecast, *Our World*, broad-cast on July 7.

Fraser were driven by Tom Keylock in Keith's Bentley from Redlands to a secret rendezvous with a police car. They arrived at the courthouse in Chichester by a back entrance, three-quarters of an hour before their hearing at West Sussex quarter sessions. About fifty people, mostly teenagers, were waiting. Police were out in force but there was no screaming welcome.

The front row of the public gallery contained several teenagers, and was full. Mick and Keith looked unconcerned as they sat in the large dock with Robert Fraser, Mick chatting amiably with the prison officer beside him. Robert had pleaded guilty to possessing heroin tablets, not guilty to possessing other tablets; Keith and Mick both pleaded not guilty to the charges against them. Robert was the first to go on trial.

Mr. Morris (prosecuting) said he had today seen a prescription made out in January by a Dr. Greenburg for the capsules, known by their commercial name, Desbutal, and he wanted the charge to remain on file and not be dealt with.

Mr. Denny (Defending) in mitigation, said that Fraser had opened his own art gallery in Mayfair five years ago, and it was an outstanding success. This was not obtained without hard work, and it may be because of this that he was more prone to the temptation that was put before him. A person employed at the gallery had offered him heroin tablets about twelve months ago. Fraser was not a drug-taker, but accepted because he believed he would be able to stop. After a comparatively short time he found that he was hooked. At no time did he supply or sell or give any other person any quantity of heroin.

Detective-Sergeant Stanley Cudmore said that in November 1966 at Marlborough Street Court, Fraser had been fined £20 and ordered to pay £50 costs, for willfully exposing, or causing to be exposed to public view, an indecent exhibition of paintings.

Mr. Denny (Defending) said: "Fraser staged a complete exhibition of the works of a famous American artist named Jim Dine at the art gallery of which he is founder and director. Some of this work was in the Tate Gallery and other galleries, but Fraser decided to give coverage to all his work. Certain exhibits offended against the Vagrancy Act. It is not uncommon these days for people possessing 'hard' drugs such as heroin to be work-shy, spineless individuals who wandered about and were delinquent. I am anxious that the court should be disabused of any such idea in the case of Fraser. Because his record shows him to be a person of quite the contrary qualities, with no little ability, some considerable spirit, and indeed courage which has shown itself in his life."

Dr. John Craigmore said that, as well as being an ordinary medical practitioner, he assisted people addicted to alcohol or drugs. He had prepared a report on Fraser which he handed to the judge. Dr. Craigmore said that nine days after the raid by police at Redlands, Fraser came to him for a cure. After traumatic treatment he relapsed and took heroin again. But once more he had the strength to telephone the doctor and ask for assistance. "At the moment he is cured of his addiction and there is no reason why he should go back to the addiction," said Dr. Craigmore.

Fraser was found guilty of illegally possessing twenty-four heroin tablets, and was remanded in custody, and later spent the night in Lewes Prison with Mick. Judge Block said he would not pass sentence until the cases of Mick and Keith had been heard.

After adjourning for lunch, Mick went on trial.

Mr. Michael Ansell (Scientific officer at Metropolitan Police Lab) said that tablets sent him by West Sussex Police contained substances known during the war as Benzedrine, nowadays prescribed for slimming.

Mr. Havers (Defending) showed Mr. Ansell a cardboard packet and a pamphlet in Italian which he agreed appeared to go with the phial. Mr. Ansell said that he had had to use three of the tablets in his analysis partly because they were so small and partly because they were unusual.

Mr. Louis Priest (Administrative assistant on the staff of the Pharmaceutical Society of Great Britain and a specialist on poison and drugs) was shown the packet and pamphlet by the Defense. He said that roughly translated the pamphlet said that the drug could be used for tiredness, physical exhaustion, convalescence, travel sickness and heights. The dosage was one to four tablets a day. Mr. Havers said the pills were also used for carsickness, sea-sickness, hayfever and even asthma.

Mr. Morris (Prosecuting): "It appears from the phial that they emanated in Milan, having the word Milano, Italian for Milan, on the label. These two drugs are not found together in any substance manufactured in this country, so far as our analysts know."

Dr. Raymond Dixon Firth said he had been Mick's doctor since July 1965, when Mick had gone to him for a complete medical check-up. Mick had since consulted him from time to time. He recollected the conversation with Mick sometime at the beginning of the year when he was told that during a period abroad he was given some tablets called Italian pep pills of the Benzedrine type. He was asked by Mick whether they were all right and he said yes, in an emergency, but not to be taken regularly.

Dr. Firth was asked: "From your point of view was he properly in possession of them?" He replied: "Certainly."

Mr. Havers submitted that Dr. Firth's verbal agreement to Mick about taking the pills amounted, legally, to issuing a prescription.

Judge Block ruled: "I have no hesitation whatever in saying that the evidence given by Dr. Firth does not in law amount to the issue of a prescription by a qualified practitioner."

Mr. Havers asked for an adjournment to consider whether he should address the jury before they retired. Returning to court, he announced he had decided not to, and the judge immediately began his summing up. Judge Block said: "The defense that is open to Mr. Jagger is that he was in possession of a prescription issued by a qualified medical practitioner. So really as a matter of law, I have to direct you to say there is no defense to the charge and ask you to retire and consider your verdict."

The all-male jury took only six minutes to return their verdict: guilty of illegal possession of four tablets containing two drug substances without authority.

Mr. Havers said: "Sometimes I wonder if all of us in this court are not too old to try this case." He then asked for a certificate to appeal on a point of law. Mick was remanded to Lewes Prison overnight. He traveled the thirty-seven miles there in the prison van with Robert Fraser and four other men. When it swung through Lewes Jail gates just on 7 p.m., he was taken to the remand wing and allowed to see his solicitors. They took him three books and a sweater. Mick asked for forty Benson and Hedges cigarettes. His request for an electric razor was refused because the prison provided razors. He was offered an evening meal before lights went out at 10 p.m. Later, after the time for lights out, a jigsaw puzzle was sent in to him.

Mick and Robert Fraser were woken up at 7 a.m. the following day and ate breakfast alone in their cells. When they arrived in court before the hearing, they were handcuffed. They waited in a cell beneath the courtroom while the trial went on.

Marianne, who had just finished her run at the Royal Court Theatre, arrived in Chichester early in the morning, entering the courthouse by a rear entrance to avoid a crowd of about a hundred teenagers. She failed to see Mick before the hearing but was told she could see him afterwards.

Mr. Morris said a young woman [Marianne Faithfull], naked except for a fur-skin rug, was sitting between two men on a sofa facing the fireplace. Between the sofa and the fireplace was a stone table. On it was a tin marked Incense. A briar pipe-bowl on the table was taken away and its contents analyzed. They were found to contain traces of cannabis resin. On that same table was some ash which was also analyzed and found to contain Indian hemp. In one of the first-floor bedrooms there was a pudding basin containing three cigarette ends and ash also found to contain cannabis.

Mr. Morris said: "Also in the drawing-room was a man, not before the court, and not now in this country whom I shall call Mr. X. He was searched and in his right-hand pocket was a tin containing two pieces of a brown substance which was analyzed and contained no less than 66 grains of cannabis resin. In another pocket was an envelope containing herbal cannabis and a substantial ball of brown substance which turned out to be 150 grains of cannabis resin. There was a pipe containing traces of cannabis resin. In all this man had very large supplies. A warrant was issued for his arrest on February 13 or 14, but he left the country on the 14th." Judge Block: "I understand this man did a quick bunk to Canada."

Detective Woman Constable Rosemary Slade said that

when she first went into the house, she saw a young woman sitting on a settee in the nude. The young woman let the rug fall from time to time, exposing her body.

Detective Woman Constable Evelyn Fuller said: "The woman was in a merry mood and one of vague unconcern."

Mr. Morris said the only significance of this young lady's behavior was that when the police arrived she remained unperturbed, apparently enjoying the situation. He alleged this was because she was smoking hemp.

Detective Woman Constable Fuller continued: "When the rug fell to the ground, she remarked, 'Look, they want to search me.'"

Mr. Havers said: " She is well-known to many. Her name is bandied around in Fleet Street. Her name has been blackened in a way that could affect her career."

Mr. Morris said: "She went upstairs to where her clothes were and was searched. When she returned she was still wearing only that rug."

Sergeant John Challon said: "She was taken upstairs and when she got to the bedroom door, she allowed the rug to fall to the ground. She had nothing on. I heard a laugh from a man in the bedroom who was using the phone. I saw her naked back."

Mr. Havers asked if it was a big rug. "Quite large," said Sergeant Cudmore. "Was it bigger than a fur coat?" "Yes," the Detective said. Mr. Havers said: "But it's a bed cover, isn't it? Six feet square. Take a look." And he stretched it out across the barristers' benches.

When the court adjourned for lunch, Keith left in his Bentley and a group of young schoolgirls ran after the car screaming. At a local hotel, he had lunch with his legal advisers. Marianne was having lunch there too but in accordance with the court's ruling they did not speak. Mick and Robert Fraser, still in the cells under the courthouse, had lunch sent in from the Globe Hotel. The meal was itemized on TV: for Mick prawn cocktail, roast lamb, strawberries and cream, while Robert had iced melon, fresh salmon and salad, and strawberries. They shared a bottle of Beaujolais. (Regulations said that prisoners on remand cannot have more than half a bottle of wine.)

While Keith's trial was going on, Chelsea police were called out to Brian's flat, on a false alarm. In his fur-collared dressing-gown, Brian went out on to the balcony at his Courtfield Road flat after police had broken in. Earlier the police had received a dramatic hoax message that the guitarist had been taken ill and an ambulance was called. Brian said he was looking for another flat because of similar annoyances recently.

The trial then reconvened.

Mr. Havers asked Detective-Sergeant Stanley Cudmore: "Was your source a well-known national newspaper?"

Sergeant Cudmore: "Yes, sir."

Mr. Havers: "A well-known national newspaper gave information which led to the raid at Redlands. Who tipped off the paper? When you hear which paper it is suggested it is, you may find difficulty in accepting them as well-known guardians of the public morals of this country. The week before the raid, it published an article. The consequences were a writ for libel served upon the *News of the World.* In the remaining five days, Mr. Jagger was subjected to being followed wherever he went or whatever he did. A van or car was constantly outside his flat. Can you think of any better way to kill off the ensuing libel action? Schneiderman was at the party loaded to the gunwhales with cannabis resin, the only man at the party found to have cannabis on him, but when the charges were made, he had gone. With a girl in this alleged euphoric state, you might expect to find cannabis ash everywhere, but this was not found. Was the girl high on cannabis? I wonder if the jury has stopped to consider that the story of the girl's movements was given so that they could draw the inference she was smoking cannabis. She is not on trial. She is a girl who remains technically anonymous, and I hope she will remain anonymous. She is described as a drug-taking nymphomaniac with no chance of saying anything in her defense. Do you expect me to force that girl to go into the witness-box with no chance to refute the allegations? I am not going to tear the blanket aside and subject her to laughter and scorn. If I can't call the girl, and Mr. Richards is in agreement with this, I will not call anyone else."

The court was then adjourned for the day. Marianne was taken down a flight of stairs to the cells where she spent twelve minutes with Mick who was awaiting an escort back to Lewes Prison for his second night in custody. She gave him newspapers, magazines, fresh fruit, a game of draughts, sixty cigarettes and a science-fiction book. Later she slipped away in a friend's car and was driven to Redlands.

Michael Cooper also visited Mick, smuggling in a miniature camera to photograph him for possible use on the next album cover, although later he said that police had confiscated his film after he took a picture of Mick through the door of his cell. Keith also went down to the cells to see him for a few minutes. Mick was taken back to Lewes Prison in a van, handcuffed to a prison officer. A Home Office official said: "It is up to the police to decide if a person should be handcuffed."

The *London Evening Standard* echoed many people's views when it wrote: "The rather grim scenes of Jagger and Fraser appearing handcuffed together are surely an unnecessary humiliation. Are the two really considered dangerous criminals liable to make trouble unless they are manacled? To the public it must seem, in this case, an act of unnecessary harshness."

On the third day of the trial Keith stepped into the witness-box, to give evidence in his own defense.

Keith said: "I left school in the summer of 1962. Success has meant a complete lack of privacy from 1963 onwards, and continual work for four years. I need an army to maintain privacy. In my private life, whether in my flat or my house, I'm never left alone. I'm often recognized when out walking, and find it necessary to employ a security man [Tom Keylock]. I've traveled in very many countries, and at parties and other functions, and I've met thousands of people. It was in such a way that I met David Henry Schneiderman in New York about a year ago, but only for five minutes. The next time I met him was in London, a week before the raid on my house. This was completely by chance, as far as I was concerned. He was on his own at the time, and I met him at a club. I hadn't visited Redlands for some weeks before the raid."

Mr. Havers said: "How did this party at Redlands come about?"

Keith said: "It was suggested to me a week previously by a friend. I agreed, and then completely forgot about it."

After giving details of the events leading up to and

including the drugs bust, Keith was asked if he had a liking for incense.

Keith: "I picked up the habit of using incense from fans, who have sent me joss sticks over the past three years. I like the smell of incense being burned."

Keith was asked if there was anything sinister attached to the burning of it by him, and was it done to cover up the smell of cannabis?

Keith: "No, sir."

Keith was then shown a briar pipe with no stem, which the prosecution alleged had contained cannabis resin. Keith said he got it from an American tour manager in Los Angeles. Keith said: "On a trip like that, one gets a mountain of stuff. My suitcases when I get back are full of the stuff. When I opened my suitcase, the pipe must have just been left lying around the place."

Mr. Havers said: "Does that demonstrate that in your house, when things are put down, they stay there. They are left?"

Keith: "They do, sir."

Keith was then asked about a basin in which cigarette ends and ash, alleged to have contained cannabis resin, were found.

Keith: "We didn't have a lot of ashtrays. I had no knowledge whatsoever that cannabis was smoked, and in no way did I permit it."

Mr. Havers said: "Had you any knowledge that during the weekend cannabis resin had been smoked?"

Keith: "None whatsoever."

Mr. Havers: "Did you in any way permit it?"

Keith: "No, sir."

Keith was then cross-examined by Mr. Morris: "Is it part of your defense that Schneiderman had been planted at your weekend party, as part of a wicked conspiracy by the *News of the World*?"

Keith: "Yes, it is."

Mr. Morris said: "Is your defense that Schneiderman was planted by the *News of the World* in order to get Jagger convicted of smoking hashish?"

Keith: "That is the suggestion. I agree it is entirely possible."

Mr. Morris: "Is this what you are saying, that because the *News of the World* did not want to pay libel damages to Jagger, which they might have to pay if what they had published about him was untrue, that they planted or arranged to have planted, Indian hemp at your party?"

Keith: "Yes, sir."

Mr. Morris: "So, if you are seriously suggesting that this was part of a plot, it is a curious plot in that nothing in fact was done to associate Jagger with Indian hemp."

Keith: "He was associated with the whole raid, which is enough, I am sure."

Mr. Morris: "Your suggestion is that that misfired and the only result of that criminal conspiracy is that you are in the dock?"

Keith: "Yes, sir. Strange things happened between the time the writ was served and the party. When I was staying with one of the Stones [meaning Brian] I noticed a brown furniture van with white side-panels. There was no name on the van. The same night I saw it outside Mick's house. In the same week, I was followed by a green florist's van, which had the same white panels."

Asked about the party, Keith said: "Most of the guests at my party were personal friends. There were a number of people there who were hangers-on, and whom we tolerate. On that particular occasion there were two or three of these people whom I did not know particularly well. Two of the guests, including Schneiderman, were in the category of hangers-on. Schneiderman had asked if he could come to the party, and was told that this would be all right."

Mr. Morris: "It is clear from the amount of Indian hemp found on him, and the fact that he had a pipe, that Schneiderman was probably somebody that smoked it."

Keith: "Definitely."

Mr. Morris: "Did you know that?"

Keith: "Not at the time, no."

Mr. Morris: "If he was a friend, you would not expect him to smoke Indian hemp at your house without telling you?"

Keith: "No."

Mr. Morris: "Do any of your friends who were there smoke Indian hemp?

Keith: "Not to my knowledge. After the party I tried to find out more about Schneiderman, but he had left the country two days after the police raid."

Mr. Morris: "There was a warrant for his arrest."

Keith: "I did not know that."

Asked if Schneiderman would have had the opportunity to plant hemp in the house while other guests were not there, Keith said: "It would have been possible."

Mr. Morris asked about the smell that police said they noticed in the house.

Keith said: "It did not strike me as unusual."

Mr. Morris: "Is that truthful? Did you not notice that there was something about it? That it was not just incense?"

Keith repeated his reply.

When Mr. Morris asked if an incense bowl could have been used for sniffing hemp, defense counsel suggested that no one had said that an impact could be got from sniffing it.

Keith said: "Incense was being burned fairly frequently throughout the whole evening. I burned it, and I know others did. Joss sticks were also being burned."

Mr. Morris then asked Keith about the young woman at the party.

Mr. Morris: "Would you agree that in the ordinary course of events you would expect a young woman to be embarrassed if she had nothing on in front of several men?"

Keith: "Not at all. We were not old men and we are not worried about petty morals. She was not under the influence of drink or anything. I wasn't surprised that she did not dress when she went up to the bedroom. As far as I know, she had been upstairs and bathed. She had taken off her dirty clothing because she had been in the country, and had not brought a fresh set of clothes with her. She came downstairs for a cup of tea and was sitting there when police arrived."

Mr. Morris pointed out that in her bedroom there was a white blouse, a brassiere and black velvet trousers that she could have used.

Keith said the girl had taken them off previously.

Mr. Morris: "Did it not come as a great surprise to you that she was prepared to go back downstairs still only wearing a rug in front of ten police officers?"

Keith said: "I thought the rug was big enough to cover

three women. There was nothing improper in the way she was wearing it."

Mr. Morris: "I wasn't talking about impropriety, but embarrassment."

Keith: "She doesn't embarrass easily. Nor do I."

Mr. Morris: "You do not think it was because she had been smoking Indian hemp and it had got rid of her inhibitions and embarrassment?"

Keith: "No, sir."

Mr. Morris: "Throughout the time she was in your presence, did she either deliberately or accidentally let fall the rug?"

Keith: "Absolutely not."

In his closing speech for the prosecution, Mr. Morris said the young lady was anonymous, but the *News of the World* was not. Allegations had been made, and unless they were repeated outside the court, the *News of the World* could not clear itself. There was not a shred of evidence to back up the allegations. He added: "It is important to remember that you are not trying the *News of the World,* as you are not trying the young lady in the rug. You are trying Keith Richards."

In his closing speech for the defense, Mr. Havers referred to prejudice clearly disclosed the previous night in newspapers with headlines like "Jagger Handcuffed on Way to Jail." He added: "The handcuffing is nothing more than Home Office regulations. But it is headlines, and there are headlines today about the fact that a girl went to see him. The curious juxtaposition of these photographs and that piece of information so close to the 'nude girl in Stones' house story' is intended to convey to the public that this is the girl whose name is not disclosed. It must put pressure on you, the jury. Whatever verdict you return there will be people who will criticize you or praise you."

In his summing-up, Judge Block told the jury of eleven men and one woman to put out of their minds any prejudice about Richards' views on "petty morals," and they should not be prejudiced by allegations about the lady who was in some condition of undress. The issue facing them was comparatively simple: "You have to be satisfied cannabis resin was being smoked in the house when the police went there, and you have to be satisfied

Richards knew it. You are trying a man who is well known in the entertainment world and inevitably in circumstances like these there has been an enormous amount of publicity. That situation was to a certain extent exacerbated by an unfortunate remark from a junior minister of the Crown, who referred to this case in detail between the committal proceedings and who now, from what I read of the report, suggested that it was impossible that Richards should have a fair trial because of the publicity attendant upon it.* That gentleman obviously didn't know the qualities of a Sussex jury."

The jury took an hour and five minutes to consider its verdict. They returned and pronounced Keith guilty of knowingly allowing cannabis resin to be smoked at his house.

In a mitigation plea, before Judge Block passed sentence on Mick, Keith and Robert, Mr. Havers urged that the case be approached in proper proportions.

On behalf of Mick, Mr. Havers said that the fact that Jagger was at the house party where cannabis was smoked by some guests should not influence his situation. He had been convicted of possessing only four pills, which were of a type of which no less than 150 million had been prescribed on National Health prescriptions in the last year.

There had been one suggestion that he had been convicted of possessing dangerous drugs, but actually the tablets he had came under the poisons schedule and were not classified as dangerous drugs legally. They were of a type known as the purple heart group, used for slimming purposes, nervous disorders and other purposes by many people, and their use in this connection was justified to

*This was a reference to extensive publicity which followed an assertion by Mr. Dick Taverne, QC, joint parliamentary undersecretary, Home Office, that Mick's and Keith's trial was an example of the need for having some committal proceedings heard in private, as proposed in the new Criminal Justice Bill. Addressing the conference of the Justices' Clerks' Society at Llandudno, Mr. Taverne said: "One cannot anticipate what the outcome of these proceedings will be. But whatever happens elsewhere, can one really say there will be no prejudice in the minds of the public against these defendants, even if they are acquitted?"

the extent of the number of NHS prescriptions. "There must be all the difference in the world between a heroin tablet and these.

"This conviction may well affect his future when it comes to seeking to accept contracts outside Britain. I do not know what the immigration rules in foreign countries are, but one supposes there may be very stringent rules about admitting people convicted of drug offenses. It may have a very grave effect on his future there."

Mr. Havers then made his plea on behalf of Keith, saying that the position was entirely different from that of Jagger. "You must try and form some idea of the sort of man we are dealing with. One sometimes wonders whether one really knows enough in the field of justice. A parent or a schoolmaster who knows a particular child knows very much more than a stranger. It may be, having seen him, that you have gained a view about him that he is a likeable young man who is perhaps very much a man who goes his own way and if his friends are fool enough to smoke cannabis, although he might discourage them, as was shown by the jury's verdict, he did not physically take the cigarette away and throw it in the fire."

Judge Block retired for ten minutes, along with three other West Sussex lay justices, to deliberate before passing sentence. When he returned, Mick and Robert Fraser were led into court to join Keith in the dock to hear their sentences.

Keith was sentenced first: to be jailed for twelve months and ordered to pay £500 towards costs. Keith raised his eyes to the ceiling, then stood down from the dock, pale and silent, as he was led to the cells. Teenagers in the public gallery almost drowned the last words of Judge Block as the sentences were announced rapidly.

Judge Block then called upon Fraser and told him: "In your case you will go to prison for six months and pay £200 costs." The second count against Robert Fraser was not to be proceeded with, but was to remain on file.

Finally it came to Mick, who had gripped the dock rail tensely as the two jail sentences were passed upon his friends. Now alone in the dock, he looked around the court nervously. Mick was jailed for three months and ordered to pay £100. He went pale at the sentence, swayed and almost collapsed, mopped his brow, remained still for a moment, turned, put his fist to his forehead and started to cry. Then he walked at almost a snail's pace, shaking his head in dismay and whistling softly, towards the staircase leading from the dock to the cells. The details of the sentences spread to the 600 outside, and there were yells of "Let them go," "Shame" and "Unfair."

Mick and Keith were granted certificates to appeal against their convictions.

"I'm his agent—I get twenty-five per cent of everything!"

Twenty minutes after they had been sentenced, Marianne, wearing dark glasses and a black trouser suit, arrived at the court in Keith's Bentley. The crowd surged forward. Pale and crying she pushed her way to the double gates guarded by police. She spent fifteen minutes with Mick in his cell, weeping as she left by a rear door, watched by more than 200 people.

The crowd waited two hours to see Mick and Keith driven from the court, and missed them. A police Land Rover emerged from the double gates as a decoy. Mick and Keith, surrounded by about ten police officers, used

Me with my new MGB outside Keston, June 1966

Summer 1966

Far left: Keith outside Redlands

Left: Charlie outside the Old Brewery, Lewes

Right: Brian in his Elm Park Lane flat

Andrew Oldham

Allen Klein

Above and left: In New York on the *Sea Panther* for a press conference, June 1966

Peter Frampton at Pye Studios, London, playing my Vox Mando guitar, 1966

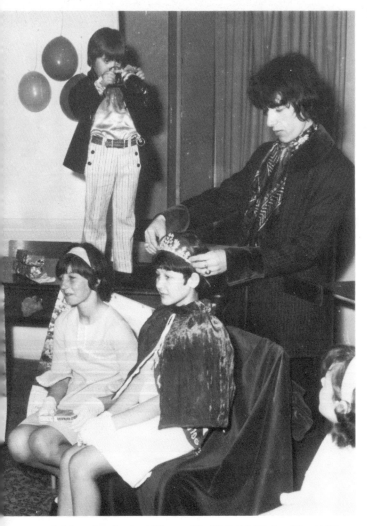

Judging a beauty competition—while Stephen takes the pictures! May 1967

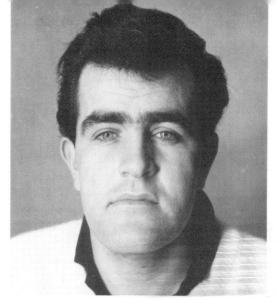

Stu—Ian Stewart, Stones founder member, road manager and friend

Mick and Robert Fraser at Redlands before their court appearances,
June 1967

Brian at the US Embassy in London, 1967, getting a visa before going to New York for the *Their Satanic Majesties* photo session

Me and Keith at the *Satanic Majesties* session

The Rock 'n' Roll Circus rehearsal, Londonderry House Hotel, December 9, 1968: Jimmy Miller and Mick; Brian; me, Keith and Brian

Rock 'n' Roll Circus: *(left to right)* Rocky Dijon, Roger Daltrey, John Entwhistle, Keith Moon, Pete Townshend, John Lennon, Yoko Ono, Keith, Mick, Charlie, Brian, me and Eric Clapton

December 1968: The *Beggars Banquet* press launch—custard pies were worn

Mick and Marianne arriving at court after their drugs bust, May 1969

Right: Astrid at Gedding Hall

Below: Stephen and Astrid in Denmark

Cotchford Farm—Brian's home—from the garden

Above: Brian's funeral, July 1969

Mick Taylor

Charlie, Mick Taylor, Mick Jagger, Keith and me just before our Hyde Park concert

the front entrance. A handful of fans watched them troop dejectedly across the pavement to a police vehicle. Fans wept and cried "We love you" as they saw the car leaving. Mick seemed to be holding back tears while Keith stared stonily ahead, biting his lower lip. Mick was handcuffed to a policeman, and Keith and Robert Fraser were handcuffed together. They were driven to a rendezvous on the outskirts of Chichester, where they were transferred to a prison van with a seven-man crew.

Allen Klein in New York was told by phone of the sentences. The Stones office sent a telegram to Rome to inform Anita of Keith's sentence.

The *Daily Mail* reported next day that: "The £1 million a year empire of pop, second only to the Beatles, is at a temporary halt. Their agents were busy ringing America to cancel a planned tour later this year. They were also anxious about whether the Stones will be allowed into America with a drug conviction against two of them." I assured a reporter that the group would not break up, but added that "unless our record company puts out an old record, we have nothing new in the bag."

That night The Who had an emergency meeting, and decided to record two Jagger–Richards songs immediately as a tribute. Their co-manager Chris Stamp flew back from New York to London to co-produce the session with Kit Lambert. John Entwistle was honeymooning on the *Queen Elizabeth*, and so Pete Townshend over-dubbed the bass parts. They recorded "The Last Time" and "Under My Thumb." The Who announced: "There was no time to consider production or arrangements, and what has emerged is a straightforward and very rough cover version of the two songs."

Kit Lambert said: "It's just a simple gesture and we are not trying to cash in. All royalties will go to charity."

The Who placed a large advert in the *Evening News* and *Evening Standard:*

Special Announcement

The Who consider Mick Jagger and Keith Richards have been treated as scapegoats for the drug problem and as a protest against the grave sentences imposed on them at Chichester yesterday, The Who are issuing today the first of a series of Jagger–Richards songs to

keep their work before the public until they are again
free to record themselves.

More than 200 chanting teenagers protested outside
Fleet Street newspaper offices against the prison sentences, beginning outside the *News of the World* offices.
Long-haired youths and miniskirted girls chanted "Free
the Stones" and "We want love." A placard, carried by
model Kim Kerrigan, Keith Moon's girlfriend, said "Free
Keith."

In a dance hall jammed with teenagers in Bognor Re-
gis, a few miles from the courtroom, the DJ stopped the
music and turned off the flashing lights. He said: "Be
cool for a moment and be serious. Cast your thoughts to
a courtroom where three young men were deprived of
their freedom. Let's have three minutes' silence for some
of the country's finest talent." He then played "The Last
Time."

Brian flew to Rome to confer with Anita while Mick
and Keith's solicitors worked until after midnight to get
their appeal forms completed. These had to be signed in
the two prisons (Brixton and Wormwood Scrubs) to which
Mick and Keith had, respectively, been sent.

Next day, Friday, the newspapers had a field day with
conjecture. The *Daily Mirror* said: "The dreamlike world
of pop music came down to earth when Jagger and Richards swapped their millionaire homes for prison cells.
Each of the Stones is worth at least £250,000 [!!!], so
Jagger and Richards can afford to take a rest. Even an
involuntary one."

Meanwhile, crowds swarmed outside the *News of the
World* building chanting "We want Mick Jagger," and
"Change the law." Minor scuffles broke out when fans
mingled with staff from a nearby printing works. Traffic
in several streets was brought to a standstill as the crowd
milled about.

At the High Court of Criminal Appeal, Lord Justice
Diplock, Mr. Justice Braben and Mr. Justice Waller heard
the pleas for bail from Mr. Michael Havers QC and Mr.
Geoffrey Leach for Mick and Keith. Dealing with Mick,
Mr. Havers said the accepted evidence was that Jagger
had been in possession of four pep pills, and a doctor had
given him moral authorization to have them: "There is no

question of peddling, no question of vast quantities and there is all the difference in the world between this case and the case of the person who has large quantities for gain as a peddler or pusher."

Mr. Havers continued that the question was whether the remarks by the doctor could be construed as the issue of a prescription, and could an oral prescription justify possession. There was a substantial point of law involved on which there was little guidance and no authority.

Dealing with Keith, Mr. Havers said that there was substantial ground of appeal against conviction with regard to the admissibility of evidence relating to the behavior of a girl at the party. The prosecution said her behavior indicated that she had taken hemp. They said Richards must have had it drawn to his attention that hemp had been smoked because of her behavior. There was no evidence that the woman had hemp on her. The evidence was merely concerned with her behavior. If Richards was found guilty, this was a first offense. There was no evidence of massive hemp smoking.

The three High Court judges granted Mick and Keith bail in their own recognizance of £5,000 each, plus two sureties each of £1,000. They would be free until their appeals against their convictions and sentences were heard in the autumn. They had to stay in England while they were on bail, and hand in their passports.

In the afternoon Les Perrin and Stan Blackbourn left the High Court in company with solicitor Peter Howard to finalize the release of Mick and Keith from prison. Mick, wearing a beige sports coat and green paisley-pattern tie, was released from Brixton prison at 4:25 p.m. He waved and smiled to a group of photographers and a handful of young girls. He then left in Keith's Bentley. At 5:08 they drove into Wormwood Scrubs to collect Keith. They drove to their counsel's chambers for discussions. A short time later they went for a quiet drink in the nearby Feathers Pub in Fleet Street. Mick told the *Daily Mail:* "I just went dead when I was sentenced. I could think of nothing. It was just like a James Cagney film except everything went black." Keith described much the same kind of reaction: "I was so stunned at the sentence that I just went limp. I thought of nothing. Later I just wept. You just don't know the feeling. When

I got to jail I was given an ill-fitting uniform and a sort of lumber-jacket. The other prisoners were great. They even shared their tobacco with me, and tobacco is the scene in there."

Mick: "We had very, very good treatment, though no different from the other prisoners. They all wanted our autographs. The other chaps showed a great interest in the case and wanted to know all the details. We do not bear a grudge against anyone for what has happened. We just think the sentences were rather harsh."

A number of top groups planned to demonstrate their support for Mick and Keith at a huge pop concert. With the proceeds they aimed to send a vast quantity of flowers to Judge Block, as a token of their forgiveness of his actions.

Meanwhile the BBC finally decided, after a lot of threats, not to cut Jagger and Richards out of a television film. The film, with Mick, Keith, Brian and Marianne in the audience, appeared in the show *Our World* for 400 million viewers; the Beatles were singing one of the anthems of that psychedelic summer, "All You Need Is Love."

Outside the offices of the *News of the World,* 200 pop fans and beatniks continued to protest against the paper. The *News of the World* responded on July 2: "A monstrous charge against the *News of the World* was made during the trial of Keith Richards. It was a charge made without a shred of evidence to support it . . . Let us make quite clear that it was [*sic!*] the *News of the World* that passed information to the police."

In Carnaby Street sets of handcuffs were on sale at Lord Kitchener's Valet at £1 a pair, with a label advertising them as similar to those worn by Mick while in custody. "Be Faithfull with a pair of Jagger's links," ran the sales slogan—and sales boomed.

But there was also support for the judge's decision. Writing in the *Evening News,* Charles Curran said: "I hold that people who break the law ought to be punished. The law that Jagger and Richards broke is not a trifle, either. For it seeks to prevent people from using dangerous drugs for fun . . . Look at Jagger and Richards. Each of them is a millionaire at twenty-three. How does it come about that they are so rich? Their wealth flows from the fact that they are manufactured pieces of wish-fulfilment . . . Their lives tend to represent, in reality, what their admirers' are in fantasy. So long as the pop idol sticks to bawling and wailing—well, we can put up with that. But once he starts to add drugs to his drivel, society must take immediate note of it."

But most public opinion was generally angry with the convictions and the severity of the sentences. A typical response came in a letter written to the *Daily Mail:* "I am a housewife in my thirties. I have had a bottle of Benzedrine tablets in a cupboard for a long time, but for the life of me I cannot remember where I got them. It is only now, after Jagger's sentence, that I realize that I, and possibly thousands of others, could also be liable up to two years' jail and a £1,000 fine."

In the ensuing national and international debate, the wider issue of the effects of smoking marijuana, and the issue of whether it should be made legally available, like alcohol and cigarettes, was debated; the concern that "where reefers are smoked, hard drugs are not far away"; and the argument over whether one should be allowed to do what one wishes in the privacy of one's own home. All the papers and television and radio programs debated the impact of drugs and the responsibilities of pop stars to their fans during a decade in which our music and that of literally hundreds of other groups around the world was a vibrant soundtrack to social change.

A measured legal response came from the *New Law Journal:* "The three-month prison sentence on Jagger for a first offense, and the introduction at this trial of evidence about a girl in a skin rug are two disturbing features of the case."

And now came the biggest shock of all: the turning point of public attitudes towards the Stones and, by implication, towards the youth culture. Pilloried for five years as the world's most hateful group, destroyers of millions of kids, unkempt, dirty and loud-mouthed, the Stones through Mick and Keith suddenly found allies in the most unlikely areas. A colossal public outcry began at the harshness of the sentences, long before the appeal was heard. National newspapers, which had enjoyed baiting and taunting us, sprang to the defense of Mick and Keith with hundreds of thousands of words tilting at the

judiciary as well as examining attitudes to soft drugs.
Their main thrust was that Mick and Keith had been
made scapegoats because of their fame and that the sentences were outrageously savage. Would they have been
jailed had they been anonymous people? *The Times,* that
bastion of the Establishment, weighed in on July 1 with
an editorial that at once set the tone of the campaign and
astonished its conservative readers and others with its
liberalism. Under the evocative headline "Who Breaks a
Butterfly on a Wheel?" the article was written by the
upper-crust William Rees-Mogg, who had been editor for
only six months. He wrote: "We have . . . a conviction
against Mr. Jagger purely on the ground that he possessed four Italian pep pills, quite legally bought but not
legally imported without a prescription. Four is not a
large number. This is not the quantity which a pusher of
drugs would have on him, nor even the quantity one
would expect in an addict.

"In any case Mr. Jagger's career is obviously one that
does involve great personal strain and exhaustion; his
doctor says that he approved the occasional use of these
drugs, and it seems likely that other drugs would have
been prescribed if there was need of them. Millions of
similar drugs are prescribed in Britain every year, and for
a variety of conditions. One has to ask, therefore, how it
is that this technical offense, divorced as it must be from
other people's offenses, was thought to deserve the penalty of imprisonment . . . particularly surprising as Mr.
Jagger's is about as mild a drug case as can ever have
been brought before the courts. It would be wrong to
speculate on the judge's reasons, which we do not know
. . . There must remain a suspicion in this case that Mr.
Jagger received a more severe sentence than would have
been thought proper of any purely anonymous young man."

Later that month *The Times* had what I thought should
have been the last word on the subject: a reader wrote:
"The question, why the handcuffs and the night in prison
for Mick Jagger, is surely answered by A. E. Housman:

*'Oh who is that young sinner with the handcuffs on his
wrists?*
*And what has he been after that they groan and shake
their fists?*

*And wherefore is he wearing such a conscience-stricken
air?
Oh they're taking him to prison for the color of his hair.' "*

The effect of all this on Brian was devastating. Believing
he was vulnerable to another bust, he moved for nearly a
week into the Royal Garden Hotel with the girlfriend
who was to be loyal and meaningful to the rest of Brian's
life. Suki Potier was another fashion model whose face
bore the now-expected resemblance to Brian's, and for
the next two years she would give him the solace he needed
as he tried to weather the problems that encircled him.

"Suki was a beauty when she started with Brian,"
Stash says, "but she became a sort of living shadow of
Brian. And she was a bad-luck person. She had been
with Tara Browne in the car when he died." (This ill luck
was to continue to the end. After Brian's death she
married Bob Ho, a prominent Hong Kong businessman.
Bob and Suki died in a car crash together in Portugal in
the late seventies.)

The pressure on Brian was now very heavy: while Mick
and Keith's trial was being aired, public attention caused
the speeding-up of the court appeals by Mick and Keith
to July 31 after the intervention of the Lord Chief Justice. Brian, however, now had to wait four months, until
the end of October, for his to be heard fully. He was
continually visiting Harley Street specialists and on July 3
he hired a car to be driven to a health clinic in Liphook,
Hampshire. Les Perrin and Stan Blackbourn accompanied him, and Brian checked in under the pseudonym of
Mr. L. Howlett. Suki Potier joined him shortly afterwards.

His psychological condition was, however, far more
serious than a health clinic could hope to cure. The
principal at the clinic wrote to Blackbourn saying it was
"sincerely felt that this is not the type of establishment
where Mr. Jones can obtain help and the specialized
treatment he requires." After forty-eight hours Brian and
Suki checked out to be driven back to London. Still
Brian would not return to Courtfield Road; when the car
arrived there Suki went in to get him some fresh clothes
and he checked into the Hilton, again as Mr. Howlett.

Stash told me of Brian's condition at this time: "Brian
was not OK within a month of us getting busted. I was at

Robert Fraser's apartment when Brian came in, and, much to my horror, he proceeded to hit about twenty objects, banging into the walls and richocheting across the room like a ping-pong ball. That was the terrible effect of those downers. He took them because he felt alienated, worried, and it was the only way he could isolate himself into some kind of security blanket. It was a one-way street. He had a disaster written in neon lights all over him and none of us could do anything about it."

Such was the focus of attention on Mick and Keith that the serious decline in Brian's condition was hardly noticed by any of us. But he was in such a state of depression, filled with anxieties and emotional instabilities, that on July 5 a Harley Street consultant arranged for his immediate admission to the Priory Clinic for psychiatric analysis. (Coincidentally it was the same place in which Beatles manager Brian Epstein had been treated two months earlier. He was to die less than six weeks later.) Suki again checked in with him. When the newspapers heard, Les Perrin pleaded with his journalist friends not to seek him out "because it may well impede his recovery."

When Astrid and I twice visited Brian at the Priory we found him in good spirits but rather confused and disturbed by recent events. He looked pale. There was again talk in some circles that the Stones might break up through the aggravation of the various busts, but if anything seemed more likely to cause the split, it was Brian's condition at that time; yet I personally could not visualize the Stones without him.

Suki left the Priory on July 12 and checked into the Richmond Hill Hotel, remaining an out-patient. That day Brian felt strong enough to venture out. He hired a chauffeured car for four hours and drove into town to a music shop, buying tortoiseshell and felt plectrums, two sets of Spanish guitar strings and two soprano sax reeds. That night he reappeared at the Olympic for our recording session as if nothing had happened, before returning to the Priory later. On other outings he went to his favorite boutique, Dandie Fashions, and to a restaurant in Maidenhead. He seemed determined not to put himself wholly under medical care.

Brian finally checked out of the Priory on July 24. Three days later he and Suki flew out on holiday, with

Nicky, Tara Browne's widow, to Marbella, to stay at her villa for nearly three weeks. "It's been a year of pressure," he told reporters at the airport. "Don't make a big thing out of this. No one is getting married or anything. We are just going on holiday, relaxing, behaving ourselves. I decided on the spur of the moment. I have been under pressure for some time and I need a rest."

Nicky Browne said: "Suki, Brian and I are old friends. He was a close friend of Tara, and he was kind to me during the difficult time after Tara's death."

When he returned, Brian checked into Skindles Hotel at Maidenhead, where he remained until September 13, when we all flew to New York. But the old problem seemed to reappear with his arrival back from Spain. There was a deep problem within Brian that none of us could reach. Sometimes he could function perfectly well on a day-to-day basis, but beneath that was a confusing mixture of complications which even he didn't seem to want to confront and deal with thoroughly.

A second phase of my own matrimonial problems came just as the other Stones' crises were unfolding. Diane, visiting her father in Sydenham from South Africa, heard that Astrid was living with me at Keston. She arrived at the house to take Stephen, insisting that she wanted to take him back to South Africa with her. I met her and her father at his flat and with a heavy heart I agreed to her demands, for Stephen's sake. I wrote her a check for Stephen's airfare and they flew out to Durban via Johannesburg on July 14. A Rolling Stone's life was anything but private by now and the press got wind of my split—rather late, considering Diane had first left for South Africa five months earlier. There were front-page articles everywhere. Diane expressed her point of view in the *Daily Express*:

> I left Bill because I am not prepared to share him with anybody, let alone thousands of strange women. How many wives would like to have their husbands crawled over by thousands of women? I know I am a jealous woman and, of course, a jealous woman should never be married to a pop star. I blame the Stones fans for breaking up our marriage. They made the success of

the Stones possible, but they also made it impossible for us to live a normal happy life. We could hardly leave our house for a family outing without being besieged by fans. I can't expect Bill to give up his career. At the same time I can't divorce him. I left him, and a divorce would have to be in his hands. While he was with a little-known group, he met the Stones and was invited to join them. In a year they were at the top of the pop music world. That was when our home life began to change. Previously we had been happy. At first I thought it wonderful to have a famous husband. Bill did not let the success go to his head, but reports about the behavior of the Stones worried him. He became very quiet and withdrawn. I'm worried over Stephen. By day he plays around quite happily, but when I put him to bed at nights, he wants his dad. Bill and I agreed that Stephen should go to him for a month every year. But when I see how Stephen frets for Bill, I know that he will have to go to him for very much longer.

I think we both knew there would have to be a more permanent solution.

The other "quiet Stone," Charlie, had his own dramatic interlude. One evening in a Chinese restaurant back in Lewes a man at the next table began jeering, calling Charlie a pansy and insulting Shirley. "He punched Shirley in the stomach," Charlie recalled. "So I punched him in the face and he hit me back." The police arrived, a truce was called, and both sides decided to take no action. Just what the Stones needed at this point!

At our recording sessions at Olympic in the next couple of weeks, Brian was conspicuously absent; Keith, too, was not present on a few occasions, which was less understandable. There was no music in the can, certainly not enough to sustain our name on records if the worst happened and Mick and Keith went to jail. The sessions at the Olympic were a bit of a hotchpotch around this time, but in America, London Records shrewdly released an album of twelve songs, some culled from hit singles. Under the title *Flowers*, capturing the mood of the period, the jacket design featured a photo of each of us individually, in over-shapes on the stem of a flower.

Some insiders later noted that Brian's picture was atop the only stem without leaves, and decided that that was a bad omen. It was certainly macabre, in retrospect, but at the time nobody commented.*

One early July day I had sat alone at the Thomas organ and wrote a song called "In Another Land," which was a bit "spacey" but interesting. I made a demo on my home tape-recorder. When I played it to Moon a couple of days later he liked it too. Although it was complete and he never contributed anything to it, we decided to register it with our songwriting company Mossy Music.

Astrid and I drove to Barnes on July 13 to attend a recording session with the Stones at Olympic with Glyn Johns as engineer. Nobody else turned up except Charlie and pianist Nicky Hopkins. We were thinking of leaving when Glyn said to me, "Do you have a song to do?" I sat at the piano and played "In Another Land" and they all liked it. We worked on putting a basic track together, and got a good master on tape. It then came time to add the vocals, which worried me. In the end I suggested tremolo on my voice. The Small Faces were recording next door, and Glyn asked Steve Marriott to come in and help me. We sang it together and it worked well. The track was given the working title "Acid in the Grass."

Next night Glyn told Mick and Keith about my session and played them what we'd done. They liked it, agreeing it was compatible with the rest of the tracks. I'd finally broken the "songwriting" stranglehold of Mick and Keith.

It was ironic that this happened at the time of Brian's estrangement from the band. Stu said: "The only time Brian looked like coming into his own was when they did that awful *Satanic Majesties*, where he got the chance to dabble with the Mellotron. It was a terrible shame. He'd do anything. He would turn up at the studio with saxophones, and he even played harp on one number. There was one in the back of the studio for an orchestra session the next day. He had the ability to actually sit down and fiddle with it, and got something out of it fairly easily. The talent and ability was there, but he just screwed himself up. It was tragic, because Brian really was a good

---

Flowers reached number three in America, staying in the charts for thirty-five weeks.

player, but all he wanted to do was fiddle about with reed instruments and Indian drums. He just dabbled and was too out of it to play anything. Being a star just got to him totally."

At another session, we completed four-track masters of "We Love You," "Lady Fair," and "Fairground," and Andy Johns, Glyn's younger brother, began working as a tape operator for us. It was at this time that John Lennon and Paul McCartney did backing vocals on "We Love You."

When it was eventually released on August 18, Mick complained that the printed lyrics for the song were totally different from those he had written and sung on the disc. Even so the single sold respectably, with a highest entry at four in the *New Musical Express*. There was an attempt to hide the fact that Lennon and McCartney were singing back-up, because by performing with the Stones without permission they were breaking their contract with EMI. Instead of being stated as a fact, John and Paul's presence on the record was simply put out as a rumor. The Beatles' office agreed that John and Paul had attended the recording session but Mick, asked point blank if they had sung, said: "Oh, they can't be on the same record as *us!* We've got different recording contracts. I don't know how that got out. We do go to each other's sessions but this sort of thing makes it more difficult for us to do that." He said Brian was away when the voice tracks were done, but added Mellotron later. "It's got a foreboding sound."

We caught some flak, particularly from American writers, for supposedly copying the Beatles style, but British critics were generally supportive. Penny Valentine wrote in *Disc:* "When are the Stones not the Stones, children? When they are the Beatles, of course. Which is another way of pointing out the remarkable similarity, not apparent before, between this single and the Beatles work on *Sergeant Pepper*."

Jimi Hendrix remarked: "Production-wise 'We Love You' is very complex. More so than their other hits, I feel. This record only really moves me towards the end. I wouldn't say it was Beatles-influenced at all."

On the day before Mick and Keith's appeal, and in case it failed, Andrew arranged for Peter Whitehead to make a film with Mick, Keith and Marianne* to promote "We Love You." It was shot in a church hall in Essex and based on scenes from the trial of Oscar Wilde. Mick appeared as Wilde in frilly-fronted shirt, tails and with a green carnation. Marianne wore a short wig to play Lord Alfred Douglas—"Bosie." Keith played the Marquis of Queensberry, Bosie's father. Color sequences showed the Stones at a recording session. Mick remarked: "We were luckier than Oscar. As for any connection between his life and the record, well, it's all there, isn't it?"

When Andrew offered the four-minute film to *Top of the Pops*, it was rejected. Producer Johnnie Stewart did not consider it suitable for the type of audience that watched the program. Peter Whitehead said: "Pop music today is a socially committed form and the BBC are being irresponsible to ignore what is happening in the whole of the pop business today. I'm very annoyed at the decision. Pop is not all sweetness and light, as the program would like to see it, and my film is a valid social comment."

There was consolation from America and Germany, where the film was televised.

The signs were ominously bad for Mick and Keith when Robert Fraser lost his appeal on July 22 and went to jail for six months.

While Brian was in Marbella with Suki and Nicky Browne, I spent the day at home in Keston with Astrid, and Charlie was in Lewes. As dawn broke, scores of teenagers began queuing outside the court in London for the seventy-six seats in the public gallery; several carried placards with the slogan, "Support the Stones."

Mick stood in the dock, while Keith, who had developed chicken pox, was kept in a separate room. Scores of teenagers, many wearing sweaters bearing Rolling Stones slogans across the chest, craned forward in the public gallery as the hearing got under way. Mick turned towards them and held his finger to his lips. Almost immediately there was silence above.

---

*This was the first of many times Mick involved his current girlfriend in Stones projects, even to the exclusion of other members of the band. No other member of the band ever did this.

Michael Havers said that Keith was appealing against his conviction, and also applied for leave to appeal against the sentence on the grounds of its severity. The appeal was on five grounds: (1) That the evidence made a cornerstone of the case by the prosecution was wrongly admitted. The evidence of the girl, her dress or undress, was "wholly inadmissible"; (2) That if it was held to be admissible, the evidence should have been excluded by the discretion of the judge, because it was so prejudicial; (3) That the chairman misdirected the jury about what the prosecution had to prove as to the meaning of the word "permitting"; (4) That he failed to detail the lack of evidence regarding the knowledge of the cannabis drug; (5) That he failed to put fully the defense to the jury.

After a two-hour hearing, the judges left the court to confer. On returning, Lord Parker said that the conviction on Richards could not be allowed to stand, and his appeal was upheld. Lord Parker said: "It would be unsafe to allow the conviction to stand. Judge Block erred in not warning the jury there was no proper evidence, other than purely tenuous evidence, that the girl clad only in a rug had smoked cannabis and that Richards must have known about it." Some girls in the public gallery screamed. Others cried. There was some commotion until the court ushers called on them to be quiet. Tears came to Mick's eyes as an official went to give Keith the decision of the court.

The court then heard Mick's appeal as he stood in the dock, his head bowed, and his face red. Mick received a conditional discharge, although his conviction would stand. The order, made at sessions, that he should pay £100 towards the prosecution costs was set aside. Lord Parker said there was no evidence of over-indulgence in drugs by Mick, and no evidence of peddling to others, adding: "If you keep out of trouble for the next twelve months, what has happened will not go on your record as a conviction. When one is dealing with somebody that has great responsibilities as you have, because, whether you like it or not, you are an idol of a large number of the young in this country, you have grave responsibilities. Accordingly, if you do come for punishment, it is only natural that those responsible will carry a higher penalty."

Outside the court a crowd of about 300 received the

news of the court's decision quietly. Mick and Keith left the building by a small door leading into the judge's quadrangle, and climbed into their car. Well-wishers rushed up. One called: "How does it feel to be free?" Mick said: "Lovely." Keith said: "I feel spotty." As the car moved off, several screaming girls threw themselves on to the vehicle. There were shouts of "Good old Mick" and "Well done, Keith." The Stones office sent Mick and Keith two garlands of flowers.

Judge Leslie Block said: "I am not shocked by this matter. After all, we make the decisions, but we always thank God for the Court of Appeal."

After the appeal result was announced, the Indica Bookshop in Southampton Row, a well-known hippie center, became the communications post for the sending out of messages about celebrations that night. London's hippies and flower children were to celebrate the result of the appeal in Westminster Abbey and Hyde Park, where they would join other hippies for an evening love-in. The Stones had been invited to attend, and the organizers were confidently expecting a big attendance.

Marianne Faithfull said: "Now it's all over all of a sudden all the things we have been worrying about have disappeared. We are going to live together. I see nothing wrong with that. We are happy in each other's company. We have been looking at homes together, but have not yet decided which one to buy. Neither John [Dunbar] nor I have talked about a divorce. I don't want one, but I can't really speak for him."

After Keith arranged to have flowers sent to his mother, he was driven to London airport where he flew to Rome to join Anita, who had returned to Italy earlier to star alongside Jane Fonda in Roger Vadim's film *Barbarella*.

Later in the day Mick and Marianne arrived at Battersea heliport, then were whisked away in a helicopter to attend a press conference, at Granada TV's West End headquarters in Golden Square. When they arrived, Marianne waited outside in a mini-car, saying: "I'm really happy that things have turned out all right. I couldn't eat anything this morning, I was so nervous."

The *Daily Telegraph* reported that the press conference was "as noisy, heated and turbulent as a bear fight. [Mick] was the most composed person there, and his clothes were the loudest part about him. He wore purple-satin plush trousers, an off-white shirt, a shirt jacket with an embroidered red, yellow and green collar and cuffs, and off-white shoes, as he sat on a window-sill facing the questioners. There was no seating accommodation, and reporters crammed under the torrid lights were streaming with sweat as technicians and cameramen weaved through them to record the scene."

Mick was reported as saying: "Technically I broke the law, but I don't think it was very serious."

After the press conference Mick and Marianne went by helicopter to Spain's Hall near Ongar, in Essex, the home of Sir John Ruggles-Brise, to record *World In Action*. Also included on the program were William Rees-Mogg, Editor of *The Times*, Lord Stow Hill, a former Home Secretary, and Dr. John Robinson, Bishop of Woolwich. Mick was wearing what appeared to be a thigh-length smock with an embroidered open neck. He said: "In the public sector, to do my work, I have responsibilities. But my personal habits are of no consequence to anyone else. Until recently attempted suicide was a crime. Anyone who takes a drug, a very bad drug such as heroin, commits a crime against himself. I cannot see how it is a crime against society."

All this time some central force beyond music or money must have held us together. The events of the previous three months would have split any other group: the girl-swapping, the management problems, the police harassment, the court cases, the disintegration of Brian, the division between those who smoked and those who didn't. If ever we were going to wrap it all up, this was the heavy period when it could have happened.

Astrid, commenting on my attitude towards drugs at this time, says: "We didn't socialize with the others much because some were starting to get into drugs and Bill certainly wasn't. He was older and more mature than they were, and probably scared of it. Everyone was judged by whether he took drugs or not. It was *that* immature! They thought people really uncool if they didn't do drugs. The reality was that the drug-takers couldn't handle feeling threatened by somebody who didn't. It takes a certain strength *not* to do drugs in that situation and it was a big gap. There was no meeting point. Bill couldn't accept Mick and Keith and they couldn't accept him. They would make fun of his straightness. We weren't part of that scene; we stayed quietly at home. I felt so shy and out of place. They indicated that I should try to 'get Bill to loosen up', which meant taking drugs; but I thought it was a bit much to say it to me.

"I think it took a heavy toll on Bill. He just internalized it all, never expressed it, didn't talk about his feelings much. But his reaction came out in many other ways much later."

One of the nastiest characteristics of the British press is that when a celebrity has problems, a reporter will put the boot in. Despite Mick and Keith's triumph and the avalanche of sympathy from the public, there was a body of people waiting for us to say we would quit under the strain of it all.

There was conjecture over our freedom to tour America after the pronouncement that Mick was "guilty." In 1965 the Drug Abuse Control Amendments were passed to the Federal Food, Drug and Cosmetics Act, adding "depressant or stimulant" drugs to the proscribed list. Thus, possession became a federal offense that could preclude a visa. And there seemed little doubt that other countries, particularly Japan, which was a future big territory for rock tours, would ban us. In fact, we didn't tour Japan until 1990 specifically because of the busts.

We all reflected on the new position, and it's amusing to recall what I said when asked if we would ever go on tour again: "It could happen—but it's such a drag now. It's all right leaping about the stage when you're twenty, but when you get to twenty-five or twenty-six it gets a bit embarrassing. Mick feels he is old enough to get into something new now. I know Charlie couldn't care less, but if Mick and Keith suddenly decided on something I suppose we would do it. The other trouble is that the people we play to now are not really our audience. Our fans have got married and turned into a record-buying public rather than one which goes to stage shows."

On August 5 it was announced that Marianne Faithfull was to star in a new film, *Girl on a Motorcycle,* opposite French actor Alain Delon. Although Marianne had had a cameo role in a French film the previous year, this would be her first major picture. Mick and Marianne flew to Ireland on August 11 for a four-day holiday and stayed with brewery heir Desmond Guinness. The next day the press caught up with them again. Upon their return to England, Mick and Marianne counted twenty-nine photographers waiting for them at London airport, a sure sign of their new notoriety. Two taxi-drivers refused to drive them into town because of the drugs trial.

Having just celebrated his twenty-fourth birthday, Mick was emerging as an eloquent speaker, telling everyone he had no regrets over what had happened and that he had not worried over the result of the appeal. This was untrue. We all knew he was petrified that he might go to jail. But Mick told *Disc*: "It was a strain, I suppose. But easy to beat. We didn't mind being at the center of everything simply because we're quite used to it now. No, I wasn't really scared about the verdict. It was just that it took up so much time, mentally and physically. I kept thinking all the time what I would have to do if Keith went to jail, or if I went to jail. I don't feel bitter. I was relieved, but I soon got over the feeling of relief. Now I'm trying to forget it. It didn't affect us that much." On the prospects of touring, Mick said: "People are offering us enormous amounts to play again but if I do a show I'd like to do it for nothing. Where the kids don't have to pay, for a change. They should be able to groove around and have a nice time for nothing."* Anyway, as he pointed out, we'd already done a tour that year and "everybody who wanted to see the Rolling Stones has seen us already. They've had ample chance because we've done an awful lot of touring." All his ideas had changed in the past few months, he continued. The Stones wanted to play outdoors, but there were presentation problems. "Something like Monterey would be great, but you can't rely on the British weather."

And finally, Mick was contemplative: "Pop music is not my life. It's a nice part of my life but nowhere near all of it. My life is nice. But I am leading a very ordered existence—too ordered."

*Mick was two years ahead of his time with this visionary plan: two of rock's first free concerts were held by Blind Faith and then by us in Hyde Park in the summer of 1969.

In rock circles, a rumor began to circulate that Brian was leaving the Stones, but Mick quashed it, saying he'd spoken to Brian in Marbella and he was expected back to record with us. In reality, though, I think we all knew deep down that it was only a matter of time before Brian would part from the Stones in some way. Jimmy Page was rumored as a possible successor.

It was good to see Mick doing his bit to unify the group during these difficult days. "I am one-fifth of the Rolling Stones," he told *New Musical Express.* "I am not deserted, lonely or apart on stage."

It seemed sad that while Mick was producing a record for Marianne, speaking so well about the Stones and himself, putting our position and his into perspective, Brian was bogged down with small problems in Marbella—worrying about how to pay his bills.

After an alarm call to the Stones office from Brian for cash, Stan Blackbourn telexed Klein in New York on July 8: "Brian has cabled a request urgently for collection by self $300 at ABNO Malaga, Marbella branch. Also requests hotel bill to be paid to New Marbella Club, Marbella. I will inform Brian to send hotel bill to New York for payment." Under pressure to settle the bill quickly, and without the funds sent immediately from Klein's office, Brian borrowed the money from a Major Dawson at the hotel, promising to repay him as soon as possible. This proved more difficult than even Brian expected. Several days after Brian had returned to London, a cable from the major to the Stones office said the cash had not arrived from New York, and that he (Major Dawson) "required it soonest" since he was leaving Spain himself. Ronnie Schneider in Klein's office telexed the Stones office in London: "I sent $300 on 10.8.67 to Brian in Spain which you said he received. Are you referring to another $300 now? If so, please give me details as I know nothing about it." Visiting the Stones office, Brian became so worried about the failure to honor his debt to Dawson that he shot off this telex to Klein's office: "Reference $300 to Major Dawson at Marbella—would you please confirm this has been done as I am extremely worried about it. Can you please answer now?" There was no reply from Klein's office. Brian telexed again: "Can you please give me an answer?" Still no reply.

"Will you please telex us as soon as you come in?" Brian asked again. He then repeated the details of his request. There was still no reply from Klein's office. Brian pleaded: "Is there any chance of an immediate reply?" At last, an answer: "No. I have to find Ronnie." Brian capitulated. "OK, thanks. Please reply as soon as poss." Eventually the matter was resolved and Major Dawson got his $300.

This pathetic episode serves as an example of the poor service given to the Stones—except Mick and Keith—by the people we employed when money was involved; and also of the low regard in which Brian particularly was held. He showed little self-esteem in allowing himself to be kicked around like that, but the actions of Andrew, Mick, Keith and now Klein had seen to it that his seniority, or at least equal status, had long been forgotten. As far as they were concerned he was just a sideman in the band . . . and by then, Brian was far too messed up to fight back even if he had wanted to.

To me it was sad that Brian was scuffling for cash from the Stones office while the same office was using the band's kitty for Mick's and Keith's expenses. So many of the trial costs had been set off against the Stones' general account, although three of us had never incurred them!

The Stones were now quite scattered, mentally and physically. Charlie and Shirley finally moved house on September 8 to Peckham. Mick and Marianne (referred to in *Private Eye* as Marijuana Faithfull) flew to Amsterdam and then to Paris, holding court at the Hotel Meurice, and I busied myself with a recording session at Olympic for my group the End, cutting "Loving Sacred Loving."

I had a heavy dose of flu (and an overdraft of £79) as we flew from various European cities to New York on September 13, for a business meeting and to shoot a picture for the cover of the new album with Michael Cooper, a friend of the band who often hung out with us.*

*Michael Cooper photographed the controversial cover for the Beatles' album *Sergeant Pepper's Lonely Hearts Club Band,* which had just been released when we commissioned him. *Satanic Majesties* was heavily criticized as a stylistic musical copy of *Pepper,* and Cooper was also under fire for our cover, described by critics as a theme too close to *Pepper.* Michael committed suicide in 1973; in 1989 I contributed to a book of his work.

The arrival of Michael Cooper marked the departure of Stones photographer Gered Mankowitz who remembers: "When the split between Andrew and the Stones appeared it was quite clear that I was on Andrew's side.

"I was very sympathetic to Andrew's problems in the recording studio. Andrew took a lot of substances but he had them totally under control. He functioned for the job of work, but increasingly it seemed the band didn't want to do anything. We'd get to the Olympic studios for sessions due to start about ten and the boys wouldn't arrive until maybe two or three in the morning, pretty much incapable of doing anything. And Andrew would be very depressed. Olympic cost around £250 a night in those days and it was just being wasted. The final split for me as their official photographer came at one such session: Mick and Michael Cooper appeared and in front of me they went up to Andrew in the control room and said: 'Andrew, this is what we're gonna do for the cover.' Nothing could have made it clearer to me what was happening: for the first time, Andrew was being *told* what was being done and I was being told, indirectly, that I wasn't taking the picture. There was no debate.

"Andrew's influence had outlived itself. Or it had grown old, they'd grown tired of it, apart from it. This was a traumatic revolution within the band, changing their music. And Andrew wasn't a party to that."

Predictably, Keith faced enormous problems getting through New York immigration on September 13. He was taken to a private room and grilled for half an hour before they allowed him a "deferred entry" examination, answering questions about his drugs trial, at the immigration offices on Broadway next morning. Mick, too, faced half an hour of questions when he arrived on a later flight. His luggage was searched extensively and he was ordered to report to the immigration authorities later that day for another quiz. Finally, they were given permission to stay for a fortnight, much longer than they needed, but the immigration men said they would "not decide whether they would be able to enter the USA again until we have studied reports of the drugs cases in Britain."

Michael Cooper's imaginative plan for the *Satanic Majesties* cover took us to a studio at Pictorial Productions, Mount Vernon, New York that night, where we helped prepare a warehouse for the session next day. We all got totally involved in doing the album cover. Michael had already laid out a basic idea and he said, "Right, I want you to decorate it because it's your picture." So we all got stuck in. Michael had got all the stuff together and there were piles of it in the studio—just like Christmas decorations. I hung up the Saturn thing to float from the ceiling. We added our own artistic little touches to it and we went out to get clothes, and down to the flower district for plants and foliage. We put the faces of the Beatles in some of the flowers. We all went to the studio with spray cans. We kept popping out and buying things when we ran out. Michael took the first 3-D pictures of us dressed up, using a 3-D camera from Japan, as well as some more normal photos.

Then next day, September 14, we met Klein to confirm the decision that had become inevitable: a split from Andrew. We'd come a long way together but neither side was happy and before acrimony set in and tore us apart (as had happened with the Beatles) it was healthier that we went different ways. "There's no ill feeling," I told the press. "We are still on good terms but we all have different ideas on record production." Leslie Perrin stated that we had "parted from our recording manager because the Stones have taken over more and more of the production of their own music." But Mick added pointedly: "I felt we were doing practically everything ourselves anyway. And we just didn't think along the same lines. But I don't want to have a go at Andrew. Allen Klein is just a financial scene. We'll really be managing ourselves."

Much more accurate would have been an admission by Mick that we were about to be virtually managed by *him*. He brought into our Maddox Street office as "personal secretary" Jo Bergman, an American girl who had been helping Brian Epstein in the running of the Beatles fan club, and had latterly been assistant to Marianne. Not surprisingly, she took all her instructions from Mick, and, with Andrew gone, it was a Jagger–Faithfull–Bergman organization, with Jo catering to Mick's every whim. She even arranged for flowers to be sent from him regularly to Marianne in Heidelberg and Geneva where she was making her film. This was once again charged to the Stones' account.

Andrew Oldham was dignified about his exit: "Everything the Stones have done has been natural," he said. "They were not puppets, they were people. Whatever else is said about them, they were as close to professionalism as any five artists can get. *We split because we had no need of each other any more. As people we went in different directions. There was no definite decision. It was just over. We split because we all got to a stage of mutual boredom.* We had made so much bread and I for one didn't want to know anything anymore." Andrew later said: "Allen Klein, contrary to popular opinion, has never, in fact, screwed me, nor the Stones. Certainly that was the situation in 1967. What happened from 1967 on I'm not interested in."

New Musical Express said the Stones "may regret parting from Andrew." I think they got it the wrong way round . . .

Charlie and I flew back to London together with the knowledge that the foundations of the Stones had been dramatically reworked. Keith had managed to alienate our close friend Scott Ross while in New York. Scott had a major role in a documentary called *You Are What You Eat,* produced by Peter Yarrow (of the group Peter, Paul and Mary). We'd been staying at the Plaza Hotel, where Keith and Scott had hung out till dawn in a room doing dope. When Scott departed, "still half stoned," he phoned Keith back at the Plaza and found, to his amazement, that Keith was angry that he had not returned to continue their time together. "I can't be running around; I'm making a movie!" Scott explained. But by the time he returned to the film set, Yarrow had closed down the film and they were searching for Scott around Greenwich Village.

Mick returned to face the news and advice from our solicitors that since his landlords at Harley House were continually receiving complaints from other tenants about fans, he should vacate the flat as soon as possible. In May Mick and Marianne had visited a forty-acre, sixteenth-century manor house near Newbury, in Berkshire. Stargroves, which was originally one of Oliver Cromwell's military headquarters, was to become one of Mick's many homes and investments.

*   *   *

Not even Brian's enemies would have wished upon him the next event, which found him under a microscope in October: in the offices of our solicitors, Joynson-Hicks, he was interviewed by a detective in connection with a murder investigation. Brian, an inveterate nightclubber even during his months of gloom, had been at a club on the same night a murder victim had last been seen alive. Brian completed a signed statement and, although he wasn't incriminated, it was another piece of aggravation.

Still the recording sessions rumbled on, with Brian intermittently going for consultations with a psychiatrist and to the Priory. The rest of us often arrived at the Olympic never quite knowing who would be present. We recorded several tracks that were never released, with odd titles like "Bathroom/Toilet" and "Gold Painted Fingernails." Once, when I dozed off on the settee in the control room, they recorded me snoring and used it on the end of one of the album tracks.

It was all getting very spaced out, and a lot of the old disciplined thrust had left the band. I think there was a realization by Mick and Keith at this time that this wasn't just a rock 'n' roll band anymore, but also an important part of western youth culture. They'd won a critical battle against authority.

All this left Brian way out on a limb as he awaited his trial. He took off on a solitary motoring tour around his beloved West Country, stopping off in Wells, Taunton, Penzance and St. Ives, and on October 26 he went with a friend to Marbella again for a few days. Before going he ordered a two-piece gray pinstripe suit with foulard tie, costing £71, to be made for his court case. It was interesting that while Mick and Keith had been to court looking fashion-conscious in a contemporary way, Brian intended to present himself formally.

Although I was strongly against drugs for myself, I was put in a vulnerable position by the pushers who were constantly around the band—in the studios, on the tour in dressing-rooms, hotels, planes, cars. They were there all the time. I dissociated myself from it, didn't want to know, but I had to keep aware because if the cops did bust us I would have been thrown in jail together with the rest of them, as would Charlie. And who would believe that we weren't involved? It worried me because

I had a family, and whenever there was a bust, the newspaper headline read: "Rolling Stone arrested . . ." rather than Mick Jagger, Keith Richards or Brian Jones.

So it was a risk. I accepted that if I was in the band, it was something that had to be tolerated. But they wouldn't lift a finger to help me in my family situation—they wouldn't cancel a recording session because it was Stephen's birthday—but when I got there despite such occasions and they hadn't shown up, that drove me mad. So the "separatism" built up: when I went on tour I went back to my room and kept myself away from the cliques, the hangers-on. In the recording studio I did the sessions, always showed up on time, and when it was finished I'd go home. I hardly socialized with the others for ten years from about 1967.

Mick and Keith couldn't accept that people had different views or tastes from theirs. If you weren't one of their gang, they thought you were *against* the gang. Childish. Anything they didn't want to do was *wrong*, and if they were in a bad mood, everyone was expected to join it. I came close to leaving on many occasions because of the various frustrations and what I considered to be selfishness. I also couldn't identify much with the music on *Satanic Majesties*. Altogether, it often felt that there really wasn't much of a future in the band for me.

Stones performances were frequently affected by the influence of drugs, and it was a wonder there wasn't a bust at the Olympic studios. At the time, they thought they played better, as people do when they have had too much, but when they listened to the playback next day, they realized it was bloody awful. And once again, what could I do about it? I was part of five people who collectively put on a bad show that night, and no matter how well Charlie or I played, we were stuck with the consequences.

Such was the impact of pop in the sixties that there were a whole host of television shows: the national *Top Of The Pops* and *Juke Box Jury* from the BBC was complemented by networked series like *Thank Your Lucky Stars*, *Ready Steady Go!* and *A Whole Scene Going*.

Jonathan King, a pundit who had a freak hit with *Everyone's Gone to the Moon*, also hosted a weekly show called *Good Evening.** Naturally, being Jonathan, he traded in gossip and delivering "exclusive" news. One piece of chat he heard about the Stones and the Beatles became international news. The rapport between Mick and Lennon and McCartney had been strengthened since they had dipped into transcendental meditation together; and the Beatles were using soft drugs, further bringing them together. Mick had sent flowers to both John out at Weybridge and to Paul at St. John's Wood to thank them for their contribution to our single "We Love You" and, since Mick's home was just around the corner from Paul's, he and Marianne were frequent visitors. A casual idea that the Stones and Beatles might link up in management to form our own record production organization was blown up by Jonathan King.

"At the moment," Paul McCartney said, "we are just exchanging views to see whether we can work something out between us." And the Beatles' office stated: "We look upon any merger as a fusion of nine people's business talents in a new and exciting project. Nothing has changed since Brian Epstein's death, but the prospect of some professional tie-up between the Beatles and the Stones is very intriguing. What the boys are contemplating is a separate business project for opening up a joint talent center that will build up on other people's talents, produce and distribute their records."

Our European booking agent, Tito Burns, thought it would be an "excellent idea" if the Stones and Beatles merged their business interests, and there was much speculation on the two groups pooling money to build or buy "the best equipped studio in London" (although precisely where our money would come from to fund such a venture was unknown, except perhaps to Allen Klein).

Naturally the music business supported the plan, particularly because it would encourage new groups. "This is a great idea," Pete Townshend declared. "Between them they should be able to get one of the best-equipped studios in London, which will immediately help small

---

*Jonathan also wrote a weekly column for *Disc* and *Music Echo,* edited by Ray Coleman in the sixties. He now writes for the *Sun.*

groups. These groups will be able to have the best instead of the rubbish they often have to put up with."

Jonathan, who saw it as "a big-business merger," described the idea as "very stimulating. It will do a lot of good things for the business. I suspect they'll go into behind-the-scenes business, setting an example to a lot of other groups. They are a unique power in pop, virtually free to do as they please, and are also close friends."

Mick stated: "We'd like to set up a label together, but that would be a long way in the future. I have decided I don't want to be a record producer. It's not very groovy." Mick instructed our solicitors to register the name Mother Earth as a possible name for our own studio.

But the premature nature of all this was emphasized by Mick through Les Perrin when on October 17 he issued a statement deflating the balloon:

> In view of the statements made over the weekend, but not emanating from the Rolling Stones, that a business merger between them and the Beatles is imminent, it is felt that the position should be clarified. Mr. Mick Jagger states that preparatory conversations of a purely exploratory nature were held between him and Mr. Paul McCartney. Discussed was the possibility, or advisability, of opening a recording studio at some unspecified future date. These conversations have not been resolved and any assumption to the contrary should be considered premature. It should also be pointed out that a report indicating that the Rolling Stones are without management is incorrect. Mr. Allen Klein of New York City has been the business manager for the Rolling Stones for the past two years. The European agent is Mr. Tito Burns of Harold Davison Ltd, Regent Street. This situation remains unaltered.

With the kind of irony that made the events of that year look more like fiction than fact, just as the Beatles–Stones merger was being mooted, our old managers were battling out their differences in the High Court.

In the dispute which began being heard on October 16, Eric Easton was suing Andrew Oldham and seeking the appointment of a temporary receiver to look after royalty payments and other assets resulting from their three-year partnership agreement, and also suing Decca Records and Nanker-Phelge Music. The Rolling Stones, Andrew Oldham and Decca Records opposed the claim.

Mr. Maurice Finer QC, for Eric Easton, said the story began early in 1963, when Mr. Easton met Mr. Oldham who was then nineteen. Mr. Easton had been in the entertainment world for twenty-five years, and had been an agent and manager of well-known artists. Mr. Oldham was a reporter on a music paper, and Mr. Easton let him a room where he could start on his own as a publicist. They heard about a new group called the Rolling Stones, who were performing at the Station Hotel, Richmond, Surrey for £1 a head a night. They went to see them and were impressed, and entered into a joint management venture. The managers' remuneration was to be 25 per cent of earnings in excess of £100 a week, and 25 per cent of the gramophone-record royalties that might be earned by the group. "The group's career was meteoric and by the autumn of 1964 their name was second only to that of the Beatles."

About the middle of 1964 relations deteriorated between the two, Mr. Easton claiming that Mr. Oldham began to show signs of wishing to exclude him from so profitable an enterprise. Since July 1965 Mr. Easton had not received a penny. On August 27, 1965, the press announced that Mr. Oldham and Mr. Klein had taken over management of the group. Mr Oldham was quoted as saying "I manage the Stones, and Allen Klein manages the Stones and me." Mr. Easton had been totally excluded from the affairs of the Stones since August 1965, following the arrival in England from America of Allen Klein.

Maurice Finer said: "You may think it is [Klein's] influence that is responsible for a great part of the trouble in this case. This gentleman is quite simply a predator in the field of pop artists. The assets consist of very large sums of money that have accrued and are accruing both here and abroad, particularly on the American continent."

As that case continued, another was about to begin.

Brian flew back from Spain on Sunday, October 29 for his court hearing next day, while Mick flew out to Frankfurt for a short visit to Marianne, who was filming. The only Stones "insider" present at Brian's hearing was Tom

Keylock, and while the case was still being heard at the Inner London Sessions, he departed to chauffeur Mick and Keith to the airport, where they met Glyn Johns and Ronnie Schneider to fly to New York for work on the remixing and mastering of new album tracks. It would have been impossible for all the Stones to have attended court with Brian because it would have turned the case into a media circus, but had one or two of us gone, we'd have learned far more about our friend and colleague in a half hour than we had managed to glean in five years.

Brian looked immaculate in a charcoal-gray suit with a thin stripe, slightly flared cuffs, and blue tie with polka dots atop a white lace shirt with long, pointed collar as he and Stash arrived in Brian's silver-gray Rolls. Scarcely any Stones fans were outside the court when they arrived.

Stash was first up, and he pleaded not guilty to being in unlawful possession of drugs.

Robin Simpson (Prosecuting) said that Prince Stanislaus Klossowski de Rola had made it clear from the outset when police searched Brian's flat that he was just a guest there. The only item which might have contained drugs was the prince's cigarette holder, but it was examined and nothing was found. "The evidence against him is exceedingly thin." Stash was discharged after the prosecution put forward no evidence. He was awarded costs of £78 15s.

Brian appeared in the dock and pleaded guilty to two drugs charges. He admitted possessing a quantity of cannabis and cannabis resin without authority, and permitting his premises to be used for the smoking of cannabis or cannabis resin. He denied two charges of unlawfully possessing Methedrine and cocaine respectively, and these pleas were accepted by the prosecution.

Robin Simpson said they regarded Brian's plea as an absolutely proper one to accept. Brian accepted the responsibility for the cannabis, but so far as the cocaine and Methedrine was concerned, the prosecution were prepared to accept that Brian did not know that they were there.

James Comyn (Defending) pleaded with the court not to send Brian to jail. He said that Brian had made it clear immediately that he had taken some cannabis, but he had nothing to do with hard drugs. "Jones has instructed me to say that he has never been an addict of hard drugs. That he was a cannabis smoker. But he has cut it and all drugs out completely. For him they solved no problems. They only created problems. No one should take an example from him. He has never peddled or pushed drugs. He had never bought them, nor carried them around. He has had many people to his flat, many parties, and he knew these people were smoking cannabis, and he, sometimes, had smoked some of it himself, getting it from them. He had taken on his shoulders the responsibility for what was found in his flat though he did not think there was a very considerable amount of drugs there. But there was another side to it. This young man has suffered very greatly from his arrest and the charges, and virtually had a breakdown shortly afterwards. He was under strict medical care and was responding to treatment, and appears to be cooperative. He is prepared to carry on treatment. There is a lot of good in him, and there is a lot of good he can do. Anybody who has seen him in the last few months can derive from it no encouragement for drug-taking nor for relaxation of the drug laws. His doctors say prison would break his career prospects, his spirit and his health."

Mr. Comyn added that Brian, a brilliant young man with an exceptional career, was a successful musician and had recently gained some fame as a composer. He had also a tremendous talent for writing. "He is a member of this group who have had their misfortunes this year. He wants to turn over a new leaf and get down to things which are really worthwhile for the future."

James Comyn cross-examined Detective-Sergeant David Patrick, who agreed that while appreciating all drugs were serious, the amount of cannabis found was comparatively small.

Dr. Leonard Henry, a psychiatrist, gave evidence for Brian. He said he had seen Brian about eight times that year. When he first saw him he was under the influence of drugs. He appeared not to have a great deal of resistance against stress situations. He was extremely agitated and in a generally depressive condition. He was quite incoherent and unable to give Dr. Henry a complete history. He had been treated with anti-depressants and tranquilizers. The doctor felt that Brian couldn't handle being in prison and should be hospitalized.

Dr. Henry said: "In my opinion he was a very sick man. By July, his condition had worsened and he was sent to a private nursing home in Roehampton, and he had been admitted for treatment. Since his discharge there has been an enormous change in his mental attitude. His treatment has obviously done him a great deal of good. He was now much less anxious and depressed, with a sensible approach to problems. I have given a great deal of thought to a prison sentence, which I feel would be completely disastrous to his health, and would mean his complete collapse. I do not think he could possibly stand the stigma of a prison sentence. There might be an attempt to injure himself."

Dr. Anthony Flood, another psychiatrist, said Brian had come under his care at the nursing home in July for nearly three weeks. When he arrived he was deeply distressed and his attitude was that of a potential suicide.

James Comyn said: "A man who was ill?"

Dr. Flood: "Indeed so."

Dr. Flood said that one could become dependent on cannabis. He believed Brian was now managing to do without it.

Brian then told the court about his position: "I was never really dependent on drugs. They had never done anything positive for me." Making a vow in court that he would have nothing further to do with drugs, he added: "I hope that this will be an example to young people who attempt to try drugs."

Brian waited ninety minutes in the cells for the court to consider his counsel's plea. The court then adjourned for lunch and Brian was taken to a room below the court. When the court reconvened, the chairman, Mr. Reginald Seaton, said: "I have given your case anxious and careful consideration. The offense of being the occupier of premises and allowing them to be used for the purpose of smoking cannabis resin is very serious indeed. This means that people can break the law in comparative privacy and so avoid detection for what is a growing canker in this country at the present moment. No blame attaches to you for the phial of cocaine, but there are people who come to this sort of party and that is how the rot starts, from cannabis to hard drugs. You occupy a position by which you have a large following of youth, and therefore it behoves you to set an example . . . Although I am moved by everything I have heard, I would be failing in my duty if I did not refer to the seriousness of the offenses by passing sentence of imprisonment.''

Brian was sentenced to nine months in jail for permitting his flat to be used for purposes of smoking cannabis. He was also sentenced to three months to run concurrently for having possession of cannabis, and ordered to pay £265 10s. costs. He winced and muttered in bewilderment at the sentence, but gave no sign of emotion. He turned away quickly and was led from the dock by two court officials.

Notice of appeal against Brian's sentence was immediately given. James Comyn asked for bail pending an appeal against sentence, but this was rejected by the chairman. Les Perrin said that an application for bail pending consideration of an appeal would be made next day before a High Court judge in chambers. Half an hour after being sentenced, Brian was driven by prison van to Wormwood Scrubs, past the Rolls-Royce in which he'd been driven to court five hours previously.

In the evening, about forty young people staged a protest march against Brian's jail sentence, many of them dressed as hippies, wearing beads, fur coats and colored jackets. They gathered at World's End in the Kings Road, where they were shepherded politely up and down by half a dozen policemen, to avoid causing an obstruction, while two police vans stood by. After ninety minutes the demonstrators moved towards Sloane Square and trouble broke out. Arrests came at the end of what had begun as a peaceful demonstration, said to be organized by Release, a body dedicated to helping those arrested for drug offenses. Police swooped after they had paraded for about two hours. Six men and two girls were arrested and taken to Chelsea police station. The eight included Mick Jagger's brother Chris, who was charged with abusive behavior and obstructing a police officer.

The sentence on Brian was generally thought by the press to be too severe. The *Daily Sketch* said that "dishing out a nine-month sentence is as likely to turn a pop star into a martyr as to deter his fans. Besides, if the

Appeal Court later reduces or quashes a harsh sentence, as happened in the case of Jagger, the authority of the law is lessened." Even the *Sun* took much the same line: "Such a sentence, far from convincing young people that cannabis (hemp) is harmful, is too likely to make a martyr of this wretched young man and invest it with false glamor."

James Comyn had planned to make an application for bail in the High Court on the 31st, but met a delay in presenting his case: many judges were absent from the law courts because of the state opening of Parliament. If his appeal failed and he qualified for full remission, Brian would serve six months.

High Court Judge Mr. Justice Donaldson, sitting in private, was asked by Mr. James Comyn QC, to grant bail to Brian, pending appeal against his sentence. Dr. Anthony Flood and Dr. Leonard Henry were summoned to repeat the evidence they had given during the trial.

Brian's lawyer then announced: "Pending appeal, in the light of further medical evidence, and on his undertaking to continue to have medical treatment meanwhile, Brian was granted bail on the recognizance of £250 and two independent sureties of £250."

After being freed on bail Brian was collected from Wormwood Scrubs by his lawyer Peter Howard. After formalities had been completed, they left by the front entrance. A score of photographers and newsreel cameras were there to see Brian smiling and waving as he was driven to the White Horse Pub at Longford, Middlesex, near London airport.

There Brian sat alone in a corner near the fire, sipping a rum and Coke, as regulars chatted at the bar. Brian was then driven to a friend's house in the country to rest before continuing medical treatment. "It's great to be on the outside again," he reflected. "But I'm not in a position to say anything. All I want now is a little peace and quiet."

News of Brian's case was phoned to Mick and Keith in New York, where they were due to attend a Hallowe'en party at the Electric Circus in Greenwich Village.* They

---

*While there they were told that *Flowers* had been awarded a gold disc in America (our seventh successive gold); it had become our fastest-selling album ever.

were there for talks with Allen Klein, who again confirmed: "There is absolutely no question of bringing in a replacement for Brian."

Les Perrin said: "The Stones have not appeared in concert since April and have not played a British date since October 1966, so you will see that they are not very interested in touring. In fact, there are no tour plans whatsoever. We will meet all the other obstacles as they present themselves, but, if necessary, the Stones can continue for an interim period as a four-man group."

Since the bust Brian had been virtually homeless, and the office had had his furniture and effects moved into storage. Now out on bail, he and Suki moved into a small new flat at 17 Chesham Street, Belgravia; the memories of Courtfield Road were too grim ever to return there.

Two weeks after Brian was bailed, a speech of astonishing tactlessness was made by Mick's and Keith's trial judge, Leslie Block. Speaking at a dinner held by the Horsham (Sussex) Ploughing and Agricultural Society, he made a scarcely veiled criticism of the Court of Appeal for their leniency: "We did our best, your fellow countrymen, I, and my fellow magistrates, to cut these Stones down to size, but alas, it was not to be, because the Court of Criminal Appeal let them roll free."

The possibility of these disgraceful, partisan remarks coloring the decision of Brian's appeal incensed us and many others. Les Perrin made a statement:

> In view of Brian Jones being on bail it seems deplorable that a member of the judiciary should so contravene the normally accepted practice in a case being *sub judice*, as to joke and poke fun. He made an unprecedented observation both on the trial he conducted at Chichester, and the subsequent findings of the Court of Criminal Appeal. Is this the kind of justice Britain expects? Is this man typical of those who hold the title, the high and esteemed office to try and sentence people? How can the public believe, in the light of this utterance by Judge Block, that the Rolling Stones can get an unbiased hearing? His statement smacks of pre-judgement, a getting-together, "to cut the Stones down to size" because of who they are. It is a pity that he did not observe the ethics of *sub judice* in a like manner to Mr. Jagger, Mr. Richards, Mr. Jones by remaining silent.

Judge Block said later: "Of course, I was being very sarcastic."

Of course.

With no management in Britain and Klein still holding the reins from New York, it seemed incomprehensible that what could happen next would be a freezing of a million dollars of our money due to us under US agreements. But that's what a judge directed as the saga of Easton versus Oldham (and by implication the Klein agreement that he entered us into) continued.

In the High Court Easton's counsel said Easton was suing Klein for damages for procuring breaches of the Rolling Stones contracts. Easton asked the judge to appoint a receiver of payments under a large number of contracts, pending the hearing of his action against Andrew Oldham. He alleged that he was wrongfully excluded from a partnership for joint management of the Stones, and was claiming payment of money due. Eric said that Oldham had told him of meeting Klein, who claimed Decca would give a better deal for the Stones. "I heard phrases like 'he eats people' used about Klein, and I did not want the group to be associated with him." He claimed he was entitled to be protected against any possibility of Oldham "unconsciously" making away with the assets of the partnership.

Mr. Justice Buckley ordered a freeze on our earnings in North America until a partnership agreement had been decided between Oldham and Easton. He banned Oldham from taking any steps to get hold of money payable under American agreements. He also accepted undertakings from Decca that it would freeze earnings in this country by suspending payments of royalties. The judge said Oldham could have behaved with a great deal more frankness than he did, and he refused to allow him any costs in the present case. He also revealed that more court battles were to follow before the group's problems were sorted out.

A newspaper reported that the Stones' world record sales had brought in £42,333,000. To whom, I still wonder! While all these millions were being bandied about, another figure of £700,000 was mentioned as being invested by us in a recording studio in London: Mick had looked at two possible sites.

But I was bitten financially in the mundane matter of buying a new car. A local dealer arrived at my Keston house and I gave him a check for £650 for an Alfa Romeo, handing over my MGB sports car in part exchange. He said he'd contact me when the car was ready for delivery. For several months I inquired with no success and when I instructed solicitors, they informed me that the company had gone bankrupt. Nothing more could be done. I never saw the Alfa, my deposit or my old MGB again. A lesson learned.

I needed a break. Astrid and I flew to New York on November 13 for five days, during which we shopped and went to Allen Klein's house for dinner. We found his house rather bizarre: everything was so "plastic," and, it seemed to me, in bad taste. He told me that the record company was releasing my track "In Another Land" as a single in America. He said, "It's the only love song on the album." We eventually got free and returned to the hotel. Astrid says of the night: "I thought he was the most appalling person I had ever met." Then on to Bermuda for a real break—nearly three weeks—to see my brother Paul and his wife Jean, who lived there. While we were there, we all went for dinner at the Four Ways Inn—which confused me because I'd only ever known three and still do!

While I was there, the Stones' sixteenth American single was released—and it was a Wyman composition, "In Another Land." Produced by me and by Glyn Johns, who also engineered it, the record had a Mick–Keith song, "The Lantern" on the B-side. "Wyman goes solo," said *Billboard* magazine, "in the off-beat piece of rock ballad material that should prove a monster . . . a weirdy that can't miss." It didn't do too badly and achieved a highest position of sixty-four. No promotion had been done on this record.

In London, Brian was busy with domestic matters, part-exchanging his Rolls-Royce Silver Cloud Mark 2 for a dawn-blue Mark 3 model, costing him £2,100. He immediately had dark windows and an eight-track stereo tape-recorder fitted. And when his ex, Linda Keith, went into the London Clinic for an operation, he took care of her with flowers and paid the bill. He went off on another sojourn to the West Country, returning to guest with Mick and Charlie on the *Top Gear* radio program, in which they introduced all the tracks on our new album, *Their Satanic Majesties Request.**

The day I flew back to England the Stones were awarded a gold record for *Satanic Majesties* in the USA—*before* its release! The final cover suggestion, which was implemented, came from Brian, whose "maze" idea was complicated. When you found your way through the maze, if you went through to the cover you came through the door of the citadel. I never tried it but I thought, knowing Brian, that it would have been one of those mazes where there was no way out—that he'd done it on purpose for people who were stoned out of their brains, to keep them out of the way for a couple of days—or that it was something he'd give to his friends when they came round for dinner!

Released on December 8, this, our seventh album in Britain, was immediately attacked as indulgent, pretentious and a catastrophic mistake. Despite all his pressures at this time, Brian was still able to pinpoint the changing moods in pop thinking—and within the Stones—that had created the concept of *Satanic Majesties:* "The album is a very personal thing, but the Beatles are just as introspective. You have to remember our entire lives have been affected lately by social–political things that come out in our work. In a way, songs like '2,000 Light Years from Home' are prophetic, not at all introverted. They are the things we believe will happen. Changes in values and attitudes. Entertainment is boring; communication is everything."

Asked why such ambitious thought had not gone into popular music before, and why groups like the Stones and Beatles had changed pop's format and approach so significantly, Brian said: "Because of the wars. Just as people began to look at life and their values, a war would break out and nothing destroys culture, art or the simple privilege of having time to think quicker than a war. And once you get the horror and terror of a war people have

---

*Decca did not like this title as it parodied the Queen's message on all British passports: "Her Britannic Majesty . . . Requests and Requires . . . ." But by now we'd persuaded Decca to live dangerously.

to escape from it. They need the escapist pop cultures that croon about moon and June and romance. I've never had to go through those times and I thank God I have not." Ballad singers, he added, were "necessary for all those people who were tired and worn out by the war."

In the heady atmosphere of 1967, when an avalanche of rock groups from America's west coast shifted the pendulum from London, *Satanic Majesties* struck the correct mood. But a subtle change of style was one thing; poor execution was another and as *Billboard* said: "If the three-dimensional cover seems far out, listen to the record, the most experimental the group has yet recorded." A writer in the *Daily Mirror* was less diplomatic: "Count me out of this scene. I can't come to grips with it. I've just been labeled a square by Mick."

Mick was quick to defend the route down which he had taken the Stones with this controversial record: "We don't write commercial music. We write what we want and if that happens to be commercial, that's fine." Making the point that the album was made under pressure— we'd begun recording it in February and work was continued on it until just before its release—Charlie commented: "Sometimes I think it was a miracle that we produced *anything* with all the emotional upheavals within the group. We had to find a new direction. The era that bred the Liverpool boom was over."

Most critics branded the album a sad, ill-conceived, "druggy" attempt to reply to the Beatles' *Sergeant Pepper*— and John Lennon was among those who disliked it. We met our strongest opposition in America. Rock writer Jon Landau said that *Satanic Majesties*, "despite moments of unquestionable brilliance, puts the status of the Rolling Stones in jeopardy. With it, the Stones abandon their capacity to lead in order to impress the impressionable. They have been far too influenced by their musical inferiors and the result is an insecure album in which they try too hard to prove that they too can say something new.

"The album is marred by poor production. In the past there has been a great gulf between production styles of the Beatles and Stones. The Beatles' production is often so 'perfect' that it sounds computerized. The Stones have never gotten hung up on that sort of thing. With the shift in pose to something nearly 'arty,' the weak guitars and confused balance merely become annoying." And my own debut didn't escape the general slaughter. "Bill Wyman's debut as a vocalist and songwriter is fairly inconspicuous." Landau summed up with his view that we had been trapped by "the familiar dilemma of mistaking the new for the advanced . . . it is an identity crisis of the first order and one that will have to be resolved more satisfactorily than it has been on *Their Satanic Majesties Request* if their music is to continue to grow." Privately, I agreed entirely.

For the first time, Mick was now forced to defend one of our projects. "It's different from the others we've done and different from the next we'll do. But it's still just an album, not a landmark or a milestone or anything pretentious like that. All we have tried to do is make an album we like with some sounds that haven't been done before. It doesn't mean we'll never release any more rock 'n' roll or R & B tracks."

While the world was discussing *Satanic Majesties,* and the death of Otis Redding in a plane crash, Brian was in a highly charged state over his appeal case, still living with the very real prospect of going to jail. The day before his case came up in the law courts on December 12, he went for treatment with another psychiatrist. Mick was in court to give Brian moral support, a vital gesture because of Brian's condition.

Medical testimony was given to Mr. Justice Parker, sitting with two other law lords, that the prison sentence had affected him so deeply that he was potentially suicidal. In addition to the evidence by Brian's own psychiatrists, another, appointed independently by the court, testified to Brian's "extremely precarious state of emotional adjustment" and his "fragile grasp of reality."

The public declaration of Brian's condition was damaging for Brian but was essential to secure the compassionate decision by Mr. Justice Parker. Brian's sentence was set aside and Brian placed on probation for three years, with the extra proviso that he should continue to receive psychiatric treatment and pay the maximum fine of £1,000. "Remember," Mr. Justice Parker told him somberly, "this is a degree of mercy which the court has shown. It's not a let-off."

Stash, noting that by that time Brian was skidding downhill, says: "An artist *can* be hounded into a state in which his mental health will deteriorate and that's what happened to Brian, I'm sure. I was very angry and blamed the authorities, but ultimately an individual has to blame himself."

For twenty-four hours, a shaken Brian tried to return to normality, eating with friends the next night at an Indian restaurant in South Kensington. On Thursday, December 14, Brian picked up a takeaway meal from the Alvaro and returned to his flat. Later that evening his new chauffeur John Coray arrived to find Brian had collapsed.

Coray made a 999 call and, after spending nearly an hour in St. George's Hospital, Hyde Park Corner, Brian ignored doctors' requests that he should stay in overnight. They said he was suffering from "mental tiredness," but Brian discharged himself and later was driven to see Dr. Flood at the Priory, Roehampton. "There is no cause for alarm," the doctor stated. "He is just tired and suffering from over-strain. I want him to go on holiday as soon as possible." Brian said that his problem was a reaction to the trial. He had also suffered raging toothache and next day went into the Harley Street nursing home for two extractions.

Despite all the battering our album received, after only ten days in the American shops, it had passed the $2-million sales mark, outselling the Beatles' *Magical Mystery Tour*. London Records sent an exultant cable to Sir Edward Lewis at Decca in London: "It's not a hit. It's an epidemic!" It entered the *Billboard* chart and stayed there for twenty-three weeks, rising to number two. In Britain it was in the charts for twelve weeks, reaching a highest position of three. Not bad performances for what many regarded as our most non-commercial record. And figures released by the Record Industries Association of America showed that our first ten albums had all been certified gold; that month we had also won the British R & B section and were second in the vocal category in *Melody Maker*. "Combined with the huge sales they have enjoyed with their hit singles, the Stones have a world-sales total to date of $100 million," said Leslie Perrin in a press statement. Of that, it was estimated that we had £3 million to share between us—before tax.

Christmas loomed. On December 17 Mick sent flowers to Marianne, who was filming in Nice, and on her return to London they flew off on holiday. Brian's activities were more predictable, even mundane: on December 22 he drove up to our accountant's office, received a parking ticket as usual in Great Castle Street, had lunch in the Alvaro with Linda and then, temporarily reunited, they flew to Colombo, Ceylon, to stay with Stash. Keith and Anita flew to Paris en route to Tangier and Marrakesh. Charlie and Shirley stayed in Sussex, and Astrid and I flew to Sweden, to meet her family and spend the holiday with Astrid's sister Karin and her boyfriend Jan in Västerås. We flew into snow and the next morning I froze while shifting twelve inches from the driveway to get the car out.

In America our seventeenth single was released, "2,000 Light Years from Home" backed by "She's a Rainbow," killing my single "In Another Land" stone dead. The new record achieved a highest position of number ten.

Back in London, 6,000 Christmas cards, designed by Charlie, went out to our fans inside the newsletter. There had been plenty of news of the Stones in the media: we had to reassure them we were all alive, well, and still very much together.

11

De-Klein

I'm not rebelling against anything! I never rebelled against my parents. Rebellion has nothing to do with it. A lot of kids of this generation have nothing in common—nothing at all—with their parents. They are totally unlike them. Everybody always talks about problems of communication, but it's more than that. Kids are not afraid of their freedom, 'cause they've had it all their lives. Older people are frightened of young people 'cause they're frightened of freedom. Parents don't really have any idea of it at all, no conception of what it is, so they are frightened and their kids aren't. They are not a bit alike. Older people don't want to know where it's at, they're frightened, and the kids are finding out and are not frightened. Parents are functioning in the system, and younger people are finding out how to function outside of it and be free.

Mick Jagger, 1968

There is a whole side of Mick's nature I do not understand. Still, when he gets older, he will learn he must give in to some things . . .

Eva Jagger, 1968

We began 1968, nearly five years after we had achieved success and were called millionaires, virtually cashless. I had £871 in the bank and was still paying all my personal expenses, while the other four Stones were continuing to have various incidentals such as flat-cleaning, taxis, food, theater tickets and domestic repairs paid out of petty-cash at the office. There, the staff comprised four: Stu, who earned £1,872 a year; Jo Bergman, personal secretary (£1,560), Maggie Phillips, secretary (£1,300) and Shirley Arnold, fan-club secretary and telephonist (£1,040).

We were still all dispersed: Astrid and I flew back from

Sweden. Still in Ceylon, Brian's expenditures on doctors' fees were added to by almost £9,000 in legal fees
for his drug bust and appeal cases; Mick and Marianne
continued their holiday abroad; and Keith returned from
Marrakesh to Paris, where he decided to take an apartment.

Jo Bergman meanwhile had quickly found new office
space for the Stones at 12 George Street and telexed
Klein in New York: "Have found new offices . . . rent is
£1,650 per annum, rates £290, rent to be paid quarterly
in advance . . . also found premises for rehearsal room,
top priority as far as Mick is concerned. Rent £650,
premium £650, soundproofing estimates £250, furnishing,
heating etc. £100, piano £150, mikes £100, speakers £100.
Will be leased by Ian Stewart. Need rent and premium
almost at once for Ian to hand over. Remaining needed
almost at once. This is obviously urgent so that we may
finally establish our little mini-empire. You are already
aware of the fact that we are destitute, the boys are
destitute, and only you can save us. P.S. It's snowing like
hell." This new office was intended as the base for the
recording studio; the band's administrative offices from
February 5, 1968, were at 46a Maddox Street, Mayfair.

Down in Sussex, blissfully oblivious to all the politics,
drugs and machinery surrounding the band, Charlie's
lifestyle bore no relation to the archetypal rock 'n' roller's. The rooms were filled with antiques and paintings,
with a fine library of books. Charlie's huge collection of
military artifacts included rifles and revolvers from the
American Civil War. What pleased Charlie about being a
Stone, then as now, was the freedom it gave him to
indulge himself in these hobbies, and build up his jazz
record collection. Charlie and Shirley's first child, Sera-
phina, was born on March 18, 1968.

Since Charlie and I were the only Stones in England,
we were asked to take on the tenancy of the new office
formally. But Charlie refused, saying he was unhappy
about putting himself in the position of having to rely on
Klein to send over the rent. However, Charlie added, if
there was no other way, he would do it. When they
approached me I refused for the same reasons. It was
incomprehensible to me that our money was still gov-
erned by Klein in New York, and sent to all of us on an
ad hoc basis. I doubt if anyone else in the entertainment

world was in such a quandary over money after so much success.

We were in a state of disarray, more preoccupied with our private affairs and schemes than with the Stones—a trend that, sadly, continued. The crises of the previous twelve months—drug busts, law suits, my marital split, bans and brawls around the band—took a heavy toll. On February 8 at home at Keston, I felt really unwell and had an "anxiety attack"—certainly caused by the loss of Stephen to Diane in South Africa; similar things occurred later to show it was stress-related. A doctor prescribed sleeping tablets which freaked me out: I paced the floor until the effects wore off. It made me feel a lot worse and I've never taken a sleeping pill since. A month later I went for a complete medical check-up, but nothing serious was diagnosed.

The rest of the Stones were socializing: when Mick and Brian (both heavily bearded), and Keith, returned to London, Mick attended the Duke of Bedford's party in honor of the Supremes, while Brian went to a reception for the group Grapefruit, together with Donovan, the Beatles (minus George) and Cilla Black.

This was a period when several Stones changed homes. The nomadic Brian, when he wasn't flying in and out of Paris, moved out of his flat in Chesham Street shortly after Linda Keith had collapsed there, prompting a typically inaccurate newspaper headline: "Stones girlfriend in drug coma." For a period Brian checked into the Lygon Arms Hotel, in Worcestershire, followed by several weeks in the Imperial Hotel, Queen's Gate, in London. During this period of hotel-hopping he caused damage to a hotel in Bayswater—£15 worth. Amazingly, considering his fame and supposed fortune, Brian Jones was without roots. While he searched for a permanent home, he finally moved into a third floor flat at Royal Avenue House, in the Kings Road, rented to him by Lord Eliot. From here, he set off to Cornwall, bidding to buy Nansladron Farm, Tremaine. "I'm a country lad from the Cotswolds, so I know a bit about farms," Brian explained. "I'll be living there more than in London and plan to buy cows, pigs and poultry. I want a place where there is security and I can be completely self-sufficient. The whole social and economic scene is such a drag that I just want to get away." Mick expressed his concern at Brian's plan to base himself so far from town, but irrational behavior was by now expected from Brian.

Mick's property moves were, predictably, more scientifically planned. He became a member of the Country Gentlemen's Association in January 1968 and in March he finally bought Stargroves, for a mere £25,000 because it was in a ruinous state and needed extensive repairs before it was habitable. Mick completed this property hunt in May with the purchase of a city home: for £50,000 he bought a house with the smartest address in town: 48 Cheyne Walk, Chelsea. Christopher Gibbs was employed by Mick to redecorate it (and while doing so he suggested the name "Beggars Banquet" as the title for our next album).

We were still targets of sniping from some quarters, and an extraordinary attack on us came at this time from Canada. Two months after the death of Otis Redding, a writer named Ritchie Yorke accused us of giving Otis neither artistic nor financial credit for the song "(I Can't Get No) Satisfaction." Yorke roared that we'd had "plenty of time and many opportunities to make a confession" but we'd remained "stubbornly and disgustingly silent." What was the core of his complaint? Yorke wrote:

> They did *NOT* write "Satisfaction," nor did they even record it first. "Satisfaction" was written by Otis Redding, who sold it to Mick for a measly $10,000. The Stones were visiting Memphis and heard Otis cutting the song at a session. They begged him to sell it to them. After much persuasion, he reluctantly agreed. Not anxious for the kind of competition Redding could give them, they also convinced the soul singer not to release his version for at least twelve months. The Stones gaily jetted back to London, recorded "Satisfaction," and the disc sold close to 5 million copies. Each of the labels on these records gave composing credits to Keith and Mick. On writing royalties alone, the Stones have earned more than $50,000 from "Satisfaction" . . . later Volt Records in Memphis decided to issue Redding's original version. One would think that the untimely death of Otis Redding would be sufficient motivation for Jagger to come out from behind his lace and ruffles and tell it like it is.

The absurdity of this concoction is easily proved. The first time we visited Memphis was on November 17, 1965, more than six months after we recorded "Satisfaction" in the RCA Studios—and more than five months after we released it as a single in America.

Further proof of the nonsensical ramblings came from Steve Cropper, of Booker T and the MGs, who told *Rolling Stone* magazine: "When we recorded the Otis version of 'Satisfaction,' we didn't know the tune . . . if you ever listened to the record, you can hardly understand the lyrics, right? I sat down to a record player and copied down what I thought the lyrics were and handed Otis a piece of paper, and before we got through with the cut he threw the paper on the floor and that was it . . . as far as the story that Otis originally wrote 'Satisfaction' goes, it's completely false because we took the Rolling Stones record and then cut our version of what we thought we heard."

On March 8 I released in England what I thought was a strong record by the End, a single on Decca titled "Shades of Orange" backed by "Loving Sacred Loving" (both Wyman/Gosling). Reviews were very good; Derek Johnson wrote in *New Musical Express:* "Here's one to watch. There's a nagging thump beat, and a fascinating backing of pipe-organ, muted trumpets and muffled saxes, and above all, an absorbing lyric that's exceptionally well-presented. If the Stones had waxed this, it would have been an immediate hit. The End must rely on high-pressure promotion."

As usual, I got none—and nothing happened to the record.

By March we were all aware that after the dubious reception of *Satanic Majesties* we would have to start planning that new album. Mick recruited a New Yorker living in London, Jimmy Miller, to produce it after his impressive production work with the Spencer Davis Group, Traffic and Spooky Tooth.

In spite of all the extra-musical activities surrounding the band, the chemistry between us was always good when we got together and were able to concentrate. As Astrid confirms: "What made them tick, and what mustn't be forgotten, was their love for music and love of playing. That was the bottom line. There was more integrity and depth in the Stones than in a lot of other bands. There was a spirit of idealism and in the sixties they didn't compromise. Later, it was different."

For the first time under Miller's supervision the juices began to flow. At the start of one session Keith took out his new Philips cassette-recorder and played us a demo of a song he'd done at home. We tried working on it but couldn't get the same sound or feeling as the demo. Charlie then took out a miniature antique box he'd just bought in town. This contained a tiny snare and small cymbal that fitted on to its side. When he started playing it on the floor, Keith sat beside him with an acoustic guitar and they played the track together. It sounded great. So they fixed up Keith's cassette player and proceeded to record the song on to cassette, using its microphone. Compared with the sophistication of normal recording techniques, even in 1968, this was a raw, "homemade" method, but it worked. We were all knocked out by the crude sound and recorded the hi-fi dub of "Primo Grande (Street Fighting Man)" from cassette on to four-track. Two nights later we transferred it from four-track to eight-track, with some more over-dubs. It was to become a Stones classic.

For two months the momentum of our music kept us productive and disciplined. After *Satanic Majesties*, we *had* to tighten up. Between March 23 and 29 we recorded masters of "Jigsaw Puzzle," "Child of the Moon," "Parachute Woman"—and "Jumpin' Jack Flash."

The crucial riff for this song was mine, and it evolved in the unorthodox way that some of the best ideas do. One night during rehearsals at Morden I was sitting at the piano waiting for Mick and Keith to arrive. Charlie and Brian came in as I began playing the electronic keyboard, messing around with a great riff I'd found. Charlie and Brian began jamming with me and it sounded really good and tough. When Mick and Keith walked in they said: "Keep playing that, and don't forget it—it sounds great."

A few weeks later when we were in the Olympic studio, out came my riff, the backbone for Mick's terrific lyrics: "I was born in a crossfire hurricane . . ." And we all worked on the music. The part I'd composed worked perfectly—but the credit for this, one of our best tracks ever, reads Jagger–Richards. I knew the important riff was my idea and so did the band, but I'd forgotten to do anything about it. Even Keith admitted in interviews that I wrote that song. At the time it didn't worry me so much as I considered it a contribution to our success.

It happened frequently that basic ideas and middle bits by Brian, Charlie and me went into the melting-pot during long studio sessions, but over a period of hours or days the origins of our suggestions disappeared. I'd say something like: "That thing I did in the middle really worked, didn't it?" And Mick would reply: "That was my idea!" I'd dismiss it with a laugh rather than argue at the time—who wants a disagreement in the studio when you are all trying to be creative?

I urged Charlie and Brian to join me in standing up for ourselves. I maintained that we had every right to earn something from songs that Mick and Keith didn't bring into the studio complete, but which were cooperative band efforts. I didn't see why we should all pay equal session money for the studio rental, get equal record royalties—the Stones income has always been a five-way split—but absolutely nothing from songwriting and publishing of songs to which we'd genuinely contributed. Many other bands shared their publishing. I had raised the issue at meetings in the past with everyone present, but Brian's and Charlie's support fell by the wayside. I was on my own against Andrew, Mick and Keith, who really slagged me off for being greedy. Yet where did the greed really lie?

Mick and Keith proposed next that we open our own rehearsal and recording studios in London, paid for by the Stones, to be used by us and others. Since we had very little money, I voted against the idea; none the less we took a five-year lease from April 1 on a ground-floor and basement at 47—49 Bermondsey Street, Southwark, to be used for rehearsals and storage only.

That was by no means the only unilateral decision taken at this time. Back in December 1967 Mick, through the Stones office, had instructed solicitors to prepare an agreement with Christopher Gibbs and Nigel Gordon giving them authority to write a treatment based on something called *The Green Knight* for a possible film involving the Stones and Sandy Lieberson.* The film would be made by Shakti Films Ltd of India. A week later, the project was put on hold, but in early April 1968 solicitors were again instructed by the Stones office to prepare an agreement with us financing the project. I was totally unaware of this investment of the group's money. A few weeks of shooting took place in various Indian cities, but nothing ever came of it.

I was also unaware of another project being discussed: a Mr. Anthony Foutz checked into the Carlton Tower Hotel in London on March 7 and met Keith and Anita. They talked about a "trippy" filmscript, to include Mick, Keith, Brian, Anita, Marianne, "Sky People" and "saucers," etc. A Carlo Ponti project, *Maxigasm,* was scheduled to be filmed in North Africa, but again never happened.

Charlie and I were obviously regarded as "too straight" and not "hip" enough for this project. Fortunately for us, this was not a Stones investment.

Describing our "incredible enthusiasm" in working on songs that formed our new album, Jimmy Miller was energized by what he called "a return to the raw, solid Stones sound . . . after *Sergeant Pepper* most groups thought: well, what can we do *now?* and got overcomplicated. It took Bob Dylan to bring simplicity back to the scene."†

Mick now conceded that the drugs affairs had "screwed us up" as far as work went, and we had become unstable. For the first time, also, he stated that our individuality had to be recognized, "but we're as much a group as we want to be."

We recruited Michael Lindsay-Hogg, a prominent television director, to shoot a promotional film of us miming to "Jumpin' Jack Flash"—quite a revolutionary move, since the video age had not yet arrived and the idea of a pop group utilizing its own visual strengths in this way was almost unique.‡

*He was later to produce *Performance.*
†This was a reference to the album *John Wesley Harding* that Dylan released in 1968 after his long silence.
‡The Beatles had begun the trend with a video to accompany their song "Strawberry Fields Forever" in 1967. Previously, we'd done only odd bits of film footage to accompany the music.

A week later we shot the promotional film for "Child of the Moon" in the country, then returned to Olympic studios where Michael Lindsay-Hogg filmed us doing "Jumpin' Jack Flash" with our faces painted. Four camera crews were used; Michael charged £670 for directing and the bill for shooting the promotional films for "Jumpin' Jack Flash" and "Child of the Moon" was £2,453.

This seemed astronomical since our financial instability continued unchecked. The band finally agreed that something had to be done about this matter, and so, at the beginning of April we appointed solicitors Berger Oliver to look into the Allen Klein situation for us, and they wrote to him asking for details of payments to us for tours of Europe in March–April 1966; America in June–July 1966; Europe in March–April 1967; as well as details of record-guarantee monies, and songwriting monies for Mick and Keith.

In the meantime we all split for short holidays. Mick, Marianne and Christopher Gibbs flew to Dublin; Keith and Anita flew to Rome; I sent a telegram to Diane in South Africa, asking for Stephen to come on holiday to Britain later that month, and then took a three-day drive in the West Country with Astrid. Brian and Linda Keith flew to Spain for four days.

On May 9—with less than £50 in my bank account—I asked our new bookkeeper, Fred Trowbridge, to get me some money from America and he telexed Klein: "Bill says he is penniless and would you please send $5,000 to his private bank account urgently. Please telex confirmation that the money has been sent."

Four days later, as if by magic, I received a $5,000 payment from Nanker-Phelge Music, New York! Another check came for me, and the same to Brian, of $1,787, covering "royalties from 7/1/67 to 12/21/67."

On May 28, just as we were gearing up for a campaign with our new single "Jumpin' Jack Flash," more checks came in from Klein's office. We each received $5,000 and $6,250, representing our guarantee payments under agreements Numbers 5 and 17 with London Records, New York; and Mick and Keith additionally received $21,250 each, guarantee payments as writers, from Gideon Music.

*   *   *

The world's pop temperature by mid 1968 was less fiery than it had been for the previous five years. The psychedelic explosion of 1967 had produced a clear division: pop music and rock music. Bands like Cream, The Band (with their debut album), Jefferson Airplane, the Nice, Pink Floyd and Jimi Hendrix represented a shift in emphasis from simple singles to virtuoso musicianship. At the other end, pop music was alive and well: Louis Armstrong's "Wonderful World" topped the British chart in April and became the year's top-selling UK single; Cliff Richard and the Shadows celebrated their tenth anniversary, while in the States Simon and Garfunkel were top with "Mrs. Robinson." A free concert in London's Hyde Park—the very first—featured Pink Floyd (Syd Barrett had just left this band to be succeeded by Dave Gilmour), Marc Bolan's T. Rex, Jethro Tull and Roy Harper.

We seemed to have a foot in both camps. *Satanic Majesties* had put us firmly in the "concept album" category but we still hankered after a chart-topping single despite Mick's public statements that it wasn't important. We hadn't topped the singles chart since May 1966 with "Paint It Black." After that came "Have You Seen Your Mother Baby" (number two in October 1966), "Let's Spend the Night Together" (number two, February, 1967) and "We Love You" (number four, August 1967).

"Jumpin' Jack Flash" simply *had* to reach the top to restore our credibility. In the fickle world we inhabited, we were being written off as veterans as a new wave of bands began to make an impact. "The group's status as pop idols depends entirely on their past reputation," taunted the *Daily Express*. Urging us to get together more as a group, Judith Simons wrote: "Things look gloomy for them. The Stones have made plenty of plans but done very little. For example, they are to build their own recording studios. So far building has not started. They are to start their own record company. No record has yet been released. They were going to make a film about Britain being controlled by teenagers. The idea was abandoned."

With the drug busts and the split from Andrew, it was easy for the critics to cast us aside as a spent force. And with the news in early May that Mick was to star in his first solo film, the unity of the band was in doubt. The movie *Performance,* starring James Fox, told the story of a pop musician who had dropped out of the social stream of contemporary life until he met a vicious gangster. Mick, who was set to sing one song in the film and write the musical score, said of his role: "It's not me, but it's not alien to me, either . . . I can see his point of view. I'm playing a very strange boy who has kind of retired into himself and lives within his mind. There have been times when I felt much older than my years but I don't feel that now."

Impulsiveness had been the benchmark of the Stones' careers, right through to our return to the stage in America in 1989—something many people believed to be impossible. But even back in the sixties we were, as Mick said, acting unpredictably. A typical example was on May 12, when we decided to do a surprise appearance on stage at the *New Musical Express* Poll-Winners Concert at the Empire Pool, Wembley. The bill included Status Quo, Lulu, Love Affair, Cliff Richard, the Shadows, Dusty Springfield, the Herd, Amen Corner, the Tremeloes, the Move and Scott Walker . . . and the compère, Jimmy Savile, kept hinting to the 10,000 crowd that a surprise act was in store.

This, our first stage show in Britain for two years, was an emotional occasion for us and for the fans, who were delirious with excitement as we premièred our new single, "Jumpin' Jack Flash," followed by "Satisfaction." Scenes from the old days were re-enacted: commissionaires fought with girls, police and attendants linking arms to hold back hysterical fans. Marianne stood chucking flowers on stage, tears streaming down her face; Mick's gymnastics were intact despite the lay-off and although hardly a note could be heard above the roar of the crowd, the excitement was tremendous. Kids were crying with joy as Mick threw his shoes among the audience. "Just like the old days," everyone said backstage. The *NME* boss and concert organizer Maurice Kinn told the crowd afterwards that the Stones had been subjected to a lot of bad publicity and he wanted to emphasize that we had appeared at his concert completely at our own suggestion. This brought renewed applause. Roger Moore presented us with our award as Best R & B Group.

This concert was Brian's last live appearance. He was

by now completely disenchanted with the general pop scene, and told everyone he was hung up on electronic and experimental sounds. He should have been encouraged in this, but Mick's possessiveness reappeared when the manufacturers of the newly invented Moog synthesizer sent a representative to London to teach him how to operate the complex instrument, with its huge variety of sounds; this was to help him write the score for the film *Performance.* Mick never mastered the instrument, which could have been very useful for the Stones, too, but no one else ever had the chance to get to grips with it when his interest dimmed. Significantly, Brian said that if there was no room for electronic and experimental sound on the Stones' new album, he would like to do something separately. Originally, he had wanted "Child of the Moon" to be the A-side of our new single, but finally capitulated to the commercial prospects of "Jumpin' Jack Flash."

Even so, there were signs of a new spirit of togetherness as we all attended a directors' meeting at 46a Maddox Street on May 16, specifically to appoint new lawyers, Berger Oliver, to represent the band, succeeding Joynson-Hicks. After this five-minute formality we all went with our wives and girlfriends to see *2001—A Space Odyssey,* buying ten tickets for £12 18s. 6d. from the office petty-cash—for once, justifiably!

Over at Olympic studios, where we had been working well under Jimmy Miller's baton, we recorded "Silver Blanket," "Stray-Cat Blues," Muddy Waters' "Still a Fool," and "No Expectations." At one session we quickly cut my song "Downtown Suzie" (later released by Klein on *Metamorphosis,* an album of out-takes) and tried demos of another of my songs. However, I noticed that if my songs did not quite gel in one or two takes, they were rejected and not tried again—whereas with Mick and Keith's songs we would play one for a week if necessary. A typical example was in Jean-Luc Godard's film *One Plus One* with the song "Sympathy for the Devil."

Two days after we recorded the last track, on the night of May 20, Brian took a sleeping-pill prescribed by his doctor and at 7:20 a.m. the next morning, as he was sleeping, four policemen knocked, rang the bell for about ten minutes and shouted through the letter-box that it was the police. Finally Detective-Constable Brian Liddell climbed into the flat and opened the door; Detective-Sergeant Robin Constable went into the bedroom, where a light was on. Brian, sitting on the floor at the far side of the room, behind the bed, had a telephone under his dressing-gown and was in the process of dialing. The detective, telling Brian who he was, said he had a warrant to search the premises for drugs. Brian said: "I was first going to telephone for my solicitor." Constable: "I've been knocking on the door for about ten minutes and speaking through the letter-box. Why didn't you open the door?" Brian: "You know the scene, man. Why do I always get bugged?"

Constable searched the bedroom but found nothing. Liddell went into the smaller bedroom and began searching it, but he found nothing either. Detective-Constable Prentice and Detective-Sergeant Thelma Wagstaff went into the lounge. Liddell then took the kitchen. Prentice, looking through a bureau, had difficulty in opening the middle top drawer. It half opened and he saw a small record by the Rolling Stones. He put his hand into the back of the drawer and found a ball of blue wool. He took it out and, feeling something hard as he pulled the wool apart, he found a piece of brown substance. He didn't take it out but called Constable into the lounge, who came in, accompanied by Brian.

Prentice: "I have just found this ball of wool in this drawer." Brian: "Oh, no. This can't happen again, just when we're getting on our feet." Prentice opened the middle of the wool, to reveal a piece of brown substance sticking out. Constable: "Is this your wool?" Brian: "It could be." Brian was then cautioned by Constable, who continued: "Well, this officer, as you have seen, has found it in this drawer with this piece of brown substance inside. Does it belong to you?" Brian shrugged his shoulders and made no reply. Constable: "When Prentice showed me the wool, you seemed to recognize it immediately." Brian: "Why do you always have to pick on me? I've been working all day and night promoting our new record and now this has to happen." Constable: "Is this your flat?" Brian: "No, I've just been staying here for two weeks while the place I bought is being decorated." Constable: "Is all the property here yours?" Brian: "No.

Some of it belongs to Lord Eliot." Constable: "Does he rent the flat to you?" Brian: "Yes."

Prentice: "In the drawer where I found the wool there is one of the Rolling Stones' records. Is it yours?" Brian: "It probably is." Constable: "I am arresting you and you will be taken to Chelsea police station where you will be charged with possessing cannabis." Brian: "I never take the stuff. It makes me so paranoid."

Prentice then went to Brian's bedroom and started searching it. He took possession of an ashtray containing cigarette ends. Constable searched the bathroom, and in a toilet bag found a used phial. In the lounge on a table he found a jar filled with colored material. He showed Brian the two items. Constable: "What are these?" Brian: "The phial was prescribed to me some time ago, and the jar was left by someone after a party the other night."

Liddell completed his search of the kitchen and went into the hallway. Brian and Constable came in from the lounge. Constable told Liddell to go with Brian to the bedroom while he got dressed. He then accompanied Brian to the front door and, together with the other officers, they left the flat.

Shortly before 10 a.m. Brian, looking pale, unshaven and haggard, arrived at Marlborough Street Magistrates' Court in a red Morris Oxford. He was wearing a dark gray striped mod-style jacket over an open-necked psychedelic shirt, red trousers and fawn boots. He was led into the court by Detective-Sergeant Constable, who held his left arm.

He denied possessing a quantity of cannabis. Detective-Sergeant Constable asked for a three-week remand, because the drug had to be sent to a laboratory for analysis.

Mr. Pirie, the magistrates' chairman, told Brian that he would be remanded in his own recognizance of £1,000, and one surety of a similar amount by our recently appointed bookkeeper, Mr. Frederick Trowbridge, until June 11. There was no objection to bail, as long as there was a surety.

The press had a jamboree and our hearts sank. On the eve of the release of such a vital new record, in the midst of making an album, and on the crest of a new wave, the timing of this bust couldn't have been worse. Outside the court police controlled a crowd of about a hundred people and cameramen but Brian left by a back entrance in a chauffeured black Humber, slumped in the back seat, a hand over his face. He was distraught because he felt utterly innocent.

Brian was "on the run" again from his flat, and went with his instruments and clothes to Redlands to stay while Keith was away in Vienna. Yet again we were waiting for the outcome of a Stone's involvement with the law.

It's strange: it's always seemed that the band bounces back and produces excellence when under pressure. From the ashes of the Redlands bust came the rise to eminence of Mick as a spokesman for our generation; now, facing flak for running out of steam, appearing jaded, losing direction, and with the departure of Andrew Oldham and Eric Easton, we needed a boost. When our fourteenth British single, "Jumpin' Jack Flash," was released on May 24, the response was tremendous. "The Stones have a unique flair for taking a basically simple formula and turning it into a miniature epic," wrote Derek Johnson in the *New Musical Express*. "It's a disc that's pungent, galvanic, insistent, utterly compelling and vital." In *Melody Maker* Bob Dawbarn agreed: "It certainly stirs memories of the group a year or two back—wild, exciting, bluesy . . . some particularly nice noises issuing from Bill's bass guitar." He wasn't to know, but *Keith* played bass on "Jack Flash." Long-time Stones watcher Roy Carr later described the single as "as near-perfect as any rock record should ever possibly be . . . one of the most important records *any* group has ever cut."

As the promotion machinery swung into action, Mick told Ray Coleman in an interview for *Disc:* "I don't care whether it gets to Number One or not; I really think it's quite a good single; now it's up to the people who buy records . . . I don't think it will be a disaster for us if it fails to reach the top." Denying he was the leader of the band, Mick said; "I am not the leader of the Stones. Charlie is the leader of the Rolling Stones and I wouldn't attempt to usurp his authority in any way. When he makes a decision, we stick by it." Mick was in the habit of stringing people along: around this time he convinced an *Evening Standard* reporter that our new single had been recorded on "an ordinary household tape-cassette machine at my house. It didn't take long."

There was no holding the record: within three days Decca reported that it had sold 93,512 in Britain and on Monday, May 27, alone it sold 10,132! It went into the chart at fourteen and kept selling steadily at the rate of 10,000 a day.* The single, our eighteenth in America, was released there on the London label on June 1, with a prediction from *Billboard* that it would put us back at the top of their Hot 100 chart.†

And right afterwards our film debut came, in a Jean-Luc Godard production, *One Plus One*. From our recording sessions on June 4 onwards, camera crews had moved in to film us. The Stones' role in this hundred-minute film was to act as a kind of backdrop to the story of a girl who arrived in London and freaked out. To Mick, particularly, the most worthwhile aspect of this film was the lucky break when Godard by chance filmed the complete evolution of the song "Sympathy for the Devil" as it changed course over several sessions.

It began as a folky song, rather like "Jigsaw Puzzle," but it didn't work, so we kept changing it until finally it evolved as a samba. The song was originally titled "The Devil is My Name," but its final title, "Sympathy for the Devil," was also used for the movie's American release.

By contrast with the earlier plans for a movie, this one progressed efficiently and didn't need too much of our attention. We received a fee in June 1968 of $50,000 (£18,878 in those years); a special clause in the contract recognized the difficulties of Brian in relation to his bust and protected his participation in the film: "The non-availability of Brian Jones to perform his services under the contract arising from the current charge against him shall not entitle us to suspend or determine the artist's services thereunder."

The band was on a high as we made plans for our new album, *Beggars Banquet*. There were grandiose plans for its cover, which went through many changes before ending up as simple script lettering on a white background.

*It reached Number One in Britain and stayed there for three weeks.
†It was top of the US chart for a week.

We hired two bays in the Cadogan Square car park for
three full days from June 7 for the purpose of painting a
grand piano. The office ordered five pairs of cricket
pads, stumps, bails, two balls and two bats from the
cricket firm of Jack Hobbs, and from theatrical costum-
iers Berman and Nathan we ordered some outlandish
gear: Mick, who dressed as a swell, wore trousers, top
hat, a tailcoat and pumps. Charlie, dressed as a stable-
groom, wore shirt, tricorn, breeches, waistcoat, boots
and stock. The rest of us wore assorted hats, boots, cord
trousers and medieval tunics. Also on hand were black
skullcaps, assorted medieval shirts, breeches, seven pairs
of tights, tunics and rough leather jerkins.

The album cover picture, as we planned it, was photographed with us dressed as tramps at a house we rented
at £45 for a day: Sarum Chase in Hampstead. A room
was decorated in medieval style, with a huge banquet
table including a suckling pig (which cost £25!).

Next day, we drove in convoy up the M1 motorway,
Astrid and me in my Mercedes 250 bumper-tailing Keith
and Tom Keylock in the Bentley at speeds of between 90
and 120 m.p.h., until we reached an old ruin near Derby.
They tried to lose us but we stayed with them, much to
their annoyance. Pictures were taken in a variety of garb,
including medieval clothing, and we also dressed in cricket
gear for pictures in a field where the grass was so long we
could hardly walk.

All-night sessions at the Olympic were the norm during
the completion of the album, and the adrenalin was flowing with the presence of Godard's film crew. His method
suited us perfectly, for he had no real master plan or firm
script. He worked from one point to another, filming a
piece and then deciding what to do next after looking at
the result. As Keith pointed out, that was precisely how
we shaped our songs and recording sessions. Nothing was
ever firmly laid down and songs went through many
changes of structure or rhythm before completion.

Nicky Hopkins, the keyboards player, was brought in
to augment the band on this album, with Glyn Johns
engineering and Jimmy Miller producing. But there was
near-disaster after an all-night session on June 10 when
the heat from the film crew's arc lamps set fire to the
studio ceiling. The rest of the boys had left and my first

thought was to save the tapes: Jimmy and I dashed in to the control room and then into the vaults to pull them clear, and *then* we ran for safety. Everyone was evacuated while three fire-engines came within minutes to extinguish the blaze. Guitars, amplifiers, a Hammond organ and photographic equipment were all soaked. After the firemen had finished, Jimmy Miller and I returned the undamaged tapes to the studio's tape vault and we left for home.

Next day Brian faced the second court appearance in his latest drugs bust. Typically, early in the morning, he went for a 3-guinea hair styling, manicure and massage: appearance was vital to Brian and his court appearances always found him looking stylish and immaculate. A chauffeured car took him and Tom Keylock to Marlborough Street Magistrates' court. A group of fifty teenagers stood in the gallery, and a court official told them that if they made any noise they would be ejected. He also warned several girls who had cameras to keep them in their bags.

Brian then appeared, wearing a gray pinstripe suit, white shirt and blue tie with large white spots. The girls in the public gallery sobbed as Brian sat motionless in the dock. He pleaded not guilty. Evidence was given in writing. This was the new procedure under the Criminal Justice Act, so that there was no need for evidence to be given in detail in court. Brian made an eight-minute appearance, and elected to go for trial by jury. Michael Havers (Defending) asked if there was any objection to unrestricted bail because Brian had "commitments abroad." A police officer said there was no objection, and that there would be no restrictions on his traveling abroad. The girls were crying again, as Brian was formally sent for trial at the Inner London Sessions, where he would appear before a jury on June 25.

Afterwards, Brian dodged about thirty fans when he left by a back exit and was driven home. Tom Keylock then went to the Priory Clinic to pick up some medicine for Brian. Later, Brian and Suki Potier were driven to London airport where they flew to Malaga, Spain for four days.

Brian's problems were played out in public, while some of us coped with difficulties privately. I had been having sleepless nights for some time, and my general tension needed a solution. I realized that I had to learn to relax. Photography provided the outlet. I'd always been interested in nature and biology and the combination of the two helped me unwind. Mick and Keith let off steam with new motorbikes they had bought to use in the countryside near their homes; Charlie seemed happy among his antiques and the latest Miles Davis and Buddy Rich records.

With "Jumpin' Jack Flash" topping the charts in *Melody Maker* and *Disc,* and with a fine album imminent, it should have been a great time for us. But the writs and terse messages continued to fly around us: on June 19 Andrew Oldham served a writ against Gideon Music, Mirage, Essex, Decca, London Records, Nanker-Phelge Music and Allen Klein. The same day, Klein received a sardonic telex from Mick: "The phones and electricity will be cut off tomorrow. Also the rent is due. I am having to run the office despite your wishes. If you would like to remedy this please do so."

That done, Mick flew to Paris and on to Rome, where he was joined by Marianne; Keith stayed at home with a bank balance showing a debit of £3,720, talking about the UFOs he had seen near Redlands.

For me there was a glimpse into rock's direction in the seventies—the birth pangs of "heavy metal." In Olympic studios to attend a session for the End on June 22, Jimmy Page came in and we chatted. He invited me to the dubbing room, where he played me three or four tracks he'd done with the Yardbirds. They sounded so powerful, a completely new style for them. He mentioned that the group was splitting up and that he might form a new group and use these tracks. Two months later he formed Led Zeppelin, with Peter Grant as their manager. These tracks became part of their debut album.

As Mick immersed himself in his role for *Performance,* with a total fee of $100,000 plus 7½ per cent of the film's net profits, our return to action was being heralded by the media as a "comeback." It was a fair comment, because we'd been off the road and devoting time to such things as losing managers and drug busts; but as Keith said: "We never felt we'd been away. We've always been around."

Jimmy Miller, whom we all rated highly as a producer,

delivered his verdict in an enlightening interview with
Penny Valentine of *Disc*. He thought we had been "musically misjudged . . . they are capable of great beauty in
their writing. Unlike the Beatles, the Stones have never
really been recognized as being in the beautiful bracket."
He said of me: "Bill is the really punctual, reliable one of
the group. I think he feels that perhaps his ideas aren't
really very good for the Stones—that's why he produces
[the End] separately. Also he doesn't offer too many
suggestions at sessions because Keith writes the songs
with Mick and Bill feels that Keith, being a guitarist,
knows exactly what bass line he wants." This was untrue:
I was constantly adding my ideas to the structure of
songs, both as a bass player and in other ways.

Brian, said Jimmy, was "probably the one I've made
most effort to get along with. When the sessions [for
Beggars Banquet] started, he came to me and said he
didn't think he would be able to contribute much. I
didn't push him. I asked Mick what the situation was and
Mick said: 'Look, you can't force him, but he'll be OK.'
And he was right. When we started working he really got
into it and started to get excited, and he apologized to
me for having had doubts at the beginning. Brian is very
insecure. He has to have people around him all the
time—and he has a lot of hang-ups. But when he's doing
something that really interests him he's almost a different
character."

Others close to the band, who saw Brian's disintegration away from the studio, testify to his problems. Astrid
says: "Brian didn't seem together enough to be able to
handle anything. He was more out of it on a daily basis,
whereas the others certainly weren't. Looking back, really, they weren't that stoned. It wasn't destructive. They
got through an awful lot of work." Shirley Arnold, our
fan-club secretary points out: "There was this friction
between them. Mick was very creative and must have felt
Brian was holding him back. Brian just couldn't cope
with it."

As the new single rose to number two in the States and
was highly placed around the world, Mick, Marianne
(newly pregnant) and Jimmy Miller flew to Los Angeles
on June 6 to join Glyn Johns and started mixing the new
album there. They flew in to find that our single was

Number One in *Cashbox* magazine. Charlie flew to Los Angeles with Shirley to help Mick and Jimmy Miller mix the album.

Brian's contribution to the new album had been minimal, though, and his psychological estrangement from the band at that time can be judged by his departure even before the album recording sessions had been finished for Gibraltar on June 3, en route to Tangier with Suki Potier and Tom Keylock. Brian was magnetically drawn to the area but, as always with him, it could never be an event-free trip: Suki overdosed on drugs. Luckily after several days in hospital she recovered. Brian's friend Brion Gysin and a local man named Hamri took Brian to the Atlas mountains, to hear the Pipes of Pan played by the Master Musicians of JouJouka.

This was an almost physical experience for Brian, one that was dramatically to shape his future and be a lasting influence on the band (though we did not know it when he returned, brimming with enthusiasm). Brian's flirtation with these Moroccan musicians, regarded by many as just a diversion back in 1968, showed how, despite all his personal problems, he still had an exceptionally fine ear; twenty-one years later, with our 1989 album *Steel Wheels*, we were still acknowledging this with our JouJouka sounds.

In mid-1968 we all seemed intent on establishing more peaceful roots. But my concern for Stephen suddenly took priority when Astrid and I met him at London airport in June after his flight from Durban for a holiday. He was thin, and looked unwell. He told us he had had really bad toothache for some time, but that his mother had informed him that he could wait until he got to England—Dad could pay for dental treatment. When he recovered from the treatment, Astrid, Stephen and I drove to the New Forest for a picnic and next day we bought him a new wardrobe in Carnaby Street. It was wonderful to have him back.

Stephen was due to return to Diane in Durban in early August, but after seeing how he'd been treated I decided to keep him in England and fight for his custody. On September 1, I received a collect call at Keston from Diane in South Africa. We had a row about Stephen and, ignoring her threat to come to England to retrieve him, I remained firm in my decision that he should not return to her.

At this time Astrid and I were trying to find a new house to replace Keston. While we were looking over a property in Essex the agent phoned to recommend us another house that would be going on the market next day. It took us an hour to reach Gedding, near Bury St. Edmunds in Suffolk and on our arrival Gedding Hall, built in 1480, struck us as so stunning that we were sure we'd arrived at the wrong place. Gathering courage, we drove up the long drive to the Hall, which was surrounded by a beautiful moat, with black swans and ducks. The park and grounds were immaculately kept but a gardener stopped us to say the owner was away and we could see the exterior only. As he showed us round, Astrid and I agreed that only if the place was falling to bits inside would we *not* try to buy it. Completely bowled over, we made an appointment to view it and returned home to Keston elated.

We went back six days later, taking Stephen, and Karin and Jan, Astrid's sister and her boyfriend. On our arrival the owner, Geoff Allen, showed us the interior of the house. On the television set, I was somewhat taken aback to see a full-sized photograph of the Kray Brothers; Geoff told me they'd been great friends for years and had often visited him at the Hall. The place was beautiful; I offered £41,000, even though I had only £1,000 in my bank account; this was accepted. Geoff said that although a member of the Queen's Household had offered more, he preferred to sell it to me, a self-made man like him. We could visit it any time before buying it, he added as we left. In the evening, Astrid, Karin, Jan, my future gardener Dennis Halfacre and his wife Joan went for dinner at our local, where we talked excitedly about the new house non-stop.

Although I had confidently made an offer for Gedding, the Stones' financial situation was going from bad to worse. After the Olympic studios fire, Stu had bought a new replacement Hammond organ, but was still waiting for reimbursement from New York. Fred Trowbridge, who received a reminder from the taxman that we owed £13,639, let fire in this angry telex to Klein's office in New York on June 19:

Embassy [our travel agents] have threatened court
action if the bills for £1,406 14s. (copies of which have
been sent to Klein) are not paid. Could you please pay
as you promised and advise me of payment. We have
made numerous attempts to contact you on the telephone. We are making a further attempt between
10:15 a.m.–11 a.m. (your time). The position has now
reached crisis point. I need money now. As follows:
Overdraft (now) £3,180 17s. 9d. Creditors as list £7,284
8s. Less paid £277. Total £7,007 8s. 10d. Plus new Les
Perrin bill £157 10s. Total £7,164 18s. 10d. Plus monthly
quota £2,610. Total pounds £12,955 10s. 7d. Yes Allen
I need £12,955.10.7 (pounds), now. Please await.

Back in London from Morocco, Brian and Suki abandoned the plan to buy a farm in Cornwall and settled on
somewhere much more romantic. Just as I'd fallen instantly in love with Gedding, Brian decided on his first
visit to buy Cotchford Farm, fifty miles southeast of
London, near Hartfield in Sussex. He got it for £28,750.
The old farmhouse, built of brick and partly hung with
tiles, with ornamental gardens, a paddock and woodland
extending for about eleven acres, had once been owned
by the author of *Winnie the Pooh,* A. A. Milne. It should
have been a haven of tranquillity.

Brian was totally immersed still in the Moroccan musicians he had discovered and on August 1 he arranged for
a car to take George Chiantz, of Olympic studios, to
Tangier, en route to Marrakesh, where he met up with
Brian and Suki at the Es Saadi Hotel. Brian had arranged for George and himself to record the local musicians; he had even had a bass guitar shipped out specially
to him from London.

Brion Gysin took Brian to a musician named G'Naoua
in Marrakesh, and also to the Maalimin musicians. Brian
and George Chiantz later recorded the Master Musicians
of JouJouka. Sadly, though, Brian did not live to enjoy
the fruits of his musical vision. Although Klein had these
tapes for some considerable time, he seemed totally unin-
terested in the project, and never got a record release
together for Brian. When Brian left us in June 1969,
Klein shipped the tapes back to the Stones office. The
album was finally put out by the Stones on October 8,

1971, three years after Brian had made the recordings, as a tribute to him, entitled *Brian Jones Presents the Pipes of Pan at JouJouka*.

Even in his beloved Morocco, Brian's health was a problem. Suddenly, on the balcony of his hotel room, he blacked out. George Chiantz was shocked but the experienced Suki assured him it was quite a regular occurrence; Brian, she said, would be back to normal if he slept for a while. They picked him up, still unconscious, and carried him to his bed. He slept soundly and later woke up remembering nothing of the incident. After this, on August 16, Brian went to the Clinique California in Tangier where a doctor prescribed sleeping tablets; four days later Brian returned to the hospital where the same doctor prescribed Valium and Laroxyl.

Soon after a cable arrived from the Stones office saying he was needed back in London to attend to the purchase of Cotchford Farm. He returned on August 23 to a "welcome home" banquet of flowers from us as he moved into Suki's flat in Hampstead, pending purchase of his country home.

Bands of our stature became used to gossip, and it wasn't surprising that Brian's habits caused people to suggest he would leave. It was also sometimes said that I was leaving, but as this had no foundation, I didn't give any other rumors much time. Eric Clapton was said to be replacing me in the Stones when his band Cream broke up at Christmas 1968, but Eric declared: "I know nothing about it. I wouldn't join unless I was asked! It's all pretty strange to me—and I'd have to play lead guitar, anyway!" Mick, speaking from Ireland where he was on holiday with Marianne, stated: "The five Rolling Stones remain the five Rolling Stones. There is to be no alteration."

Mick had wanted *Beggars Banquet* to be released on his twenty-fifth birthday, July 26, but it was impossible. The actual music and the mixing were the least of several problems: Keith joined Mick, Charlie and Jimmy Miller in Hollywood, and they jumped from studio to studio to ensure the best sound for each track. We were all confident that this would be a milestone album, and it remains a favorite of ours.

The biggest hurdle for the record's release became the cover design. The photographic sessions with us dressed as tramps and in medieval costumes didn't inspire Mick and in Los Angeles, Mick, Keith and Anita had a brainwave. They brought in Barry Feinstein to photograph a lavatory, adding graffiti to make a more dramatic impact. Back in London, the completed artwork showed a view of a lavatory wall and a drawing of a nude girl on a drainpipe. Graffiti on the wall of the toilet included: "Lyndon loves Mao," "John loves Yoko," "Bob Dylan's Dream," "God rolls his own" and "I sit broken-hearted." Inside the album cover was a picture of the band sitting around a banquet table, with Mick taking a bite of an apple speared on the blade of Keith's knife, and the words: "Beggars Banquet, RSVP."

The graffiti on the toilet wall caused Decca to erupt. While London Records in America insisted that the cover *had* to have the name of the band to ensure maximum sales, Decca's chairman Sir Edward Lewis told Mick that he considered the graffiti picture in "dubious taste." "We don't find it at all offensive, so we must stand by it," Mick replied. "Decca have put out a record with an atom bomb exploding on the cover *[Atomic Tom Jones]*. I find *that* more offensive than graffiti."

Mick later said: "We really have tried to keep the album within the bounds of good taste. I mean, we haven't shown the whole lavatory! That *would* have been rude. We've only shown the top half! We did not deliberately go out to produce a cover of this kind for sensationalism, or to offend 'them'. It was simply an idea that had not been done before and we chose to put the writing on a lavatory wall because that's where you see most writings on walls."

Mick said the music on the album was definitely the kind that we could play on stage, and named "Sympathy for the Devil" and "No Expectations" as his favorites. Asked why nothing was released as a single in advance of the album ("Jumpin' Jack Flash" was way ahead of the LP and was never intended as a trailer), Mick said the Stones were "too busy doing other things to find time to promote a single." This was not so: we were all fairly inactive at the time. It was actually *Mick* who was too busy with other pursuits, notably preparing the filming of *Performance*.

The battle with Decca carried wider implications than were immediately apparent. Record companies were facing a sales slump and the accent had shifted from singles to albums. "Jumpin' Jack Flash" had failed to sell a quarter of a million in Britain, which was depressing news for a chart topper, and the Beatles' singles were suffering similarly. If it was a thin time for the Beatles and the Stones, imagine what it was like for the rest. Artists could now achieve a chart position with a sale of a mere 5,000 singles, and it needed only 80,000 copies to get to the Number One position. Our commitment to a thematic album was therefore correct. In America, "Street Fighting Man" and "No Expectations" were released as a single trailer for the album on August 31, our nineteenth single in the US (where it reached forty-eight in the charts). But it aroused a storm of controversy and was quickly banned by some radio stations, particularly in Chicago, the scene of street violence and controversial police brutality during the Democratic presidential convention. "Street Fighting Man" depicted the violence that took place in cities during long, hot summers around the world; purely by coincidence it was the month of the invasion by Russian troops of Czechoslovakia.*

Although the delay in the album release, and the banned single, were irritating, they sustained the controversial aura of the Stones—which we never had to try hard to do! It was a period of intense political awareness by pop musicians. On the B-side of the Beatles' chart topping single "Hey Jude" was John Lennon's "Revolution"; he'd fought vainly to make it the A-side. Pop stars who had been around for about five years were now in their mid to late twenties, with strong social, political and cultural awareness that was bound to be conveyed in songs. I'm sure Mick knew this, and though the confrontations caused him to expend a lot of energy, he battled intelligently to ensure that the Stones came over strongly.

---

*In the USA the original color sleeve had a photo of a street demonstration. There is no telling how many real copies do exist, since it was in stores less than a week before being recalled and banned. This is the most sought-after Stones item ever. Collectors have been known to pay over $500 for it and there are many counterfeit copies in circulation.

On the "Street Fighting Man" problem, and censorship generally, he said: "What it all comes down to is that we design the sleeves and make the records—just like we have been doing for the last five years. We'll get this album distributed somehow even if I have to go down the end of Greek Street and Carlisle Street at two o'clock on Saturday morning and sell them myself.

"What really worries me is the principle of being dictated to over our product by our distributors. I am opposed to all forms of censorship. The only censorship one can have is by the artists themselves, which we do subconsciously anyway."

As the battle over the album cover reached deadlock, mammoth color posters of the picture inside the sleeve (the Mick–Keith apple-eating scene) went up on hoardings in London, Manchester and Birmingham. Costing £450 a month, quite expensive, this was the first time a rock band had used such a promotion technique, and it was a source of great interest to the advertising industry. The only problem was that we were advertising an album that could not be bought. And the word back from our fans was that they were getting restless.

Our activities, personally as well as professionally, continued to be turbulent, amazingly so considering we were "off the road." Diane arrived in England in early September to contest custody of Stephen, staying with her relations in Warminster. Things were complicated by a bout of nervous tension which hit me on September 10, for which a doctor gave me an injection. Newspapers were soon knocking on my door at Keston, having got wind of the custody disagreement. Astrid, described by journalists as "a blonde in a red velvet suit," answered the door and said I could not discuss the matter of Stephen without my solicitor's advice; but Walter Cory, Diane's father, went on record with this: "Diane came over to England about three weeks ago to try to get custody of Stephen. She hasn't contacted me since she arrived in this country because we don't see eye to eye over Stephen's future. I went to Durban to see Diane at Christmas and thought it would be better if Bill were to look after Stephen. I arranged for Stephen to come for a holiday in June. You couldn't find a better father. He

really dotes on Stephen and I can't praise him enough."
The issue of custody was eventually put aside until our
divorce proceedings.

Over at 48 Cheyne Walk, the noted interior designer
David Mlinaric began work for Mick, who had delivered to
the house such exotic items as a Regency bed and a Louis
XV bath (c.1770), which he bought in Ireland for £900.
Despite such trappings and his adoption by the Establishment, Mick was never shy of media combat. When Marianne
told the press that she was pregnant and was divorcing her
husband, but that she and Mick did not plan to marry, the
moralists were outraged. Mick went on the *David Frost Show*
to defend their decision, and had a heated exchange of
views with Mary Whitehouse, who led a chorus of criticism.

But Mick's thoughts were mostly on movies as he
started work on *Performance;* shooting in London called
for ten weeks of his exclusive services from September 3.
The high spot of the film as far as the press was concerned was that the script required Mick to make love to
a lady now part of Stones folklore, Anita Pallenberg.
Observers did not miss the point that this meant Anita
had now "been involved" with three of the Stones, and
this fueled rumors of an affair between Mick and Anita.
"We're all one big family," Mick quipped drily.

On September 12 there was the world première of *Girl
on a Motorcycle,* starring Alain Delon and Marianne.
This was far from being Marianne's screen debut: she
had appeared in a Jean-Luc Goddard film, quickly followed by a role in *I'll Never Forget What's 'Is Name,* with
Oliver Reed, in which she took off her clothes. *Girl on a
Motorcycle* continued her "look of dreamy sensuality,"
according to one reviewer, and the *Illustrated London
News* recommended her latest film "if you relish the
prospect of seeing Marianne Faithfull clad only in a skin-
hugging black leather suit, riding a motorbike for hours
on end around the European countryside . . ."

We won the single of the year category in the *Melody
Maker* readers' 1968 Pop Poll Awards: in the top group,
both British and international section, we were second to
you-know-who.

While Mick was busy filming, Marianne was in Ireland,
holidaying with her mother in Tuam, County Galway.
Ever the gentleman, Mick sent her flowers (he also sent

orchids to Anita Pallenberg in London). After Marianne had been in Ireland for nearly a month, Mick went to see her, flying to Shannon with a Harley Street specialist, Dr. Victor Bloom. Marianne was obviously going through problems; had she freaked out over the rumored affair between Mick and Anita, or was she having difficulties with her pregnancy? At one point, she had treatment at Portiuncula Hospital, Ballinasloe.

On the *Performance* set, meanwhile, according to Donald Cammell: "Keith was trying to sabotage my movie because he was jealous of Mick with Anita. He didn't want Anita to do the film and wouldn't speak to me for a long time and wouldn't perform on the track of the music; but Anita was having the time of her life. She'd go home to Keith, who'd be terribly jealous when he heard she'd been in bed with Mick."

Back from Morocco, Suki needed specialist medical attention, and Anita briefly entered King's College Hospital, London. Astrid and Shirley were fine!

Then there were the court appearances. Brian truly poured his heart out when he appeared at the Inner Sessions at Marylebone Street magistrates' court on September 26. And it worked. Looking pale and tired, with rings under his eyes, he wore a dark single-breasted suit, white shirt and red tie. Tom Keylock and Suki Potier were in the public gallery, which was packed with teenage girls.

Brian was charged with having in his possession 144 grains of cannabis without lawful authority. He gave his address as Redlands, West Wittering, Sussex. His face sickly white and in a trembling voice which could scarcely be heard, he pleaded not guilty. The jury was made up of ten men and two women.

Brian said that he had taken over the furnished flat while a house he had bought was being decorated. American actress Joanna Pettet, the previous tenant, had been there for about six months, and had moved out only two hours before he moved in. He knew nothing of the cannabis. He examined the flat the day he moved in and found a stocking, a sock and a bottle of marking ink with the initials J. M. on it in the bureau.* Brian said that

*When Joanna Pettet was questioned by the FBI she said that the ball of wool had been left by her, but denied knowledge of the cannabis found inside it.

later the same day he had left to spend some days in Cornwall. He had been recording at night and sleeping during the day. He spent some time at a friend's house and only stayed at the Chelsea flat half the time.

Brian continued: "The first thing I heard one morning was a loud knocking on the door. I did not immediately become aware of what this banging was. Then I put on a sort of kimono-type dressing gown and tiptoed to the front door and looked through the spy-hole. I remember seeing three men of the type I do not usually see through the spy-hole. I panicked. There had been a number of raids previously in the Chelsea area and I believed it was in fact the police on my doorstep that morning. I was frightened of them. I seem to have formed a fear of the police. I tiptoed back to the bedroom and tried to decide whether or not to call my solicitor."

Some time elasped before the police actually entered the flat. The prosecution alleged that the drug was found in a ball of wool. Brian said: "I would easily have had time to dispose of anything I should not have had. When the ball of wool was shown to me I was absolutely shattered. I felt everything swim. I don't knit. I don't darn socks, and I don't have a girlfriend who darns socks. I did not have the slightest knowledge that the ball of wool was in the flat. It was such an important time in the group's life. We had not had a record out in a long time and we were just promoting one. We had the feeling that this new record was going to lead us on the road back to success. The trouble involving me and two other members of the group had set us back. I have friends in the flat and friends of friends, but I don't suspect any of them putting the cannabis there. Last year the Lord Chief Justice made it clear to me what would happen if I were ever convicted again on this sort of charge. Last year's affair made me very frightened of the drug. I explained here last year that I used it only experimentally. To take it now would make me very paranoid indeed. I have not touched the stuff since then. I don't touch it. I had no difficulty in giving it up."

When the court reconvened after lunch, Brian said he had been having medical treatment since last year's case. Dr. Anthony Flood (psychiatrist) said: "Nothing suggested to me that Jones was playing around with cannabis. If I put a reefer cigarette by this young man, he would run a mile."

Michael Havers asked Brian about the effect of the drug. "It heightens an experience," Brian replied, "and if one is not feeling very happy—and at the time I was not, because I had personal difficulties—it makes one much more unhappy. I have had absolutely nothing to do with the drug since then."

At this point Mick and Keith entered the gallery, and spectators, counsel and jury turned to look. They sat down at the front with the schoolgirls.

Chairman Reginald Seaton, in his final address to the jury, said the burden of proof rested not on Brian, but on the police, and that their case was completely circumstantial. No evidence of using cannabis had been found—no ashes, no cigarette ends. There was only the cannabis itself, which the jury had seen and could decide for themselves whether it might have been disposed of before the police entered. "If you think the prosecution has proved without a doubt that the defendant, Brian Jones, knew the cannabis was in his flat, you must find him guilty. Otherwise, he is innocent."

The jury then retired to consider its verdict, returning forty-five minutes later. As the foreman announced "guilty," Brian, near to collapse, staggered back, muttering. Girls in the public gallery gasped; one began to cry. Suki started to cry and Keith was visibly trembling. Brian slumped to his seat in the dock, his head in his hands, mumbling: "No, no, no. It can't be true." The chairman said: "I think this was a lapse and I don't want to interfere with the probation order that already applies to this man. I am going to fine you according to your means. You must keep clear of this stuff. You really must watch your step. You will be fined £50 with 100 guineas [£105] costs. For goodness sake, don't get into trouble again or you really *will* be in serious trouble."

Fans in the public gallery rushed into the main corridor, hugging and kissing each other. Brian left the court, hand in hand with Suki, and then danced a jig with her and Mick. He grinned at the schoolgirls and posed for photographs. Suki Potier said: "I had resigned myself to not seeing Brian for a long time. I think everyone had. That judge is one beautiful man." In the car after the hearing, Cynthia Stewart put her arms round Brian as he sobbed uncontrollably. "He definitely couldn't have taken prison," she said.

Brian said: "When the jury announced the guilty verdict, I was sure I was going to jail for at least a year. It was such a wonderful relief when I heard I was only going to be fined. I'm happy to be free. It's wonderful. This summer has been one long worry to me. Someone planted the drug in my flat, but I don't know who. I will state till my death that I did not commit this offense."

Although we were not involved directly in their litigation, it was odd to watch Andrew Oldham and Eric Easton in the High Court. Their lengthy battle began on October 2, Eric and Andrew fighting over whether they should get their share of money if there was success in other actions involving music publishing companies run by Klein and others. Although we were mercifully not implicated, we suffered because while the case went on an estimated £417,000 in royalties was frozen. The battle was simplified when on the second day Andrew signed all his interests in the Stones over to Klein. On October 25 Andrew was told by a judge that he was in "manifest contempt" of a court requirement to pay £5,000, received from his management of the Stones, into court; he was given three weeks to pay this into a joint bank account. When on November 15 Judge Buckley noted that Andrew had purged his contempt by paying in the money, the heat was taken out of the case by a dramatic concession by Andrew: he no longer denied that there was a partnership between himself and Eric—who had sought a prison committal order against Andrew for failing to comply with an undertaking to produce a list of documents or to pay into an account money he received in respect of Stones joint management. Oldham was ordered to pay the costs, Judge Buckley adding: "The important matter is that Mr. Oldham has indicated that he is prepared to submit broadly to the relief claimed by Mr. Easton. He no longer denies that there was a partnership and will submit to its dissolution." And the Beatles thought *they* had troubles with Apple!

I could never fathom why, in the midst of all the complications and telex messages about money for the

Stones, people who had nothing to do with us became involved. Jo Bergman cabled Allen Klein on October 29 about Mick's brother: "The $200 sent by you for Chris Jagger is at the Nepal Bank, Kathmandu. Chris is now in Calcutta and cannot get money transferred to him because of postal strike. Mick requests you write to Nepal Bank, Kathmandu and get money returned to you which Chris will confirm from Calcutta. Will you then please send further $200 to Chris care of First National City Bank of New York, Calcutta. Do not send American Express. Please send today as this is urgent and confirm to us that money has gone."

Three days later:

Bergman: "What happened to Chris Jagger's money?"

Klein: "It is located at the Bank of Kathmandu."

Bergman: "Chris Jagger requested they send it back to you. Please send him $200 to First National City Bank of New York in Calcutta."

The situation with the band was not much better. A handful of examples from this date: A request on August 14 for £125,000 to be sent by the Klein office to Mick's account, for the purchase of some property, did not seem to have been acted upon by October 21, when a further telex from Fred Trowbridge in Maddox Street to Kenny Salinsky in Klein's office said: "What is happening on Mick's checks re his properties . . . these are most urgent."

On October 14 Brian cabled to ask for £6,000 "urgently" to cover his court case fees, and Charlie cabled Klein's office on October 21: "I have not yet received my $5,000. Please telephone me back. The number is Halland, Sussex, 215."

Five days later, an exasperated Trowbridge again cabled Salinsky saying: "Berger Oliver [solicitors] are screaming for the balance of Bill's money. What is happening to those checks? What about Brian's £6,000? Has Mick's film contract been sorted out yet?"

And on October 28 a letter from accountants Laurence Myers to Klein said:

Before you left London on 10/12/68, I explained to you the absolute urgency of dealing with the outstanding information that we require to complete the Stones' personal Income Tax Returns to date and the Partnership Accounts for year ending Jun 67. Allen, I must stress that our clients' best interests are being prejudiced by their failure to return this outstanding information which only you can provide. I am today sending you a telex in connection with this matter and trust that, by the time you receive this letter, I will have heard from you. P.S. We are still awaiting, also, funds in order to settle the £13,000 tax liability that is now overdue in respect of the past remunerations for Rolling Stones Ltd.

I finally moved into Gedding Hall on October 30, 1968, six days after my thirty-second birthday.* The furniture from Keston had been moved in the previous week by Dennis Halfacre, who agreed to become my resident gardener (essential for fourteen acres). Upon taking possession of the hall, I officially became Lord of the Manor of Gedding and Thormwood. Six bedrooms, three bathrooms and an eight-car garage made it enormously comfortable and spacious for Astrid, Stephen and me. And as I told a Johannesburg newspaper in a telephone interview at the time: "The most important thing in my life right now is that I have Stephen back with me. He is everything to me and I know he will be happy in Suffolk." And indeed he was.

The year had given me little time to devote to private projects but two of my diversions from the Stones did wind up as record releases. Mick, Eric Clapton, Jimmy Page, Ian Stewart (piano) and his friend Chris Winters (drums) were lured into a studio by Andrew Oldham to overdub on to a bunch of demonstration songs written by Eric and Jimmy. This was released by Andrew's Immediate label as *Blues Anytime, Volume 1,* the tracks being "Snake Drive," "Tribute to Elmore" and "West Coast Idea."

Charlie was active with a group of musicians called the People Band. At Olympic studios, they cut an album, finally released on Transatlantic in 1970.

What often seemed uncanny was the coincidence of events in the Beatles' lives, which ran parallel to ours. While we faced the Decca problem over the album cover, they were having problems with Apple; two weeks after

*I had taken out two mortgages of £20,000 each.

Brian's court bust, John Lennon and Yoko were busted at their London flat; and on November 11, three days after Lennon and his first wife Cynthia were divorced, I went to see my solicitor to start divorce proceedings and I hired a private detective to report on Diane's movements in South Africa.

By November 19 Marianne was in a nursing home in Avenue Road, St. John's Wood. Mick sent her roses and visited; we all sent her flowers, fruit and chocolates, but on November 22 she miscarried. She was seven months pregnant with a girl, whom they had planned to name Carina. (The previous day, Yoko Ono too had a miscarriage.)

By the end of November we had agreed to have a "good" book written about the Stones. Stanley Booth, a writer for *Rolling Stone* magazine, was recommended. We eventually signed a letter, during our American tour of 1969, giving Booth permission to go ahead. *Dance with the Devil* was finally published in 1984.*

Meanwhile the commotion over the album cover had to be resolved and, after meetings at Decca House between various Stones, Allen Klein and Sir Edward Lewis, we agreed to dump the graffiti design. Rather symbolically, the song called "You Can't Always Get What You Want," written by Mick and Keith, had been recorded on November 17 at Olympic with the addition of the noted American keyboardist Al Kooper; this was an extremely long session, running from 10 p.m. until 6:15 a.m., and proof that when the mood took the band, the motivation and music was always there . . . for most of us, anyway. Brian's contribution to that session was to lie on his stomach most of the night, reading an article on botany.

Following the invitation theme of the album title, we agreed on a simple white cover with the name of the band, and *Beggars Banquet*, with RSVP at the bottom. The design came dangerously close to the Beatles' recently released *White Album*, something we could have done without after the comparison of *Satanic Majesties*

---

*I loaned Stanley Booth many of my own photos and scrapbooks, and did extensive interviews. After repeated requests I finally got my scrapbooks back from him in the late 1980s.

and *Sergeant Pepper*. But we'd already been bruised by a two-month delay and it was vital to get the LP out in time to catch Christmas sales. Mick, sore about the way we had been messed around, lost no chance to give Decca a kick on a different score. On November 28 he wrote to them: "Since the commencement of our relationship with Decca Records, we have specifically requested the exclusion of all Rolling Stones' records from your 'Bulk Advertisements.' We are therefore most sorry to see that you have included *Beggars Banquet* along with a number of other Decca LPs in *Record Retailer* on November 17. Much as we do appreciate your (doubtlessly) well-meant intentions, we do not share the same ideals in 'how to advertise.' This is, in fact, a contravention of a clause in our contract. *Please make sure this will never ever happen again—never ever.*"

A media party was essential to make some impact. Maggie Phillips in our office tried to book the Tower of London, to continue the medieval theme, but this was not available for commercial events. Instead, the "Beggars Banquet" was held in the Elizabethan Room at the Gore Hotel, Kensington, on December 4. Brian, Charlie, Mick and I were all dressed as beggars for the seven-course Elizabethan banquet, served by cleavage-showing wenches; 120 media people dined by candlelight on such delicacies as boar's head and cucumber and artichokes in Canary wine, washed down with claret and mead.

Then, as toasts were drunk and clay pipes distributed, plus snuff, Mick, wearing a frock-coat, starched but collarless evening shirt, gray top hat and white plastic fork in his button-hole, welcomed the guests with a formal toast: "Right, have you all had enough to eat and drink? Thank you all for coming. I hope you've had a nice time. I hope you've had your After Eights because we didn't invite you here to eat and drink and enjoy yourself, did we?" With that, Mick took one of the gold confectionery boxes given to all guests, who had been instructed not to open them until the following Wednesday. Opening a box in full view, Mick took the plastic foam custard pie out and plunged it into the face of Brian, sitting next to him. The scenes that followed were like something from a Laurel and Hardy film. All the guests, who had been served with pies as Mick spoke, hurled them at Mick,

Brian, Charlie and me. We ducked to avoid them, and one pie sailed across the banqueting hall into the face of Lord Harlech, who tried but failed to protect himself with a copy of the album. Then he joined in the battle. "Not quite the sort of party I'm accustomed to," said Lord Harlech, former British Ambassador to the USA, "but thoroughly enjoyable. I'm here because Mick is a friend of mine. He has been very kind to my children."

Most rejoiced in the revelry. Others grinned grudgingly as their immaculate suits were smothered in crazy foam which was supposed to clean off but unfortunately stained. Some saw it as a bit of Stones revenge for the way in which journalists had reported our antics over the past five years. This wasn't true; it was just a lark; we were surrounded by friendly writers.

A notable absentee was Keith, who did not arrive until the end of the party, for a reason we never discovered.

We all had a ball and there was a bonus: the party reached the night's independent television news, with scenes from the pie-throwing . . . and they even played a snatch of "Street Fighting Man," a track that would never have got any attention. Mick wrote a charming letter of thanks to the Gore Hotel, apologizing for the mess.

After a delay of six months, the album was released on December 6.* The powerful lyrics of this album, plus its swing to acoustic rather than electronic sounds, made it instantly popular among the critics. Indeed, some writers named it one of the best rock 'n' roll albums of the sixties. While Mick described the material as "just a hazy mirror of what we were thinking last summer when we wrote the songs," the *International Times* declared it our best-ever record, "retaining the cynicism and drive of earlier albums but replacing the roughness with intrinsic thematic simplicity." Perhaps our finest work, it encompassed the populist consciousness of "Factory Girl," the "hymn of praise" to hardworking people in "Salt of the Earth" (in which Mick and Keith picked a team of gospel girl singers from the streets of Watts, Los Angeles), the bluesy ballad "No Expectations' and the straight blues "Parachute Woman," which recalled our "Little Red Rooster" period.

*The inside cover picture was by Michael Joseph and the album design was by Tom Wilkes. It reached number three in Britain and number five in the USA.

In retrospect *Beggars Banquet* was a microcosm of the time in which it was recorded. The short psychedelic dream had withered and was being replaced by a back-to-basics outlook in everyday life. Introspection was replaced by clearly defined, roots-inspired sounds and lyrics, and Mick and Keith's writing captured the moment accurately. Ironically, the delay in the album's release worked to its timely advantage, and the neutrality of the spartan, white front cover placed a heavier, more significant emphasis on the inside picture depicting us at the aftermath of a feast in a decaying baronial hall. The image and message was one of dangerous human indulgence.

When the album was released in America, Jann Wenner wrote in *Rolling Stone* magazine: "The Stones have returned and they are bringing back rock 'n' roll with them. Their new album will mark a point in the short history of rock and roll: the formal end of all the pretentious, nonmusical, boring, insignificant, self-conscious and worthless stuff that has been tolerated during the past year in the absence of any standards set by the several great figures in rock and roll. *Beggars Banquet* should be the mark of this change, for it was *Their Satanic Majesties Request* which was the prototype of junk masquerading as meaningful."*

Once again, we found ourselves compared with the Beatles. Several writers pointed out that while the Beatles' focus had usually been love and beauty, ours was violence and a release of frustration. The rawness of the songs on our album was contrasted favorably with the softness of many of the new Beatles songs.

Cheered by all this, we plunged into a lengthy project which will always be remembered as a quirky, incomplete chapter in rock history. *The Rolling Stones Rock 'n' Roll Circus Show,* conceived by Mick, and produced and financed by the band, was a terrific idea for a color TV spectacular for world distribution, bringing in a battalion of major rock stars alongside circus performers, acrobats, clowns, animals and dwarfs from Sir Robert Fossett's

Rolling Stone later voted this the best rock album of the year, "Sympathy for the Devil" track of the year and the Stones best band. We also kept our crown as top British R & B group in the *New Musical Express* annual readers' poll.

Circus. Sanford Lieberson was executive producer, as he was for *Performance;* Michael Lindsay-Hogg was brought in as director; and camera-work was to be by Tony Richmond, who had worked alongside Jean-Luc Godard on *One Plus One.*

With an investment of about £50,000, we recruited a huge cast of major artists, flying in the four-man top blues band Taj Mahal from Los Angeles (and in the end they did not perform as they could not get a work permit!) and adding John Lennon and Yoko, Eric Clapton, Jethro Tull and The Who. Johnny Cash declined our invitation to fly in to participate; the Isley Brothers could not come; and Traffic, whom we asked, were disbanding. Cream had just split, leaving Clapton free to appear as a solo guitarist.

Astrid and I stayed at the Londonderry House Hotel to be more accessible to working in town; Keith and Anita took a suite there while he looked for a London flat.

Rock 'n' Roll Circus was a lavish affair: at the first soundtrack recording session at the Olympic studios on December 8, Jimmy Miller was producing along with Glyn Johns and Tony Visconti conducted a full orchestra. Costumes, ordered from a variety of sources, promised a truly visual extravaganza: 400 ponchos and hats for the audience; a crêpe Jean Harlow dress for Marianne; a red satin top, trousers and cap, with red and black stockings and shoes for me; a magician's cloak and cap for Brian; a rainbow suit and shoes for Charlie; military outfit for Keith; and for Mick, a ringmaster's outfit, plus two sweaters, a sequinned dress, cloak, false front, trousers and tails; an acrobat costume for Keith Moon; and even a long beard for Anita!

Cowboys and rodeo horses, trapeze acts, plate spinners, midgets, a fire-eater and a strong man were expected to join the invited audience of 800 at Wembley studios when we began filming on December 10. "We decided to put up the money for the spectacular ourselves so that we had complete control of the production. We have never tried producing a show before. If we aren't pleased with the result, we will scrap it," Mick said. Brian, wearing gold-colored tight trousers and a thick, long-haired fur coat, added: "There's a latent clown in all of us. We had the idea of doing a show set in a circus for a long time."

As rehearsals began it was clear that this was going to be as much a parade of pop families as a circus show. Five-year-old Julian Lennon walked in with John holding one of his hands and Yoko, dressed as a witch, his other. John was wearing a silver and black diagonal-striped body-clinging cat suit, leering through National Health wire-framed glasses and brandishing a trumpet. He explained that the Beatles were to have made their television film *Magical Mystery Tour* before the Stones but it had been postponed. "No, the Stones haven't stolen our thunder," he said to somebody. "Our rivalry with them was always a myth."

We had hired a Steinway grand piano and four-track mobile recording equipment was set up at the studios, at a cost of more than £1,000. Every guest had a chauffeured car on hand for the three-day shoot. We were learning the hard way—like the Beatles over at Apple—that financing a project with so many "taps turned on" was a severe strain on resources, but the resulting film could, of course, have been lucrative. However, I found it irritating that while Mick's Marianne, Keith's Anita, and John's Yoko were absorbed into the filming, neither Astrid, Shirley Watts nor Suki Potier were even considered as participants. This attitude by Mick and Keith continued to polarize the band.

Keith's ego also demanded that he joined the "super-group," which effectively elbowed me out. This line-up already had two guitarists (Clapton on lead and Lennon on rhythm), so the only way Keith could get in was by playing bass. This he did. A woman trapeze artist swung overhead while pianist Julius Katchen played Brahms, before the super-group swung into the Lennon composition "Yer Blues." Then clowns, a fire-eater and a cowboy on horseback led on to The Who, who performed an excerpt from their opera *Tommy* during which a monocled and top-hatted Keith Moon spilled beer on his snare drum. After "A Song for Jeffrey" from Jethro Tull, it was the Stones' turn. Augmented by Rocky Dijon on bongos,* we went on at 3 a.m. on the final night and performed "Route 66," "Confessin' the Blues," "Jumpin'

---

*Rocky Dijon later played congas on our albums *Sticky Fingers* and *Let It Bleed*.

Jack Flash," "Parachute Woman," "You Can't Always Get What You Want," "No Expectations," ending with "Sympathy for the Devil."

There was a load of laughs and a great spirit at the circus. Mick wrestled with a tiger; the grand parade in the circus ring was a photographer's paradise. When someone asked Lennon what kind of amplifier he wanted he replied: "One that plays." (Many people commented on his new mellowness since meeting Yoko.) Clapton, noting a midget's huge, red crêpe bowtie, said: "I'd give anything for that." Keith advised him: "Nick it!" At an impromptu jam session backstage, the Clapton-led supergroup swung into "Hound Dog" and "Peggy Sue," Eric saying: "I'm still a rocker and there's nothing I can do about it!" Yoko provided a strange diversion to one side with a dance she invented in which she contrived to wiggle inside her voluminous black dress so that neither her head nor her limbs were exposed.

Inevitably, some of the events planned for the circus didn't happen. Marianne was going to sing but didn't; Anita, cast as a bearded lady, did not appear; and the boxing kangaroo didn't show. Later, Ian Anderson of Jethro Tull slammed the circus as a show. "It was a good idea initially but badly produced and badly run," he asserted. "I felt it was just thrown together. With a little more time and planning it would have been much better."

Jo Bergman wrote to all the artists to thank them for their cooperation, and also to their managers to seek permission for them to be featured on a soundtrack album of the Rock 'n' Roll Circus, with proceeds going to charity. Requests went to Kit Lambert and Chris Stamp for The Who, Terry Ellis for Jethro Tull, Mike Jeffries for Mitch Mitchell, Robert Paterson for Julius Katchen and Robert Stigwood for Eric Clapton. Stigwood's reply seemed to sum up the whole woolly concept and execution of the project: "Before discussing Eric Clapton's availability for your LP, I would like somebody to discuss with me the question of the contract for his appearance in the TV show."

The show was exhausting and exhilarating—but it was never shown. When Mick saw the rushes of the shoot, he insisted that our appearances were below standard, since we'd gone on so late and so tired; the audience, too, lacked spark in the film for the same reason. He had a re-shoot costed, but this came in at £10,300, and nothing was done. *Rock 'n' Roll Circus* gathers dust, another costly indulgence.*

*When The Who were compiling footage for their 1971 film *Quadrophenia*, they requested their segment from this show. We gave it to them, and they included it in their film. At the time of writing (1990), we're still awaiting its return! In 1989, during our American tour, we included one song from *Circus* "You Can't Always Get What You Want"—in a two-hour retrospective television program, titled *25 × 5*.

12

Little Boy Blues

It was a miracle we produced *anything,* under the pressures and emotional upheavals within the group. We had to find a switch of direction. The era that bred the Liverpool boom in pop music was over—if the Beatles returned to Liverpool now they would have no need of police cordons or roads blocked off to ensure their safety. They had sensed the times and made the change. There were just a handful of kids outside the studios when we recorded recently, where there had been hundreds before. More than ever . . . you must stand or fall by your product.

—Charlie Watts, February 1969

Roots have always been essential to me, and to a lesser extent to Charlie. Mick, Keith and Brian were much more nomadic; to this day, Mick doesn't seem content to stay in one location for more than a couple of weeks.

As Christmas neared Brian and Suki went to his much-loved Ceylon for the holiday. Mick and Marianne, Keith and Anita flew to Lima, Peru. For some time Keith had been reading about magic, and wanted to visit an expert in Rio de Janeiro. "I'm not frightened of any consequences," he said. "I believe magic is only a combination of natural forces." They flew out on Keith's twenty-fifth birthday, December 18. Mick had always been interested in other cultures and had been studying comparative mythology, he said. He wanted to look at the Incas of Peru and contemporary Indians. They stayed in Lima where Mick and Keith ran into trouble at the luxurious Crillon Hotel. They entered a public room of the hotel wearing brightly colored trousers and no shirts. Refusing the manager's request to dress more soberly, they were asked to leave. They moved to a more welcoming place;

from there they hired a jeep to travel around the country.

For Charlie and Shirley and Astrid and me, it was a British Christmas Day, complete with snow. Astrid's family arrived from Sweden, and together with my parents we all enjoyed a real white Christmas.

My life in the country at Gedding Hall was calm. Gazing out of the kitchen window on New Year's Day I spotted a big pheasant across the moat. That night, I took pictures of the almost-full moon from the tower. We enjoyed feeding and photographing the ducks. I applied myself to getting the house together for the return later in January of Stephen, who was staying with Diane over Christmas.

There seemed more concentration on solo projects and private lives than on the Stones at this time. The Beatles, too, were in turmoil as they played their final live appearance on the roof of their Apple headquarters in Savile Row on January 30; on February 3 Allen Klein took control of their company to the dismay of Paul McCartney, who opposed his arrival but was out-voted by John, George and Ringo.

We took possession in February 1969 of a mobile recording studio that we'd had built specially for us. *Beggars Banquet* was still in the Top Ten both in Britain and America as we reconvened at the Olympic studios with Jimmy Miller for a series of recording sessions from February 9.

Despite his holiday, Brian looked pale and seemed to be "floating" mentally and physically: he was drifting around London even though he had his Sussex home, Cotchford Farm. He was spending a lot of time at the Playboy Club.

His appeal against conviction on the drugs charge had been dismissed by the appeals court on January 13, while he was in Ceylon. Three judges said there were no grounds for interfering with the verdict of the London Sessions.

A further example of "separatism" in the Stones came when, in February, a Jaguar saloon car was bought by the band as a "group car," to be used when needed. However, whenever I, Brian or Charlie required it, it was being used by Mick or Keith, who took turns in commandeering it for their own personal use most of the time.

Brian, Charlie and I were also irritated by the procrastination of the Klein office on our individual projects. Charlie had produced a jazz album by the People Band but the inertia of the Klein office on this prompted a letter from Peter Swales in our office to Al Steckler in the Klein New York office on January 7:

> We all know you're doing a great job folks but Charlie has not heard what's happening and naturally wants to get the album out. He has asked me to do what I can in Europe to get it released but I don't want to tread on your ground. I realize Klein would want to finalize the deal but I am eager to sound out people over here.
>
> (1) Are you selling this LP to an American company? (E.S.P.?) and if so to which countries will they license it?
>
> (2) Dependent on the above shall I try to sell it to a company here and/or some European companies, to start with?
>
> Charlie would be very pleased to get just the cost of it back. I can't honestly envisage any incredible sales. In fact people might go as far as to saying it's crap. But remember there is a large market for these sort of sales in Germany . . . Also what is happening with Brian's *JouJouka* LP? Shall I try and sell that?

There was considerable interest in Charlie's, Brian's and my projects by Bob Krasnow of Blue Thumb Records but, with great reluctance from us, he had to be stalled because we were tied to Klein. On February 11 Jo Bergman cabled Steckler: "Elektra wants Brian's album. What's happening? Brian hysterical."

Everyone was becoming uptight about the situation. A London friend of Brion Gysin telephoned and wrote to Jo Bergman inquiring about the fate of the record on Gysin's behalf. Jo replied direct to Gysin in Morocco on February 18 showing frustration and diplomacy:

> Brian has asked me to write to you about the progress of the *JouJouka* album. When Brian returned from Morocco last year he edited the album and prepared the art-work together with designer, Al Vandenburg. The cover looks beautiful and has Hamri's painting on the front and one of his son's paintings on the inside

cover. Brian spent a considerable time in the studio editing the material and this was finished about the end of September. The art-work and the tapes for the album were then sent to our New York office. Klein, who looks after business affairs for the Stones in America, promised to handle negotiations for this album and to make sure that it was released in the best possible way and with the right sort of promotion. During the time that Brian was in Ceylon, we made repeated inquiries to Klein to find out what was happening, and since Brian has been back, he also has been in touch with Klein. Klein's office keep telling us that they are arranging everything, that it will be done etc., but we have heard no concrete facts about what label will release the album and when. I know that Brian is most anxious that Hamri and the musicians should be aware of the state of the album, and that Brian has been trying to arrange its release. Brian sends his regards and will be contacting you soon himself.

I was equally vexed about Klein's failure to push ahead with the release of an album by the End. I cabled Klein on February 18: "The End are fed up with waiting for their album to be released and with promises I have given them. In the next two days they are telling Decca that they no longer exist, to get out of their contract. They will sign with RCA immediately. Please advise."

Klein responded: "Try to hold them off. I will be arriving in London Monday 24th."

Though we were recording tracks (with no specific aim towards an album or a single), I missed touring. The band was in a strange vacuum and with so many loose ends around our private projects, we were all restless. My pleasure was my home and in spending time with Astrid and Stephen. At Gedding, I called in the interior designer David Hicks, but his estimate of almost £6,000 for curtains and carpets alone was far more than I could afford, since I had had a bank overdraft of between £10,000 and £12,000 for some time. In the 1970s I was to turn to David Mlinaric.

Looking for a different album cover idea, Mick wrote in January to the painter, M. C. Escher: "Dear Maurits,

For quite a time now I have had in my possession your
book and it never ceases to amaze me . . . In fact I think
your work is quite incredible and it would make me very
happy for a lot more people to see and know and understand exactly what you are doing. In March or April this
year we have scheduled our next LP record for release,
and I am most eager to reproduce one of your works on
the cover-sleeve. Would you please consider either
designing a 'picture' for it, or have you any unpublished
works which you might think suitable?"

A reply from Escher to the Stones said: "Some days
ago I received a letter from Mr. Jagger asking me either
to design a picture or to place at his disposal unpublished
work to reproduce on the cover-sleeve for a LP record.
My answer to both questions must be no, as I want to
devote all my time and attention to the many commitments made; I cannot possibly accept any further assignments or spend any time on publicity. By the way, please
tell Mr. Jagger I am not Maurits to him, but very sincerely, [signed] M. C. Escher."

New albums for the Stones were far from Brian's mind.
There was a credit of less than £4,000 in his bank account
as he celebrated his twenty-seventh birthday on February
28. Mick arranged to have the Stones office send him a
bowl of flowers, but by March 18 Brian was "down" and
back in the Priory Clinic, suffering from depression. He
stayed there until March 20, missing a series of band
rehearsals and recording sessions. Jack Nitzsche flew in
from Los Angeles to supervise arrangements for completion of "You Can't Always Get What You Want." At
the recording session at Olympic on March 15, there was
a huge 50-piece choir.

Brian's rudderless life twisted and turned in every way,
that strange spring of 1969. His health and state of mind
were still unpredictable and we could never be sure whether
he'd make a session, but our loyalty to him was strong if
unspoken. Unexpectedly, he split with Suki at the beginning of April, although he continued to see her occasionally.
We were surprised, since it had seemed a good relationship and they appeared suited. He began seeing Linda
Keith again and a new girlfriend, Anna Wohlin, a twenty-
two-year-old Swedish student and model, who bore the
by-now expected, physical resemblance to Suki and Anita.

Mick, meanwhile, was dipping into the world of publishing. He had become friendly with Jann Wenner, editor and publisher of America's *Rolling Stone* magazine, then based in San Francisco. Wenner flew into London on March 26 for talks about the setting up of the Trans-Oceanic Comic Company (*Rolling Stone* magazine USA) to publish his magazine in Britain. A lease on offices at 19 Hanover Square was taken; Mick was the only Stone involved in this project. Wenner had named his magazine after us, as his favorite band; a British operation with Mick at the helm would have been a great coup. But it proved difficult to transplant Wenner's publishing philosophy into a British edition. Mick, who had expressed a wish to be involved in the editorial content, never had the time, and after a few months publishing operations ceased. Britain already had enough music papers.

After a two-week visit with Astrid and Stephen to Bermuda to visit my brother Paul, my divorce from Diane got under way with a preliminary hearing in the London Divorce Court on April 21, 1969. It continued at the High Court on July 9, where I wore a specially made fawn suit. I hadn't worn a suit since my wedding day back in 1959! Matching the style of the time, my hair was shoulder-length.

My solicitor, Mr. J. J. David, told Judge Willis that Diane and I had parted in early 1967 and had entered into financial arrangements. The judge approved these terms. I then petitioned for a divorce, citing Victor Gummow, a South African, as co-respondent. He was neither present nor represented. My inquiry agent, George Devlin, gave evidence in support of my allegations of adultery.

A statement by Diane placed before the court said she did not contest my petition. Judge Willis exercised discretion in respect of my admitted adultery after being told that I wished to marry the woman concerned. I was granted a decree nisi because of Diane's adultery, with custody of Stephen granted to me, with agreed access by Diane.

Next day's *Daily Express* quoted me as saying: "Diane and I were reasonably happy up to 1963, the year it all started happening for the Stones. As the Stones became more successful, our marriage started to go wrong. It was the touring really . . . that meant Diane and I obviously saw less and less of each other. During the next three years there was a terrible strain between us and it was impossible." The press reported that the divorce case had revealed my best-kept secret: "His fans have always believed he was five years younger." My divorce was made absolute on October 10, 1969.

Despite the fact that we were off the road, there were plenty of plans being made by the office to keep our names in people's minds. The schedule drawn up called for a new single by early May; *Through the Past Darkly* (*Big Hits Vol. Two*), a compilation for the third week in May; a brand new album for the first week in June; the *Rock 'n' Roll Circus* soundtrack album "before September 1969 or whenever the show is screened;" a second new single by early September; a second brand new album by November; and by the third week in November, a third new single. The note giving these schedules was sent to all of us, so whatever Brian's state he must have known at this difficult stage in his life that the wheel was still turning and the Stones machine was plowing on. Perhaps he was miffed at the charging to his account of a chauffeured car by Al Steckler of the Allen Klein office when Steckler arrived in London—to be driven to Redlands! As for the *Rock 'n' Roll Circus* project—it took a lawyer's letter to claim £10,540 as the balance of £19,935 due from us to the company, Colourtel. The problem with the Stones, as ever, was that too many people were nominally "in charge"—but nobody had the complete authority or time to tie all our activities together smoothly.

Stu was busy with running our mobile studio and rehearsal rooms: in April being used by Rod Stewart and the Faces. Ian MacLagan, their keyboard player (he toured and recorded with us in the 1970s and early 1980s) remembers Stu insisting: "It can't be blues if there's a minor chord in it." "He played me 'In the Ghetto' from the first Delaney and Bonnie album. He said: 'You know, I played this to Nicky Hopkins and he went, "Oh yeah, let's see," and he played the whole tune straight off. I don't like that about Nicky.' "

Mick had been experiencing some frustration in putting together the sleeve for the album that eventually appeared in a hexagonal shape, *Through the Past Darkly*. Finally, he erupted in a cable to Ronnie Schneider at the Klein office on May 13: "Your inefficiency is a drag. What the fuck did you do with all the photographs, not the press cuttings, the photographs? They were supposed to be delivered to Andy Warhol. We await your reply."

I knew precisely how Mick felt. My own project with the End was still thwarted by lack of action from Klein's office. I cabled Klein's office on May 12 asking what was happening about the album, the money advance and added: "Advise immediately as promised. Very urgent." Two days later, having received no reply, I sent another cable saying: "Whole situation getting entirely out of hand. Need to know urgently." The following day I cabled saying the advance was needed for new van and equipment for the End, "without which they can't work. We would like $5,000 if possible but must have minimum of $2,500. Six great new tracks already recorded and album and single will be ready early July. Biogs and pix en route to you. Please treat advance as top priority and make me very happy."

We all seemed to be locked into the same problem: Keith had run into hassles over the purchase of property he wanted, a Queen Anne house formerly owned by a Conservative minister, Anthony Nutting, at 3 Cheyne Walk, Chelsea, 200 yards from Mick. With all the money controlled tightly from New York, he had to seek the 10 per cent deposit of £5,500 by cable and point out to them that the balance of £49,500 would be required within two weeks. Our cash requirements were so difficult to grapple with; Ronnie Schneider cabled Jo Bergman: "Please give this telex to David Platz [Essex Music]. Have Fred Trowbridge as one of the signatures on the account but don't write any checks without me knowing." From Bergman to Ronnie Schneider on May 14 went this plea: "Where are you? Need to have answer to my today's telex rather immediately. Colourtel are coming to see me this afternoon. Please recognize my panic."

While we continued recording offers came in from Zambia and Nigeria for us to do concerts, but these, plus a contract for us to appear at the Memphis Country Blues Festival, went unanswered in the general confusion that surrounded us. Luckily, in our desire to be seen and heard as breaking new ground artistically, we attracted people with original ideas, such as the photographer Ethan Russell. For the cover of *Through the Past Darkly* technicians had been at St. Katharine's Dock, next to Tower Bridge, from 8:30 a.m. on May 21, setting up a hydraulic platform. We lay on the ground in a star shape for the shots, which we used on the inside cover. Back in Ethan's studio, he had set up a huge sheet of glass and took pictures of us with our faces pressed up against it. He later had us throw chairs and a brick at it until it cracked to enable another imaginative shot.

Plans for a Stones film seemed to have evaporated but Mick was constantly in demand for solo roles. His most ambitious and controversial part was announced on May 18: a big-budget movie to be made on location in Australia in July. Mick would play the swashbuckling nineteenth-century folk-hero, bandit Ned Kelly, who terrorized the early Australian townships for more than ten years. Mick was also being asked to write the score of the film, in which Marianne would also star.

Four days later, the police took the shine off Mick's announcement by busting him and Marianne at Cheyne Walk. They had just finished tea when half a dozen police led by Detective-Sergeant Robin Constable from Chelsea police station arrived. They took substances from the house for examination and Mick and Marianne were allowed to make their way to the police station in his new bright yellow Morgan car. Formally charged with possessing cannabis, they appeared at Marlborough Street Magistrates' Court next morning and were released on £50 bail each until next day.

With their arms around each other, they walked up the same court steps next morning, Marianne in a fawn suede-and-python-skin two-piece suit, Mick in a purple suit and a violet shirt. Both prosecution and defense asked for a remand; outside, a crowd of about 200 blocked the road, waiting to see Mick and Marianne leave.

Their sartorial splendor continued when they re-appeared on June 23. This time they walked in separately looking pale and serious, Mick in a dark cloak over a pin-striped suit, white shirt, patterned tie and black boots; Marianne in an oatmeal-colored cape. Michael Havers,

defending them, said the prosecution had agreed to a
further remand until September 29 since Mick and Marianne had contracts to begin filming in Australia in a few
weeks. "I shall then know from Australia how much
longer filming will take," he added. John O'Keeffe (prosecuting) said that although the request was "somewhat
unusual," there was no objection to the three-month
delay.

The customary flowers to a Stone in trouble were sent
to Mick and Marianne at Cheyne Walk. The bust hung
over them for six months until December 19, when Mick
was fined £200 with £52 costs for possessing cannabis and
Marianne was acquitted. More serious, perhaps, was the
eighteen-month ban Mick received on his US visa, meaning that we couldn't travel to the States.

The time-bomb that had been ticking under Brian simply had to be detonated. For some two years not only
had he been physically vulnerable and battered by his
drug busts, but within the Stones he was sad, isolated and
obviously unhappy.

He loved his new rural home where he and Anna
Wohlin bought an Afghan hound; but his inner trauma,
aggravated by the loss of Anita and the assumption of
band leadership by Mick and Keith, found Brian totally
marooned. Pictures of him taken in the garden at his
home showed him looking bloated and sickly. Towards
the end of May, during a recording session, Brian inti-
mated that he was thinking of leaving to pursue his own
career. Nobody was particularly surprised. Intoxicated by
fame and success, he paradoxically had no empathy with
the direction in which Mick and Keith's commercial songs
had taken us. He felt we had deserted our roots. The
purist bluesman and instrumental experimenter inside Brian
clashed with the hard-headed songwriting machine of
Mick and Keith, who knew how to steer the Stones
upwards. A split was inevitable. It had been mooted as a
possibility two years earlier, but Mick was said to have
been against Brian's departure, since it might destroy our
image. Whatever Brian's debits, he was a great visual
attraction; now, though, we were securely established
and it seemed to me Mick and Keith felt we could afford
to lose him. He had become unreliable.

The decision on Brian's successor was dealt with before his departure was finalized. Stu, who understood the chemistry of the group, recommended Mick Taylor, a stalwart guitarist with John Mayall's Bluesbreakers. Mick had been only fourteen, and a year away from leaving school, when we had our first small hit with "Come On," but his pedigree since as a blues-based musician was exemplary; it was known that anyone (like Eric Clapton) who came through the Mayall band had strong roots. Mick Jagger phoned Mick Taylor on Stu's advice and invited him to come to our recording session at the Olympic on May 30. Taylor sat in with us for the first time and his empathy was clear; he was a superb natural player.

His arrival coincided with the recording of one of our finest tracks. We returned on June 1 to Olympic with Jimmy Miller. Brian was not there. The new song marked Taylor's debut and was quite an entry for him. We listened to playbacks, did some rough mixing, and Stu ordered food. At 11 p.m., after eating, we started recording a song called "Honky-Tonk Women." We tried various ways before Jimmy Miller sat down at the drums and showed Charlie a rhythm. Jimmy then picked up a cowbell and played it, giving the track the distinctive edge that made it so successful. By 3:15 we had a great master; we then did a rough mix, finishing at four. We dispersed with the knowledge that we had completed a winning single.

There was irony and tragedy in the imminent departure of Brian at the moment we'd cut such a triumphant track. He knew, of course, of the "trial" of Mick Taylor, and considered it deceitful since he had not yet formally left. Down in Sussex he was striving to regain better health, swimming regularly and taking enormous pride in the history of the place. He showed everyone who visited the life-sized statue of Christopher Robin in the garden and the sundial with Pooh, Piglet and other animals carved on it. He visited the local pub and seemed on course for a more stable chapter in his life, once he could find a respectable way of leaving the Stones.

Brian was the most sensitive musician I've known and for him to depart from the Stones must have caused much anguish. Not surprisingly, he identified strongly with a song that summer written by another iconoclast who found the going hard: John Lennon ran into a number of personal crises once he took up with Yoko Ono, and the lyrics he wrote in "The Ballad of John and Yoko" were played repeatedly by a smiling, knowing Brian at Cotchford Farm:

> *Christ, you know, it ain't easy*
> *You know how hard it can be;*
> *The way things are going*
> *They're gonna crucify me.*

In the early hours of Saturday, June 7, Keith crashed his Mercedes on the A286, eight miles from Redlands. The car was a write-off but Keith escaped unhurt. Anita went to St. Richards Hospital, Chichester, with a broken collarbone, and next day went for specialist treatment in Harley Street. Keith rented a London apartment in Park Lane for ten days; the man who has skirted disaster all his life breathed again.

Next day, he had to shake off the shock and, with Mick, deal decisively with the departure of Brian. They worked from 2 p.m. until 6:30 p.m., listening to play-backs, and, after mixing "Honky-Tonk Women" until 7:15, they drove to Cotchford Farm. Knowing that Brian viewed them as plotters against him, they shrewdly took Charlie along as peacemaker in case the meeting became ugly. But the thirty-minute conversation was friendly and all parties were relieved that matters were reaching a conclusion. Mick and Keith told Brian that the group could not go on working with him the way he was; there was a violent disagreement over the music. Brian agreed. That night, the split was officially announced by both Brian and Mick.

Brian said: "I no longer see eye to eye with the others over the discs we are cutting. We no longer communicate musically. The Stones' music is not to my taste anymore. The work of Mick and Keith has progressed at a tangent, at least to my way of thinking. I have a desire to play my own brand of music rather than that of others, no matter how much I appreciate their musical concepts. We had a friendly meeting and agreed that an amicable termination, temporary or permanent, was the only answer. The only solution was to go our separate ways, but we shall still remain friends. I love those fellows."

Mick said: "The only solution to our problem was for Brian to leave us. He wants to play music which is more his own rather than always playing ours. We have decided that it is best for him to be free to follow his own inclinations. We have parted on the best of terms. We will continue to be friends and we're certainly going to meet socially in future. There's no question of us breaking up a friendship. Friendships like ours just don't break up like that."

Mick Taylor seemed custom-built for the Stones.* Yet there were some similarities with Brian: he was shy, sensitive and bluesy. "When I was with John Mayall's Bluesbreakers I was playing the blues. I'd always been writing music but it wasn't the kind of music that the group could use. Now I can write numbers that will have a better chance of being used. Since I am a lead guitarist, both Keith and I will be playing lead more or less. A rhythm guitarist is expendable; you don't really need one, so in effect there will be two leads."

Jagger said: "I'd never heard him live, only on records. He'd been through the John Mayall school of guitarists, people like Peter Green and Eric Clapton. I didn't want to go through the whole bit of auditioning guitarists so I spoke to John Mayall, a man whose judgement I respect in these matters. John just grunted when I told him we'd like to see Mick Taylor, so I took it as a yes." What would Brian do? "He's gotta do his own thing, man," Jagger told a reporter. "You'll really have to ask him what he's got in his mind. He hasn't said anything to us."

For several weeks, Brian's old mentor and friend Alexis Korner had been visiting Cotchford Farm with his wife and children. When the split happened, the wise bluesman was a willing listener and ally, just as he had been in

---

*Born Michael Kevin Taylor in Welwyn Garden City, Hertfordshire on January 17, 1948, the son of an aircraft worker, Mick taught himself guitar while still at school. Leaving school at fifteen, he worked as a commercial artist/engraver for three months. He joined a local group, the Gods, and sat in with John Mayall's Bluesbreakers when Eric Clapton failed to turn up. After he'd left the Gods, Mick was contacted by Mayall when guitarist Peter Green left. He left Mayall in the spring of 1969 to go solo.

1962. Brian indicated that he'd like to join Alexis's latest band, New Church, but Korner knew Brian too well to believe that this would succeed after the heights Brian had reached. Better, he advised him, to form a new band. "He was probably more sane at that period than I'd known him for a very long time," Korner recalled later. "He was in a calmer frame of mind; there were things he wanted to do musically and he loved the house. The villagers liked him, almost took it upon themselves to protect him from the world. He said to us that the house was where he would like to have his children." He devoted a lot of time to renovations and landscaping, hiring a builder named Frank Thoroughgood to live in the cottage while supervising structural alterations to the house and the laying of a drainage system.

In the downstairs music-room at Cotchford Farm, looking out on walled gardens and trim lawns, Brian began composing and planning for his new group, asking disc jockey John Peel to recommend musicians. Micky Waller was an early visitor to Sussex; the respected ex-drummer with Jeff Beck was all set to join the new band. Brian's home studio equipment included three tape-machines and microphones, two organs, a piano and other instruments on which he enjoyed experimenting. The basic model for his new band was America's resounding contemporary blues band Creedence Clearwater Revival: Brian was obsessed with their hit "Proud Mary," which boomed around his house at that time. Mentally free of the Stones, physically improving, with Anna Wohlin and two new spaniel dogs at his side, Brian was certainly capable of re-emerging with musical significance. At the end of June he looked poised for a rebirth: the moment he left the Stones, Brian had renounced drugs, telling all those around him that they were destructive. He was paranoid about allowing them in his house, lest the police should seek him out again. And he ensured that all his visitors arrived "clean."

It was twenty-four hours before the amicable departure of Brian that Mick pointed the Stones towards an event that would become enshrined in our history. Blind Faith, the super-group that starred Eric Clapton and Steve Winwood, played a unique free concert in the summer sunshine at Hyde Park. About 150,000 fans were there, and amid the euphoria and camaraderie of the musicians, Mick and Marianne were also impressed with the organization. Recently there had been plans for us to appear at the Colosseum in Rome, where Italian TV cameras were to film us. The venue was irresistible, and caught everyone's imagination: gladiators had fought there, Christians were torn to pieces by the lions there, Nero held decadent court there—and now in the 1960s the Rolling Stones would take rock 'n' roll there. Perfect theater! The spectacle could be captured on film, and sold to the world in place of the dormant *Rock 'n' Roll Circus* film, in which our performance had been mediocre. However, the two shows scheduled for the Colosseum were suddenly canceled (despite the *Sunderland Echo*'s report on June 28 that "This week saw the Stones take Rome by storm in two concerts at the city's ancient Colosseum!") and Mick's thoughts turned elsewhere.

After seeing the spectacular Hyde Park concert, he approached the organizers, Blackhill Enterprises.* The response was positive. As Blind Faith performed "Under My Thumb" as a gesture to the arrival of Mick, he visualized our new-look band, with a new guitarist, making a glittering debut under the summer skies in a similar free concert that would outshine the now-abandoned Rome concerts. The date was set for our first live show since the previous year's random appearance at the *New Musical Express* Pollwinners concert: Hyde Park, July 5.

Les Perrin then seized every media opportunity to push Mick Taylor and the Hyde Park concert into the headlines. Brian's departure was a downer, and Mick still had the drugs bust hanging over him; here was daylight again. A photo call and press conference at the bandstand at Hyde Park on June 13 introduced Mick Taylor and announced the forthcoming free show.

The Stones were on the way back, forcefully, Perrin stated. Fans as well as journalists came to glimpse Taylor for the first time. In a white coat, and described as

---

*While he was backstage Mick was approached by a security guard, Jim Callaghan, who asked if he had a job for him. He later joined the Stones as our security chief on every tour from 1973 to the present day.

having "Byronic" looks, he looked over-awed as cameras flashed all around him. Rather like Charlie and me, Taylor was not an extrovert like Mick and Keith, and it showed. "I'm not nervous about joining the Stones. I'm just getting used to all the fuss," he told reporters. "Stories about the boys don't worry me. I'm sure I will fit in very well. I can tell you that I'm very happy about my pay." (He was hired for £150 a week initially, until he was confirmed as a fully fledged member of the band when, like all of us, he would receive one-fifth of the band's income from concerts and record sales.)

Jagger, who had arrived with the short hair-style needed for the Ned Kelly film, declared the new Stone to be "one of us . . . he gets on well with Keith and he is a blues player who wants to play rock 'n' roll, so that's OK."

Mick Taylor may have been happy with his pay, but my bank account showed a £10,000 debit at this juncture, and despite my receipt of $15,000 as our annual guarantee payment from Klein, and $5,000 from London Records on June 2, and Keith and Mick's receipt of $42,000 as their annual guarantee payment at the same time, I walked into the Stones office on June 12 to find a testy Mick and Keith's on the telex to Klein's office in New York. Keith said: "Allen Klein promised me £55,000 and I must have it by Tuesday at the outside. Get it together. No, repeat *no* excuses, will be accepted for any delay whatsoever." Mick said: "Will I also be getting my $72,000 for my country-house repairs on Monday too? Jo [Bergman] wants to know about Rome as she is going crazy over here. Please reply."

Bibi in Klein's office responded: "Ronnie says he will get back to you after he speaks to Rome." Mick: "Will you ask him about my money?" Bibi: "I did." Mick: "What did he say?" There was no answer. Mick: "I want an answer." Bibi: "He says he will take care of all problems when he arrives Monday morning. Many thanks, Bibi."

We went on to the basement of the Beatles' Apple studios to rehearse for the Hyde Park concert. Looking back, it was a curious place for us to work, since Klein's control had spread to both the Beatles and the Stones and caused ripples of dissent in both camps. The interaction between the two groups generated anticipation that some Beatles might guest at our Hyde Park show, particularly since Keith had worked with George Harrison on recording sessions for the singer-keyboardist Billy Preston. There was always a "movement" wanting to put the Stones and Beatles together in any way possible. The rehearsals, particularly with a new guitarist, were long, heavy and successful. We were conscious that there was a risk of our being rusty after such a long lay-off. So we went through "Satisfaction," "Stray-Cat Blues," "I'm Free," "Down-Home Girl," "Sympathy for the Devil," Otis Redding's "I've Been Loving You Too Long"—the list went on. Twelve songs were the target, including "Jumpin' Jack Flash," of course, and the new single, "Honky-Tonk Women." Mick could hardly wait to get back on stage; that was obvious.

Simultaneously, at Olympic we were recording tracks that would eventually go on *Let It Bleed*. Nanette Workman sang back-up vocals on one track, "Country Honk," which also featured a fiddler named Byron Berline. Preferring a natural sound, Berline went outdoors to record his fiddle part; a car drove by during the recording and its "honk" was retained in the song, which went on to the album. One track I vividly recall was "I Don't Know Why," which we worked on at Olympic from midnight to 4:45 a.m. on June 30—having finished a four-hour rehearsal at Apple at 8 p.m.! We finally got a good take of the song, which wound up on *Metamorphosis* in 1975; it was a good example of the band's determination to see a good song through to completion whatever the difficulties. They could say plenty (and plenty did) about the Stones, but we could never be accused of laziness.

The night of Wednesday, July 2, 1969, was humid and cloudy in Sussex and since Brian suffered from asthma and hayfever, he was using his inhaler liberally: the rural setting of Cotchford Farm near Hartfield was not the best place for him to live since the pollen count was possibly twice as high there as in the city. But it was Brian's haven and nothing could shift him. He told friends he wanted to live there forever and be buried there.

Reverting to the love of his jazzy youth in Cheltenham, Brian had bought a saxophone and during the evening he played this and other instruments casually, alone in his oak-beamed music-room in the basement. "In limbo" between leaving the Stones and forming his new band, Brian was in a relaxed frame of mind.

At around 8:30 p.m., Brian joined Anna, the builder Frank Thoroughgood and Janet Lawson, a nurse who was staying with Frank, for dinner. Janet described Brian's conversation as "garbled"; he had been drinking and taking sleeping tablets. Frank recalled: "He was not really under the influence of drink but he staggered slightly. We watched TV and Brian remarked on the heat. We had had quite a bit to drink." At 10:30, Brian asked Frank and Janet to join him and Anna for a swim. Janet declined. "He had been drinking. He was a bit unsteady on his feet. They were in no condition to swim. I felt strongly about this and mentioned it to both of the men. They disregarded my warning."

In his multi-colored swimming trunks, Brian went with Anna, in a black bikini, and Frank, towards the flood-lit, blue-tiled pool which would present them with no vast temperature shock since it was heated to around 80°F.

"I went to the pool to keep an eye on them," Janet said. "Brian had trouble getting on to the springboard, so Frank helped him and Brian flopped into the water. The two men appeared sluggish in the water but I decided they could look after themselves." Anna did not spend long in the water. After about twenty minutes Janet and Anna left the pool area for a while, returning to the house. Ten minutes later Frank left the water for a few minutes and went indoors for a cigarette and a towel.

At that point, Janet "immediately went to the pool and saw Brian at the bottom, quite motionless. I sensed the worst and shouted to Anna and Frank." Returning to the pool Frank called out and Anna dashed from the house; they both dived in and pulled Brian out. They laid him on his back, a towel propping up his head, and Janet, with her nursing experience, pumped a little water out of him and massaged his heart. (Anna told Astrid and me a few days later that when they got Brian out of the pool and laid him down, he was still alive and had a pulse.) Anna and Frank applied artificial respiration but there was no reaction. They phoned for an ambulance and a local doctor. When ambulancemen arrived, they tried to revive him and used a pump for about half an hour to try to coax back the spark of life. (Anna maintained to Astrid and me that nobody seemed to take the incident seriously enough in her opinion.)

When the police, including Detective-Chief Inspector Ron Marshall, head of East Grinstead CID, arrived, ambulancemen were applying artificial respiration. Then a local doctor arrived and after examination pronounced Brian dead.

Leslie Perrin and Tom Keylock were the first Stones people on the scene at 3:30 a.m. I'd left the others at Olympic studios just before 2 a.m. where they were mixing tracks for *Let It Bleed.* The news was broken to Mick Jagger in a phone call from Tom Keylock's wife. He, Keith and Charlie sat around, dazed and disbelieving. Charlie called me at the Londonderry House Hotel at 3 a.m., half an hour after we had gone to bed. Astrid and I were stunned, in tears. It was hard to speak. We sat for a long while, unable to comprehend what had happened.

Back in Sussex, police took statements from Frank, Anna and Janet as Brian's body was taken by ambulance to a mortuary. Brian's father was informed. Les Perrin, who alerted his best friend in newspapers, Don Short of the *Daily Mirror,* said: "Anna, who is in a shocked state and terribly upset, did not get to bed until about 5 a.m. When it was light, Tom Keylock and I inspected the pool. We found Brian's puffer [inhaler] on the side of the pool. We gave it to the police." Brian's death could have been caused by a number of things: a bad asthma attack? A lethal combination of pills and alcohol? Or was it an epileptic fit? Anita Pallenberg believes he died because there was no one around who knew what was really wrong with him: "He had been in that condition many times before, but there had always been people around to turn him on his side and take care of him."

The news of Brian's death bounced across the world and appalled everyone who had been remotely touched by him: former girlfriends, musicians, old schoolfriends and particularly those close to the Stones who knew of his crucial contribution to our early years. Some reacted callously, others with heartfelt pain. In Lambeth, Brian's former girlfriend Pat Andrews was living with Brian's son in a bleak reception center run by the local council.

"They woke me up at 6:30 in the morning and told me: 'We've just heard on the news, Brian's dead—now you'll be able to get some money.' It did not sink in till about ten o'clock when I heard it myself. I just broke down and cried. Even with all the arguments and trouble we had, I didn't wish this on him. He had to have girls around him because of his insecurity. He had to prove his male instincts. The funny thing is, I think that we all still love him in one way or another. He was the hardest boy in the world to understand. I think we all believed we could understand him if we tried long enough. But really, no one ever could. It just does not seem fair that he's dead before he really got a chance to grow up. Well, at least now he does not have to work so hard at living."

Suki Potier said: "When my boyfriend Tara Browne was killed Brian gave me a shoulder to cry on. He picked up the pieces and made me feel a woman again. I will never forget him. He was a wonderful, incredible person."

Pete Townshend of The Who said to the *London Evening News:* "Well, today's a pretty normal day for Brian. He always seemed to be losing out one way or another. I used to see a lot of the Stones' success lying with him but the rest of the Stones never really dug him. He was always under some drug or other, a very druggy sort of person." George Harrison, the Beatle with whom Brian had most empathy, said: "I don't think he had enough love or understanding."

A former Stones secretary said: "The sadness of his dying is somehow not so bad as the sadness of seeing him try to live. Even with millions of girls clamoring to meet him, and ready to do anything for him, he was lonely. He just couldn't communicate with people. Brian couldn't love anybody except himself or his own music. Kindness, yes—but love, no. That was his problem. He used to use drugs and drink to try to overcome his deep loneliness."

We were all numbed as we gathered at the office that afternoon. As we met, Brian's spaniels and his Afghan hound were being taken from his home to boarding kennels. During the day, the pathologist carried out a post mortem, reporting drowning, drugs and "liver degeneration." Among the band and the office staff only one subject was talked about, but with the need for discipline that mourners somehow feel, we had to press on with a visit to Lime Grove Studios to film our segment for *Top of the Pops*. The day after Brian's death brought the release of our fifteenth single in Britain and our twentieth in America: "Honky-Tonk Women" backed by "You Can't Always Get What You Want." This was so commercial that it was issued as a double-A-side to attract maximum promotion.* With the spotlight on the Stones now for the worst reason, the attention gained by the record was phenomenal and the response to its impact was ecstatic, many regarding it as a quintessential Stones track.

That night, a recording session had been booked for us at Olympic, but nobody attended. Mick and Marianne went instead to a party thrown by Prince Rupert Loewenstein. Held in a marquee in the garden of his Kensington home, it featured three groups, Yes, Stalactites, and Al Wynn; the police had sixty complaints and visited several times, but the event continued. Other guests included Princess Margaret, actors Peter Sellers and Peter Wyngarde, fashion designer Hardy Amies, Lord Harlech and Lord and Lady Tavistock. Mick wore a "white dress' from Mr. Fish—the dress he would immortalize at our Hyde Park concert—and danced the night away.

The euphoria of planning the Hyde Park concert for two days after Brian's death was now overshadowed. It was Charlie who suggested it should become a memorial and tribute to Brian, but it was Mick whom the press approached for a decision. "We will do the concert—for Brian," Mick told the newspapers. "We have thought about it an awful lot and feel he would have wanted it to go on. He *was* music. I understand how many people will feel, but we are now doing it because of him."

And so on Friday July 4, we duly reported for rehearsals at the Apple studios for three hours from 5 p.m. When I returned to the hotel, I found Astrid in my suite with Anna Wohlin. Tom Keylock had "rescued" her from the press and brought her here to hide away for a few days. It made sense because Astrid, being Swedish too, could take care of her. She stayed with us, successfully avoiding the baying media, until the afternoon of

---

*This topped the British charts for five weeks and the American charts for four.

July 7 when, looking stylish in a fawn coat over a white mini dress and a floppy, white-brimmed hat, she was driven to Cotchford Farm. After collecting her possessions she went on to the inquest at East Grinstead, where she gave evidence with Frank Thoroughgood and Janet Lawson.

The coroner, Dr. Angus Sommerville, asked Anna if she had ever seen Brian have an asthma attack. Anna: "No, but he often used his inhaler, particularly when he was in the pool, and had difficulty in breathing." She thought he also used it for hayfever.

Asked by the coroner if she had ever seen him take a black pill called Duraphit, Anna replied: "Yes, once." She added that the night he died, Brian and Frank were under the influence of drink.

Dr. Albert Sachs, consultant pathologist, said Brian had all the signs of natural disease. He had pleurisy and his heart was larger than it should have been for his age. His liver was twice the normal weight. There was no evidence of an asthmatic attack, though there were indications of chronic bronchial trouble. Brian had taken a fairly large quantity of a drug.

Recording a verdict of misadventure, the coroner stated: "He would not listen. So he drowned, under the influence of alcohol and drugs."

Two days later, Anna took a chauffeured car, charged to Brian's account, from East Grinstead to London and flew home to Stockholm, never to be heard from again. So quickly, so prematurely, with the same dazzling speed with which he lived, Brian had gone, and to many a chapter had closed. But the sadness of his departure, and the rare talent he contributed to the world of music, ensured that his memory would remain for ever.

"I hope," said Alexis Korner, "that people give him a better deal in death than they did in life."

It was utterly incredible that, on the eve of our biggest concert, the air was thick with tributes to a Stone who had so recently departed. Jimmy Miller described him as "entirely a musician who never quite adapted to the commercial and image aspect of being a Stone. As lead guitarist, ideally he should have had more to say but he would prefer not to play rather than feel he was ruining the original conception of a number. Mick and Keith had evolved as the composers and Brian was the sidesman to their ideas. I was looking forward to seeing him to discuss producing his records when he had formed his own group."

I felt it was essential to point out what a pioneer Brian was: Brian was the first person in England to play bottleneck guitar when nobody knew what it was. He had continued to develop his interest in different instruments and brought to our attention a great deal we might otherwise have missed. As for his personality, for all his weaknesses and hang-ups, his impertinence and terrible behavior, he was a pivotal figure. As a symbol of the sixties that helped to shape us, he was entitled to a free pardon.

Keith was typically both gentle and tough: "Brian was a cat who could play any instrument. It was like: 'There it is. Music comes out of it. If I work at it for a bit, I can do it.' It's him on marimbas on 'Under My Thumb' and Mellotron on quite a few things on *Satanic Majesties*. He was the strings on '2,000 Light Years from Home.' Brian on Mellotron and the brass on 'We Love You,' all that Arabic riff. He was one of those people who are so beautiful in one way, and such an asshole in another." Keith had once said to Brian: "You'll never make thirty, man." Sadly, Brian's reply was simple: "I know."

Mick was bitterly upset and it showed: "I am wordless, sad and shocked. Something has gone. We were like a pack, like a family, we Stones. I just say my prayers for him. I hope he becomes blessed. I hope he is finding peace; I really want him to. I wasn't ever really close to him."

Rolling Stone summed up my feelings precisely: "If Keith and Mick were the mind and body of the Stones, Brian was clearly the soul."

More than 500 people, mostly women, gathered outside the Cheltenham parish church to say their last goodbyes to the local pop star at his funeral on July 10. It was a fitting setting, just a few steps from the Jones family house in Hatherley Road where the young Brian had nurtured his love of music, and in the church where, as a boy, he had sung in the choir and been confirmed.

Astrid and I were collected from our London hotel and driven to Mr. and Mrs. Jones's house in Cheltenham.

Here we met all his family plus Charlie and Shirley Watts, Stu and Cynthia, and Tom Keylock. We were all choked up. It was hard to take in much except the masses of flowers among which was a wreath of red roses shaped like a guitar from Brian's parents and sister Barbara. There, too, was a wreath from Mick and Marianne, and one from the Stones as a group, eight-feet tall with "The Gates of Heaven" in red and yellow roses. Jo Bergman and Peter Swales had sent a rose each.

The fourteen-car cortège drove through the Cheltenham streets to the church, and hundreds of people out shopping stopped to watch and crowd the pavements. Many had handkerchiefs to their faces. In gently falling rain, we finally arrived at the church where typists and shopgirls interrupted their lunch-hour to attend the service. Dozens of girls, many dressed in black and carrying red roses, had converged on the town. Many were crying as the bronze metal casket was carried into the church. We entered and took our seats. Others present included Eric Easton, Suki Potier, Linda Lawrence and Brian's son Julian, aged five, who had flown in from America.*

Canon Hugh Evan Hopkins said he had "immediately and gladly" agreed when Mr. and Mrs. Jones had asked "with some understandable diffidence" whether Brian's funeral service could take place in the parish church. It was a quiet, dignified fifteen-minute service. But we thought Canon Hopkins was very cynical, and didn't like many of the things he said about Brian: "He had little patience with authority, convention and tradition. In this he was typical of many of his generation who have come to see in the Stones an expression of their whole attitude to life. Much that this ancient church has stood for in 900 years seems totally irrelevant to them." The scripture reading was the story of the prodigal son.

As the funeral procession left for the town's cemetery near Prestbury, extra police controlled the crowds on the three-mile drive. Hundreds lined the route and filled

---

*Mick and Marianne had just left for Australia to film *Ned Kelly*, but I was saddened by the absence of Keith, Anita, Allen Klein, Andrew Oldham, Jo Bergman and everyone else associated with Brian and the Stones, and all his other professional, as well as his personal friends.

the quiet cemetery nestling in a fold of the Cotswolds. The orderly crowd, mostly youngsters, stood quietly and sadly as the huge solid bronze casket, which had been flown over from New York, was lowered into the green carpeted grave. Many girls tossed roses in after it.

Shamefully, press photographers pushed mourners out of the way so they could hang over the grave to take photos. Long-haired hippies curled up in yoga-style contemplation. Nearby, nearly 500 wreaths and floral tributes, mostly of red and yellow roses, covered the lawns.

The pollen count was particularly high that summer and by a strange quirk during these days of tension, Mick Jagger developed hayfever—something he had not suffered since he was fifteen. His eyes reddened, his nose was wet and he began sneezing continually; finally, on the night before the Hyde Park concert, he developed laryngitis.

Luckily, Mick's entire life has run on his exceptionally high adrenalin; there was nothing more certain to me than that he would defy any medical problem to get on that stage next day. "There's no money to be made out of concert tours in Britain so we might as well do it for nothing," he said, explaining the concept of the free concert. "People think there's a fortune in touring but I never made any money out of it. The expenses are phenomenal. We want to do it. It's fun to play. It only becomes work when we have to do it day in, day out."

The night before the show, hundreds of young people began bedding down in the park, under the stars. At about 11 p.m. there came a touching moment when someone called for two minutes' silence for Brian. Some 500 stood in silent tribute and the scene was set for the next day's emotional requiem. By midnight, with the numbers growing every minute, about 300 had camped in the cockpit, a dip in the heart of the park scheduled to be the stage. The park normally closes at midnight, but the police, noting the quiet behavior of the fans, left it open.

Throughout the night couples, many barefoot and wearing jeans, kaftans, sweaters, beads and with ribbons in their hair, trickled into the park. Many spent the night singing to guitars. A lunatic fringe, determined, as al-

ways, to spoil a cheerful occasion for everyone else,
smashed up deck chairs, tore up fencing and stripped
branches from trees to feed about fifty fires. Police controlled them and firemen were called only once. Youths
who danced while brandishing flaming torches were pelted
with empty beer cans by angry fans. One, who sustained
a cut head, was taken away by ambulance. Police arrested twelve people and charged five of them.

The day of the concert, Saturday July 5, coincided with
Marianne filing a petition for divorce against John Dunbar. John filed a petition in return in which he cited Mick
Jagger. Mick had many other things on his mind. He told
friends he was terrified of taking the stage for this concert. He had ordered a carpet to be put on stage so that
he could dance barefoot, and he wanted the stage decorated with plastic palm trees, parakeets and special flowers. Hundreds of palm trees were found but no parakeets.
Beneath the stage was a first-aid center resembling a
World War I casualty point. If the weather was fine,
250,000 fans were expected, which would make it the
biggest gathering anywhere since the death of Rudolph
Valentino.

The concert was anything but free, though: organized
by Blackhill Enterprises in association with the Stones, it
cost much more than the £600 or so needed to put on an
average free pop show. Blackhill reckoned they were
shelling out £3,000. There was the running of their office
and the hire of caravans for this. The normal stage in the
park was three feet high, but a special ten-foot one had
to be constructed so that more people could see the
performers, and a special dais on stage for the amplifiers
raised them twenty feet above the ground to ensure that
the sound carried into the depths of the huge crowd.

By 11 a.m. police estimated that 20,000 fans were
sweltering in the hot sunshine. Hundreds cooled off by
bathing in the Serpentine and others snapped up every
available ice-cream or soft drink. Others sang, strummed
guitars or played tom-toms. And still they came, throughout the day, thousands and thousands swarming into the
park. Beaded, bangled, bejeweled, they included men
who looked like birds, and birds who looked like men.
Some girls showed their breasts in see-through dresses.

The fans waited patiently, policed by fifty Hell's Angels, called in at the suggestion of the promoters to act as "heavy men." You never saw a police force like it. Black leather suits, studded to the eyeballs, Nazi helmets, swastikas, crosses and bizarre brass insignia everywhere. Tattooed arms, thick leather belts with ornate buckles, and a million metal badges and buttons retrieved from the junk shops of Europe to bring back memories of World War II. The Angels had come from all over: Forest Gate, Birmingham, Brighton, Gosport, riding their Harley Davidsons. One had his face painted like a peacock with reds and blues, eyeballs surrounded by lipstick and mascara. But they were mostly gentle with the crowd, and overall an asset. They were very effective, the sight of their terrifying uniforms and their very numbers ensuring firm control.

It was so peaceful. Looking out, the fans stretched as far as anyone could see. From the air they looked like a swarm of bees.

At the Londonderry House Hotel, my son Stephen, now seven years old, arrived from Gedding to attend the concert. Our suite had been chosen as the meeting place for the band and entourage. As people began to arrive there, all the talk was about Brian's death and the coming concert. Mick, still suffering from laryngitis, was very upset, and found it difficult to talk about Brian without showing his emotions. I told him that we should try to feel positive about it.

The concert started at 1 p.m. The running order was: The Third Ear Band, King Crimson, Screw, Alexis Korner's New Church, Family, Battered Ornaments and the Stones. The crowd were perfectly controlled, and the vibes were wonderful.

The scent of burning joss sticks wafted on the summer breeze, and bearded, beaded hippies swayed to the music. There were marijuana-smokers, a few LSD-trippers and the sound of cow-bells. Older people wandered along to listen and stayed to marvel at the volume and diversity of sound that came in waves from the stage. The mammoth crowd was orderly, highly appreciative of the almost non-stop music. A riotous mass of color stretched out and away from the palm-bedecked stage.

People started to suffer from the heat. Hell's Angels hoisted fainting girls through the throng to first-aid tents.

The compère, Sam Cutler, said: "Take off your vests and put them over your heads." Boys and girls alike took his advice, and nobody thought the consequent exposure worth a second glance. Cutler added: "If you feel faint, please don't come to the stage to collapse. It wasn't built to take so many."

Meanwhile, at the Londonderry House Hotel, a huge army ambulance pulled up. We left my suite and were ushered into it. Allen Klein was here, acting as "chief of security," and looking the part.

At 4:15, in anticipation of the Stones' arrival, the leather militia began preparing a way through the crowds for us by standing shoulder to shoulder. We drove into the park and slowly made our way through throngs of people, arriving dramatically in our dark green ambulance. Klein got out first and helped to hustle us into caravans. We looked out of the windows to see faces everywhere. There, at one window, was my old girlfriend Doreen Samuels. We chatted for a few minutes but it was impossible to hear anything properly.

It was near time for us to go onstage. We hurriedly tuned up in a caravan, using a harmonica with great difficulty. The din outside made nonsense of our efforts.

The British are wonderful! Around half a million fans waited with stolid respectability for our appearance. The crowd, restrained and well-behaved, burst into a frenzy of applause when Sam Cutler spoke. "The Stones want to play tonight for Brian," he said simply.

In the musicians' enclosure in front of the stage, Hell's Angels kept order for camp followers: beautiful girlfriends and wives, some in transparent blouses, feeding their children in what at times did feel like a gypsy encampment. Guests included Paul and Linda McCartney with their children, Eric Clapton and girlfriend Alice Ormsby Gore, Ginger Baker and daughter, Tony Hicks (Hollies), Donovan, Chris Barber, Marsha Hunt, Kenny Lynch, Mama Cass and husband, David Gilmour (Pink Floyd), actress Miranda Hampton.

Onstage were Marianne in a long white dress, carrying her son Nicholas; she said she felt terrible—"dope sick"; photographer Michael Cooper; and Julie Felix. Stu and Tom Keylock were there too, helping us. Astrid, with

Karin and Jan, kept away, side-stage, while Klein looked after my son Stephen onstage.

We eventually went on at 5:25, the welcoming roar reaching Wembley proportions. Mick wore his cool and summery button-through mini dress, with bows and bishop sleeves over a mauve vest and white trousers. Mick had asked Ossie Clark to run him up a snakeskin suit for the show, but the day was so hot that Mick decided to wear the Michael Fish "dress" atop white trousers which he had worn at Prince Rupert's ball two nights earlier. He made fashion history and surely established another "first" by being the first man to take off a dress in public.*

His face pale and drawn as he battled with his dry throat, Mick stepped forward. "Cool it and listen," he urged the crowd. And they did. "Cool it for a minute because I would really like to say something about Brian. I don't know how to do this thing but I'm going to try. I'm just going to say something that was written by Shelley . . ."

Mick then launched, with considerable courage, into his reading of the thirty-ninth stanza from *Adonais* by Percy Bysshe Shelley:

Peace, peace! He is not dead, he doth not sleep—
He has awakened from the dream of life—
'Tis we, who lost in stormy visions, keep
With phantoms an unprofitable strife,
And in mad trance, strike with our spirit's knife
Invulnerable nothings.—We decay
Like corpses in a charnel; fear and grief
Convulse us and consume us day by day,
*   And cold hopes swarm like worms within our living clay.*

He slipped his page to continue with Stanza 52:

The One remains, the many change and pass;
Heaven's light forever shines, Earth's shadows fly;
Life, like a dome of many-coloured glass,
Stains the white radiance of Eternity,

*When I visited Sammy Davis Jr. in Los Angeles in the mid-1970s, he told me that he had ordered this dress and was to collect it but that it was "loaned" to Mick. Sammy later ordered three others to be made for him in black, brown and champagne.

Until Death tramples it to fragments.—Die,
If thou wouldst be that which thou dost seek!

The massive throng heard the poem in silence and as
we all stood listening, the dust of the day rose into the
sultry air amid the oaks and the elms and the beeches of
a city's expanse of green. Anyone would be forgiven for
thinking this great gathering had come to hear a famous
religious leader or some eastern mystic. The carnival
atmosphere became appropriately tranquil, a gracious
memorial to Brian.

When he finished reading, Hyde Park erupted again,
and rock 'n' roll was back. As we began to blast into
"I'm Yours, She's Mine," 3,500 butterflies were released
into the sky from cardboard boxes. Later it was said that
many had died through being stifled in boxes without air,
but from where I stood, thousands seemed to be flutter-
ing and landing in the crowd and on the stage. It was a
beautiful sight.*

Mick was away in our first concert for fourteen months:
leaping into the air, pouting, blowing kisses, dancing,
jumping, swaying, going down on his haunches like a
small animal. He pranced across the stage, set his hand
on his hip, and sold himself as if he'd never been away.
He smoothed his hair, quickly discarding the white dress.
We moved through hits, old favorites, new songs, but
the sound wasn't good. We were dragging. We were
off-form. Mick whined at us: "Tempo! Get the tempo
together!" We were not at our best, perhaps because the
sheer weight of the occasion got to us.

But the crowd—between 250,000 and 500,000, depend-

---

*At a cost of £300, most of the butterflies were supplied by
Brian Gardiner, a Cambridge researcher to the unit of inverte-
brates, chemical physiology, who bred them as a hobby. He said
a number of them were sterilized but others were not. A further
500 came from World Wide Butterflies, run by Robert Gooden,
who said they were all unsterilized. Blackhill Enterprises had
cleared the release of sterilized butterflies with the Ministry of
Public Building and Works, who agreed, provided no cabbage
whites were released. But a butterfly expert, Hugh Newman,
asserted later that his son was at the concert and there had been
cabbage whites. "It's a shocking business. They cause irrepara-
ble damage."

ing on who you listen to—was getting off on the event anyway. They went wild, hundreds dancing, everyone on their feet. We soon went out of tune in the hot sun, but performed for fifty minutes with the amplification so powerful that we were told we could be heard half a mile away, against the wind, at Marble Arch.

Our one-hour set proceeded with "Jumpin' Jack Flash," "Mercy Mercy," "Down-Home Girl," "Lovin' Cup," "Honky-Tonk Women," "Midnight Rambler," "(I Can't Get No) Satisfaction," "Street Fighting Man," "Sympathy for the Devil," "Love in Vain," "I'm Free," "Stray-Cat Blues" and "No Expectations."

Granada paid a large sum to Blackhill Enterprises for the television rights. Produced by Jo Durden Smith and Leslie Woodhead, their extensive filming operation included a staff of fifty with seven top camera crews. The music was recorded on eight-track for Granada TV using equipment worth about £30,000. The TV soundtrack for *Stones in the Park* was "Midnight Rambler," "Satisfaction," "I'm Free," "I'm Yours, She's Mine," "Jumpin' Jack Flash," "Honky-Tonk Women," "Love in Vain" and "Sympathy for the Devil"—which was not in the order we worked on stage. The program was first shown on British TV in September 1969.

A silent film of the concert, made by Peter Ungerleiden and titled *Under My Thumb*, was shown in March 1970 at the New Arts Lab in Robert Street, Camden, London. And Kenneth Anger filmed parts of the concert and included them in his movie *Invocation of My Demon Brother*.

More than 400 fans who had fainted in the heat went to hospital. Police confiscated several knives and made twelve arrests. Encouraged by offers of a free record for every three sacks of rubbish collected, fans cleared up fifteen tons of debris—and left the park cleaner than on a normal Saturday!

If it wasn't our most musical performance, it was certainly the most heartfelt, and Hyde Park on July 5, 1969, remains the biggest open-air free concert ever held in Britain—breathtaking, stunning, spectacular in its impact. And sad. For Brian Jones had died, signaling the end of an era. The Rolling Stones could never be the same. The band changed, but the band went on—drawing strength from our troubles, taking risks, leading the way, and always *The Stones* . . .

Appendix 1

LETTER AGREEMENT (8/1/65) from Allen Klein to the Rolling Stones said:

"Gentlemen,

(1) Reference is made to a number of agreements of even date between you, Andrew Loog Oldham, London Records Inc., and the undersigned (which agreements were numbered for reference) pursuant to which, among other things, the undersigned became the manufacturer of all phonographic records (embodying your performances) in the USA, pursuant to Agreement No. 9.

(2) To induce you to execute the aforementioned agreements, and in particular, Agreement No. 9, the undersigned agreed to make certain guarantees to you which are contained herein. You have advised the undersigned that so long as Andrew Loog Oldham produces and continues to produce your recordings the one-half (½) of the applicable guarantees contained herein are to be paid directly to him and one-half (½) of the applicable royalties contained herein are to be paid directly to him.

(3) Notwithstanding anything to the contrary contained in either Agreement No. 5, or 9 or any other agreement to which you were either a party or to which you have signed as a consent party, and as an inducement for you to execute such agreements above-mentioned, the following constitutes the undersigned's obligation to you:

(a) During the period of 8/1/65 through 7/31/66, the undersigned guarantees that the minimum aggregate royalties (computed at 18½% of wholesale in accordance with the agreement between Nanker Phelge Music Limited, and London Records Inc.) which are presently deemed earned and payable to you shall be One Million ($1,000,000) Dollars.

(b) In the event there are sufficient sales of records in the USA embodying your performances so that the undersigned recoups (from royalties computed at 18½%) the Million Dollars provided for in subparagraph (a) above, on or prior to 7/31/66, then and in such event the minimum guarantee to you shall be escalated from One Million ($1,000,000) Dollars to Three Million ($3,000,000) Dollars.

(c) In the event there are sufficient sales of records in the USA embodying your performances so that the undersigned recoups (from royalties computed at 18½%) and aggregate of Two Million ($2,000,000) Dollars on or prior to 7/31/67, then and in such event the minimum guarantee to you shall be escalated from Three Million ($3,000,000) Dollars to Four Million ($4,000,000) Dollars.

(4) As part of the consideration for our entering in Agreement No. 9 with London Records Inc., London Records Inc. has agreed to undertake to make that portion of the guarantee set forth in Paragraph (3) subdivision (a) above, part of the guarantee herein contained to-wit: the sum of One Million ($1,000,000) Dollars to be paid Five Hundred Thousand ($500,000) Dollars to you (pursuant to Agreement No. 5) and Five Hundred Thousand ($500,000) Dollars to Andrew Loog Oldham pursuant to Agreement No. 6.

(5) The foregoing guarantee has been given to you by the undersigned as an inducement for you to have executed the agreements aforementioned and as an inducement for the negative covenants you have entered into so that no one other than the undersigned will receive any recording rights for the period mentioned in the agreements to the undersigned in the USA.

(6) That portion of the guarantees contained herein which come into effect and which are not paid to you in our behalf by London Records Inc., shall be paid to you in twenty (20) equal annual instalments commencing with 6/1/66, and annually thereafter on the 6/1/67, and on June 1st in each year thereafter until the total guarantees are paid to you. In the event the royalties exceed all of the guarantees contained herein, such sum which exceeds the guarantees shall be deemed excess royalties and shall be

paid to you on 6/1/86. Each of you shall furnish us with the addresses to which payments are to be made and payments shall be made directly to you, your heirs or assigns in the ratio of one-fifth (⅕) each of all payments referred to herein except for those payments which have been directed to be made to Andrew Loog Oldham or Andrew and/or Eric Easton. Very truly yours, Nanker Phelge Music Ltd." (Signed by Allen Klein.)

LETTER AGREEMENT (7/30/65) from Andrew Oldham (really Allen Klein) to The Rolling Stones said:

"Gentlemen,

(1) We have this date entered into several agreements wherein I as the Producer of your recordings have granted to you fifty per cent (50%) of all royalties due and/or payable to me from 1963 until 1970.

(2) I have further for our mutual benefit and in order for all of us to participate in a proposed capital gains transaction assigned all masters of your performances for the USA and Canada to a corporation that we jointly own named Nankerphelge.

(3) It is our understanding that on the sale of the assets or stock of Nankerphelge you are to receive collectively fifty per cent (50%) of the proposed selling price for your stock which will be at least $1,300,000 payable over 20 years and I am to receive twenty-five per cent (25%) for my stock and the other twenty-five per cent (25%) of the $1,300,000 shall be determined at a later date.

(4) Your royalty earnings in the USA and Canada shall be computed as follows: (a) For sales up to 2/28/65 a royalty of 7% of wholesale; (b) For sales after 2/28/65 a royalty of 9¼%. At such time as your one half share of the $1,300,000 has been earned against the foregoing royalties you will then continue to receive nine and one-quarter per cent (9¼%) of all sales in the USA and Canada of the wholesale selling price.

(5) Payments will be made to you directly by the American Record Company.

(6) In pursuit of the foregoing I will immediately enter into and consummate all agreements and documents nec-

essary to effectuate this $1,300,000 agreement in our joint behalf. Please indicate your acceptance. Very truly yours, Andrew Loog Oldham." (Signed by The Rolling Stones and Andrew Oldham.)

LETTER AGREEMENT (7/30/65) from Andrew Oldham (really Allen Klein) and The Rolling Stones to The Decca Record Company Ltd. said:

"Dear Sirs, In consideration of your entering at our request into certain Agreements with Andrew Loog Oldham whereby you have the exclusive right to accept recordings/tapes embodying performances by us for the world excluding the USA and Canada, we hereby jointly and severally undertake to make our services exclusively available to the said Andrew Loog Oldham for recording purposes until 5/10/70, and to make available to you during each year new recordings for at least three LPs and four singles. If for any reason whatsoever the said Andrew Loog Oldham is not able or does not perform the said agreement, we the undersigned jointly and severally undertake to provide you if so required with our exclusive recording services for any unexpired period of the said Agreement at the same schedule of payments and at our net rate of royalty as is now existing under the Agreements with Decca and the said Andrew Loog Oldham, and in such event you (Decca) will be obliged to continue to make all payments and royalties to Andrew Loog Oldham as is provided in such Agreements between Decca and Andrew Loog Oldham as long as Decca continues to sell records containing our performances. The costs of such recordings to be deducted from sums due to Andrew Loog Oldham. Yours faithfully." (Signed by The Rolling Stones and Andrew Oldham.)

LETTER AGREEMENT (7/30/65) from Andrew Oldham (really Allen Klein) and The Rolling Stones to the Decca Record Company Ltd. said:

"Gentlemen,
(1) Reference is made to an Agreement dated as of

5/14/63, between Andrew Loog Oldham and The Decca Record Company Ltd., for the period 5/14/63 through 2/28/65, hereinafter referred to as Agreement No. 1; an Agreement dated as of 5/14/63 for the period 5/14/63 through 8/1/65 between Nanker Phelge Music Ltd. and The Decca Record Company Ltd. hereinafter referred to as Agreement No. 2; an Agreement dated as of 2/28/65 for the period 2/28/65 through 5/10/66 between Andrew Loog Oldham and The Decca Record Company Ltd. hereinafter referred to as Agreement No. 3, and an Agreement dated as of 5/10/66 through 5/9/70 between Andrew Loog Oldham and The Decca Record Company Ltd. hereinafter referred to as Agreement No. 4.

(2) The Decca Record Company Ltd. hereby agrees to make minimum advance payments against your share of royalties coming due to you under Agreements 1, 3 and 4 of an aggregate amount of $350,000 (Three hundred and fifty thousand dollars) to be paid in ten (10) equal annual instalments the first instalment of $35,000 (Thirty five thousand dollars), which shall be paid on 7/30/65, and yearly thereafter for nine (9) succeeding years. Such payments shall be made in the equivalent pound sterling at $2.80 to the pound.

(3) The Decca Record Company Ltd. has been advised and instructed by Andrew Loog Oldham to pay to you directly and in your name an aggregate of fifty per cent (50%) of the earned royalties as defined and set forth under the Agreement referred to above which are numbered and referred to as Agreements 1, 3 and 4. Your share of such royalties are as follows:

(a) For sales in UK until 2/28/65—7% of wholesale. For sales in UK after 2/28/65—12% of wholesale.

(b) For all sales in foreign countries (outside USA and Canada)—7% of wholesale.

(c) For sales in USA and Canada until 2/28/65—7% of wholesale. For sales in USA and Canada after 2/28/65—9¼% of wholesale (royalties in USA and Canada are not recouped hereunder).

Decca shall have the right to withhold your share of the earned royalties under sub-paragraph (a) and (b) above until Decca has recouped the aforementioned aggregate minimum advance payments referred to in paragraph 2 above. In the event your share of royalty earnings under sub-paragraph (a) and (b) above exceed the aggregate minimum advance payments to be made under paragraph 1 above, then and in such event we shall pay to you such excess royalties on 7/30/76.

(4) The foregoing minimum guarantee advance payments shall be pro rata and sent to each of you at such address as each of you shall notify us of so that each of you will receive separate payments of one-fifth of the aggregate share of the guaranteed advance payments and one-fifth of The Rolling Stones portion of the excess earned royalties as is provided for herein, after recoupment by us of the guarantee set forth in paragraph 2 above from royalties under sub-paragraph (a) and (b) of clause 3 above.

(5) We have requested Andrew Loog Oldham to consent to this Agreement and his signature together with that of The Decca Record Company Ltd. and yourselves shall constitute this as our binding agreement." (Signed by Decca, Andrew Oldham and The Rolling Stones.)

LETTER AGREEMENT (7/30/65) from Andrew Oldham (really Allen Klein) and The Rolling Stones to The Decca Record Company Ltd. which said:

"Gentlemen,

(1) Reference is made to an Agreement dated as of 5/14/63, between Andrew Loog Oldham and The Decca Record Company Ltd., for the period 5/14/63 through 2/28/65, hereinafter referred to as Agreement No. 1; an Agreement dated as of 5/14/63 for the period 5/14/63 through 8/1/65 between Nanker Phelge Music Ltd. and The Decca Record Company Ltd. hereinafter referred to as Agreement No. 2; an Agreement dated as of 2/28/65 for the period 2/28/65 through 5/10/66 between Andrew Loog Oldham and The Decca Record Company Ltd. hereinafter referred to as Agreement No. 3, and an Agreement dated as of 5/10/66 through 5/9/70 between Andrew Loog Oldham and The Decca Record Company Ltd. hereinafter referred to as Agreement No. 4.

(2) Reference is made to a letter of even date by you to The Decca Record Company Ltd. whereby you have assigned 50% of all royalties under Agreements 1, 3 and 4 to The Rolling Stones.

(3) The Decca Record Company Ltd. hereby agrees to make minimum advance payments against all royalties due and coming due to you under Agreements 1, 3 and 4 of an aggregate amount of $350,000 (Three hundred and fifty thousand dollars) to be paid in ten (10) equal annual instalments of $35,000 (thirty five thousand dollars) the first of which shall be paid on 7/30/65, and yearly thereafter for nine (9) succeeding years. Such payments shall be made in the equivalent pound sterling at $2.80 to the pound. Until further notice by you one half of said guarantee is to be paid to you at the rate of $17,500 (seventeen thousand five hundred dollars) per year.

(4) The foregoing minimum advance payments as set forth in paragraph 3 above shall be offset by us against your net share of any and all earned royalties becoming due to you after deducting The Rolling Stones's share under the Agreements referred to as Agreements 1, 3 and 4 above with respect to your share of such royalties. In the event your net share of royalty earnings under Agreements 1, 3 and 4 exceed the aggregate minimum advance payments to be made under paragraph 3 above then and in such event we shall pay to you such excess royalties on 7/30/76.

(5) Kindly confirm your agreement with the above by signing the note at the foot of the accompanying duplicate of this letter and this will constitute our binding agreement. Yours very truly." (Signed by Decca and Andrew Oldham.)

LETTER AGREEMENT (7/30/65) from Andrew Oldham (really Allen Klein) to The Decca Record Company Ltd. said:

"Gentlemen,

(1) Reference is made to an Agreement dated as of 5/14/63, between Andrew Loog Oldham and The Decca Record Company Ltd., for the period 5/14/63 through 2/28/65, hereinafter referred to as Agreement No. 1; an Agreement dated as of 5/14/63 for the period 5/14/63 through 8/1/65 between Nanker Phelge Music Ltd. and The Decca Record Company Ltd. hereinafter referred to

as Agreement No. 2; an Agreement dated as of 2/28/65 for the period 2/28/65 through 5/10/66 between Andrew Loog Oldham and The Decca Record Company Ltd. hereinafter referred to as Agreement No. 3, and an Agreement dated as of 5/10/66 through 5/9/70 between Andrew Loog Oldham and The Decca Record Company Ltd. hereinafter referred to as Agreement No. 4.

(2) You are hereby authorized and directed to pay fifty per cent (50%) of all earned royalties under Agreements 1, 3 and 4 as referred to in Paragraph 1 above directly to and in the name of The Rolling Stones or each of them as they may desire." (Signed by Andrew Oldham.)

AGENDA (9/20/65) for the meeting of the directors of Rolling Stones Ltd. read:

(1) To appoint Mr. Michael Philip Jagger as Chairman of the company in place of Mr. E. C. Easton.

(2) To appoint Mr. C. Watts as Secretary of the company in place of Mr. B. Boreham.

(3) To consider the letter dd. 9/11/65 received from M. Jagger, K. Richards, C. Watts, B. Jones and W. Wyman requiring the directors of the company to convene an extraordinary General Meeting.

(4) To change the Bankers, at present Lloyds Bank Ltd., Kingsway to Westminster Bank Ltd., 133 Baker St., London W1.

(5) To change the registered office of the company from la Little Argyle St., London W1 to 138 Ivor Ct., Gloucester Place, London NW1.

(6) To request that Eric Easton Ltd. pay to the company the amounts held in respect of taxation reserve deducted.

(7) To remove the financial and statutory books to the new registered office.

Appendix 2

An asterisk indicates that there is some question concerning the date, the recording or transmission date or the station concerned.

Records: 1963–69

6/7/63   1st single in UK   "Come On"/"I Want to be Loved"

8/28/63   single in UK   "Poison Ivy" (1)/"Fortune Teller" (WITHDRAWN)

9/63   album in UK   *Thank Your Lucky Stars* ("Come On")

11/1/63   2nd single in UK   "I Wanna Be Your Man"/"Stoned"

1/10/64   1st EP in UK   *The Rolling Stones*
1 Tracks: "Bye-Bye Johnny"/"Money"/"You Better Move On"/"Poison Ivy" (2)

1/64   single in US   "I Wanna Be Your Man"/"Come On (WITHDRAWN)

1/24/64   album in UK   *Ready Steady Go!* ("Come On"/"I Wanna Be Your Man")

1/24/64   album in UK   *Saturday Club* ("Poison Ivy" (1)/"Fortune-Teller")

2/64   Single in US   "Not Fade Away/Stoned" (WITH-DRAWN)

2/21/64   3rd single in UK   "Not Fade Away"/"Little by Little"

3/6/64   1st single in US   "Not Fade Away"/"I Wanna Be Your Man"

4/17/64   1st album in UK   *The Rolling Stones*
Tracks: "Route 66"/"I Just Wanna Make Love to You"/"Honest I Do"/"Mona (I Need You Baby)"/"Now I've Got a Witness"/"Little by Little"/"I'm a King Bee"/"Carol"/"Tell Me"/"Can I Get a Witness"/"You Can Make It If You Try"/"Walking the Dog"

5/64   1st album in US   *England's Newest Hitmakers— The Rolling Stones*
Tracks: "Not Fade Away"/"Route 66"/"I Just Wanna Make Love to You,"/"Honest I Do"/"Now I've Got a Witness"/"Little by Little"/"I'm a King Bee,"/"Carol"/"Tell Me"/"Can I Get a Witness"/"You Can Make It If You Try"/"Walking the Dog"

5/22/64   album in UK   *Fourteen* ("Surprise Surprise")

6/13/64   2nd single in US   "Tell Me'/"I Just Wanna Make Love to You"

6/26/64   4th single in UK   "It's All Over Now"/"Good Times, Bad Times"

7/25/64   3rd single in US   "It's All Over Now"/"Good Times, Bad Times"

8/14/64   2nd EP in UK   *Five by Five*
Tracks: "If You Need Me"/"Empty Heart"/"2120 South Michigan Avenue"/"Confessing the Blues"/"Around and Around"

9/26/64 4th single in US "Time is on My Side"/"Congratulations"

10/24/64 2nd album in US *12 × 5*
Tracks: "Around and Around"/"Confessing the Blues"/"Empty Heart"/"Time is on My Side"/ "Good Times, Bad Times"/"It's All Over Now"/ "2120 South Michigan Avenue"/"Under the Boardwalk"/"Congratulations"/"Grown Up Wrong"/"If You Need Me"/"Susie Q"

11/13/64 5th single in UK "Little Red Rooster"/"Off the Hook"

12/19/64 5th single in US "Heart of Stone"/"What a Shame"

1/15/65 2nd album in UK *The Rolling Stones No. 2*
Tracks: "Everybody Needs Sombody to Love"/ "Down-Home Girl"/"You Can't Catch Me"/ "What a Shame"/"Grown Up Wrong"/"Down the Road Apiece"/"Under the Boardwalk"/"I Can't be Satisfied"/"Pain in My Heart"/"Off the Hook"/"Susie Q"

2/13/65 3rd album in US *The Rolling Stones, Now!*
Tracks: "Everybody Needs Somebody to Love"/ "Down-Home Girl"/"You Can't Catch Me"/ "Heart of Stone"/"What a Shame"/"Mona (I Need You Baby)"/"Down the Road Apiece"/ "Off the Hook"/"Pain in My Heart"/"Oh Baby"/ "Little Red Rooster"/"Surprise Surprise"

2/26/65 6th single in UK "The Last Time"/"Play With Fire"

3/13/65 6th single in US "The Last Time"/"Play With Fire"

6/5/65 7th single in US "(I Can't Get No) Satisfaction"/ "The Under-Assistant West Coast Promotion Man"

6/11/65   3rd EP in UK   *Got Live If You Want It*
Tracks: "We Want the Stones"/"Everybody Needs Somebody to Love"/"Pain in My Heart"/ "Route 66"/"I'm Moving On"/"I'm Alright"

7/30/65   4th album in US   *Out of Our Heads*
Tracks: "Mercy Mercy"/"Hitch-Hike"/"The Last Time"/"That's How Strong My Love Is"/"Good Times"/"I'm Alright"/"(I Can't Get No) Satisfaction"/"Cry to Me,"/"The Under-Assistant West Coast Promotion Man"/"Play With Fire"/ "The Spider and the Fly"/"One More Try"

8/20/65   7th single in UK   "(I Can't Get No) Satisfaction"/"The Spider and the Fly"

9/24/65   3rd album in UK   *Out of Our Heads*
Tracks: "She Said Yeah"/"Mercy Mercy"/"Hitch-Hike"/"That's How Strong My Love Is"/"Good Times"/"Gotta Get Away"/"Talkin' 'Bout You,/ "Cry to Me"/"Oh Baby"/"Heart of Stone"/"The Under-Assistant West Coast Promotion Man"/ "I'm Free"

9/25/65   8th single in US   "Get Off of My Cloud"/"I'm Free"

10/22/65   8th single in UK   "Get Off of My Cloud"/"The Singer Not the Song"

12/4/65   5th album in US   *December's Children (and Everybody's)*
Tracks: "She Said Yeah"/"Talkin' 'Bout You" /"You Better Move On"/"Look What You've Done"/"The Singer Not the Song"/"Route 66"/ "Get Off of My Cloud"/"I'm Free"/"As Tears Go By"/"Gotta Get Away"/"Blue Turns to Grey"/"I'm Moving On"

12/18/65   9th single in US   "As Tears Go By"/"Gotta Get Away"

2/4/66   9th single in UK   "19th Nervous Breakdown"/
"As Tears Go By"

2/12/66   10th single in US   "19th Nervous Breakdown"/
"Sad Day"

4/2/66   6th album in US   *Big Hits (High Tide and Green Grass)*
Tracks: "(I Can't Get No) Satisfaction"/"The Last Time"/"As Tears Go By"/"Time is on My Side"/"It's All Over Now"/"Tell Me"/"19th Nervous Breakdown"/"Heart of Stone"/"Get Off of My Cloud"/"Not Fade Away"/"Good Times, Bad Times"/"Play with Fire"

4/15/66   4th album in UK   *Aftermath*
Tracks: "Mother's Little Helper"/"Stupid Girl"/"Lady Jane"/"Under My Thumb"/"Doncha Bother Me"/"Goin' Home"/"Flight 505"/"High and Dry"/"Out of Time"/"It's Not Easy"/"I am Waiting"/"Take It or Leave It"/"Think"/"What to Do"

5/7/66   11th single in US   "Paint It Black"/"Stupid Girl"

5/13/66   10th single in UK   "Paint It Black"/"Long Long While"

7/2/66   12th single in US   "Mother's Little Helper"/
"Lady Jane"

7/2/66   7th alburn in US   *Aftermath*
Tracks: "Paint It Black"/"Stupid Girl"/"Lady Jane"/"Under My Thumb"/"Doncha Bother Me"/"Think"/"Flight 505"/"High and Dry"/"It's Not Easy"/"I Am Waiting"/"Goin' Home"

9/23/66   11th single in UK   "Have You Seen Your Mother Baby"/"Who's Driving Your Plane"

9/24/66   13th single in US   "Have You Seen Your Mother Baby"/"Who's Driving Your Plane"

11/4/66   5th album in UK   *Big Hits (High Tide and Green Grass)*
          Tracks: "Have You Seen Your Mother Baby"/ "Paint It Black"/"It's All Over Now"/"The Last Time"/"Heart of Stone"/"Not Fade Away"/ "Come On"/"(I Can't Get No) Satisfaction"/ "Get Off of My Cloud"/"As Tears Go By"/"19th Nervous Breakdown"/"Lady Jane"/"Time is on My Side"/"Little Red Rooster"

12/10/66 8th album in US   *Got Live If You Want It*
          Tracks: "Under My Thumb"/"Get Off of My Cloud"/"Lady Jane"/"Not Fade Away"/"I've Been Loving You Too Long"/"Fortune-Teller"/ "The Last Time"/"19th Nervous Breakdown"/ "Time is on My Side"/"I'm Alright"/"Have You Seen Your Mother Baby"

1/13/67   12th single in UK   "Let's Spend the Night Together"/"Ruby Tuesday"

1/14/67   14th single in US   "Ruby Tuesday"/"Let's Spend the Night Together"

1/20/67   6th album in UK   *Between the Buttons*
          Tracks: "Yesterday's Papers"/"My Obsession"/ "Back Street Girl"/"Connection"/"She Smiled Sweet"/"Cool, Calm and Collected"/"All Sold Out"/"Please Go Home"/"Who's Been Sleeping Here"/"Complicated"/"Miss Amanda Jones"/ "Something Happened to Me Yesterday"

2/11/67   9th album in US   *Between the Buttons*
          Tracks: "Let's Spend the Night Together"/"Yesterday's Papers"/"Ruby Tuesday"/"Connection"/ "She Smiled Sweetly"/"Cool, Calm and Collected"/"All Sold Out"/"My Obsession"/"Who's Been Sleeping Here"/"Complicated"/"Miss Amanda Jones"/"Something Happened to Me Yesterday"

7/15/67   10th album in US   *Flowers*
          Tracks: "Ruby Tuesday"/"Have You Seen Your

Mother Baby"/"Let's Spend the Night Together"/
"Lady Jane"/"Out of Time"/"My Girl"/"Back
Street Girl"/"Please Go Home"/"Mother's Little
Helper"/"Take It or Leave It"/"Ride On Baby"/
"Sitting on a Fence"

8/18/67 13th single in UK "We Love You"/"Dandelion"

9/2/67 15th single in US "Dandelion"/"We Love You"

12/2/67 16th single in US "In Another Land" (Wyman)/
"The Lantern"

12/8/67 7th album in UK *Their Satanic Majesties
Request*
Tracks: "Sing This All Together"/"Citadel"/
"In Another Land"/"2000 Man"/"Sing This All
Together (See What Happens)"/"She's a Rain-
bow"/"The Lantern"/"Gomper"/"Complicated"/
"2,000 Light Years from Home"/"On with the
Show"

12/9/67 11th album in US *Their Satanic Majesties
Request*
(Tracks as above)

12/23/67 17th single in US "She's a Rainbow"/"2,000
Light Years from Home"

5/24/68 14th single in UK "Jumpin' Jack Flash"/"Child
of the Moon"

6/1/68 18th single in US "Jumpin' Jack Flash"/"Child
of the Moon"

8/31/68 19th single in US "Street Fighting Man"/"No
Expectations"

12/6/68 8th album in UK *Beggars Banquet*
Tracks: "Sympathy for the Devil"/"No Expec-
tations"/"Dear Doctor"/"Parachute Woman"/
"Jigsaw Puzzle"/"Street Fighting Man"/"Prodigal

Son"/"Stray-Cat Blues"/"Factory Girl"/"Salt of the Earth"

12/7/68   12th album in US   *Beggars Banquet*
(Tracks as above)

7/4/69   15th single in UK   "Honky-Tonk Women"/
"You Can't Always Get What You Want"

7/5/69   20th single in US   "Honky-Tonk Women"/
"You Can't Always Get What You Want"

9/12/69   9th album in UK   *Through the Past Darkly
(Big Hits Vol. 2)*
Tracks: "Jumpin' Jack Flash"/"Mother's Little Helper"/"2,000 Light Years from Home"/"Let's Spend the Night Together"/"You Better Move On"/"We Love You"/"Street Fighting Man"/"She's a Rainbow"/"Ruby Tuesday"/"Dandelion"/"Sitting on the Fence"/"Honky-Tonk Women"

9/13/69   13th album in US   *Through the Past Darkly
(Big Hits Vol. 2)*
Tracks: "Honky-Tonk Women"/"Ruby Tuesday"/"Jumpin' Jack Flash"/"Paint It Black"/"Street Fighting Man"/"Have You Seen Your Mother Baby"/"Let's Spend the Night Together"/"2,000 Light Years from Home"/"Mother's Little Helper"/"She's a Rainbow"/"Dandelion"

10/69   Promotional album for DJs in UK   *The Promotional Album*
Tracks: "Route 66"/"Walking the Dog"/"Around and Around"/"Everybody Needs Somebody to Love"/"Off the Hook"/"Suzie Q"/"I'm Free"/"She Said Yeah"/"Under My Thumb"/"Stupid Girl"/"2000 Man"/"Sympathy for the Devil"/"Prodigal Son"/"Love in Vain" (200 copies only)

12/5/69   10th album in UK   *Let It Bleed*
Tracks: "Gimme Shelter"/"Love in Vain"/"Country Honk"/"Live with Me"/"Let it Bleed"

/"Midnight Rambler"/"You Got the Silver"/
"Monkey Man"/"You Can't Always Get What
You Want"

12/6/69 14th album in US *Let It Bleed*
(Tracks as above)

Awards: 1964–69

GOLD DISCS (*all in US unless otherwise indicated*)

9/64 1st "It's All Over Now"
12/64 2nd "Time is on My Side"

6/65 3rd "The Last Time"
7/2/65 4th "(I Can't Get No) Satisfaction"
10/12/65 5th *Out of Our Heads*
11/65 6th "Get Off of My Cloud"

1/27/66 7th (Holland) "(I Can't Get No) Satisfaction"
2/66 8th *December's Children (and Everybody's)*
2/66 9th "As Tears Go By"
3/66 10th "19th Nervous Breakdown"
4/27/66 11th *Big Hits (High Tide and Green Grass)*
6/66 12th "Paint It Black"
8/9/66 13th *Aftermath*
9/66 14th "Mother's Little Helper"
11/66 15th "Have You Seen Your Mother Baby"

2/4/67 16th *Got Live If You Want It*
2/22/67 17th *Between the Buttons*
3/25/67 18th "Ruby Tuesday"
10/28/67 19th *Flowers*
11/67 20th "Dandelion"
12/6/67 21st *Their Satanic Majesties Request*

8/68 22nd "Jumpin' Jack Flash"

2/69 23rd *Beggars Banquet*
8/26/69 24th "Honky-Tonk Women"
10/69 25th *Through the Past Darkly (Big Hits Vol. 2)*
12/69 26th *Let It Bleed*

SILVER DISCS (*all in UK*)

3/12/65   1st "Not Fade Away"

7/7/64   2nd "It's All Over Now"
9/30/64   3rd *Five by Five*
12/12/64 4th "Little Red Rooster"

3/65   5th "The Last Time"
9/3/65   6th "(I Can't Get No) Satisfaction"
11/13/65 7th "Get Off of My Cloud"

2/19/66   8th "19th Nervous Breakdown"
6/4/66   9th "Paint It Black"

Shows: 1962–69

7/12/62   Marquee Jazz Club, London (1st time) (without Bill and Charlie)
*7/62   Ealing Jazz Club, London (1st time) (without Bill and Charlie). 1

*8/62   Ealing Jazz Club, London (without Bill and Charlie)

*9/62   Ealing Jazz Club, London (without Bill and Charlie)
*9/62   Ealing Jazz Club, London (without Bill and Charlie)
*9/62   Ealing Jazz Club, London (without Bill and Charlie)
*9/62   Marquee Jazz Club, London (without Bill and Charlie)

10/5/62   Woodstock Hotel, North Cheam, Surrey
*10/62   Ealing Jazz Club, London (without Bill and Charlie)
*10/62   Ealing Jazz Club, London (without Bill and Charlie)
*10/62   Marquee Jazz Club, London (without Bill and Charlie)

 *11/62   Ealing Jazz Club, London (without Bill and Charlie)
 *11/62   Flamingo Jazz Club, London (1st show) (without Bill and Charlie)
 *11/62   Red Lion Pub, Sutton, Surrey (lst show)? (without Bill and Charlie)
 *11/62   Ealing Jazz Club, London (without Bill and Charlie)
 *11/62   Flamingo Jazz Club, London (1st show) (without Bill and Charlie)
*11/30/62 Piccadilly Jazz Club, London (1st show) (without Bill and Charlie)

 *12/4/62 Ealing Jazz Club, London (without Bill and Charlie)
  12/62   Red Lion Pub, Sutton, Surrey (without Charlie)
  12/62   South Oxhey, Nr. Watford, Hertfordshire (without Charlie)
 12/12/62 Sidcup Art College, Sidcup, Kent (without Bill and Charlie)
 12/15/62 Youth Club, Church Hall, Putney, London (without Charlie)
 12/21/62 Piccadilly Jazz Club, London (without Charlie)
 12/22/62 Ealing Jazz Club, London (without Charlie)

  1/5/63   Ealing Jazz Club, London (without Charlie)
  1/7/63   Flamingo Jazz Club, London (without Charlie)
  1/9/63   Red Lion Pub, Sutton, Surrey (without Charlie)
 1/10/63   Marquee Jazz Club, London (without Charlie)
 1/11/63   Ricky Tick Club, Star and Garter Pub, Windsor, Berkshire
 1/14/63   Flamingo Jazz Club, London
 1/17/63   Marquee Jazz Club, London
 1/19/63   Ealing Jazz Club, London
 1/21/63   Flamingo Jazz Club, London
 1/23/63   Red Lion Pub, Sutton, Surrey
 1/24/63   Marquee Jazz Club, London
 1/25/63   Ricky Tick Club, Star and Garter Pub, Windsor, Berkshire
 1/26/63   Ealing Jazz Club, London
 1/28/63   Flamingo Jazz Club, London (last gig)
 1/31/63   Marquee Jazz Club, London (last gig)

2/1/63	Ricky Tick Club, Star and Garter Pub, Windsor, Berkshire
2/2/63	Ealing Jazz Club, London
2/5/63	Ealing Jazz Club, London
2/6/63	Red Lion Pub, Sutton, Surrey
2/7/63	Haringey Jazz Club, Manor House Pub, London (1st time)
2/8/63	Ricky Tick Club, Star and Garter Pub, Windsor, Berkshire
2/9/63	Ealing Jazz Club, London
2/12/63	Ealing Jazz Club, London
2/14/63	Haringey Jazz Club, Manor House Pub, London
2/16/63	Ealing Jazz Club, London
2/19/63	Ealing Jazz Club, London
2/20/63	Red Lion Pub, Sutton, Surrey
2/22/63	Ricky Tick Club, Star and Garter Pub, Windsor, Berkshire
2/23/63	Ealing Jazz Club, London
2/24/63	Station Hotel, Richmond, Surrey (1st time)
2/28/63	Haringey Jazz Club, Manor House Pub, London
3/2/63	Ealing Jazz Club, London (last gig)
3/3/63	Studio 51, Ken Colyer Club, London (1st time) Station Hotel, Richmond, Surrey
3/6/63	Red Lion Pub, Sutton, Surrey
3/7/63	Haringey Jazz Club, Manor House Pub, London
3/8/63	Ricky Tick Club, Star and Garter Pub, Windsor, Berkshire
3/9/63	Wooden Bridge Hotel, Guildford, Surrey (1st time)
3/10/63	Studio 51, Ken Colyer Club, London Station Hotel, Richmond, Surrey
3/14/63	Haringey Jazz Club, Manor House Pub, London
3/15/63	Ricky Tick Club, Star and Garter Pub, Windsor, Berkshire
3/17/63	Studio 51, Ken Colyer Club, London Station Hotel, Richmond, Surrey
3/20/63	Red Lion Pub, Sutton, Surrey
3/22/63	Ricky Tick Club, Star and Garter Pub, Windsor, Berkshire
3/24/63	Studio 51, Ken Colyer Club, London Station Hotel, Richmond, Surrey

3/29/63 Ricky Tick Club, Star and Garter Pub, Windsor, Berkshire
3/30/63 Wooden Bridge Hotel, Guildford, Surrey
3/31/63 Studio 51, Ken Colyer Club, London
         Station Hotel, Richmond, Surrey

4/3/63   Red Lion Pub, Sutton, Surrey
4/7/63   Studio 51, Ken Colyer Club, London
         Station Hotel, Richmond, Surrey
4/13/63 Antelope Hotel, Poole, Dorset (cancelled)
4/14/63 Studio 51, Ken Colyer Club, London
         Crawdaddy Club, Station Hotel, Richmond, Surrey
4/19/63 Wooden Bridge Hotel, Guildford, Surrey
4/21/63 Crawdaddy Club, Station Hotel, Richmond, Surrey
4/24/63 Eel Pie Island, Twickenham, Surrey (1st time)
4/26/63 Ricky Tick Club, Star and Garter Pub, Windsor, Berkshire
4/28/63 Studio 51, Ken Colyer Club, London
         Crawdaddy Club, Station Hotel, Richmond, Surrey

5/1/63   Eel Pie Island, Twickenham, Surrey
5/3/63   Ricky Tick Club, Star and Garter Pub, Windsor, Berkshire
5/4/63   *News of the World* Charity Gala, Battersea Park, London
5/5/63   Studio 51, Ken Colyer Club, London
         Crawdaddy Club, Station Hotel, Richmond, Surrey
5/8/63   Eel Pie Island, Twickenham, Surrey
5/12/63 Studio 51, Ken Colyer Club, London
         Crawdaddy Club, Station Hotel, Richmond, Surrey
5/15/63 Eel Pie Island, Twickenham, Surrey
5/17/63 Wooden Bridge Hotel, Guildford, Surrey
5/19/63 Studio 51, Ken Colyer Club, London
         Crawdaddy Club, Station Hotel, Richmond, Surrey
5/22/63 Eel Pie Island, Twickenham, Surrey
5/24/63 Ricky Tick Club, Star and Garter Pub, Windsor, Berkshire

5/26/63	Studio 51, Ken Colyer Club, London
	Crawdaddy Club, Station Hotel, Richmond, Surrey
5/29/63	Eel Pie Island, Twickenham, Surrey
5/31/63	Ricky Tick Club, Star and Garter Pub, Windsor, Berkshire
6/2/63	Studio 51, Ken Colyer Club, London
	Crawdaddy Club, Station Hotel, Richmond, Surrey
6/3/63	Studio 51, Ken Colyer Club, London
6/5/63	Eel Pie Island, Twickenham, Middlesex
6/7/63	Wooden Bridge Hotel, Guildford, Surrey
6/9/63	Studio 51, Ken Colyer Club, London
	Crawdaddy Club, Station Hotel, Richmond, Surrey
6/10/63	Studio 51, Ken Colyer Club, London
6/12/63	Eel Pie Island, Twickenham, Middlesex
6/14/63	Ricky Tick Club, Star and Garter Pub, Windsor, Berkshire
6/16/63	Studio 51, Ken Colyer Club, London
	Crawdaddy Club, Station Hotel, Richmond, Surrey (last gig)
6/17/63	Studio 51, Ken Colyer Club, London
6/19/63	Eel Pie Island, Twickenham, Middlesex
6/20/63	Scene Club, London
6/21/63	Ricky Tick Club, Star and Garter Pub, Windsor, Berkshire
6/22/63	Wooden Bridge Hotel, Guildford, Surrey
6/23/63	Studio 51, Ken Colyer Club, London
6/24/63	Studio 51, Ken Colyer Club, London
6/26/63	Eel Pie Island, Twickenham, Middlesex
6/27/63	Scene Club, London
6/28/63	Ricky Tick Club, Star and Garter Pub, Windsor, Berkshire
6/30/63	Studio 51, Ken Colyer Club, London
	Crawdaddy Club, Athletic Ground, Richmond, Surrey (1st time)
7/1/63	Studio 51, Ken Colyer Club, London
7/3/63	Eel Pie Island, Twickenham, Middlesex
7/4/63	Scene Club, London

7/5/63	Ricky Tick Club, Star and Garter Pub, Windsor, Berkshire
7/6/63	Kings Lynn (cancelled)
7/8/63	Studio 51, Ken Colyer Club, London
7/10/63	Eel Pie Island, Twickenham, Middlesex
7/11/63	Scene Club, London
7/12/63	Twickenham Design College, Eel Pie Island, Twickenham, Middlesex
7/13/63	Alcove Club, Middlesborough, Yorkshire
7/14/63	Studio 51, Ken Colyer Club, London
	Crawdaddy Club, Athletic Ground, Richmond, Surrey
7/15/63	Studio 51, Ken Colyer Club, London
7/17/63	Eel Pie Island, Twickenham, Middlesex
7/19/63	Deb Dance, Hastings, Sussex (cancelled—Brian ill)
7/20/63	Corn Exchange, Wisbech, Cambridgeshire (1st ballroom gig)
7/21/63	Studio 51, Ken Colyer Club, London
	Crawdaddy Club, Athletic Ground, Richmond, Surrey
7/22/63	Studio 51, Ken Colyer Club, London
7/24/63	Eel Pie Island, Twickenham, Middlesex
7/26/63	Ricky Tick Club, Star and Garter Pub, Windsor, Berkshire (last gig)
7/27/63	California Ballroom, Dunstable, Bedfordshire
7/28/63	Studio 51, Ken Colyer Club, London
	Crawdaddy Club, Athletic Ground, Richmond, Surrey
7/29/63	Studio 51, Ken Colyer Club, London
7/30/63	Ricky Tick Club, Thames Hotel, Windsor, Berkshire (1st time)
7/31/63	Eel Pie Island, Twickenham, Middlesex
8/2/63	Wooden Bridge Hotel, Guildford, Surrey
8/3/63	St Leonard's Hall, Horsham, Sussex
8/4/63	Studio 51, Ken Colyer Club, London
	Crawdaddy Club, Athletic Ground, Richmond, Surrey
8/5/63	Botwell House, Hayes, Middlesex
8/6/63	Ricky Tick Club, Thames Hotel, Windsor, Berkshire
8/7/63	Eel Pie Island, Twickenham, Middlesex

8/9/63	California Ballroom, Dunstable, Bedfordshire
8/10/63	Plaza Theatre, Handsworth, Birmingham, Warwickshire Plaza Theatre, Oldhill, Birmingham, Warwickshire
8/11/63	Studio 51, Ken Colyer Club, London 3rd Richmond Jazz Festival, Athletic Grounds, Richmond, Surrey
8/12/63	Studio 51, Ken Colyer Club, London
8/13/63	Town Hall, High Wycombe, Buckinghamshire
8/14/63	Eel Pie Island, Twickenham, Middlesex
8/15/63	Dreamland Ballroom, Margate, Kent
8/16/63	Winter Gardens, Banbury, Oxfordshire
8/17/63	Memorial Hall, Northwich, Cheshire
8/18/63	Studio 51, Ken Colyer Club, London Crawdaddy Club, Athletic Ground, Richmond, Surrey
8/19/63	Atlanta Ballroom, Woking, Surrey
8/20/63	Ricky Tick Club, Thames Hotel, Windsor, Berkshire
8/21/63	Eel Pie Island, Twickenham, Middlesex
8/23/63	Worplesdon Village Hall, Guildford, Surrey (cancelled)
8/24/63	Il Rondo Ballroom, Leicester, Leicestershire
8/25/63	Studio 51, Ken Colyer Club, London Crawdaddy Club, Athletic Ground, Richmond, Surrey
8/26/63	Studio 51, Ken Colyer Club, London
8/27/63	Ricky Tick Club, Thames Hotel, Windsor, Berkshire (without Brian—ill)
8/28/63	Eel Pie Island, Twickenham, Middlesex (without Brian—ill)
8/30/63	Oasis Club, Manchester, Lancashire
8/31/63	Royal Lido Ballroom, Prestatyn, Wales
9/1/63	Studio 51, Ken Colyer Club, London Crawdaddy Club, Athletic Ground, Richmond, Surrey
9/2/63	Studio 51, Ken Colyer Club, London
9/3/63	Ricky Tick Club, Thames Hotel, Windsor, Berkshire
9/4/63	Eel Pie Island, Twickenham, Middlesex (without Brian 2nd set—ill)

9/5/63	Strand Palace Theatre, Walmer, Kent (without Brian—ill)
9/6/63	Grand Hotel Ballroom, Lowestoft, Suffolk (without Brian—ill)
9/7/63	Kings Hall, Aberystwyth, Wales (without Brian—ill)
9/9/63	Studio 51, Ken Colyer Club, London
9/10/63	Ricky Tick Club, Thames Hotel, Windsor, Berkshire
9/11/63	Eel Pie Island, Twickenham, Middlesex
9/12/63	Cellar Club, Kingston-upon-Thames, Surrey
9/13/63	California Ballroom, Dunstable, Bedfordshire
9/14/63	Ritz Ballroom, Kings Heath, Birmingham, Warwickshire Plaza Theatre, Oldhill, Birmingham, Warwickshire
9/15/63	Great Pop Prom, Royal Albert Hall, London Crawdaddy Club, Athletic Ground, Richmond, Surrey
9/16/63	Studio 51, Ken Colyer Club, London
9/17/63	British Legion Hall, Harrow-on-the-Hill, London
9/18/63	Eel Pie Island, Twickenham, Middlesex
9/19/63	St John's Hall, Watford, Hertfordshire
9/20/63	Savoy Ballroom, Southsea, Hampshire
9/21/63	Corn Exchange, Peterborough, Northamptonshire
9/22/63	Studio 51, Ken Colyer Club, London Crawdaddy Club, Athletic Grounds, Richmond, Surrey (last resident performance)
9/23/63	Studio 51, Ken Colyer Club, London (last resident performance)
9/24/63	Ricky Tick Club, Thames Hotel, Windsor, Berkshire (last resident performance)
9/25/63	Eel Pie Island, Twickenham, Middlesex (last resident performance)
9/27/63	Floral Hall, Morecambe, Lancashire
9/28/63	Assembly Hall, Walthamstove, London
9/29/63	New Victoria Theatre, London (2 shows) (Everly Brothers)
9/30/63	Ballroom, Cambridge, Cambridgeshire
10/1/63	Odeon Theatre, Streatham, London (2 shows) (Everly Brothers)

10/2/63	Regal Theatre, Edmonton, London (2 shows) (Everly Brothers)
10/3/63	Odeon Theatre, Southend, Essex (2 shows) (Everly Brothers)
10/4/63	Odeon Theatre, Guildford, Surrey (2 shows) (Everly Brothers)
10/5/63	Gaumont Theatre, Watford (2 shows) (Everly Brothers)
10/6/63	Capitol Theatre, Cardiff, Wales (2 shows) (Everly Brothers)
10/8/63	Odeon Theatre, Cheltenham, Gloucestershire (2 shows) (Everly Brothers)
10/9/63	Gaumont Theatre, Worcester, Worcestershire (2 shows) (Everly Brothers)
10/10/63	Gaumont Theatre, Wolverhampton, Staffordshire (2 shows) (Everly Brothers)
10/11/63	Gaumont Theatre, Derby, Derbyshire (2 shows) (Everly Brothers)
10/12/63	Gaumont Theatre, Doncaster, Yorkshire (2 shows) (Everly Brothers)
10/13/63	Odeon Theatre, Liverpool, Lancashire (2 shows) (Everly Brothers)
10/15/63	Majestic Ballroom, Kingston-upon-Hull, Yorkshire
10/16/63	Odeon Theatre, Manchester, Lancashire (2 shows) (Everly Brothers)
10/17/63	Odeon Theatre, Glasgow, Scotland (2 shows) (Everly Brothers)
10/18/63	Odeon Theatre, Newcastle-upon-Tyne, Northumberland (2 shows) (Everly Brothers)
10/19/63	Gaumont Theatre, Bradford, Yorkshire (2 shows) (Everly Brothers)
10/20/63	Gaumont Theatre, Hanley, Staffordshire (2 shows) (Everly Brothers)
10/22/63	Gaumont Theatre, Sheffield, Yorkshire (2 shows) (Everly Brothers)
10/23/63	Odeon Theatre, Nottingham, Nottinghamshire (2 shows)
10/24/63	Odeon Theatre, Birmingham, Warwickshire (2 shows) (Everly Brothers)
10/25/63	Gaumont Theatre, Taunton, Somerset (2 shows)
10/26/63	Gaumont Theatre, Bournemouth, Hampshire (2 shows) (Everly Brothers)

10/27/63 Gaumont Theatre, Salisbury, Wiltshire (2 shows) (Everly Brothers)

10/29/63 Gaumont Theatre, Southampton, Hampshire (2 shows) (Everly Brothers)

10/30/63 Odeon Theatre, St Albans, Hertfordshire (2 shows) (Everly Brothers)

10/31/63 Odeon Theatre, Lewisham, London (2 shows) (Everly Brothers)

11/1/63 Odeon Theatre, Rochester, Kent (2 shows) (Everly Brothers)

11/2/63 Gaumont Theatre, Ipswich, Suffolk (2 shows) (Everly Brothers)

11/3/63 Odeon Theatre, Hammersmith, London (2 shows) (Everly Brothers) (last night)

11/4/63 Top Rank Ballroom, Preston, Lancashire

11/5/63 Cavern Club, Liverpool, Lancashire

11/6/63 Queens Hall, Leeds, Yorkshire

11/8/63 Club à Go-Go, Newcastle-upon-Tyne, Northumberland

11/9/63 Club à Go-Go, Whitley Bay, Northumberland

11/10/63 Town Hall, Crewe, Cheshire

11/11/63 Pavilion Ballroom, Bath, Somerset

11/12/63 Town Hall, High Wycombe, Buckinghamshire

11/13/63 City Hall, Sheffield, Yorkshire

11/15/63 Co-op Ballroom, Nuneaton, Warwickshire (matinee)
Co-op Ballroom, Nuneaton, Warwickshire (evening)

11/16/63 Matrix Ballroom, Coventry, Warwickshire

11/19/63 State Ballroom, Kilburn, London

11/20/63 Chiswick Polytechnic Dance, Athletic Club, Richmond, Surrey

11/21/63 McIlroys Ballroom, Swindon, Wiltshire

11/22/63 Town Hall, Greenwich, London

11/23/63 The Baths, Leyton, London
Chez Don Club, Dalston, London

11/24/63 Studio 51, Ken Colyer Club, London
Majestic Ballroom, Luton, Bedfordshire

11/25/63 Ballroom, Warrington, Lancashire

11/26/63 Ballroom, Altrincham, Cheshire

11/27/63 Ballroom, Wigan, Lancashire
Memorial Hall, Northwich, Cheshire

11/28/63	Amble, Northumberland (cancelled)
11/29/63	The Baths, Urmston, Lancashire
11/30/63	Kings Hall, Stoke-on-Trent, Staffordshire
12/1/63	Oasis Club, Manchester, Lancashire
12/2/63	Assembly Rooms, Tamworth, Staffordshire
12/3/63	Floral Hall, Southport, Lancashire
12/4/63	The Baths, Doncaster, Yorkshire
12/5/63	Theatre, Worcester, Worcestershire (2 shows)
12/6/63	Odeon Theatre, Romford, Essex (2 shows)
12/7/63	Fairfield Halls, Croydon, Surrey (2 shows)
12/8/63	Olympia Ballroom, Reading, Berkshire Gaumont Theatre, Watford, Hertfordshire (2 shows)
12/10/63	Chester, Cheshire (cancelled)
12/11/63	Bradford Arts Ball, King and Queens Hall, Bradford, Yorkshire
12/12/63	Locarno Ballroom, Liverpool, Lancashire
12/13/63	Ballroom, Hereford, Herefordshire
12/14/63	The Baths, Epsom, Surrey
12/15/63	Civic Hall, Guildford, Surrey
12/17/63	Town Hall, High Wycombe, Buckinghamshire
12/18/63	Corn Exchange, Bristol, Gloucestershire
12/20/63	Lido Ballroom, Winchester, Hampshire
12/21/63	Kayser Bondor Ballroom, Baldock, Hertfordshire
12/22/63	St Mary's Hall, Putney, London
12/24/63	Town Hall, Leek, Staffordshire
12/26/63	Selby's Restaurant, London
12/27/63	Town Hall, Reading, Berkshire
12/28/63	Club Noreik, Tottenham, London
12/30/63	Studio 51, Ken Colyer Club, London
12/31/63	Drill Hall, Lincoln, Lincolnshire
1/3/64	Glenlyn Ballroom, Forest Hill, London
1/4/64	Town Hall, Oxford, Oxfordshire
1/5/64	Olympia Ballroom, Reading, Berkshire
1/6/64	Granada Theatre, Harrow-on-the-Hill, London (2 shows) (Ronettes)
1/7/64	Adelphi Theatre, Slough, Buckinghamshire (2 shows) (Ronettes)
1/8/64	Granada Theatre, Maidstone, Kent (2 shows) (Ronettes)

1/9/64   Granada Theatre, Kettering, Northamptonshire (2 shows) (Ronettes)

1/10/64   Granada Theatre, Walthamstow (2 shows) (Ronettes)

1/11/64   The Baths, Epsom, Surrey

1/12/64   Granada Theatre, Tooting, London (2 shows) (Ronettes)

1/13/64   Barrowlands Ballroom, Glasgow, Scotland

1/14/64   Granada Theatre, Mansfield, Nottinghamshire (2 shows) (Ronettes)

1/15/64   Granada Theatre, Bedford, Bedfordshire (2 shows) (Ronettes)

1/16/64   McIlroys Ballroom, Swindon, Wiltshire

1/17/64   City Hall, Salisbury, Wiltshire

1/18/64   Pier Ballroom, Hastings, Sussex

1/19/64   The Theatre, Coventry, Warwickshire (2 shows) (Ronettes)

1/20/64   Granada Theatre, Woolwich, London (2 shows) (Ronettes)

1/21/64   Granada Theatre, Aylesbury, Buckinghamshire (2 shows) (Ronettes) (without Brian)

1/22/64   Granada Theatre, Shrewsbury, Shropshire (2 shows) (Ronettes)

1/23/64   Pavilion, Lowestoft, Suffolk

1/24/64   The Palais, Wimbledon, London

1/25/64   California Ballroom, Dunstable, Bedfordshire

1/26/64   De Montfort Hall, Leicester, Leicestershire (2 shows) (Ronettes)

1/27/64   Colston Hall, Bristol, Gloucestershire (2 shows) (Ronettes)

1/31/64   Public Hall, Preston, Lancashire

2/1/64   Valentine Charity Pop Show, Royal Albert Hall, London

2/2/64   Country Club, Hampstead, London

2/5/64   Ballroom, Willenhall, Staffordshire

2/8/64   Regal Theatre, Edmonton, London (2 shows) (John Leyton) Club Noreik, Tottenham, London

2/9/64   De Montfort Hall, Leicester, Leicestershire (2 shows) (John Leyton)

2/10/64   Odeon Theatre, Cheltenham, Gloucestershire (2 shows) (John Leyton)

2/11/64 Granada Theatre, Rugby, Warwickshire (2 shows) (John Leyton)

2/12/64 Odeon Theatre, Guildford, Surrey (2 shows) (John Leyton)

2/13/64 Granada Theatre, Kingston-upon-Thames, Surrey (2 shows) (John Leyton)

2/14/64 Gaumont Theatre, Watford, Hertfordshire (2 shows) (John Leyton)

2/15/64 Odeon Theatre, Rochester, Kent (2 shows) (John Leyton)

2/16/64 The Guildhall, Portsmouth, Hampshire (2 shows) (John Leyton)

2/17/64 Granada Theatre, Greenford, Middlesex (2 shows) (John Leyton)

2/18/64 Rank Theatre, Colchester, Essex (2 shows) (John Leyton)

2/19/64 Rank Theatre, Stockton-on-Tees, Durham (2 shows) (John Leyton)

2/20/64 Rank Theatre, Sunderland, Durham (2 shows) (John Leyton)

2/21/64 Gaumont Theatre, Hanley, Staffordshire (2 shows) (John Leyton)

2/22/64 Winter Gardens, Bournemouth, Hampshire (2 shows) (John Leyton)

2/23/64 Hippodrome Theatre, Birmingham, Warwickshire (2 shows) (John Leyton)

2/24/64 Odeon Theatre, Southend, Essex (2 shows) (John Leyton)

2/25/64 Odeon Theatre, Romford, Essex (2 shows) (John Leyton)

2/26/64 Rialto Theatre, York, Yorkshire (2 shows) (John Leyton)

2/27/64 City Hall, Sheffield, Yorkshire (2 shows) (John Leyton)

2/28/64 Sophia Gardens, Cardiff, Wales (2 shows) (John Leyton)

2/29/64 Hippodrome, Brighton, Sussex (2 shows) (John Leyton)

3/1/64 Empire Theatre, Liverpool, Lancashire (2 shows) (John Leyton)

3/2/64 Albert Hall, Nottingham, Nottinghamshire (2 shows) (John Leyton)

3/3/64   Opera House, Blackpool, Lancashire (2 shows) (John Leyton)

3/4/64   Gaumont Theatre, Bradford, Yorkshire (2 shows) (John Leyton)

3/5/64   Odeon Theatre, Blackburn, Lancashire (2 shows) (John Leyton)

3/6/64   Gaumont Theatre, Wolverhampton, Staffordshire (2 shows) (John Leyton)

3/7/64   Winter Gardens, Morecambe, Lancashire (2 shows) (John Leyton)

3/15/64   Invicta Ballroom, Chatham, Kent (without Charlie—on holiday)

3/17/64   Assembly Hall, Tunbridge Wells, Kent

3/18/64   City Hall, Salisbury, Wiltshire

3/21/64   Whitehall, East Grinstead, Sussex

3/22/64   Pavilion, Ryde, Isle of Wight, Hampshire

3/23/64   Guildhall, Southampton, Hampshire

3/25/64   Town Hall, Birmingham, Warwickshire (2 shows)

3/26/64   Town Hall, Kidderminster, Worcestershire (2 shows)

3/27/64   Ex-Serviceman's Club, Windsor, Berkshire

3/28/64   Wilton Hall, Bletchley, Buckinghamshire
        Club Noreik, Tottenham, London

3/30/64   Ricky Tick Club, Plaza Ballroom, Guildford, Surrey
        Olympia Ballroom, Reading, Berkshire

3/31/64   West Cliff Hall, Ramsgate, Kent

4/1/64   Locarno Ballroom, Stevenage, Hertfordshire

4/3/64   The Palais, Wimbledon, London

4/4/64   Leas Cliff Hall, Folkestone, Kent

4/5/64   Gaumont Theatre, Ipswich, Suffolk (2 shows)

4/6/64   Royal Hotel Ballroom, Lowestoft, Suffolk

4/8/64   Mod Ball, Empire Pool, Wembley, Middlesex

4/9/64   McIlroy's Ballroom, Swindon, Wiltshire

4/10/64   The Baths, Leyton, London

4/11/64   Pier Ballroom, Hastings, Sussex

4/12/64   Fairfield Halls, Croydon, Surrey (2 shows)

4/16/64   Cubi-Club, Rochdale, Lancashire (abandoned)

4/17/64   Locarno Ballroom, Coventry, Warwickshire

4/18/64   Royalty Theatre, Chester, Cheshire

4/22/64   Carlton Ballroom, Slough, Buckinghamshire

4/24/64   Gaumont Theatre, Norwich, Norfolk (2 shows)

4/25/64	Odeon Theatre, Luton, Bedfordshire (2 shows)
4/26/64	*NME* Poll-Winners Concert, Empire Pool, Wembley, Middlesex (afternoon)
	Empire Pool, Wembley, Middlesex (evening)
4/27/64	Pop Prom, Royal Albert Hall, London (2 shows)
4/28/64	Public hall, Wallington, Surrey
4/30/64	Majestic Ballroom, Birkenhead, Cheshire
5/1/64	Imperial Ballroom, Nelson, Lancashire
5/2/64	Spa Royal Hall, Bridlington, Yorkshire
5/3/64	Palace Theatre, Manchester, Lancashire
5/7/64	Savoy Ballroom, Southsea, Hampshire
5/8/64	Town Hall, Hove, Sussex
5/9/64	Savoy Ballroom, Catford, London
5/10/64	Colston Hall, Bristol, Gloucestershire (2 shows) (without Brian 1st show)
5/11/64	Winter Gardens, Bournemouth, Hampshire (2 shows)
5/13/64	City Hall, Newcastle-upon-Tyne, Northumberland (2 shows)
5/14/64	St Georges Hall, Bradford, Yorkshire (2 shows)
5/15/64	Trentham Gardens, Stoke-on-Trent, Staffordshire (2 shows)
5/16/64	Regal Theatre, Edmonton, London (2 shows)
5/17/64	Odeon Theatre, Folkestone, Kent (2 shows)
5/18/64	Chantinghall Hotel, Hamilton, Lanarkshire, Scotland
5/19/64	Capitol Theatre, Aberdeen, Scotland (2 shows)
5/20/64	Caird Hall, Dundee, Scotland (2 shows)
5/21/64	Regal Theatre, Edinburgh, Scotland (2 shows)
5/23/64	The University, Leicester, Leicestershire
5/24/64	The Theatre, Coventry, Warwickshire (2 shows)
5/25/64	Granada Theatre, East Ham, London (2 shows)
5/26/64	Town Hall, Birmingham, Warwickshire (2 shows)
5/27/64	Danilo Theatre, Cannock, Staffordshire (2 shows)
5/28/64	Essoldo Theatre, Stockport, Cheshire (2 shows)
5/29/64	City Hall, Sheffield, Yorkshire (2 shows)
5/30/64	Adelphi Theatre, Slough, Buckinghamshire (2 shows)
5/31/64	Pop Hit Parade, Empire Pool, Wembley, Middlesex (afternoon)

Empire Pool, Wembley, Middlesex (evening)

6/5/64	Swing Auditorium, San Bernardino, California (1st US tour)
6/6/64	State Fair, San Antonio, Texas (afternoon)
	State Fair, San Antonio, Texas (evening)
6/7/64	State Fair, San Antonio, Texas (afternoon)
	State Fair, San Antonio, Texas (evening)
6/12/64	Ballroom, Excelsior Fair, Minneapolis, Minnesota
6/13/64	Music Hall, Omaha, Nebraska
6/14/64	Olympia Stadium, Detroit, Michigan
6/17/64	Westview Park, Pittsburgh, Pennsylvania
6/19/64	State Farm Arena, Harrisburg, Pennsylvania
6/20/64	Carnegie Hall, New York (afternoon)
	Carnegie Hall, New York (evening)
6/22/64	Magdalen College, Oxford, Oxfordshire
6/26/64	Alexandra Palace, London
7/11/64	Spa Royal Hall, Bridlington, Yorkshire
7/12/64	Queens Hall, Leeds, Yorkshire (2 shows)
7/18/64	Beat City Club, London
7/19/64	Hippodrome, Brighton, Sussex (2 shows)
7/24/64	Empress Ballroom, Blackpool, Lancashire
7/25/64	Imperial Ballroom, Nelson, Cheshire
7/26/64	De Montfort Hall, Leicester, Leicestershire (2 shows)
7/31/64	Ulster Hall, Belfast, Northern Ireland
	Flamingo Ballroom, Ballymena, Northern Ireland
8/1/64	Pier Ballroom, Hastings, Sussex
8/2/64	Longleat House, Warminster, Wiltshire
8/8/64	Kurhaus, Scheveningen, The Hague, Holland
8/9/64	New Elizabethan Ballroom, Belle Vue, Manchester, Lancashire
8/10/64	Tower Ballroom, New Brighton, Cheshire
8/11/64	Winter Gardens, Blackpool, Lancashire (cancelled)
8/13/64	Palace Ballroom, Douglas, Isle of Man
8/14/64	Palais, Wimbledon, London
8/18/64	St Georges Hall, New Theatre Ballroom, Guernsey, Channel Islands

8/19/64	St Georges Hall, New Theatre Ballroom, Guernsey, Channel Islands
8/20/64	St Georges Hall, New Theatre Ballroom, Guernsey, Channel Islands
8/21/64	Springfield Hall, St Helier, Jersey, Channel Islands
8/22/64	Springfield Hall, St Helier, Jersey, Channel Islands
8/23/64	Gaumont Theatre, Bournemouth, Hampshire (2 shows)
8/24/64	Gaumont Theatre, Weymouth, Dorset (2 shows)
8/25/64	Odeon Theatre, Weston-super-Mare, Somerset (2 shows)
8/26/64	Odeon Theatre, Exeter, Devon (2 shows)
8/27/64	ABC Theatre, Plymouth, Devon (2 shows)
8/28/64	Gaumont Theatre, Taunton, Somerset (2 shows)
8/29/64	Town Hall, Torquay, Devon (2 shows)
8/30/64	Gaumont Theatre, Bournemouth, Hampshire (2 shows)
9/5/64	Astoria Theatre, Finsbury Park, London (2 shows) (Inez Foxx)
9/6/64	Odeon Theatre, Leicester, Leicestershire (2 shows) (Inez Foxx)
9/8/64	Odeon Theatre, Colchester, Essex (2 shows) (Inez Foxx)
9/9/64	Odeon Theatre, Luton, Bedfordshire (2 shows) (Inez Foxx)
9/10/64	Odeon Theatre, Cheltenham, Gloucestershire (2 shows) (Inez Foxx)
9/11/64	Capitol Theatre, Cardiff, Wales (2 shows) (Inez Foxx)
9/13/64	Empire Theatre, Liverpool, Lancashire (2 shows) (Inez Foxx)
9/14/64	ABC Theatre, Chester, Cheshire (2 shows) (Inez Foxx)
9/15/64	Odeon Theatre, Manchester, Lancashire (2 shows) (Inez Foxx)
9/16/64	ABC Theatre, Wigan, Lancashire (2 shows) (Inez Foxx)
9/17/64	ABC Theatre, Carlisle, Cumberland (2 shows) (Inez Foxx)

9/18/64 Odeon Theatre, Newcastle-upon-Tyne, North-umberland (2 shows) (Inez Foxx)

9/19/64 Usher Hall, Edinburgh, Scotland (2 shows) (Inez Foxx)

9/20/67 ABC Theatre, Stockton-on-Tees, Durham (2 shows) (Inez Foxx)

9/21/64 ABC Theatre, Kingston-upon-Hull, Yorkshire (2 shows) (Inez Foxx)

9/22/64 ABC Theatre, Lincoln, Lincolnshire (2 shows) (Inez Foxx)

9/24/64 Gaumont Theatre, Doncaster, Yorkshire (2 shows) (Inez Foxx)

9/25/64 Gaumont Theatre, Hanley, Staffordshire (2 shows) (Inez Foxx)

9/26/64 Odeon Theatre, Bradford, Yorkshire (2 shows) (Inez Foxx)

9/27/64 Hippodrome Theatre, Birmingham, Warwick-shire (2 shows) (Inez Foxx)

9/29/64 Odeon Theatre, Guildford, Surrey (2 shows) (Inez Foxx)

10/1/64 Colston Hall, Bristol, Gloucestershire (2 shows) (Inez Foxx)

10/2/64 Odeon Theatre, Exeter, Devon (2 shows) (Inez Foxx)

10/3/64 Regal Theatre, Edmonton, London (2 shows) (Inez Foxx)

10/4/64 Gaumont Theatre, Southampton, Hampshire (2 shows) (Inez Foxx)

10/5/64 Gaumont Theatre, Wolverhampton, Stafford-shire (2 shows) (Inez Foxx)

10/6/64 Gaumont Theatre, Watford, Hertfordshire (2 shoves) (Inez Foxx)

10/8/64 Odeon Theatre, Lewisham, London (2 shows) (Inez Foxx)

10/9/64 Gaumont Theatre, Ipswich, Suffolk (2 shows) (Inez Foxx)

10/10/64 Odeon Theatre, Southend, Essex (2 shows) (Inez Foxx)

10/11/64 Hippodrome, Brighton, Sussex (2 shows) (Inez Foxx) (last night)

10/20/64 Olympia Theatre, Paris, France

10/24/64	Academy of Music, New York (afternoon) (2nd US tour)
	Academy of Music, New York (evening)
10/26/64	Memorial Auditorium, Sacramento, California
10/28/64	*Tami* Show, Civic Auditorium, Santa Monica, California
10/29/64	*Tami* Show, Civic Auditorium, Santa Monica, California
10/31/64	Swing Auditorium, San Bernardino, California
11/1/64	Civic Auditorium, Long Beach Arena, California (afternoon)
	Balboa Park Bowl, San Diego, California (evening)
11/3/64	Public Hall, Cleveland, Ohio
11/4/64	Loews Theatre, Providence, Rhode Island
11/11/64	Auditorium, Milwaukee, Wisconsin (without Brian—ill)
11/12/64	Coliseum, Fort Wayne, Indiana (without Brian —ill)
11/13/64	Hara Arena, Dayton, Ohio (without Brian— ill)
11/14/64	Memorial Auditorium, Louisville, Kentucky (without Brian—ill)
11/15/64	Arie Crown Theatre, McCormick Place, Chicago, Illinois
11/20/64	Glad Rag Ball, Empire Pool, Wembley, Middlesex
12/4/64	Fairfield Halls, Croydon, Surrey (2 shows)
1/6/65	ABC Theatre, Belfast, Northern Ireland (2 shows)
1/7/65	Adelphi Theatre, Dublin, Eire (2 shows)
1/8/65	Savoy Theatre, Cork, Eire (2 shows)
1/10/65	Commodore Theatre, Hammersmith, London (2 shows)
1/22/65	Manufacturers Auditorium, Agricultural Hall, Sydney, Australia (2 shows)
1/23/65	Manufacturers Auditorium, Agricultural Hall, Sydney, Australia (afternoon)
	Manufacturers Auditorium, Agricultural Hall, Sydney, Australia (evening) (2 shows)

1/25/65   City Hall, Brisbane, Australia (2 shows)
1/26/65   City Hall, Brisbane, Australia (2 shows)
1/27/65   Manufacturers Auditorium, Agricultural Hall, Sydney, Australia (evening) (2 shows)
1/28/65   Palais Theatre, St Kilda, Melbourne, Australia (2 shows)
1/29/65   Palais Theatre, St Kilda, Melbourne, Australia (afternoon)
          Palais Theatre, St Kilda, Melbourne, Australia (evening) (2 shows)

2/1/65   Theatre Royal, Christchurch, New Zealand (2 shows)
2/2/65   Civic Theatre, Invercargill, New Zealand (2 shows)
2/3/65   Town Hall, Dunedin, New Zealand (2 shows)
2/6/65   Town Hall, Auckland, New Zealand (afternoon)
          Town Hall, Auckland, New Zealand (evening) (2 shows)
2/8/65   Local venue, Wellington, New Zealand (2 shows)
2/10/65   Palais Theatre, St Kilda, Melbourne, Australia (2 shows)
2/12/65   Centennial Hall, Adelaide, Australia (2 shows)
2/13/65   Capitol Theatre, Perth, Australia (afternoon)
          Capitol Theatre, Perth, Australia (evening) (2 shows)
2/16/65   Badminton Stadium, Singapore (2 shows)

3/5/65   Regal Theatre, Edmonton, London (2 shows) (1st night) (Hollies)
3/6/65   Empire Theatre, Liverpool, Lancashire (2 shows) (Hollies)
3/7/65   Palace Theatre, Manchester, Lancashire (2 shows) (Hollies)
3/8/65   Futurist Theatre, Scarborough, Yorkshire (2 shows) (Hollies)
3/9/65   Odeon Theatre, Sunderland, Durham (2 shows) (Hollies)
3/10/65   ABC Theatre, Huddersfield, Yorkshire (2 shows) (Hollies)
3/11/65   City Hall, Sheffield, Yorkshire (2 shows) (Hollies)

3/12/65	Trocadero Theatre, Leicester, Leicestershire (2 shows) (Hollies)
3/13/65	Granada Theatre, Rugby, Warwickshire (2 shows) (Hollies)
3/14/65	Odeon Theatre, Rochester, Kent (2 shows) (Hollies)
3/15/65	Odeon Theatre, Guildford, Surrey (2 shows) (Hollies)
3/16/65	Granada Theatre, Greenford, Middlesex (2 shows) (Hollies)
3/17/65	Odeon Theatre, Southend, Essex (2 shows) (Hollies)
3/18/65	ABC Theatre, Romford, Essex (2 shows) (Hollies)
3/26/65	Fyns Forum, Odense, Denmark (2 shows)
3/28/65	Koncert Sal, Tivoli Gardens, Copenhagen, Denmark (2 shows)
3/30/65	Koncert Sal, Tivoli Gardens, Copenhagen, Denmark (2 shows)
3/31/65	Masshallen, Gothenberg, Sweden (2 shows)
4/1/65	Kungliga Tennishallen, Stockholm, Sweden (2 shows)
4/2/65	Kungliga Tennishallen, Stockholm, Sweden
4/3/65	Open-air venue, Helsinki, Finland
4/11/65	*NME* Poll-Winners Concert, Empire Pool, Wembley, Middlesex (afternoon)
4/16/65	Olympia Theatre, Paris, France
4/17/65	Olympia Theatre, Paris, France
4/18/65	Olympia Theatre, Paris, France
4/23/65	Maurice Richard Arena, Montreal, Canada (1st night)
4/24/65	YMCA Auditorium, Ottawa, Canada
4/25/65	Maple Leaf Gardens, Toronto, Canada
4/26/65	Treasure Island Gardens, London, Canada
4/29/65	Palace Theatre, Albany, New York (2 shows)
4/30/65	Auditorium, Worcester, Massachusetts
5/1/65	Academy of Music, New York (afternoon) Convention Hall, Philadelphia, Pennsylvania (evening)
5/4/65	Georgia Southern College Auditorium, Statesboro, Georgia

5/6/65   Jack Russell Stadium, Clearwater, Florida

5/7/65   Legion Field Stadium, Birmingham, Alabama

5/8/65   Coliseum, Jacksonville, Florida

5/9/65   Arie Crown Theatre, McCormick Place, Chicago, Illinois

5/14/65   New Civic Auditorium, San Francisco, California

5/15/65   Swing Auditorium, San Bernardino, California

5/16/65   Civic Auditorium, Long Beach, California (afternoon)

5/17/65   Community Concourse, Convention Hall, San Diego, California

5/21/65   Civic Auditorium, San Jose, California

5/22/65   Convention Hall, Ratcliffe Stadium, Fresno, California (afternoon)
Municipal auditorium, Sacramento, California (evening)

5/29/65   Academy of Music, New York (afternoon)
Academy of Music, New York (2 shows) (evening) (last night)

6/15/65   Odeon Theatre, Glasgow, Scotland (2 shows)

6/16/65   Usher Hall, Edinburgh, Scotland (2 shows)

6/17/65   Capitol Theatre, Aberdeen, Scotland (2 shows)

6/18/65   Caird Hall, Dundee, Scotland (2 shows)

6/24/65   Messhallen, Oslo, Norway

6/25/65   Yyteri Beach, Pori, Finland

6/26/65   R. B. Hallen Copenhagen, Denmark (2 shows)

6/29/65   Baltiska Hallen, Malmö, Sweden (2 shows)

7/16/65   Odeon Theatre, Exeter, Devon (2 shows)

7/17/65   The Guildhall, Portsmouth, Hampshire (2 shows)

7/18/65   Gaumont Theatre, Bournemouth, Hampshire (2 shows)

7/25/65   ABC Theatre, Great Yarmouth, Norfolk (2 shows)

7/26/65   Local venue, Leicester, Leicestershire

8/65   Odeon Theatre, Blackpool, Lancashire (cancelled)

8/1/65   London Palladium, London (2 shows)

8/22/65   Futurist Theatre, Scarborough, Yorkshire (2 shows)

9/3/65	Adelphi Theatre, Dublin, Eire (2 shows)
9/4/65	ABC Theatre, Belfast, Northern Ireland (2 shows)
9/8/65	Palace Ballroom, Douglas, Isle of Man
9/11/65	Münsterland Halle, Münster, West Germany (2 shows) (1st night)
9/12/65	Gruga Halle, Essen, West Germany (2 shows)
9/13/65	Ernst Merck Halle, Hamburg, West Germany (2 shows)
9/14/65	Circus-Krone-Bau, Munich, West Germany (2 shows)
9/15/65	Waldbühne Halle, West Berlin, West Germany
9/17/65	Wiener Stadthalle, Vienna, Austria
9/24/65	Astoria Theatre, Finsbury Park, London (2 shows) (Spencer Davis) (1st night)
9/25/65	Gaumont Theatre, Southampton, Hampshire (2 shows) (Spencer Davis)
9/26/65	Colston Hall, Bristol, Gloucestershire (2 shows) (Spencer Davis)
9/27/65	Odeon Theatre, Cheltenham, Gloucestershire (2 shows) (Spencer Davis)
9/28/65	Capitol Theatre, Cardiff, Wales (2 shows) (Spencer Davis)
9/29/65	Granada Theatre, Shrewsbury, Shropshire (2 shows) (Spencer Davis)
9/30/65	Gaumont Theatre, Hanley, Staffordshire (2 shows) (Spencer Davis)
10/1/65	ABC Theatre, Chester, Cheshire (2 shows) (Spencer Davis)
10/2/65	ABC Theatre, Wigan, Lancashire (2 shows) (Spencer Davis)
10/3/65	Odeon Theatre, Manchester, Lancashire (2 shows) (Spencer Davis)
10/4/65	Gaumont Theatre, Bradford, Yorkshire (2 shows) (Spencer Davis)
10/5/65	ABC Theatre, Carlisle, Cumberland (2 shows) (Spencer Davis)
10/6/65	Odeon Theatre, Glasgow, Scotland (2 shows) (Spencer Davis)
10/7/65	City Hall, Newcastle, Northumberland (2 shows) (Spencer Davis)

10/8/65	ABC Theatre, Stockton-on-Tees, Durham (2 shows) (Spencer Davis)
10/9/65	Odeon Theatre, Leeds, Yorkshire (2 shows) (Spencer Davis)
10/10/65	Empire Theatre, Liverpool, Lancashire (2 shows) (Spencer Davis)
10/11/65	Gaumont Theatre, Sheffield, Yorkshire (2 shows) (Spencer Davis)
10/12/65	Gaumont Theatre, Doncaster, Yorkshire (2 shows) (Spencer Davis)
10/13/65	De Montfort Hall, Leicester, Leicestershire (2 shows) (Spencer Davis)
10/14/65	Odeon Theatre, Birmingham, Warwickshire (2 shows) (Spencer Davis)
10/15/65	Regal Theatre, Cambridge, Cambridgeshire (2 shows) (Spencer Davis)
10/16/65	ABC Theatre, Northampton, Northampton-shire (2 shows) (Spencer Davis)
10/17/65	Granada Theatre, Tooting, London (2 shows) (Spencer Davis) (last night).
10/29/65	Forum, Montreal, Canada (1st night)
10/30/65	Barton Hall, Cornell University, Ithaca, New York (afternoon) War Memorial Hall, Syracuse, New York (evening)
10/31/65	Maple Leaf Gardens, Toronto, Canada
11/1/65	Memorial Auditorium, Rochester, New York
11/3/65	Auditorium, Providence, Rhode Island
11/4/65	Arena, Newhaven, Connecticut (2 shows)
11/5/65	The Gardens, Boston, Massachusetts
11/6/65	Academy of Music, New York (afternoon) Convention Hall, Philadelphia, Pennsylvania (evening)
11/7/65	Mosque Theatre, Newark, New Jersey (2 shows)
11/10/65	Reynolds Coliseum, Raleigh, North Carolina
11/12/65	Memonal Auditorium (War Memorial Hall), Greensboro, North Carolina
11/13/65	Coliseum, Washington, DC (afternoon) Civic Center, Baltimore, Maryland (evening)
11/14/65	Civic Coliseum (Auditorium), Knoxville, Tennessee
11/15/65	Coliseum, Charlotte, North Carolina

11/16/65	Municipal Auditorium, Nashville, Tennessee
11/17/65	Mid South Coliseum, Memphis, Tennessee
11/20/65	State Fair Youth Center, Shreveport, Louisiana
11/21/65	Will Rogers Stadium, Fort Worth, Texas (after-noon)
	Memorial Auditorium, Dallas, Texas (evening)
11/23/65	Assembly Center, Tulsa, Oklahoma
11/24/65	Civic Center (Arena), Pittsburgh, Pennsylvania
11/25/65	Arena (Auditorium), Milwaukee, Wisconsin
11/26/65	Cobo Hall, Detroit, Michigan
11/27/65	Hara Arena, Dayton, Ohio (afternoon)
	The Gardens, Cincinnati, Ohio (evening)
11/28/65	Arie Crown Theater, McCormick Place, Chi-cago, Illinois (2 shows)
11/29/65	Coliseum, Denver, Colorado
11/30/65	Veterans Memorial Coliseum, Phoenix, Arizona
12/1/65	Agrodrome, Vancouver, Canada
12/2/65	Coliseum, Seattle, Washington
12/3/65	Memorial Auditorium, Sacramento, California
12/4/65	Civic Auditorium, San Jose, California (2 shows)
12/5/65	Convention Hall, San Diego, California (after-noon)
	Sports Arena, Los Angeles, California (eve-ning) (last night)
2/18/66	Commemorative Auditorium, Showgrounds, Sydney, Australia (2 shows) (1st night)
2/19/66	Commemorative Auditorium, Showgrounds, Sydney, Australia (afternoon)
	Commemorative Auditorium, Showgrounds, Sydney, Australia (2 shows) (evening)
2/21/66	City Hall, Brisbane, Australia (2 shows)
2/22/66	Centennial Hall, Adelaide, Australia
2/23/66	Palais Theatre, St. Kilda, Melbourne, Australia (2 shows)
2/24/66	Palais Theatre, St. Kilda, Melbourne, Australia (2 shows)
2/25/66	Palais Theatre, St. Kilda, Melbourne, Australia (2 shows)
2/26/66	Palais Theatre, St. Kilda, Melbourne, Australia (2 shows)
2/28/66	Town Hall, Wellington, New Zealand (2 shows)

3/1/66   Civic Theatre, Auckland, New Zealand
3/2/66   Capitol Theatre, Perth, Australia (last night)
3/26/66   Braband Hall, Den Bosche, The Hague, Holland (lst night)
3/27/66   Palais des Sports, Brussels, Belgium
3/29/66   Olympia Theatre, Paris, France (2 shows)
3/30/66   Salle Vallier, Marseilles, France
3/31/66   Palais d'Hiver, Lyon, France (2 shows)

4/3/66   Kungliga Tennishallen, Stockholm, Sweden (2 shows)
4/5/66   K. B. Hallen, Copenhagen, Denmark (2 shows) (last night)

5/1/66   *NME* Poll-Winners Concert, Empire Pool, Wembley, Middlesex (afternoon)
6/24/66   Manning Bowl, Lynn, Massachusetts
6/25/66   Local venue, Cleveland, Ohio (afternoon)
          Civic Arena, Pittsburgh, Pennsylvania (evening)
6/26/66   Coliseum, Washington DC (afternoon)
          Civic Center Baltimore, Maryland (evening)
6/27/66   Dillon Stadium, Hartford, Connecticut
6/28/66   Local venue, Buffalo, New York
6/29/66   Maple Leaf Gardens, Toronto, Canada
6/30/66   Forum, Montreal, Canada

7/1/66   Stadium, Atlantic City, New Jersey
7/2/66   Forest Hills Tennis Stadium, Queens, New York
7/3/66   Asbury Park, New Jersey
7/4/66   Local venue, Virginia Beach, Virginia
7/6/66   War Memorial Hall, Syracuse, New York
7/8/66   Cobo Hall, Detroit, Michigan
7/9/66   State Fairgrounds Coliseum, Indianapolis, Indiana
7/10/66   Arie Crown Theatre, McCormick Palace, Chicago, Illinois
7/11/66   Sam Houston Coliseum, Houston, Texas
7/12/66   Kiel Convention Hall, St. Louis, Missouri
7/14/66   Local venue, Winnipeg, Canada
7/15/66   Civic Auditorium, Omaha, Nebraska
7/19/66   PNE Forum, Vancouver, Canada
7/20/66   Local venue, Seattle, Washington
7/21/66   Memorial Coliseum, Portland, Oregon

7/22/66	Auditorium, Sacramento, California
7/23/66	Lagoon, Davis County, Salt Lake City, Utah (afternoon)
	Local venue, Phoenix, Arizona (evening)
7/24/66	Local venue, Bakersfield, California (2 shows)
7/25/66	Hollywood Bowl, Los Angeles, California
7/26/66	Local venue, San Francisco, California
7/28/66	International Sports Center, Honolulu, Hawaii

9/23/66	Royal Albert Hall, London (2 shows) (1st night) (Tina Turner)
9/24/66	Odeon Theatre, Leeds, Yorkshire (2 shows) (Tina Turner)
9/25/66	Empire Theatre, Liverpool, Lancashire (2 shows) (Tina Turner)
9/28/66	Apollo Theatre, Ardwick, Manchester, Lancashire (2 shows) (Tina Turner)
9/29/66	ABC Theatre, Stockton-on-Tees, Durham (2 shows) (Tina Turner)
9/30/66	Odeon Theatre, Glasgow, Scotland (2 shows) (Tina Turner)

10/1/66	City Hall, Newcastle-upon-Tyne, Northumberland (2 shows) (Tina Turner)
10/2/66	Gaumont Theatre, Ipswich, Suffolk (2 shows) (Tina Turner)
10/6/66	Odeon Theatre, Birmingham, Staffordshire (2 shows) (Tina Turner)
10/7/66	Colston Hall, Bristol, Gloucestershire (2 shows) (Tina Turner)
10/8/66	Capitol Theatre, Cardiff, Wales (2 shows) (Tina Turner)
10/9/66	Gaumont Theatre, Southampton, Hampshire (2 shows) (Tina Turner) (last night)

3/25/67	Indoor Hall, Malmö, Sweden (2 shows) (1st night)
3/27/67	Indoor Hall, Örebro, Sweden (2 shows)
3/29/67	Stadthalle, Bremen, West Germany (2 shows)
3/30/67	Sporthalle, Cologne, West Germany (2 shows)
3/31/67	Westfullenhalle, Dortmund, West Germany

4/1/67	Ernst Merck Halle, Hamburg, West Germany (2 shows)
4/2/67	Stadthalle, Vienna, Austria (2 shows)
4/5/67	Palazzo dello Sport, Bologna, Italy (2 shows)
4/6/67	Palazzo dello Sport, Rome, Italy (2 shows)
4/8/67	Palazzo dello Sport, Milan, Italy (2 shows)
4/9/67	Palazzo dello Sport, Genoa, Italy (2 shows)
4/11/67	Olympia Theatre, Paris, France (2 shows)
4/13/67	Sala Kongresowej, Palace of Culture, Warsaw, Poland (2 shows)
4/14/67	Hallenstadion, Zurich, Switzerland
4/15/67	Hautreust Hall, The Hague, Holland
4/17/67	Panathinaikos Football Stadium, Athens, Greece
5/12/68	*NME* Poll-Winners Concert, Empire Pool, Wembley, Middlesex
6/25/69	Coliseum, Rome, Italy (cancelled)
6/26/69	Coliseum, Rome, Italy (cancelled)
7/5/69	Free concert, Hyde Park, London
11/7/69	State University, Fort Collins, Colorado (1st night)
11/8/69	Forum, Los Angeles, California (2 shows)
11/9/69	Coliseum, Oakland, California
11/10/69	Sports Arena, San Diego, California
11/11/69	Coliseum, Phoenix, Arizona
11/13/69	Moody Coliseum, Dallas, Texas
11/14/69	University Coliseum, Auburn, Alabama
11/15/69	Assembly Hall, University of Illinois, Champagne, Illinois (2 shows)
11/16/69	International Amphitheatre, Chicago, Illinois
11/20/69	Forum, Los Angeles, California
11/24/69	Olympia Stadium, Detroit, Michigan (2 shows)
11/25/69	Spectrum, Philadelphia, Pennsylvania
11/26/69	Civic Center, Baltimore, Maryland
11/27/69	Madison Square Garden, New York
11/28/69	Madison Square Garden, New York (2 shows)
11/29/69	The Gardens, Boston, Massachusetts (2 shows)
11/30/69	Festival, International Raceway, West Palm Beach, Florida

12/6/69	Free Concert, Altamont Speedway, Livermore, California
12/14/69	Saville Theatre, London (2 shows)
12/21/69	Lyceum Theatre, London (2 shows)

Film and Television 1957–69

1957	ATV *Seeing Sport* (Mick and Father) (taped '57)
7/7/63	ATV *Thank Your Lucky Stars* (same day) Birmingham
8/28/63	ARTV *Ready Steady Go!* (same day) London
8/29/63	Granada *Scene at 6:30* (same day) Manchester
9/8/63	ATV *Thank Your Lucky Stars* (same day) Birmingham
11/22/63	ARTV *Ready Steady Go!* (same day) London
11/23/63	ATV *Thank Your Lucky Stars* (taped 11/17/63) Birmingham
*n/d.	BBC Pilot Show (taped 12/19/63) London
12/27/63	ARTV*Ready Steady Go!* (same day) London
1/2/64	BBC *Top of the Pops* (taped 1/1/64) Manchester
1/30/64	BBC *Top of the Pops* (taped 1/29/64) Manchester
2/64	BBC *Town and Around* (taped 1/30/64) London
2/8/64	ATV *Arthur Haynes Show* (taped 2/7/64) Elstree
2/14/64	ARTV *Ready Steady Go!* (same day) London
2/29/64	ABC *Thank Your Lucky Stars* (taped 2/23/64) Birmingham
3/5/64	BBC *Top of the Pops* (taped 3/4/64) Manchester
3/64	Granada *Scene at 6:30* (taped 3/4/64) Manchester

3/12/64 BBC *Top of the Pops* (taped 2/22/64) Weymouth

4/3/64 ARTV *Ready Steady Go!* (same day) London
4/8/64 BBC *Top of the Pops* (taped 3/4/64) (Repeat)

4/64 ARTV *Ready Steady Go! Mod Ball* (taped 8.4.64) Wembley
4/20/64 ARTV *Ready Steady Go!* (same day) Montreux, Switzerland
4/30/64 BBC *Top of the Pops* (taped 4/29/64) Manchester

5/3/64 ABC *NME Poll-Winners Concert* (taped 4/26/64) Wembley
5/4/64 Granada *Scene at 6:30* (taped 5/4/64) Manchester
5/64 BBC *Top Beat Pop Prom* (taped 4/27/64) London
5/64 Southern *Two Go Round* (taped 5/6/64) Southampton
5/64 BBC2 *Open House* (taped 5/9/64) London
5/30/64 ABC *Thank Your Lucky Stars* (taped 5/24/64) Birmingham

*6/1/64 US TV Newsreel interview (same day) New York
*6/2/64 US TV *Les Crane Show* (same day) New York
*6/64 US TV (tape 6/10/64) Chicago
*6/11/64 US TV Newsreel (same day) Chicago
6/13/64 ABC *Hollywood Palace Show* (taped 6/3/64) Los Angeles
*6/64 U S TV Interview (taped 6/13/64) Omaha, Nebraska
*6/64 US TV (taped 6/18/64) Cleveland *Ohio*
*6/64 US TV (taped 6/19/64) Harrisburg, Pennsylvania
6/20/64 WPIX Ch.11 *Clay Cole Show* (same day) New York
*6/64 UK TV Newsreel interview (taped 6/22/64) London
6/26/64 ARTV *Ready Steady Go!* (same day) London

7/1/64   BBC   *Top of the Pops* (taped 6/27/64) London
7/4/64   BBC   *Juke Box Jury* (taped 6/27/64) London
7/6/64   ARTV   *Ready, Steady, Win (n.d.)* London (Brian, interview)
7/16/64   BBC   *Top of the Pops* (taped 7/15/64) Manchester
7/31/64   BBC   *Six Ten* (same day) Belfast, Northern Ireland (without Keith)

8/64   UK TV?   Newsreel (taped 8/2/64) Warminster
8/7/64   ARTV   *Ready Steady Go!* (same day) London
8/8/64   ABC   *Thank Your Lucky Stars* (taped 7/28/64) Teddington
8/64   Dutch TV   Newsreel interview (taped 8/8/64) The Hague
8/64   Dutch TV?   Newsreel of riot (taped 8/8/64) The Hague
8/64   TV?   Interview (taped 8/13/64) Douglas, Isle of Man
8/64   TV?   Interview (taped 8/20/64) Guernsey, Channel Isles
8/64   TWW   Interview (taped 8/24/64) Dorchester
8/25/64   TWW   *Here Today* (taped 8/25/64) Weston-super-Mare
8/26/64   ARTV   *The Man They Call Genius* (taped 7/20/64) Croydon (Bill, Keith and Charlie in audience)
9/64   Border   Interview (taped 9/17/64) Carlisle
9/22/64   US TV   *Red Skelton Hour* (taped 8/5/64) London

*10/64   Belgian TV   Special (taped 10/18/64) Brussels
*10/64   French TV   Special (taped 10/19/64) Paris
10/25/64   CBS   *Ed Sullivan Show* (same day) New York
10/31/64   WPIX Ch. 11   *Clay Cole Show* (taped 10/24/64) New York

*11/10/64   US TV   *Red Skelton Hour* (taped 8/5/64) (Repeat)
11/64   WANE Ch. 15   Interview (taped 11/12/64) Fort Wayne, Texas
11/20/64   ARTV   *Ready Steady Go!* (same day) London

11/25/64   ARTV   *Glad Rag Ball* (taped 11/20/64) Wembley

12/5/64   ABC   *Thank Your Lucky Stars* (taped 11/29/64) Birmingham

US TV   *Shindig* (2 shows) (taped 12/15/64) Shepperton

12/31/64   ARTV   *Ready Steady Go!* (same day) London

1/6/65   BBC   *Six Five* (same day) Belfast, Northern Ireland

1/15/65   ARTV   *Ready Steady Go!* (same day) London

*1/65   Australian TV   Interview (taped 1/21/65) Sydney

*1/65   Australian TV   Interview (taped 1/21/65) Sydney

*1/65   Australian TV   Interview (taped 1/28/65) Melbourne

1/30/65   ABC   *Thank Your Lucky Stars* (taped 1/13/65) Teddington

*2/65   New Zealand TV   Ads and plugs for Shows (taped 1/30/65) Melbourne

2/12/65   ATVO   *Rolling Stones Special* (taped 1/29/65) Melbourne

*2/65   Japanese TV   Interview (taped 2/17/65) Tokyo

2/26/65   ARTV   *Ready Steady Go!* (same day) London

2/28/65   ABC   *Eamonn Andrews Show* (same day) Teddington

3/11/65   BBC   *Top of the pops* (taped 3/4/65) Manchester

3/11/65   Granada   *Scene at 6:30* (same day) Manchester

3/65   Granada   *In the North* (taped 3/11/65) Manchester

3/18/65   BBC   *Top of the Pops* (taped 3/4/65) (Repeat)

3/25/65   BBC   *Top of the Pops* (taped 3/23/65) London

*3/65   Danish TV   Interview (taped 3/25/65) Copenhagen

3/27/65   ABC   *Thank Your Lucky Stars* (taped 3/21/65) Birmingham

*4/8/65   Swedish TV   30 min. Special (taped 3/2/65) Stockholm

4/9/65	ARTV *Ready Steady Goes Live* (same day) Wembley	
4/18/65	ABC *Big Beat 65* (taped 3/11/65) Wembley	
*4/65	Canadian TV Interview (taped 4/22/65) Montreal	
*4/65	Canadian TV Interview (taped 4/25/65) Toronto	
*4/65	Canadian TV Interview (taped 4/26/65) London, Ontario	

5/2/65	CBS *Ed Sullivan Show* (same day) New York
*5/65	US TV *Clay Cole Show* (taped 5/3/65) New York
*5/65	US TV *Hollywood à Go-Go* (taped 5/15/65) Los Angeles
*5/65	US TV *Shivaree* (taped 5/16/65) Los Angeles
5/65	ABC US *Shindig* (taped 5/20/65) Los Angeles

6/4/65	ARTV *Ready Steady Goes Live* (same day) Wembley
6/10/65	BBC *Top of the Pops* (same day) London
6/12/65	ABC *Thank Your Lucky Stars* (taped 6/6/65) Birmingham
6/65	Norwegian TV Newsreel (taped 6/23/65) Oslo

7/13/65	BBC1 *The World of Jimmy Savile* (taped 7/65) London
7/13/65	BBC1 *The World of Jimmy Savile* (taped 7/65) London (Brian, interview)
*7/19/65	US TV *Shivaree* (taped 5/16/65) (Repeat)

8/1/65	ABC *Thank Your Lucky Stars* (taped 7/26/65) Birmingham
8/9/65	ABC US *Shindig* (1) (taped 7/28/65) Twickenham
8/65	ABC US *Shindig* (2) (taped 7/28/65) Twickenham
8/23/65	Granada *Scene at 6:30* (same day) Manchester
8/27/65	ARTV *Ready Steady Go!* (same day) Wembley
*8/28/65	US TV? *Shivaree* (taped 5/16/65) (Repeat)

9/2/65	BBC *Top of the Pops* (taped 8/19/65) London

9/4/65	ABC	*Thank Your Lucky Stars* (taped 8/29/65) Birmingham
9/9/65	BBC	*Top of the Pops* (taped 8/19/65) (Repeat)
9/10/65	ARTV	*Ready Steady Go!—The Rolling Stones Special Show* (taped 9/2/65) Wembley
9/16/65	BBC	*Top of the Pops* (taped 8/19/65) (Repeat)
9/23/65	BBC	*Top of the Pops* (same day) London
9/30/65	BBC	*Top of the Pops* (taped 8/19/65) (Repeat)
10/14/65	BBC	*Top of the Pops* (clip of 'Charlie is My Darling')
10/22/65	ARTV	*Ready Steady Go!* (same day) Wembley
*10/65	US TV	Interview (taped 10/28/65) New York
11/4/65	BBC	*Top of the Pops* (taped 10/19/65) London
*11/65	US TV	Interview (taped 11/6/65) Philadelphia
11/11/65	BBC	*Top of the Pops* (taped 10/19/65) (Repeat)
*11/15/65	US TV	*Hullabaloo* (taped 11/11/65) New York
11/18/65	BBC	*Top of the Pops* (taped 10/19/65) (Repeat)
*12/11/65	US TV	*Shivaree* (taped 5/16/65) (Repeat)
12/23/65	BBC	*Top of the Pops* (n.d.) (Repeat)
12/25/65	BBC	*Top of the Pops* Xmas Show (n.d.) (Repeat)
12/26/65	BBC	*Top of the Pops* (Repeat of 12/25/65)
12/30/65	BBC	*Top of the Pops* (taped 10/19/65) (Repeat)
*12/30/65	UK TV	*Man Alive (n.d.)* London (some of Stones interview)
12/31/65	ARTV	*Ready Steady Go!* (same day) Wembley
1/20/66	BBC	*Top of the Pops* (same day) London
*2/6/66	UK TV	*Eamonn Andrews Show* (same day) London
*2/6/66	UK TV	*Eamonn Andrews Show* (same day) London (Mick, interview)
2/10/66	BBC	*Top of the Pops* (taped 2/3/66) London
2/13/66	CBS	*Ed Sullivan Show* (same day) New York
2/66	Australian TV?	Interview (taped 2/16/66) Sydney
2/17/66	BBC	*Top of the Pops* (taped 2/3/66) London (Repeat)

3/3/66   BBC *Top of the Pops* (taped 2/22/66) Brisbane
3/21/66   BBC *Carl Alan Awards Show* (same day) London (no Stones)

4/66   ARTV *Ready Steady Go!* (taped 4/1/66) Paris (Brian and me in audience)
4/14/66   BBC *Top of the Pops* (same day) London

5/66   BBC NME *Poll-Winners Concert Live* (taped 5/1/66) Wembley
5/8/66   ABC *Thank Your Lucky Stars* (same day) Birmingham
5/12/66   BBC *Top of the Pops* (taped 4/14/66) (Repeat)
5/19/66   BBC *Top of the Pops* (taped 4/14/66) (Repeat)
5/26/66   BBC *Top of the Pops* (taped 4/14/66) (Repeat)
5/27/66   ARTV *Ready Steady Go!* (same day) Wembley

6/15/66   BBC *A Whole Scene Going* (n.d.) London (Mick, interview)

9/10/66   ARTV *Ready Steady Go!* (n.d.) Wembley
9/11/66   CBS *Ed Sullivan Show* (taped 9/9/66) New York
9/22/66   BBC *Top of the Pops* (taped 9/12/66) (film of New York)
9/29/66   BBC *Top of the Pops* (taped 9/23/66) Kensington (film of gold disc presentation party)

10/7/66   ARTV *Ready Steady Go!* (taped 10/4/66) Wembey
10/66   ARTV *David Frost Show* (taped 10/14/66) London (Mick, interview)
12/22/66   BBC *Top of the Pops* (taped 12/17/66) London
12/23/66   ARTV *Ready Steady Go!* (final show) (same day) Wembley (Mick only)
12/26/66   BBC *Top of the Pops* (taped 2/3/66) (Repeat)
12/26/66   BBC *Top of the Pops* (taped 4/14/66) (Repeat)

1/15/67   CBS *Ed Sullivan Show* (same day) New York
1/22/67   ITV *Sunday Night at the London Palladium* (same day) London
1/26/67   BBC *Top of the Pops* (taped 1/25/67) London

2/2/67   BBC   *Top of the Pops* (taped 1/25/67) (Repeat)

2/5/67   ABC   *Eamonn Andrews Show* (same day) London

2/5/67   ABC   *Eamonn Andrews Show* (same day) London (Mick, interview)

5/2/67   BBC   *Look of the Week* (taped) London (Mick, interview)

*7/6/67   UK TV   *Our World* (taped 6/25/67) London (Beatles: 'All You Need Is Love') (Mick, Keith and Brian in audience)

8/67   ITV   *World in Action* (taped 7/31/67) Essex (Mick, interview)

12/21/67   BBC   *Top of the Pops* (featured tracks from *Satanic Majesties)*

12/26/67   BBC   *Top of the Pops* (taped 1/25/67) (Repeat)

2/5/68   ABC   *Eamonn Andrews Show* (taped 2/5/68) London (Mick, interview)

5/68   Southern NME *Poll-Winners Concert* (taped 5/12/68) Wembley (Stones 'Live')

5/18/68   ITV   *Time for Blackburn* (taped 5/12/68) Wembley (Stones 'Live')

5/18/68   ITV   *Time for Blackburn* (taped 5/12/68) Wembley (Mick, interview)

5/23/68   BBC   *Top of the Pops* (Jumpin' Jack Flash promo film)

5/26/68   BBC   *Line Up* (same day) London (Charlie, interview)

6/6/68   BBC   *Top of the Pops* (Jumpin' Jack Flash Promo film) (Repeat)

6/27/68   BBC   *Top of the Pops* (Jumpin' Jack Flash with still pictures of us and dancers in studio)

7/68   BBC   *Top of the Pops* (taped 6/26/68) London

9/6/68   ARTV   *David Frost Show* (taped 9/3/68) London (Mick, interview)

10/12/68   LWT   *Frost on Saturday* (live) London (Mick, interview)
11/30/68   BBC2   *Release* (n.d.) London (Mick, interview)
11/30/68   LWT   *Frost on Saturday* (taped 11/29/68) London

12/5/68   ITN   News (same day) London (*Beggars Banquet* press reception)

*7/5/69   UK TV   Newsreel of Hyde Park Concert (same day) London
*7/69   US TV   *David Frost Show* (US) (taped 6/16/69) London
*7/69   US TV   *David Frost Show* (US) (taped 6/16/69) London (Mick, interview)
*7/10/69   UK TV   Newsreel of Brian's funeral (same day) Cheltenham
7/10/69   BBC   *Top of the Pops* (taped 7/3/69) London
7/17/69   BBC   *Top of the Pops* (taped 7/3/69) (Repeat)
7/31/69   BBC   *Top of the Pops* (taped 7/3/69) (Repeat)

8/8/69   BBC   *Top of the Pops* (n.d.) (Mick, interview)

9/2/69   Granada   *The Stones in the Park* (taped 7/5/69) London

10/23/69   CBS   *Ed Sullivan Show* (n.d.) New York

12/21/69   CBS (Ch. 2)   *Ed Sullivan Show—The Swinging Soulful Sixties* (n.d.) (Repeat)
12/25/69   BBC1   *Top of the Pops* (Pt. 1) (n.d.) (Repeat?)
12/25/69   BBC1   *Top of the Pops Christmas Special* (taped 12.12.69) London
12/27/69   LWT   *A Child of the Sixties* (n.d.) (Repeat)
12/28/69   BBC2   *Ten Years of What* (n.d.) (Repeat)
12/31/69   BBC1   *Pop Go the Sixties* (n.d.) (Repeat)

Radio: 1963–69

5/13/63   BBC   Audition for *Jazz Club* (rejected) (taped 4/23/63) London (without Bill or Charlie)

10/5/63 BBC *Saturday Club* (taped 9/23/63) (London) (Bill, Brian and Charlie backing Bo Diddley)
10/26/63 BBC *Saturday Club* (n.d.) London

2/18/64 BBC *Saturday Club* (taped 2/3/63) London
2/18/64 BBC *Pop Inn* (same day) London

64 BBC 1st *Stereo Show* (taped 3/19/64) London

4/10/64 BBC *Joe Loss Radio Show* (same day) London
4/17/64 Radio Luxembourg: *Nestlés' Top Swinging Groups* (taped 3/18/64) London
4/18/64 BBC *Saturday Club* (taped 4/13/64) London
4/24/64 Radio Luxembourg: *Nestlés' Top Swinging Groups* (taped 3/18/64) London
4/64 WINS New York *Murray the K Show New York*—NME *Poll-Winners* Concert (taped 4/26/64) Wembley, Middlesex

5/1/64 Radio Luxembourg: *Nestlés' Top Swinging Groups* (taped 3/18/64) London
5/64 BBC *Top Beat Pop Prom* (taped 4/27/64) London
5/8/64 Radio Luxembourg: *Nestlés' Top Swinging Groups* (taped 3/18/64) London
5/30/64 BBC *Saturday Club* (taped 5/25/64) London

*6/1/64 US radio Interview (same day) New York
WINS New York *Murray the K's Swinging Soirée* (same day) New York
*6/7/64 US radio Interview (same day) San Antonio, Texas
* US radio Interview (same day) San Antonio, Texas
6/10/64 WMAQ Chicago *Jack Eigen Show* (same day) Chicago, Illinois
6/64 US radio (taped 6/10/64) Chicago, Illinois
*11/6/64 US radio (same day) Chicago, Illinois
*12/6/64 US radio (taped 6/12/64) Minneapolis, Minnesota
*12/6/64 US radio (taped 6/12/64) Minneapolis, Minnesota

*6/64   US radio   (taped 6/14/64) Detroit, Michigan
*6/64   US radio   (taped 6/17/64) Pittsburgh, Pennsylvania
6/64   US radio   (taped 6/18/64) Cleveland, Ohio
6/18/64   WHK Cleveland   *Mike Douglas Show* (same day) Cleveland, Ohio
*6/64   US radio   (taped 6/19/64) Harrisburg, Pennsylvania

7/12/64   Radio Luxembourg   *This is Their Life*
7/64   Radio Luxembourg   *Teen and Twenty Disc Club* (taped 7/16/64) London
7/17/64   BBC   *Joe Loss Radio Show* (same day) London
7/23/64   BBC   *Top Gear* (taped 7/17/64) London

*8/64   Radio   Interview (taped 8/13/64) Douglas, Isle of Man

9/28/64   North Staffs. Hospital Broadcasting Service Interview (taped 9/25/64) Hanley, Staffordshire
10/5/64   Radio Luxembourg   *Battle of the Giants— Stones v Animals* (Pt. 1)
10/9/64   Radio Luxembourg   *Battle of the Giants— Stones v Animals* (Pt. 2)
*10/64   French radio   Interview (taped 10/20/64) Paris
10/64   Europe No. 1   Live show (taped 10/20/64) Paris
*10/64   US radio   *Ed Rudy* (taped 10/23/64) New York
10/24/64   WINS New York   *Murray the K's Swinging Soirée* (same day) New York
10/64   KRLA LA   *Gary Mack* (taped 10/27/64) Los Angeles, California (Mick and Keith, interview)
*10/64   US radio   (taped 10/28/64) Santa Monica, California (Brian, interview)
10/31/64   BBC   World Service *Rhythm and Blues* (taped 10/8/64) London

11/22/64   BBC   *Teen Scene* (taped 11/22/64) London
11/24/64   BBC   *Pop Inn* (taped 11/23/64) London (Bill, interview)
   BBC   *Saturday Club* (cancelled by Andrew Oldham)
   BBC   *Top Gear* (cancelled by Andrew Oldham)

BBC *The Joe Loss Show* (cancelled by Andrew Oldham)

12/18/64 Radio Luxembourg London (Brian, interview)
12/28/64 Radio Luxembourg *Battle of the Giants—Stones v Gene Pitney*

1/65 BBC Interview (taped 1/6/65) Belfast
*1/65 Australian radio Interview (taped 1/21/65) Sydney
1/65 2UE Sydney Interview (taped 1/21/65) Sydney
*1/65 Australian radio Interview (taped 1/28/65) Melbourne
*2/65 New Zealand radio Interview (taped 1/31/65) Christchurch
*2/65 Japanese radio Interview (taped 2/17/65) Tokyo

3/2/65 BBC *Pop Inn* (same day) London (some of Stones)
3/6/65 BBC *Top Gear* (taped 3/1/65) London
3/18/65 BBC *Melody Fair* (taped 3/16/65) Greenford, Middlesex (Brian, interview)

4/65 Europe No. 1 Live show (taped 4/18/65) Paris
*4/65 Canadian radio Interview (taped 4/22/65) Montreal
*4/65 Canadian radio Interview (taped 4/25/65) Toronto
*4/65 Canadian radio Interview (taped 4/26/65) London, Ontario
4/65 WTRY Albany Interview (taped 4/29/65) Albany, New York
4/65 WDIC Hartford Interview (taped 4/30/65) Hartford, Connecticut
5/9/65 BBC World Service *Sights and Sounds of London* (taped 3/11/65) Wembley, Middlesex (Brian, interview)

5/65 KHJ LA Interview (taped 5/11/65) Los Angeles, California
5/15/65 KMEN San Bernardino Interview (taped 5/15/65) San Bernardino, California

6/21/65 BBC *Teen Scene* (same day) London

6/65 BBC *Woman's Hour* (taped 6/21/65) London

6/65 Radio SYD (pirate radio) Interview (taped 6/27/65) Denmark

*6/65 Swedish radio (taped 6/29/65) Malrnö (Charlie, interview)

7/10/65 Radio Luxembourg *Battle of the Giants* Stones v. Beatles

8/30/65 BBC *Yeh Yeh* (taped 8/20/65) London

9/18/65 BBC *Saturday Club* (taped 8/20/65) London

10/65 KHJ LA Radio promos (taped 10/18/65) London

10/65 US radio Interview (taped 10/28/65) New York

*11/65 Boston radio Radio promos (taped 11/1/65) New York

2/66 BBC (taped 2/1/66) London (Mick and Keith, interview)

*2/66 Australian radio Interview (taped 2/16/66) Sydney

2/66 3UZ Melbourne Show (taped 2/23/66) Melbourne

3/29/66 Europe No. 1 *Olympia Show Live* (same day) Paris

7/7/66 Radio Luxembourg *Battle of the Giants*-Beatles vs. Stones

7/16/66 Radio Luxembourg *Battle of the Giants*-Stones v. Walker

8/15/66 Radio Luxembourg *Battle of the Giants*-Cliff Richard v. Stones

9/66 Radio Luxembourg (taped 9/19/66) London (Mick and Keith, interview)

9/66 BBC (taped 9/27/66) London (Mick, interview)

12/3/67 BBC *Top Gear* (taped 11/30/67) London (Mick, Brian and Charlie, interview)

*3/16/68 BBC *Scene and Heard* (n.d.) London (Brian and Mick interview)

5/15/68   BBC   *Top Gear* (same day) London (Mick and Brian, interview)

5/15/68   BBC   *Scene and Heard* (same day) London (Brian, interview)

5/18/68   BBC   *Scene and Heard* (taped 5/15/68) (Repeat) (Brian, interview)

*6/6/68   UH radio   Interview with John Peel (Mick)

7/17/68   BBC   *Scene and Heard* (taped 5/15/68) (Repeat) (Brian, interview)

9/14/68   BBC   *Scene and Heard* (n.d.) London (Mick, interview)

9/21/68   BBC   *The Voice of Pop* (n.d.) London (Mick, interview)

12/14/68   BBC   *Scene and Heard* (n.d.) London (Mick, interview)

7/6/69   BBC   *Scene and Heard (live)* London (Mick, interview)

7/69   Australian radio   (taped 7/15/69) Sydney (Mick, interview)

Index

Note: Entries for the original Stones—Mick Jagger, Keith Richards, Brian Jones and Charlie Watts—are not comprehensive and do not cover their activities as part of the overall group. The references are selected to point to individual characteristics, achievements, incidents, etc.